AutoCAD 2026

A Power Guide for Beginners and Intermediate Users

CADArtifex

A premium provider of learning products and solutions

www.cadartifex.com

AutoCAD 2026: A Power Guide for Beginners and Intermediate Users
Author: Sandeep Dogra
Email: info@cadartifex.com

Published by
CADArtifex
www.cadartifex.com

ISBN: 978-9394074989

NOTICE TO THE READER

The publisher and the author make no representations or warranties with respect to the accuracy or completeness of the contents of this work/text and specifically disclaim all warranties, including without limitation warranties of fitness for a particular purpose. The publisher neither guarantees any of the products described in the text nor has performed any independent analysis in connection with any of the product information contained in the text. No warranty may be created or extended by sales or promotional materials. This work is published with the understanding that the publisher is not engaged in rendering legal, accounting, or other professional services. Neither the publisher nor the author shall be liable for damages arising herefrom. Further, readers should be aware that Websites listed in this work may have changed or may have been removed in the time between the writing and the publishing of this work.

Examination Copies

Textbooks received as examination copies in any form such as paperback or eBooks are for review only and may not be made available for the use of the student. These files may not be transferred to any other party. Resale of examination copies is prohibited.

Electronic Files

The electronic file/eBook in any form of this textbook is licensed to the original user only and may not be transferred to any other party.

Disclaimer

The author has made sincere efforts to ensure the adequacy of the material described herein, however the author makes no warranty (expressed or implied), with respect to the quality, precision, accuracy, or freedom from error of this document or the products it describes.

www.cadartifex.com

Dedication

First and foremost, I would like to thank my parents for being a great support throughout my career and while writing this book.

Heartfelt gratitude goes to my wife and my sisters for their patience and endurance in supporting me to take up and successfully accomplish this challenge.

I would also like to acknowledge the efforts of the employees at CADArtifex for their dedication in editing the contents of this textbook.

Contents at a Glance

Table of Contents

Preface

AutoCAD, a product of Autodesk Inc., is one of the biggest providers of technology to engineering, architecture, construction, manufacturing, media, and entertainment industries. It is a complete software that lets you design, visualize, simulate, and publish your ideas before they are built or created. Moreover, Autodesk continues to develop a comprehensive portfolio of state-of-the-art 3D software for the global market.

AutoCAD delivers a rich set of high productivity tools and commands that allow you to create stunning designs, speed up the documentation work, and add precision to your engineering and architectural drawings. AutoCAD is extremely versatile in its ability to create 2D and 3D drawings. With AutoCAD, you can share your designs with your clients, sub-contractors, and colleagues in more efficient ways.

AutoCAD 2026: A Power Guide for Beginners and Intermediate Users textbook is designed for instructor-led courses as well as for self-paced learning. It is intended to help engineers, designers, and CAD operators interested in learning AutoCAD to create 2D engineering drawings as well as 3D Models. This textbook is a great help for new AutoCAD users and a great teaching aid for classroom training. The textbook consists of 13 chapters, and a total of 552 pages covering major workspaces of AutoCAD such as Drafting & Annotation and 3D Modeling, teaching you to use AutoCAD software for creating, editing, plotting, and managing real world 2D engineering drawings and 3D Models.

This textbook not only focuses on the usage of the tools/commands of AutoCAD but also the concept of design. Every chapter of this textbook contains tutorials that provide users with step-by-step instructions on how to easily create mechanical designs and drawings. Moreover, every chapter ends with hands-on test drives allowing users to experience AutoCAD's user-friendly and powerful capabilities.

Who Should Read This Textbook

This textbook is written to benefit a wide range of AutoCAD users, varying from beginners to advanced users as well as AutoCAD instructors. The easy-to-follow chapters of this book allow you to understand different design techniques and AutoCAD tools/commands easily.

What Is Covered in This Textbook

AutoCAD 2026: A Power Guide for Beginners and Intermediate Users textbook is designed to help you learn everything you need to know to start using AutoCAD 2026 with straightforward, step-by-step tutorials. This book covers the following topics:

Chapter 1, "***Introduction to AutoCAD,***" introduces system requirements for installing AutoCAD and explains how to start a new drawing file. It also introduces screen components, workspaces, and sheet sets of AutoCAD. Additionally, it explains how to change the color theme, background color, and how to open, save, and share drawing files in AutoCAD.

*Chapter 2, "**Creating Drawings - I**,"* introduces how to set drawing units, drawing limits, and grid and snap settings. It also introduces various coordinate systems and explains how to create a line, circle, and arc entities in AutoCAD. Additionally, it explains how to cancel, erase, undo, and navigate 2D drawings.

*Chapter 3, "**Working with Drawing Aids and Layers**,"* introduces Ortho mode, Polar Tracking, Object Snap, and Object Snap Tracking. It also explains how to specify grids and snaps settings, how to work with layers and assign objects to layers.

*Chapter 4, "**Creating Drawings - II**,"* introduces how to create rectangles, polygons, polylines, ellipses, elliptical arcs, splines, donuts, construction lines, ray lines, and points. It also describes how to define point style/size.

*Chapter 5, "**Modifying and Editing Drawings - I**,"* introduces various object selection methods and methods for trimming and extending drawing entities. It also explains how to mirror, fillet, chamfer, offset, move, copy, rotate, scale, stretch, and lengthen drawing entities, and create arrays.

*Chapter 6, "**Working with Dimensions and Dimension Styles**,"* introduces various components of a dimension, methods for creating a new dimension style, modifying the existing dimension style, and overriding dimension style. It also explains how to apply various types of dimensions such as linear dimension, aligned dimension, angular dimension, diameter dimension, and radius dimension.

*Chapter 7, "**Editing Dimensions and Adding Text**,"* introduces methods for modifying dimensions by using the DIMEDIT command, DIMTEDIT command, DDEDIT command, dimension grips, Properties palette, and editing tools. It also explains how to add text/notes to drawings, create and modify text style, and add text by using the Single Line and Multiline Text tools. Moreover, it also describes how to edit single line and multiline texts, and how to convert a single line text to multiline text.

*Chapter 8, "**Modifying and Editing Drawings - II**,"* introduces methods for editing drawing entities by using the grips and the Properties palette. It also discusses about matching the properties of an object with the other drawing objects, and how to identify the coordinates of a point in a drawing.

*Chapter 9, "**Creating Hatches and Gradients**,"* introduces methods for creating different types of hatch patterns and gradients in enclosed areas of a drawing.

*Chapter 10, "**Working with Blocks and Xrefs**,"* introduces methods for creating and inserting a Block and WBlock into a drawing alongwith, methods for editing Blocks and making Dynamic Blocks. It also explains how to work with external reference files (Xrefs).

*Chapter 11, "**Working with Layouts**,"* explains how to get started with a Paper space/layout and introduces different components of a layout (Paper space). It also explains how to set up sheet/paper size of a layout, how to add, rename, and delete a layout. It also discusses how to work with viewports, access the Model space within a viewport, clip a viewport, lock the object scale in a viewport, control the display of objects in a viewport, and control layer properties of a viewport. Additionally, it explains how to switch between the Model space and layout, and how to create viewports in the Model space.

*Chapter 12, "**Printing and Plotting**,"* introduces methods for configuring a plotter (output device) in AutoCAD. It also explains how to create a plot style and set up the default plot style for plotting/printing. Additionally, it introduces how to plot/print drawings in AutoCAD.

*Chapter 13, "**Introducing 3D Basics and Creating 3D Models**,"* discusses about creating 3D Models in the 3D Modeling workspace. It explains how to create various 3D primitives such as box, cylinder, sphere, cone, and torus. The chapter introduces World Coordinate System (WCS) and User Coordinate System (UCS). It also explains how to set the work plane to a predefined orthographic view, work with Dynamic UCS, and control the display of UCS. Besides, it describes how to create extrude, revolve, sweep, loft, and 3D wall-like polysolid features of a 3D model. It also introduces methods for performing various boolean operations, checking interference, and copying edges of a solid feature.

Icons/Terms used in this Textbook

The following icons and terms are used in this textbook:

Note

Note: Notes highlight information which requires special attention.

Tip

Tip: Tips provide additional advice, which increases the efficiency of the users.

Flyout

A flyout is a pop-up in which a set of tools is grouped together, see Figure 1.

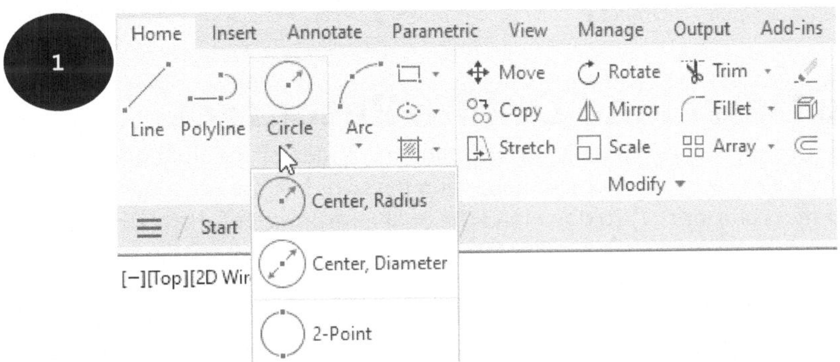

Drop-down List

A drop-down list is a pop-up in which a set of options is grouped together to perform a task, see Figure 2.

Field

A field allows you to enter a new value, or modify the existing value, as per your requirement, see Figure 2.

Check box

A check box allows you to turn on or off the use of a particular option. It is used for selecting an appropriate option to turn it on, see Figure 2.

Button

A button appears as a 3D icon and is used for confirming or discarding an action. It is also used for turning on or off the uses of a particular option or command, see Figure 2.

2

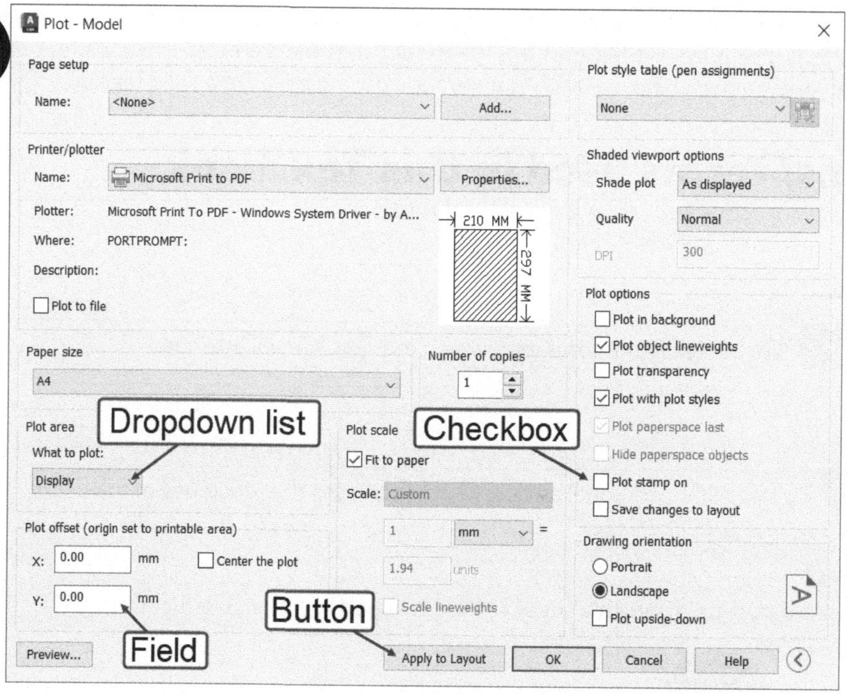

How to Download Online Resources

To download the free online teaching and learning resources of the textbook, log in to our website (*cadartifex.com/login*) by using your username and password. If you are a new user, you need to first register (*cadartifex.com/register*) to download the online resources of the textbook.

Interactive Learning Support

Tutorials are supported by **QR codes** that provide instant access to video demonstrations for additional help, making it easier to follow each step visually.

How to Contact the Author

We value your feedback and suggestions. Please e-mail us at ***info@cadartifex.com***. You can also log on to our website ***cadartifex.com*** and write your comments about the textbook.

We would like to express our sincere gratitude to you for purchasing **AutoCAD 2026: A Power Guide for Beginners and Intermediate Users** textbook. We hope that the information and concepts introduced in this book will help you to accomplish your professional goals.

CHAPTER

1

Introduction to AutoCAD

In this chapter, the following topics will be discussed:

- Installing AutoCAD
- Getting Started with AutoCAD
- Starting a New Drawing File
- Working with Various Components of a Drawing
- Starting a New Drawing File by using the Create New Drawing dialog box
- Changing the Color Theme
- Changing the Background Color
- Working with Workspaces
- Working with Sheet Sets
- Opening a Drawing File
- Saving a Drawing File
- Sharing a Drawing File

Welcome to the world of Computer-aided design (CAD) with AutoCAD. AutoCAD, a product of Autodesk Inc., is one of the biggest providers of technology to engineering, architecture, construction, manufacturing, media, and entertainment industries. It is a complete software that lets you design, visualize, simulate, and publish your ideas before they are built or created. Moreover, Autodesk continues to develop a comprehensive portfolio of its state-of-the-art 3D software for the global market.

AutoCAD delivers a rich set of high productivity tools and commands that allow you to create stunning designs, speed up the documentation work, and add precision to your engineering and architectural drawings. AutoCAD is extremely versatile in its ability to create 2D and 3D drawings. With AutoCAD, you can share your designs with your clients, sub-contractors, and colleagues in more efficient ways.

Owing to its capabilities in creating 2D and 3D drawings, AutoCAD is used across a wide range of industries by engineers, architects, project managers, graphic designers, and many other professionals.

Installing AutoCAD

If you do not have AutoCAD installed on your system, you first need to get it installed. However, before you do so, you need to check the system requirements and ensure that you have a system capable of running AutoCAD adequately. Below are the system requirements for installing AutoCAD 2026.

1. **Operating Systems:** 64-bit OS that follows Autodesk's Product Support Lifecycle policy.
2. **Processor**: Basic processor 2.5-2.9 GHz and recommended processor 3+ GHz.
3. **RAM:** Basic memory 8 GB and recommended memory 32 GB.
4. **Display Card:** 2 GB GPU with 29 GB/s Bandwidth and DirectX 11 compliant and recommended 8 GB GPU with 106 GB/s Bandwidth and Directx 12 compliant.
5. **Disk Space:** 10.0 GB (suggested SSD)

For more information about the system requirements for AutoCAD 2026, visit the AutoCAD website *at https://knowledge.autodesk.com/support/autocad/learn-explore/caas/sfdcarticles/sfdcarticles/System-requirements-for-AutoCAD-2026-including-Specialized-Toolsets.html.*

Once the system is ready, install AutoCAD using the AutoCAD DVD or the downloaded AutoCAD data.

Getting Started with AutoCAD

Once the AutoCAD 2026 is installed on your system, start by double-clicking on the **AutoCAD 2026** icon available on the desktop of your system. As soon as you double-click on the **AutoCAD 2026** icon, the system prepares to start AutoCAD by loading all the required files. Once all the necessary files are loaded, the startup user interface of AutoCAD 2026 appears, see Figure 1.1.

1.1

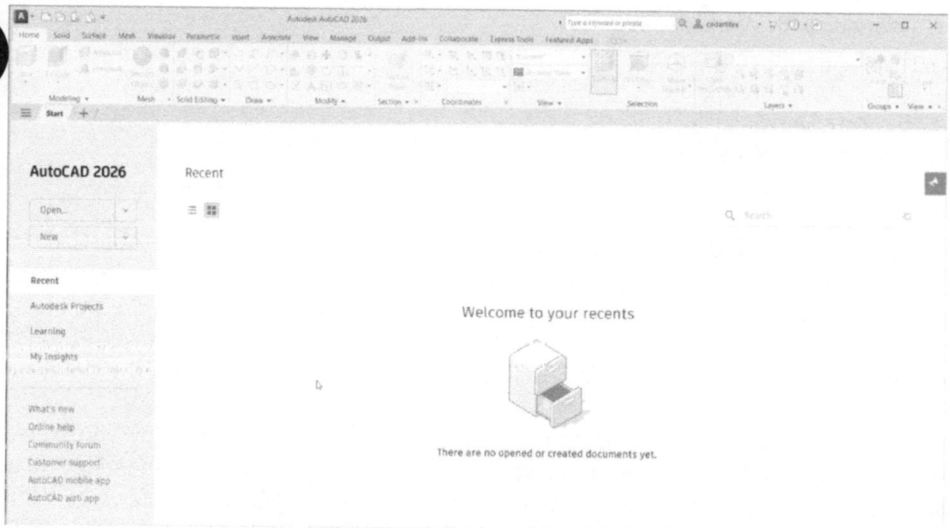

If you are starting AutoCAD for the first time after installing the software, the **Sign in** window appears, see Figure 1.2. In this window, enter your E-mail and then click on the **NEXT** button. The **Welcome** page of the **Sign in** window appears, see Figure 1.3. In this **Welcome** window, enter your password and then click on the **SIGN IN** button. The startup user interface of AutoCAD 2026 appears, refer to Figure 1.1.

1.2

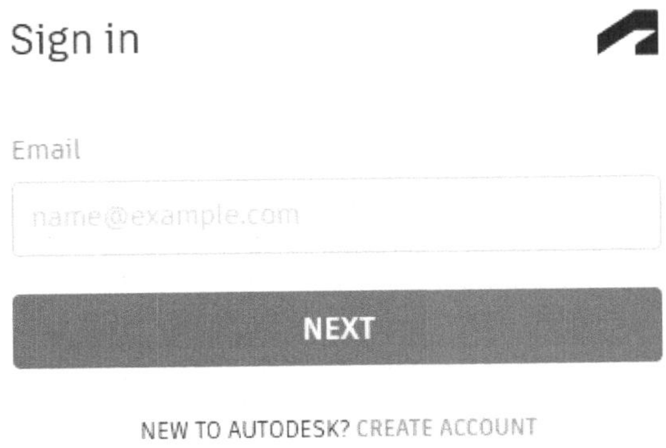

1.3

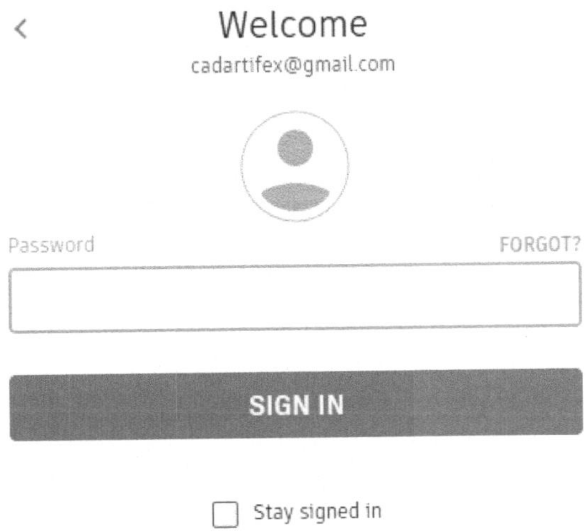

The startup user interface of AutoCAD is provided with the **Start** tab which gives quick access to start a new drawing, open an existing drawing, learn about various featured topics, and so on, see Figure 1.4. The **Start** tab is also provided with four sub-tabs: **Recent**, **Autodesk Docs**, **Learning**, and **My Insights**. By default, the **Recent** sub-tab is activated. As a result, a list of recently opened documents is displayed on the screen, see Figure 1.4. The various options available in the **Start** tab of the startup user interface are discussed next.

1.4

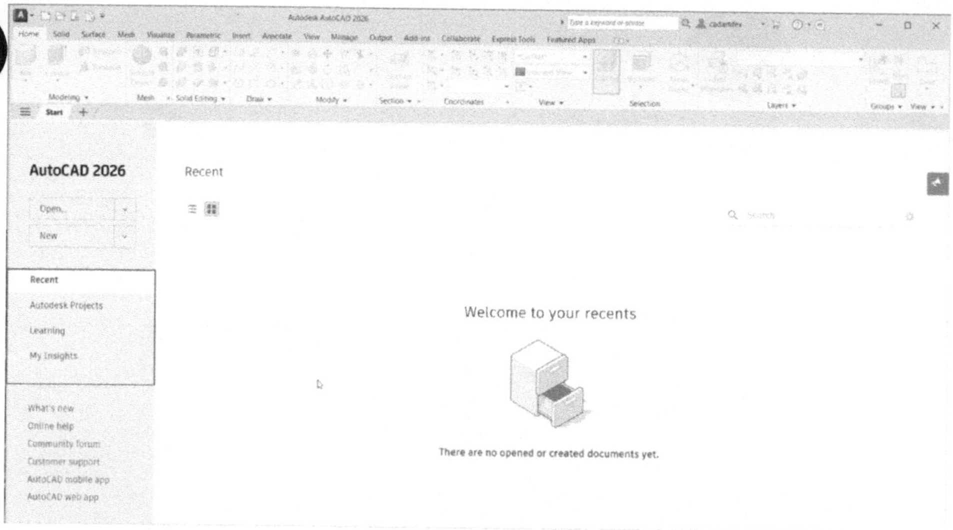

Open

The **Open** tool is used for opening an existing drawing file. To do so, click on the **Open** tool in the **Start** tab, see Figure 1.5. The **Select File** dialog box appears. In this dialog box, browse to the location where the drawing file is saved. Next, select the drawing file to be opened and then click on the **Open** button in the **Select File** dialog box. The selected drawing file gets opened in AutoCAD.

1.5

Open a sheet set

The **Open a sheet set** tool is used for opening an existing sheet set file. A sheet set manages multiple drawings (sheets) of a project in a tree view for performing operations such as plotting and publishing in an easier and faster way. You will learn about creating a new sheet set later in this chapter.

To open an existing sheet set, click on the down arrow next to the **Open** tool in the **Start** tab and then click on the **Open a sheet set** tool in the drop-down list that appears, see Figure 1.6. The **Open Sheet Set** dialog box appears. This dialog box displays a list of all the existing sheet sets. Select the required sheet set and then click on the **Open** button.

1.6

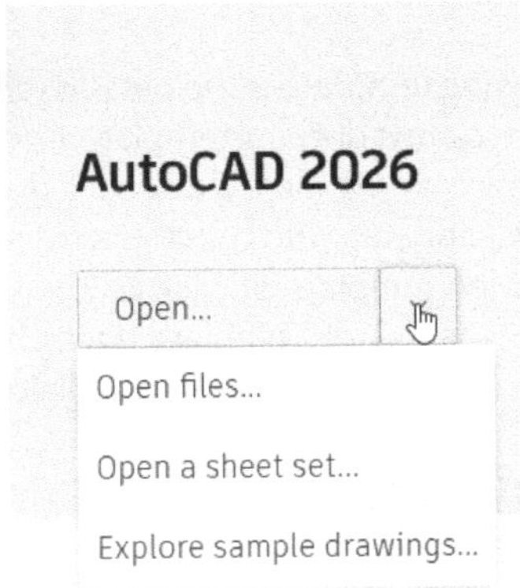

Explore sample drawings

The **Explore sample drawings** tool is used for opening a sample drawing file of AutoCAD. To do so, click on the down arrow next to the **Open** tool in the **Start** tab and then click on the **Explore sample drawings** tool in the drop-down list that appears, refer to Figure 1.6. The **Select File** dialog box appears. In this dialog box, browse to the required sub-folder of the **Sample** folder and then select a sample file to be opened. Next, click on the **Open** button in the dialog box.

New

The **New** tool is used for starting a new drawing file with the default drawing template (*acad.dwt*). To do so, click on the **New** tool in the **Start** tab of the startup user interface of AutoCAD. A new drawing file with a default template (*acad.dwt*) gets invoked and appears in a new tab with the default name '**Drawing 1**', see Figure 1.7. Note that in this figure, the color theme has been set to light, the background color of the drawing area has been changed to white and the display of grids has been turned off for better clarity. You will learn about changing the color theme, background color, and grid settings later in this chapter. Also, the various components of a new drawing file are discussed later in this chapter.

1.7

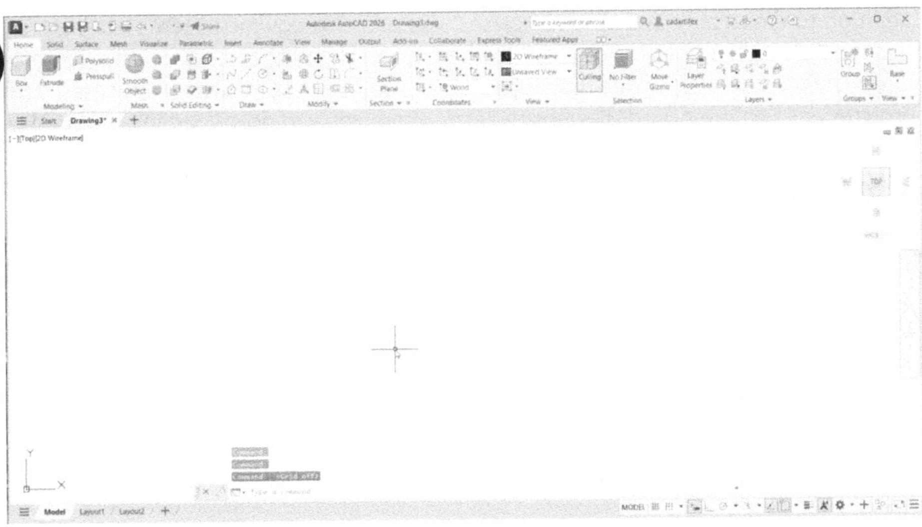

Browse Templates

In AutoCAD, the *acad.dwt* drawing template is the default template. As a result, when you start a new drawing file, it gets started with *acad.dwt* drawing template, by default. However, you can select any other available template to start a new drawing file. To do so, click on the down arrow next to the **New** tool in the **Start** tab. A drop-down list appears with the display of recently opened templates, see Figure 1.8. You can choose a recently opened template or click on the **Browse templates** tool in the drop-down list, see Figure 1.8. On doing so, the **Select Template** dialog box appears with a list of all the available drawing templates. Click on the required template in this dialog box and then click on the **Open** button.

1.8

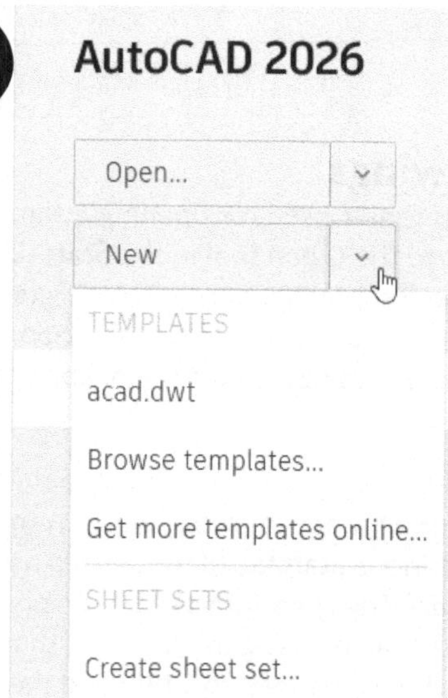

Get more templates online

In addition to the default available templates, you can also download templates online, as required. To do so, click on the down arrow next to the **New** tool and then click on the **Get more templates online** tool in the drop-down list that appears, refer to Figure 1.8. You are redirected to the AutoCAD Templates page on the Autodesk website, from where you can download the required templates.

Create sheet set

The **Create sheet set** tool is used for creating a new sheet set. As discussed earlier, a sheet set is used for managing multiple drawings (sheets) of a project in a tree view, see Figure 1.9. It helps in plotting, publishing, opening, e-transmitting, and zipping many drawing files in an easier and faster way. You will learn about creating a sheet set later in this chapter.

1.9

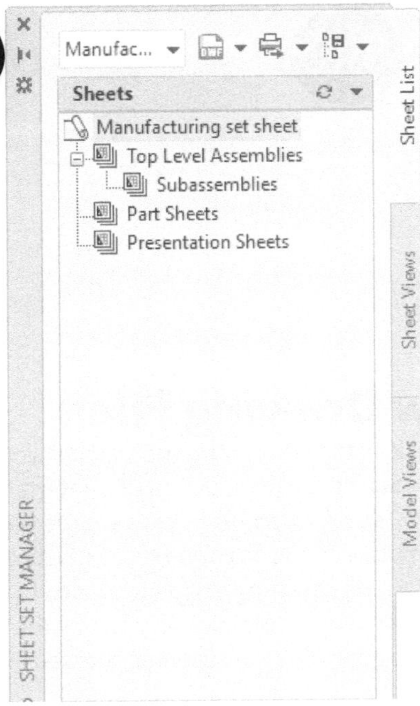

Recent Sub-tab

As discussed earlier, the **Recent** sub-tab is activated in the **Start** tab, by default. As a result, a list of recently opened documents is displayed on the screen. You can click on any recently opened drawing file in the list to open it again.

Autodesk Docs Sub-tab

The **Autodesk Docs** sub-tab is used for accessing a connected drive to manage the files of a project easily. Note that you need to have a Desktop connector installed on your system to access the connected drives on Autodesk Docs. It is a service that integrates an Autodesk data management source with a desktop folder (connected drive) of your system for easy file management.

Learning Sub-tab

The **Learning** sub-tab allows you to access various learning resources in the form of tips and video tutorials.

My Insights Sub-tab

The **My Insights** sub-tab provides information and suggests features based on your usage.

Connect

The **Connect** section on the right panel of the startup user interface is used for logging into **Autodesk** account to access online services. In this section, you can also access an online form to provide feedback.

In addition to the above, the **Start** tab of the startup user interface also provides some of the important links to access resources such as what's new, online help, community forum, customer support, AutoCAD mobile app, and AutoCAD web app, see Figure 1.10.

1.10

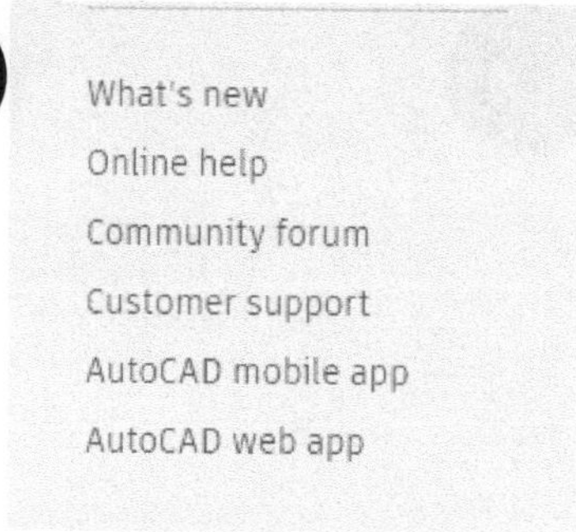

Starting a New Drawing File

To start a new drawing file, click on the **New** tool in the startup user interface, see Figure 1.11. Alternatively, click on the **+sign**, next to the **Start** tab in the startup user interface of AutoCAD to start a new drawing file with the default template (see Figure 1.12) or click on the **New** tool in the **Quick Access Toolbar**, see Figure 1.13. The **Select template** dialog box appears, see Figure 1.14. In this dialog box, select the *acad.dwt* drawing template. The *acad.dwt* drawing template is used for starting the 2D drawing environment whereas the *acad3D.dwt* drawing template is used for starting the 3D modeling environment. Next, click on the **Open** button in the dialog box. The new drawing gets started with the *acad.dwt* drawing template.

1.11

1.12

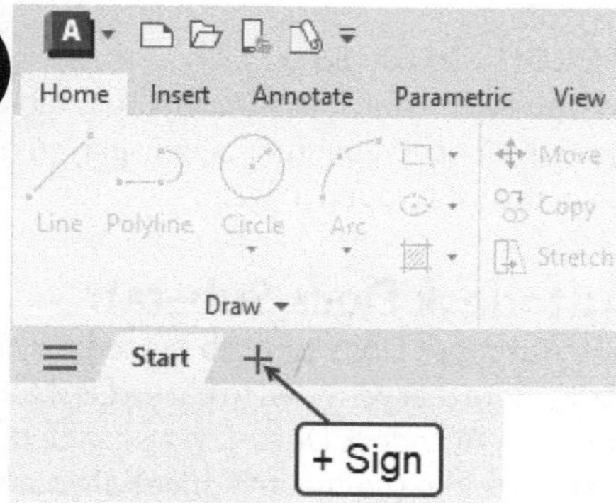

1.13

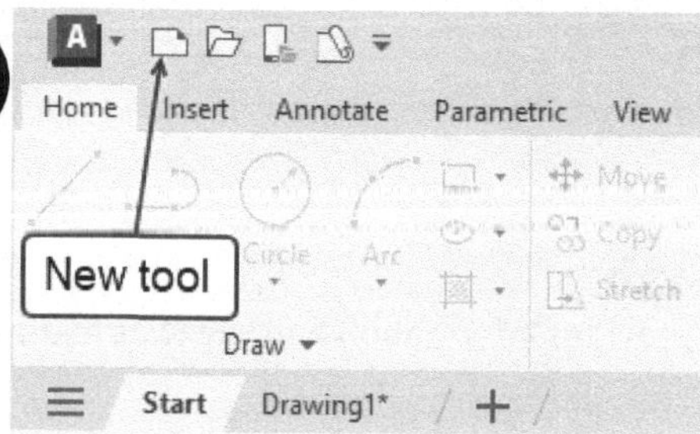

1.14

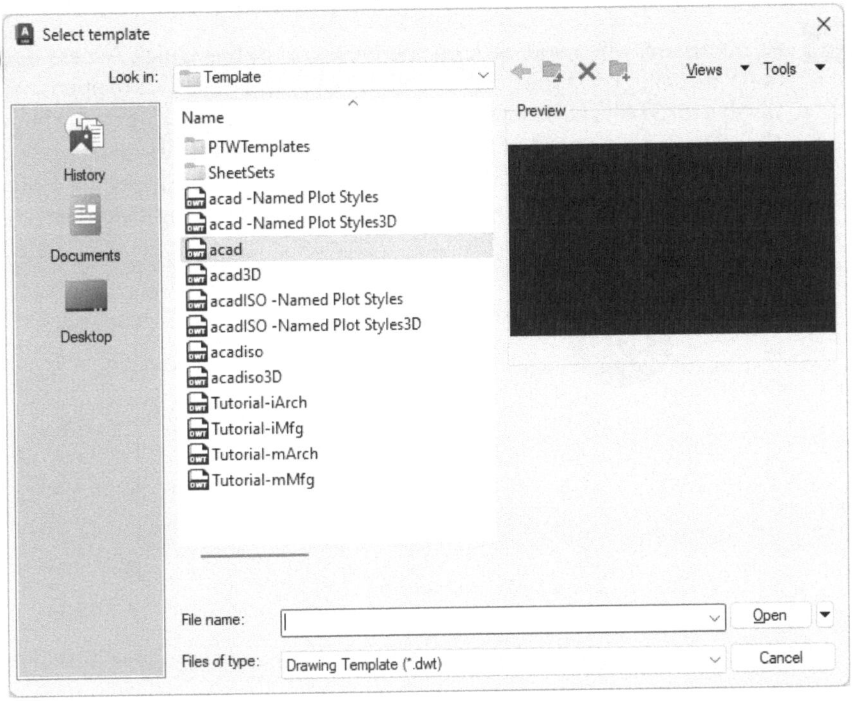

You can also start a new drawing file without a drawing template either in metric or imperial unit system by using the **Select template** dialog box. To do so, click on the down arrow, next to the **Open** button in the **Select template** dialog box, see Figure 1.15. A drop-down list appears. In this drop-down list, the **Open with no Template - Imperial** and **Open with no Template - Metric** options are available. You can click on the required option to start a new drawing file.

1.15

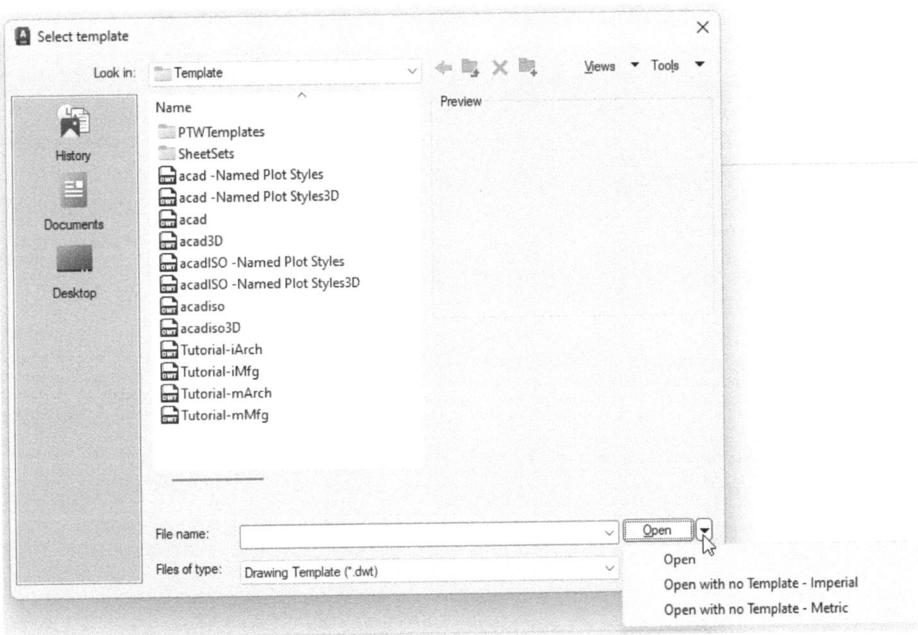

Note: As discussed, when you click on the **New** tool in the **Quick Access Toolbar**, the **Select template** dialog box appears for starting a new drawing file. This happens because the system variable for STARTUP is set to 3. If you set it to 1 then by clicking on the **New** tool, the **Create New Drawing** dialog box appears, see Figure 1.16. You can also start a new drawing by using this **Create New Drawing** dialog box. You will learn about setting system variables and starting a new drawing file by using the **Create New Drawing** dialog box later in this chapter.

1.16

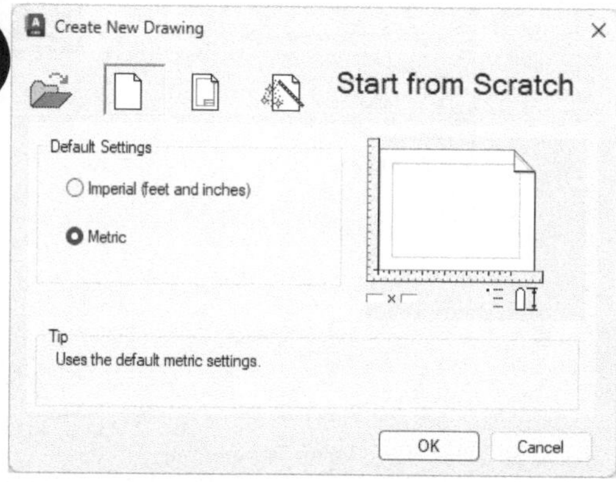

Figure 1.17 shows various components of a new drawing file such as **Application Menu**, **Quick Access Toolbar**, **Ribbon**, **ViewCube**, Command Line window, **Navigation Bar**, and Status Bar. Note that the color theme has been set to light, the background color of the drawing area has been changed to white, and the display of grids is turned off for better clarity. You will learn about changing the color theme, background color of the drawing area, and controlling the display of grids later in this chapter.

1.17

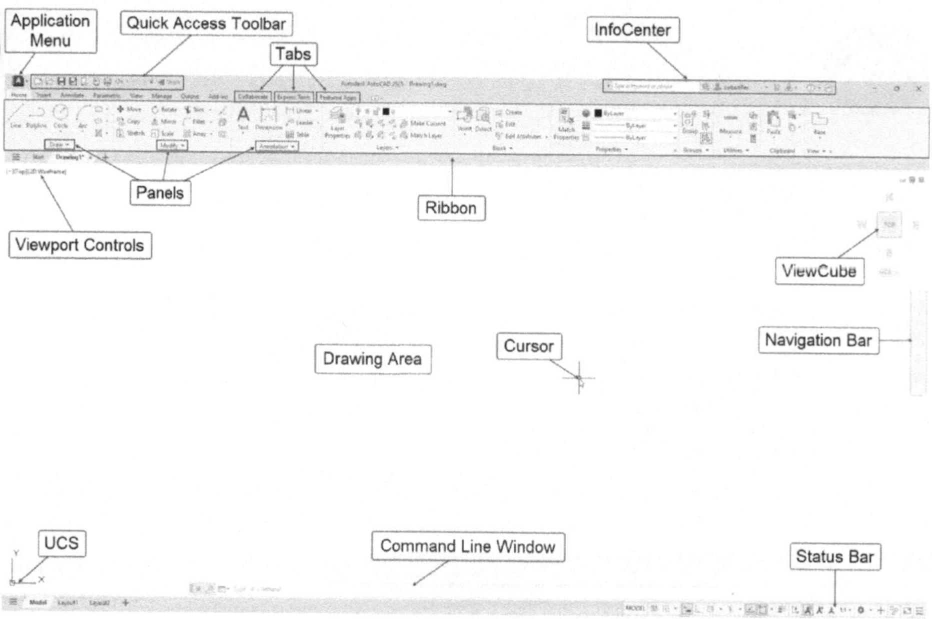

Note that the availability of tools in the **Ribbon** depends upon the activated workspace. By default, the **Drafting and Annotation** workspace is the active workspace of a new drawing. As a result, the tools related to drafting and annotation are available in the **Ribbon**. You can switch among the **Drafting and Annotation**, **3D Basics**, and **3D Modeling** workspaces by using the **Workspace Switching** flyout, see Figure 1.18. You will learn more about workspaces later in this chapter.

1.18

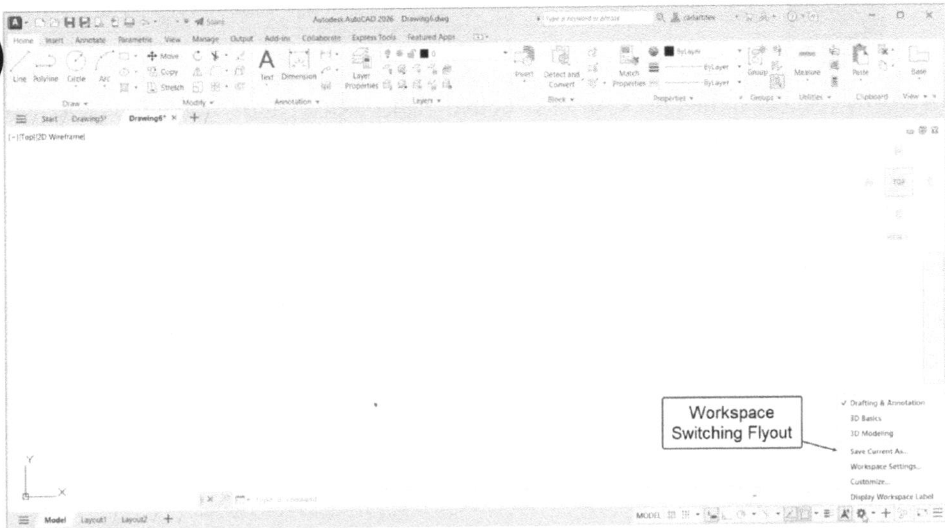

Working with Various Components of a Drawing

The various components of a new drawing such as **Application Menu**, **Quick Access Toolbar**, **Ribbon**, **ViewCube**, Command Line window, **Navigation Bar**, and Status Bar are discussed next.

Application Menu

The **Application Menu** is used for accessing the commonly used tools for starting, opening, saving, exporting, and printing/publishing a drawing file. To invoke the **Application Menu**, click on the **Application** button (red AutoCAD icon) at the upper left corner of the screen, see Figure 1.19.

1.19

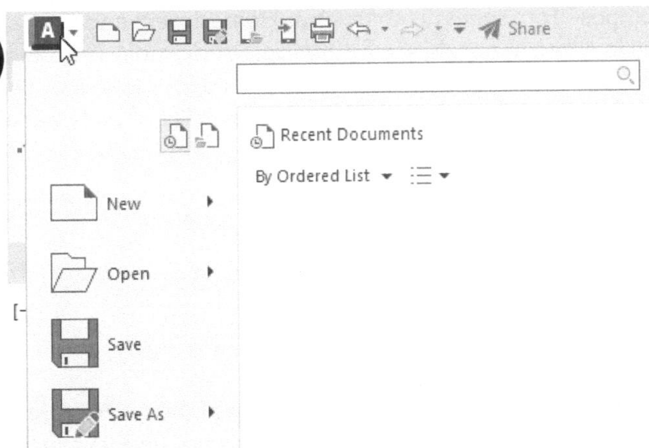

Quick Access Toolbar

The **Quick Access Toolbar** is provided with frequently used tools such as **New, Open, Save, Save As, Plot, Undo, Redo,** and **Share Drawing**, see Figure 1.20. It is available in the upper left corner of the screen. In addition to the default tools, you can customize to add or remove tools in the **Quick Access Toolbar**.

1.20

To add more tools in the **Quick Access Toolbar**, right-click on a tool in the **Quick Access Toolbar**. A flyout appears, see Figure 1.21. In this flyout, click on the **Customize Quick Access Toolbar** option. The **Customize User Interface** window appears. This window displays a list of all the available tools/commands in AutoCAD. Move the cursor over the tool/command to be added to the **Quick Access Toolbar** and then press and hold the left mouse button on it. Next, drag the cursor where you want to add this tool in the **Quick Access Toolbar** and then release the left mouse button. The selected tool gets added to the specified location in the **Quick Access Toolbar**. Similarly, you can add multiple tools by dragging them one by one from the **Customize User Interface** window to the **Quick Access Toolbar**. You can also drag and drop multiple tools at a time in the **Quick Access Toolbar** from the **Customize User Interface** window by pressing and holding the CTRL key. After adding the required tools to the **Quick Access Toolbar**, click on the **OK** button to exit the **Customize User Interface** window.

1.21

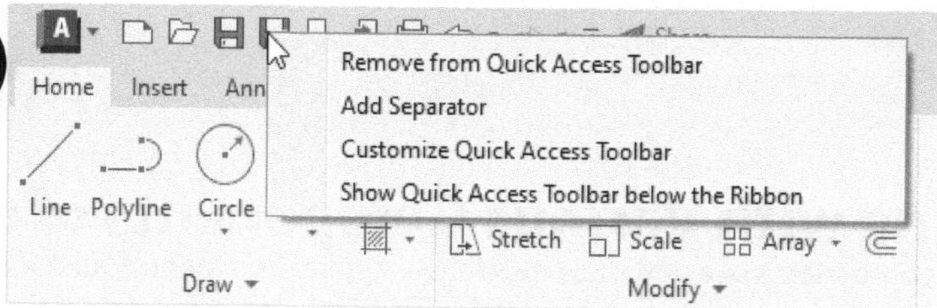

To remove a tool from the **Quick Access Toolbar**, move the cursor over the tool to be removed and then right-click. A flyout appears, see Figure 1.21. In this flyout, click on the **Remove from Quick Access Toolbar** option. The selected tool gets removed from the **Quick Access Toolbar**.

Ribbon

The **Ribbon** is composed of a series of tabs such as **Home, Insert,** and **Annotate** in which a set of similar tools are grouped in different panels, see Figure 1.22. For example, the tools used for creating drawing objects are arranged in the **Draw** panel, and the tools used for modifying or editing objects are grouped in the **Modify** panel, see Figure 1.22. Note that the availability of tools, panels, and tabs in the **Ribbon** depends upon the activated workspace.

1.22

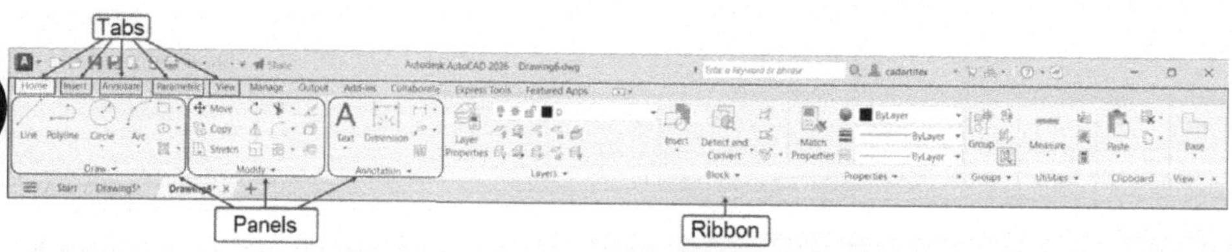

By default, the **Ribbon** is docked horizontally at the top of the drawing area. You can dock the **Ribbon** vertically to the right or left of the drawing area. You can also undock the **Ribbon** such that it can float within the drawing area. To dock the **Ribbon** vertically to the right or left of the drawing area, right-click on a tab in the **Ribbon**. A shortcut menu appears, see Figure 1.23. In this shortcut menu, click on the **Undock** option. The **Ribbon** gets undocked and appears in a floating state in the drawing area. Next, right-click on the title bar of the undocked **Ribbon**. A shortcut menu appears. In this shortcut menu, click on either the **Anchor Left** < or the **Anchor Right** > option. To dock the **Ribbon** back to the default position (horizontally at the top of the drawing area), press and hold the left mouse button on the title bar of the **Ribbon** and then drag the **Ribbon** toward the top of the drawing area. Next, release the left mouse button when the outline of a window appears at the top of the drawing area.

1.23

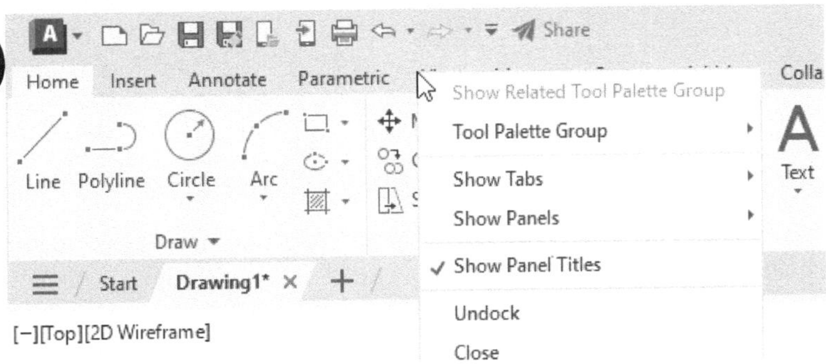

You can also change the default display state of the **Ribbon** (**Full Ribbon**) to three minimized states: **Minimize to Tabs**, **Minimize to Panel Titles**, and **Minimize to Panel Buttons**. To do so, click on the down arrow available at the end of the last tab in the title bar of the **Ribbon**, see Figure 1.24. A flyout appears. In this flyout, click on the required display state. In the **Minimize to Tabs** display state, the **Ribbon** gets minimized such that only the tab titles appear in the **Ribbon**. In the **Minimize to Panel Titles** display state, only the tab and panel titles appear in the **Ribbon**. In the **Minimize to Panel Buttons** display state, only the tab titles and panel buttons appear in the **Ribbon**.

1.24

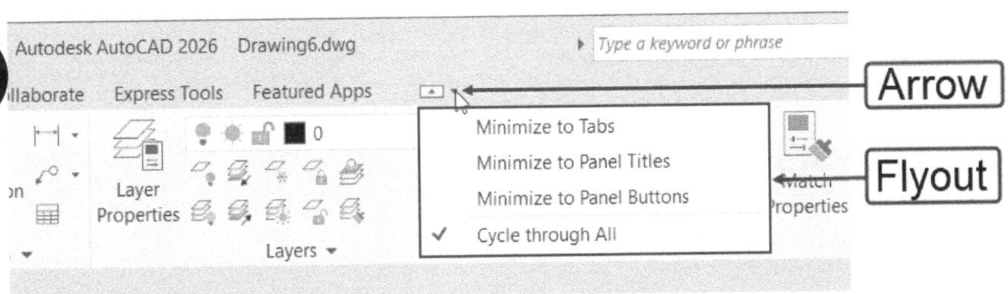

You can also cycle through different states of the **Ribbon** by clicking on the small rectangular button with a black arrow in it, located at the end of the last tab in the **Ribbon**, see Figure 1.25. On clicking this rectangular button, you can cycle through all four display states of the **Ribbon** in a sequence, **Full Ribbon**, **Minimize to Panel Buttons**, **Minimize to Panel Titles**, and **Minimize to Tabs**.

1.25

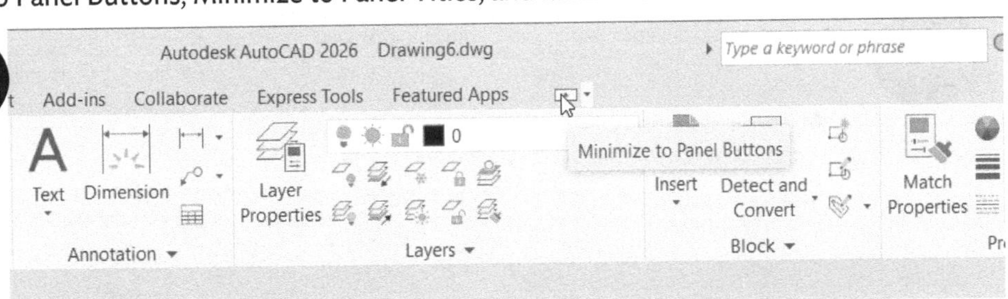

InfoCenter

The **InfoCenter** is available at the upper right corner of the AutoCAD window, see Figure 1.26. It is used for accessing help documents for finding information related to a topic. Also, it provides tools to access the Autodesk App Store, Sign In to an Autodesk account, Autodesk YouTube/Facebook/Twitter channels, and so on. The various components of the **InfoCenter** are discussed next.

1.26

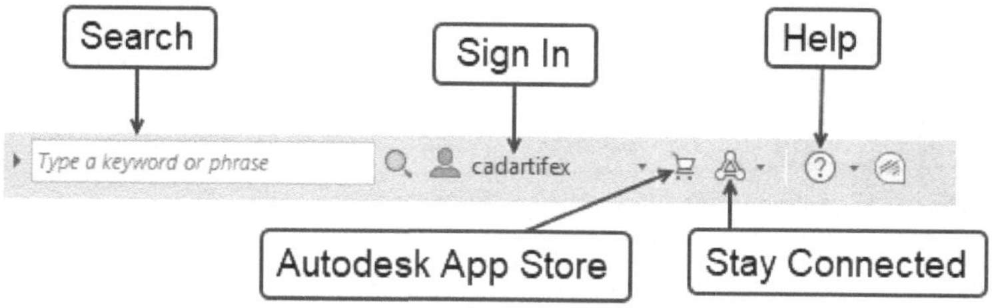

Search

The **Search** field is used for entering a keyword of a topic or a command/tool to find information related to it in the help documents.

Sign In

The **Sign In** area of the **InfoCenter** displays your name. When you click on your name, a flyout appears, see Figure 1.27. The options in this flyout are used for accessing your account details, exploring purchase options, managing licenses, privacy settings, and signing out of your Autodesk account.

1.27

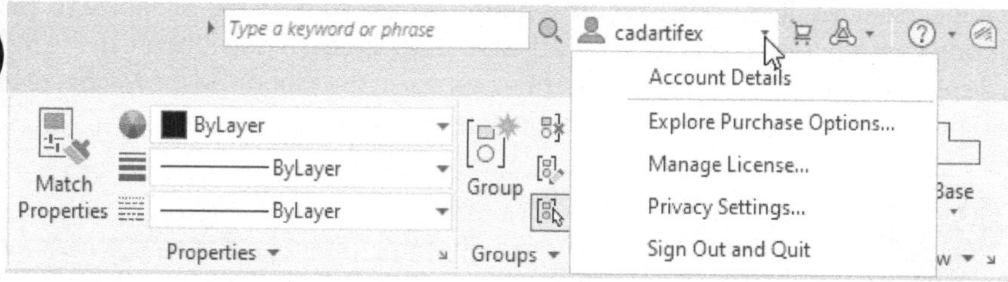

Autodesk App Store

The **Autodesk App Store** tool is used for accessing the Autodesk App Store web page for downloading plug-ins and Autodesk applications.

Stay Connected

The **Stay Connected** tool is used for staying connected with the Autodesk online community. When you click on **Stay Connected** in the **InfoCenter**, a flyout appears, see Figure 1.28. This flyout provides various options to stay connected with Autodesk.

1.28

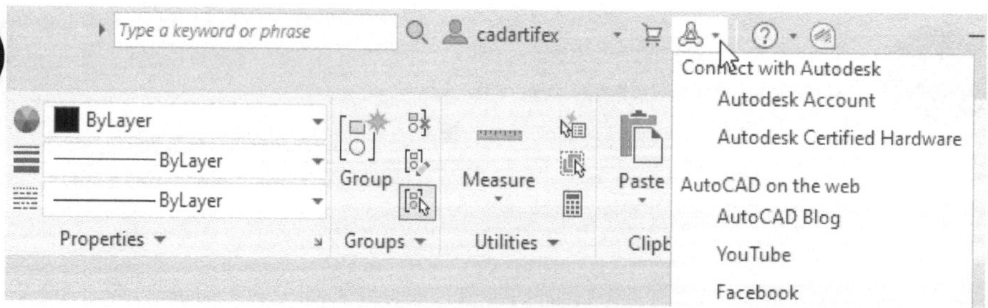

Help

The **Help** tool is used for accessing online help documents. When you click on the **Help** tool in the **InfoCenter**, the online help document gets opened. If you click on the down arrow next to the **Help** tool in the **InfoCenter**, a flyout appears, see Figure 1.29. By using the tools in this flyout, you can access online help documents, download offline help documents, send feedback, get product information, and so on.

1.29

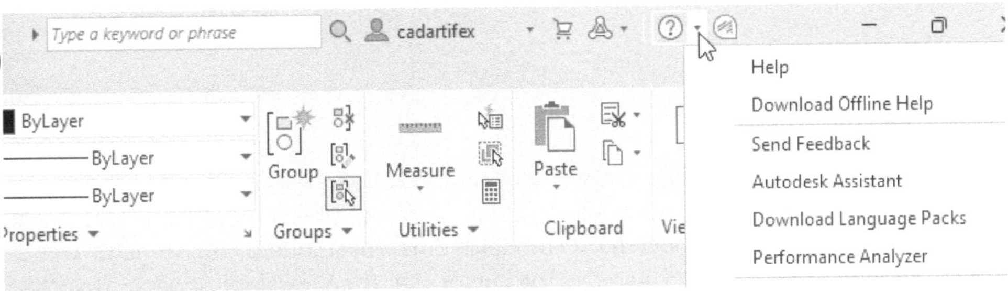

Command Line Window

A small horizontal window appears at the bottom of the drawing area and is known as the Command Line window, see Figure 1.30.

1.30

The Command Line window is used for entering commands and displays subsequent command prompt sequence. By default, the Command Line window displays one line of text (command prompt), which provides information about the action to be taken and various options based on the currently active command or tool. Notice that as you continue working through a command or tool, the previous command prompts get scrolled up and appear in the faded background just above the Command Line window, see Figure 1.31. Note that by default, only the last three command prompt lines appear above the Command Line window. To display all the previous command prompt lines, press the F2 key. You can also increase or decrease the display area of the Command Line window to show the previous command prompts. To do so, move the cursor over the top edge of the Command Line window and then drag it by pressing and holding the left mouse button.

1.31

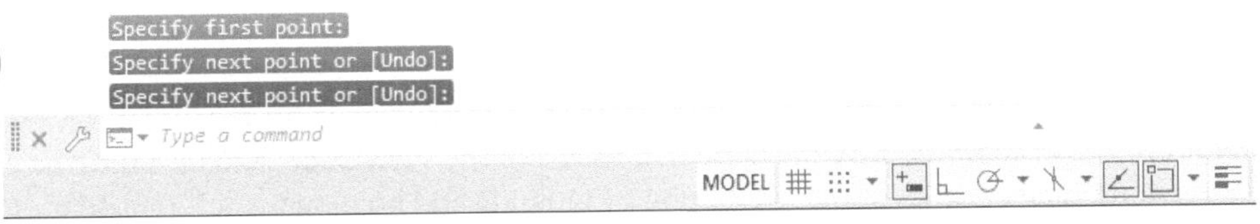

Tip: It is recommended for new users to pay attention to the command prompt as through it, AutoCAD communicates with you and informs you about the action to be taken.

Note: If the display of the Command Line window is turned off or it does not appear in the drawing area, then press the CTRL + 9 key to display it again in the drawing area.

ViewCube

The **ViewCube** is available at the upper right corner of the drawing area, see Figures 1.32 and 1.33.

1.32

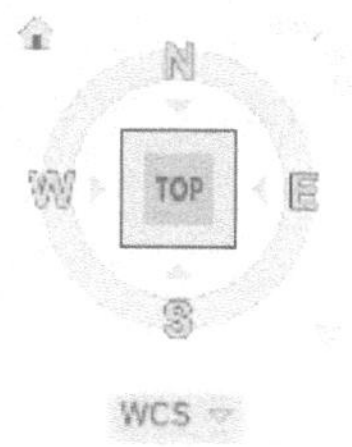

The **ViewCube** is used for changing the view/orientation of a drawing or model. You can switch between standard and isometric views of a model by using the **ViewCube**. It is primarily used in a 3D modeling environment where you can view the 3D model in different standard and isometric views. By default, it is in an inactive state. When you move the cursor over the **ViewCube**, it becomes active and works as a navigation tool. You can navigate a drawing by using the **ViewCube** components, see Figure 1.33. The various **ViewCube** components are discussed next.

1.33

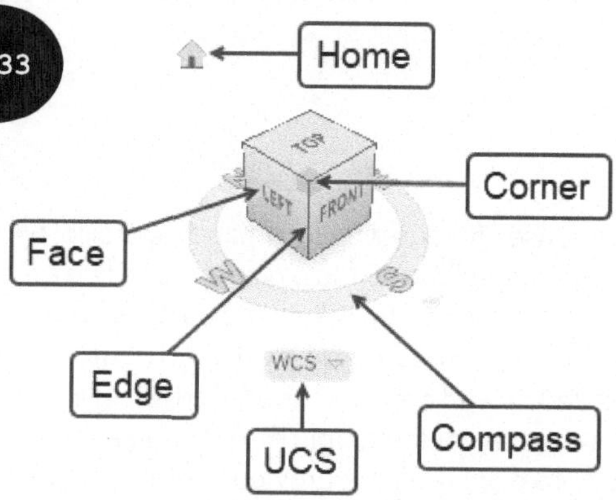

Home

The **Home** icon of the **ViewCube** is used for bringing the current view of the drawing to the default home position.

Corner

A corner of the **ViewCube** is used for getting an isometric view or for rotating the view freely in all directions. To get an isometric view, click on a corner of the **ViewCube**, and to rotate the view freely in all directions, drag a corner of the **ViewCube** by pressing and holding the left mouse button.

Compass

The **Compass** is used for rotating the view. To do so, press and hold the left mouse button on the **Compass** ring and then drag the cursor.

Edge

An edge of the **ViewCube** is used for getting an edge-on view or for rotating the view freely in all directions. To get an edge-on view, click on the edge of the **ViewCube**, and to rotate the view freely in all directions, drag an edge of the **ViewCube** by pressing and holding the left mouse button.

Face
A face of the **ViewCube** is used for getting an orthogonal view such as a top, front, or right. For example, to get a top view of the drawing or model, click on the top face of the **ViewCube**.

UCS
When you click on the down arrow available in the **UCS** option of the **ViewCube**, the **UCS** drop-down list appears, see Figure 1.34. By using the options in this drop-down list, you can select an existing UCS or create a new UCS, see Figure 1.34. The term UCS stands for User Coordinate System, which is used for defining points in 2D and 3D environments. By default, AutoCAD is provided with a World Coordinate System (WCS), which is a global system. You will learn more about coordinate systems in later chapters.

1.34

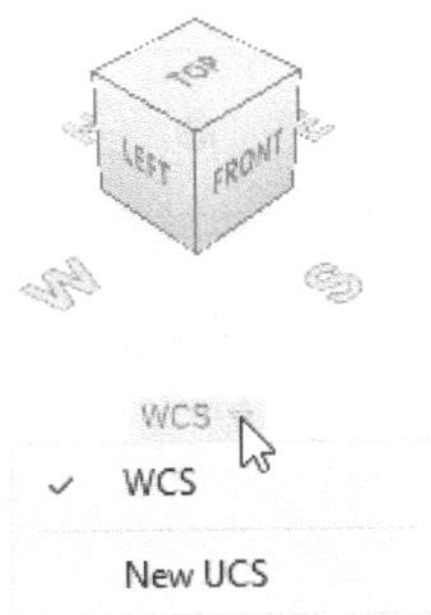

Note: If the **ViewCube** is not displayed on the right corner of the drawing area, then click on the **View Cube** tool in the **Viewport Tools** panel of the **View** tab in the **Ribbon**, see Figure 1.35.

1.35

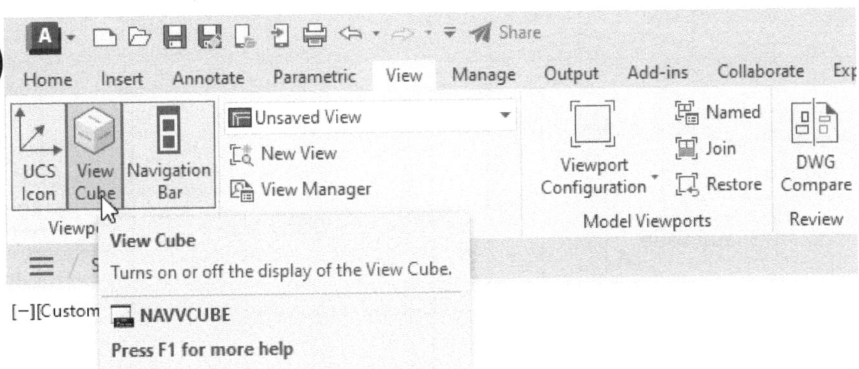

Navigation Bar
The **Navigation Bar** is used for accessing navigation tools such as **Zoom** and **Pan**, see Figure 1.36. It is available to the right of the drawing area. You can turn on or off the display of the **Navigation Bar** by clicking on the **Navigation Bar** tool in the **Viewport Tools** panel of the **View** tab in the **Ribbon**, see Figure 1.37. The various navigation tools of the **Navigation Bar** are discussed in Chapter 2.

1.36

1.37

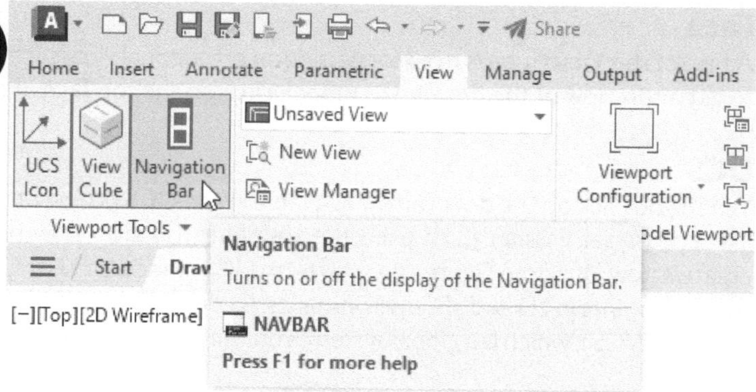

Status Bar

The Status Bar provides quick access to some of the commonly used drawing tools, which allow you to toggle settings such as grid, snap, dynamic input mode, ortho mode, polar tracking, and object snap, see Figure 1.38. In addition to the default tools in the Status Bar, you can customize to add or remove tools in it, as per the requirement. To customize the Status Bar, click on the **Customization** tool in the Status Bar, see Figure 1.38. The **Customization** menu appears, see Figure 1.39.

1.38

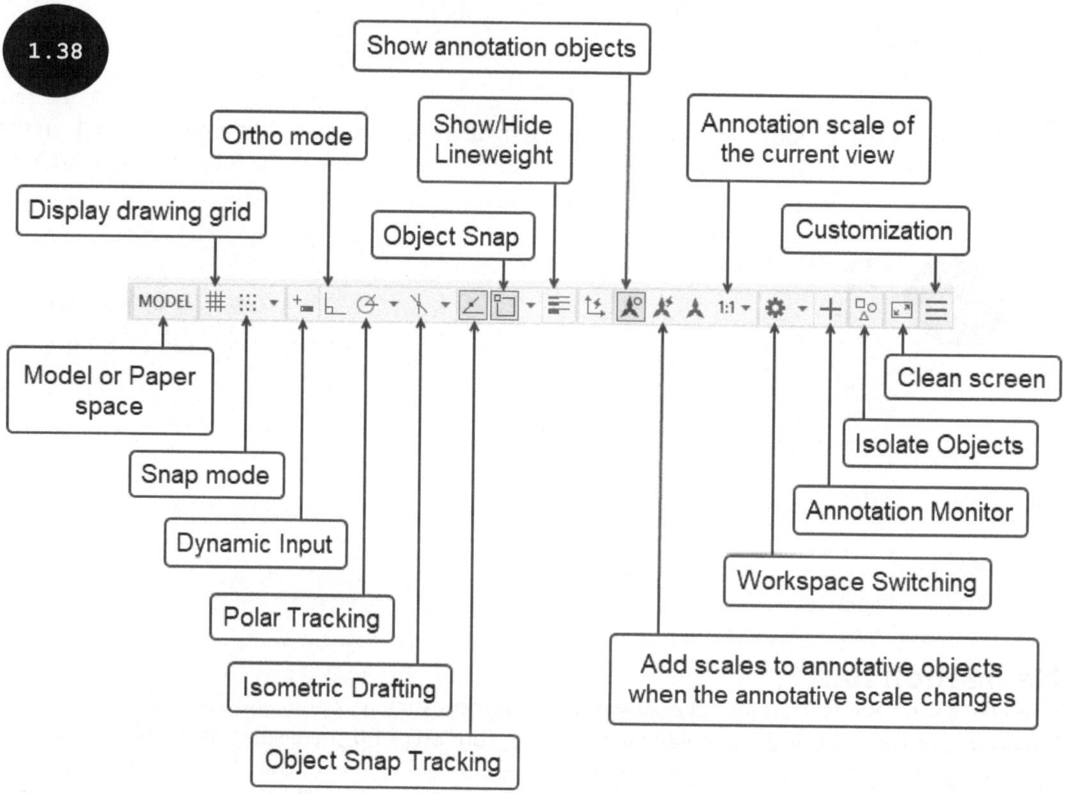

1.39

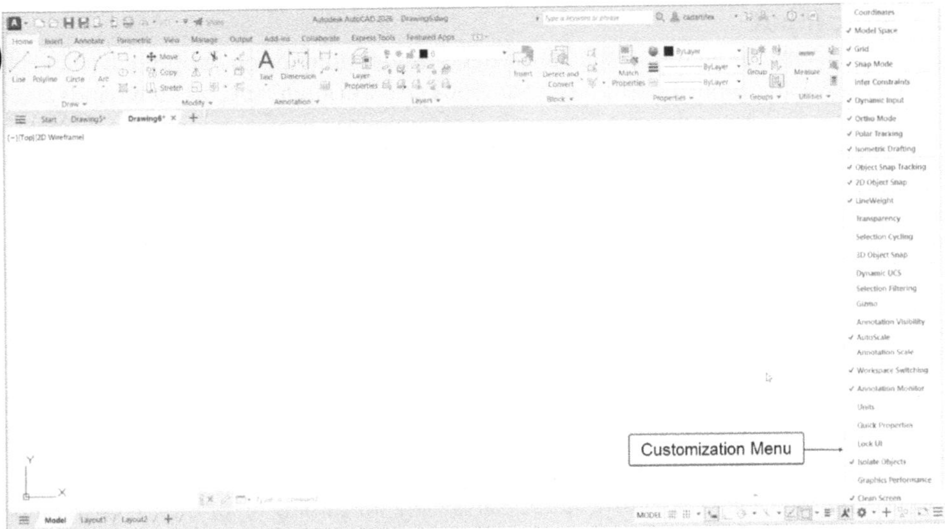

In the **Customization** menu, a tick mark in front of the tools indicates that they are currently available in the Status Bar. Click on the tools in the **Customization** menu to add or remove them from the Status Bar. Some of the tools in the Status Bar are discussed next.

Model or Paper space

The **Model or Paper space** tool of the Status Bar is used for toggling between the Model space and Paper space environments. When you start AutoCAD, the Model space is the default activated environment for creating drawings. You can create drawings in the Model space, whereas the Paper space is used for plotting drawings and generating different drawing views. You will learn more about the Model space and Paper space in Chapter 11.

Display drawing grid

The **Display drawing grid** tool of the Status Bar is used for turning on or off the display of grids in the drawing area. To turn on or off the display of grids, click on the **Display drawing grid** tool in the Status Bar or press the F7 key. You can also change the grid settings by using this tool. To do so, right-click on the **Display drawing grid** tool in the Status Bar. The **Grid Settings** option appears. Click on the **Grid Settings** option. The **Drafting Settings** dialog box appears. By using the options in the **Snap and Grid** tab of this dialog box, you can change the grid settings as required. You will learn more about specifying the grid settings in Chapter 2.

Snap Mode

The **Snap mode** tool of the Status Bar is used for turning on or off the snap mode. You can also press the F9 key to turn it on or off. The snap mode allows the cursor to move at a fixed incremental distance in the drawing area. For example, if the snap mode setting is specified to 1 unit in both the X and Y directions, then the cursor will move 1 unit incremental distance in the X-direction as well as in the Y-direction. To specify the snap mode settings, right-click on the **Snap mode** tool in the Status Bar and then click on the **Snap Settings** option in the shortcut menu that appears. The **Drafting Settings** dialog box appears. By using the options in the **Snap and Grid** tab of this dialog box, you can specify the snap settings as required. You will learn more about specifying the snap settings in Chapter 2.

Dynamic Input

The **Dynamic Input** tool of the Status Bar is used for turning on or off the Dynamic Input mode. If the Dynamic Input mode is turned on, you can enter inputs such as commands and coordinates near the cursor tip in the drawing area instead of entering in the Command Line window. It acts as an alternative method of entering commands in AutoCAD. For example, when a command is in progress, the Dynamic Input boxes appear near the cursor tip which allows you to enter coordinates and specify options, see Figure 1.40. You will learn more about entering coordinates and commands by using the Dynamic Input boxes and Command Line window in later chapters.

1.40

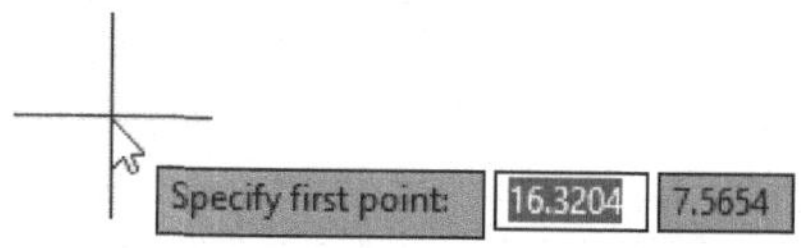

Ortho Mode

The **Ortho Mode** tool of the Status Bar is used for turning on or off the Ortho mode. You can also press the F8 key to turn on or off the Ortho mode. When the Ortho mode is turned on, the movement of the cursor gets restricted to horizontal and vertical only. As a result, you can only draw straight lines at right angles.

Polar Tracking

The **Polar Tracking** tool of the Status Bar is used for turning on or off the Polar tracking mode. When the Polar tracking mode is activated, the movement of the cursor gets snapped to the specified increment angle in the drawing area. To specify an incremental angle value, right-click on the **Polar Tracking** button in the Status Bar. A flyout appears, see Figure 1.41. This flyout displays a list of pre-defined incremental angles. You can select the required increment angle in this flyout. You can also specify a new increment angle other than the increment angles listed in the flyout. To specify a new increment angle, click on the **Tracking Settings** option in the flyout. The **Drafting Settings** dialog box appears. In this dialog box, specify the increment angle in the **Increment angle** field of the **Polar Tracking** tab and then click on the **OK** button. The new increment angle for polar tracking gets specified.

1.41

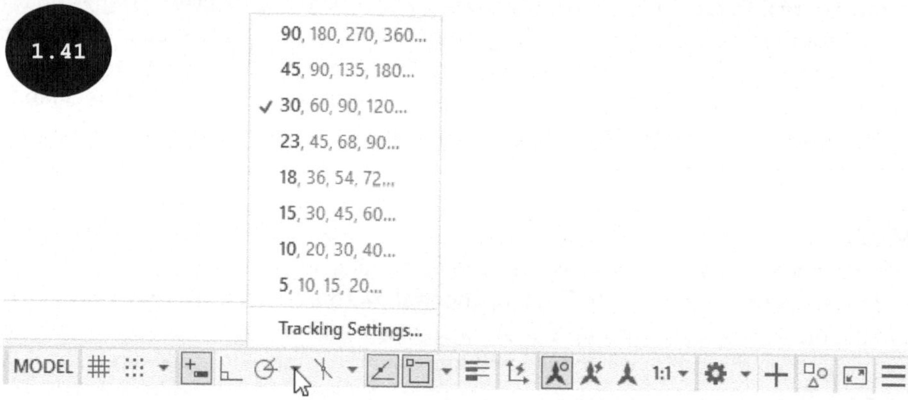

Isometric Drafting

The **Isometric Drafting** tool of the Status Bar is used for turning on or off the Isometric Drafting mode. When the Isometric Drafting mode is turned on, you can easily create the 2D isometric representation of a 3D model. You can select the **isoplane Left, isoplane Top**, or **isoplane Right** as the current 2D isometric drafting plane for creating the 2D isometric drawing. By default, the **isoplane Left** drafting plane is selected as the current 2D isometric drafting plane. To select the required 2D isometric drafting plane, click on the down arrow next to the **Isometric Drafting** tool in the Status Bar. A flyout appears, see Figure 1.42. In this flyout, click on the required 2D isometric drafting plane for creating an isometric drawing.

1.42

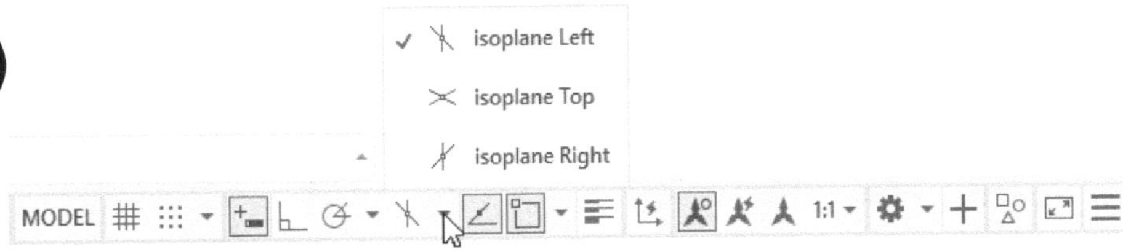

Object Snap Tracking

The **Object Snap Tracking** tool of the Status Bar is used for turning on or off the Object Snap Tracking mode. The Object Snap Tracking mode works in conjunction with the Object Snap mode and is used for specifying new points aligned to the existing points or locations in a drawing. For example, to draw a circle at the center of a rectangle, move the cursor over the midpoint of the horizontal line 'A' (see Figure 1.43) and then move the cursor vertically downward when the cursor snaps to the midpoint of the horizontal line. A vertical tracking line appears, see Figure 1.43. Next, move the cursor over the midpoint of the vertical line 'B' and then move the cursor horizontally toward right. A horizontal tracking line appears, see Figure 1.44. Next, move the cursor at the intersection of both the tracking lines and then click to specify the midpoint of the circle, see Figure 1.45.

1.43

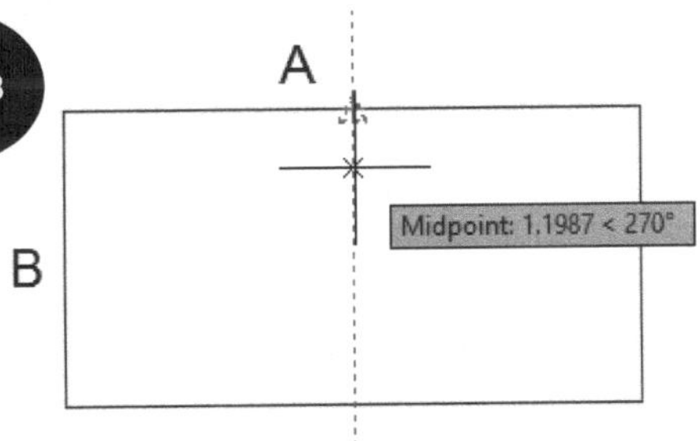

1.44

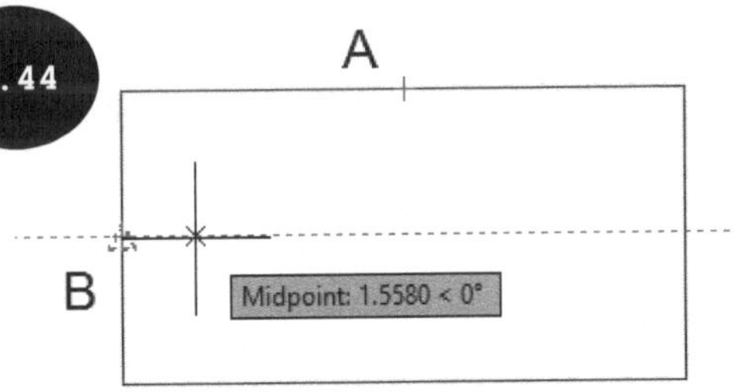

1.45

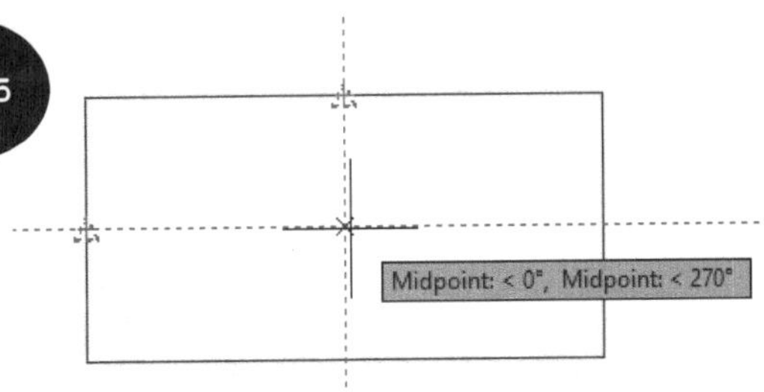

Object Snap

The **Object Snap** tool of the Status Bar is used for turning on or off the Object Snap mode. The Object Snap mode is used for snapping the cursor over the existing objects of the drawing such as midpoint, endpoint, and intersection. It is a very useful method for specifying exact points in the drawing area. When the Object Snap mode is turned on, the cursor snaps to the existing objects of the drawing as per the specified object snap settings. To specify or control the object snap settings, right-click on the **Object Snap** tool in the Status Bar. A flyout appears, see Figure 1.46. This flyout displays a list of all the object snaps. Note that a tick mark in the front of the object snaps in the flyout indicates that they are activated. You can click on the required object snaps to activate or deactivate them in the flyout. Note that the cursor snaps to the objects in the drawing area depending upon the activated object snaps. For example, if only the **Endpoint** object snap is activated then the cursor only snaps to the endpoints of the existing objects in the drawing area, see Figure 1.47.

1.46

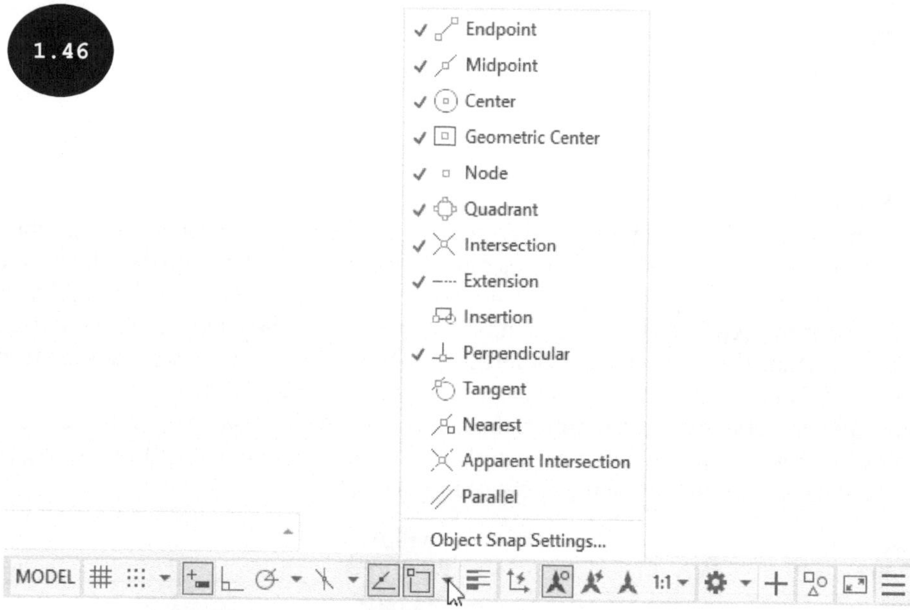

1.47

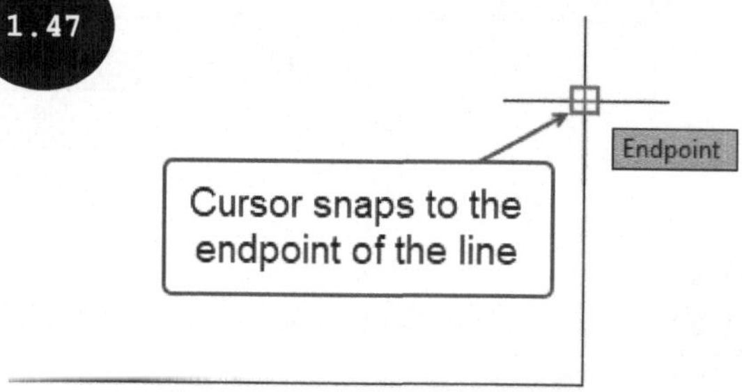

You can also invoke the **Drafting Settings** dialog box by clicking on the **Object Snap Settings** option in the flyout to control the object snap setting, see Figure 1.48. In the **Object Snap** tab of the dialog box, select the required object snap check boxes to activate them. For example, on selecting the **Endpoint** check box, the Endpoint object snap is activated, and the cursor snaps to the endpoints of the existing drawing objects in the drawing area. Similarly, on selecting the **Midpoint** check box, the Midpoint object snap is activated, and the cursor snaps to the midpoints of the drawing objects in the drawing area. To select all the object snap check boxes, click on the **Select All** button in the dialog box. Similarly, to uncheck all the object snap check boxes, click on the **Clear All** button in the dialog box. After selecting the required object snap check boxes in the dialog box, and click on the **OK** button.

1.48

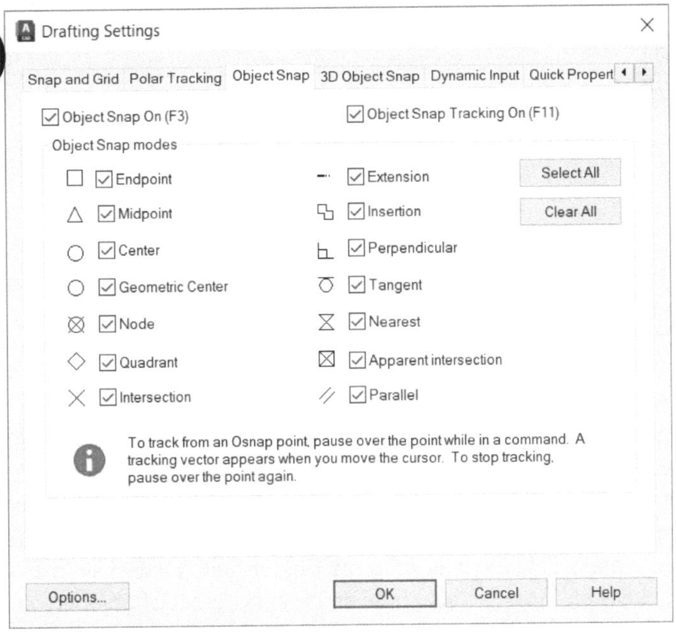

Show/Hide Lineweight

The **Show/Hide Lineweight** tool is used for turning on or off the display of the object lineweight in the drawing area. You will learn more about specifying lineweight to drawing objects in later chapters.

Show annotation objects

The **Show annotation objects** tool is used for turning on or off the display of annotative objects in the drawing area.

Annotation scale of the current view

1:1 The **Annotation scale of the current view** flyout is used for selecting the annotation scale for the annotative objects in the Model space. To invoke this flyout, click on the down arrow next to the **Annotation scale of the current view** button in the Status Bar.

Workspace Switching

The **Workspace Switching** flyout is used for switching between the AutoCAD workspaces: **Drafting & Annotation**, **3D Basics**, and **3D Modeling**. To invoke the **Workspace Switching** flyout, click on the down arrow next to the **Workspace Switching** button in the Status Bar, see Figure 1.49. Note that the availability of tools in the **Ribbon** depends upon the currently active workspace.

1.49

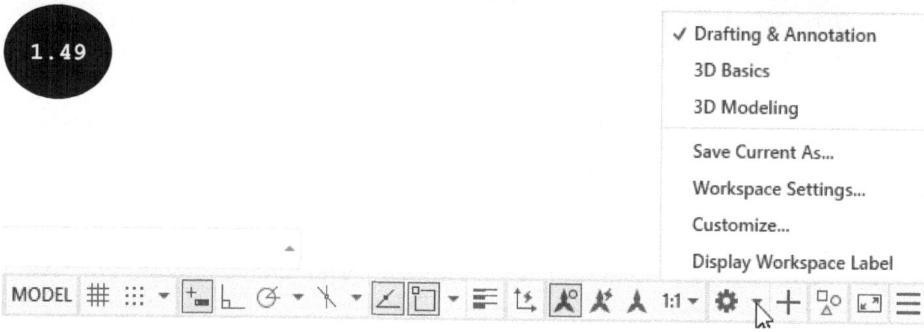

Isolate Objects

The **Isolate Objects** tool is used for isolating objects in the drawing area. You can isolate an object or a set of objects in the drawing area. To isolate objects, click on the **Isolate Objects** tool in the Status Bar. A flyout appears, see Figure 1.50. In this flyout, click on the **Isolate Objects** tool. You are prompted to select objects to be isolated in the drawing area. Select the objects to be isolated and then right-click or press ENTER. The selected objects get isolated such that the remaining drawing objects become invisible. You can also hide an object or a set of objects in the drawing area by using the **Hide Objects** tool of the flyout. To hide objects in the drawing area, click on the **Hide Objects** tool in the flyout, see Figure 1.50. You are prompted to select objects to be hidden. Select the objects to be hidden and then right-click or press ENTER. The selected objects are hidden in the drawing area. To display all the drawing objects back in the drawing area or to end the object isolation, click on the **End Object Isolation** tool in the flyout, see Figure 1.51.

1.50

1.51

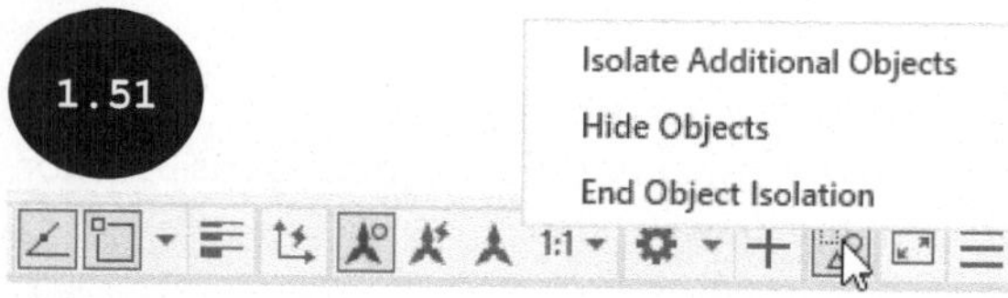

Clean Screen

The **Clean screen** tool of the Status Bar is used for expanding the drawing display area by hiding the **Ribbon** and all the available toolbars except the Command Line window, Status Bar, and Quick Access Toolbar.

Customization

The **Customization** tool is used for customizing the Status Bar such that you can add or remove tools in it. To customize the Status Bar, click on the **Customization** tool in the Status Bar. The **Customization** menu appears, which displays a list of all the tools that can be added to the Status Bar. Note that a tick mark in front of the tools in the **Customization** menu indicates that they are currently available in the Status Bar. You can click on the tools in the **Customization** menu to add or remove them in the Status Bar.

Starting a New Drawing File by using the Create New Drawing dialog box

As discussed, when you click on the **New** tool in the **Quick Access Toolbar** for starting a new drawing file, the **Select template** dialog box appears, by default. This happens because the system variable for STARTUP is set to 3. If you set up the system variable for STARTUP to 1, then on clicking the **New** tool in the **Quick Access Toolbar**, the **Create New Drawing** dialog box appears for starting a new drawing file. To do so, enter **STARTUP** in the Command Line window and then press ENTER. You are prompted to enter a new value for STARTUP.

```
Enter new value for STARTUP <3>:
```

Next, enter **1** in the Command Line window and then press ENTER. The new system variable for the STARTUP is set to 1. Now, when you click on the **New** tool in the **Quick Access Toolbar** for starting a new drawing file, the **Create New Drawing** dialog box appears, see Figure 1.52. By using the **Create New Drawing** dialog box, you can start a new drawing file from scratch, using a template, or a wizard. The methods for starting a new drawing file by using the **Create New Drawing** dialog box are discussed next.

1.52

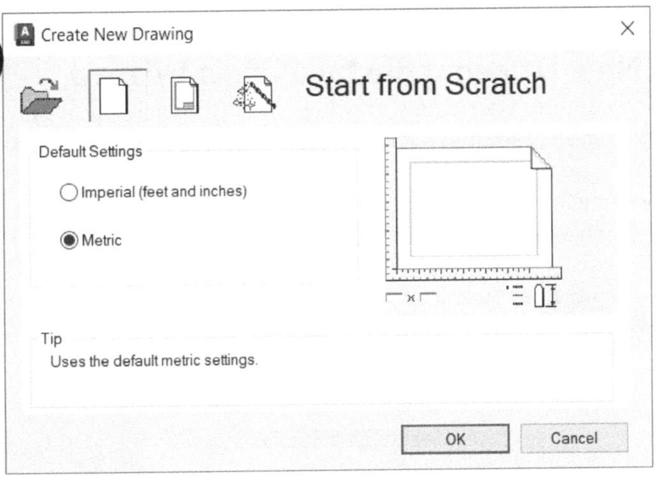

Starting a New Drawing file from Scratch

To start a new drawing file from scratch by using the **Create New Drawing** dialog box, ensure that the **Start from Scratch** button is activated in the dialog box, see Figure 1.52. You can start a new drawing file from scratch either with the default imperial (*acad.dwt*) or metric (*acadiso.dwt*) settings. By default, the **Metric** radio button is selected in the dialog box. As a result, on clicking the **OK** button, a new drawing file with default metric settings is invoked. To start a new drawing file with default imperial settings, select the **Imperial (feet and inches)** radio button in the dialog box and then click on the **OK** button.

Starting a New Drawing file by using a Template

To start a new drawing file by using a standard drawing template, click on the **Use a Template** button in the **Create New Drawing** dialog box. A list of drawing templates appears in the dialog box, see Figure 1.53. By default, the *Acad.dwt* drawing template is selected in the dialog box. Note that the selection of the default template depends on the settings specified while installing AutoCAD. Select the required template in this dialog box to start a new drawing file. Note that a drawing template contains drawing settings such as units, limits, text height, and scale factor. After selecting the required drawing template, click on the **OK** button. The new drawing file gets invoked.

1.53

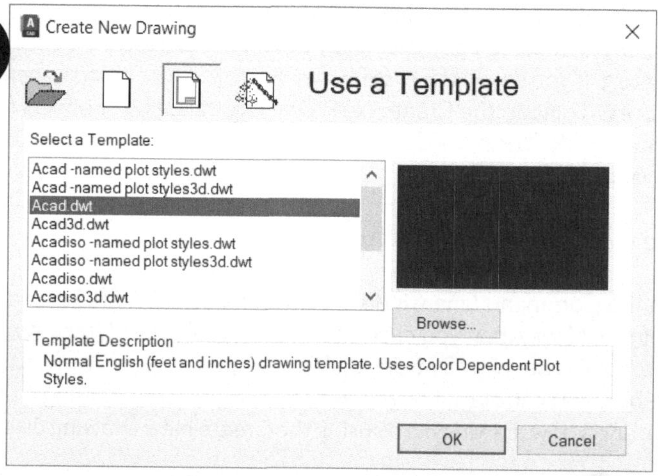

Starting a New Drawing file by using a Wizard

In AutoCAD, you can also start a new drawing with the **Advanced Setup** and **Quick Setup** wizards which allow you to specify settings such as unit, angle, angle measurement, angle direction, and area for the new drawing. To start a new drawing file by using a wizard, click on the **Use a Wizard** button in the **Create New Drawing** dialog box, see Figure 1.54. The **Advanced Setup** and **Quick Setup** options appear in the **Select a Wizard** area of the dialog box, see Figure 1.54.

1.54

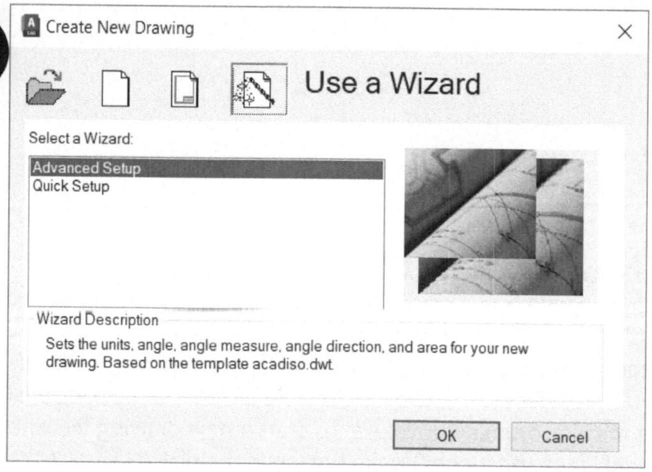

The **Advanced Setup** option allows you to specify a unit, angle, angle measurement, angle direction, and so on for the new drawing file, whereas the **Quick Setup** option only allows you to specify unit and area settings for the drawing file.

To start a new drawing with the **Advanced Setup** wizard, select the **Advanced Setup** option in the **Select a Wizard** area of the dialog box and then click on the **OK** button. The **Advanced Setup** dialog box appears on the **Units** page, see Figure 1.55. The options in the **Units** page of the **Advanced Setup** dialog box are used for setting the unit format of measurement in the drawing. Select the required unit format: Decimal, Engineering, Architectural, Fractional, or Scientific by choosing the respective radio button. You can also specify the precision for the measurement by using the **Precision** drop-down list on the **Units** page. After selecting the unit and precision, click on the **Next** button. The **Angle** page of the **Advanced Setup** dialog box appears, see Figure 1.56.

1.55

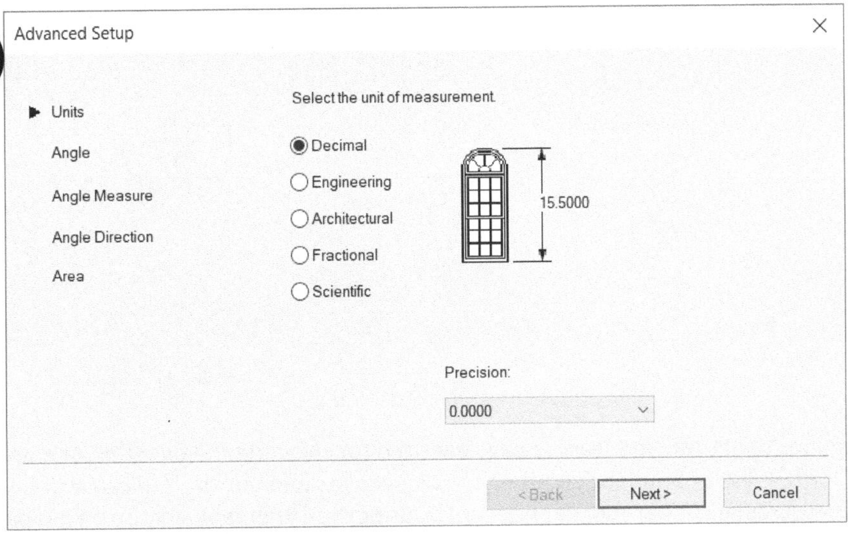

1.56

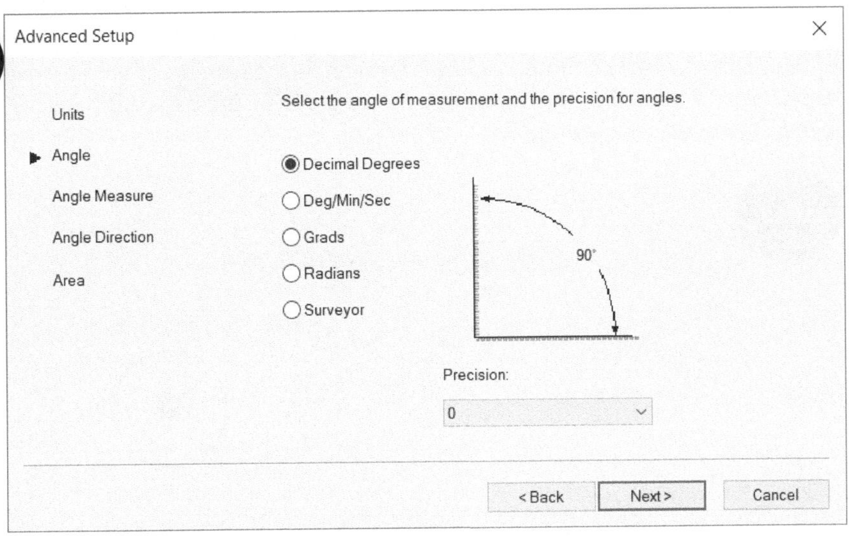

The options in the **Angle** page of the **Advanced Setup** dialog box are used for setting the angle of measurement and the precision of angle measurement for the drawing. Select the required angle of measurement: Decimal Degrees, Deg/Min/Sec, Grads, Radians, or Surveyor by choosing the respective radio button. Also, select the precision of the angle measurement by using the **Precision** drop-down list on the **Angle** page. After selecting the required angle and precision, click on the **Next** button. The **Angle Measure** page of the **Advanced Setup** dialog box appears, see Figure 1.57.

1.57

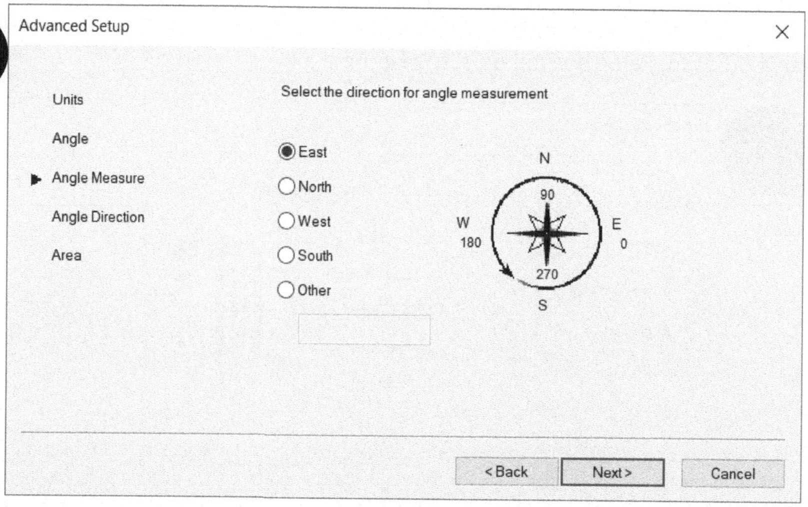

The options on the **Angle Measure** page are used for selecting the direction of angle measurement: East, North, West, or South by choosing the respective radio button. You can also set the direction of angle measurement as per your requirement by using the **Other** radio button on this page. On selecting the **Other** radio button, the field below gets enabled. In this field, you can specify the direction of angle measurement, as required. Note that by default, the **East** radio button is selected on this page. As a result, the angle measures from the east (0-degrees) in the counter-clockwise orientation. You can set the orientation (clockwise or counter-clockwise) for angle measurement on the **Angle Direction** page which appears on clicking the **Next** button on the **Angle Measure** page after specifying the direction of angle measurement, see Figure 1.58.

1.58

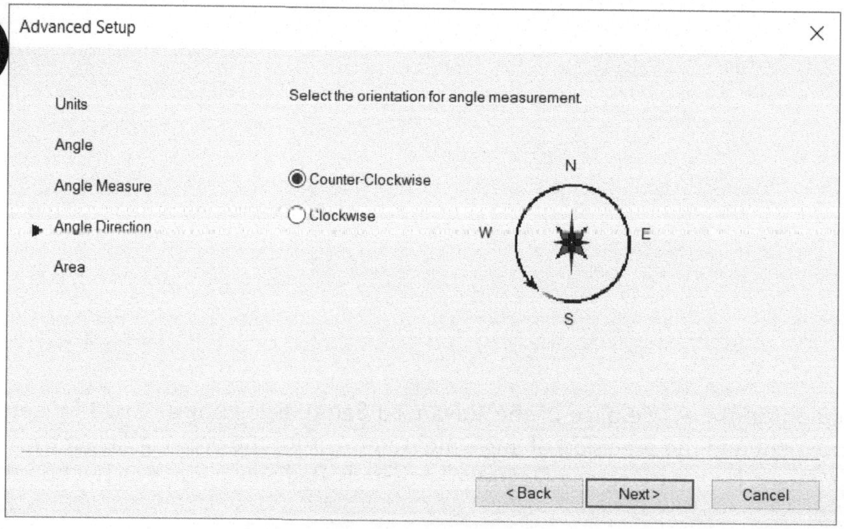

The **Angle Direction** page of the **Advanced Setup** dialog box is used for specifying the orientation for the angle measurement. You can select either a counter-clockwise or clockwise orientation for the angle measurement by selecting the respective radio button on this page. After selecting the orientation for angle measurement, click on the **Next** button. The **Area** page of the **Advanced Setup** dialog box appears, see Figure 1.59.

1.59

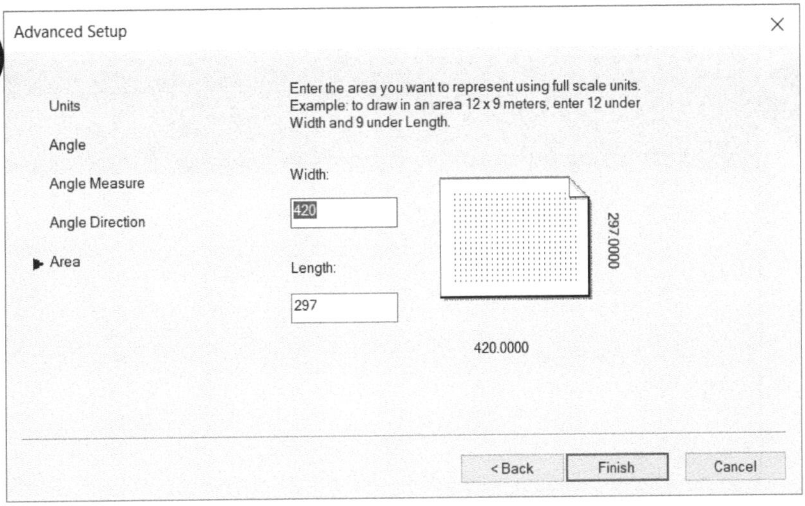

The **Area** page of the **Advanced Setup** dialog box is used for specifying the drawing area for creating the drawing. You can specify the drawing area by entering the width and length in the **Width** and **Length** fields of the page, respectively. After specifying all the drawing settings, click on the **Finish** button. A new drawing with the specified settings is invoked.

Similar to the **Advanced Setup** wizard, you can also start a new drawing with the **Quick Setup** wizard of the **Create New Drawing** dialog box. The only difference is that the **Quick Setup** wizard allows you to specify only unit and area settings of the dialog box, see Figure 1.60.

1.60

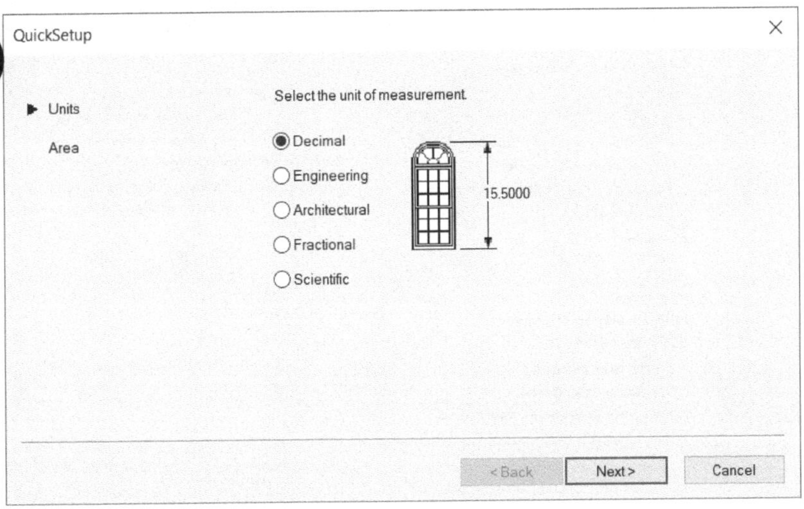

Changing the Color Theme

AutoCAD is provided with two color themes: dark color theme and light color theme. The dark color theme is the default color theme of AutoCAD. As a result, the **Ribbon**, **Palettes**, and several other interface components of AutoCAD appear in the dark color theme, see Figure 1.61. You can change the color theme by using the **Options** dialog box. To invoke the **Options** dialog box, enter **OP** in the Command Line window and then press ENTER. Figure 1.62 shows the **Options** dialog box.

1.61

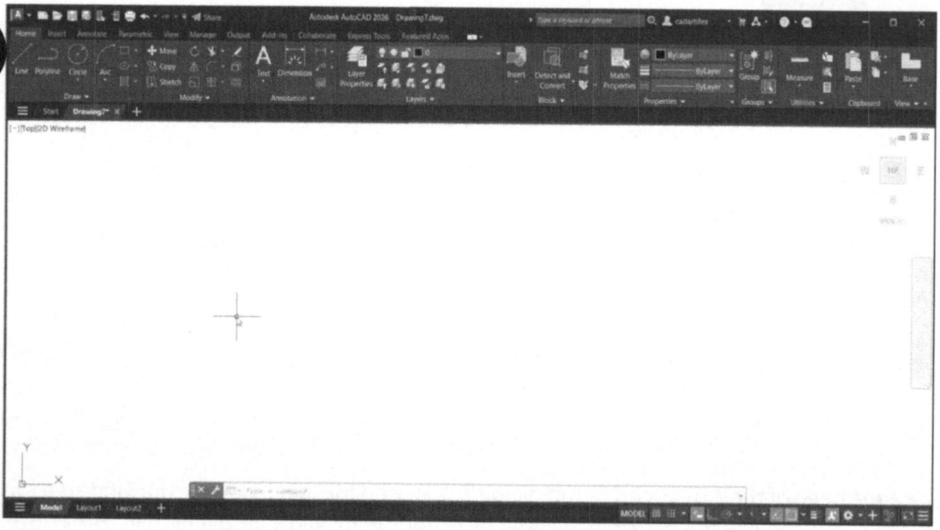

1.62

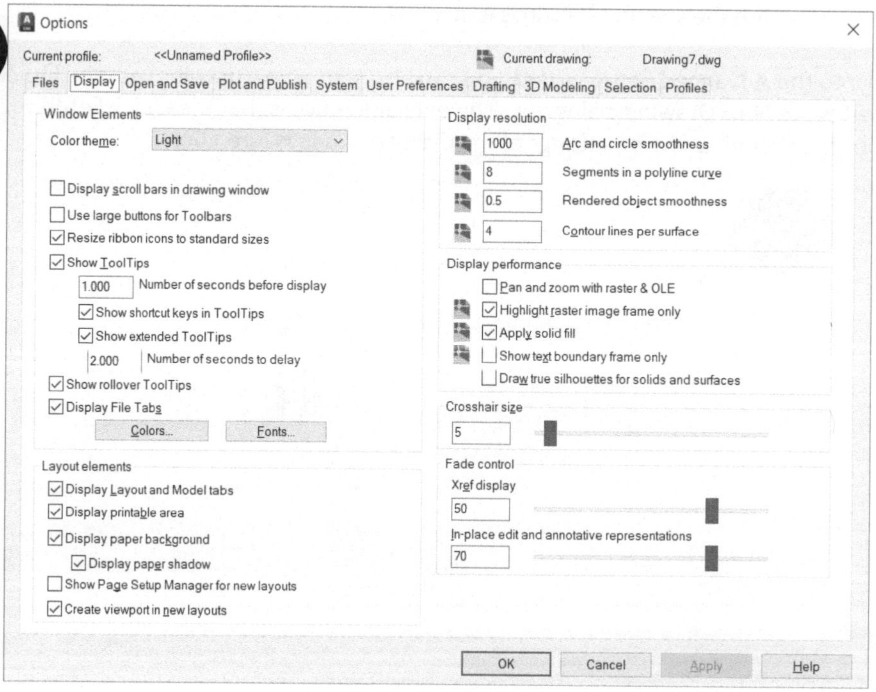

In the **Options** dialog box, click on the **Display** tab. The options related to the display settings of AutoCAD appear in the dialog box, see Figure 1.62. Next, select either the **Light** or **Dark** option in the **Color theme** drop-down list of the **Window Elements** area in the dialog box to display the AutoCAD elements/components in a light color theme or dark color theme, respectively.

Note: In this textbook, light color theme is used for clarity of images.

Changing the Background Color

In AutoCAD, you can change the background color of the drawing area/screen, sheet/layout, Command Line window, plot preview, and so on by using the **Options** dialog box. To change the background color of the drawing area/screen, enter **OP** in the Command Line window and then press ENTER. The **Options** dialog box appears. In the **Options** dialog box, click on the **Display** tab. The options related to the display settings of AutoCAD appear in the dialog box. Next, click on the **Colors** button in the **Window Elements** area of the dialog box. The **Drawing Window Colors** dialog box appears, see Figure 1.63.

1.63

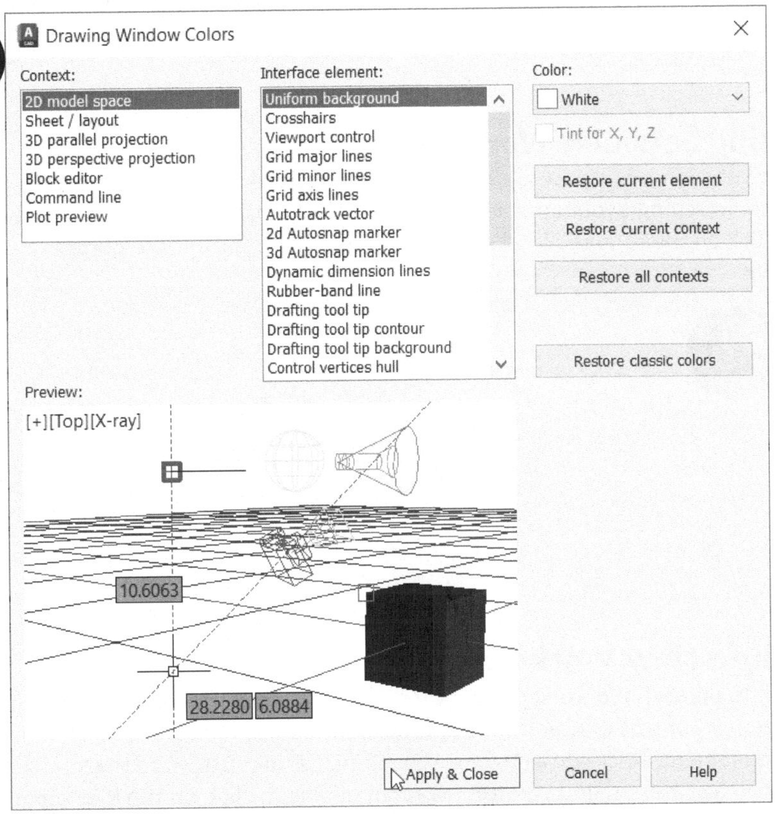

In this dialog box, ensure that the **2D model space** option is selected in the **Context** area, and the **Uniform background** option is selected in the **Interface element** area of the dialog box, see Figure 1.63. Next, select the color to be assigned to the background of the drawing area/screen in the **Color** drop-down list. Similarly, you can specify the background color of other drawing contexts such as sheet/layout,

Command Line window, and plot preview by using the **Drawing Window Colors** dialog box. After selecting the color to be assigned to the background, click on the **Apply & Close** button in the dialog box. The selected color gets assigned to the background of the drawing area, and the dialog box gets closed.

Note: In this textbook, background color of the drawing area has been changed to white for clarity of images.

Working with Workspaces

A workspace is defined as a task-oriented drawing environment in which you can control or organize the display of sets of user interface elements such as **Ribbon**, toolbars, menus, and palettes as per the requirement for accomplishing tasks. By default, AutoCAD has three pre-defined workspaces: **Drafting & Annotation**, **3D Basics**, and **3D Modeling**. When you start a new drawing file in AutoCAD, the **Drafting & Annotation** workspace is the default active workspace for creating the drawing. The **Drafting & Annotation** workspace displays the necessary tools, menus, and palettes that are used for creating and annotating 2D drawings. The **3D Basics** and **3D Modeling** workspaces provide the necessary tools, menus, and palettes that are used for creating 3D drawings. You can switch between the pre-defined workspaces and create a new workspace as per requirement. The methods for switching between workspaces and creating a new workspace are discussed next

Switching between Workspaces

To switch between workspaces, click on the **Workspace Switching** button in the Status Bar. The **Workspace Switching** flyout appears, see Figure 1.64. It displays a list of all the available workspaces. You can click on the required workspace in this flyout to make it the currently active workspace for the drawing.

1.64

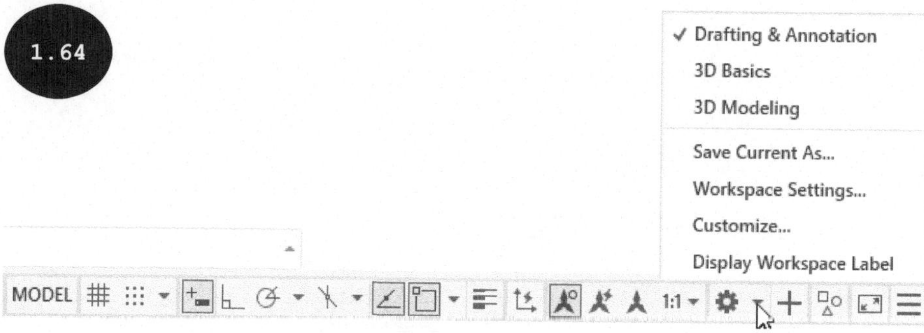

Creating a New Workspace

In addition to pre-defined workspaces, you can create a new workspace in which you can customize the arrangement of sets of user interface elements such as **Ribbon**, toolbars, menus, and palettes as per the requirement. To create a new workspace, first of all, customize the arrangement of tools in the **Ribbon**, toolbars, menus, and palettes, as required. Next, click on the **Workspace Switching** button in the Status Bar. The **Workspace Switching** flyout appears, see Figure 1.64. In this flyout, click on the **Save Current As** option. The **Save Workspace** window appears, see Figure 1.65. In this window, enter the name of the workspace and then click on the **Save** button. The new workspace is created and added to the list of workspaces in the **Workspace Switching** flyout. Also, it becomes the currently active workspace of the drawing.

1.65

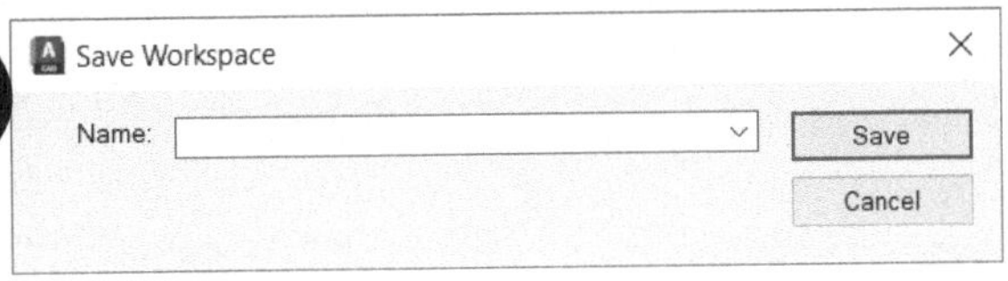

Working with Sheet Sets

Most of the real-world projects require multiple drawing sheets, sometimes running into hundreds. Cross-referencing between multiple drawing sheets of a project is a very time-consuming process. Also, plotting, publishing, and opening multiple drawing sheets of a project requires considerable time. To manage multiple drawing sheets of a project easily and efficiently, AutoCAD provides the sheet set feature. A sheet set is a very powerful feature of AutoCAD, which is used for managing or organizing a set of multiple drawings (sheets) of a project in proper order. All drawings of a sheet set act as a single unit and are displayed in a tree view. In AutoCAD, you can create different types of sheet sets: Example sheet set, Existing Drawings sheet sets, and Cloud Example sheet set. An Example sheet set uses a sample sheet set with default settings to create a new sheet set in a well-organized structure. An Existing Drawings sheet set is used for creating a new sheet set to organize existing drawings. A Cloud Example sheet set uses an existing sample sheet set with default settings to create a new cloud-based sheet set in a well-organized structure. You can create these different types of sheet sets by using the **SHEET SET MANAGER** palette. The methods for creating different types of sheet sets are discussed next.

Creating an Example Sheet Set

To create an Example sheet set, click on the **Sheet Set Manager** tool in the **Palettes** panel of the **View** tab in the **Ribbon**. The **SHEET SET MANAGER** palette appears, see Figure 1.66. Alternatively, enter **SHEETSET** in the Command Line window and then press ENTER to invoke the **SHEET SET MANAGER** palette. In the **SHEET SET MANAGER** palette, ensure that the **Sheet List** tab is activated, see Figure 1.66. Next, click on the down arrow next to the **Open** button in the **SHEET SET MANAGER** palette. A drop-down list appears, see Figure 1.67. In this drop-down list, click on the **New Sheet Set** option. The **Create Sheet Set** dialog box appears with the **Begin** page, see Figure 1.68.

1.66

1.67

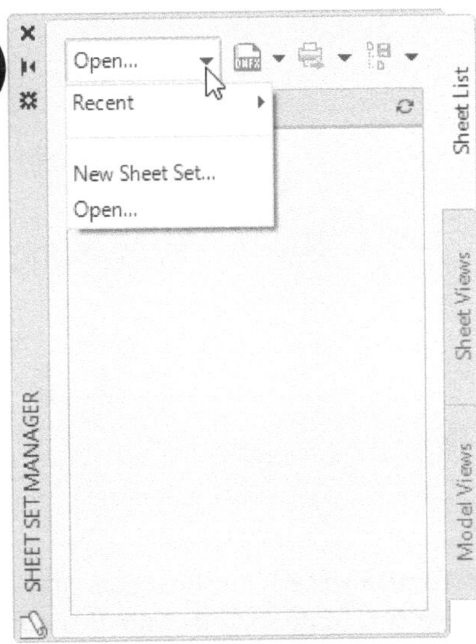

1.68

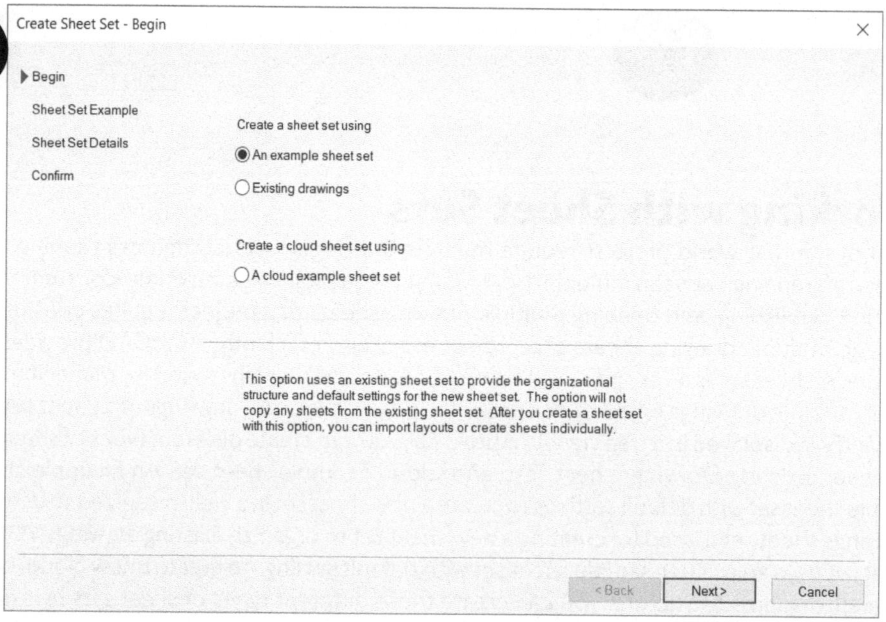

In the **Begin** page of the **Create Sheet Set** dialog box, ensure that the **An example sheet set** radio button is selected. Next, click on the **Next** button in the dialog box. The **Sheet Set Example** page of the **Create Sheet Set** dialog box appears, see Figure 1.69. On this page, the **Select a sheet set to use as an example** radio button is selected, by default. As a result, a list of all the available sample sheet sets is displayed below this radio button, see Figure 1.69. Select a required example sheet set in this field for creating a new sheet set.

1.69

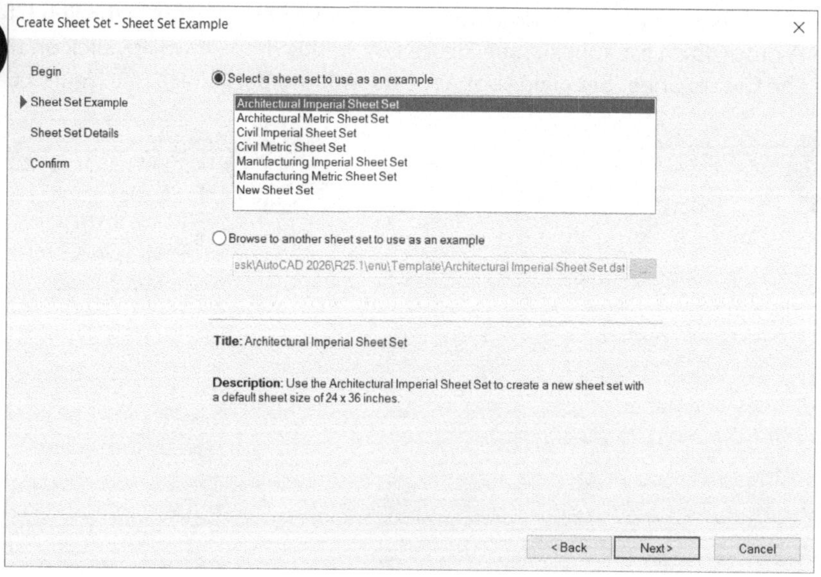

You can also select a sheet sets that is in a different location and not available in the list of example sheet set. To do so, select the **Browse to another sheet set to use as an example** radio button in the **Sheet Set Example** page of the dialog box and then click on the **Browse** button [...]. The **Browse for**

Sheet Set dialog box appears. In this dialog box, browse to a location where the required sheet set is saved and then select it. Next, click on the **Open** button. After selecting the required example sheet set for creating a new sheet set on this page, click on the **Next** button. The **Sheet Set Details** page of the dialog box appears. On this page, enter the name of the new sheet set, description, and location to save the file by using the **Name of new sheet set**, **Description**, and **Store sheet set data file (.dst) here** fields, respectively. Next, click on the **Next** button. The **Confirm** page of the dialog box appears, see Figure 1.70. This page displays the structure of the sheet set and details of the sheet set properties. Review all the sheet set properties and then click on the **Finish** button. A new sheet set gets created with the specified properties and is displayed in the **SHEET SET MANAGER** palette, see Figure 1.71.

1.70

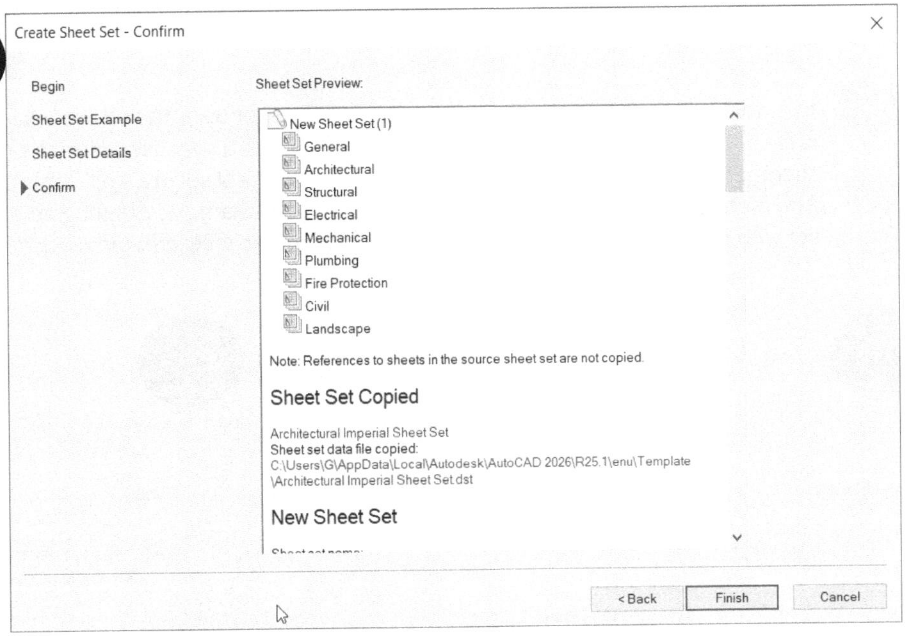

1.71

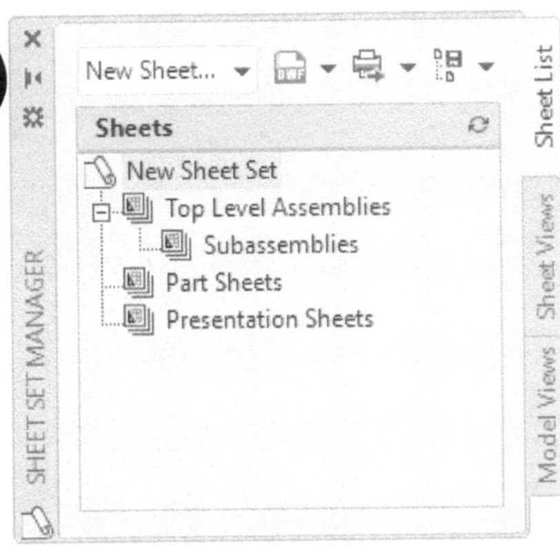

Now, you can add multiple drawing sheets in different subsets of the newly created sheet set and then create drawings in it. To add a new drawing sheet in a subset, right-click on a subset and then click on the **New Sheet** option in the shortcut menu that appears, see Figure 1.72. The **New Sheet** window appears. In this window, specify the sheet number, title, and file name, and then click on the **OK** button. A new drawing sheet gets added and displayed under the selected subset, see Figure 1.73. Similarly, you can add multiple drawing sheets under different subsets. You can also add a new subset to the main sheet set. To do so, right-click on the name of the sheet set in the **SHEET SET MANAGER** palette and then click on the **New Subset** option in the shortcut menu that appears. The **Subset Properties** window appears. In this window, specify the subset name and other properties. Next, click on the **OK** button. A new subset with the specified name and properties gets added to the sheet set. After adding the required drawing sheets and subsets, you can open a drawing sheet and then create the drawing in it. To open a drawing sheet for creating the drawing, right-click on the drawing sheet in the **SHEET SET MANAGER** palette and then click on the **Open** option in the shortcut menu that appears. The drawing sheet gets opened in a separate window with the default drawing template. Now, you can create the drawing in this sheet by using the drawing tools. You will learn about creating drawings by using the drawing tools in later chapters.

Note: In AutoCAD 2026, you can also create a cloud sheet set by using the **A cloud example sheet set** radio button of the **Create Sheet Set** dialog box. A cloud sheet set uses an existing sample sheet set with default settings to create a new cloud sheet set in a well-organized structure. The method for creating a new cloud sheet set is the same as creating an example sheet set with the only difference being that the cloud sheet set is created on the cloud.

1.72

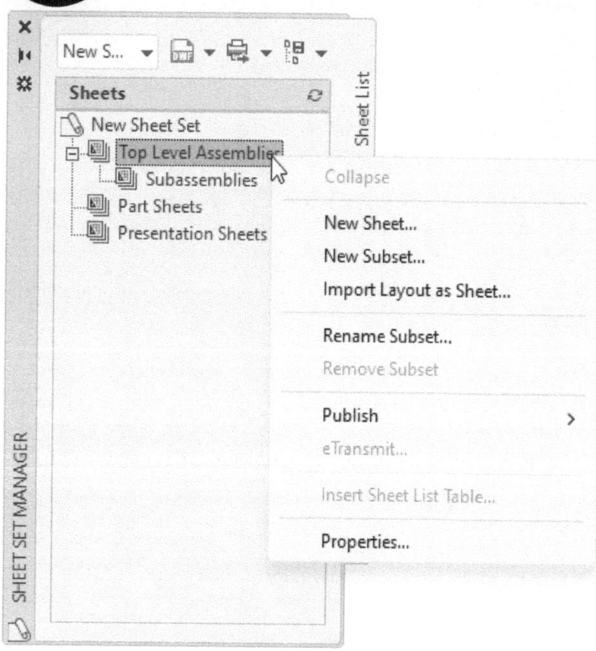

1.73

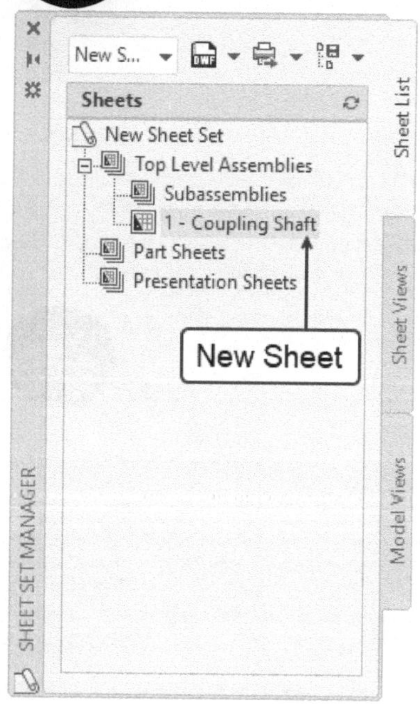

Creating an Existing Drawing Sheet Set

An Existing Drawing sheet set is created by using the existing drawings of a project. To create a sheet set by using the existing drawings, invoke the **SHEET SET MANAGER** palette and then click on the down arrow next to the **Open** button. A drop-down list appears. In this drop-down list, click on the **New Sheet Set** option. The **Create Sheet Set** dialog box appears with the **Begin** page, see Figure 1.74.

1.74

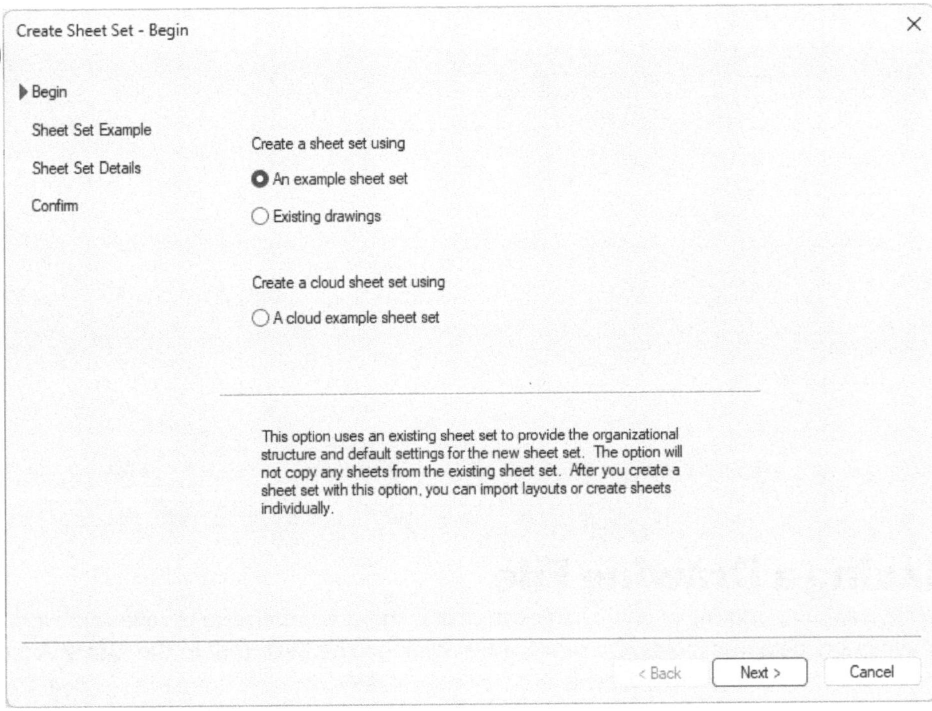

In the **Begin** page of the **Create Sheet Set** dialog box, select the **Existing drawings** radio button and then click on the **Next** button. The **Sheet Set Details** page of the dialog box appears. On this page, enter the sheet set details such as name, description, and location to save the file. Next, click on the **Next** button. The **Choose Layouts** page of the dialog box appears, see Figure 1.75. Click on the **Browse** button on this page. The **Browse for Folder** window appears. In this window, browse to the folder in which drawing files to be added to the sheet set are saved and then select it. Next, click on the **OK** button. All the drawing files of the selected folder with their initial layouts are listed in the box available on the **Choose Layouts** page. You can browse multiple folders one by one to add the drawing files.

Note that the drawing files and their first layouts listed in the box of the **Choose Layouts** page have a tick mark in front of them. You can uncheck the drawing files and layouts which you do not want to include in the sheet set. After selecting the drawing files and layouts to be included in the sheet set, click on the **Next** button. The **Confirm** page of the dialog box appears. This page displays the information about the layouts included in the sheet set. Next, click on the **Finish** button. A sheet set is created by using the existing drawing files and is displayed in the **SHEET SET MANAGER** palette.

1.75

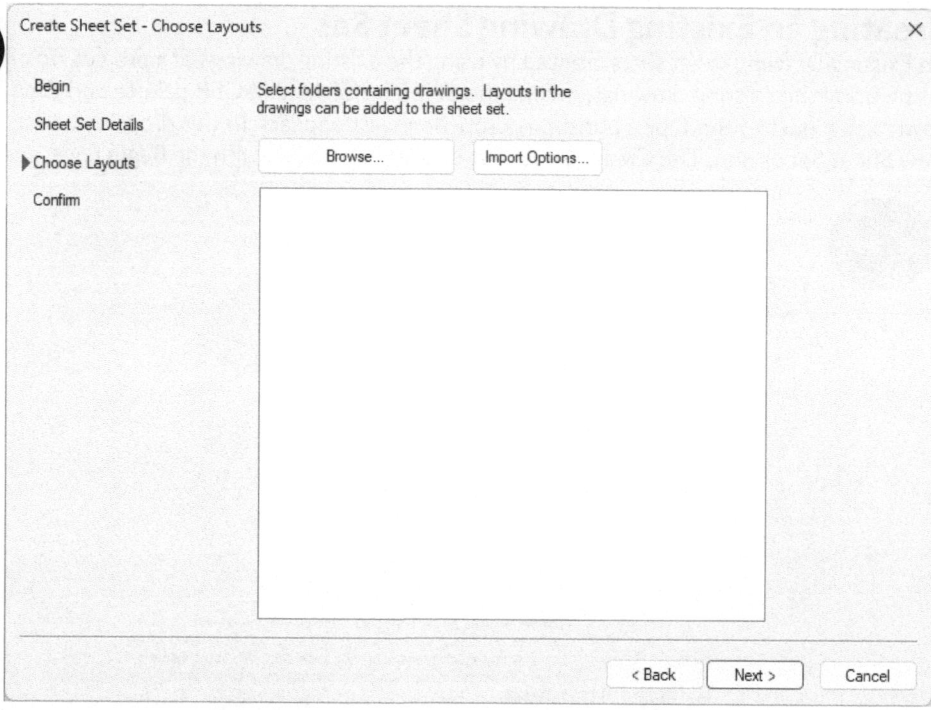

Saving a Drawing File

While creating a drawing or editing an existing drawing, it is imperative to save your work periodically to avoid any data loss. To save a drawing file, click on the **Save** tool in the **Quick Access Toolbar**, see Figure 1.76. Alternatively, press CTRL + S or enter **SAVE** in the Command Line window. Note that if you are saving a drawing for the first time then on clicking the **Save** tool, the **Save Drawing As** dialog box appears. In this dialog box, browse to a location where you want to save the drawing file and then enter the name of the drawing file in the **File name** field of the dialog box. Next, click on the **Save** button.

1.76

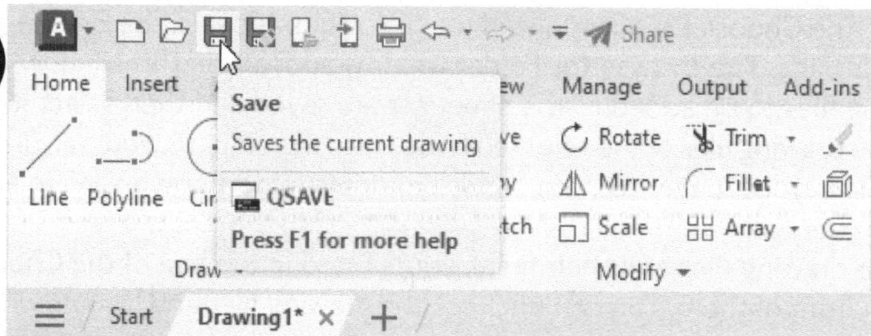

The drawing file gets saved in the specified location of your computer with the specified name in the *.dwg* file extension. The *.dwg* is the file extension of AutoCAD. Note that if the drawing has already been saved with a particular name on your computer and you have made modifications to it then by clicking the **Save** tool, the drawing gets saved directly without the display of **Save Drawing As** dialog box.

You can also save an already saved drawing file with a different name. To save an already saved drawing file with a different name, click on the **Save As** tool in the **Quick Access Toolbar**, see Figure 1.77.

Alternatively, enter SAVEAS in the Command Line window and then press ENTER. The **Save Drawing As** dialog box appears. In this dialog box, enter a new name for the drawing file in the **File name** field and then click on the **Save** button. The drawing file gets saved with the newly specified name without affecting the original drawing file.

1.77

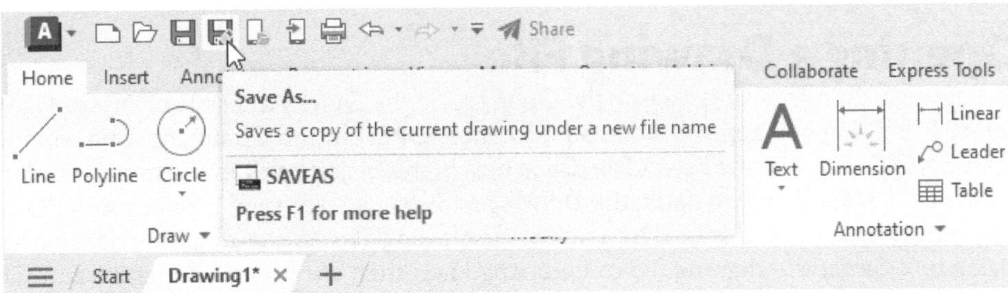

Note: AutoCAD allows you to save your drawing file in previous versions of AutoCAD. For doing so, select the required version of AutoCAD in the **Files of type** drop-down list of the **Save Drawing As** dialog box, see Figure 1.78 and then click on the **Save** button.

1.78

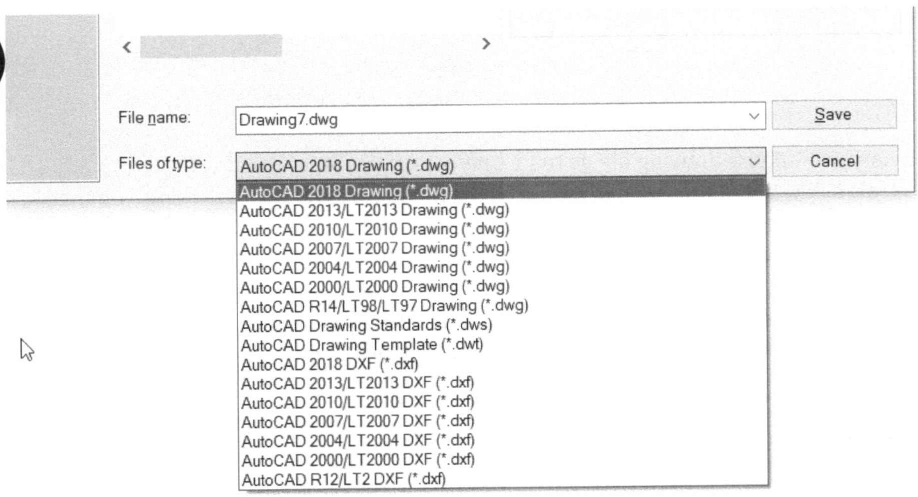

In addition to saving a drawing file by using the **Save** or **Save As** tools, AutoCAD automatically saves your drawing file after every 10 minutes. You can change the default time interval for automatically saving drawing files by using the **Options** dialog box. To do so, enter **OP** in the Command Line window and press ENTER. The **Options** dialog box appears. In this dialog box, click on the **Open and Save** tab and then enter the time interval in the **Minutes between saves** field of the **File Safety Precautions** area in the dialog box. Next, click **OK** to accept the change and exit the dialog box.

In AutoCAD, you can also save your drawings to the AutoCAD Web and Mobile folder in your Autodesk Account (Autodesk Cloud), which allows you to access your drawings anywhere in the world with internet access and on any desktop, web, or mobile device. To do so, click on **Save As > Drawing to**

AutoCAD Web & Mobile in the **Application Menu**. Alternatively, enter SAVETOWEBMOBILE in the Command Line Window. The **Save to AutoCAD Web & Mobile** dialog box appears. In this dialog box, enter the name of the drawing file in the **File name** field. Next, click on the **Save** button. The drawing gets saved in the cloud with the specified name.

Opening a Drawing File

To open an existing drawing, click on the **Open** tool in the **Quick Access Toolbar**, see Figure 1.79. The **Select File** dialog box appears. You can also enter **OPEN** in the Command Line window and then press ENTER to invoke the **Select File** dialog box. In this dialog box, browse to the location where the file is saved. Note that by default, the **Drawing (*.dwg)** file extension is selected in the **Files of type** drop-down list in the dialog box. As a result, the drawing files having *.dwg* file extension appear in the dialog box. Select the drawing file to be opened and then click on the **Open** button. The selected drawing gets opened in AutoCAD. You can also open the *.dws*, *.dxf* files or *.dwt* (template) files by selecting the **Standards (*.dws)**, **DXF (*.dxf)**, or **Drawing Template (*.dwt)** file extension in the **Files of type** drop-down list, respectively.

1.79

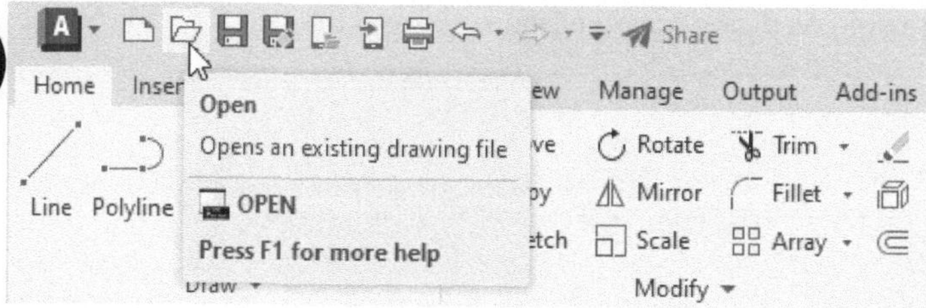

You can also open a drawing file as read-only which protects the drawing from any change, and it is used for review only. Note that AutoCAD does not restrict you from making a change in the read-only file, however, it does not allow you to save the changes made in the read-only file. To open a drawing as a read-only file, click on the **Open** tool in the **Quick Access Toolbar** to invoke the **Select File** dialog box. Next, select the drawing to be opened and then click on the down arrow next to the **Open** button in the **Select File** dialog box. The **Open** drop-down list appears, see Figure 1.80. In this drop-down list, select the **Open Read-Only** option. The selected drawing gets opened as a read-only file.

1.80

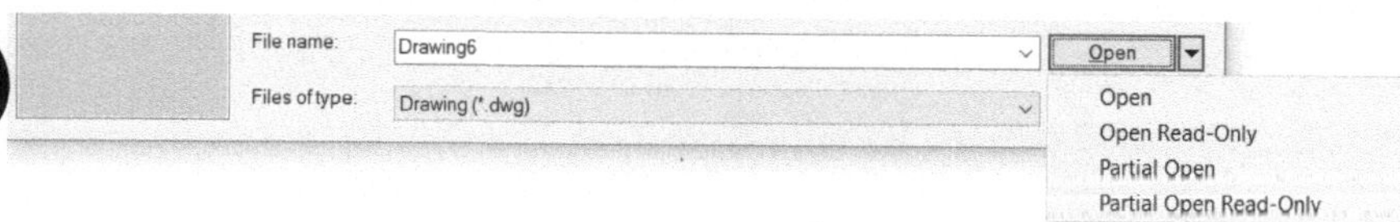

Note: When you save the read-only file after making some modifications or changes, the **AutoCAD Message** window appears, which informs you that the current drawing file is write protected. However, you can save the modified read-only file with a different name by using the **Save As** tool.

In AutoCAD, you can also open a partial view or a small portion of a drawing instead of opening the entire drawing by using the **Partial Open** option of the **Open** drop-down list, see Figure 1.80. This option is very useful if you want to modify a small portion of a big complex drawing. To open a partial view of a drawing, select the drawing in the **Select File** dialog box and then invoke the **Open** drop-down list, see Figure 1.80. Next, click on the **Partial Open** option. The **Partial Open** dialog box appears, which displays different views and layers of the selected drawing. Select the check boxes corresponding to the layers whose geometries are to be opened. Next, click on the **Open** button in the dialog box. The geometries/objects associated with the selected layers are displayed in the drawing area.

In AutoCAD, you can open drawings that are saved in Autodesk Cloud (AutoCAD Web and Mobile folder in your Autodesk Account), anywhere and from different devices. To do so, click on **Open > Drawing from AutoCAD Web & Mobile** in the **Application Menu**. Alternatively, enter OPENFROMWEBMOBILE in the Command Line Window. The **Open from AutoCAD Web & Mobile** dialog box appears. In this dialog box, select the drawing file to be opened and click on the **Open** button. The drawing gets opened.

Sharing a Drawing File

AutoCAD allows you to share a copy of your drawing including its external references with anyone by using a link. To do so, save the drawing and then click on the **Share Drawing** tool in the **Quick Access Toolbar**, see Figure 1.81. The **Share a link to this drawing** window appears, see Figure 1.82.

1.81

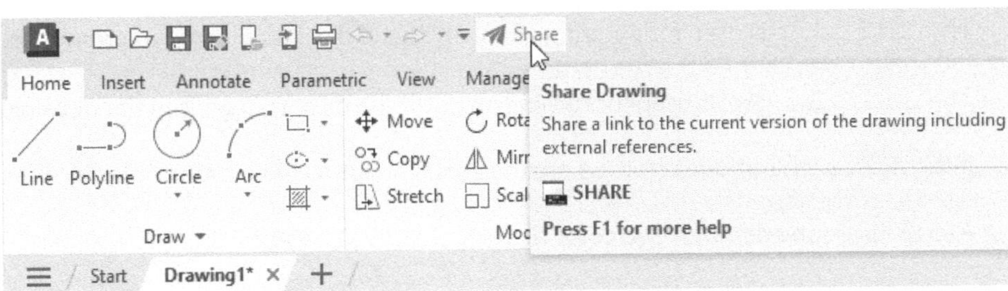

1.82

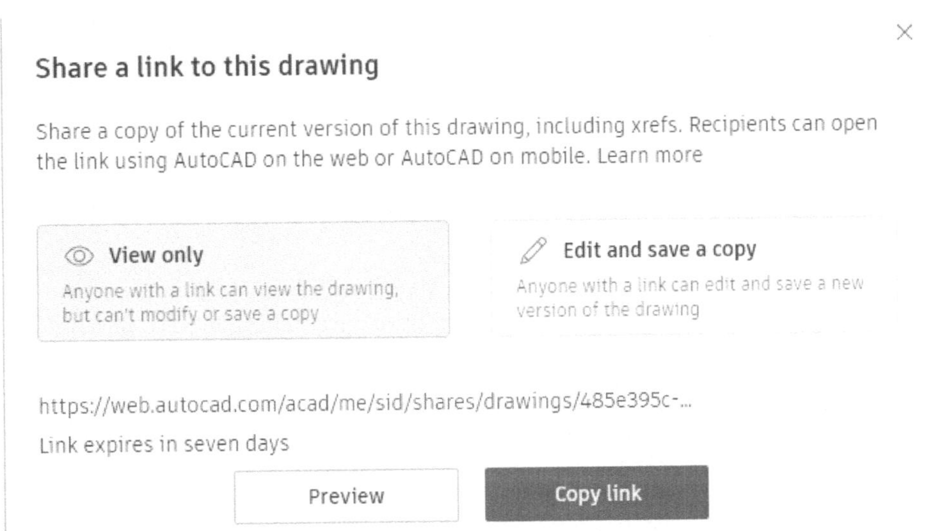

To share a read-only copy where the file can only be viewed and no editing, saving, or downloading of the file is allowed, select the **View only** option in the **Share a link to this drawing** window and then copy the link that is generated in the window. On the other hand, to share an editable copy where the file can be viewed, edited, and saved, select the **Edit and save a copy** option in the **Share a link to this drawing** window and then copy the link that is generated in the window. Now, you can give this link to anyone to access a copy of your drawing. The drawing file can also be opened in the AutoCAD web app by using the link. Note that the changes made in the edited copy of the drawing will not reflect in the original file.

Summary

The chapter introduced system requirements for installing AutoCAD and explained how to start a new drawing file. It also introduced screen components, workspaces, and sheet sets of AutoCAD while also explaining how to change the color theme, background color, and open, save, and share drawing files in AutoCAD.

Questions

Complete the following sentences:

- The ________ is used for entering commands and displays command prompt sequence.
- The ________ tool is used for turning on or off the display of grids in the drawing area.
- If the ________ mode is turned on, the cursor snaps to the existing objects of the drawing.
- AutoCAD is provided with two color themes: ________ and ________ .
- The ________ tool is used for sharing a copy of a drawing with anyone by using a link.
- By default, AutoCAD has three predefined workspaces: ________ , ________, and ________ .

CHAPTER

2

Creating Drawings - I

In this chapter, the following topics will be discussed:

- Setting up Drawing Units
- Setting Drawing Limits
- Specifying Grid and Snap Settings
- Understanding Coordinate Systems
- Creating a Drawing
- Drawing a Line
- Drawing a Circle
- Drawing an Arc
- Canceling, Erasing and Restoring Objects
- Navigating 2D Drawings

Before you start creating drawings in AutoCAD, it is important to first focus on drawing units, limits, grids, and snap settings. You should also be familiar with the coordinate systems used in AutoCAD.

Setting up Drawing Units

The first and foremost step to creating a drawing is to set up the units of measurement for the drawing. As discussed in Chapter 1, when starting a new drawing in AutoCAD, you can define a unit system for measurement; Architectural, Decimal, Engineering, Fractional, or Scientific. Besides, you can also change or modify the unit settings at any given point in time during the process of creating a drawing by using the UNITS command.

To set up a unit for the current drawing, type **UNITS** in the Command Line window and then press ENTER, see Figure 2.1. The **Drawing Units** dialog box appears, see Figure 2.2.

2.1

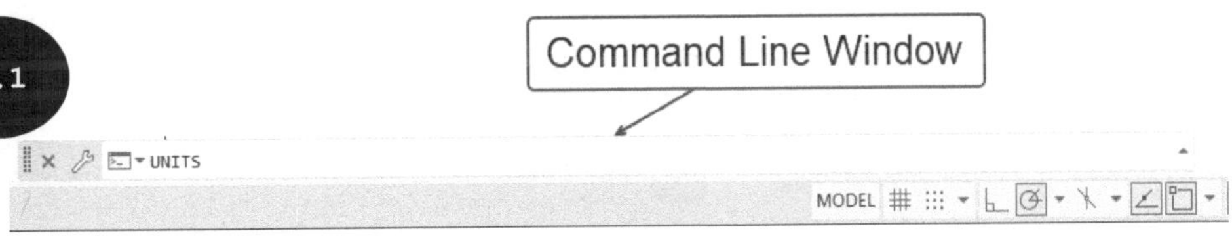

2.2

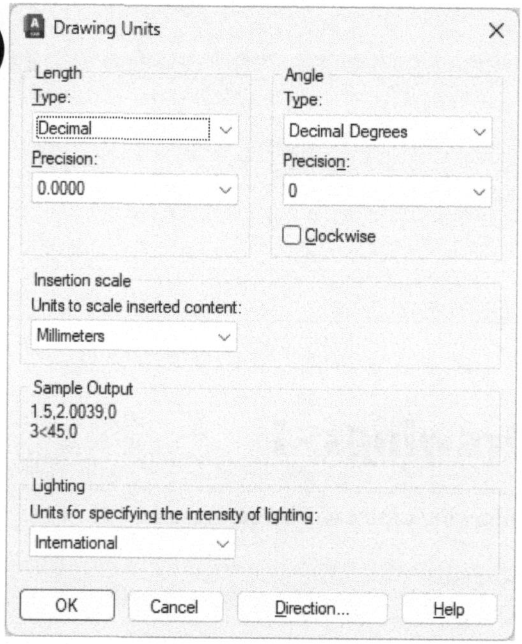

Tip: You can also type **UN** instead of **UNITS** in the Command Line window for invoking the **Drawing Units** dialog box. **UN** is a shortcut for the **UNITS** command.

After invoking the **Drawing Units** dialog box, you can set the required unit format for the measurement of length and angle. The options in the **Drawing Units** dialog box are discussed below:

Length

The options in the **Length** area of the **Drawing Units** dialog box are used for setting the required unit format and precision for the measurement of length. The options of the **Length** area are discussed next.

Type

The **Type** drop-down list of the **Length** area is used for selecting the required unit format. You can select the architectural, decimal, engineering, fractional, or scientific unit format for the measurement of length from this drop-down list. Different unit formats are discussed below:

Architectural

As the name suggests, this unit format is mostly used by architects to specify units in feet and inches. In this unit format, inches are represented in fractional form.

Note: The **Sample Output** area of the dialog box displays examples of the current unit format selected in the **Type** drop-down list of the dialog box.

Decimal
The **Decimal** unit format is used for specifying units in the metric unit system. This format is mostly used by users who work with the metric unit system for measurement.

Engineering
Similar to the **Architectural** unit format, the **Engineering** unit format is used for specifying units in feet and inches. The only difference between these two unit formats is that inches, in the **Engineering** unit format, are represented in the decimal form.

Fractional
This unit format is used for specifying units in the fractional unit system. For example, 5 feet, 6½ inches means 66-1/2 inches in the fractional unit system.

Scientific
This unit format is used for specifying units in the scientific units system. For example, 10 million parsecs means 10E+06 in the scientific units system, where 10 represents ten accurate and E+06 represents the exponential function to the sixth power.

Precision
The **Precision** drop-down list of the **Length** area is used for setting the precision of units. The availability of options in the **Precision** drop-down list depends on the type of unit format selected in the **Type** drop-down list.

Angle
The options of the **Angle** area are used for specifying a unit format and precision for the measurement of the angle. You can select the **Decimal Degrees, Deg/Min/Sec, Grads, Radians,** or **Surveyor's Units** format for the measurement of an angle by using the **Type** drop-down list of the **Angle** area. The **Precision** drop-down list of the **Angle** area is used for specifying precision for angle measurements.

If you have selected the **Decimal Degrees, Deg/Min/Sec, Grads,** or **Radians** unit format for the measurement of angle, the angle is specified in decimal degrees, degrees/minutes/seconds, grads, or radians, respectively. Whereas, if you have selected the **Surveyor's Units** format, the angle is specified based on deviation from north or south, see Figure 2.3. Note that the angle value used in the surveyors units format is not greater than 90 degrees. For example, to set an angle that measures 40 degrees from the north and 30 minutes toward the east, you need to specify **N40d30'E**.

2.3

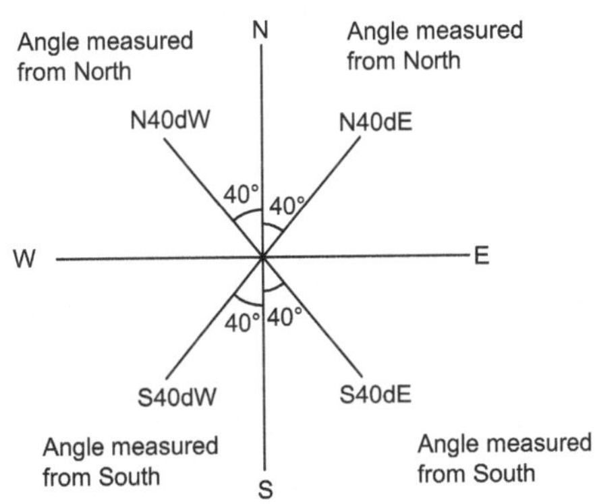

Clockwise

By default, the **Clockwise** check box is unchecked in the **Angle** area of the dialog box. As a result, a positive angle is measured in the counter-clockwise direction, see Figure 2.4. To measure a positive angle in the clockwise direction, select the **Clockwise** check box, see Figure 2.5.

2.4

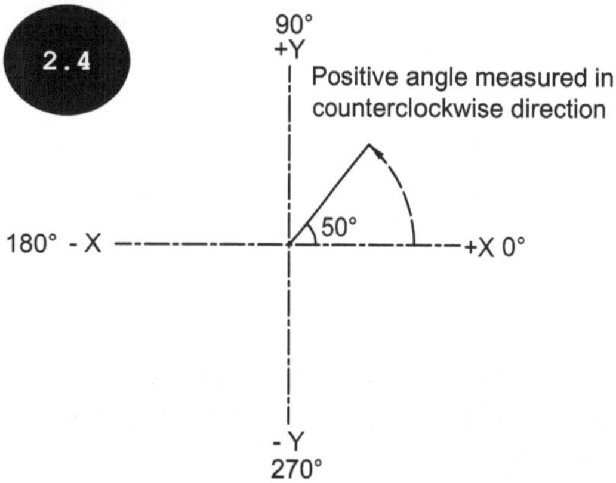

2.5

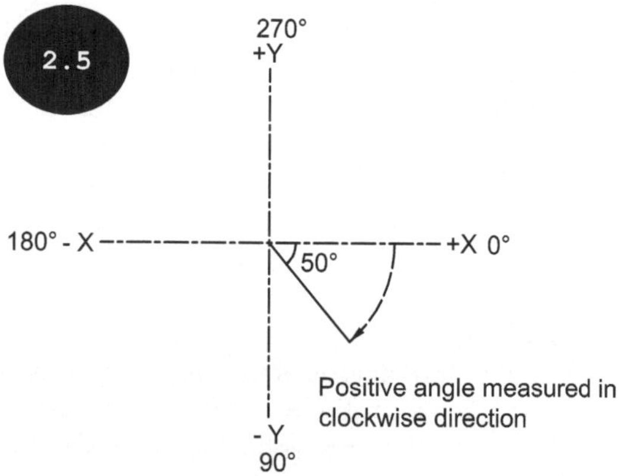

Note: It is evident from Figures 2.4 and 2.5 that the position of 0-degree is set at East position, by default. You can change the position of zero degrees from East to other positions, such as north, south, or west by using the **Direction** button in the **Drawing Units** dialog box. To set the position of zero degrees, click on the **Direction** button in the **Drawing Units** dialog box. The **Direction Control** dialog box appears, see Figure 2.6. Using this dialog box, you can set a base angle (zero degrees) at any position by selecting the appropriate radio button. You can also specify an angle value other than 0 (zero) by selecting the **Other** radio button and then entering the required angle value in the **Angle** field.

2.6

Insertion scale

The **Units to scale inserted content** drop-down list of the **Insertion Scale** area is used for setting units for the blocks and drawings that are inserted in the current drawing. Note that the unit selected in this drop-down list is applied automatically to the blocks or drawings inserted in the current drawing. If the blocks and drawings inserted in the current drawing have different units, then AutoCAD may scale them to correct the mismatch and set the unit specified in the **Units to scale inserted content** drop-down list.

Sample Output

The **Sample Output** area of the **Drawing Units** dialog box is used for displaying the sample output or an example of the unit settings for the current length and angle specified in the dialog box.

Lighting

The **Units for specifying the intensity of lighting** drop-down list of the **Lighting** area is used for setting the unit of measurement for the intensity of photometric light in the current drawing.

After specifying the desired settings for the measurement of units in the **Drawing Units** dialog box, click on the **OK** button to accept the settings and close the dialog box.

Setting Drawing Limits

After defining drawing units, it is important to set drawing limits (work area) in the drawing area. A drawing limit is an invisible and imaginary rectangular boundary in the drawing area, which defines the size of the workspace. Setting a drawing limit helps in defining the grid display within the boundary, zooming into or out of a drawing within the boundary, and plotting the drawing. You can set a drawing limit for a drawing depending on the overall size of the drawing. For example, if you are drawing a plan view of a building that is roughly around 28 feet x 36 feet then you can set the drawing limit around 56 feet x 72 feet. Note that the drawing limit is the size of your work area that accommodates the entire drawing and dimensions with some extra space, see Figure 2.7.

2.7

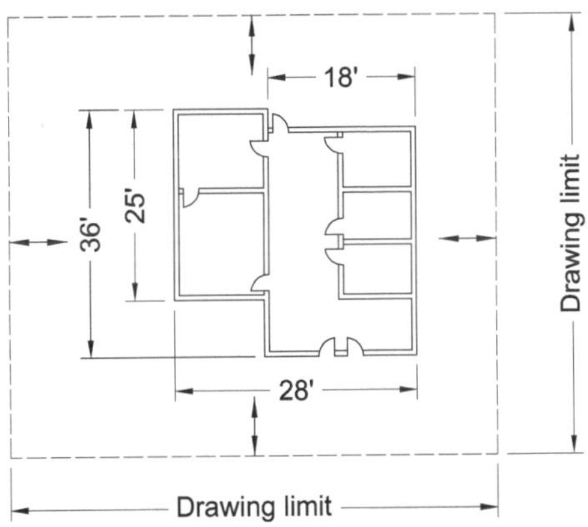

To define the drawing limit for a drawing, enter **LIMITS** in the Command Line window and then press ENTER. The command prompt for setting the drawing limit is discussed next.

Command: **LIMITS**
Reset Model space limits:
Specify lower left corner or [ON/OFF] <0.0000,0.0000>: **0,0**
Specify upper right corner <420.0000,297.0000>: **56,72**

Note: If the display of grids is turned on, the grids appear in the entire drawing area by default. To display grids within the drawing limit, enter **GRIDDISPLAY** in the Command Line window and then enter **0** in the command prompt. Next, press ENTER. You will learn more about grid settings later in this chapter.

Specifying Grid and Snap Settings

The grid is a rectangular pattern of lines or dots, which is intended to speed up the creation of drawings by aligning objects and visualizing the distance between drawing entities. Grid lines can be used as reference lines for creating drawings. Also, grid lines appear similar to a sheet of graph paper for creating a drawing, see Figure 2.8.

2.8

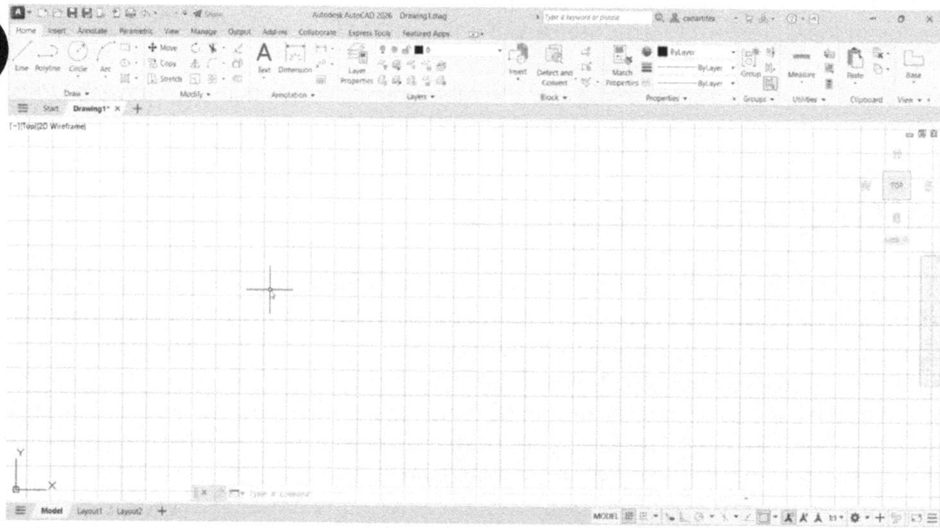

Note: The background color of the drawing area shown in Figure 2.8 has been changed to white for clear visualization. The method for changing background color has been discussed in Chapter 1.

You can control the spacing, angle, and alignment of grid lines. You can also restrict the movement of the cursor over grid lines by specifying the grid and snap settings.

To define the grid and snap settings in AutoCAD, right-click on the **Display drawing grid** button in the Status Bar, see Figure 2.9. The **Grid Settings** option appears. Next, click on the **Grid Settings** option. The **Drafting Settings** dialog box appears, see Figure 2.10.

2.9

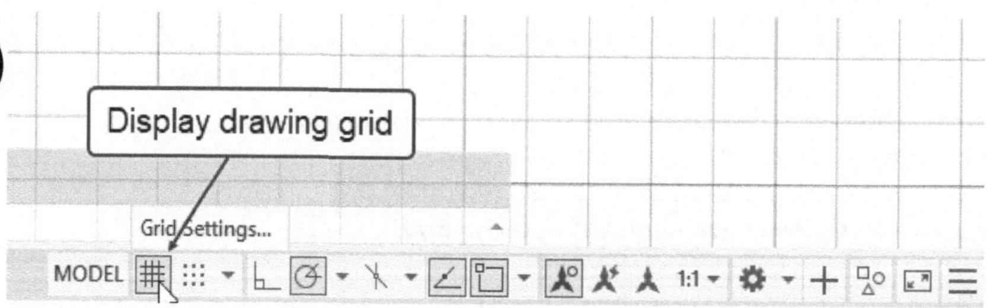

2.10

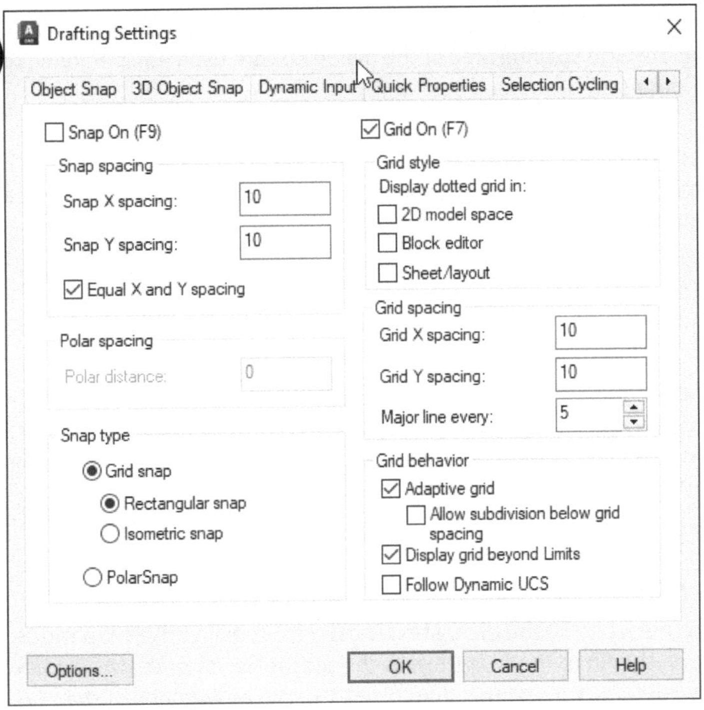

Ensure that the **Snap and Grid** tab is activated in the **Drafting Settings** dialog box, see Figure 2.10. The options in the **Snap and Grid** tab of the dialog box are used for specifying snap and grid settings. Some of these options are discussed next.

Grid On (F7)

The **Grid On** check box of this dialog box is used for toggling the display of grid lines in the drawing area. Alternatively, you can click on the **Display drawing grid** button in the Status Bar or press the **F7** key to toggle the display of grid lines.

Grid style

The options in the **Grid style** area of the dialog box are used for specifying grid styles in a 2D context. These options are discussed next.

2D model space

The **2D model space** check box of the **Grid style** area is used for setting grid style to dotted grid lines in the 2D model space (drawing area).

Block editor

The **Block editor** check box is used for setting grid style to dotted grid lines in the Block editor. You will learn more about the Block editor in later chapters.

Sheet/layout

The **Sheet/layout** check box is used for setting grid style to dotted grid lines in sheet and layout. You will learn more about sheet and layout in later chapters.

Grid spacing

The options in the **Grid spacing** area of the dialog box are used for specifying the spacing between grid lines. These options are discussed below:

Grid X spacing

The **Grid X spacing** field of the **Grid spacing** area is used for specifying the spacing between grid lines along the X direction.

Grid Y spacing

The **Grid Y spacing** field is used for specifying the spacing between grid lines along the Y direction.

Major line every

Grid lines are of two types: major grid lines and minor grid lines. The major grid lines appear darker than the minor grid lines. The **Major line every** field is used for specifying the display of the major grid lines concerning minor grid lines. For example, if you enter 5 in this field, the major grid lines will appear on every 5 counts of minor grid lines.

Snap On (F9)

The **Snap On** check box of the dialog box is used for toggling the snap mode on or off. Alternatively, you can click on the **Snap mode** button in the Status Bar or press the **F9** key to turn the snap mode on or off. Note that, by turning the snap mode on, the movement of the cursor gets restricted in the specified X and Y intervals. You can specify the X and Y intervals in the **Snap spacing** area of this dialog box, which is discussed next.

Snap spacing

The options of the **Snap spacing** area are used for snapping the movement of the cursor at the specified X and Y intervals along the X and Y directions, respectively. These options are discussed below.

Snap X spacing

The **Snap X spacing** field is used for specifying the snap spacing along the X direction. For example, if you enter 5 in this field then the cursor will snap after every 5 units along the X direction.

Snap Y spacing

The **Snap Y spacing** field is used for specifying the snap spacing along the Y direction. For example, if you enter 5 in this field then the cursor will snap after every 5 units along the Y direction.

Equal X and Y spacing

The **Equal X and Y spacing** check box is used for making the snap spacing the same along the X and Y directions.

Once you have specified the grid and snap settings in the **Drafting Settings** dialog box, click on the **OK** button to accept changes and exit from the dialog box.

Tip: In AutoCAD, you are provided with shortcuts to toggle the display of grids and snap settings. To toggle the display of grids in the drawing area, you can click on the **Display drawing grid** button # in the Status Bar or press the **F7** key. Similarly, to toggle the snap settings on and off, you can click on the **Snap mode** button ::: in the Status Bar or press the **F9** key.

Understanding Coordinate Systems

In AutoCAD, the Cartesian and Polar coordinate systems are used for specifying points in the drawing area. The Cartesian coordinate system is also known as the rectangular coordinate system, and it consists of two perpendicular lines (x-axis and y-axis) that intersect at a point called origin, see Figure 2.11. The origin has coordinate values of X = 0 and Y = 0. In the Cartesian coordinate system, the location of every point is specified by entering the X and Y coordinates values that are measured from perpendicular lines (x-axis and y-axis), see Figure 2.11. Note that in a two-dimensional space (2D plane), the Cartesian coordinate system has two perpendicular axes. Whereas, in a three-dimensional space (3D), the system has three mutually perpendicular axes (x-axis, y-axis, and z-axis).

2.11

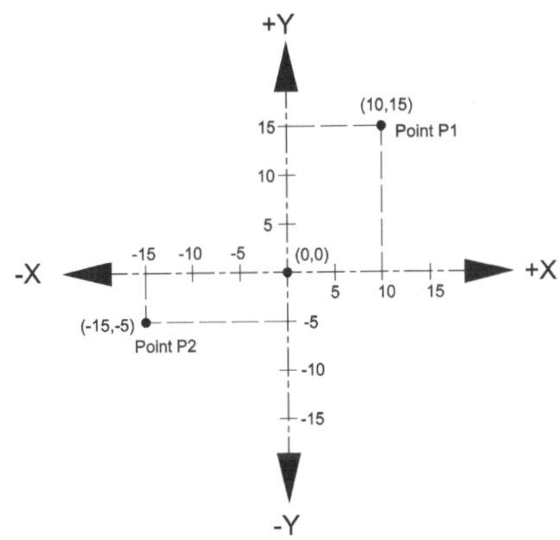

It is evident from Figure 2.11 that in the Cartesian coordinate system, you need to specify the X and Y coordinates concerning the X and Y axes for defining a point.

In the Polar coordinate system, to define the position of a point, you need to specify the distance and angle values rather than the X and Y coordinates, see Figure 2.12. Note that in the Polar coordinate system, the distance is measured from the origin, and the angle is measured from an axis representing zero degrees, see Figure 2.12. In AutoCAD, the +X axis (East) represents zero degrees for measuring the angle, by default. You can change the position of zero degrees to an axis other than the +X axis (East) as discussed earlier in this chapter.

2.12

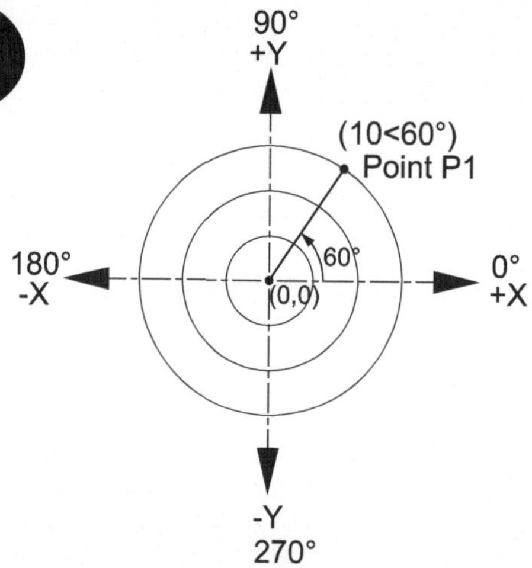

The different types of Cartesian and Polar coordinate systems are discussed next.

Cartesian Coordinate System

The Cartesian coordinate system is of two types:

1. Absolute Cartesian coordinate system
2. Relative Cartesian coordinate system

Absolute Cartesian Coordinate System

In the Absolute Cartesian coordinate system, every point you specify in the drawing area is measured from the origin (0,0) and the location of a point is defined by the X and Y coordinates, see Figure 2.13. Note that a comma should separate the X and Y coordinates you specify for locating a point. In Figure 2.13, Point P1 has coordinates (X=10, Y=15) that measure 10 units along the X axis and 15 units along the Y axis from the origin. Similarly, Point P2 has coordinates (X=25, Y=20) that measure 25 units along the X axis and 20 units along the Y axis from the origin.

2.13

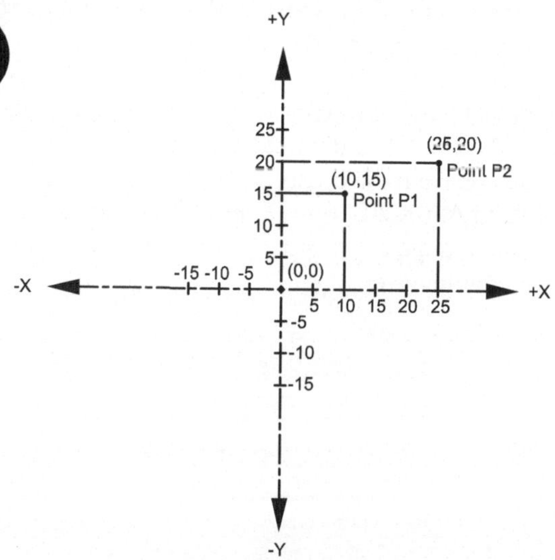

Note: In AutoCAD, you can specify coordinates either by using the Command Line window or by using the Dynamic Input boxes. As discussed, the Command Line window is available at the bottom of the drawing area, see Figure 2.14. The Dynamic Input boxes appear near the cursor in the drawing area, when the Dynamic Input mode is turned on, see Figure 2.15. To turn on or off the Dynamic Input mode, click on the **Dynamic Input** button in the Status Bar. If the **Dynamic Input** button is not available in the Status Bar by default, click on the **Customization** button in the Status Bar. A flyout appears. In this flyout, click on the **Dynamic Input** option. The **Dynamic Input** button becomes available in the Status Bar.

In the Absolute Cartesian coordinate system, the methods for specifying the X and Y coordinates of a point in the Command Line window as well as in the Dynamic Input boxes are discussed next.

Specifying a Point in the Command Line Window

To specify a point, according to the Absolute Cartesian coordinate system in the Command Line window, enter the X and Y coordinates, separated by a comma, see Figure 2.14. In this figure, the coordinates (**25, 20**) specified in the Command Line window measure 25 units along the X axis and 20 units along the Y axis for defining the start point of a line.

2.14

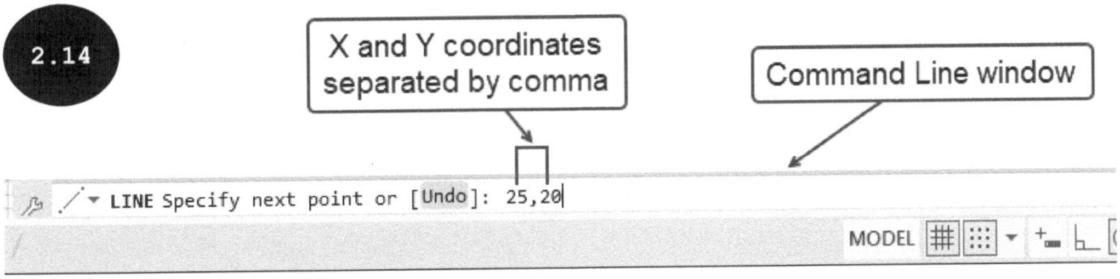

Specifying a Point in the Dynamic Input Boxes

To specify a point, according to the Absolute Cartesian coordinate system in the Dynamic Input boxes, enter # as a prefix to the X coordinate followed by the Y coordinate, see Figure 2.15. In this figure, the coordinates (**#25, 20**) specified in the Dynamic Input boxes measure 25 units along the X axis and 20 units along the Y axis for defining the start point of a line.

2.15

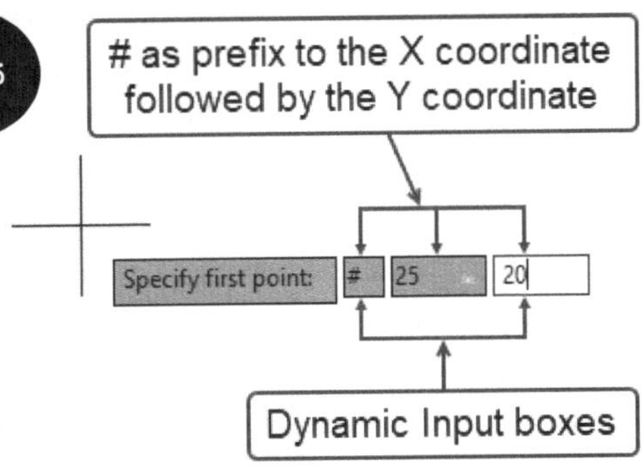

Tip: To switch between the Dynamic Input boxes for specifying the coordinates (X and Y), you need to press the TAB key. Alternatively, press the COMMA (,) key after specifying the X coordinate to switch to the next Dynamic Input box for specifying the Y coordinate.

Note: In the Absolute coordinate system, whether you specify coordinates in the Command Line window or the Dynamic Input boxes, the coordinates are measured from the origin.

Relative Cartesian Coordinate System

In the Relative Cartesian coordinate system, every point you specify in the drawing area is measured from the last specified point in the drawing area, and the location of the point is defined by the X and Y coordinates, see Figure 2.16. In Figure 2.16, the coordinates (X=10, Y=15) of the point 'P2' measure 10 units along the X axis and 15 units along the Y axis from the last specified point (point P1).

2.16

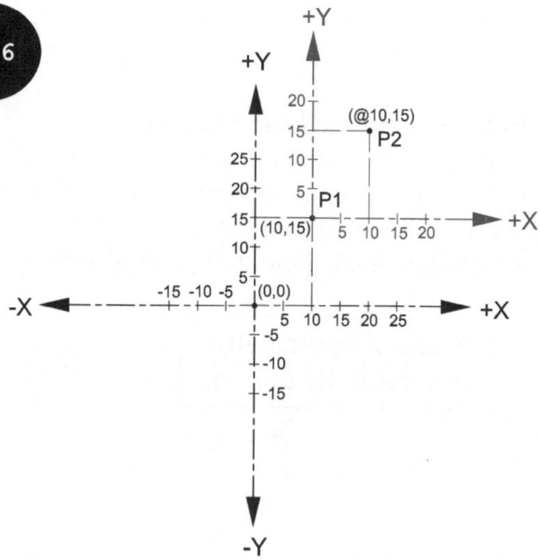

In the Relative coordinate system, the methods for specifying the X and Y coordinates of a point in the Command Line window as well as in the Dynamic Input boxes are discussed next.

Specifying a Point in the Command Line Window

To specify a point according to the Relative coordinate system in the Command Line window, enter @ as a prefix to the X coordinate followed by the Y coordinate separated by a comma, see Figure 2.17. Note that the coordinates (@10, 15) of a point (Point 2) specified in the Command Line window are measured from the last specified point, refer to Figure 2.16.

2.17

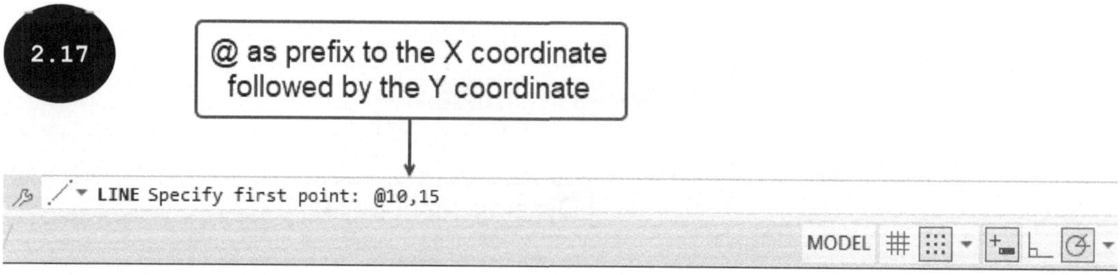

Specifying a Point in the Dynamic Input Boxes

To specify a point, according to the Relative coordinate system in the Dynamic Input boxes, enter the coordinates (X and Y) of the point in the Dynamic Input boxes, without any prefix.

Note: As discussed, in the Relative coordinate system, whether you specify coordinates in the Command Line window or the Dynamic Input boxes, coordinates are measured from the last specified point in the drawing area.

Polar Coordinate System

The Polar coordinate system is of two types as discussed below:

1. Absolute Polar coordinate system
2. Relative Polar coordinate system

Absolute Polar Coordinate System

In the Absolute Polar coordinate system, to define a point, you need to specify the distance and angle values separated by an angle bracket (<). Note that in the Absolute Polar coordinate system, the distance value measures from the origin, and the angle value measures from an axis which represents zero degree, see Figure 2.18.

2.18

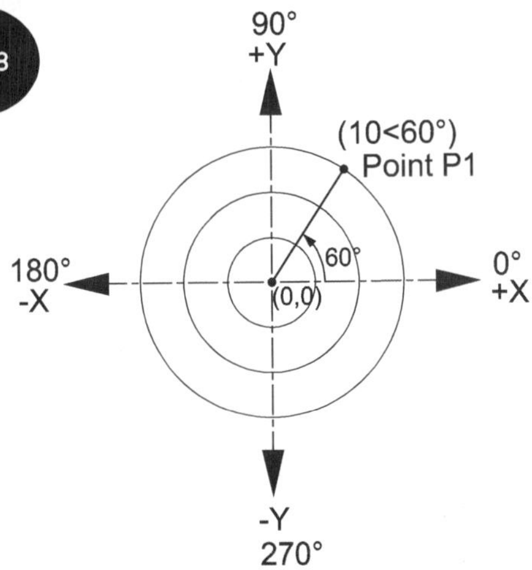

In the Absolute Polar coordinate system, the method for specifying a point in the Command Line window as well as in the Dynamic Input boxes are discussed below.

Specifying a Point in the Command Line Window

To specify a point, according to the Absolute Polar coordinate system in the Command Line window, enter the distance and angle values separated by an angle bracket (<), see Figure 2.19. In this figure, the distance and angle values (10<60°) specified in the Command Line window measure 10 units distance from the origin and 60 degrees angle from the X axis, refer to Figure 2.18.

2.19

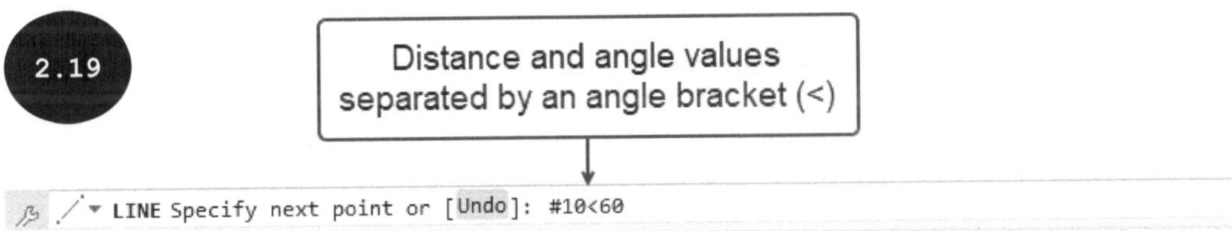

Specifying a Point in the Dynamic Input Boxes

To specify a point according to the Absolute Polar coordinate system in the Dynamic Input boxes, enter # as a prefix to the distance value followed by the angle value, see Figure 2.20. In this figure, the coordinates (#10<60) specified in the Dynamic Input boxes measure 10 units distance from the origin and 60 degrees angle from the X axis, which represents zero degrees.

2.20

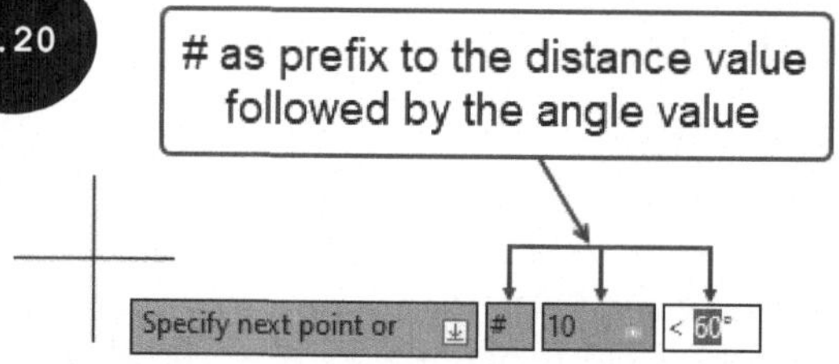

Relative Polar Coordinate System

In the Relative Polar coordinate system, every point you specify in the drawing area measures from the last specified point in the drawing area, and the location of a point is defined by entering the distance and angle values, see Figure 2.21. In Figure 2.21, the distance and angle values (10<25°) of the point 'P2" measure from the last specified point (P1).

2.21

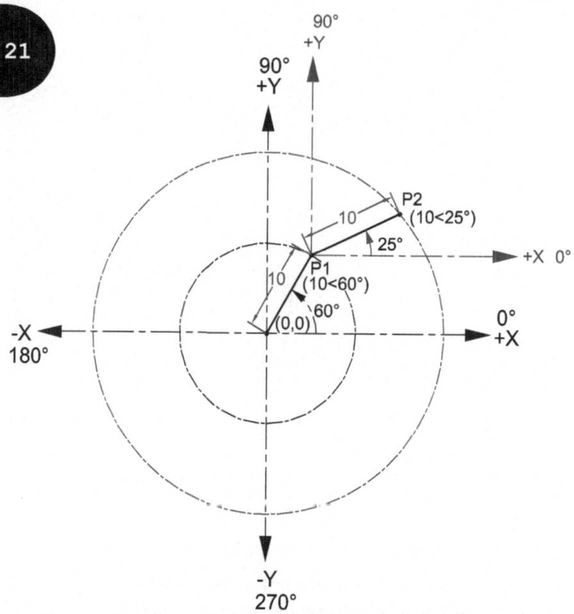

In the Relative Polar coordinate system, the methods for specifying a point in the Command Line window as well as in the Dynamic Input boxes are discussed next.

Specifying a Point in the Command Line Window

To specify a point, according to the Relative Polar coordinate system in the Command Line window, enter @ as a prefix to the distance value followed by the angle value separated by an angle bracket (<), see Figure 2.22. In this figure, the distance and angle values (@25<60) are specified for a point that measures 25 units distance from the last specified point and 60 degrees angle from the X axis originating from the last specified point.

2.22

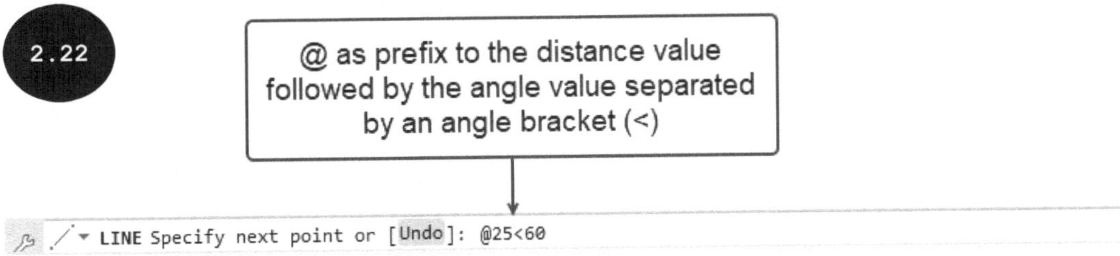

Specifying a Point in the Dynamic Input Boxes

To specify a point, according to the Relative Polar coordinate system in the Dynamic Input boxes, enter distance and angle values in the Dynamic Input boxes, without any prefix, see Figure 2.23.

2.23

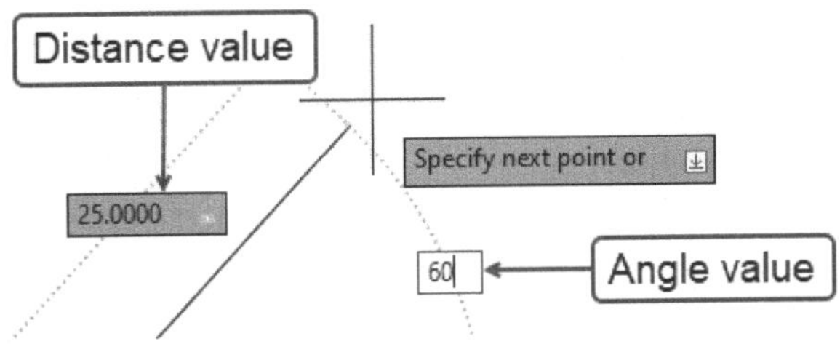

The following table summarizes the different coordinate systems discussed above.

Coordinate System		Command Line	Dynamic Input
Cartesian Coordinate System	Absolute Cartesian Coordinate System	X,Y *For example: 10,25*	# X,Y *For example: #10,25*
	Relative Cartesian Coordinate System	@X,Y *For example: @10,25*	X,Y *For example: 10,25*
Polar Coordinate System	Absolute Polar Coordinate System	**distance<angle** *For example: 25<60*	**#distance<angle** *For example: #25<60*
	Relative Polar Coordinate System	**@distance<angle** *For example: @25<60*	**distance<angle** *For example: 25<60*

Creating a Drawing

2.24

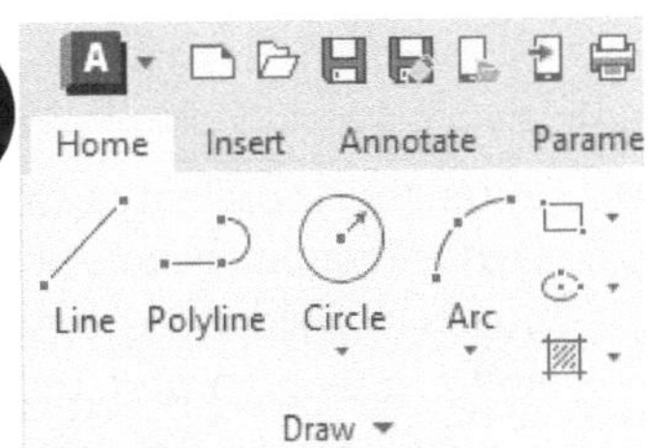

Once you have set up drawing units, limits, grid, and snap settings, and understood different coordinate systems, you can start creating a drawing in AutoCAD. In AutoCAD, the tools used for creating drawings are grouped in the **Draw** panel of the **Home** tab, see Figure 2.24. To activate a tool, click on it in the **Draw** panel or enter its shortcut key/command in the Command Line window. For example, to activate the **Line** tool, click on the **Line** tool in the **Draw** panel or enter **L** in the Command Line window and then press ENTER.

Drawing a Line

A line is defined as the shortest distance between two points. You can draw a line by specifying its start point and endpoint. The method for drawing a line is discussed below:

1. Click on the **Line** tool in the **Draw** panel of the **Home** tab, see Figure 2.25. Alternatively, enter **L** in the Command Line window and then press ENTER. The **Line** tool gets activated and you are prompted to specify the first point of the line.

```
Specify first point:
```

2.25

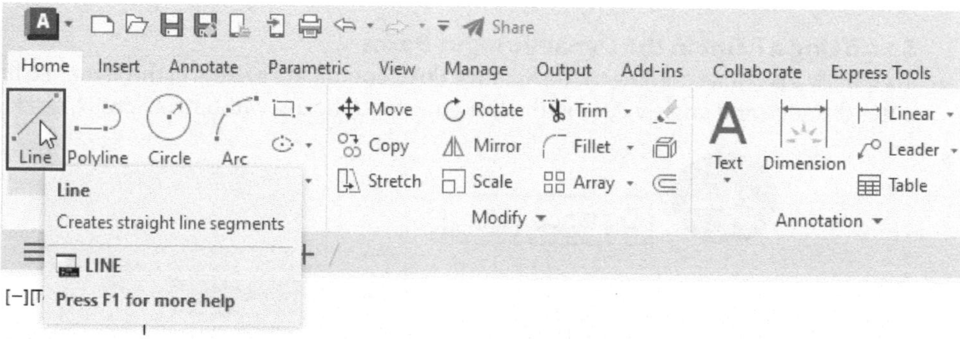

Note: As discussed, you can specify points by entering their coordinates according to the Cartesian coordinate system, or Polar coordinate system in the Command Line window or the Dynamic Input boxes. You can also pick points directly in the drawing area by clicking the left mouse button.

2. Enter the coordinates (X and Y) of the first point in the Command Line window or the Dynamic Input boxes. Alternatively, click in the drawing area to specify the first point of the line. As soon as you specify the first point of the line, you are prompted to specify the next (second) point of the line.

```
Specify next point or [Undo]:
```

Note: To specify coordinates in the Command Line window, you may need to turn off the Dynamic Input mode. You can turn on or off the Dynamic Input mode by clicking on the **Dynamic Input** button in the Status Bar.

3. Enter the coordinates (X and Y) of the second point in the Command Line window or the Dynamic Input boxes, or click in the drawing area. A line is drawn between the two specified points in the drawing area, see Figure 2.26. Also, a rubber band line gets attached to the cursor, and you are prompted to specify the next (third) point of the line.

```
Specify next point or [Undo]:
```

2.26

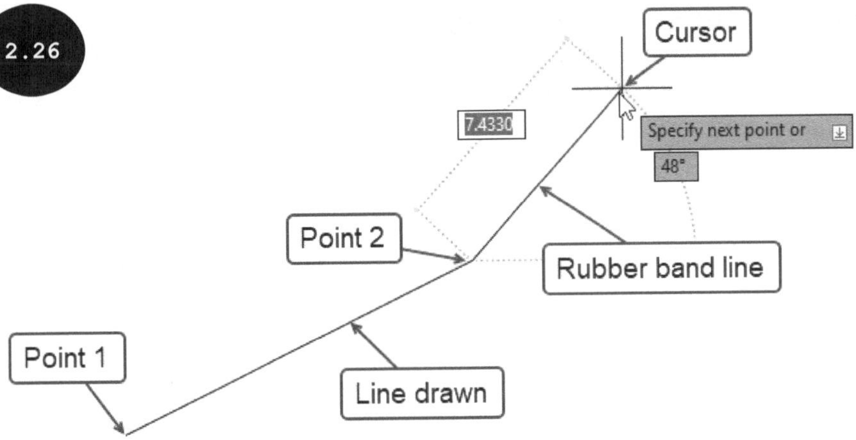

4. Similarly, you can continue specifying points in the drawing area for creating a chain of lines.

Note: After specifying the third point of the line, the command sequence appears as "`Specify next point or [Close Undo]:`" By using the options (Close and Undo) of the command sequence, you can create a closed loop of the line entities, and undo the last specified point.

To undo or cancel the last specified point, click on the **Undo** option that appears in the command sequence. Alternatively, enter **U** in the Command Line window and then press ENTER. You can undo or cancel multiple points one after another by continuously using this option.

To create a closed loop of the line entities where the last point joins to the first specified point, click on the **Close** option that appears in the command sequence or enter **C** in the Command Line window and then press ENTER, see Figure 2.27.

5. Once all the line entities have been drawn, exit from the **Line** tool by pressing the ENTER key. You can also press the **ESC** or **SPACEBAR** key to exit from the **Line** tool. Alternatively, right-click in the drawing area and then click on the **Enter** or **Cancel** option in the shortcut menu that appears to exit from the **Line** tool, see Figure 2.28.

2.27

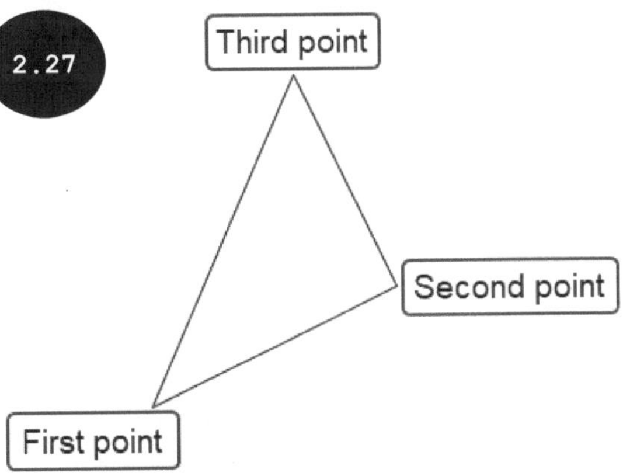

2.28

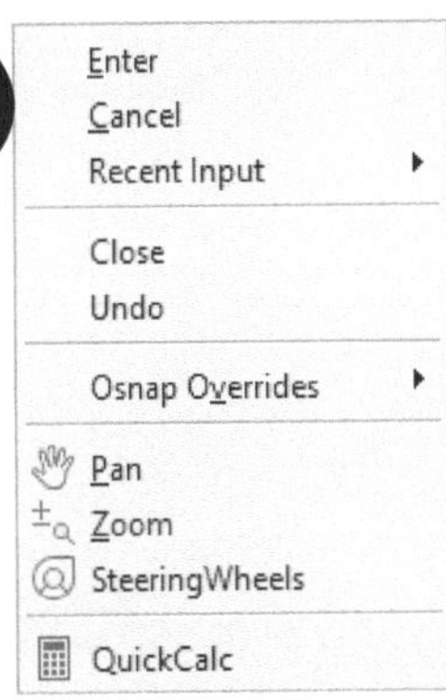

Command Sequence for Drawing a Line

```
Tool/Command: Line or L (ENTER)
Specify first point: (Specify X, Y coordinates)
Specify next point or [Undo]: (Specify X, Y coordinates)
Specify next point or [Undo]: (Specify X, Y coordinates)
Specify next point or [Close Undo]: ENTER
```

Note: While creating a drawing, it does not matter which coordinate system you use for specifying points in the drawing area. You can use any of the coordinate systems or a combination of coordinate systems to specify points in the drawing area as per your convenience.

Tutorial 1

Create the drawing shown in Figure 2.29 by using the Absolute Cartesian coordinate system. Also, specify the coordinates of the points by using the Command Line window.

2.29

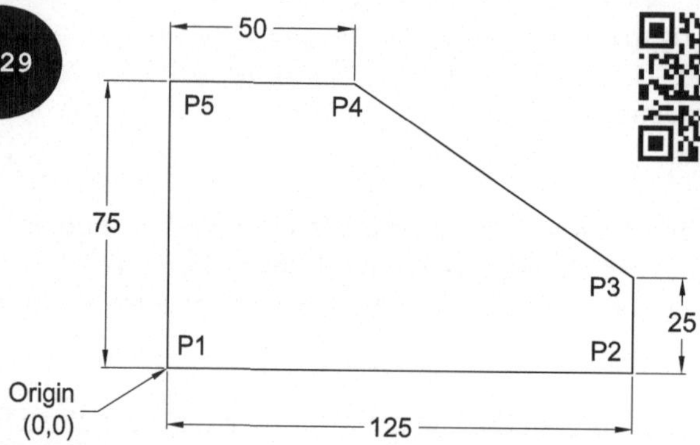

Section 1: Starting AutoCAD

1. Double-click on the AutoCAD icon on your desktop. The startup user interface of AutoCAD appears with the **Start** tab, see Figure 2.30.

2.30

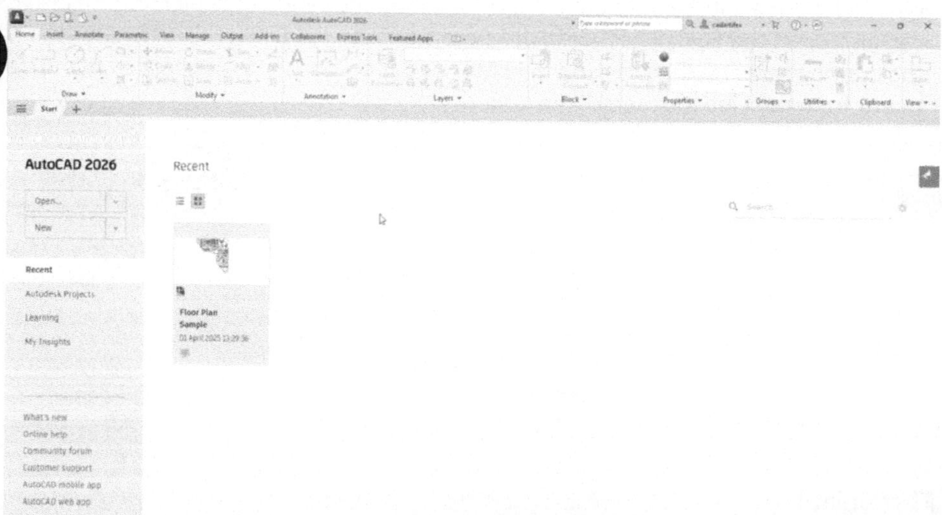

2. Click on the **New** tool in the **Start** tab, see Figure 2.30. A new drawing file with the default drawing template gets invoked.

   Alternatively, to invoke a new drawing file, click on the **New** tool in the **Quick Access Toolbar**, which is located at the top left corner of AutoCAD. The **Select template** dialog box appears. In this dialog box, choose the ***acad.dwt*** template and then click on the **Open** button. A new drawing file with ***acad.dwt*** template gets invoked. You can also right-click on the **Start** tab and then click on the **New** option in the shortcut menu that appears to invoke a new drawing file. Additionally, you can click on the + sign available next to the **Start** tab to invoke a new drawing file.

Section 2: Selecting Workspace for Creating Drawing

1. Click on the **Workspace Switching** button in the Status Bar. A flyout appears, see Figure 2.31.

2.31

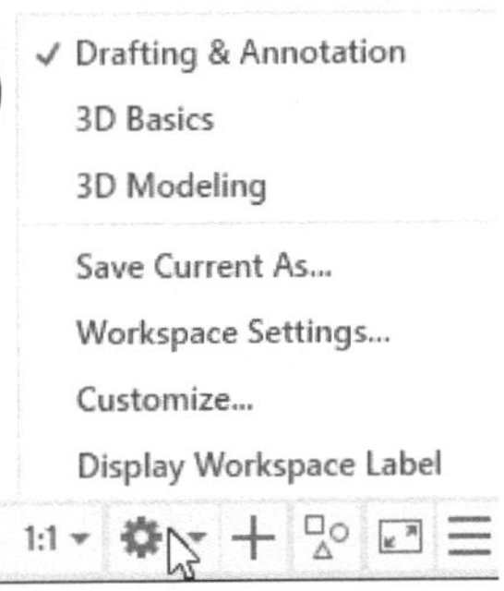

2. In this flyout, ensure that the **Drafting & Annotation** option is tick-marked to create drawings in the Drafting & Annotation workspace.

Note: A tick-mark next to a workspace indicates that it is selected as the current workspace for creating drawings. By default, the Drafting & Annotation workspace is selected as the current workspace for creating drawings.

Section 3: Defining Limits for Drawing

1. Follow the command sequence given below to define the limits of the drawing.

```
Command: LIMITS (ENTER)
Specify lower left corner or [ON/OFF]<0.0000,0.0000>: 0,0 (ENTER)
Specify upper right corner <12.0000,9.0000>: 250,150 (ENTER)
```

Section 4: Creating Drawing

As stated in the description of the tutorial, you need to enter coordinates in the Command Line window according to the Absolute Cartesian coordinate system for specifying points. It is recommended to turn off the Dynamic Input mode to enter coordinates in the Command Line window.

1. Click on the **Dynamic Input** button in the Status Bar to turn off the Dynamic Input mode. Note that it is a toggle button.

2. Click on the **Line** tool in the **Draw** panel of the **Home** tab. The **Line** tool gets activated, and you are prompted to specify the first point of the line. You can also enter **L** in the Command Line window and then press ENTER to activate the **Line** tool.

3. Follow the command sequence given below for creating the drawing.

```
Specify first point: 0,0 (ENTER)
Specify next point or [Undo]: 125,0 (ENTER)
Specify next point or [Undo]: 125,25 (ENTER)
Specify next point or [Close Undo]: 50,75 (ENTER)
Specify next point or [Close Undo]: 0,75 (ENTER)
Specify next point or [Close Undo]: C or Close
```

Tip: To specify points in the Dynamic Input boxes according to the Absolute coordinate system, you need to enter # as a prefix to the X coordinate followed by the Y coordinate in the Dynamic Input boxes.

Note: To fit the drawing completely in the drawing area, enter **ZOOM** in the Command Line window and then press ENTER. Next, enter **All** in the Command Line window and then press ENTER. The drawing fits entirely inside the drawing area.

Hands-on Test Drive 1

Create the same drawing created in Tutorial 1 by using the Relative Cartesian coordinate system, see Figure 2.32. Also, specify the coordinates of the points by using the Command Line window.

2.32

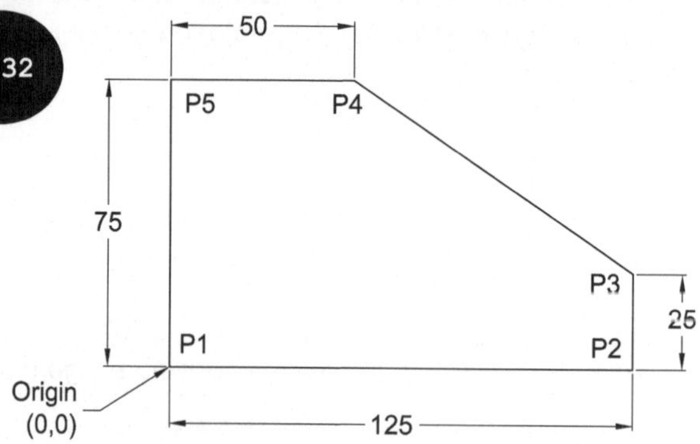

Hint: *In the Relative Cartesian coordinate system, every point you specify in the drawing area measures from the last specified point in the drawing area.*

The command sequence for creating a drawing with some of the coordinates of the points is as follows:

```
Tool/Command: Line or L (ENTER)
Specify first point: 0,0 (ENTER)
```

```
Specify next point or [Undo]: @125,0  (ENTER)
Specify next point or [Undo]: @0,25   (ENTER)
Specify next point or [Close Undo]: _______  (ENTER)
Specify next point or [Close Undo]: _______  (ENTER)
Specify next point or [Close Undo]: C or Close
```

Tutorial 2

Create the drawing shown in Figure 2.33 by using the Relative Polar coordinate system. Also, specify the coordinates of the points by using the Command Line window.

2.33

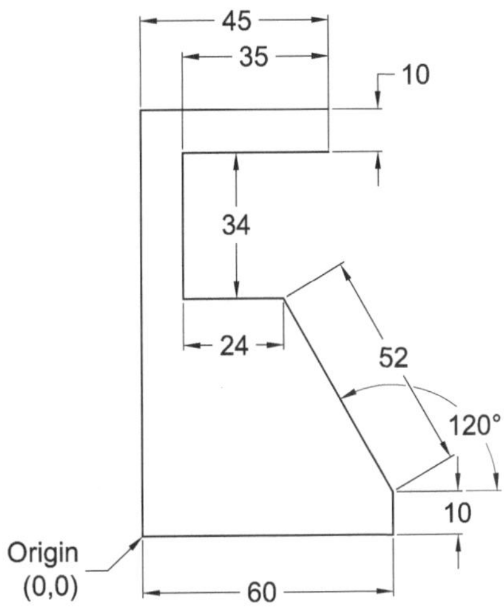

Section 1: Starting AutoCAD

1. Start AutoCAD by double-clicking on the AutoCAD icon on your desktop, if not already started.

2. In the Get Started section of the startup user interface, click on **Start Drawing**. A new drawing file with the default drawing template gets invoked.

Section 2: Selecting Workspace for Creating Drawing

1. Click on the **Workspace Switching**  button in the Status Bar. A flyout appears, see Figure 2.34.

2.34

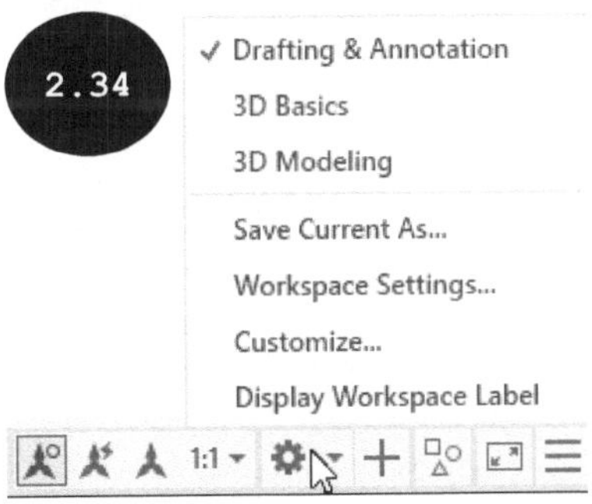

2. Ensure that the **Drafting & Annotation** option is tick-marked in this flyout.

Section 3: Defining Limits for Drawing

1. Follow the command sequence given below to define the limits of the drawing.

```
Command: LIMITS (ENTER)
Specify lower left corner or [ON/OFF]<0.0000,0.0000>: 0,0 (ENTER)
Specify upper right corner <12.0000,9.0000>: 120,200 (ENTER)
```

Section 4: Creating Drawing

As stated in the description of the tutorial, you need to enter coordinates in the Command Line window according to the Relative Polar coordinate system for specifying points. It is recommended to turn off the Dynamic Input mode to enter coordinates in the Command Line window.

1. Click on the **Dynamic Input** button in the Status Bar to turn off the Dynamic Input mode. Note that it is a toggle button.

2. Click on the **Line** tool in the **Draw** panel of the **Home** tab. The **Line** tool gets activated, and you are prompted to specify the first point of the line. Alternatively, you can enter **L** into the Command Line window and then press ENTER to activate the **Line** tool.

Note: In the Relative Polar coordinate system, you need to enter @ as a prefix to the distance value followed by the angle value separated by an angle bracket (<) in the Command Line window. Note that in the Relative Polar coordinate system, every point you specify in the drawing area by defining its distance and angle values, measures from the last specified point in the drawing area.

3. Follow the command sequence given below for creating the drawing.

```
Specify first point: 0,0 (ENTER)
Specify next point or [Undo]: @60<0 (ENTER)
Specify next point or [Undo]: @10<90 (ENTER)
Specify next point or [Close Undo]: @52<120 (ENTER)
Specify next point or [Close Undo]: @24<180 (ENTER)
Specify next point or [Close Undo]: @34<90 (ENTER)
Specify next point or [Close Undo]: @35<0 (ENTER)
Specify next point or [Close Undo]: @10<90 (ENTER)
Specify next point or [Close Undo]: @45<180 (ENTER)
Specify next point or [Close Undo]: C or Close
```

Hands-on Test Drive 2

Create the same drawing created in Tutorial 2, by using the Relative Polar coordinate system, see Figure 2.35. You need to specify the coordinates of the points by using the Dynamic Input boxes.

2.35

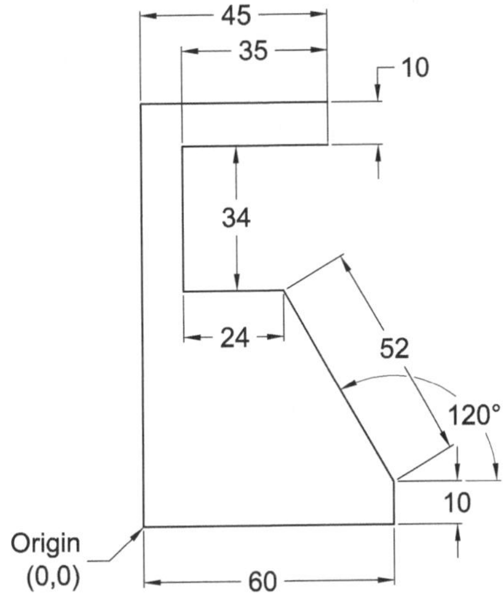

Hint: For specifying points by using the Relative Polar coordinate system in the Dynamic Input boxes, you first need to turn on the Dynamic Input mode by clicking on the ***Dynamic Input*** *button in the Status Bar. Next, you can directly enter the distance and angle values without any prefix in the respective Dynamic Input boxes, which appear near the cursor tip.*

Drawing a Circle

In AutoCAD, you can draw a circle by using the following methods:

- Defining center point and radius
- Defining center point and diameter
- Defining two diametrically opposite points on the circumference of the circle
- Defining three points on the circumference of the circle
- Defining two tangent points and radius
- Defining three tangent points

2.36

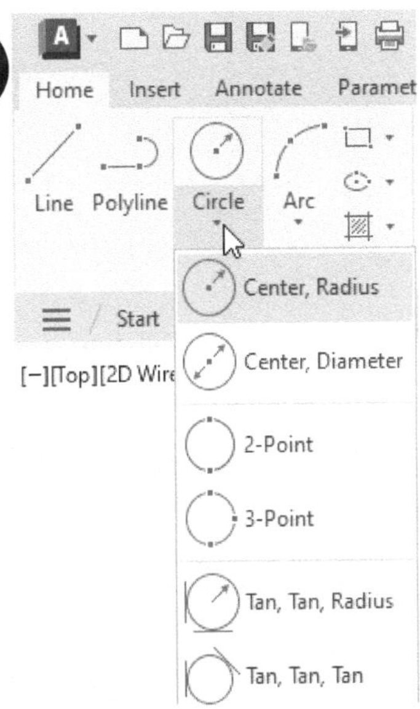

In AutoCAD, the tools for drawing a circle are available in the **Circle** flyout of the **Draw** panel in the **Home** tab, see Figure 2.36. Alternatively, you can invoke the **Circle** command for drawing a circle by entering **CIRCLE** or **C** in the Command Line window and then pressing ENTER. Different methods for drawing a circle are discussed next.

Drawing a Circle by Defining Center Point and Radius

You can draw a circle by defining its center point and radius by using the **Center, Radius** tool of the **Circle** flyout. For doing so, once the **Center, Radius** tool has been activated, you can specify the coordinates (X, Y) of the center point of the circle either in the Command Line window or the Dynamic Input boxes. The method for drawing a circle by defining center point and radius is discussed below:

1. Invoke the **Circle** flyout (see Figure 2.36) and then click on the **Center, Radius** tool. The **Center, Radius** tool gets activated, and you are prompted to specify the center point of the circle. Alternatively, you can enter **C** or **CIRCLE** in the Command Line window and then press ENTER to activate this tool.

   ```
   Specify center point for circle or [3P 2P Ttr (tan tan radius)]:
   ```

2. Specify the coordinates (X, Y) of the center point either in the Command Line or the Dynamic Input boxes, and then press ENTER. You are prompted to specify the radius of the circle. Alternatively, you can click in the drawing area to specify the center point of the circle.

   ```
   Specify radius of circle or [Diameter]:
   ```

Tip: To create a circle by defining its diameter, click on the **Diameter** option in the command prompt or enter **D** in the Command Line window and then press ENTER. Next, specify the diameter of the circle in the Command Line window.

3. Enter the radius value of the circle and then press ENTER. A circle with a specified radius is created in the drawing area, see Figure 2.37.

2.37

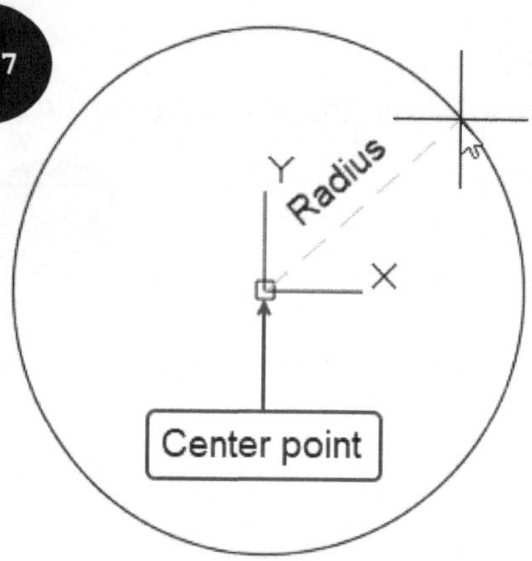

Drawing a Circle by Defining Center Point and Diameter

You can draw a circle by defining its center point and diameter by using the **Center, Diameter** tool of the **Circle** flyout, see Figure 2.38. The method for drawing a circle by defining its center point and diameter is discussed below:

2.38

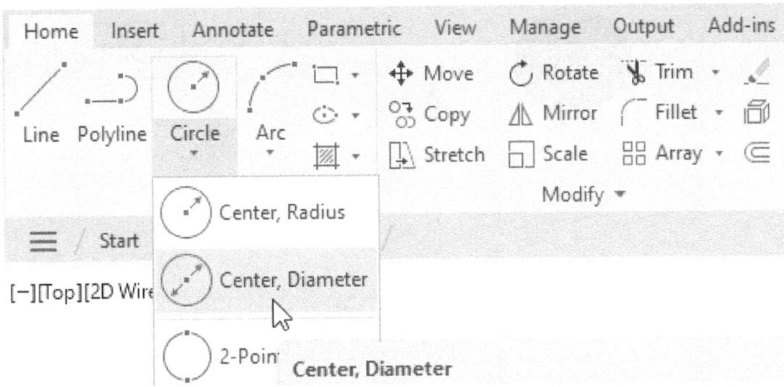

1. Invoke the **Circle** flyout and then click on the **Center, Diameter** tool. You are prompted to specify the center point of the circle. Alternatively, enter **C** in the Command Line window and then press ENTER.

```
Specify center point for circle or [3P 2P Ttr (tan tan radius)]:
```

2. Specify the coordinates (X, Y) of the center point either in the Command Line window or the Dynamic input boxes and then press ENTER. You are prompted to specify the diameter of the circle.

```
Specify radius of circle or [Diameter]:_d Specify diameter of circle:
```

Note: If you invoke the tool for creating a circle by entering C or **CIRCLE** in the Command Line window, then after specifying the center point of the circle, you need to click on the **Diameter** option in the command prompt for specifying the diameter of the circle.

3. Enter the diameter of the circle and then press ENTER. A circle with a specified diameter is created, see Figure 2.39.

2.39

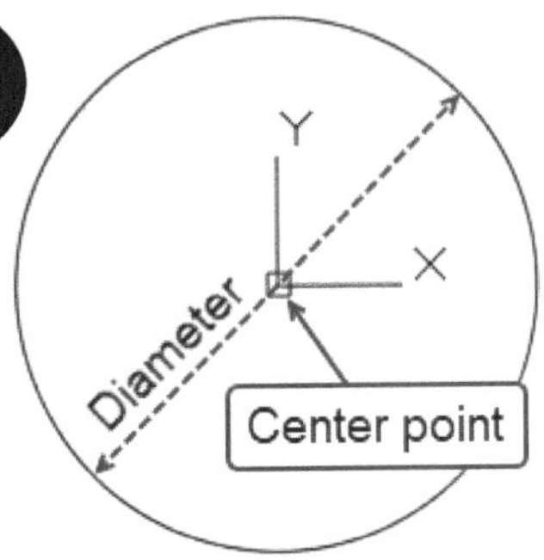

Drawing a Circle by Defining 2 Points

You can draw a circle by defining two diametrically opposite points on the circumference of the circle by using the **2-Point** tool, see Figure 2.40. You can also enter **C** or **CIRCLE** into the Command Line window and then click on the **2P** option in the command prompt that appears for creating the circle by defining two points on the circumference of the circle. The method for drawing a circle by defining two points is discussed below:

2.40

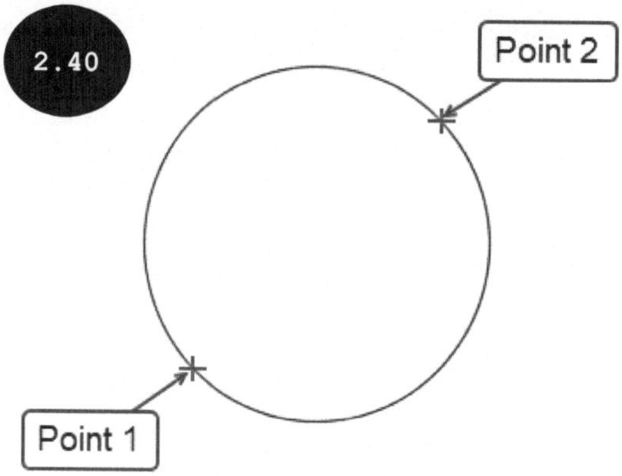

1. Invoke the **Circle** flyout and then click on the **2-Point** tool. You are prompted to specify the first point on the circumference of the circle. Alternatively, enter **C** in the Command Line window and then press ENTER. Next, click on the **2P** option in the command prompt that appears.

```
Specify center point for circle or [3P 2P Ttr (tan tan radius)]:_2p
Specify first endpoint of circle's diameter:
```

2. Enter the coordinates (X, Y) of the first point either in the Command Line window or in the Dynamic Input boxes, and then press ENTER. Alternatively, click in the drawing area to define the first point of the circle. After specifying the first point, you are prompted to specify the second point of the circle.

```
Specify second endpoint of circle's diameter:
```

3. Enter the coordinates (X, Y) of the second point on the circumference of the circle either in the Command Line window or in the Dynamic Input boxes, and then press ENTER. The circle is drawn, see Figure 2.40. You can also click directly in the drawing area to define the second point on the circumference of the circle.

Drawing a Circle by Defining 3 Points

In AutoCAD, you can draw a circle by defining three points on the circumference of the circle, see Figure 2.41. The method for drawing a circle by defining three points is discussed below:

2.41

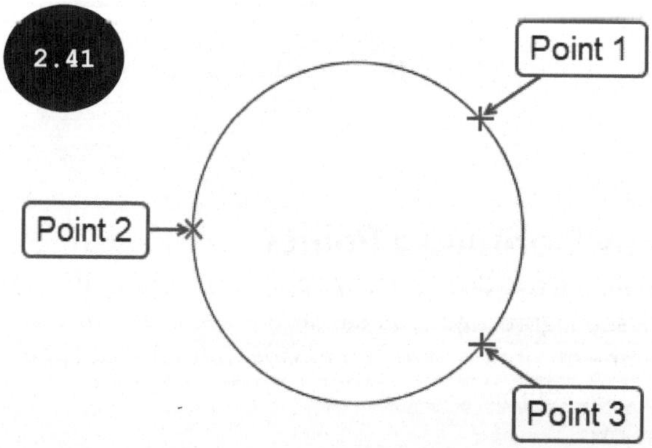

1. Invoke the **Circle** flyout and then click on the **3-Point** tool. You are prompted to specify the center point of the circle. Alternatively, enter **C** or **CIRCLE** in the Command Line window and then press ENTER. Next, click on the **3P** option in the command prompt or enter **3P** in the Command Line window.

```
Specify center point for circle or [3P 2P Ttr (tan tan radius)]:_3p
Specify first point on circle:
```

2. Enter the coordinates (X, Y) of the first point either in the Command Line window or in the Dynamic Input boxes, and then press ENTER. Alternatively, you can click directly in the drawing area to define the first point. As soon as you specify the first point, you are prompted to specify the second point of the circle.

```
Specify second point on circle:
```

3. Enter the coordinates (X, Y) of the second point. You are prompted to specify the third point. Also, a preview of the circle appears such that it has passed through the two specified points.

```
Specify third point on circle:
```

4. Enter the coordinates (X, Y) of the third point. The circle is drawn, see Figure 2.41.

Drawing a Circle by Defining Two Tangent Points and Radius

In AutoCAD, you can draw a circle that is tangent to two objects/entities. To draw a circle tangent to two objects/entities, you need to define two tangent objects and the radius of the circle by using the **Tan, Tan, Radius** tool, see Figure 2.42. The method for drawing a circle by defining two tangent points and radius is discussed below:

1. Invoke the **Circle** flyout and then click on the **Tan, Tan, Radius** tool. You are prompted to specify the first tangent object. Alternatively, enter **C** in the Command Line window and then press ENTER. Next, click on the **Ttr (tan tan radius)** option in the command prompt or enter **ttr** in the Command Line window.

```
Specify point on object for first tangent of circle:
```

2. Click on the first tangent object in the drawing area, see Figure 2.42. You are prompted to specify the second tangent object.

```
Specify point on object for second tangent of circle:
```

3. Click on the second tangent object in the drawing area, see Figure 2.42. You are prompted to specify the radius of the circle.

```
Specify radius of circle:
```

4. Enter the radius value of the circle either in the Command Line window or in the Dynamic Input boxes and then press ENTER. A circle tangent to the two selected objects is drawn, see Figure 2.42.

2.42

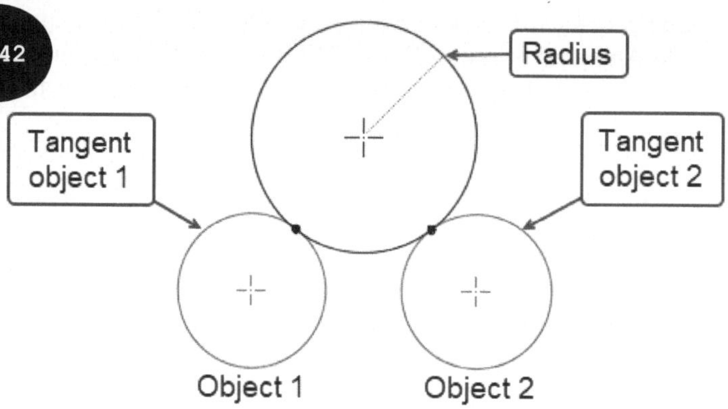

Drawing a Circle by Defining Three Tangent Points

In AutoCAD, you can draw a circle that is tangent to three objects/entities. To draw a circle tangent to three objects/entities, you need to define three tangent objects by using the **Tan, Tan, Tan** tool, see Figure 2.43. The method for drawing a circle by defining three tangent points is discussed below:

1. Invoke the **Circle** flyout and then click on the **Tan, Tan, Tan** tool. You are prompted to specify the first tangent object.

```
Specify center point for circle or [3P 2P Ttr (tan tan radius)]:_3p
Specify first point on circle:_tan to
```

2. Click on the first tangent object in the drawing area, see Figure 2.43. You are prompted to specify the second tangent object.

```
Specify second point on circle:_tan to
```

3. Click on the second tangent object in the drawing area, see Figure 2.43. You are prompted to specify the third tangent object.

```
Specify third point on circle:_tan to
```

2.43

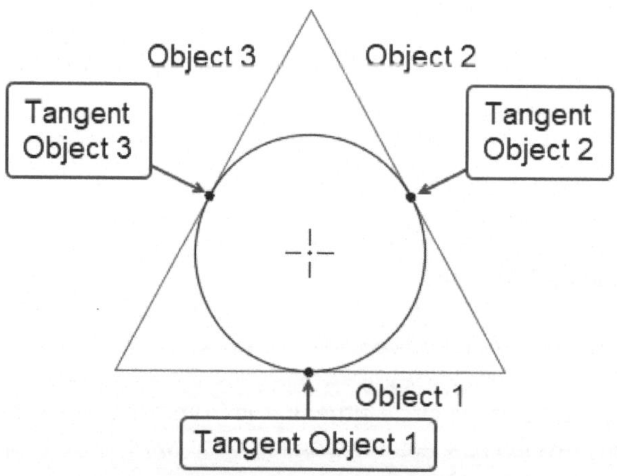

4. Click on the third tangent object, see Figure 2.43. A circle tangent to the three selected objects is drawn, see Figure 2.43.

Drawing an Arc

In AutoCAD, you can draw an arc by using different methods. The tools for drawing an arc are available in the **Arc** flyout of the **Draw** panel in the **Home** tab, see Figure 2.44. Alternatively, you can enter **ARC** or **A** in the Command Line window and then press ENTER to draw an arc. Different methods for creating an arc are discussed next.

Drawing an Arc by Defining 3 Points

You can draw an arc by defining three points on the circumference of the arc by using the **3-Point** tool, see Figure 2.45. The method for drawing an arc by defining three points is discussed below:

2.44

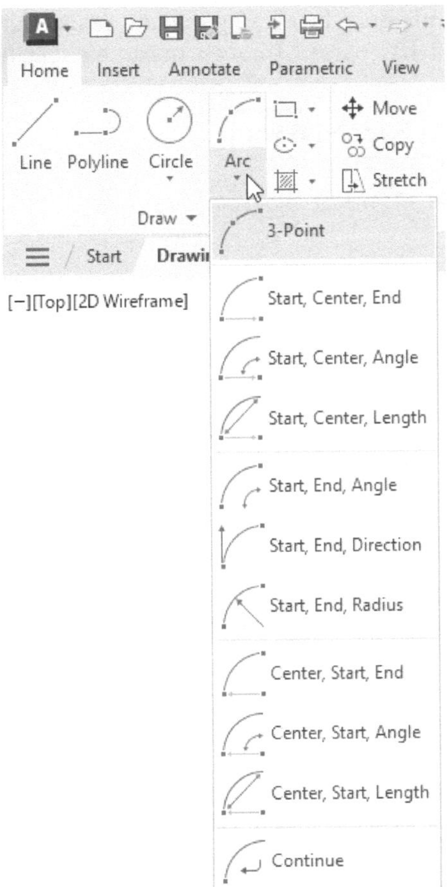

2.45

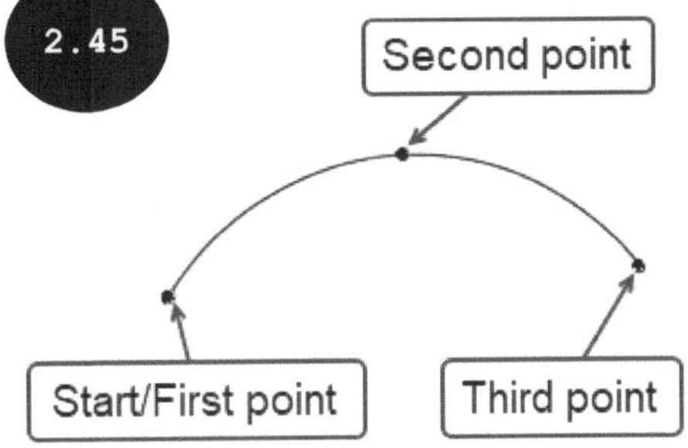

1. Click on the down arrow in the arc tool of the **Draw** panel to invoke the **Arc** flyout, see Figure 2.44. Next, click on the **3-Point** tool. You are prompted to specify the start point of the arc. Alternatively, enter **A** or **ARC** in the Command Line window and then press ENTER to invoke the **3-Point** tool.

```
Specify start point of arc or [Center]:
```

2. Enter the coordinates (X, Y) of the start point and then press ENTER. You are prompted to specify the second point of the arc. You can also click in the drawing area to specify the start point of the arc.

```
Specify second point of arc or [Center End]:
```

3. Move the cursor counter-clockwise or clockwise in the drawing area and then click the left mouse button to specify the second point of the arc on its circumference. You can also specify the second point of the arc by entering its coordinates (X, Y). As soon as you specify the second point, you are prompted to specify the endpoint of the arc. Also, the preview of the arc appears such that it has passed through the first and second points specified in the drawing area.

```
Specify end point of arc:
```

4. Specify the endpoint of the arc on its circumference by clicking the left mouse button in the drawing area. The arc is drawn such that it has passed through the three specified points, see Figure 2.46.

2.46

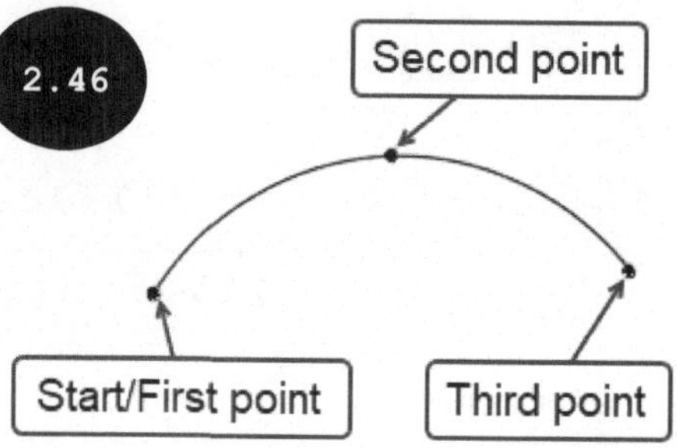

Drawing an Arc by Defining Start, Center, and EndPoints

You can draw an arc by defining the start, center, and endpoints using the **Start, Center, End** tool of the **Arc** flyout, see Figure 2.47. The method for drawing an arc by defining start, center, and endpoints is discussed below:

1. Invoke the **Arc** flyout and then click on the **Start, Center, End** tool. You are prompted to specify the start point of the arc. Alternatively, enter **A** in the Command Line window and then press ENTER.

```
Specify start point of arc or [Center]:
```

2. Enter the coordinates (X, Y) of the start point and then press ENTER. You are prompted to specify the center point of the arc. You can also click the left mouse button in the drawing area to specify the start point of the arc.

```
Specify center point of arc:
```

Note: If you invoke the tool for creating an arc by entering **A** or **ARC** in the Command Line window then after specifying the start point of the arc, you need to click on the **Center** option in the command prompt for specifying the center point of the arc.

3. Move the cursor to the required location in the drawing area and then click to specify the center point of the arc. You can also enter the coordinates (X, Y) for specifying the center point of the arc. As soon as you specify the center point, you are prompted to specify the endpoint of the arc. Also, the preview of the arc appears in the counter-clockwise direction in the drawing area.

```
Specify end point of arc (hold Ctrl to switch direction) or [Angle chord Length]:
```

Note: By default, an arc is created in the counter-clockwise direction. To change the direction of the arc from counter-clockwise direction to clockwise direction, press and hold the CTRL key and then specify the endpoint of the arc.

4. Specify the endpoint of the arc by clicking the left mouse button. The arc is drawn, see Figure 2.47.

2.47

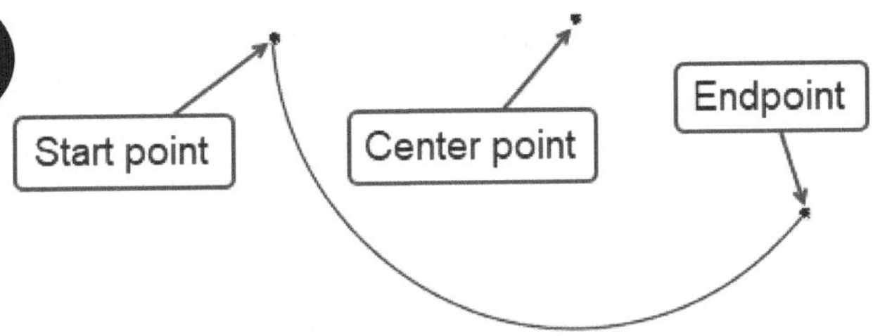

Drawing an Arc by Defining Start Point, Center Point, and Angle

You can draw an arc by defining start point, center point, and angle using the **Start, Center, Angle** tool of the **Arc** flyout, see Figure 2.48. Below is the command sequence for drawing an arc.

`Tool/Command:` *Click on the **Start, Center, Angle** tool in the **Arc** flyout.*
`Specify start point of arc or [Center]:` *Specify the start point of the arc.*
`Specify center point of arc:` *Specify the center point of the arc.*
`Specify included angle (hold Ctrl to switch direction):` *Specify the angle of the arc (see Figure 2.48).*

2.48

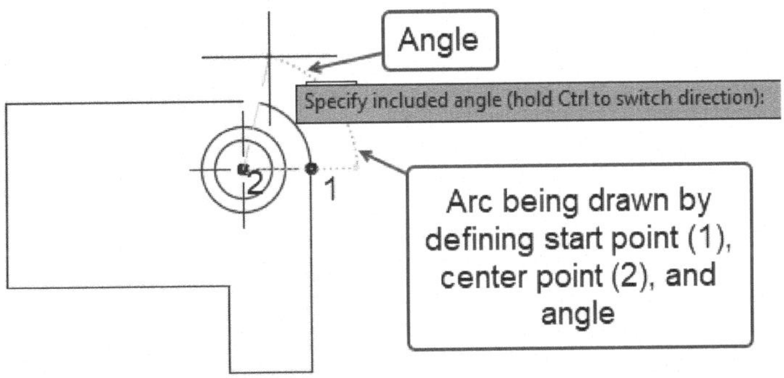

Tip: As discussed, you can specify coordinates (X, Y) either in the Command Line window or in the Dynamic Input boxes. Alternatively, you can also click the left mouse button in the drawing area for specifying points.

Drawing an Arc by Defining Start Point, Center Point, and Length

You can draw an arc by defining start point, center point, and length using the **Start, Center, Length** tool of the **Arc** flyout, see Figure 2.49. Below is the command sequence for drawing an arc by specifying the start point, center point, and length.

`Tool/Command:` *Click on the **Start, Center, Length** tool in the **Arc** flyout.*
`Specify start point of arc or [Center]:` *Specify the start point of the arc.*
`Specify center point of arc:` *Specify the center point of the arc.*
`Specify length of chord (hold Ctrl to switch direction):` *Specify the length of the chord (see Figure 2.49).*

2.49

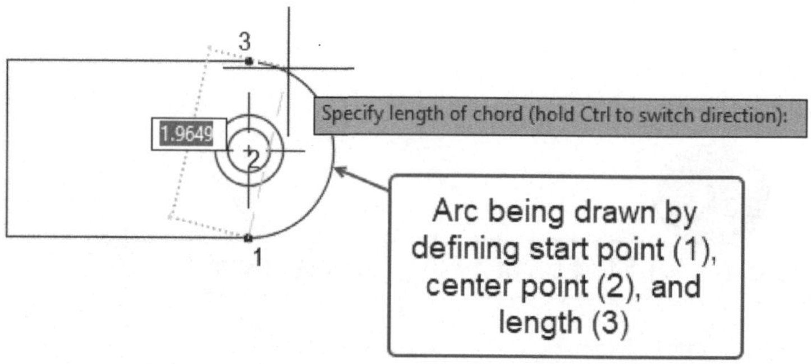

Drawing an Arc by Defining Start Point, EndPoint, and Angle

You can draw an arc by defining start point, endpoint, and angle using the **Start, End, Angle** tool of the **Arc** flyout, see Figure 2.50. Below is the command sequence for drawing an arc by specifying the start point, endpoint, and angle.

`Command/Tool:` *Click on the **Start, End, Angle** tool in the **Arc** flyout.*
`Specify start point of arc or [Center]:` *Specify the start point of the arc.*
`Specify end point of arc:` *Specify the endpoint of the arc.*
`Specify included angle (hold Ctrl to switch direction):` *Specify the angle of the arc (see Figure 2.50).*

2.50

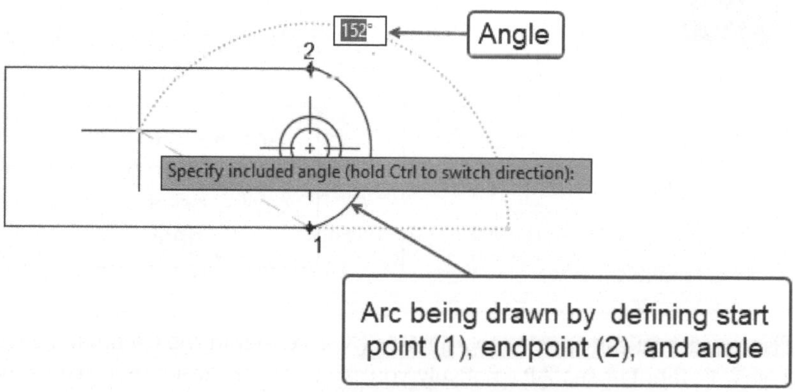

Drawing an Arc by Defining Start Point, EndPoint, and Direction

You can draw an arc by defining start point, endpoint, and direction using the **Start, End, Direction** tool of the **Arc** flyout, see Figure 2.51. Below is the command sequence for drawing an arc by specifying the start point, endpoint, and direction.

`Tool/Command:` *Click on the* ***Start, End, Direction*** *tool in the* ***Arc*** *flyout.*
`Specify start point of arc or [Center]:` *Specify the start point of the arc.*
`Specify end point of arc:` *Specify the endpoint of the arc.*
`Specify tangent direction for the start point of arc (hold Ctrl to switch direction):` *Specify the direction of the arc (see Figure 2.51).*

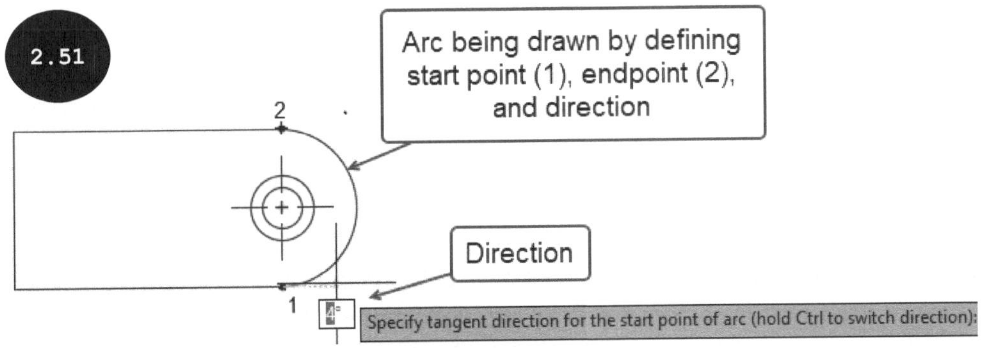

Drawing an Arc by Defining Start Point, EndPoint, and Radius

You can draw an arc by defining start point, endpoint, and radius using the **Start, End, Radius** tool of the **Arc** flyout, see Figure 2.52. Below is the command sequence for drawing an arc by specifying the start point, endpoint, and radius.

`Tool/Command:` *Click on the* ***Start, End, Radius*** *tool in the* ***Arc*** *flyout.*
`Specify start point of arc or [Center]:` *Specify the start point of the arc.*
`Specify end point of arc:` *Specify the endpoint of the arc.*
`Specify radius of arc (hold Ctrl to switch direction):` *Specify the radius of the arc (see Figure 2.52).*

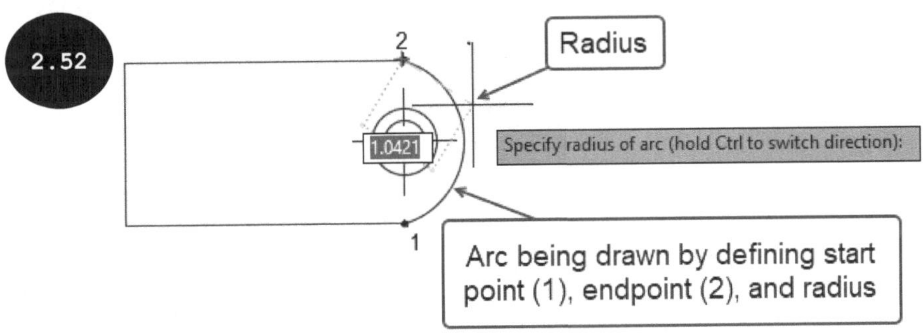

Drawing an Arc by Defining Center Point, Start Point, and EndPoint

You can draw an arc by defining the center point, start point, and endpoint using the **Center, Start, End** tool of the **Arc** flyout, see Figure 2.53. Below is the command sequence for drawing an arc by specifying the center point, start point, and endpoint.

`Tool/Command:` *Click on the **Center, Start, End** tool in the **Arc** flyout.*
`Specify center point of arc:` *Specify the center point of the arc (see Figure 2.53).*
`Specify start point of arc:` *Specify the start point of the arc (see Figure 2.53).*
`Specify end point of arc (hold Ctrl to switch direction) or [Angle chord Length]:` *Specify the endpoint of the arc (see Figure 2.53).*

2.53

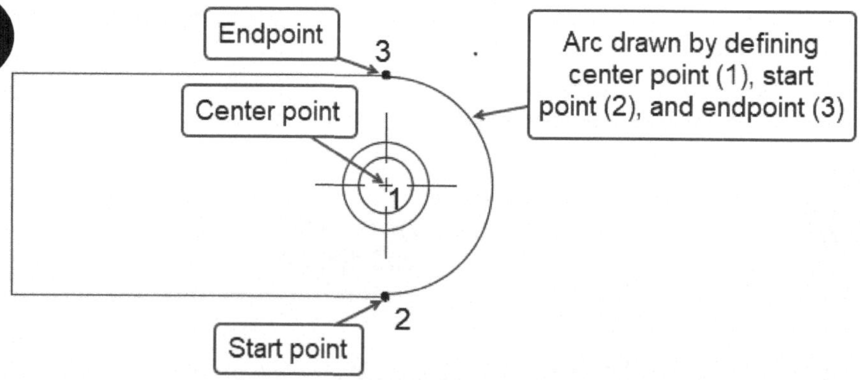

Drawing an Arc by Defining Center Point, Start Point, and Angle

You can draw an arc by defining the center point, start point, and angle using the **Center, Start, Angle** tool of the **Arc** flyout, see Figure 2.54. Below is the command sequence for drawing an arc by specifying the center point, start point, and angle.

`Tool/Command:` *Click on the **Center, Start, Angle** tool in the **Arc** flyout.*
`Specify center point of arc:` *Specify the center point of the arc (see Figure 2.54).*
`Specify start point of arc:` *Specify the start point of the arc (see Figure 2.54).*
`Specify included angle (hold Ctrl to switch direction):` *Specify the angle of the arc (see Figure 2.54)*.

2.54

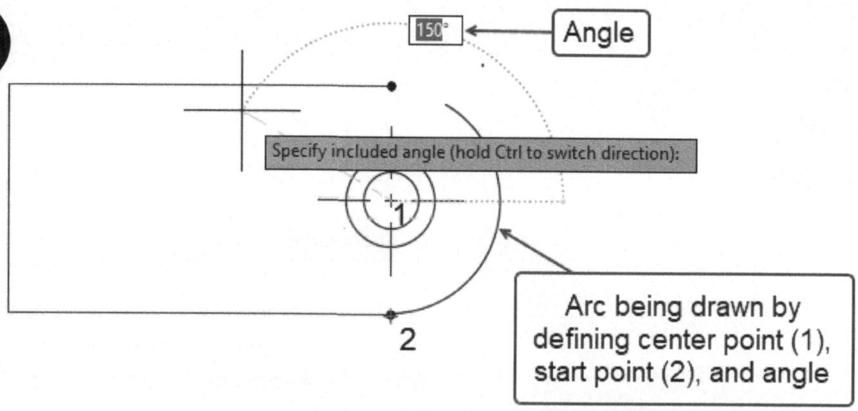

Drawing an Arc by Defining Center Point, Start Point, and Length

You can draw an arc by defining the center point, start point, and length using the **Center, Start, Length** tool of the **Arc** flyout, see Figure 2.55. Below is the command sequence for drawing an arc by specifying the center point, start point, and length.

`Command/Tool:` *Click on the **Center, Start, Length** tool of the **Arc** flyout.*
`Specify center point of arc:` *Specify the center point of the arc.*
`Specify start point of arc:` *Specify the start point of the arc.*
`Specify length of chord (hold Ctrl to switch direction):` *Specify length to draw an arc (see Figure 2.55).*

2.55

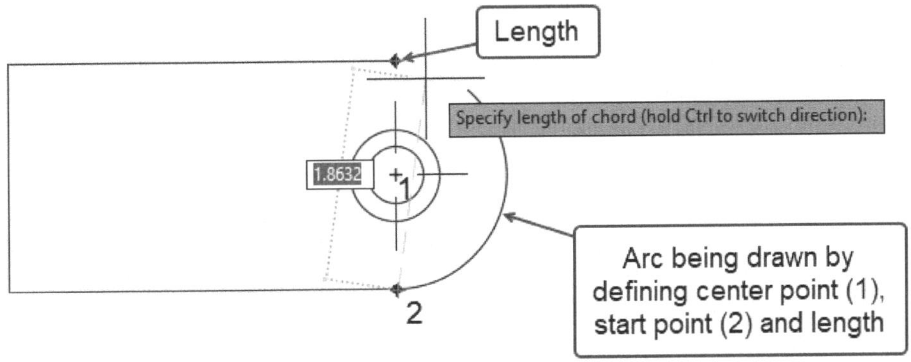

Drawing an Arc by using the Continue Tool

You can draw an arc tangent to the last drawn line or arc entity by using the **Continue** tool of the **Arc** flyout. Below is the command sequence for drawing an arc tangent to the last drawn line or arc entity.

`Tool/Command:` *Click on the **Continue** tool in the **Arc** flyout. The preview of a tangent arc appears such that its start point is fixed at the endpoint of the last drawn entity.*
`Specify end point of arc (hold Ctrl to switch direction):` *Click to specify the endpoint of the arc.*

Canceling, Erasing and Restoring Objects

In AutoCAD, you can cancel or exit the currently active command/tool, erase or delete unwanted entities, and restore the erased or deleted entities in the drawing area. To cancel or exit the currently active command/tool, press the ESC or ENTER key. Alternatively, right-click in the drawing area and then click on the **Cancel** or **Enter** option in the shortcut menu displayed. For example, if you are creating line entities by using the **Line** tool then press the ESC or ENTER key to terminate the creation of lines and exit from the **Line** tool. Refer to the command sequence given below:

`Tool/Command:` *Line or L* (***ENTER***)
`Specify first point:` *Specify X, Y coordinates or click in the drawing area.*
`Specify next point or [Undo]:` *Specify X, Y coordinates or click in the drawing area.*
`Specify next point or [Undo]:` *ESC or ENTER.*

To erase the drawing entities that are drawn by mistake, enter **E** or **ERASE** in the Command Line window and then press ENTER. The erase command gets activated, and you are prompted to select the objects to be erased. Click on the objects to be erased from the drawing. You can click on multiple objects one by one to erase them. Next, press the ENTER key or right-click in the drawing area. The selected objects get deleted from the drawing. Refer to the command sequence given below:

```
Command: ERASE or E (ENTER).
Select objects: Click on the first object to be erased.
Select objects: Click on the second object to be erased.
Select objects: ENTER.
```

Tip: You can also click on the **ERASE** tool in the **Modify** panel of the **Home** tab to erase the drawing entities.

To erase all objects/entities of a drawing at a time, invoke the **ERASE** tool/command and then enter **All** in the Command Line window.

You can restore an object that has accidentally been deleted in a drawing. To do so, enter **Undo** or **U** in the Command Line window and then press ENTER. The undo command gets activated, and the previously deleted object gets restored in the drawing area. You can use the undo command multiple times to restore the previously deleted objects one by one. Alternatively, press CTRL + Z to restore the previously deleted objects.

Navigating 2D Drawings

In AutoCAD, you can navigate a drawing by using the navigating tools. The navigating tools such as **Zoom** and **Pan** can be accessed from the **Navigation Bar**, which is on the right side of the drawing area, see Figure 2.56. Different navigating tools are discussed next.

Zoom

AutoCAD has many powerful tools to zoom into or zoom out of the drawing for better control over it. These tools are available in the **Zoom** flyout of the **Navigation Bar**. To invoke the **Zoom** flyout, click on the down arrow in the zoom tool of the **Navigation Bar**, see Figure 2.57. Some of the zoom tools are discussed next.

2.56

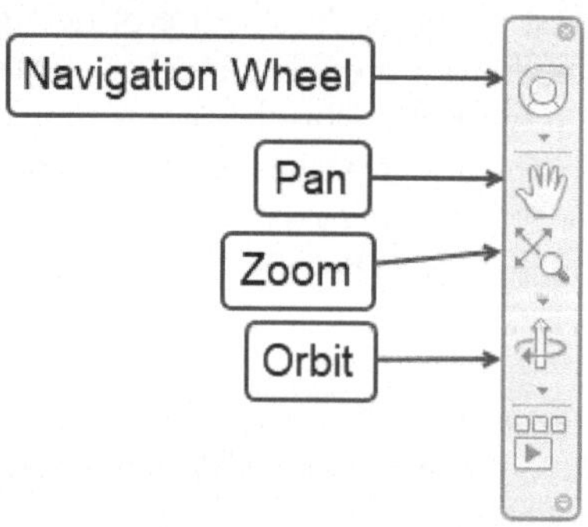

2.57

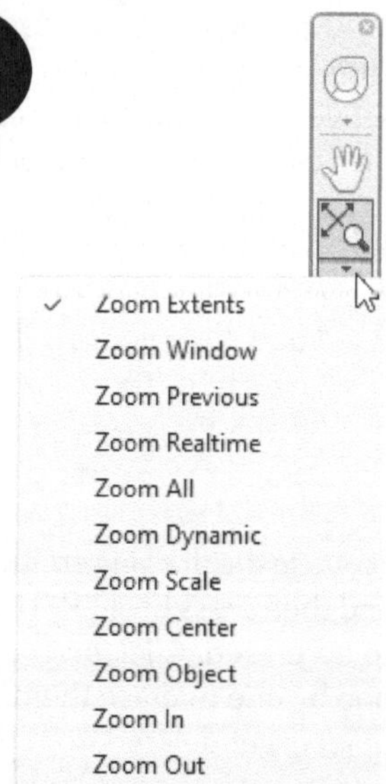

Zoom Realtime

The **Zoom Realtime** tool is used for zooming into or zooming out of the drawing area, dynamically. In other words, you can dynamically enlarge or reduce the view of the drawing area by using the **Zoom Realtime** tool. To invoke the **Zoom Realtime** tool, click on the down arrow in the zoom tool of the **Navigation Bar**.

The **Zoom** flyout appears, see Figure 2.57. In this flyout, click on the **Zoom Realtime** tool, see Figure 2.58. Alternatively, to invoke the **Zoom Realtime** tool, enter Z or ZOOM in the Command Line window and then press ENTER twice. Refer to the command sequence given below:

2.58

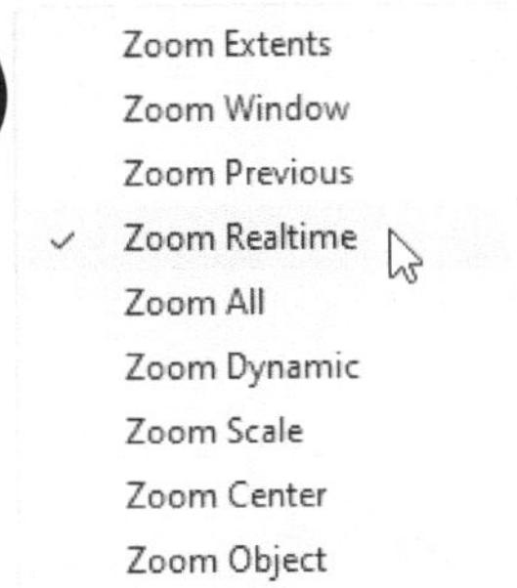

Tool/Command: *Zoom or Z* (***ENTER***).
Specify corner of window, enter a scale factor (nX or nXP), or [All/Center/Dynamic/Extents/Previous/Scale/Window/Object]<real time>: ***ENTER***.

After invoking the **Zoom Realtime** tool, press and hold the left mouse button in the drawing area and then drag the cursor upward or downward in the drawing area. On dragging the cursor upward, the drawing view starts enlarging, and on dragging the cursor downward, the drawing view starts shrinking. Note that in the process of enlarging or shrinking the drawing view, the scale of the drawing remains the same; only the viewing distance changes to enlarge or shrink the view.

Zoom All

The **Zoom All** tool is used for zooming the entire drawing or drawing limit to fit inside the drawing area. If the drawing is large and goes outside the drawing limit, then the entire drawing fits inside the drawing area by using the **Zoom All** tool, see Figure 2.59. However, if the drawing is smaller than the drawing limit, then the drawing limit fits inside the drawing area using the **Zoom All** tool, see Figure 2.60. To invoke the **Zoom All** tool, click on the down arrow in the zoom tool of the **Navigation Bar**. The **Zoom** flyout appears. In this flyout, click on the **Zoom All** tool. Alternatively, enter Z or ZOOM in the Command Line window and then press ENTER. Next, enter **A** or **ALL** to invoke the **Zoom All** tool. Refer to the command sequence given below:

2.59

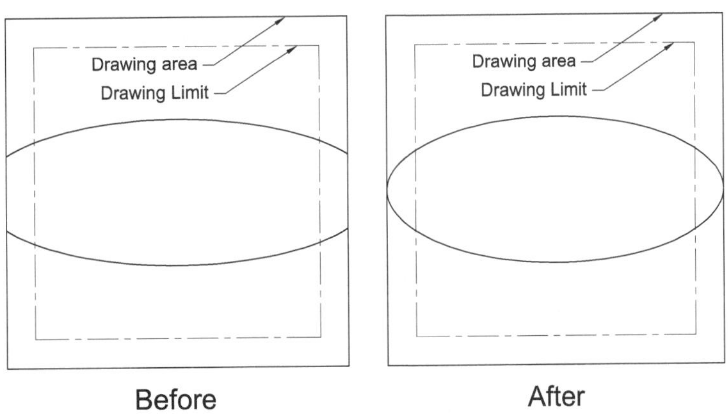

2.60

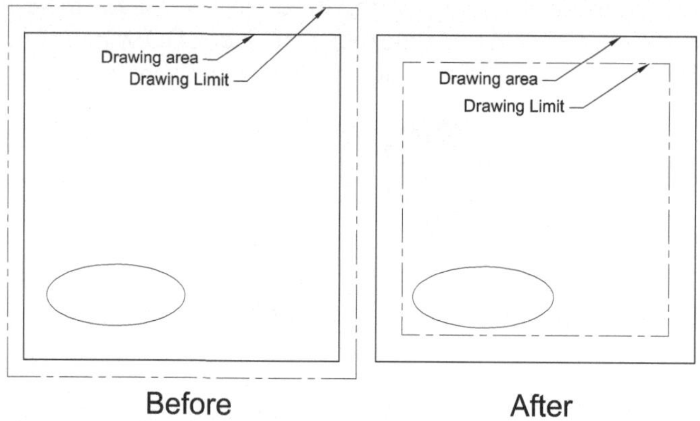

Command: *Z or Zoom* (***ENTER***).
Specify corner of window, enter a scale factor (nX or nXP), or [All/Center/Dynamic/Extents/Previous/Scale/Window/Object]<real time>: *A or ALL* (***ENTER***).

As soon as you invoke the **Zoom All** tool/command, the entire drawing or drawing limit fits inside the drawing area.

Zoom Window

The **Zoom Window** tool is used for zooming into an area of a drawing. You can specify an area of a drawing to be zoomed into by drawing a rectangular window around it. To invoke the **Zoom Window** tool, invoke the **Zoom** flyout of the **Navigation Bar** and then click on the **Zoom Window** tool. Alternatively, enter Z or ZOOM in the Command Line window and then press ENTER. Next, enter W in the Command Line window to invoke the **Zoom Window** tool. Refer to the command sequence given below:

Command: *Z or Zoom* (***ENTER***).
Specify corner of window, enter a scale factor (nX or nXP), or [All/Center/Dynamic/Extents/Previous/Scale/Window/Object]<real time>: *W* (***ENTER***).
Specify first corner: *Click to specify the first corner of the rectangular window in the drawing area.*
Specify first corner: Specify opposite corner: *Click to specify the opposite corner of the rectangular window.*

After drawing a rectangular window, the area lying inside it gets magnified and fits in the drawing area.

Zoom Previous

The **Zoom Previous** tool is used for displaying the previously zoomed view of a drawing. To invoke the **Zoom Previous** tool, invoke the **Zoom** flyout of the **Navigation Bar** and then click on the **Zoom Preview** tool. Alternatively, enter **Z** or **Zoom** in the Command Line window and then press ENTER. Next, enter **P** in the Command Line window to invoke the **Zoom Previous** tool. Refer to the command sequence given below:

```
Command: Z or Zoom (ENTER).
Specify corner of window, enter a scale factor (nX or nXP), or
[All/Center/Dynamic/Extents/Previous/Scale/Window/Object]<real
time>: P (ENTER).
```

Zoom Extents

The **Zoom Extents** tool is used for fitting a drawing completely inside the drawing area by expanding or shrinking the drawing view. By using this tool, all the entities in the drawing get magnified to their largest capacities in the drawing area. To invoke the **Zoom Extents** tool, invoke the **Zoom** flyout of the **Navigation Bar** and then click on the **Zoom Extents** tool. Alternatively, enter Z or ZOOM in the Command Line window and then press ENTER. Next, enter **E** to invoke this tool. Refer to the command sequence given below:

```
Command: Z or Zoom (ENTER).
Specify corner of window, enter a scale factor (nX or nXP), or
[All/Center/Dynamic/Extents/Previous/Scale/Window/Object]<real
time>: E (ENTER).
```

Zoom In

The **Zoom In** tool is used for zooming into a drawing by doubling its size in the drawing area. To invoke the **Zoom In** tool, invoke the **Zoom** flyout of the **Navigation Bar** and then click on the **Zoom In** tool. Alternatively, enter Z or ZOOM in the Command Line window and then press ENTER. Next, enter **2X** to invoke this tool. Refer to the command sequence given below:

```
Command: Z or Zoom (ENTER).
Specify corner of window, enter a scale factor (nX or nXP), or
[All/Center/Dynamic/Extents/Previous/Scale/Window/Object]<real
time>: 2X (ENTER).
```

Zoom Out

The **Zoom Out** tool is used for zooming out of the drawing by decreasing its size to half of the current size of the drawing. To invoke the **Zoom Out** tool, invoke the **Zoom** flyout of the **Navigation Bar** and then click on the **Zoom Out** tool. Alternatively, enter Z or ZOOM in the Command Line window and then press ENTER. Next, enter **.5X** in the Command Line window to invoke this tool. Refer to the command sequence given below:

```
Command: Z or Zoom (ENTER).
Specify corner of window, enter a scale factor (nX or nXP), or
[All/Center/Dynamic/Extents/Previous/Scale/Window/Object]<real
time>: .5X (ENTER).
```

Note: You can turn on or off the display of the **Navigation Bar** in the drawing area by using the **Navigation Bar** tool in the **Viewport Tools** panel of the **View** tab in the **Ribbon**, see Figure 2.61. By default, this tool is activated in the **Viewport Tools** panel of the **View** tab. As a result, the display of **Navigation Bar** is turned on in the drawing area.

2.61

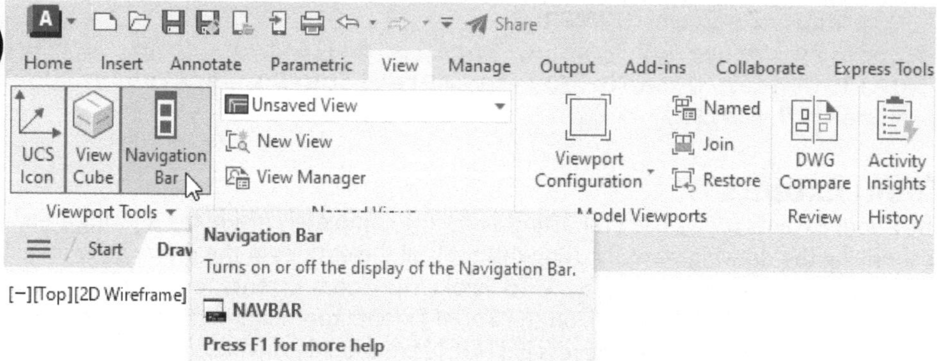

Pan

The **Pan** tool is used for panning/moving a drawing in the drawing area. To invoke the **Pan** tool, click on the **Pan** tool in the **Navigation Bar**, see Figure 2.62. After invoking the **Pan** tool, you can pan the drawing by pressing and holding the left mouse button and then dragging the cursor.

2.62

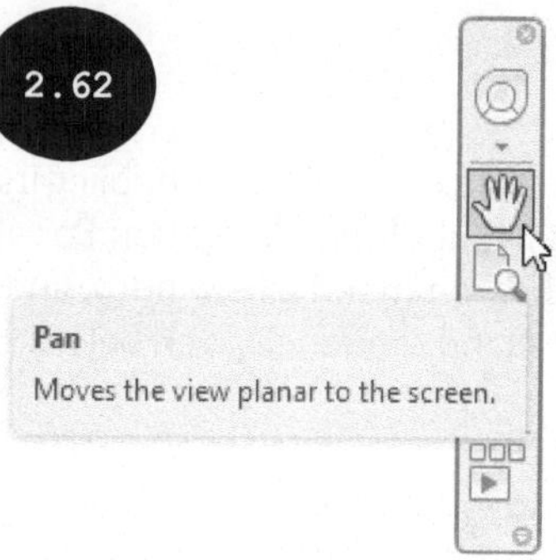

Tutorial 3

Create the drawing shown in Figure 2.63, by specifying points using the Absolute Cartesian coordinate system. Also, use the Dynamic Input boxes for specifying coordinates. The dimensions shown in this figure are for your reference only. You will learn about applying dimensions in the later chapters.

2.63

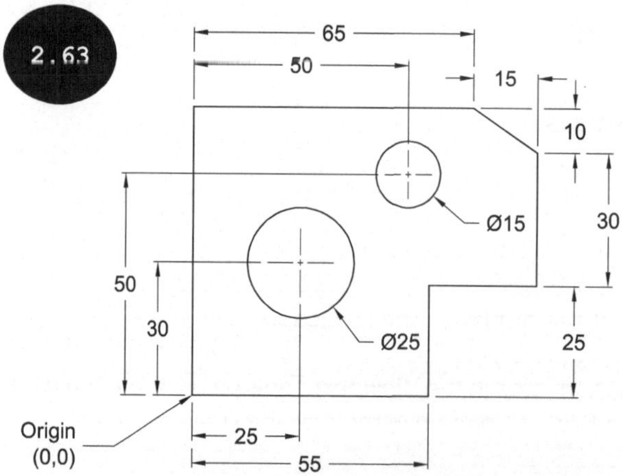

Section 1: Starting AutoCAD

1. Double-click on the AutoCAD icon on your desktop. The startup user interface of AutoCAD appears with the **Start** tab, see Figure 2.64.

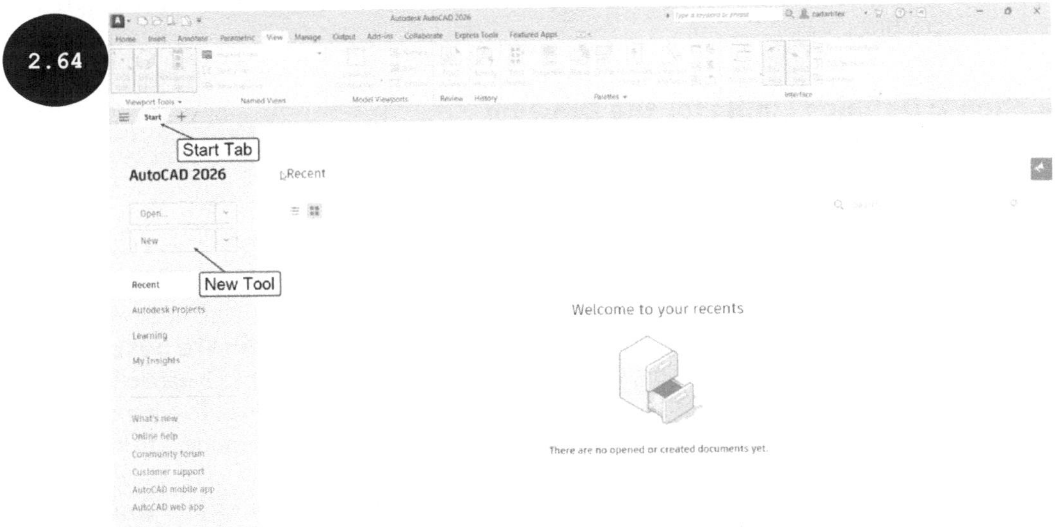

2. Click on the **New** tool in the **Start** tab, see Figure 2.64. A new drawing file with the default drawing template gets invoked.

Note: Alternatively, to invoke a new drawing file, click on the **New** tool in the **Quick Access Toolbar**, which is at the top left corner of AutoCAD. The **Select template** dialog box appears. In this dialog box, choose the ***acad.dwt*** template and then click on the **Open** button. A new drawing file with the ***acad.dwt*** template gets invoked. You can also right-click on the **Start** tab and then click on the **New** option in the shortcut menu that appears. Additionally, you can click on the **+** sign available next to the **Start** tab to invoke a new drawing file.

Section 2: Selecting Workspace for Creating Drawing

1. Click on the **Workspace Switching** button in the Status Bar. A flyout appears, see Figure 2.65.

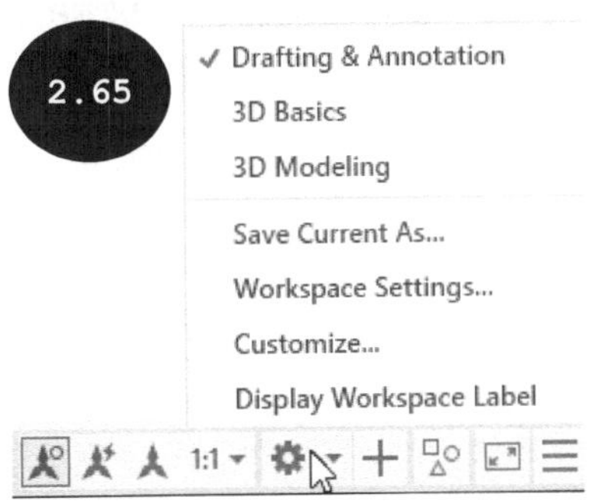

2. In this flyout, ensure that the **Drafting & Annotation** option is tick-marked to create drawings in the Drafting & Annotation workspace.

Note: A tick-mark next to a workspace indicates that it is selected as the current workspace for creating drawings. By default, the Drafting & Annotation workspace is selected as the current workspace for creating drawings. You can click on any workspace to make it current for creating drawings.

Section 3: Defining Limits for the Drawing

1. Follow the command sequence given below for defining limits for the drawing.

`Command:` *LIMITS* (***ENTER***).
`Specify lower left corner or [ON/OFF]<0.0000,0.0000>:` *0,0* (***ENTER***).
`Specify upper right corner <12.0000,9.0000>:` *160,130* (***ENTER***)

Section 4: Creating a Drawing by Using the Absolute Coordinate System

As stated in the tutorial description, you need to enter coordinates in the Dynamic Input boxes according to the Absolute Cartesian coordinate system for specifying points. To enter coordinates in the Dynamic Input boxes, you need to ensure that the Dynamic Input mode is turned on.

1. Ensure that the Dynamic Input mode is turned on. You can turn on or off the Dynamic Input mode by clicking on the **Dynamic Input** button in the Status Bar. It is a toggle button.

2. Click on the **Line** tool in the **Draw** panel of the **Home** tab. The **Line** tool gets activated, and you are prompted to specify the first point of the line. Alternatively, you can enter **L** in the Command Line window and then press ENTER to activate the **Line** tool.

Note: In the Absolute coordinate system, the coordinate values measure from the origin. To specify coordinates in the Dynamic Input boxes according to the Absolute coordinate system, you need to enter # as a prefix to the X coordinate followed by the Y coordinate.

3. Follow the command sequence given below for creating the drawing.

`Specify first point:` *0,0* (***ENTER***)
`Specify next point or [Undo]:` *#55,0* (***ENTER***)
`Specify next point or [Undo]:` *#55,25* (***ENTER***)
`Specify next point or [Close Undo]:` *#80,25* (***ENTER***)
`Specify next point or [Close Undo]:` *#80,55* (***ENTER***)
`Specify next point or [Close Undo]:` *#65,65* (***ENTER***)
`Specify next point or [Close Undo]:` *#0,65* (***ENTER***)
`Specify next point or [Close Undo]:` *C or Close (See Figure 2.66)*

`Command:` *Z or Zoom* (***ENTER***)
`Specify corner of window, enter a scale factor (nX or nXP), or [All/Center/Dynamic/Extents/Previous/Scale/Window/Object]<real time>:` *A or ALL* (***ENTER***)

2.66

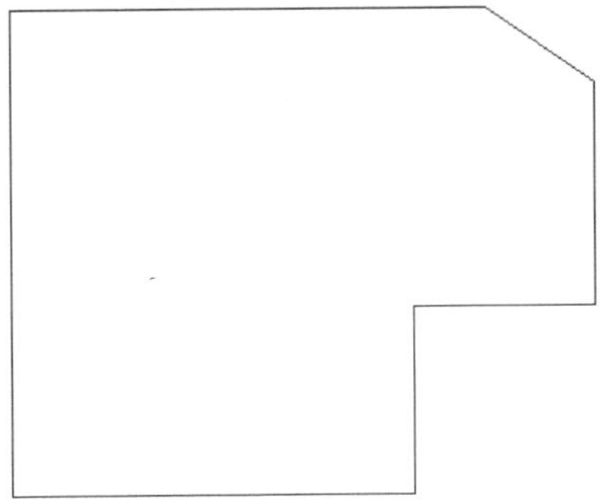

Command: *C or Circle* (***ENTER***)
Specify center point for circle or [3P 2P Ttr (tan tan radius)]: **25,30** (***ENTER***)
Specify radius of circle or [Diameter] : *D* (***ENTER***)
Specify diameter of circle : **25** (***ENTER***) *(See Figure 2.67)*

Command: *C or Circle* (***ENTER***)
Specify center point for circle or [3P 2P Ttr (tan tan radius)]: **50,50** (***ENTER***)
Specify radius of circle or [Diameter] <12.5000>: *D* (***ENTER***)
Specify diameter of circle <25.0000>: **15** (***ENTER***) *(See Figure 2.68)*

2.67

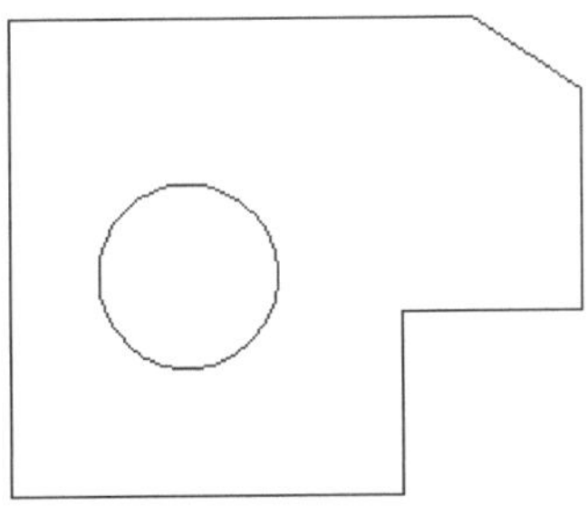

2.68

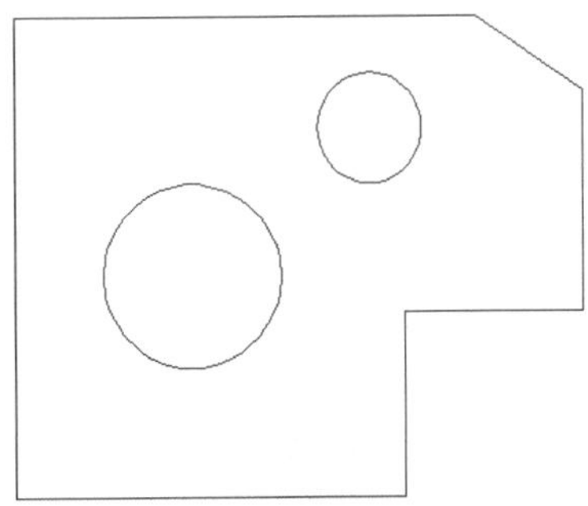

Section 5: Saving the Drawing

After creating the drawing, you need to save it.

1. Click on the **Save** tool in the **Quick Access Toolbar**. The **Save Drawing As** dialog box appears.

2. Browse to a local drive of your system and then create a folder with the name *AutoCAD*.

3. Create another folder with the name *Chapter 2* inside the *AutoCAD* folder. Next, enter **Tutorial 3** in the **File name** field of the dialog box.

4. Click on the **Save** button in the dialog box. The drawing gets saved with the name Tutorial 3.

Tutorial 4

Create the drawing shown in Figure 2.69 by using the Relative Polar coordinate system. Also, use the Dynamic Input mode for specifying coordinate points. The dimensions shown in this figure are for your reference only. You will learn about applying dimensions in later chapters.

2.69

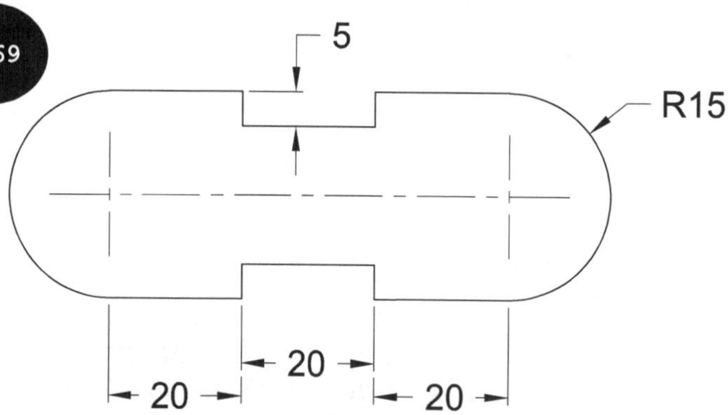

Section 1: Starting AutoCAD

1. Start AutoCAD and then click on the **New** tool in the **Quick Access Toolbar**, which is at the top left corner of the screen, see Figure 2.70. The **Select template** dialog box appears, see Figure 2.71.

2.70

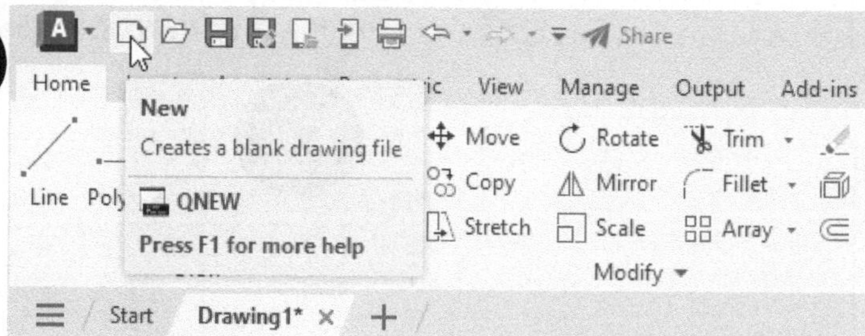

2.71

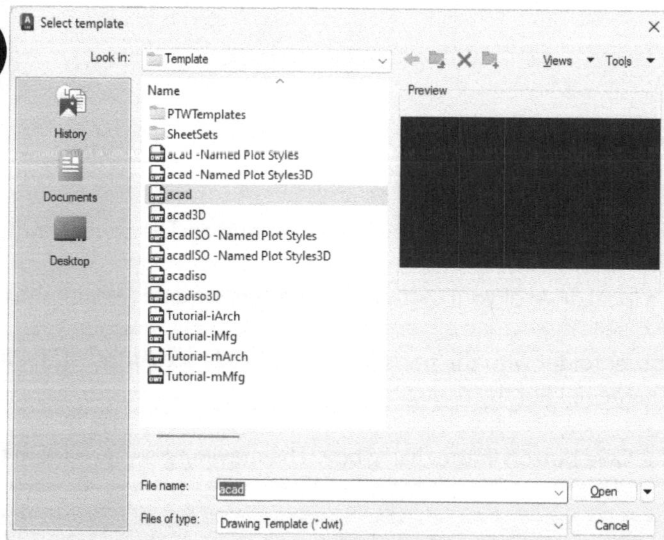

2. In the dialog box, click on the ***acad.dwt*** template and then click on the **Open** button. A new drawing file with the ***acad.dwt*** template gets invoked.

3. Ensure that the Drafting & Annotation workspace is selected as the current workspace for creating the drawing.

Section 2: Drawing Line Entities

As stated in the tutorial description, you need to enter coordinates in the Dynamic Input boxes as per the Relative Polar coordinate system for specifying points.

1. Ensure that the Dynamic Input mode is turned on. You can turn on or off the Dynamic Input mode by clicking on the **Dynamic Input** button in the Status Bar. It is a toggle button.

2. Click on the **Ortho Mode** button in the Status Bar or press the **F8** key to turn on the Ortho mode. By activating the Ortho mode, you can create horizontal or vertical straight lines only.

3. Click on the **Line** tool in the **Draw** panel of the **Home** tab. The **Line** tool gets invoked, and you are prompted to specify the first point of the line.

Note: In the Relative Polar coordinate system, the distance and angle values are measured from the last specified point in the drawing area.

4. Follow the command sequence given below for creating the drawing.

`Specify first point:` *Click the left mouse button in the drawing area to specify the first point.*
`Specify next point or [Undo]:` *Move the cursor horizontally toward right and then enter* ***20*** *in the Dynamic Input box* (***ENTER***) *(See Figure 2.72).*
`Specify next point or [Undo]:` *Move the cursor vertically upward and then enter* ***5*** (***ENTER***).
`Specify next point or [Close Undo]:` *Move the cursor horizontally toward right and then enter* ***20*** (***ENTER***).
`Specify next point or [Close Undo]:` *Move the cursor vertically downward and then enter* ***5*** (***ENTER***).
`Specify next point or [Close Undo]:` *Move the cursor horizontally toward right and then enter* ***20*** (***ENTER***).
`Specify next point or [Close Undo]:` *Move the cursor vertically upward and then enter* ***30*** (***ENTER***) *(See Figure 2.73).*

2.72

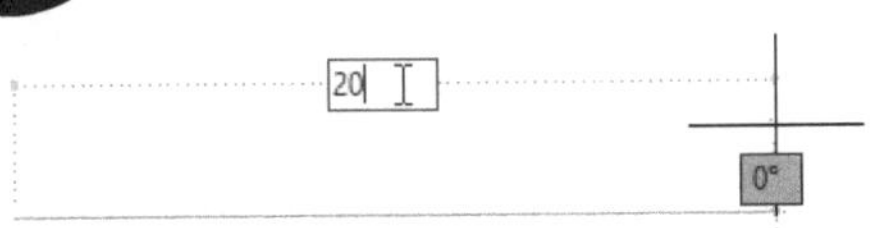

2.73

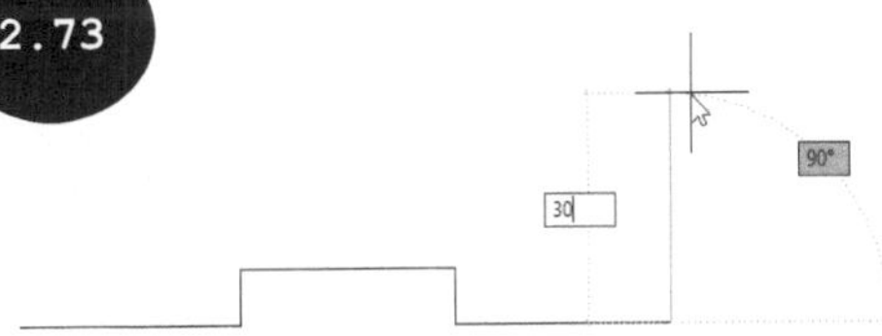

`Specify next point or [Close Undo]:` *Move the cursor horizontally toward left and then enter* ***20*** (***ENTER***).

`Specify next point or [Close Undo]:` *Move the cursor vertically downward and then enter 5* `(`***ENTER***`).`
`Specify next point or [Close Undo]:` *Move the cursor horizontally toward left and then enter 20* `(`***ENTER***`).`
`Specify next point or [Close Undo]:` *Move the cursor vertically upward and then enter 5* `(`***ENTER***`).`
`Specify next point or [Close Undo]:` *Move the cursor horizontally toward left and then enter 20* `(`***ENTER***`).`
`Specify next point or [Close Undo]:` *C or Close (See Figure 2.74).*

2.74

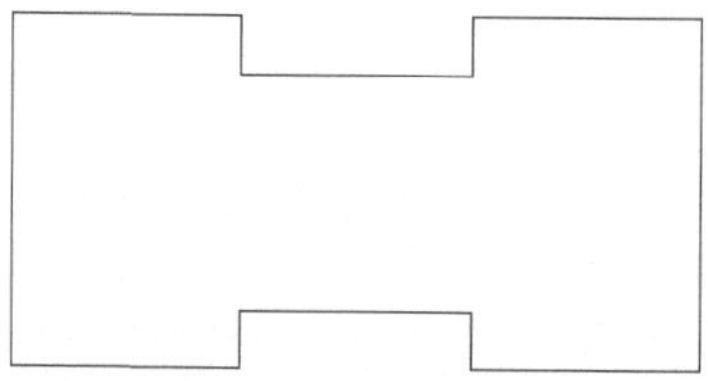

`Command:` *Z or Zoom* `(`***ENTER***`).`
`Specify corner of window, enter a scale factor (nX or nXP), or [All/Center/Dynamic/Extents/Previous/Scale/Window/Object]<real time>:` *A or ALL* `(`***ENTER***`).`

Section 3: Erasing the Unwanted Entities of the Drawing

1. Click on the **Erase** tool of the **Modify** panel of the **Home** tab or enter **E** in the Command Line. The **Erase** tool gets activated, and you are prompted to select the objects to be erased.

   `Select objects:`

2. Click on the right and left most vertical entities one after the other as the entities to be erased, see Figure 2.75. Next, press ENTER. The selected entities are deleted, see Figure 2.76.

2.75

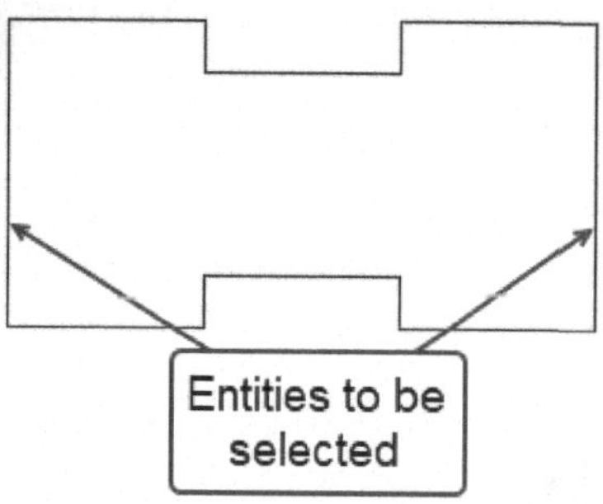

2.76

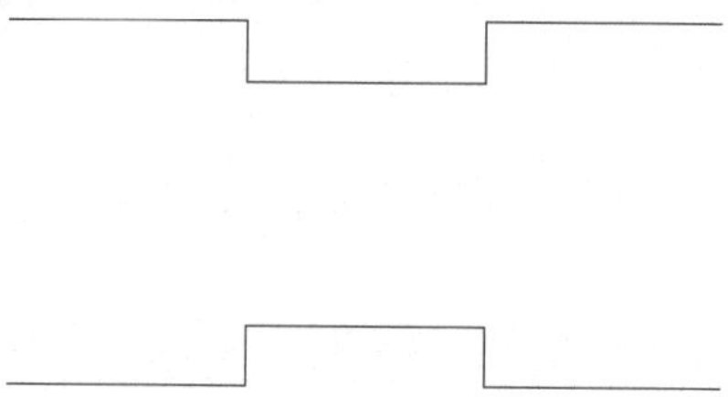

Section 4: Drawing Arcs

1. Click on the down arrow at the bottom of the arc tool. The **Arc** flyout appears, see Figure 2.77.

2. In this flyout, click on the **Start, End, Radius** tool, see Figure 2.77. The **Start, End, Radius** tool is activated, and you are prompted to specify the start point of the arc.

   `Specify start point of arc or [Center]:`

2.77

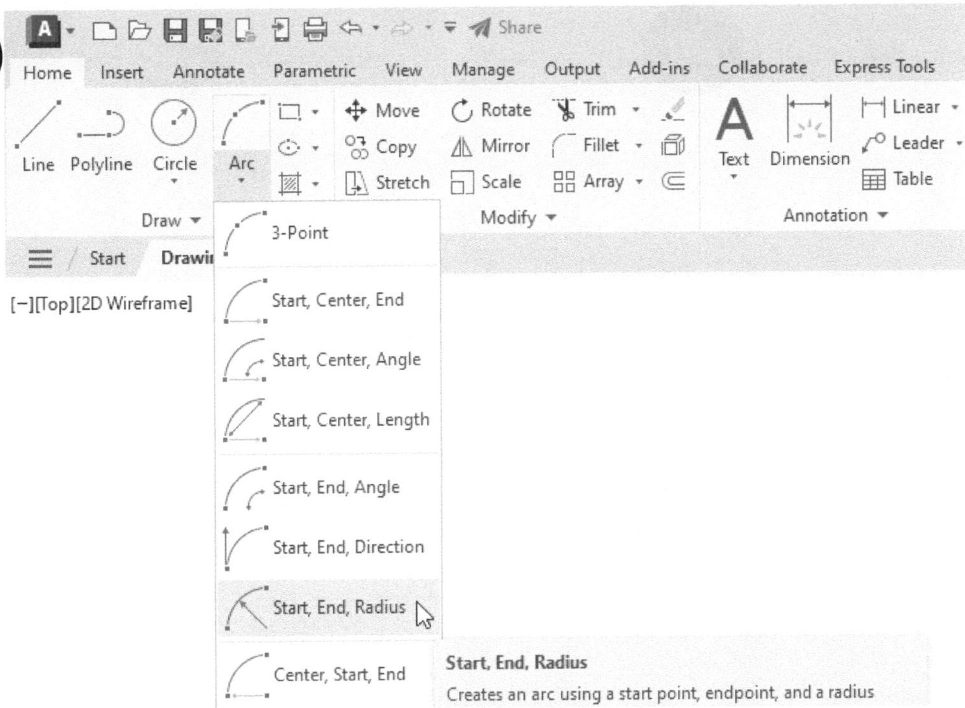

3. Click on the **Object Snap** button in the Status Bar to activate the Object Snap mode. You will learn more about Object Snap mode in later chapters.

Note: You need to ensure that the Endpoint snap mode is activated so that the cursor can snap to the endpoint of an entity. For doing so, right-click on the Object Snap button in the Status Bar and then ensure that the Endpoint option is tick-marked in the flyout that appears.

4. Move the cursor over the endpoint of the lower right-most horizontal line and then click to specify the start point of the arc when the cursor snaps to the endpoint of the line, see Figure 2.78.

```
Specify end point of arc:
```

2.78

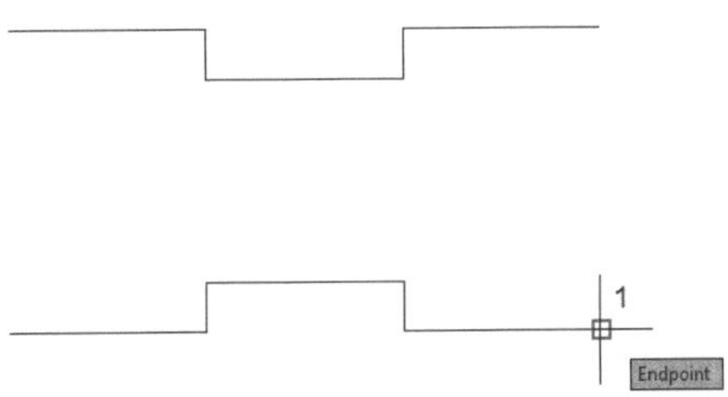

5. Move the cursor over the endpoint of the upper right-most horizontal line and then click to specify the endpoint of the arc when the cursor snaps to it, see Figure 2.79.

```
Specify radius of arc (hold Ctrl to switch direction) :
```

2.79

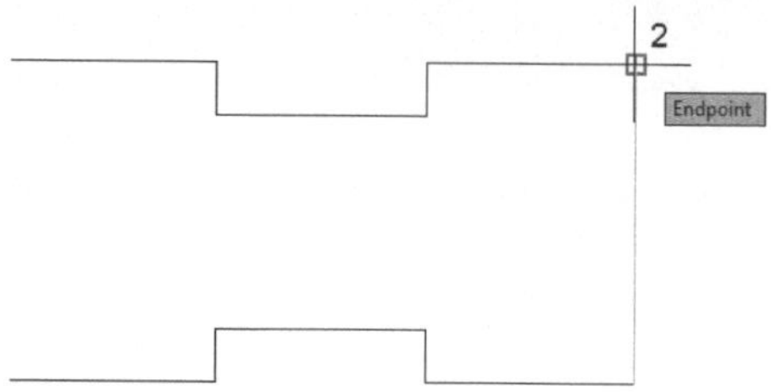

6. Move the cursor horizontally toward the right and then enter **15** as the radius of the arc in the **Dynamic Input** box, which appears near the cursor in the drawing area. The arc is drawn, see Figure 2.80.

2.80

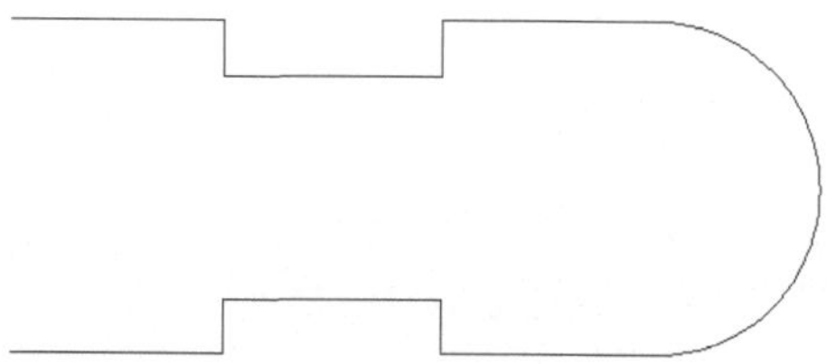

7. Similarly, draw an arc on the left side of the drawing by using the **Start, End, Radius** tool, see Figure 2.81.

2.81

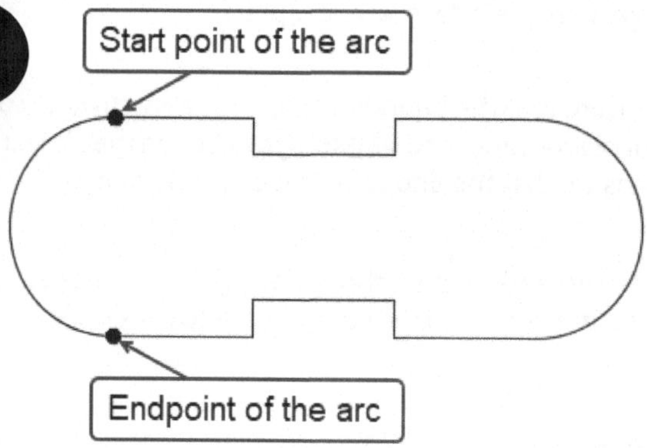

Section 5: Saving the Drawing

After creating the drawing, you need to save it.

1. Click on the **Save** tool in the **Quick Access Toolbar**. The **Save Drawing As** dialog box appears.

2. Browse to the *Chapter 2* folder, inside the *AutoCAD* folder. If the folders are not created in Tutorial 3 of this chapter, then you need to first create these folders on a local drive of your system.

3. Enter **Tutorial 4** in the **File name** field of the dialog box and then click on the **Save** button. The drawing gets saved with the name Tutorial 4.

Hands-on Test Drive 3

Create the drawing shown in Figure 2.82 by using the Relative Cartesian coordinate system. Also, use the Dynamic Input boxes for specifying coordinate points. The dimensions shown in this figure are for your reference only. You will learn about applying dimensions in later chapters.

2.82

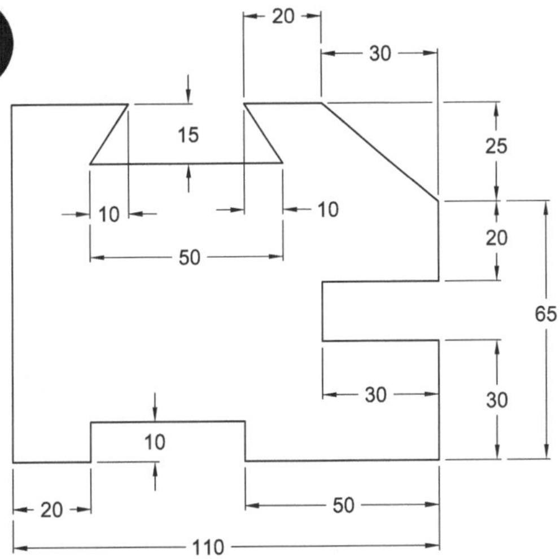

Hands-on Test Drive 4

Create the drawing shown in Figure 2.83 by using the Relative Cartesian coordinate system. Also, use the Dynamic Input boxes for specifying coordinate points.

2.83

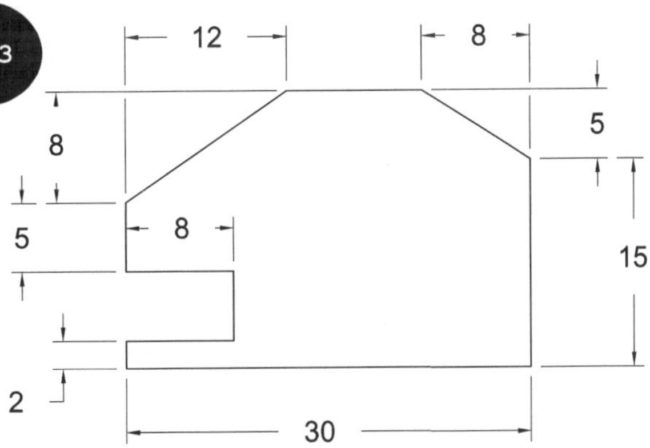

Summary

The chapter introduced the setting of drawing units, drawing limits, and grid and snap settings. It also introduced various coordinate systems used in AutoCAD and explained how to create line, circle, and arc entities in AutoCAD. Further, it discussed methods for canceling, erasing, undoing, and navigating 2D drawings.

Questions

Complete the following sentences:

- The _________ is a shortcut for the UNITS command.
- In the _________ coordinate system, every point you specify in the drawing area measures from the origin (0,0), and the location of the point is specified by the X and Y coordinates.
- In AutoCAD, you can specify coordinates either by using the _________ or _________.
- In the _________ coordinate system, every point you specify in the drawing area measures from the last specified point in the drawing area, and the location of the point is specified by the X and Y coordinates.
- In the _________ coordinate system, to define a point, you need to specify the distance and angle values separated by an angle bracket (<).
- The _________ tool is used for drawing a circle by defining two points on the circumference of the circle.
- The _________ tool is used for drawing an arc by defining the start, center, and endpoints.
- The _________ tool is used for displaying the previously zoomed view of a drawing.

CHAPTER

3

Working with Drawing Aids and Layers

In this chapter, the following topics will be discussed:

- Working with Ortho Mode
- Working with Polar Tracking
- Working with Object Snap
- Working with Object Snap Tracking
- Working with Layers
- Assigning Objects to a Layer

Drawing aids such as grid and snap, ortho, polar tracking, and object snap tracking are highly essential for creating drawings accurately and quickly in AutoCAD. Of all these drawing aids, the grid and snap settings have already been discussed in Chapter 2. The remaining drawing aids have been discussed in this chapter.

Working with Ortho Mode

The Ortho mode is used for creating horizontal or vertical straight lines. You can turn on the Ortho mode to create horizontal or vertical lines (lines at an incremental angle of 90 degrees). By doing so, you can quickly and accurately draw the horizontal or vertical line entities of a drawing. To activate the Ortho mode, click on the **Ortho Mode** button in the Status Bar, see Figure 3.1. Note that it is a toggle button. You can also press the F8 key to turn on or off the Ortho mode to create horizontal or vertical lines.

3.1

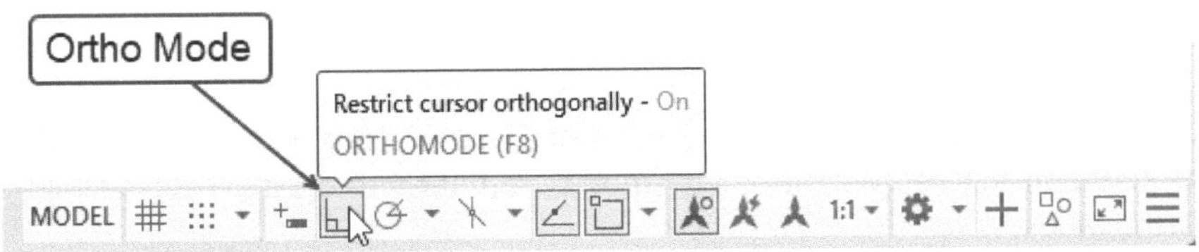

Tutorial 1

Create the drawing shown in Figure 3.2, by turning on the Ortho mode.

3.2

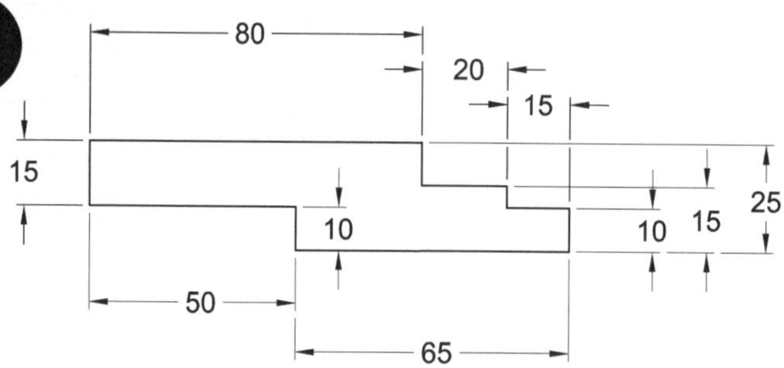

Section 1: Starting AutoCAD

1. Double-click on the AutoCAD icon on your desktop to start AutoCAD. The initial screen of AutoCAD appears with the **Start** tab, see Figure 3.3.

3.3

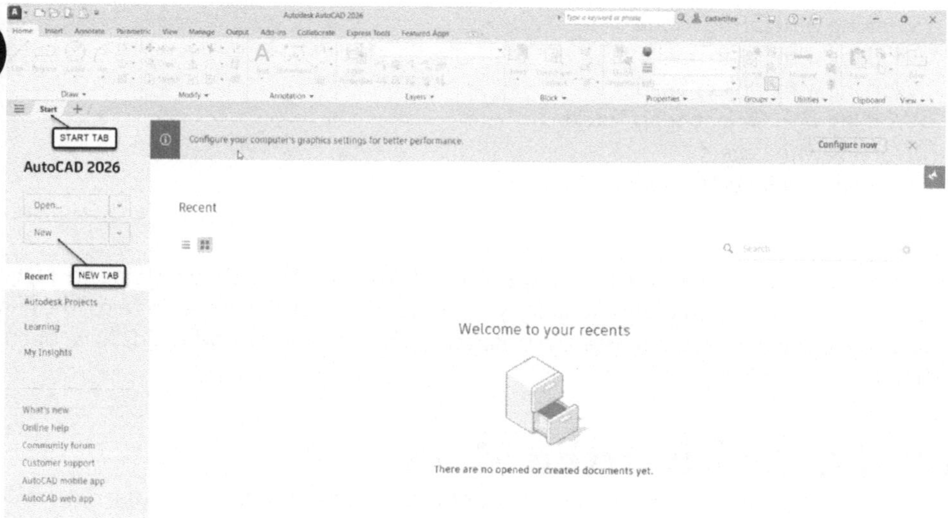

2. Click on the **New** tool in the **Start** tab, see Figure 3.3. The new drawing file with the default drawing template gets invoked. Alternatively, click on the **New** tool in the **Quick Access Toolbar**, which is at the top left corner of the AutoCAD screen. The **Select template** dialog box appears. In this dialog box, choose the **acad.dwt** template and then click on the **Open** button. A new drawing file with the **acad.dwt** template gets invoked.

Section 2: Creating a Drawing by Using the Ortho Mode

As stated in the description of the tutorial, you need to create the drawing by turning on the Ortho mode.

1. Click on the **Ortho Mode** button in the Status Bar to turn on the Ortho mode, see Figure 3.4. Alternatively, press the F8 key to activate it.

3.4

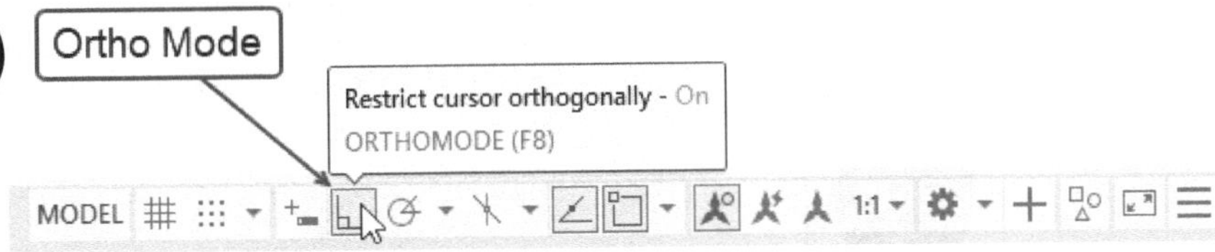

2. Ensure that the Dynamic Input mode is activated. You can turn on the Dynamic Input mode by clicking on the **Dynamic Input** button in the Status Bar.

Note: If the **Dynamic Input** button is not available in the Status Bar by default, then click on the **Customization** button in the Status Bar. A flyout appears. In this flyout, click on the **Dynamic Input** option. The **Dynamic Input** button becomes available in the Status Bar.

3. Click on the **Line** tool in the **Draw** panel of the **Home** tab. The **Line** tool is activated, and you are prompted to specify the first point of the line. Alternatively, enter **L** in the Command Line window and then press ENTER to activate the **Line** tool.

`Specify first point:`

4. Follow the command sequence given below for creating the drawing:

`Specify first point:` *Click in the drawing area to specify the first point of the line.*
`Specify next point or [Undo]:` *Move the cursor horizontally toward right and then enter* ***65*** *in the Dynamic Input box* (***ENTER***) *(See Figure 3.5).*

3.5

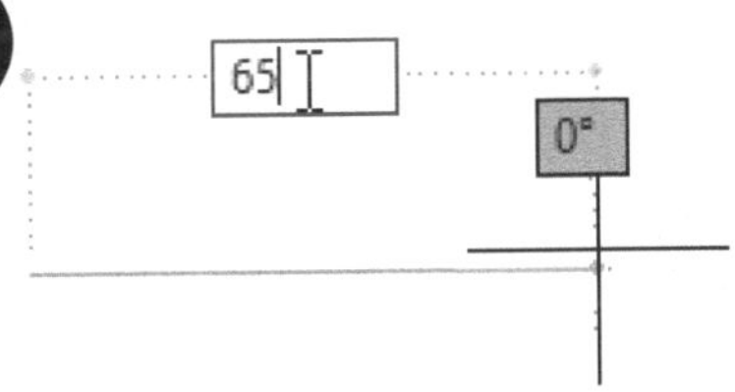

`Specify next point or [Undo]:` *Move the cursor vertically upward and then enter* ***10*** (***ENTER***).
`Specify next point or [Close Undo]:` *Move the cursor horizontally toward left and then enter* ***15*** (***ENTER***).
`Specify next point or [Close Undo]:` *Move the cursor vertically upward and then enter* ***5*** (***ENTER***).
`Specify next point or [Close Undo]:` *Move the cursor horizontally toward left and then enter* ***20*** (***ENTER***).
`Specify next point or [Close Undo]:` *Move the cursor vertically upward and then enter* ***10*** (***ENTER***).
`Specify next point or [Close Undo]:` *Move the cursor horizontally toward left and then enter* ***80*** (***ENTER***).
`Specify next point or [Close Undo]:` *Move the cursor vertically downward and then enter* ***15*** (***ENTER***).

`Specify next point or [Close Undo]:` *Move the cursor horizontally toward right and then enter 50* (***ENTER***).
`Specify next point or [Close Undo]:` *C or Close* (***ENTER***) *(See Figure 3.6).*

3.6

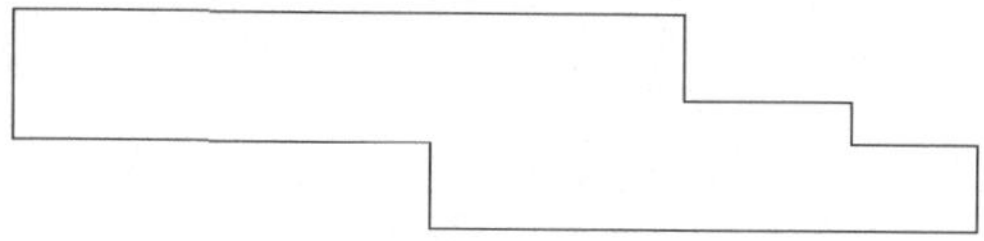

Tip: If the drawing has horizontal/vertical lines as well as inclined line entities, then you can create horizontal/vertical lines by turning on the Ortho mode. For creating inclined lines, you need to deactivate the Ortho mode. You can turn on or off the Ortho mode at any point while creating a drawing.

Working with Polar Tracking

The Polar Tracking mode is used for creating line entities at a predefined incremental angle. To do so, turn on the Polar Tracking mode by clicking on the **Polar Tracking** button in the Status Bar, see Figure 3.7. Alternatively, press the F10 key. Once the Polar Tracking mode has been turned on, the cursor snaps at the predefined incremental angle for creating a line, see Figure 3.8. For example, if the incremental angle is defined as 45 degrees then the cursor snaps at 0 degrees, 45 degrees, 90 degrees, 135 degrees, 180 degrees, and so on, for creating line entities. Figure 3.8 shows the preview of a line at an angle of 45 degrees, which is defined as the incremental angle.

3.7

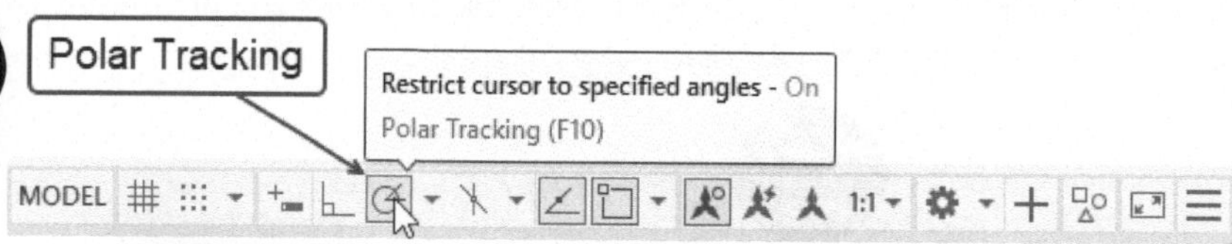

3.8

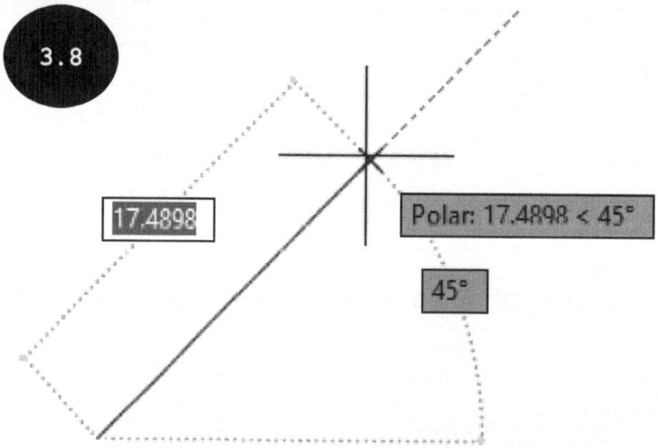

You can specify an incremental angle by using the **Drafting Settings** dialog box. To invoke the **Drafting Settings** dialog box, right-click on the **Polar Tracking** button in the Status Bar. A flyout appears, see Figure 3.9. In this flyout, click on the **Tracking Settings** option. The **Drafting Settings** dialog box appears with the **Polar Tracking** tab activated in it, see Figure 3.10. In the **Increment angle** field of the **Drafting Settings** dialog box, you can enter an incremental angle value for polar tracking, as required.

3.9

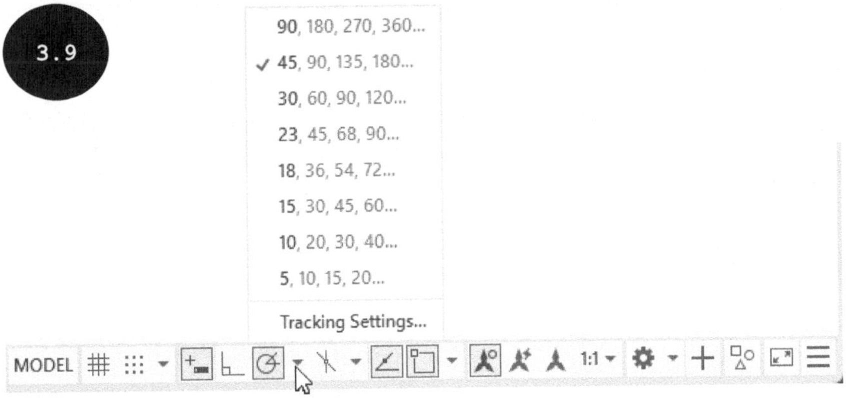

Note: In addition to specifying an incremental angle for polar tracking in the **Drafting Settings** dialog box, you can also select the predefined incremental angle directly from the flyout, see Figure 3.9. The flyout shows a list of commonly used increment angles, such as **90,180, 270, 360** and **45, 90, 135, 180** degrees.

3.10

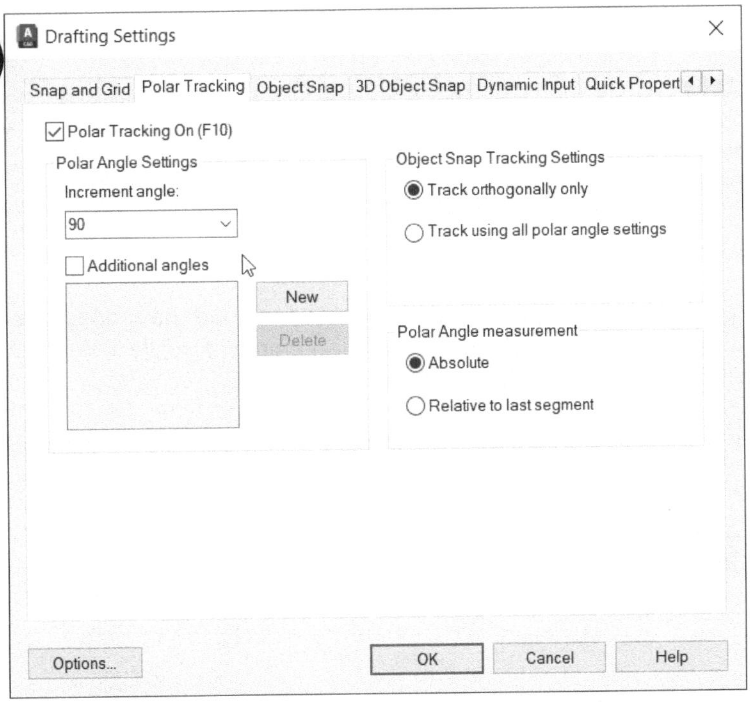

Note: Among the Ortho and Polar Tracking modes, only one mode can be activated at a time. If you turn on the Ortho mode, the Polar Tracking mode automatically gets deactivated, and vice-versa.

Tutorial 2

Create the drawing shown in Figure 3.11 by using the Polar Tracking mode.

3.11

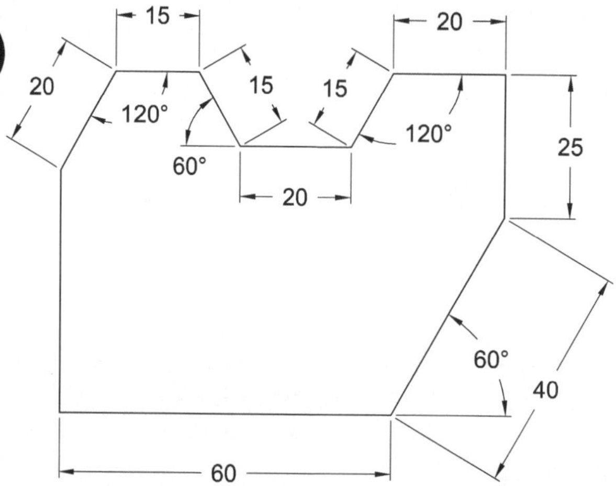

Section 1: Starting AutoCAD

1. Start a new AutoCAD drawing file.

Section 2: Creating a Drawing by Using the Polar Tracking Mode

1. Click on the **Line** tool in the **Draw** panel of the **Home** tab. The **Line** tool is activated, and you are prompted to specify the first point of the line. Alternatively, enter **L** in the Command Line window and then press ENTER to activate the **Line** tool.

    ```
    Specify first point:
    ```

    It is clear from the drawing of this tutorial that the inclined line entities have an incremental angle of 60 degrees. Therefore, you need to set the incremental angle for Polar Tracking to 60 degrees to create these entities quickly and easily.

2. Move the cursor over the **Polar Tracking** button in the Status Bar and then right-click to display a flyout, see Figure 3.12.

3.12

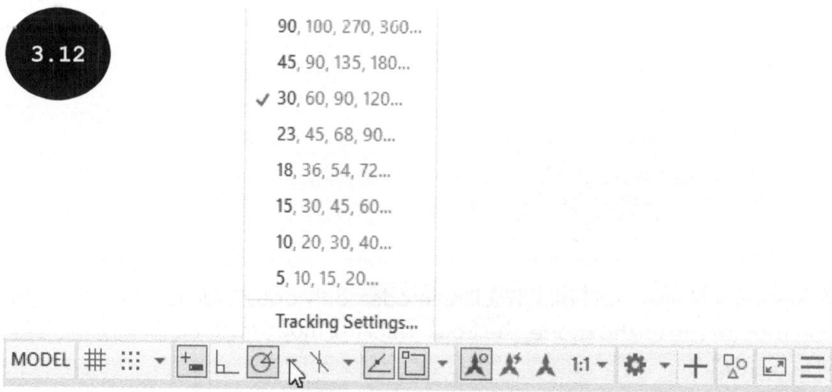

3. Click on the **30, 60, 90, 120** option in the flyout. 30 degrees is specified as the incremental angle for polar tracking.

4. Ensure that the Dynamic Input mode is activated. If not, click on the **Dynamic Input** button in the Status Bar to activate it.

5. Follow the command sequence given below for creating the drawing:

`Specify first point:` *Click in the drawing area to specify the first point of the line.*
`Specify next point or [Undo]:` *Move the cursor horizontally toward right and then enter* ***60*** *in the Dynamic Input box* (***ENTER***) *(See Figure 3.13).*
`Specify next point or [Undo]:` *Move the cursor at an angle and then enter* ***40*** *when the cursor snaps at an angle of 60 degrees* (***ENTER***) *(See Figure 3.14).*

3.13

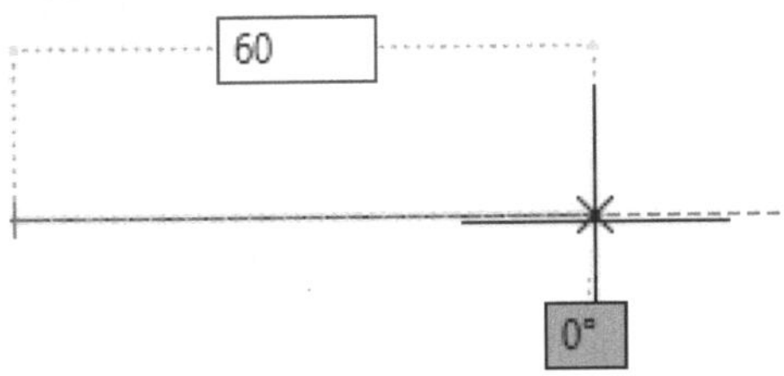

3.14

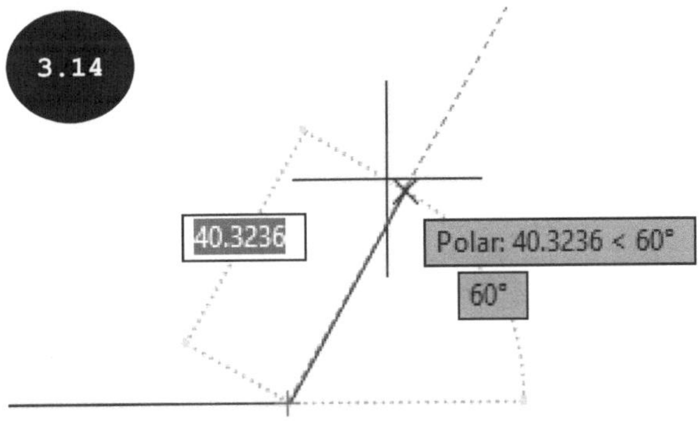

`Specify next point or [Close Undo]:` *Move the cursor vertically upward and then enter* ***25*** (***ENTER***) *(See Figure 3.15).*
`Specify next point or [Close Undo]:` *Move the cursor horizontally toward left and then enter* ***20*** (***ENTER***).
`Specify next point or [Close Undo]:` *Move the cursor clockwise and then enter* ***15*** *when the cursor snaps at an angle of 120 degrees* (***ENTER***) *(See Figure 3.16).*

3.15

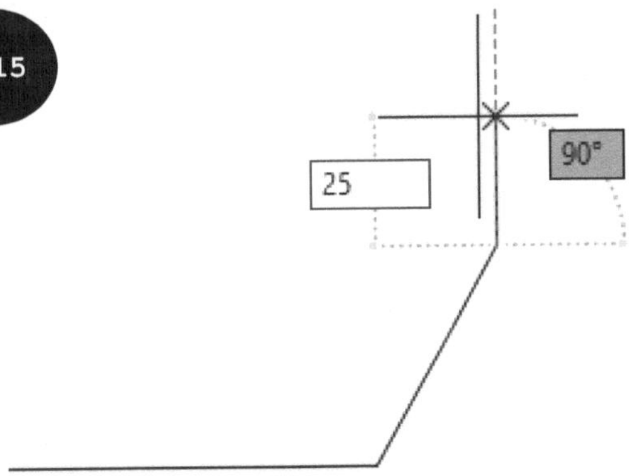

3.16

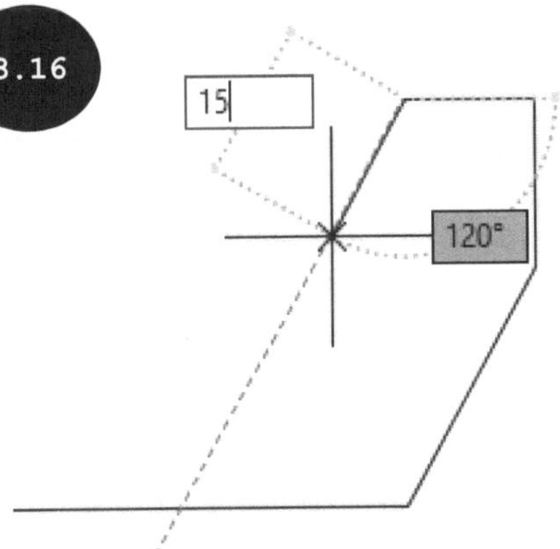

`Specify next point or [Close Undo]:` *Move the cursor horizontally toward left and then enter* ***20*** (***ENTER***).

`Specify next point or [Close Undo]:` *Move the cursor counter-clockwise and then enter* **15** *when the cursor snaps at an angle of 120 degrees* (**ENTER**) *(See Figure 3.17).*
`Specify next point or [Close Undo]:` *Move the cursor horizontally toward left and then enter* **15** (**ENTER**).
`Specify next point or [Close Undo]:` *Move the cursor clockwise and then enter* **20** *when the cursor snaps at an angle of 120 degrees* (**ENTER**) *(See Figure 3.18).*
`Specify next point or [Close Undo]:` *C or Close* (**ENTER**) *(See Figure 3.19).*

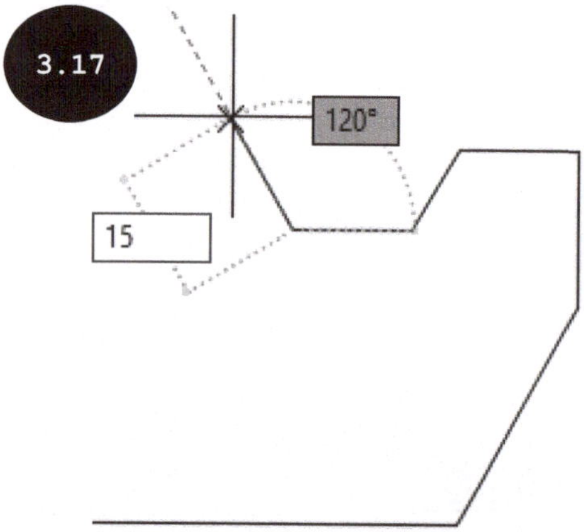

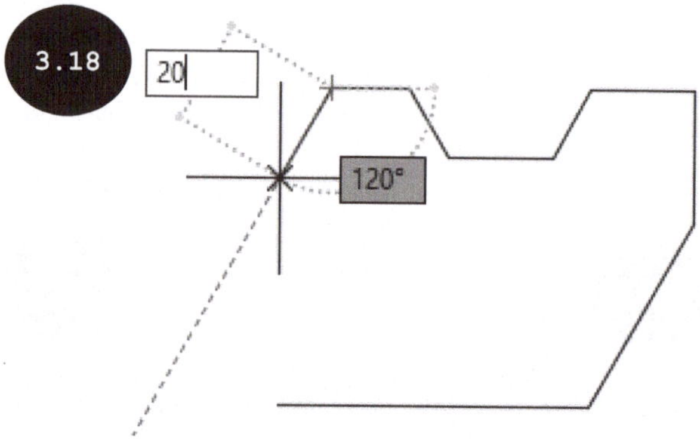

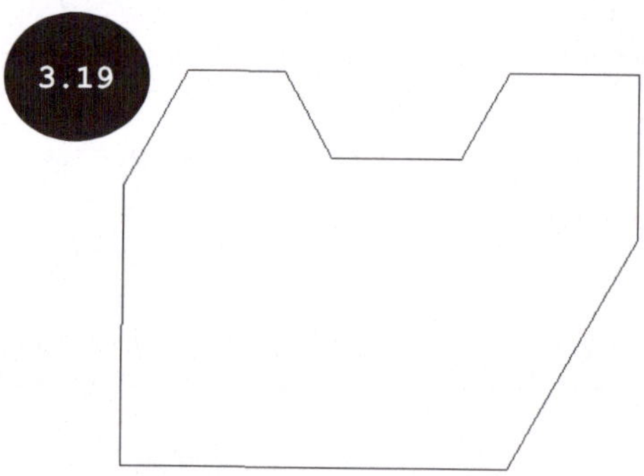

Working with Object Snap

The Object Snap mode is used for specifying points on the existing geometry of a drawing. To do so, you need to turn on the Object Snap mode, so that points can be defined quickly and accurately on the existing geometry of the drawing. The Object Snap mode is one of the most important features of AutoCAD. On turning on the Object Snap mode, the cursor snaps to the existing geometries, such as midpoint, center, node, insertion, and endpoint, which helps in specifying exact points in the drawing area. For example, if you want to create a line starting from the endpoint of an arc then first invoke the **Line** tool and then turn on the Object Snap mode. Next, move the cursor over the endpoint of the arc and then click the left mouse button when the cursor snaps to the endpoint of the arc, see Figure 3.20.

3.20

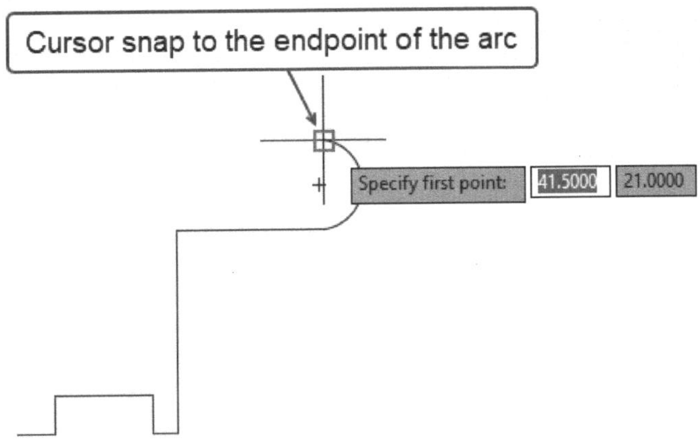

To turn on or off the Object Snap mode, click on the **Object Snap** button in the Status Bar or press the **F3** key, see Figure 3.21.

3.21

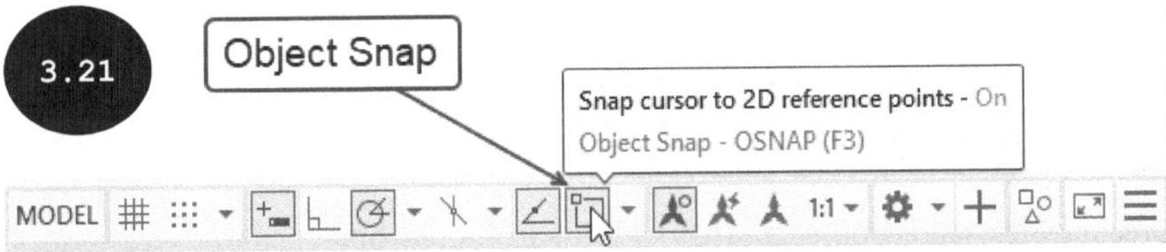

In the Object Snap mode, the cursor snaps to the geometries depending upon the Object snap settings specified in the **Drafting Settings** dialog box. To define the Object snap settings, move the cursor over the **Object Snap** button in the Status Bar and then right-click. A flyout appears, see Figure 3.22. You can also click on the down arrow next to the **Object Snap** button in the Status Bar to display this flyout. In this flyout, click on the **Object Snap Settings** option. The **Drafting Settings** dialog box appears with the **Object Snap** tab activated in it, see Figure 3.23.

3.22

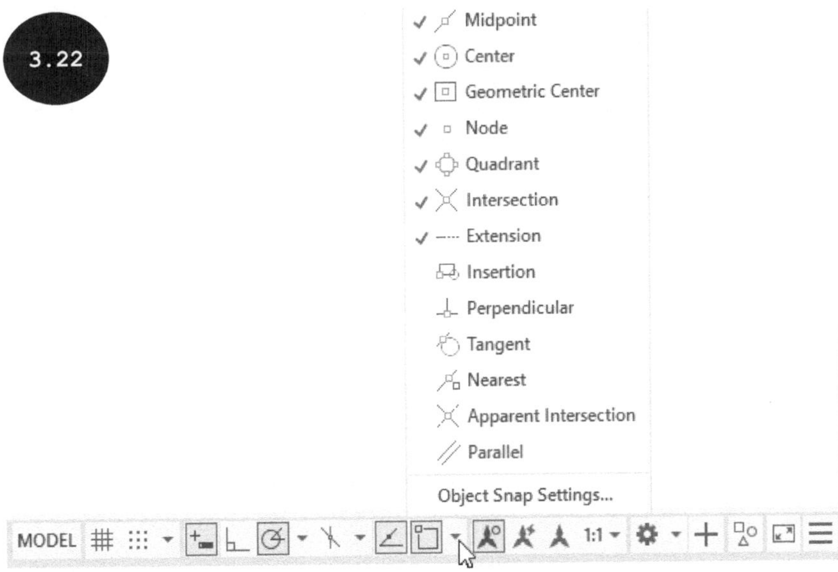

3.23

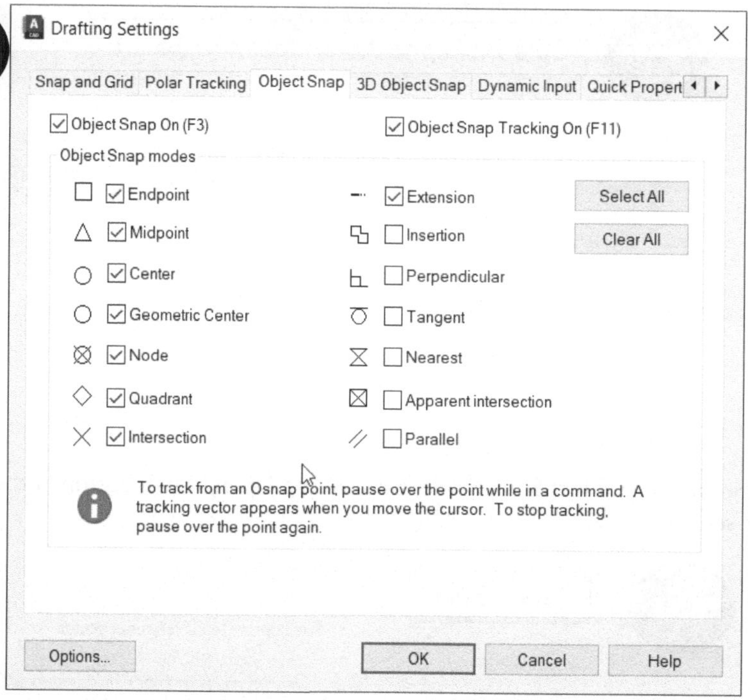

In the **Drafting Settings** dialog box, you can select the respective object snap check boxes for snapping the cursor while specifying points in the drawing area. For example, if you want to define points on the midpoint, endpoint, and center point of a geometry then you can select their respective check boxes in this dialog box. Note that the cursor snaps only to the geometries/points that are selected in the **Drafting Settings** dialog box. Figures 3.24 through 3.27 show geometries with different object snaps.

3.24

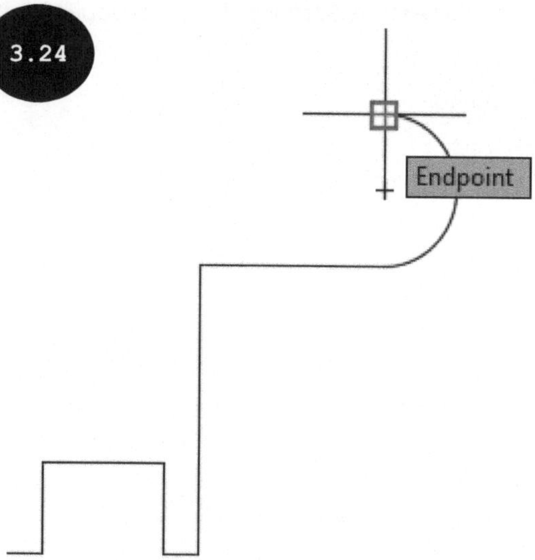

3.25

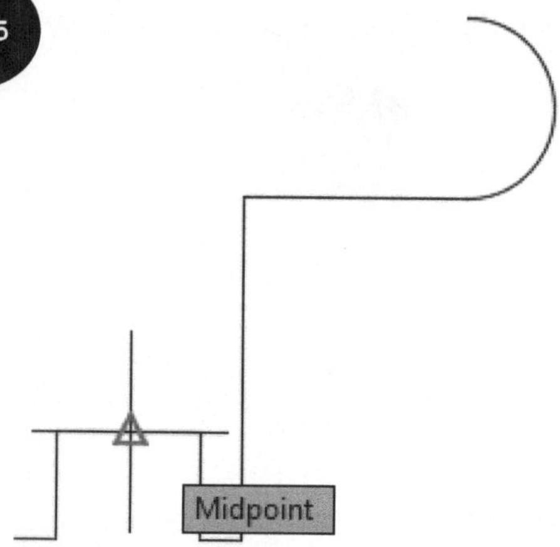

3.26

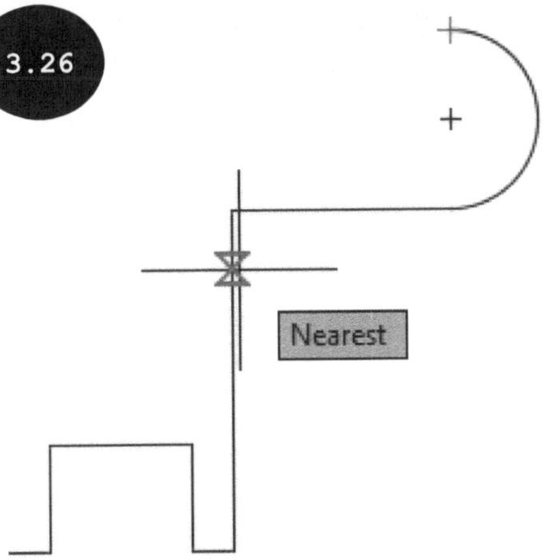

3.27

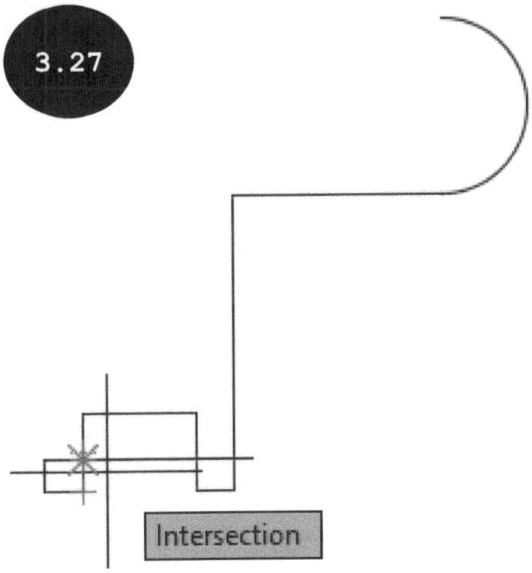

You can also select the **Select All** button in the dialog box to select all the object snap check boxes. To remove all the existing selected check boxes, click on the **Clear All** button in the **Drafting Settings** dialog box. After selecting the required object snap check boxes, click on the **OK** button in the dialog box to accept the change made as well as to exit the dialog box.

Note: In addition to specifying Object snap settings in the **Drafting Settings** dialog box, you can also select the required object snap, such as **Endpoint**, **Midpoint**, and **Center** directly from the flyout, which appears on right-clicking on the **Object Snap** button in the Status Bar, refer to Figure 3.22.

Working with Object Snap Tracking

The Object Snap Tracking mode is used for specifying new points aligned to the existing points of a drawing, see Figure 3.28. In this figure, the center point of the circle is being defined by aligning it to the endpoints of the inclined line entity of the drawing. Note that the Object Snap Tracking mode works in conjunction with the Object Snap. When the Object Snap Tracking is turned on, reference/tracking lines appear originating from the existing points of the drawing, which guide the pointer of the cursor to specify a new point in the drawing area, see Figure 3.28.

3.28

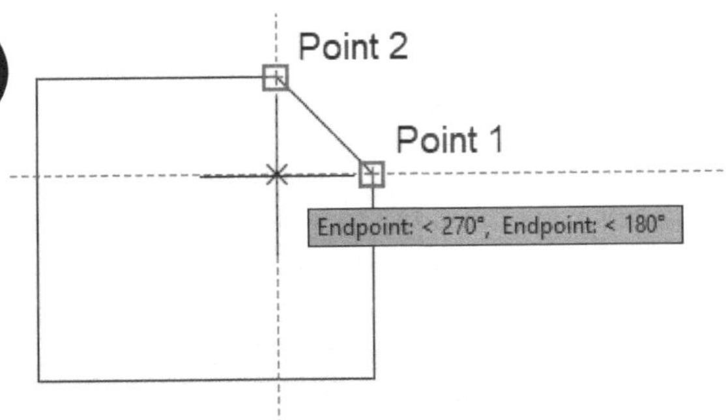

To specify points in the drawing by using the Object Snap Tracking mode, click on the **Object Snap Tracking** button in the Status Bar to turn it on. Alternatively, press the F11 key to turn on the Object Snap Tracking mode, see Figure 3.29. It is a toggle button.

3.29

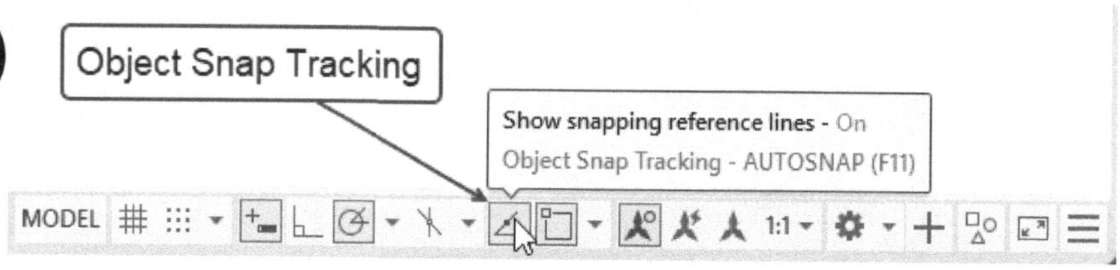

Once the Object Snap Tracking has been turned on, move the cursor to a reference point in the drawing area. When the cursor snaps to the reference point, move the cursor to a distance in the drawing area. A reference/tracking line appears, which originates from the reference point. You can use this reference/tracking line for specifying new points in the drawing area. For example, to draw a circle as shown in Figure 3.30 whose center point is at the intersection of endpoints: Point 1 and Point 2, you need to first move the cursor to Point 1, and then move it horizontally toward the left. A reference/tracking line appears. Next, move the cursor to Point 2 and when the cursor snaps to it, move the cursor vertically downward. A reference/tracking line appears. Continue moving the cursor vertically downward until the cursor snaps to the intersection of both endpoints with the help of reference/tracking lines, see Figure 3.31. Next, click the left mouse button to specify the center point of the circle at the intersection of the endpoints, see Figure 3.31.

3.30

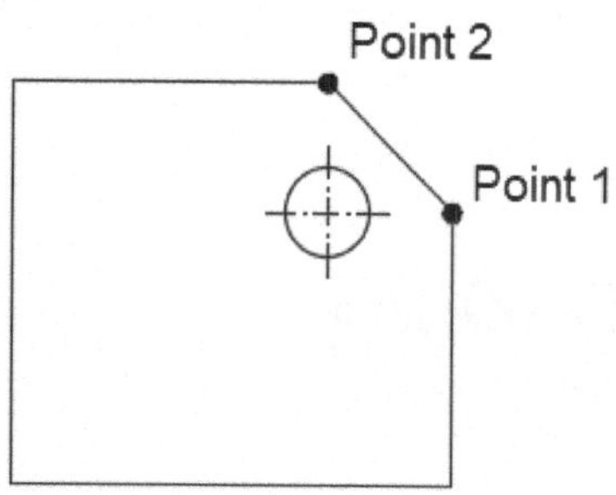

3.31

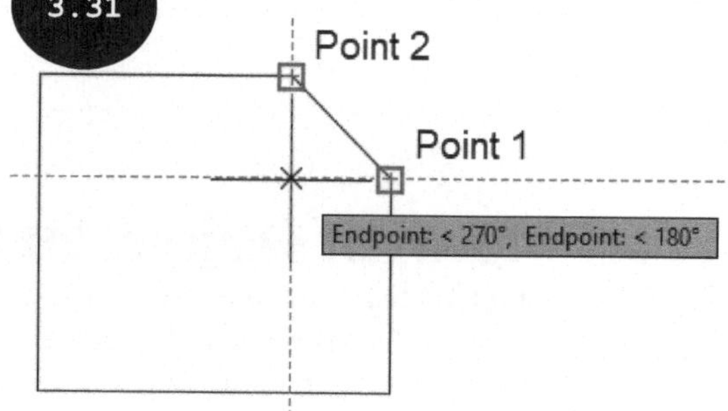

Working with Layers

In AutoCAD, you need to understand the concept of layers to create drawings in an easier and faster way. With layers, you can have better control over a drawing and create complex drawings accurately and more efficiently. Layers work in a way that is similar to tracing overlays on a drawing board, see Figure 3.32. You can have multiple layers in a drawing and organize your drawing by assigning different sets of drawing objects to different layers. For example, all dimensions are in one layer, and all hidden entities are in another layer. You can also assign different properties such as color, linetype, and lineweight to different layers of a drawing. For example, you can assign a hidden linetype to a hidden layer with a different lineweight. Note that in AutoCAD, all layers of a drawing give you a combined look as you view them from the top and appear as if you are working on a single sheet, see Figure 3.33. In this figure, object entities are in one layer with a different lineweight, dimensions are in another layer with a different color and lineweight, and center marks are in a different layer with a different color and lineweight.

3.32

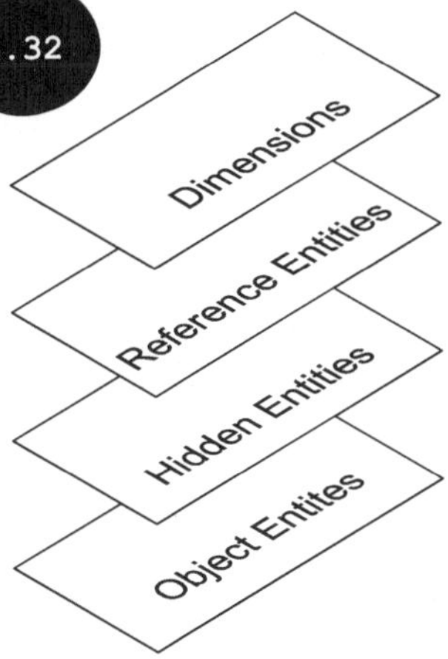

3.33

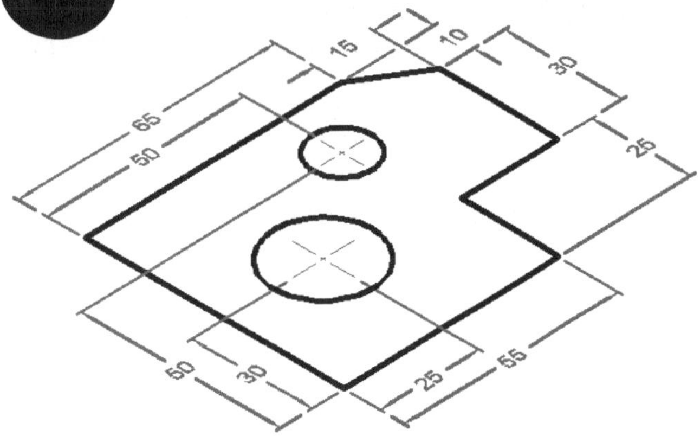

In AutoCAD, you can control the visibility, color, linetype, and lineweight of layers, independently. As a result, you can work with intricate drawings very efficiently. For example, while working on a complicated drawing, you may have to create many reference/construction lines, which you do not want to be a part of the final drawing. In such a case, you can create a layer with the name "Reference layer" and assign all the reference lines to this layer. When the drawing is complete, you can just turn off the "Reference layer" to hide all reference entities of the drawing. Note that you can turn on or off layers at any point of your drawing as per your requirement. It is always recommended to use layers functionally when working with AutoCAD. The correct use of layers is considered a good practice and is essential for creating efficient drawings.

In AutoCAD, whenever you start a new drawing, only one layer is provided with default parameters. This default layer is named as "0" (zero) layer. The "0" layer acts as the current layer, by default. This means that anything you draw in the drawing area is assigned automatically to this "0" layer.

All the operations of a layer such as creating a new layer, specifying layer properties, and so on, can be performed by using the **LAYER PROPERTIES MANAGER**. To invoke the **LAYER PROPERTIES MANAGER**, click on the **Layer Properties** tool in the **Layers** panel of the **Home** tab, see Figure 3.34. Alternatively, you can invoke the **LAYER PROPERTIES MANAGER** by entering **LAYER** or **LA** in the Command Line window. Figure 3.35 shows the **LAYER PROPERTIES MANAGER** invoked with the default "0" layer. Different operations that can be performed by using the **LAYER PROPERTIES MANAGER** are discussed next.

3.34

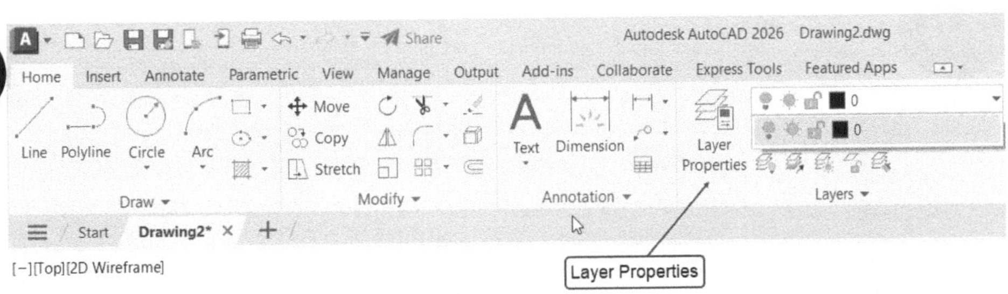

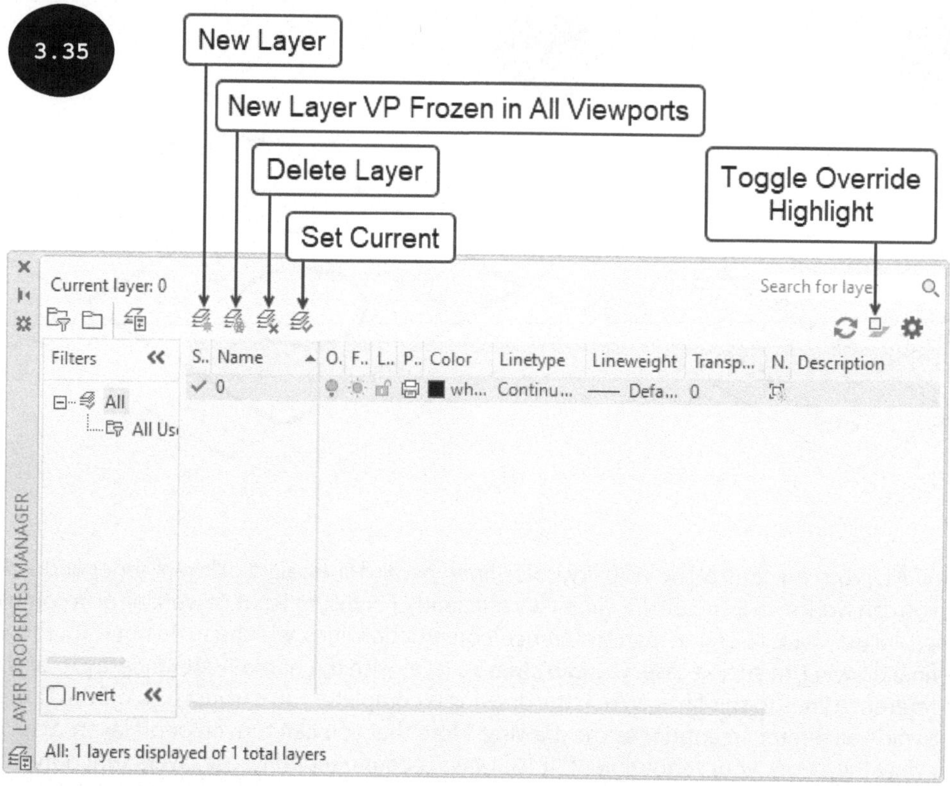

3.35

Creating a New Layer

You can create a new layer by clicking on the **New Layer** button in the **LAYER PROPERTIES MANAGER**, see Figure 3.35. Alternatively, you can press the ALT + N key after invoking the **LAYER PROPERTIES MANAGER** to create a new layer. As soon as you click on the **New Layer** button, a new layer with the default name "**Layer 1**" is created with the default properties, see Figure 3.36. Note that the name of the newly created layer appears in an edit field, which indicates that the default name of the layer can be changed as per requirement.

Note: The default properties of the newly created layer are the same as those of the currently selected layer.

3.36

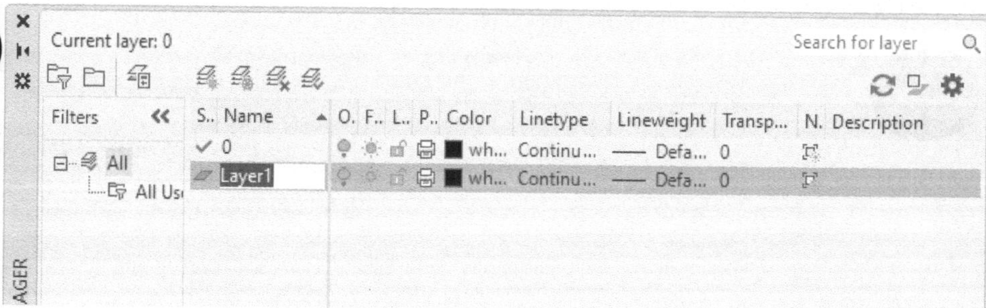

Similarly, you can create multiple layers in a drawing one by one by using the **New Layer** button of the **LAYER PROPERTIES MANAGER**. Figure 3.37 shows the **LAYER PROPERTIES MANAGER** with multiple layers.

3.37

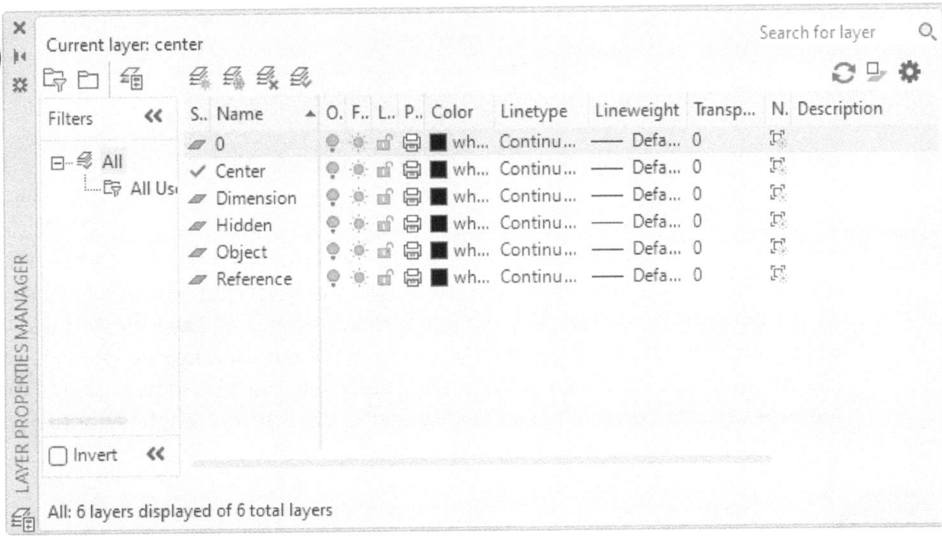

Setting the Current Layer

In AutoCAD, by default, the "0" layer is set as the current layer for a drawing. As a result, anything drawn in AutoCAD is assigned automatically to the "0" layer. Also, properties such as color, linetype, and lineweight of the "0" layer get assigned to the objects drawn. Note that a green tick mark in the **Status** field of the layer, under the **Status** column indicates that the layer is specified as the current layer of the drawing, see Figure 3.38.

3.38

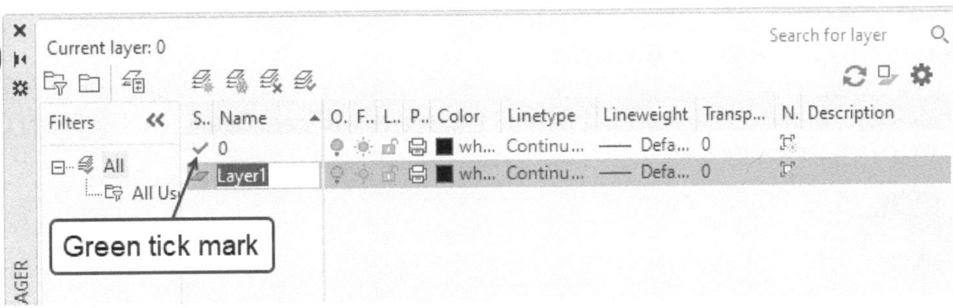

You can set a layer as the current layer for a drawing by double-clicking either on the **Status** or **Name** field of the layer to be made current. Alternatively, you can select a layer to be made current and then click on the **Set Current** button available at the top of the **LAYER PROPERTIES MANAGER**, see Figure 3.39. You can also right-click on the layer and then click on the **Set current** option in the shortcut menu that appears. As discussed, the objects/entities drawn in the drawing area automatically get assigned to the currently active layer of the drawing. However, you can further transfer the objects of one layer to another layer. The method for transferring objects from one layer to another is discussed later in this chapter.

3.39

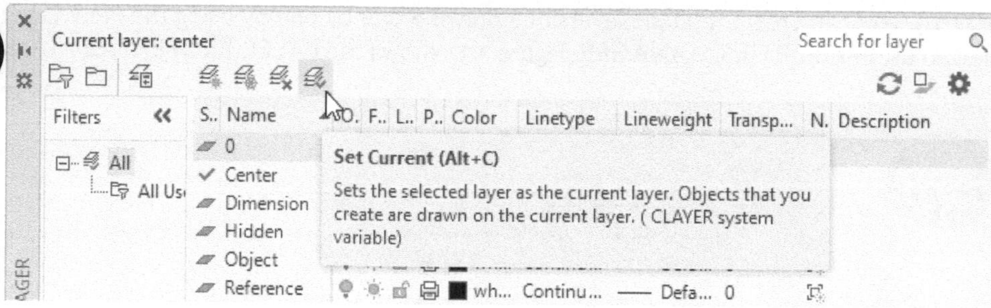

Note: You can also set a layer as the current layer without invoking the **LAYER PROPERTIES MANAGER**. For doing so, move the cursor over the **Layer** drop-down list in the **Layers** panel of the **Home** tab and then click the left mouse button. The **Layer** drop-down list appears, which displays a list of all the layers created in the current drawing, see Figure 3.40. Next, move the cursor over the layer to be made current in the drop-down list, and then click the left mouse button on it. The selected layer becomes the current layer of the drawing.

3.40

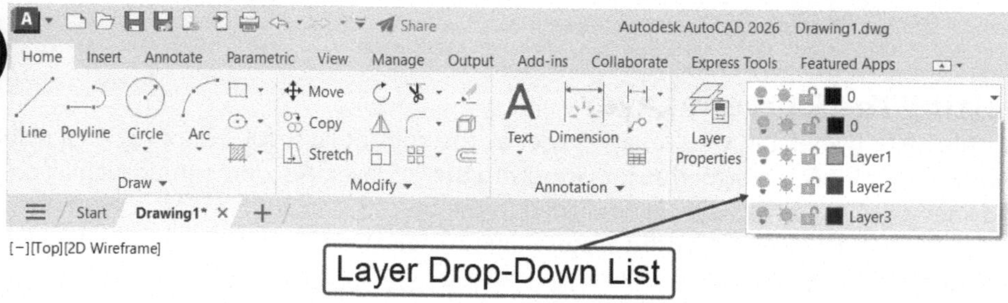

Assigning Color to a Layer

You can assign unique colors to different layers of a drawing. To assign a color to a layer, click on the **Color** field of the layer in the **LAYER PROPERTIES MANAGER**, see Figure 3.41. The **Select Color** dialog box appears, see Figure 3.42.

3.41

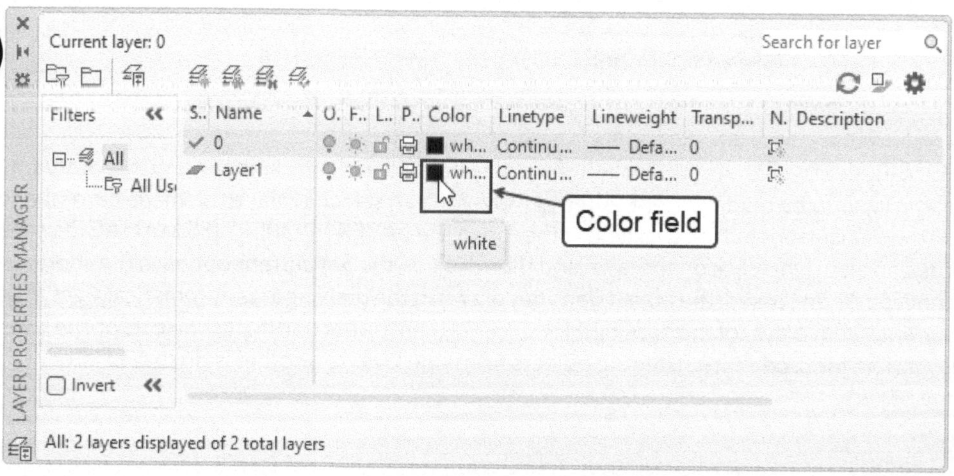

3.42

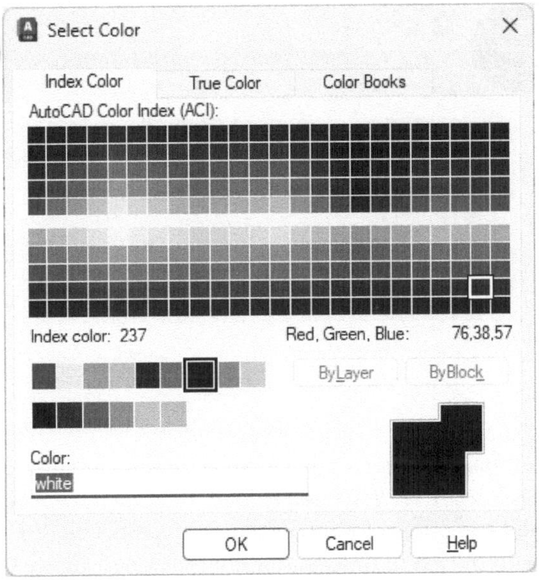

In the **Select Color** dialog box, click on the required color swatch to be assigned to the layer. Next, click on the **OK** button. The chosen color gets assigned to the layer. Similarly, you can assign different colors to different layers of a drawing.

Note: All entities/objects in the drawing area appear in the color assigned to their respective layers.

Assigning Linetype to a Layer

You can assign different linetypes to different layers of a drawing according to your requirements. For example, you can assign the **Center** linetype to a layer that is associated with the centerlines of a drawing and the **Hidden** linetype to a layer that is associated with hidden lines. To assign a linetype to a layer, click on the **Linetype** field of the layer in the **LAYER PROPERTIES MANAGER**, see Figure 3.43. The **Select Linetype** dialog box appears, see Figure 3.44.

3.43

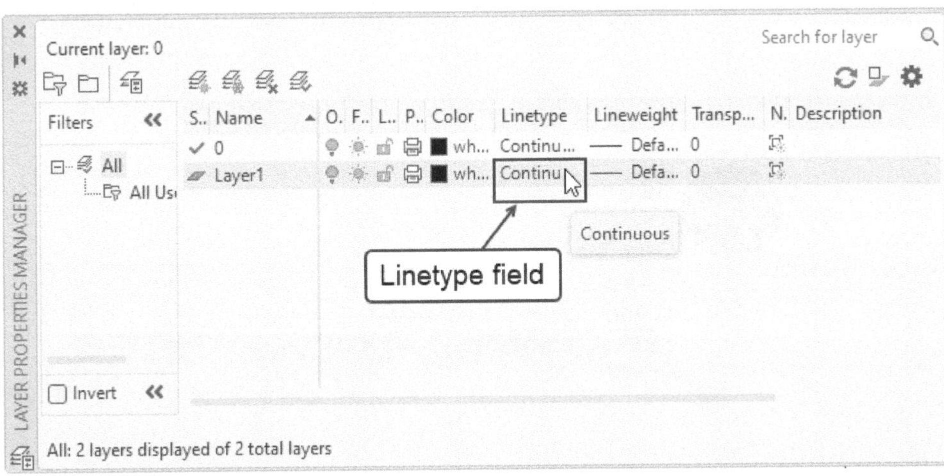

3.44

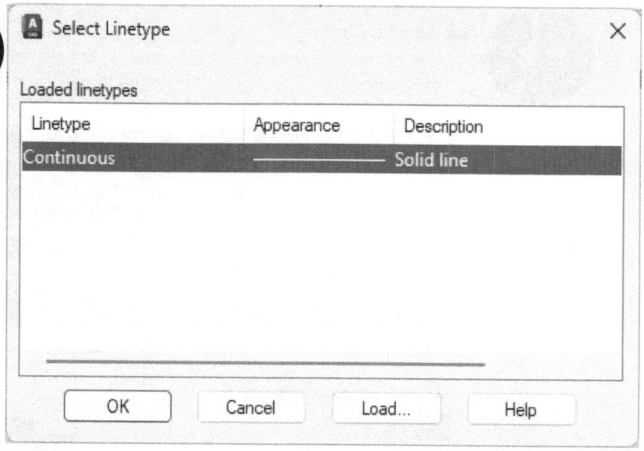

In case the **Select Linetype** dialog box appears similar to the one shown in Figure 3.44, in which only the Continuous linetype is listed, then you need to load the required linetypes into this dialog box. To load linetypes, click on the **Load** button in the **Select Linetype** dialog box. The **Load or Reload Linetypes** dialog box appears with the list of all available linetypes, see Figure 3.45. Next, click on the linetype to be loaded. You can select multiple linetypes by pressing the CTRL key. Once you have selected the linetypes to be loaded, click on the **OK** button. All the selected linetypes are listed or loaded into the **Select Linetype** dialog box. Figure 3.46 shows the **Select Linetype** dialog box with the **Center** and **Hidden** linetypes loaded.

3.45

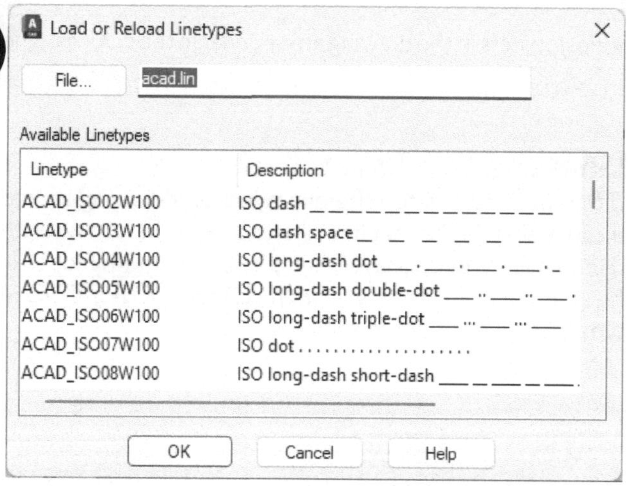

3.46

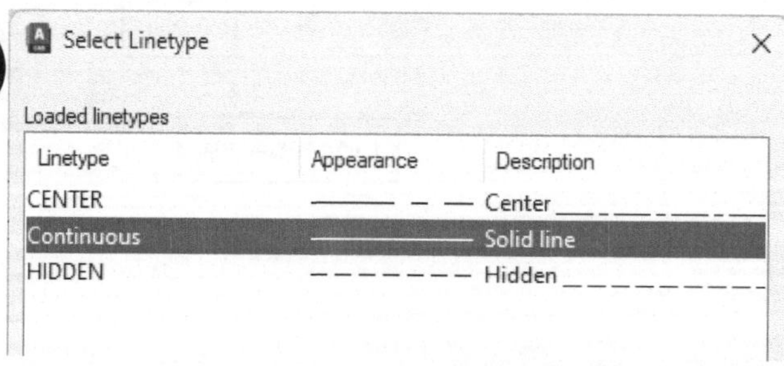

Once the required linetypes are loaded in the **Select Linetype** dialog box, click on the linetype to be assigned to the layer. Next, click the **OK** button in the **Select Linetype** dialog box. The selected linetype gets assigned to the layer. Similarly, you can assign the required linetype to other layers of the drawing.

Assigning Lineweight to a Layer

Similar to assigning color and linetype to a layer, you can assign the lineweight/thickness to a layer. To do so, click on the **Lineweight** field of the layer in the **LAYER PROPERTIES MANAGER**, see Figure 3.47. The **Lineweight** dialog box appears, see Figure 3.48.

3.47

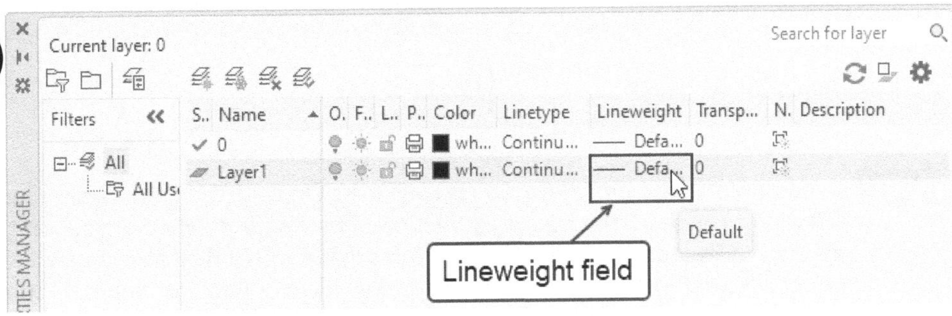

3.48

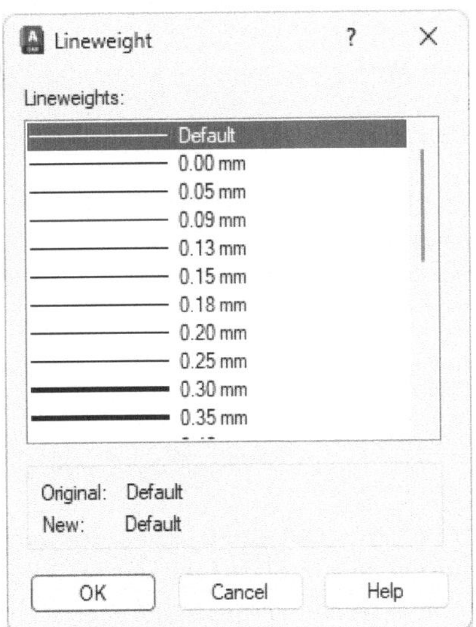

In this **Lineweight** dialog box, click on the lineweight to be assigned and then click on the **OK** button. The selected lineweight/thickness gets assigned to the layer. You can similarly assign the required lineweight to other layers of the drawing.

Note: You can turn on or off the display of the lineweight/thickness of objects in the drawing area by using the **Show/Hide Lineweight** button. It is a toggle button available in the Status Bar.

Turning a Layer On or Off

You can turn on or off a layer by clicking on the **On** field of a layer, see Figure 3.49. Note that when you turn off a layer, the objects assigned to the layer become hidden or invisible in the drawing area. Also, if you plot the drawing, the objects of the hidden layer will not be plotted.

3.49

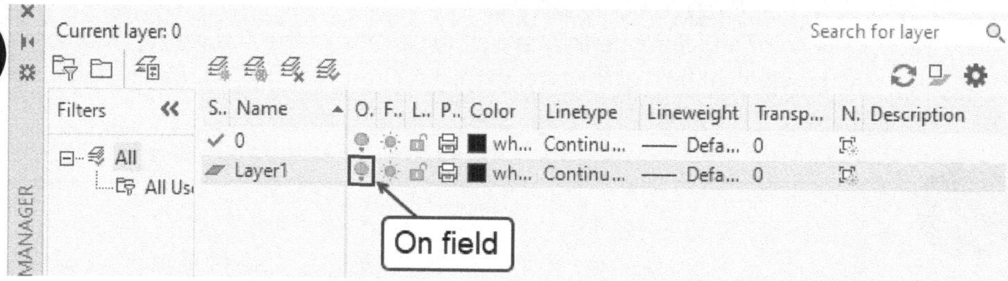

Note: If you turn off the current layer by clicking on its **On** field, then the **Layer - Current Layer Off** window appears, see Figure 3.50. This window confirms whether you want to turn off the current layer or keep it on. Also, it informs that if you turn off the current layer, then the objects drawn further will not be visible in the drawing area until you have turned on the layer.

3.50

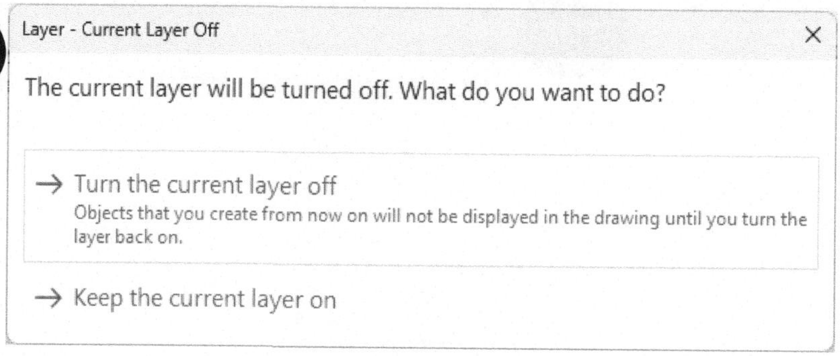

Freezing a Layer

Similar to turning a layer on or off, you can also freeze or thaw a layer by clicking on the **Freeze** field of the layer, see Figure 3.51. When you freeze a layer, the respective objects assigned to the layer get hidden in the drawing area and cannot be plotted. Note that freezing/thawing of a layer is the same as turning off/on a layer with the only difference being that on freezing a layer, the frozen layer is not considered while regenerating a drawing. As a result, the regeneration time of the drawing gets reduced. Also, it improves the system's overall performance and speeds up the zoom, pan, and other drawing operations.

3.51

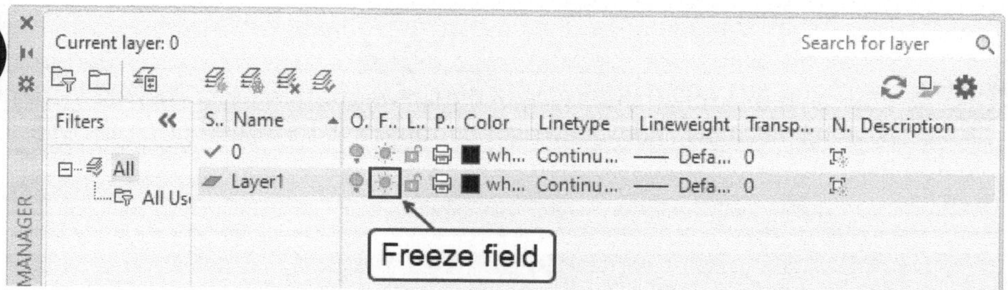

Note: You cannot freeze the current layer. If you click on the **Freeze** field of a current layer, the **Layer - Cannot Freeze** window appears (see Figure 3.52), which informs you that this layer cannot be frozen.

3.52

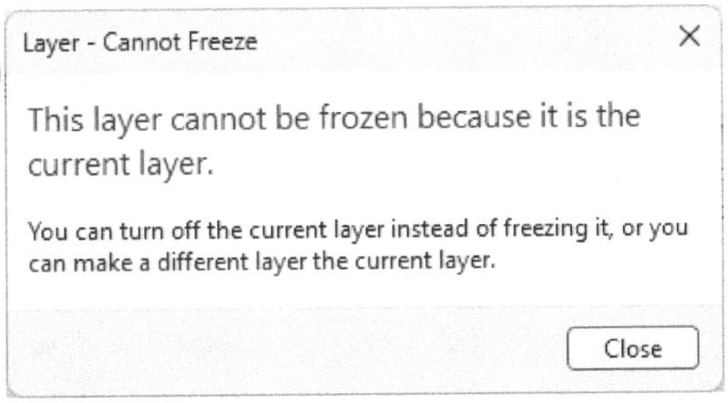

Locking or Unlocking a Layer

You can lock or unlock a layer by clicking on the **Lock** field of a layer, see Figure 3.53. The objects assigned to the locked layer cannot be edited or modified. Also, the objects of the locked layer appear faded in the drawing area. Locking a layer is very useful if you do not want any editing or modification to be done by mistake in the objects of a layer.

3.53

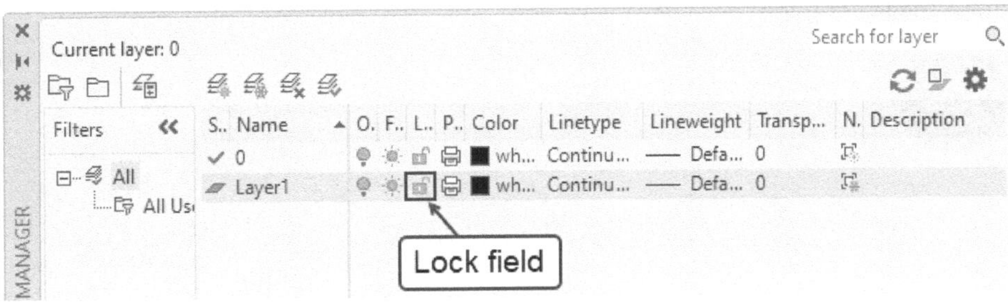

Deleting a Layer

You can delete an unwanted layer of a drawing. To do so, select the layer to be deleted in the **LAYER PROPERTIES MANAGER** and then click on the **Delete Layer** button, see Figure 3.54. Alternatively, press ALT + D to delete the selected layer. Note that you cannot delete the default '0' layer, Defpoints layer (the Defpoints layer is created automatically as soon as you apply dimensions to objects in the drawing area), current layer, layers containing objects, and Xref-dependent layers.

3.54

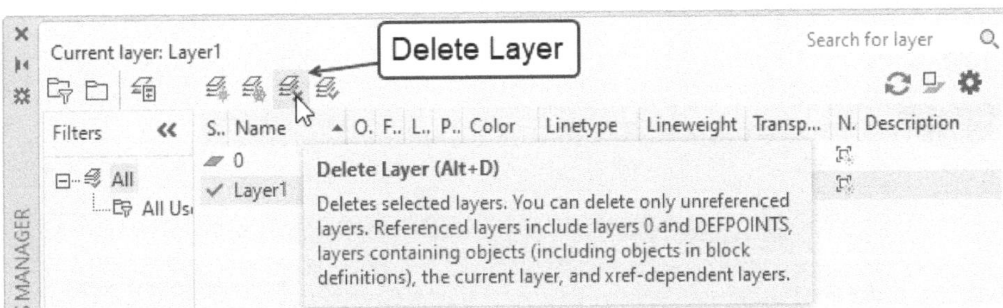

Setting Transparency of a Layer

You can define transparency for the objects of a layer by using the **Transparency** field in the **LAYER PROPERTIES MANAGER**. On clicking the **Transparency** field of the layer, the **Layer Transparency** dialog box appears, see Figure 3.55. By using the drop-down list of this dialog box, you can select transparency for the layer from "0" to "90". The objects assigned to the layer become faded in the drawing area when the transparency of the layer is defined as 10 or higher. The higher the transparency, the more faded the appearance of the objects in the drawing area.

3.55

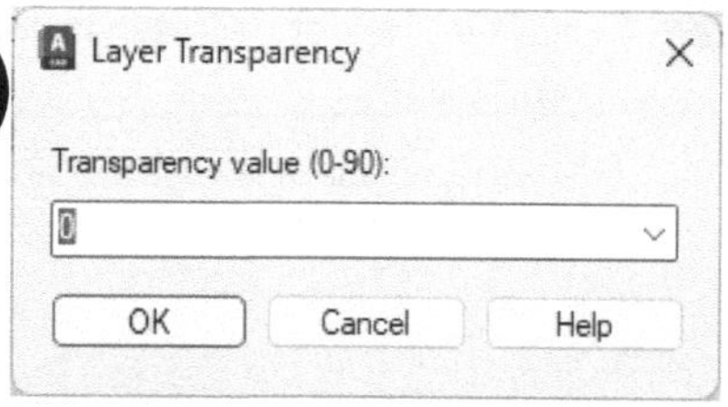

Restricting a Layer from Plotting

You can restrict a layer from plotting by using the **LAYER PROPERTIES MANAGER**. If you do not want the objects of a layer to be plotted, then you can restrict the layer from plotting. To do so, click on the **Plot** field of the layer, see Figure 3.56. A red-colored symbol appears in the **Plot** field, which indicates that the layer has been restricted from plotting. You can click again on the **Plot** field of the layer to remove the restriction.

3.56

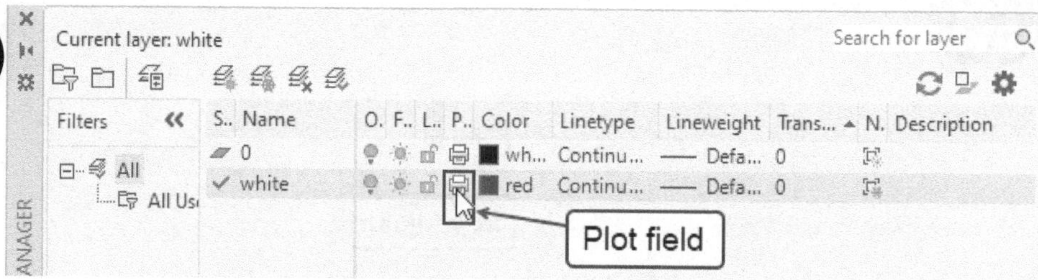

Freezing a Layer in New Viewports

You can freeze a layer in the newly created viewports by using the **New VP Freeze** field of a layer, see Figure 3.57. After freezing a layer by clicking on the **New VP Freeze** field, when you create a new viewport, all the objects of the layer become hidden/invisible in the newly created viewport. You can create multiple viewports of a drawing in the **Layout** tab. You will learn about the **Layout** tab and creating viewports in later chapters.

3.57

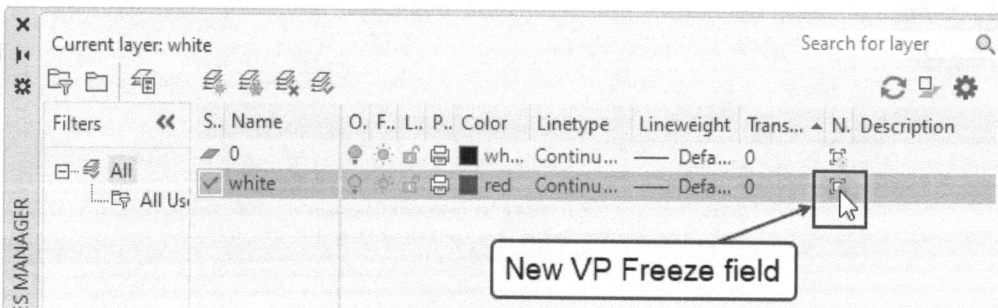

Freezing the New Layer in All Viewports

You can also freeze the newly created layer in all viewports by using the **New Layer VP Frozen in All Viewports** button of the **LAYER PROPERTIES MANAGER**, Figure 3.58. When you click on the **New Layer VP Frozen in All Viewports** button, a new layer gets created such that it becomes frozen in all viewports.

3.58

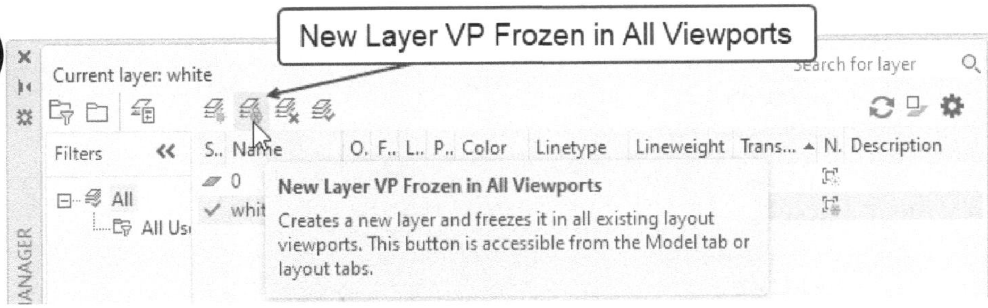

Toggle Override Highlight

You can highlight the overrides of the Xrefs (external references) layers in the drawing by using the **Toggle Override Highlight** button of the **LAYER PROPERTIES MANAGER**, see Figure 3.59. This functionality is used to easily identify the Xrefs layers of the drawing that are modified in the current drawing, see Figure 3.59. In this figure, the **External|Center** and **External|Object** layers are modified. The method for attaching external references to a drawing is discussed in Chapter 10.

3.59

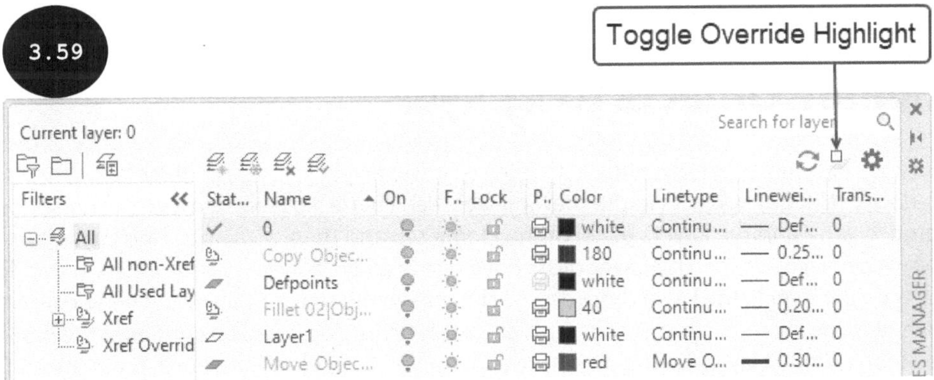

Note that when you move the cursor over the Status icon of an override Xref layer, all the applied overrides of the Xref layer appear near the cursor, see Figure 3.60.

3.60

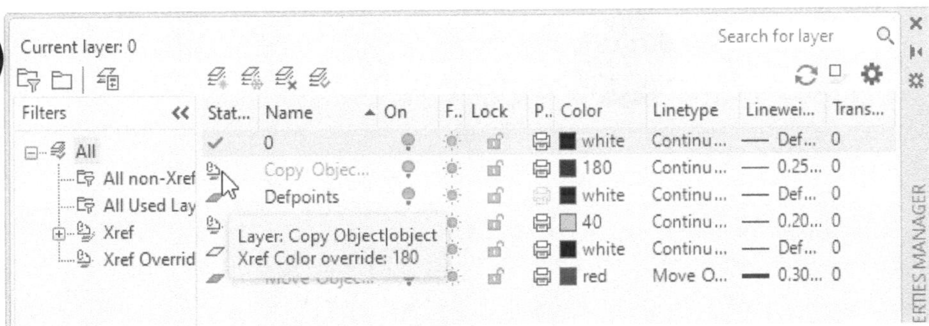

You can also reset the Xref layer properties. To do so, right-click on the layer and then click on **Reset Xref Layer Properties > Selected layer> All Properties** in the shortcut menu that appears, see Figure 3.61. All the overrides of the selected layer get reset to their original state.

3.61

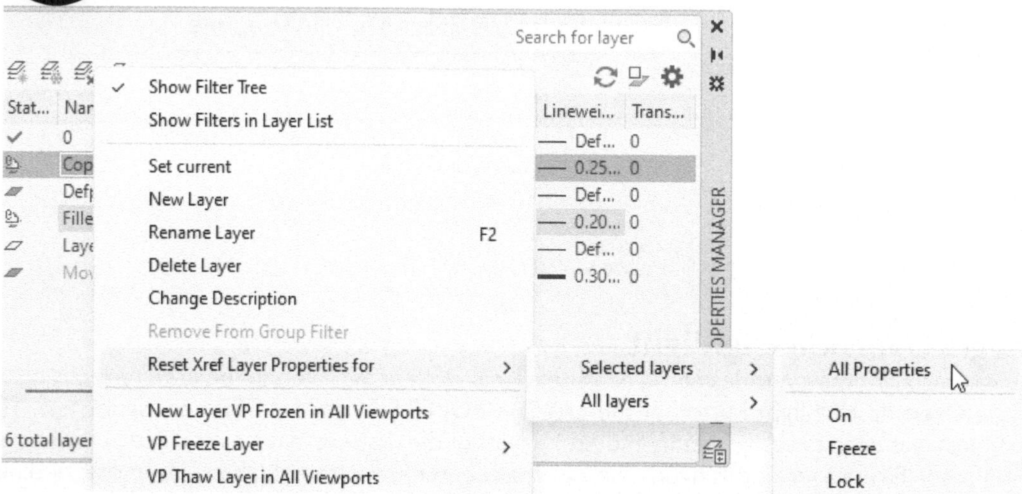

Once you have created layers and assigned layer properties, you can close the **LAYER PROPERTIES MANAGER** by clicking on the cross mark on the title bar of the **LAYER PROPERTIES MANAGER**.

Assigning Objects to a Layer

As discussed earlier, when you draw objects in the drawing area, by default, all the objects drawn get assigned automatically to the currently active layer. However, you can assign objects to other layers as well. To do so, select the objects in the drawing area, see Figure 3.62. Next, move the cursor over the **Layer** drop-down list in the **Layers** panel of the **Home** tab and then click on it. The **Layer** drop-down list appears, see Figure 3.63. The **Layer** drop-down list displays all the layers created in the drawing. Next, click on the layer in the **Layer** drop-down list to assign the selected objects. The selected objects are assigned to the layer selected, see Figure 3.64. In this figure, the selected entities of the drawing are assigned to the Hidden layer. As a result, the entities appear as hidden lines. Next, press the ESC key to exit from the current selection set. You can similarly assign a different set of objects to different layers. In Figure 3.65, the hidden lines of the drawing are assigned to the Hidden layer and the centerline is assigned to the Centerline layer.

3.62

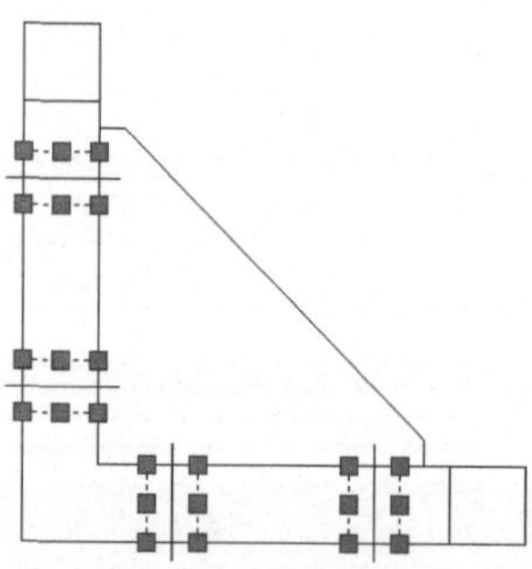

3.63

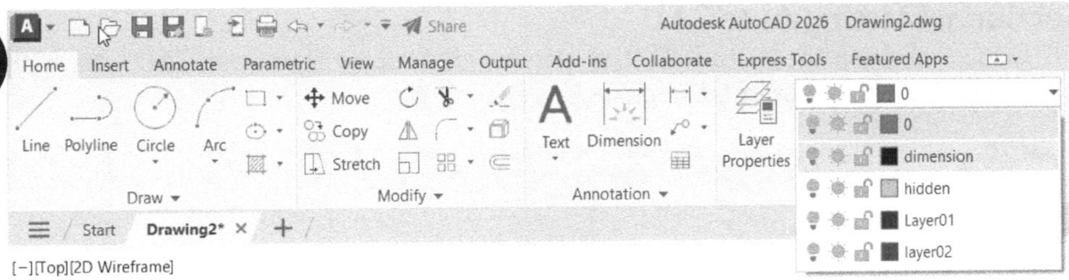

3.64

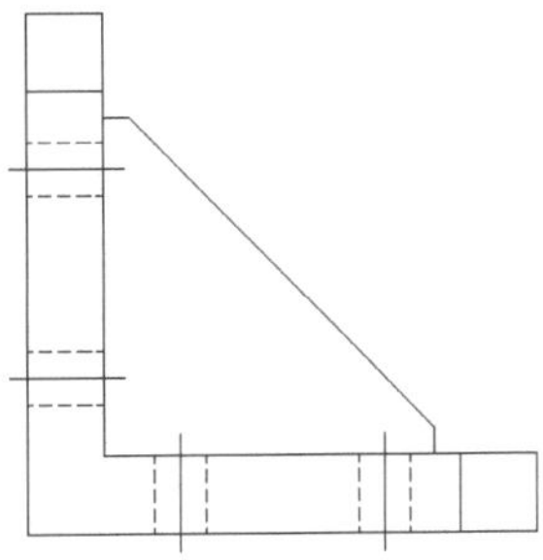

3.65

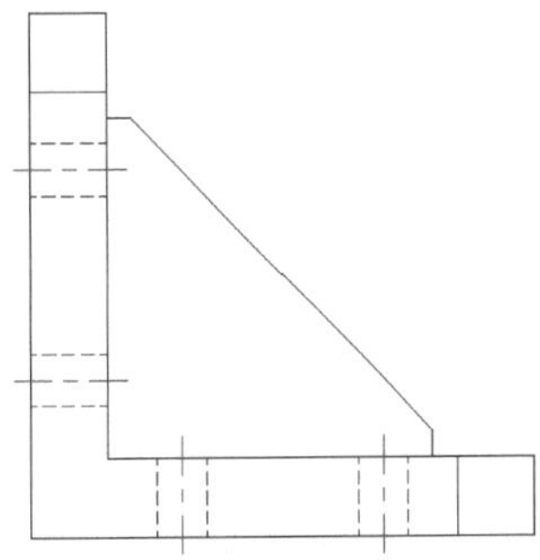

Tutorial 3

Create the drawing shown in Figure 3.66. The dimensions shown in this figure are for your reference only. You will learn about applying dimensions in the later chapters. Also, create three layers: Object, Hidden, and Centerline with the layer properties given below:

Layer Name	Color	Linetype	Lineweight
Object	Black	Continuous	0.40 mm
Hidden	Blue	Hidden	0.30 mm
Centerline	Red	Center	0.25 mm

3.66

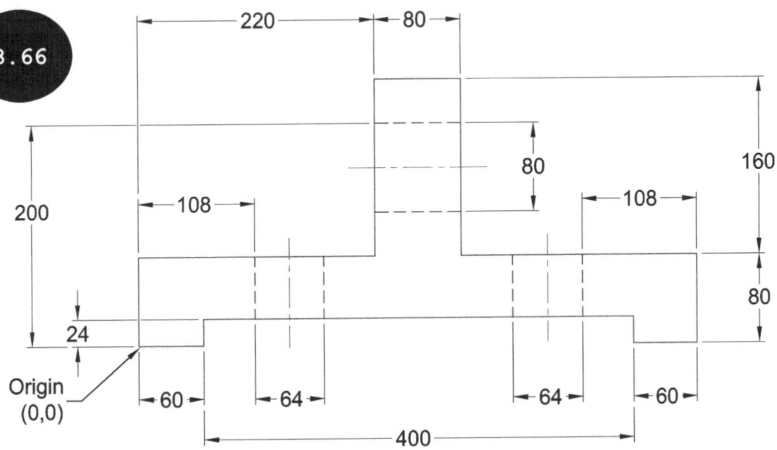

Section 1: Starting AutoCAD

1. Double-click on the AutoCAD icon on your desktop to start AutoCAD. The initial screen of AutoCAD with the **Start** tab appears, see Figure 3.67.

3.67

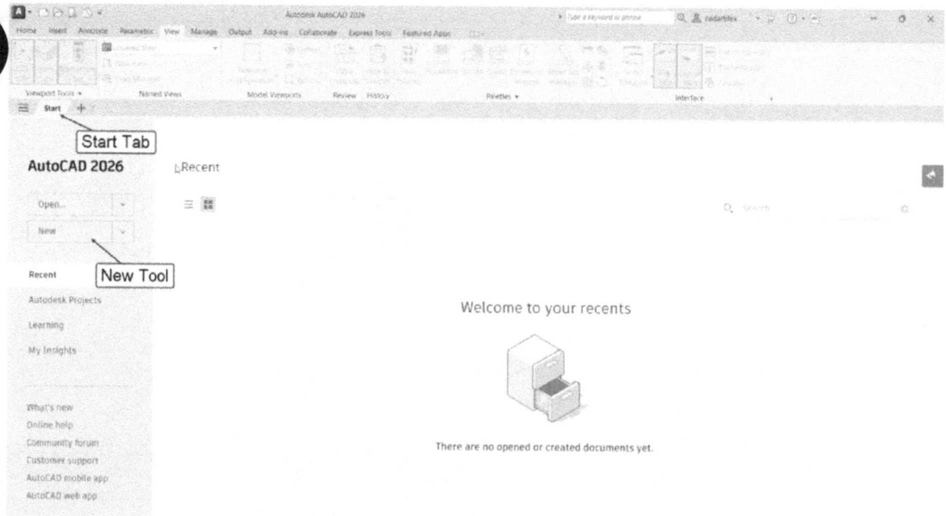

2. Click on the + sign next to the **Start** tab, see Figure 3.67. A new drawing file with the default drawing template gets invoked. Alternatively, click on the **New** tool of the **Start** tab to start a new drawing file with the default template. You can also start a new drawing file by using the **New** tool of the **Quick Access Toolbar**, which is at the top left corner of AutoCAD.

Section 2: Selecting Workspace for Creating a Drawing

1. Click on the **Workspace Switching** button in the Status Bar. A flyout appears, see Figure 3.68.

3.68

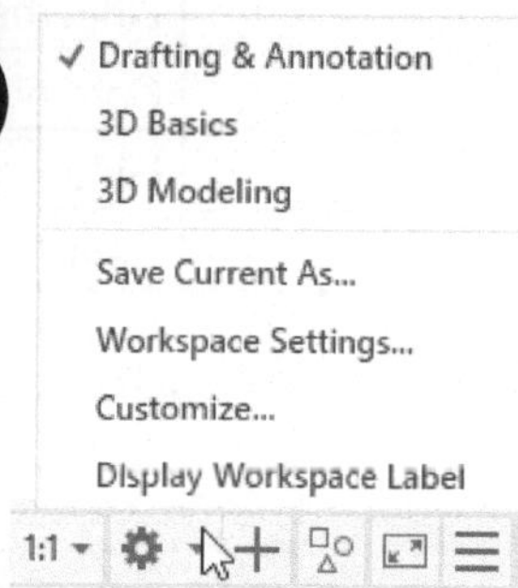

2. In this flyout, ensure that the **Drafting & Annotation** option is tick-marked to create drawings in the Drafting & Annotation workspace.

Note: A tick-mark next to the workspace indicates that it is selected as the current workspace for creating drawings. By default, the Drafting & Annotation workspace is chosen as the current workspace for creating drawings. You can click on any workspace to make it current for creating drawings.

Section 3: Creating Layer and Assigning Layer Properties

1. Click on the **Layer Properties** tool in the **Layers** panel, see Figure 3.69. The **LAYER PROPERTIES MANAGER** appears, see Figure 3.70. Alternatively, enter **LAYER** or **LA** in the Command Line window and then press ENTER to invoke the **LAYER PROPERTIES MANAGER**.

3.69

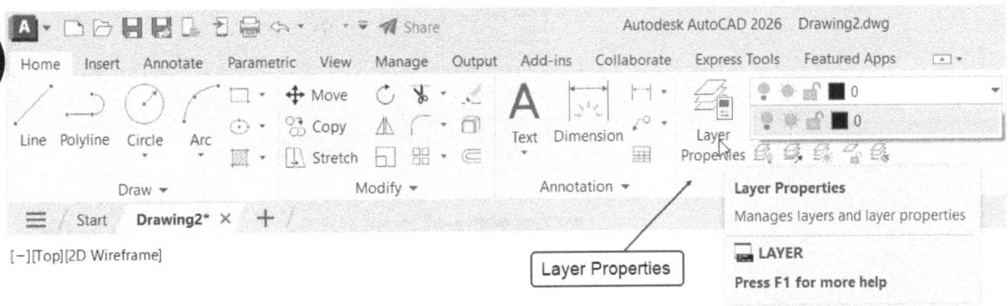

3.70

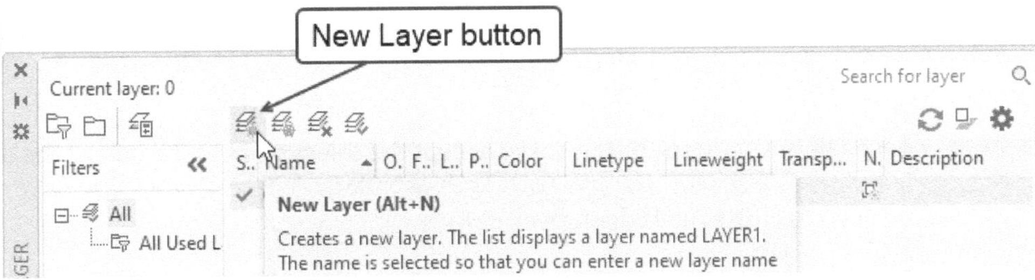

2. Click on the **New Layer** button in the **LAYER PROPERTIES MANAGER**. A new layer with the default name "**Layer 1**" is created.

3. Enter **Object** as the name of the newly created layer in the **LAYER PROPERTIES MANAGER**.

   After creating the **Object** layer, you need to define its properties such as color and lineweight. Note that the default color and linetype of the **Object** layer are the same as those mentioned in the tutorial description. Therefore, you need to only assign lineweight for the **Object** layer.

4. Click on the **Lineweight** field in the **Object** layer, see Figure 3.71. The **Lineweight** dialog box appears, see Figure 3.72.

3.71

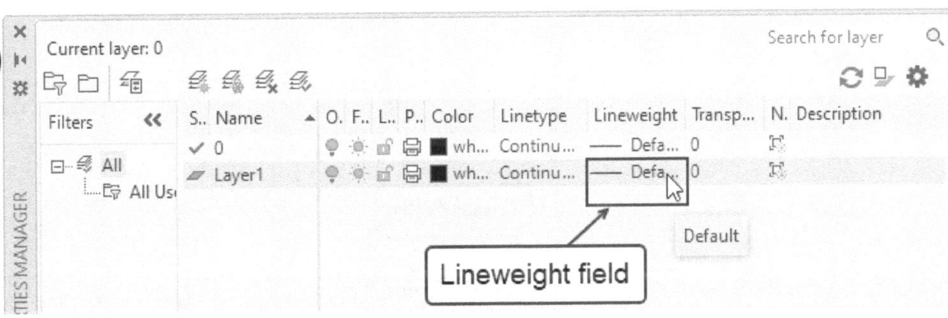

5. Click on the **0.40 mm** lineweight in the **Lineweight** dialog box, see Figure 3.72.

3.72

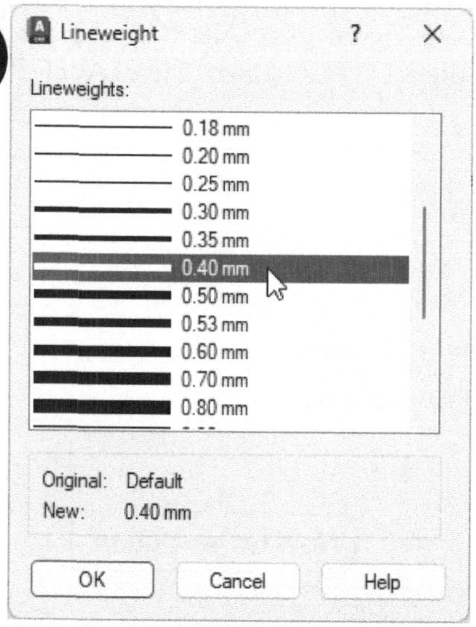

6. Click on the **OK** button in the dialog box to accept the selection as well as to exit the dialog box.

   Now, you need to create the Hidden layer.

7. Click on the **New Layer** button in the **LAYER PROPERTIES MANAGER**. A new layer with the default name "**Layer 1**" is created.

8. Enter **Hidden** as the name of the newly created layer in the **LAYER PROPERTIES MANAGER**.

   After creating the Hidden layer, you need to assign color, linetype, and lineweight to it.

9. Click on the **Color** field of the Hidden layer, see Figure 3.73. The **Select Color** dialog box appears, see Figure 3.74.

3.73

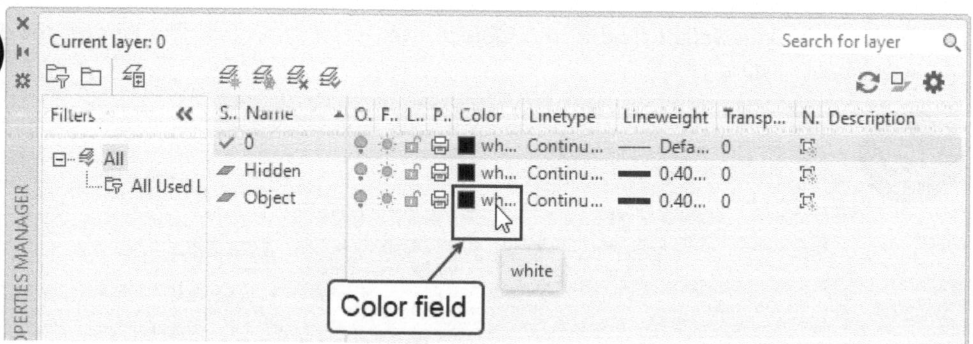

10. Click on the **Blue** color swatch in the **Select Color** dialog box (see Figure 3.74), and then click on the **OK** button in the **Select Color** dialog box. The color blue is assigned to the layer.

3.74

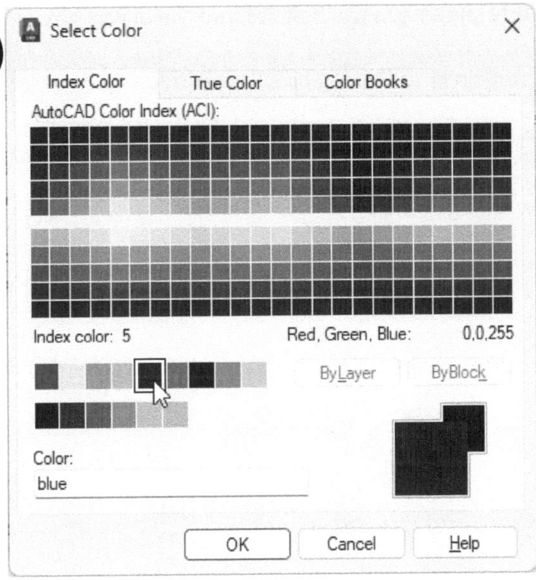

After assigning a color to the Hidden layer, you need to define Linetype and Lineweight.

11. Click on the **Linetype** field of the Hidden layer. The **Select Linetype** dialog box appears.

    If the Hidden linetype is not available in the **Select Linetype** dialog box, then you first need to load it in the dialog box.

12. Click on the **Load** button in the **Select Linetype** dialog box. The **Load or Reload Linetypes** dialog box appears, see Figure 3.75.

13. Click on the **HIDDEN** linetype in the **Load or Reload Linetypes** dialog box, see Figure 3.75.

3.75

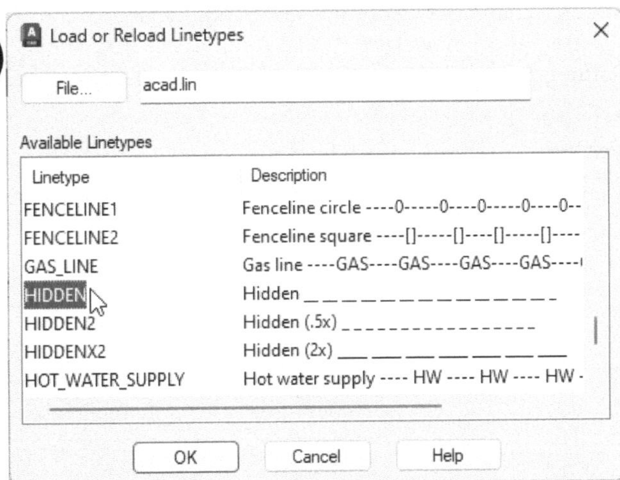

14. Click on the **OK** button in the **Load or Reload Linetypes** dialog box. The Hidden linetype is loaded in the **Select Linetype** dialog box.

15. Select the **HIDDEN** linetype in the **Select Linetype** dialog box.

16. Click on the **OK** button in the dialog box. The Hidden linetype gets assigned to the layer.

    Now, you need to assign Lineweight to the Hidden layer.

17. Click on the **Lineweight** field of the **Hidden** layer. The **Lineweight** dialog box appears, see Figure 3.76.

18. Click on the **0.30 mm** lineweight in the **Lineweight** dialog box, see Figure 3.76.

19. Click on the **OK** button in the dialog box to accept the selection as well as to exit the dialog box.

3.76

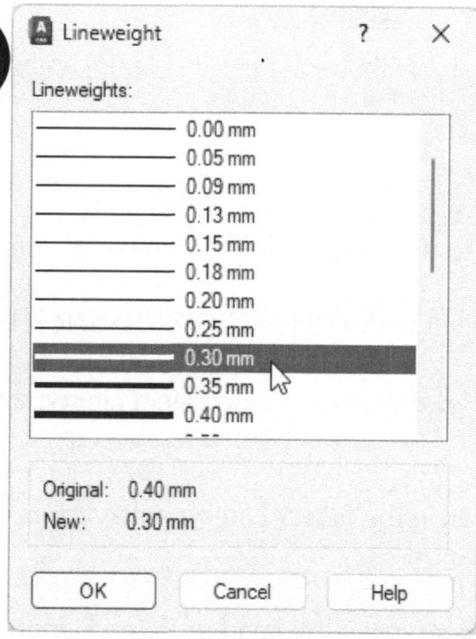

20. In a similar manner, create the Centerline layer and then assign the layer properties: Color = Red, Linetype = Center, and Lineweight = 0.25 mm. Figure 3.77 shows the **LAYER PROPERTIES MANAGER** after creating the layers: Object, Hidden, and Centerline.

3.77

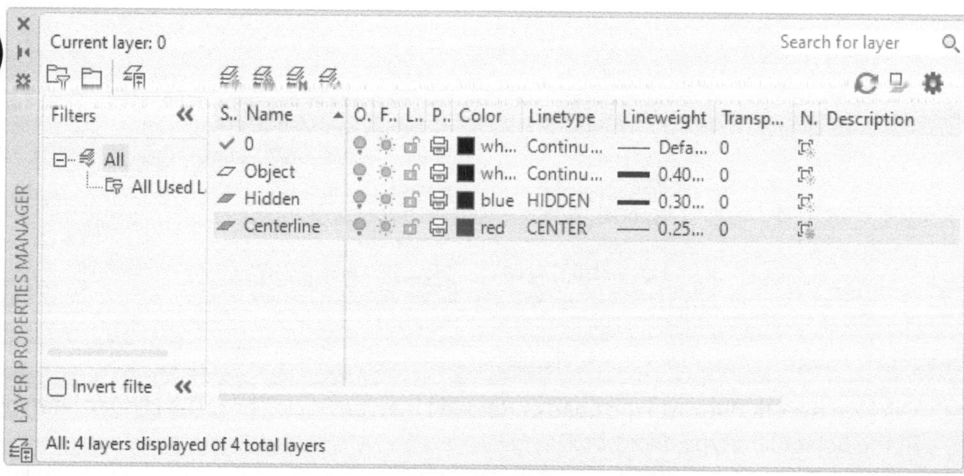

21. After creating the layers and assigning the layer properties, close the **LAYER PROPERTIES MANAGER** by clicking on the cross mark ✕ in the title bar of the **LAYER PROPERTIES MANAGER**.

Section 4: Defining Limits for Drawing

1. Follow the command sequence given below for defining limits for the drawing.

```
Command: LIMITS (ENTER)
Specify lower left corner or [ON/OFF]<0.0000,0.0000>: 0,0 (ENTER)
Specify upper right corner <12.0000,9.0000>: 820,540 (ENTER)
```

Section 5: Creating Object Entities in the Object Layer

Before creating the entities of the Object layer, you need to make the Object layer as the current layer so that the entities you create in the drawing area get assigned automatically to the Object layer.

1. Move the cursor over the **Layer** drop-down list in the **Layers** panel of the **Home** tab and then click the left mouse button to display the **Layer** drop-down list, see Figure 3.78.

3.78

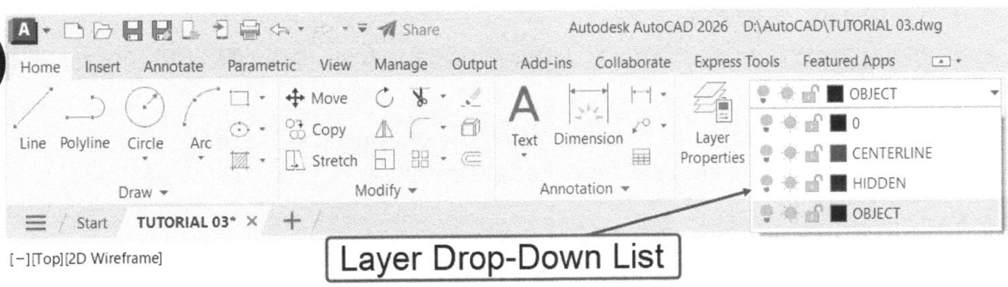

2. Click on the **Object** layer in the **Layer** drop-down list to make it the current layer.

   Now, you can create the entities of the Object layer.

3. Click on the **Line** tool in the **Draw** panel of the **Home** tab. You are prompted to specify the first point of the line.

```
Specify first point:
```

4. Click on the **Ortho Mode** button in the Status Bar or press the F8 key to turn on the Ortho mode. Note that this is a toggle button.

5. Ensure that the Dynamic Input mode is activated. You can turn on the Dynamic Input mode by clicking on the **Dynamic Input** button in the Status Bar.

6. Follow the command sequence given below for creating the drawing entities.

```
Specify first point: 0,0 (ENTER)
Specify next point or [Undo]: Move the cursor horizontally toward right and then enter 60 in the Dynamic Input box (ENTER).
```

`Specify next point or [Undo]:` *Move the cursor vertically upward and then enter* ***24*** `(`***ENTER***`).`
`Specify next point or [Close Undo]:` *Move the cursor horizontally toward right and then enter* ***400*** `(`***ENTER***`).`
`Specify next point or [Close Undo]:` *Move the cursor vertically downward and then enter* ***24*** `(`***ENTER***`).`
`Specify next point or [Close Undo]:` *Move the cursor horizontally toward right and then enter* ***60*** `(`***ENTER***`).`
`Specify next point or [Close Undo]:` *Move the cursor vertically upward and then enter* ***80*** `(`***ENTER***`).`
`Specify next point or [Close Undo]:` *Move the cursor horizontally toward left and then enter* ***220*** `(`***ENTER***`).`
`Specify next point or [Close Undo]:` *Move the cursor vertically upward and then enter* ***160*** `(`***ENTER***`).`
`Specify next point or [Close Undo]:` *Move the cursor horizontally toward left and then enter* ***80*** `(`***ENTER***`).`
`Specify next point or [Close Undo]:` *Move the cursor vertically downward and then enter* ***160*** `(`***ENTER***`).`
`Specify next point or [Close Undo]:` *Move the cursor horizontally toward left and then enter* ***220*** `(`***ENTER***`).`
`Specify next point or [Close Undo]:` *C or Close* `(`***ENTER***`)` *(See Figure 3.79).*

Tip: You may need to fit the drawing within the drawing area. To fit the drawing into the drawing area, follow the command sequence given below.

`Command:` *Z or ZOOM* `(`***ENTER***`)`
`Specify corner of window, enter a scale factor (nX or nXP), or [All/Center/Dynamic/Extents/Previous/Scale/Window/Object]<real time>:` *A or ALL* `(`***ENTER***`)`

3.79

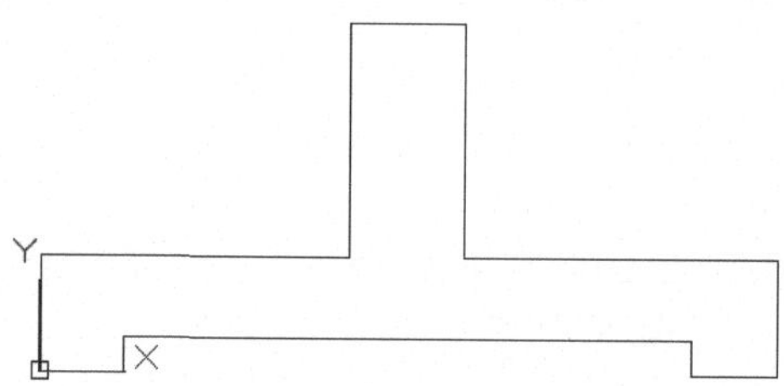

Note: To display entities in the drawing area with the lineweight/thickness assigned to the **Object** layer, click on the **Show/Hide Lineweight** button in the Status Bar to activate it.

Section 6: Creating Hidden Entities in the Hidden Layer

1. Invoke the **Layer** drop-down list in the **Layers** panel of the **Home** tab and then click on the **Hidden** layer. The Hidden layer becomes the current layer.

   Now, you can create the entities of the Hidden layer.

2. Click on the **Line** tool in the **Draw** panel of the **Home** tab. You are prompted to specify the first point of the line.

   `Specify first point:`

3. Ensure that the Ortho mode is activated. You can activate/deactivate the Ortho mode by clicking on the **Ortho Mode** button in the Status Bar or by pressing the F8 key.

4. Ensure that the Object Snap mode is activated. You can activate/deactivate the Object Snap mode by clicking on the **Object Snap** button in the Status Bar or by pressing the F3 key.

5. Ensure that the Dynamic Input mode is activated. You can activate/deactivate the Dynamic Input mode by clicking on the **Dynamic Input** button in the Status Bar or by pressing the F12 key.

6. Follow the command sequence given below for creating the entities of the Hidden layer.

   `Specify first point:` ***108,24*** (***ENTER***)
   `Specify next point or [Undo]:` *Move the cursor vertically upward and then click to specify the endpoint of the line when the cursor snaps to the upper horizontal object entity* (***ENTER***) *(see Figure 3.80).*

Note: If the cursor does not snap to the upper horizontal entity as shown in Figure 3.80, then you need to change the Object Snap settings. To change the Object Snap settings, right-click on the **Object Snap** button in the Status Bar. A flyout appears. In this flyout, click on the **Object Snap Settings** option. The **Drafting Settings** dialog box appears. In this dialog box, ensure that the **Perpendicular** check box is selected.

3.80

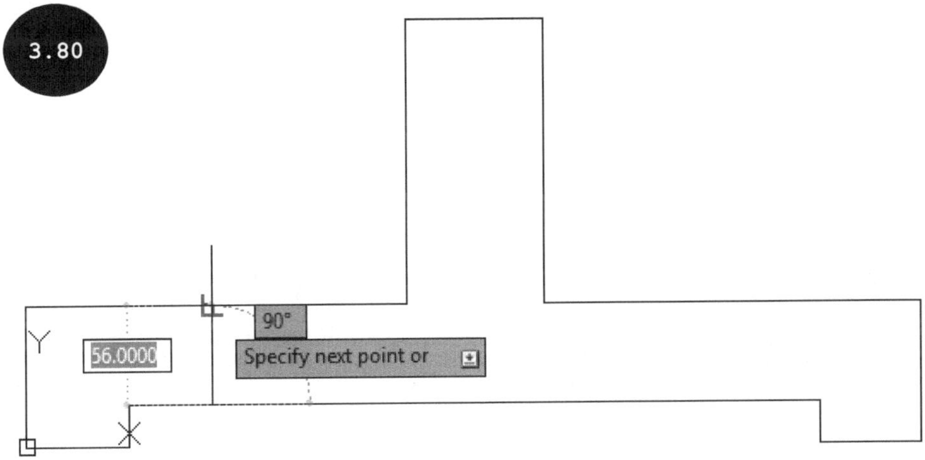

`Tool/Command:` *Line or L* (***ENTER***)
`Specify first point:` *172,24* (***ENTER***)
`Specify next point or [Undo]:` *Move the cursor vertically upward and then click to specify the endpoint of the line when the cursor snaps to the upper object line* (***ENTER***) *(see Figure 3.81).*

3.81

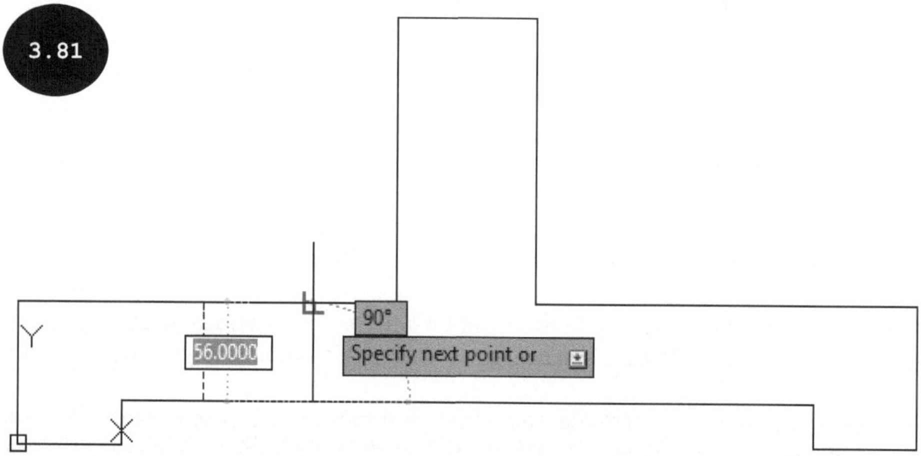

Note: If the entities of the Hidden layer appear as continuous linetype in the drawing area, then you need to increase or decrease its linetype scale by using the **Properties** panel. To increase or decrease the linetype scale, enter **PR** in the Command Line window and then press ENTER. The **Properties** panel appears to the left of the drawing area. Next, select the entity of the Hidden layer whose linetype scale is to be changed in the drawing area. The **Properties** panel displays the properties of the selected entity. Next, enter **15** in the **Linetype scale** field of the **Properties** panel. If linetype scale 15 does not work, you can try any value as the linetype scale to match the display of the hidden line, as required.

`Tool/Command:` *Line or L* (***ENTER***)
`Specify first point:` *412,24* (***ENTER***)
`Specify next point or [Undo]:` *Move the cursor vertically upward and then click to specify the endpoint of the line when the cursor snaps to the upper object line* (***ENTER***) *(see Figure 3.82).*

3.82

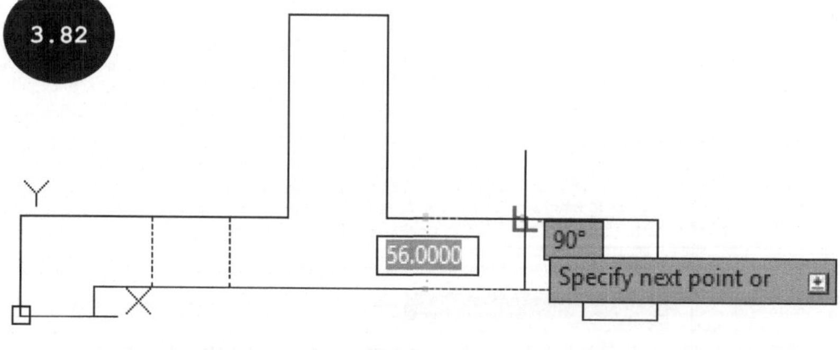

`Tool/Command:` *Line or L* (***ENTER***)
`Specify first point:` ***348,24*** (***ENTER***)
`Specify next point or [Undo]:` *Move the cursor vertically upward and then click to specify the endpoint of the line when the cursor snaps to the upper object line* (***ENTER***) *(see Figure 3.83).*

3.83

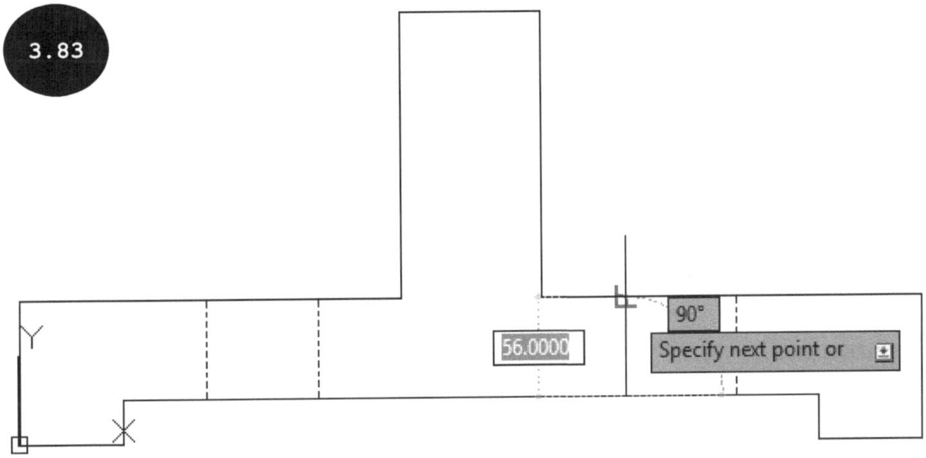

`Command:` *Line or L* (***ENTER***)
`Specify first point:` ***220,200*** (***ENTER***)
`Specify next point or [Undo]:` *Move the cursor horizontally toward the right and then click to specify the endpoint of the line when the cursor snaps to the next object line* (***ENTER***).

`Command:` *Line or L* (***ENTER***)
`Specify first point:` ***220,120*** (***ENTER***)
`Specify next point or [Undo]:` *Move the cursor horizontally toward the right and then click to specify the endpoint of the line when the cursor snaps to the next object line* (***ENTER***) *(see Figure 3.84).*

Figure 3.84 shows the drawing after creating the object and hidden line entities.

3.84

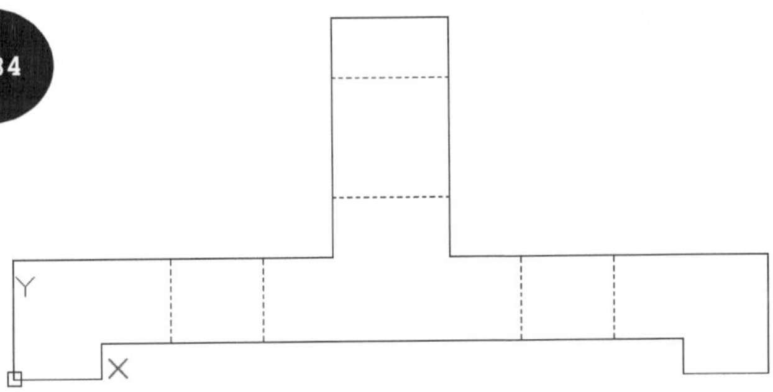

Section 7: Creating Centerlines in the Centerline Layer

1. Invoke the **Layer** drop-down list in the **Layers** panel and then click on the **Centerline** layer. The Centerline layer becomes the current layer.

After making the Centerline layer as the current layer, you can create the centerline entities of the drawing.

2. Click on the **Line** tool in the **Draw** panel of the **Home** tab. You are prompted to specify the first point of the line.

```
Specify first point:
```

3. Move the cursor toward the midpoint of the first drawn hidden line and then click to specify the first point of the line when the cursor snaps to it, see Figure 3.85.

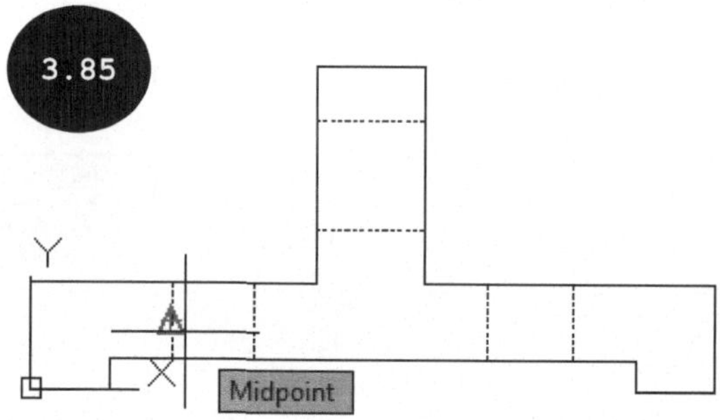

Note: If the cursor does not snap to the midpoint as shown in Figure 3.85, then you need to change the Object Snap settings. For doing so, right-click on the **Object Snap** button in the Status Bar. A flyout appears. In this flyout, click on the **Midpoint** option. Next, click anywhere in the drawing area to exit the flyout.

4. Move the cursor horizontally toward the right and then click to specify the endpoint of the line when the cursor snaps to the midpoint of the next hidden line, see Figure 3.86. Next, press ENTER.

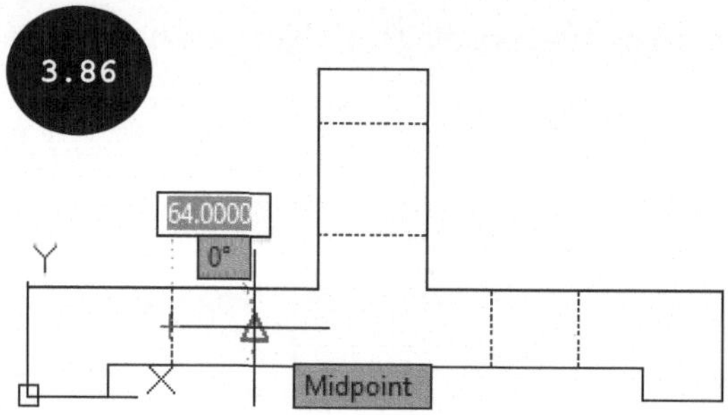

Note that the line entity drawn in the above three steps will be used as the reference line for creating the centerline.

5. Click on the **Line** tool in the **Draw** panel of the **Home** tab.

```
Specify first point:
```

6. Move the cursor toward the midpoint of the previously drawn reference line and when the cursor snaps to it (see Figure 3.87), move the cursor vertically upward to a distance outside the drawing. A reference/tracking line appears, see Figure 3.88.

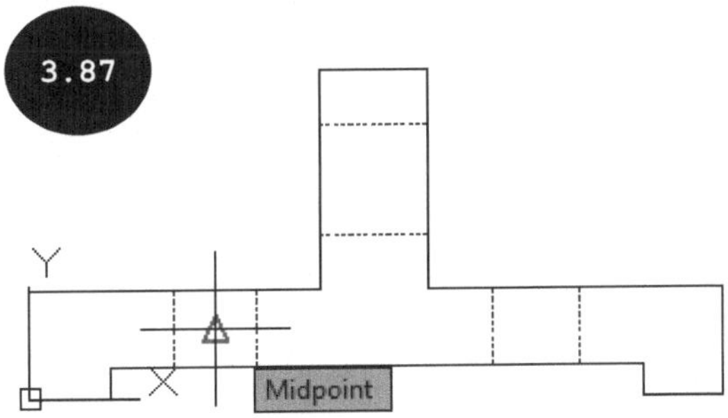

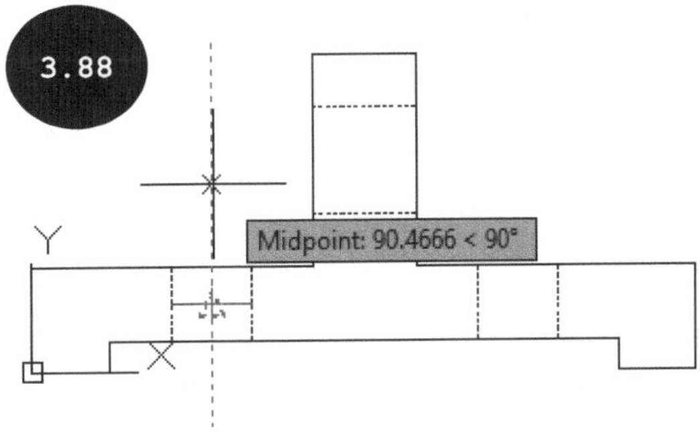

7. Click to specify the first point of the centerline somewhere near the upper horizontal line entity of the drawing, see Figure 3.88. Next, move the cursor vertically downward and click to specify the endpoint of the centerline somewhere outside the lower horizontal line entity of the drawing, see Figure 3.89.

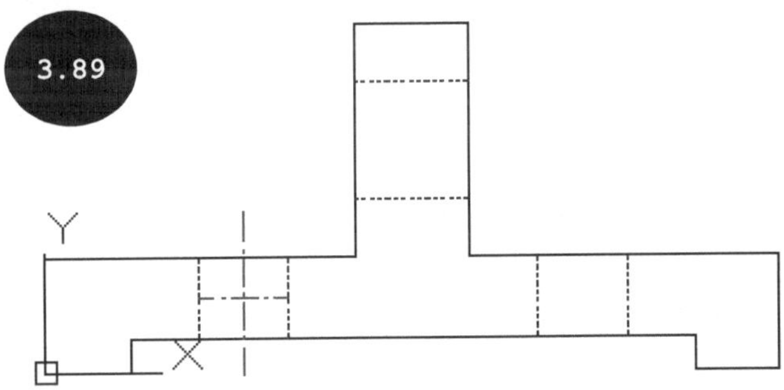

Note: If the centerline appears as continuous linetype in the drawing area, then you need to increase or decrease its linetype scale by using the **Properties** panel. For doing so, enter **PR** in the Command Line window and then press ENTER. The **Properties** panel appears to the left of the drawing area. Next, select the centerline in the drawing area. The **Properties** panel displays the properties of the selected centerline. Next, in the **Linetype scale** field of the **Properties** panel, enter the linetype scale for the centerline. You can try any value as the linetype scale to match the display of the centerline, as required.

After creating the centerline, you need to delete the reference line drawn for creating the centerline.

8. Click on the reference line in the drawing area. The reference line gets selected, see Figure 3.90. Next, press the DELETE key. The reference line gets deleted. Figure 3.91 shows the drawing after deleting the reference line.

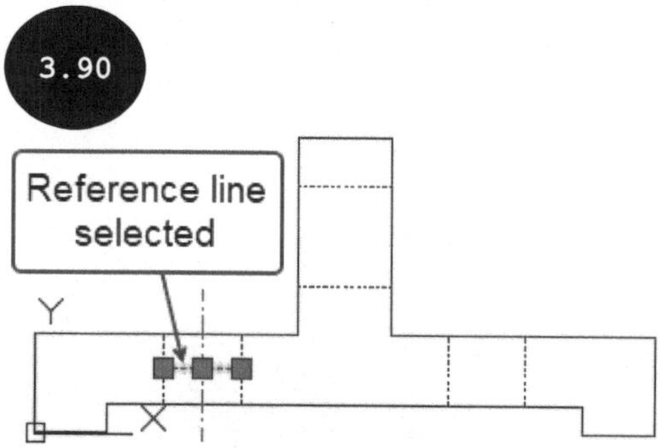

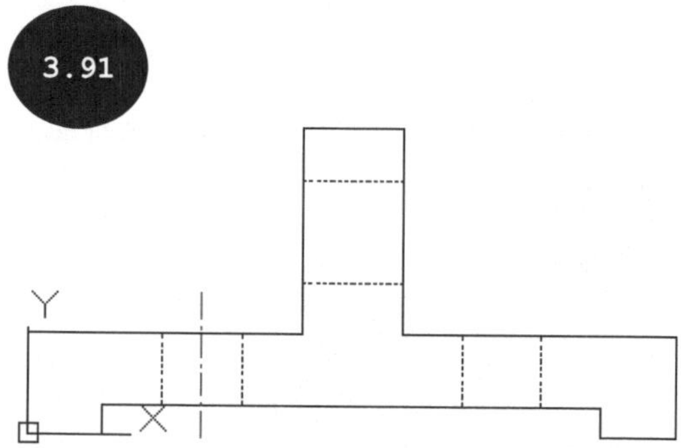

9. In a similar manner, draw the other centerlines of the drawing, see Figure 3.92. Figure 3.92 shows the final drawing after creating all the drawing entities.

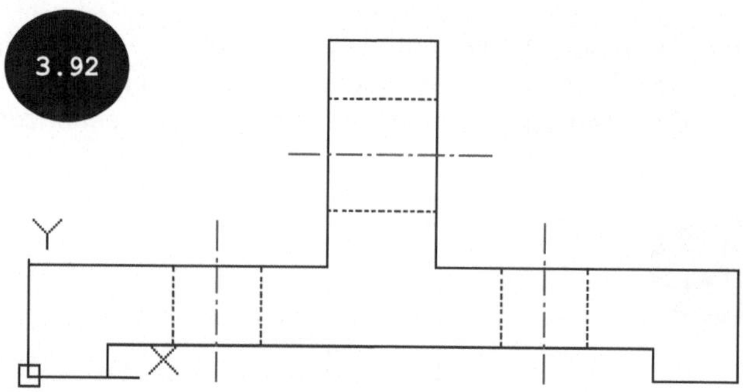

Section 8: Saving the Drawing

After creating the drawing, you need to save it.

1. Click on the **Save** tool in the **Quick Access Toolbar**. The **Save Drawing As** dialog box appears

2. Browse to the *AutoCAD* folder and then create another folder with the name *Chapter 3* inside the *AutoCAD* folder. If the *AutoCAD* folder was not created in Chapter 2, then you need to first create this folder on a local drive of your system.

3. Enter **Tutorial 3** in the **File name** field of the dialog box and then click on the **Save** button. The drawing gets saved with the name Tutorial 3 in the *Chapter 3* folder.

Tutorial 4

Create the drawing shown in Figure 3.93. The dimensions shown in this figure are for your reference only. You will learn about applying dimensions in the later chapters. Also, create three layers: Object, Hidden, and Centerline with the layer properties given below.

Layer Name	Color	Linetype	Lineweight
Object	Black	Continuous	0.50 mm
Hidden	Blue	Hidden2	0.40 mm
Centerline	Red	Center2	0.30 mm

3.93

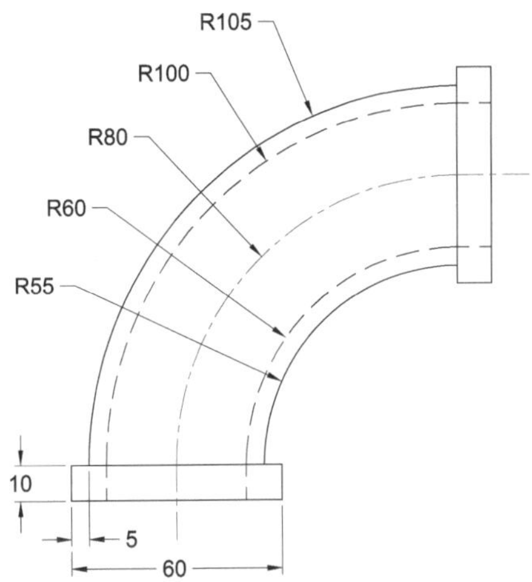

Section 1: Starting AutoCAD

1. Start AutoCAD by double-clicking on the AutoCAD icon on your desktop, if not started already.

2. Click on the **New** tool in the **Quick Access Toolbar**, which is at the top left corner of AutoCAD. The **Select template** dialog box appears. In this dialog box, choose the ***acad.dwt*** template and then click on the **Open** button. A new drawing file with the ***acad.dwt*** template gets invoked.

Section 2: Creating Layers and Assigning Properties to Layers

1. Click on the **Layer Properties** tool in the **Layers** panel of the **Home** tab, see Figure 3.94. The **LAYER PROPERTIES MANAGER** appears, see Figure 3.95.

3.94

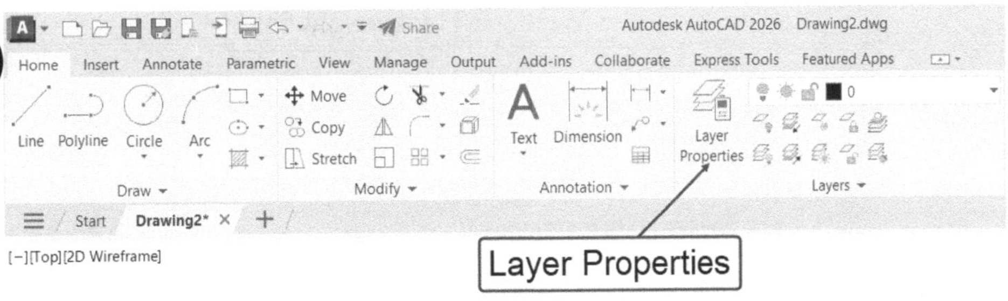

3.95

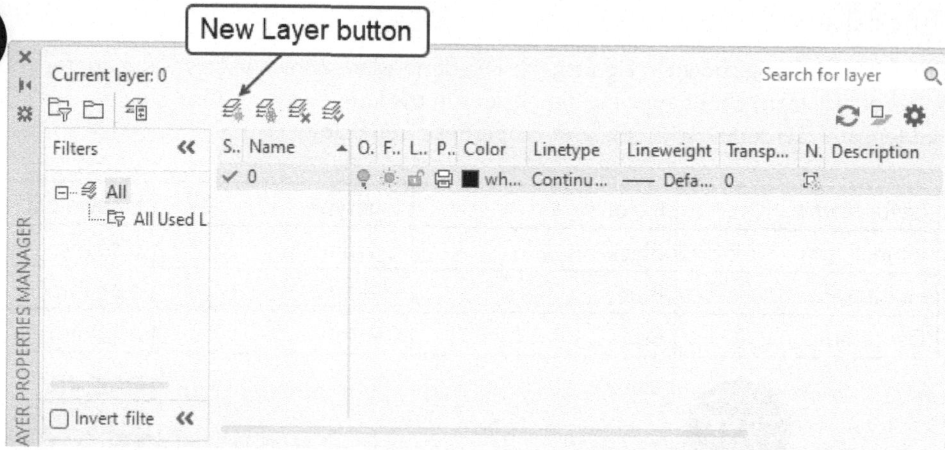

Tip: You can also enter **LAYER** or **LA** in the Command Line window to invoke the **LAYER PROPERTIES MANAGER**.

2. Click on the **New Layer** button in the **LAYER PROPERTIES MANAGER**. A new layer with the default name "**Layer 1**" is created.

3. Enter **Object** as the name of the newly created layer in the **LAYER PROPERTIES MANAGER**.

   After creating the Object layer, you need to define its properties such as color and lineweight. Note that the default color and linetype assigned to the Object layer are the same as those mentioned in the tutorial description. Therefore, you need to assign only the lineweight to the Object layer.

4. Click on the **Lineweight** field in the Object layer, see Figure 3.96. The **Lineweight** dialog box appears, see Figure 3.97.

3.96

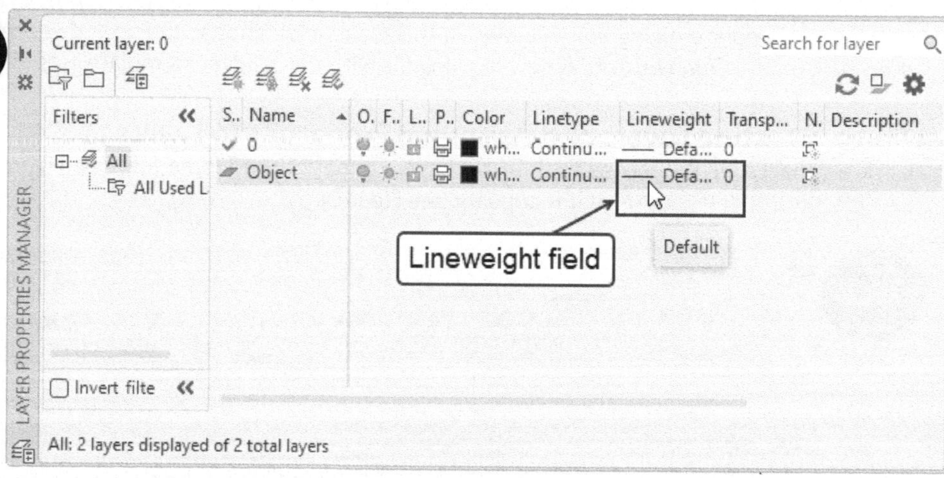

5. Click on the **0.50 mm** lineweight in the **Lineweight** dialog box, see Figure 3.97.

3.97

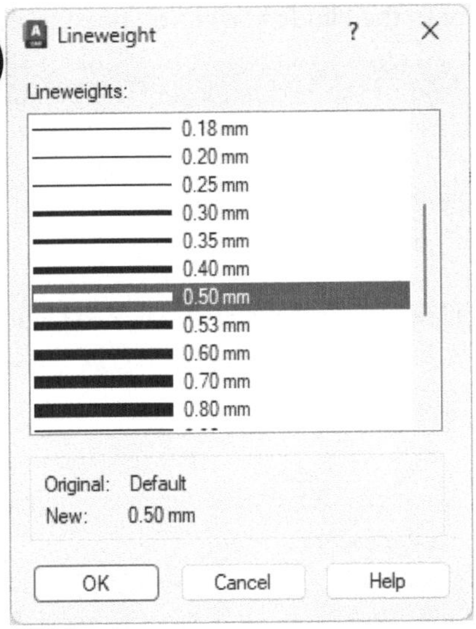

6. Click on the **OK** button in the dialog box to accept the selection as well as to exit the dialog box.

   Now, you need to create the Hidden layer.

7. Click on the **New Layer** button in the **LAYER PROPERTIES MANAGER**. A new layer with the default name "**Layer 1**" is created.

8. Enter **Hidden** as the name of the newly created layer in the **LAYER PROPERTIES MANAGER**.

   After creating the Hidden layer, you need to assign color, linetype, and lineweight to it.

9. Click on the **Color** field of the Hidden layer, see Figure 3.98. The **Select Color** dialog box appears.

3.98

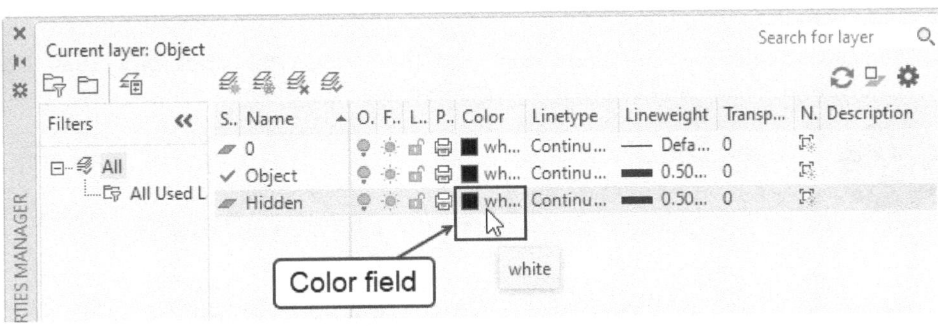

10. Click on the **Blue** color swatch in the **Select Color** dialog box and then click on the **OK** button. The chosen color gets assigned to the Hidden layer.

After assigning the color to the Hidden layer, you need to define linetype and lineweight.

11. Click on the **Linetype** field of the Hidden layer. The **Select Linetype** dialog box appears. In this dialog box, if the Hidden2 linetype is not available then you need to first load it in the dialog box.

12. Click on the **Load** button in the **Select Linetype** dialog box. The **Load or Reload Linetypes** dialog box appears, see Figure 3.99.

13. Click on the **HIDDEN2** linetype in the dialog box, see Figure 3.99. Next, click on the **OK** button. The Hidden2 linetype is loaded in the **Select Linetype** dialog box.

3.99

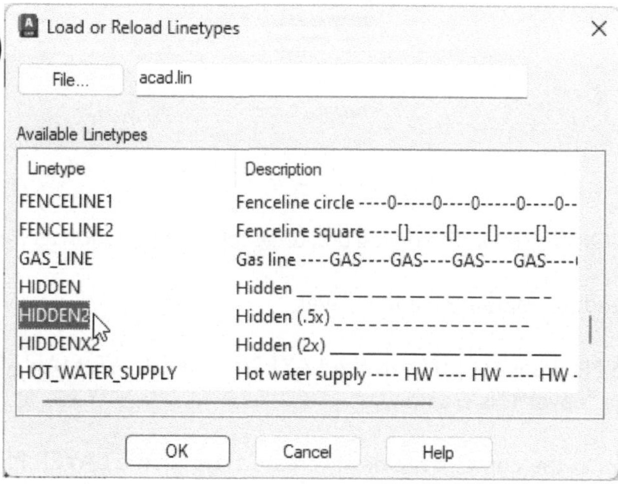

14. Click on the **HIDDEN2** linetype in the **Select Linetype** dialog box and then click on the **OK** button. The Hidden2 linetype is assigned to the Hidden layer.

15. Assign 0.40 mm lineweight to the Hidden layer.

16. Similarly, create the Centerline layer and then assign the layer properties: Color = Red, Linetype = Center2, and Lineweight = 0.30 mm, see Figure 3.100.

3.100

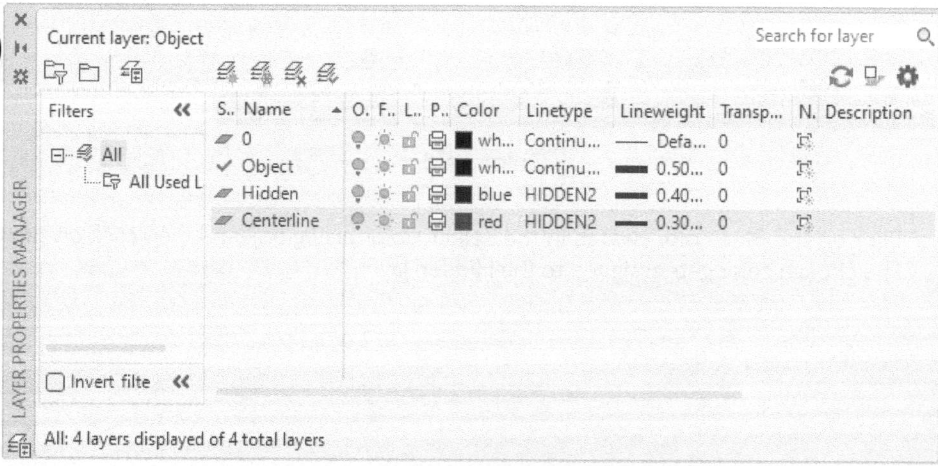

17. After creating layers and assigning properties, close the **LAYER PROPERTIES MANAGER** by clicking on the cross mark ✕ in the title bar of the **LAYER PROPERTIES MANAGER**.

Section 3: Creating Object Entities in the Object Layer

Before creating the entities of the Object layer, you need to make the Object layer as the current layer so that the entities you create in the drawing area get assigned automatically to the Object layer.

1. Move the cursor over the **Layer** drop-down list in the **Layers** panel of the **Home** tab and then click the left mouse button on it to display the **Layer** drop-down list, see Figure 3.101.

3.101

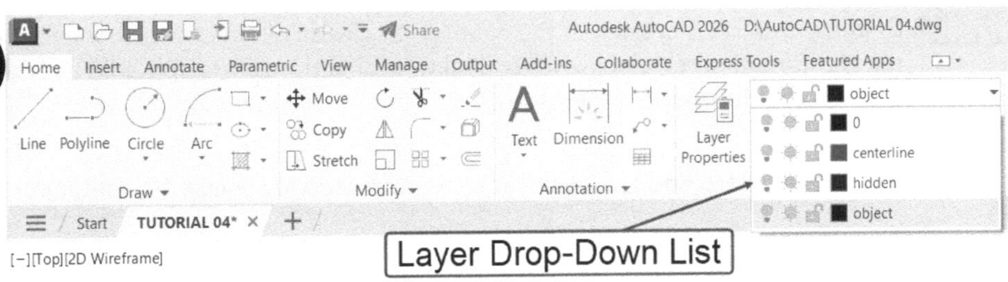

2. Click on the **Object** layer in the **Layer** drop-down list to make it the current layer.

   Now, you can create the entities of the Object layer.

3. Invoke the **Arc** flyout and then click on the **Center, Start, End** tool. You are prompted to specify the center point of the arc.

   ```
   Specify center point of arc:
   ```

4. Click anywhere in the drawing area to specify the center point of the arc. You are prompted to specify the start point of the arc.

   ```
   Specify start point of arc:
   ```

5. Ensure that the Ortho mode and the Dynamic Input mode are activated.

6. Move the cursor horizontally toward left and then enter **105** in the Dynamic Input box as the radius of the arc. Next, press ENTER. You are prompted to specify the endpoint of the arc.

   ```
   Specify end point of arc (hold Ctrl to switch direction) or [Angle
   chord Length]:
   ```

7. Press and hold the CTRL key and then move the cursor in the clockwise direction. Next, click to specify the endpoint of the arc when the angle value appears as 90 degrees near the cursor, see Figure 3.102.

3.102

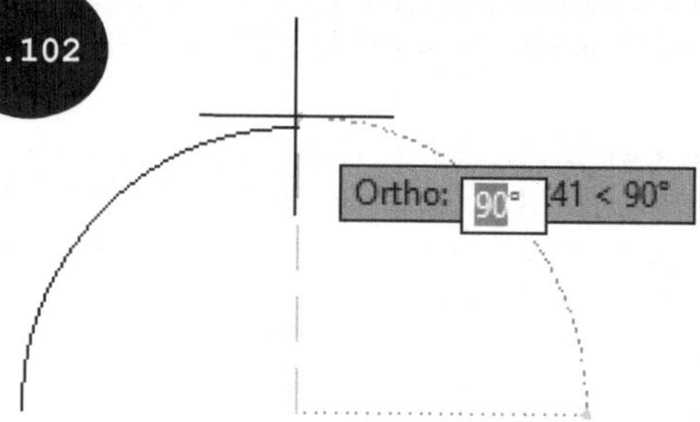

Note: By default, an arc is created in the counter-clockwise direction. To change the direction of the arc from counter-clockwise to clockwise direction, press and hold the CTRL key and then specify the endpoint of the arc.

8. Invoke the **Center, Start, End** tool again. You are prompted to specify the center point of the arc.

```
Specify center point of arc:
```

9. Move the cursor over the arc drawn earlier in the drawing area, see Figure 3.103. The center point of the arc gets highlighted in the drawing area, see Figure 3.103.

3.103

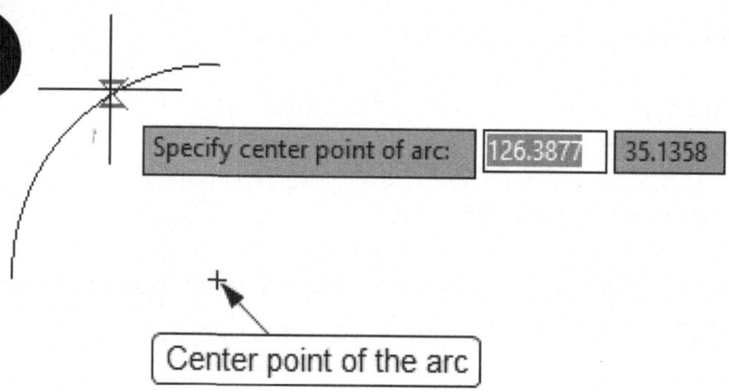

10. Move the cursor over the highlighted center point and then click the left mouse button when the cursor snaps to the center point of the arc. The center point of the arc is specified.

Note: If the cursor does not snap to the existing entities, you need to specify the Object Snap settings by using the **Drafting Settings** dialog box. For doing so, right-click on the **Object Snap** button in the Status Bar. A flyout appears. Next, click on the **Object Snap Settings** option in the flyout. The **Drafting Settings** dialog box appears. In this dialog box, click on the **Select All** button to select all the check boxes.

11. Move the cursor horizontally toward left and then enter **55** in the Dynamic Input box as the radius of the arc. You are prompted to specify the endpoint of the arc.

```
Specify end point of arc (hold Ctrl to switch direction) or [Angle
chord Length]:
```

12. Press and hold the CTRL key and then move the cursor in the clockwise direction. Next, click to specify the endpoint of the arc when the angle value appears as 90 degrees near the cursor, see Figure 3.104.

3.104

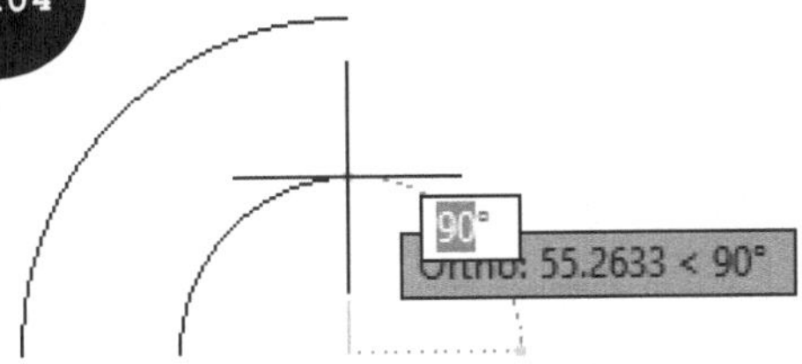

13. Click on the **Line** tool in the **Draw** panel. You are prompted to specify the first point of the line.

    `Specify first point:`

14. Move the cursor toward the start point of the first created arc and then click to specify the first point of the line when the cursor snaps to it, see Figure 3.105.

    `Specify next point or [Undo]:`

15. Move the cursor horizontally toward left and then enter **5** in the Dynamic Input box as the length of the line, see Figure 3.106. Next, press ENTER.

3.105

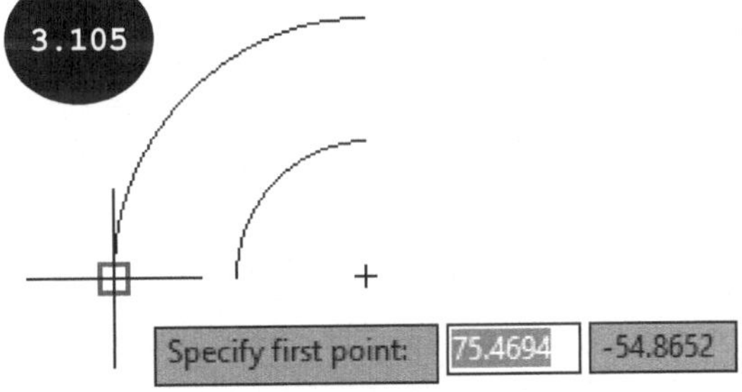

3.106

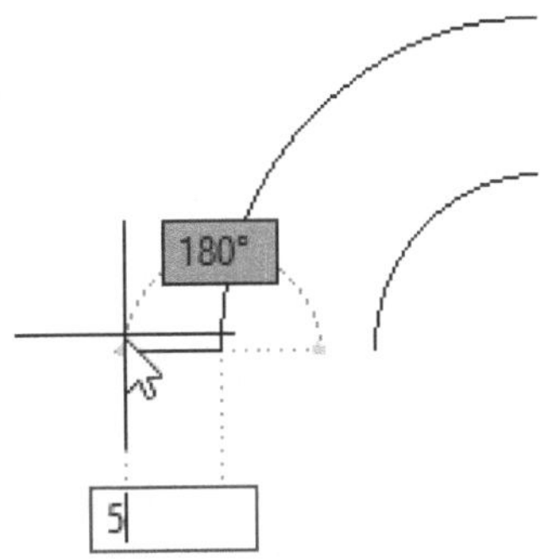

16. Follow the command sequence given below for creating the remaining line entities.

    `Specify next point or [Undo]:` *Move the cursor vertically downward and then enter* ***10*** *in the Dynamic Input box* (***ENTER***).
    `Specify next point or [Close Undo]:` *Move the cursor horizontally toward right and then enter* ***60*** (***ENTER***).
    `Specify next point or [Close Undo]:` *Move the cursor vertically upward and then enter* ***10*** (***ENTER***).
    `Specify next point or [Close Undo]:` *Move the cursor horizontally toward left and then click to specify the endpoint of the line when the cursor snaps to the start point of the first drawn arc* (***ENTER***) *(See Figure 3.107).*

3.107

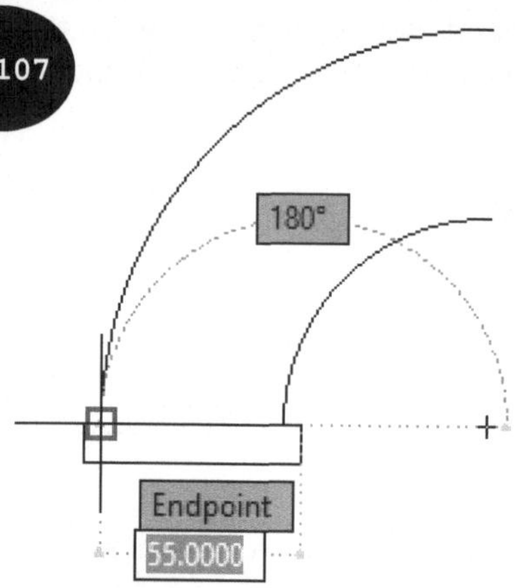

`Tool/Command:` *Line or L* (***ENTER***)
`Specify first point:` *Move the cursor toward the endpoint of the first drawn arc and then click to specify the first point of the line when the cursor snaps to it* *(See Figure 3.108).*
`Specify next point or [Undo]:` *Move the cursor vertically upward and then enter* ***5*** *in the Dynamic Input box* (***ENTER***).
`Specify next point or [Undo]:` *Move the cursor horizontally toward right and then enter* ***10*** (***ENTER***).
`Specify next point or [Close Undo]:` *Move the cursor vertically downward and then enter* ***60*** (***ENTER***).
`Specify next point or [Close Undo]:` *Move the cursor horizontally toward left and then enter* ***10*** (***ENTER***).
`Specify next point or [Close Undo]:` *C or Close* (***ENTER***) *(See Figure 3.109).*

Tip: You may need to fit the drawing within the drawing area. To do so, follow the command sequence given below.

> `Command:` *Z or Zoom* (***ENTER***)
> `Specify corner of window, enter a scale factor (nX or nXP), or [All/Center/Dynamic/Extents/Previous/Scale/Window/Object]<real time>:` *A or ALL* (***ENTER***)

3.108

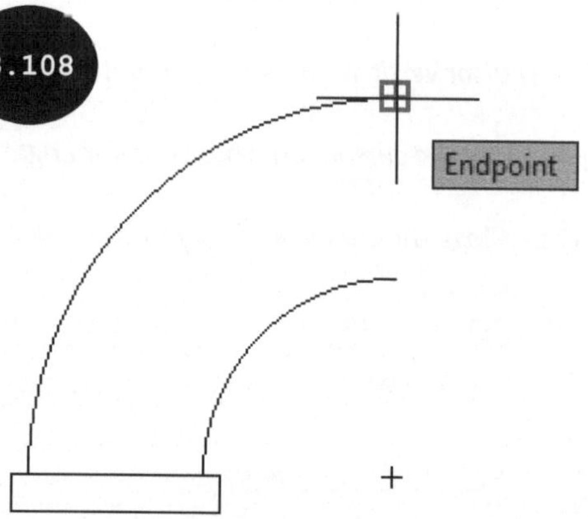

3.109

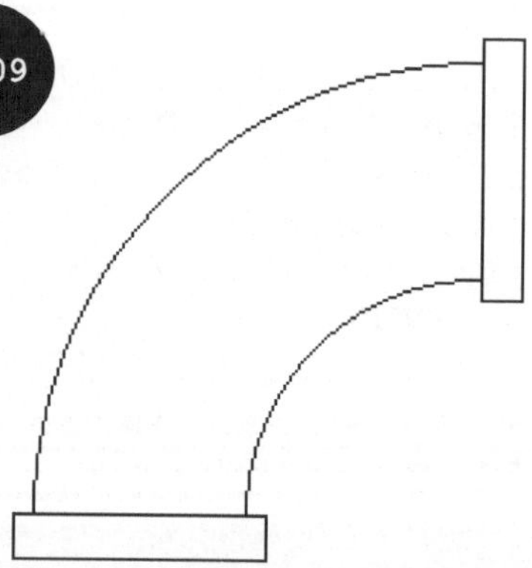

Section 4: Creating Hidden Entities in the Hidden Layer

1. Invoke the **Layer** drop-down list in the **Layers** panel of the **Home** tab and then click on the **Hidden** layer. The Hidden layer becomes the current layer of the drawing.

2. Click on the **Line** tool in the **Draw** panel. You are prompted to specify the first point of the line.

```
Specify first point:
```

3. Ensure that the Ortho mode, Dynamic Input mode, and Object Snap mode are activated.

4. Move the cursor toward the lower left vertex of the drawing and then click to specify the first point of the line when the cursor snaps to it, see Figure 3.110.

```
Specify next point or [Undo]:
```

5. Move the cursor horizontally toward right and then enter **10** in the Dynamic Input box as the length of the line. Next, press ENTER.

6. Move the cursor vertically upward and then click to specify the endpoint of the line when the cursor snaps to the next object line entity, see Figure 3.111. Next, press ENTER.

3.110

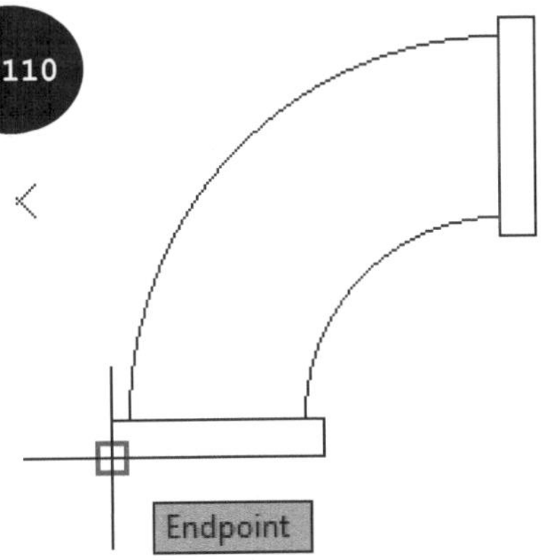

3.111

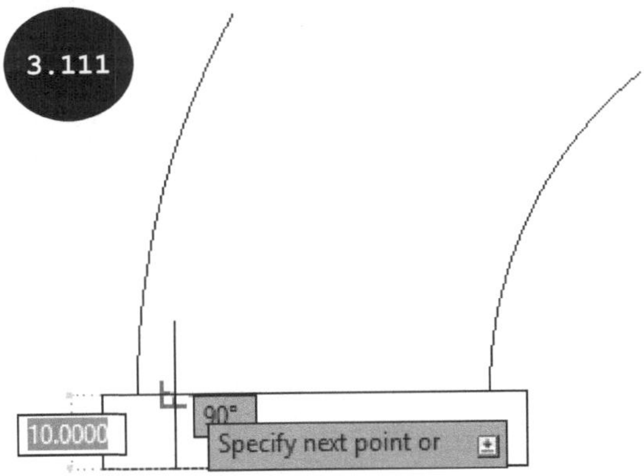

Note: If hidden line entity appears as continuous linetype in the drawing area, then you need to increase or decrease its linetype scale by using the **Properties** panel. To increase or decrease the linetype scale, enter **PR** in the Command Line window and then press ENTER. The **Properties** panel appears on the left of the drawing area. Next, select the hidden entity in the drawing area. The **Properties** panel displays the properties of the selected entity. Next, enter **10** in the **Linetype scale** field of the **Properties** panel. If linetype 10 does not work, you can try any value as the linetype scale to match the display of the hidden line, as required.

7. Click on the first drawn hidden line in the drawing area to select it, see Figure 3.112. Next, press the DELETE key. The line gets deleted. This line entity was drawn as a reference line for measuring 10 units from the lower left vertex of the drawing to create the hidden line of the drawing.

8. Similarly, draw other hidden line entities by using the **Line** tool. Figure 3.113 shows the drawing after creating the hidden line entities of the drawing.

3.112

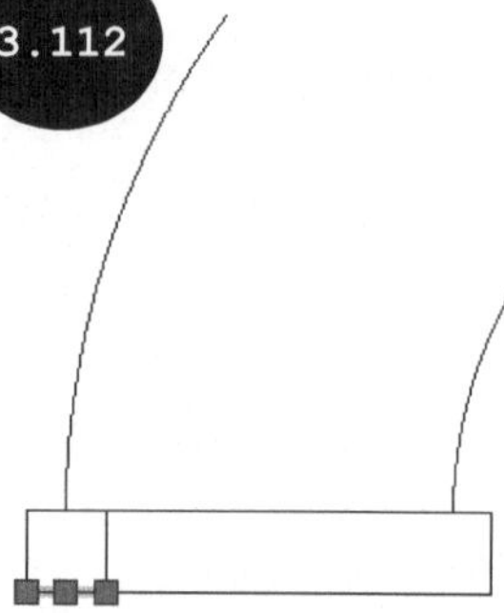

3.113

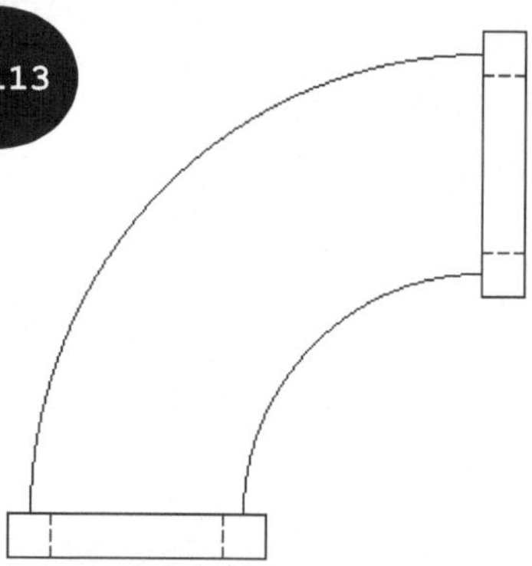

Now, you need to draw the hidden arcs of the drawing by using the **Center, Start, End** arc tool.

9. Invoke the **Arc** flyout in the **Draw** panel of the **Home** tab and then click on the **Center, Start, End** tool. You are prompted to specify the center point of the arc.

```
Specify center point of arc:
```

10. Move the cursor over the first drawn arc in the drawing area. The center point of the first drawn arc gets highlighted in the drawing area, see Figure 3.114.

11. Move the cursor over the highlighted center point and then click the left mouse button when the cursor snaps to it. The center point of the hidden arc is specified.

```
Specify start point of arc:
```

12. Move the cursor over the endpoint of the first drawn hidden line entity and then click to specify the start point of the arc when the cursor snaps to it, see Figure 3.115.

```
Specify end point of arc (hold Ctrl to switch direction) or [Angle
chord Length]:
```

3.114

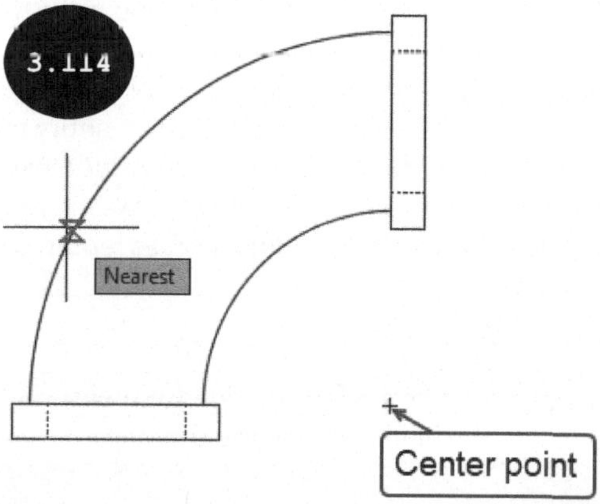

3.115

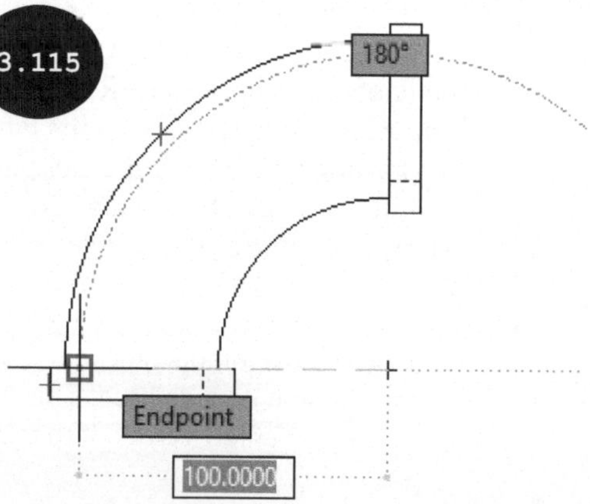

13. Press and hold the CTRL key and then move the cursor in the clockwise direction. Next, click to specify the endpoint of the arc when the cursor snaps to the endpoint of next hidden line entity, see Figure 3.116.

14. Similarly, draw another hidden arc entity of the drawing by using the **Center, Start, End** arc tool. Figure 3.117 shows the drawing after drawing the hidden arc entities.

3.116

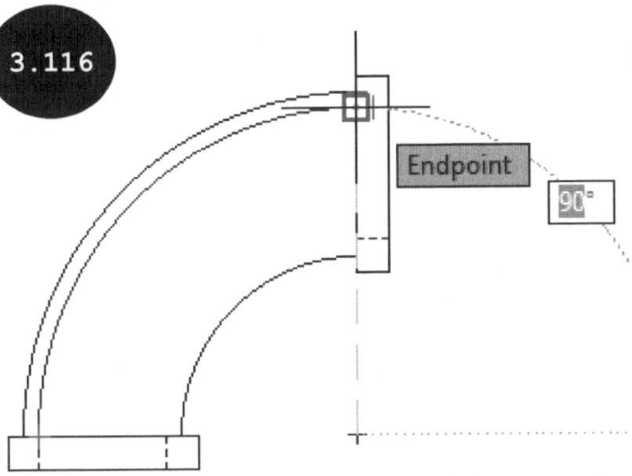

3.117

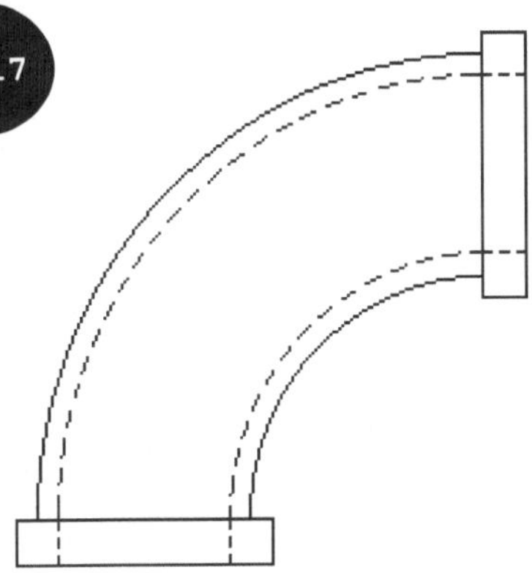

Section 5: Creating Centerlines in the Centerline Layer

1. Invoke the **Layer** drop-down list in the **Layers** panel of the **Home** tab and then click on the **Centerline** layer. The Centerline layer becomes the current layer of the drawing.

2. Invoke the **Arc** flyout in the **Draw** panel of the **Home** tab and then click on the **Center, Start, End** tool.

```
Specify center point of arc:
```

3. Move the cursor over the first drawn arc in the drawing area, see Figure 3.118. The center point of the arc gets highlighted in the drawing area, see Figure 3.118.

4. Move the cursor over the highlighted center point and then click to specify the center point of the arc when the cursor snaps to it.

```
Specify start point of arc:
```

5. Move the cursor horizontally toward left and then enter **80** in the Dynamic Input box. Next, press ENTER.

```
Specify end point of arc (hold Ctrl to switch direction) or [Angle chord Length]:
```

6. Press and hold the CTRL key and then move the cursor in the clockwise direction. Next, click to specify the endpoint of the arc when the cursor snaps to the next intersection, see Figure 3.119.

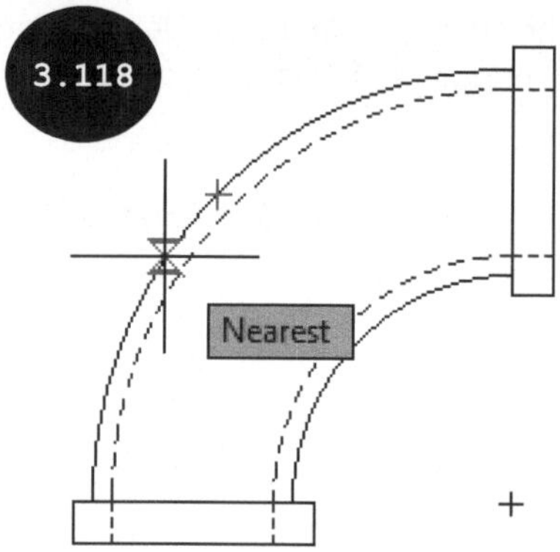

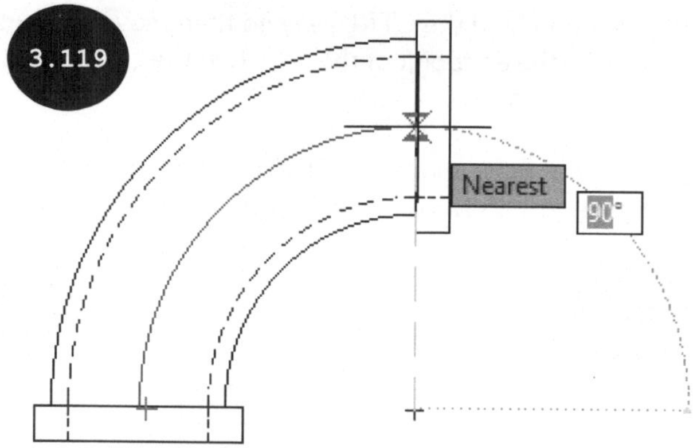

7. Click on the **Line** tool in the **Draw** panel of the **Home** tab. The **Line** tool is invoked.

```
Specify first point:
```

8. Move the cursor toward the start point of the previously drawn arc and then click to specify the start point of the line when the cursor snaps to it, see Figure 3.120.

9. Move the cursor vertically downward to a small distance and then click to specify the endpoint of the line below the horizontal line of the drawing, see Figure 3.121.

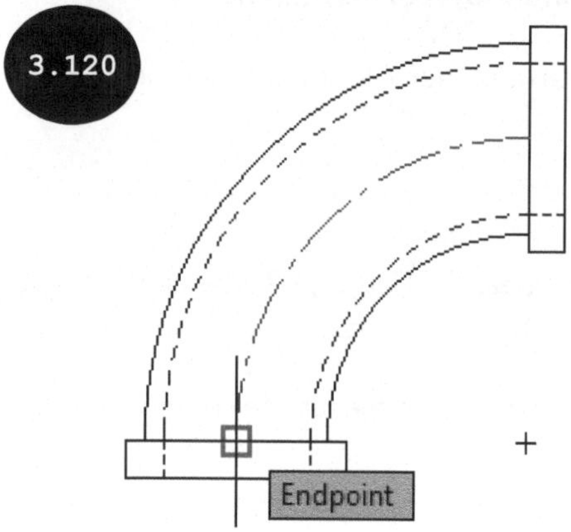

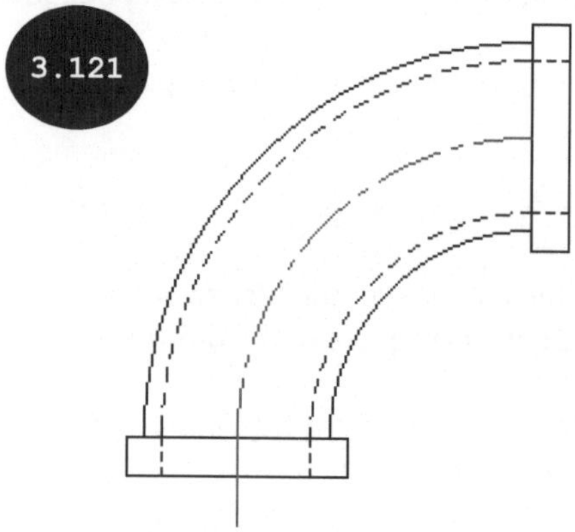

10. Similarly, draw a line on the other side of the arc. Figure 3.122 shows the final drawing.

Note: To display entities in the drawing area with the lineweight/thickness assigned to the layers, click to activate the **Show/Hide Lineweight** button in the Status Bar. Figure 3.123 shows the drawing with the lineweight/thickness turned on.

3.122

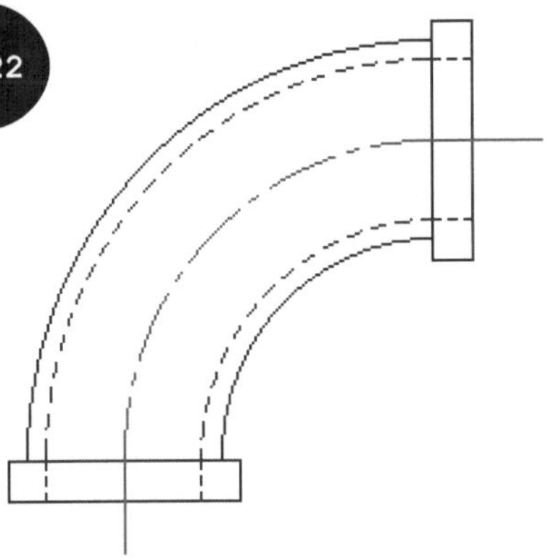

3.123

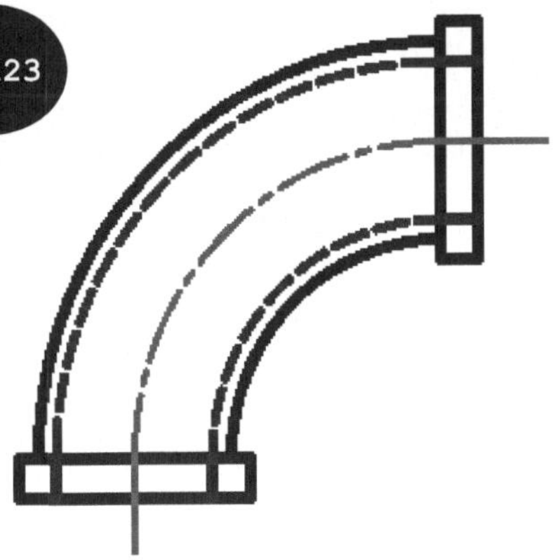

Section 6: Saving the Drawing

After creating the drawing, you need to save it.

1. Click on the **Save** tool in the **Quick Access Toolbar**. The **Save Drawing As** dialog box appears.

2. Browse to the *Chapter 3* folder, inside the *AutoCAD* folder. If these folders are not created in Tutorial 1 of this chapter, then you need to first create these folders.

3. Enter **Tutorial 4** in the **File name** field of the dialog box and then click on the **Save** button. The drawing gets saved with the name Tutorial 4 in the *Chapter 3* folder.

Hands-on Test Drive 1

Create the drawing shown in Figure 3.124. Also, create three layers: Object, Hidden, and Centerline with the layer properties given below.

Layer Name	Color	Linetype	Lineweight
Object	Blue	Continuous	0.50 mm
Hidden	Green	Hidden	0.35 mm
Centerline	Red	Center	0.30 mm

3.124

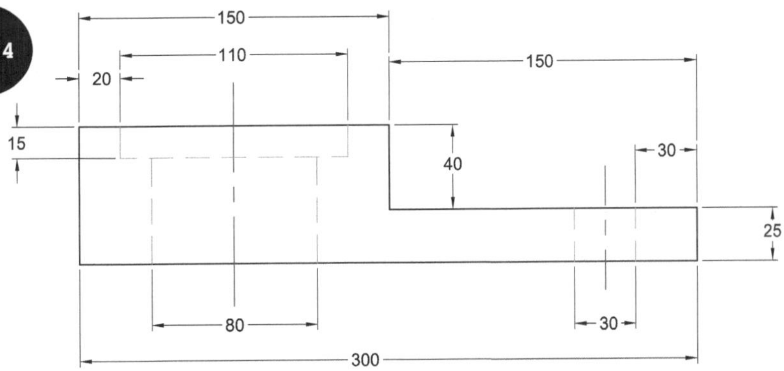

Hands-on Test Drive 2

Create the drawing shown in Figure 3.125. The dimensions shown in this figure are for your reference only. You will learn about applying dimensions in the later chapters.

3.125

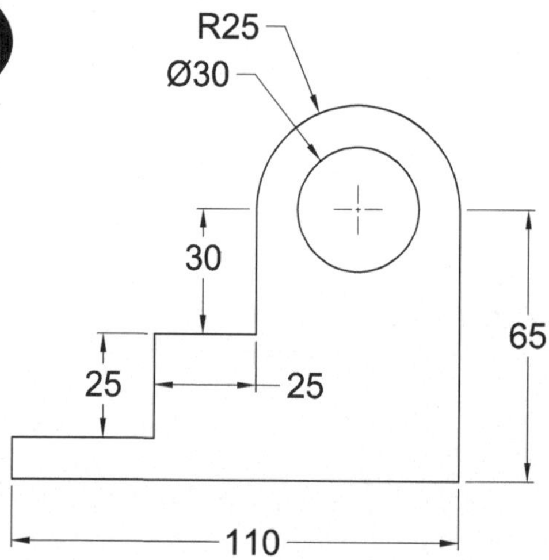

Summary

The chapter introduced the concepts of Ortho mode, Polar Tracking, Object Snap, and Object Snap Tracking. It also explained how to specify grids and snap settings in addition to working with layers and assigning objects to layers.

Questions

Complete the following sentences:

- The _________ mode is used for creating horizontal or vertical straight lines.
- The _________ mode is used for creating line entities at an increment of a set angle.
- When the _________ mode is turned on, the cursor snaps to the existing geometries of the drawing such as midpoint, center, node, insertion, perpendicular, and tangent.
- The _________ is used for creating new layers, specifying layer properties, and so on.
- The _________ tool is used for invoking the **LAYER PROPERTIES MANAGER**.
- You can set the transparency for the objects of a layer by using the _________ field in the **LAYER PROPERTIES MANAGER**.
- The objects drawn in the drawing get assigned automatically to the _________ layer.

CHAPTER

4

Creating Drawings - II

In this chapter, the following topics will be discussed:

- Drawing a Rectangle
- Drawing a Polygon
- Drawing a Polyline
- Drawing an Ellipse
- Drawing an Elliptical Arc
- Drawing a Spline
- Drawing Donuts
- Drawing Construction and Ray lines
- Drawing Points and Defining Point Style/Size

In this chapter, you will learn about drawing rectangles, polygons, polylines, ellipses, elliptical arcs, splines, donuts, construction lines, ray lines, and points.

Drawing a Rectangle

A rectangle comprises four line segments treated as a single object. In AutoCAD, you can draw a rectangle by different methods using the **Rectangle** tool in the **Draw** panel of the **Home** tab, see Figure 4.1. Various methods for creating a rectangle by using the **Rectangle** tool are discussed next.

4.1

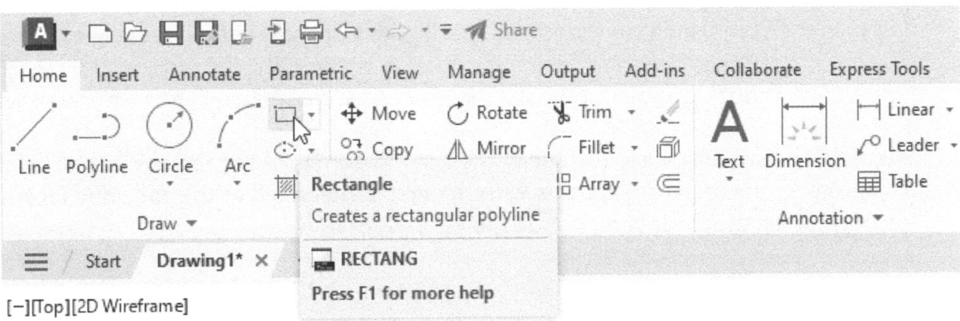

1. Drawing a rectangle by specifying diagonally opposite corners
2. Drawing a rectangle by specifying its area and one side
3. Drawing a rectangle by specifying its dimensions
4. Drawing a rectangle at an angle
5. Drawing a rectangle with chamfer
6. Drawing a rectangle with fillet
7. Drawing a rectangle with elevation
8. Drawing a rectangle with thickness
9. Drawing a rectangle with width

Drawing a Rectangle by Specifying Diagonally Opposite Corners

In AutoCAD, you can draw a rectangle by specifying its diagonally opposite corners. The first specified corner defines the position of the rectangle and the second specified corner defines the length and width of the rectangle, see Figure 4.2. The method is discussed below:

4.2

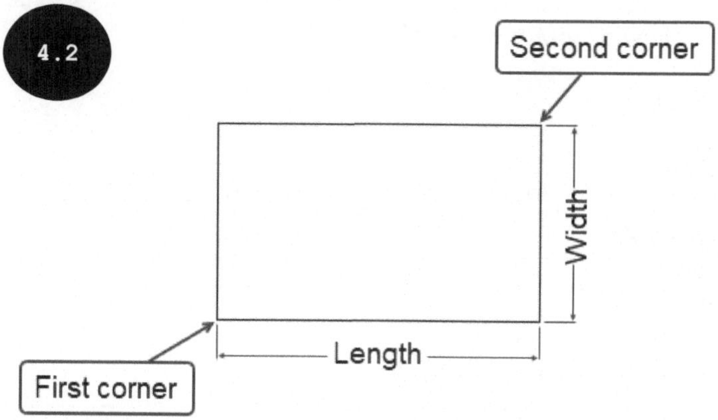

1. Click on the **Rectangle** tool in the **Draw** panel of the **Home** tab. Alternatively, enter **REC** in the Command Line window and then press ENTER. The **Rectangle** tool is activated and you are prompted to specify the first corner of the rectangle.

```
Specify first corner point or [Chamfer Elevation Fillet Thickness
Width]:
```

2. Click the left mouse button in the drawing area to specify the first corner of the rectangle. You are prompted to specify the second corner of the rectangle. Alternatively, you can enter coordinates (X, Y) in the Command Line window to specify the first corner of the rectangle.

```
Specify other corner point or [Area Dimensions Rotation]:
```

3. Move the cursor diagonally to specify the second corner of the rectangle in the drawing area. A preview of the rectangle appears with the first corner fixed at the specified location and the second corner attached to the cursor, see Figure 4.3.

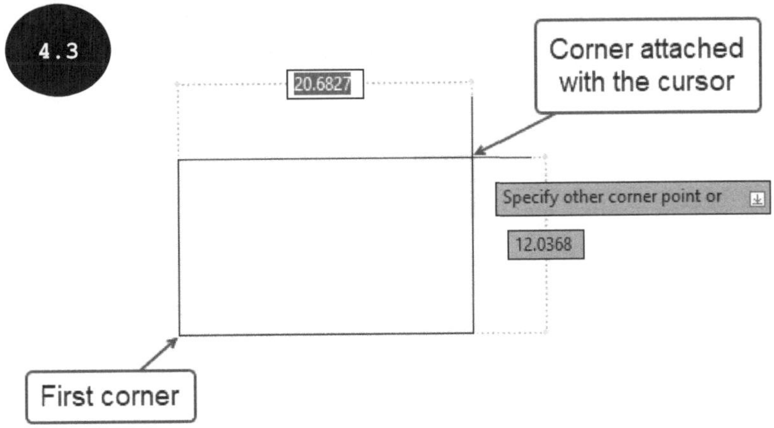

4. Enter the length and width values of the rectangle in the Dynamic Input boxes that appear near the cursor for defining the second corner of the rectangle. You can press the TAB key to switch from one Dynamic Input box to another for specifying the values. After entering the length and width values, press ENTER. The rectangle is created in the drawing area.

Note: If the Dynamic Input boxes do not appear near your cursor for specifying the length and width values of the rectangle, you need to turn on the Dynamic Input mode by clicking on the **Dynamic Input** button in the Status Bar.

Drawing a Rectangle by Specifying its Area and One Side

You can draw a rectangle by specifying its area and one side (length or width) by using the **Rectangle** tool. The method is discussed below:

Note: On specifying the area and one side (length/width) of the rectangle, AutoCAD automatically calculates the other side of the rectangle by using the formula: ***Area of rectangle = Length X Width***. For example, if you specify the Area of rectangle as 500 units and length as 50 units then the width will be equal to ***500/50*** i.e. 10 units.

1. Click on the **Rectangle** tool in the **Draw** panel of the **Home** tab. Alternatively, enter **REC** in the Command Line window and then press ENTER. The **Rectangle** tool is activated and you are prompted to specify the first corner of the rectangle.

```
Specify first corner point or [Chamfer Elevation Fillet Thickness
Width]:
```

2. Click the left mouse button in the drawing area or enter coordinates (X, Y) to specify the first corner of the rectangle. You are prompted to specify the second corner of the rectangle.

```
Specify other corner point or [Area Dimensions Rotation]:
```

3. Enter **A** in the Dynamic Input box or the Command Line window and then press ENTER. You are prompted to specify the area of the rectangle. Alternatively, click on the **Area** option in the command prompt to specify the area of the rectangle.

```
Enter area of rectangle in current units <10.0000>:
```

4. Enter the area of the rectangle and then press ENTER. You are prompted to specify either the length or width of the rectangle.

```
Calculate rectangle dimensions based on [Length Width] <Length>:
```

5. Enter **L** and then press ENTER to define the length of the rectangle. You are prompted to specify the length of the rectangle. Note that for defining the width of the rectangle, you need to enter W in the Command Line window.

```
Enter rectangle length <5.0000>:
```

6. Enter the length value of the rectangle and then press ENTER. A rectangle with the defined area and length is drawn in the drawing area, see Figure 4.4.

4.4

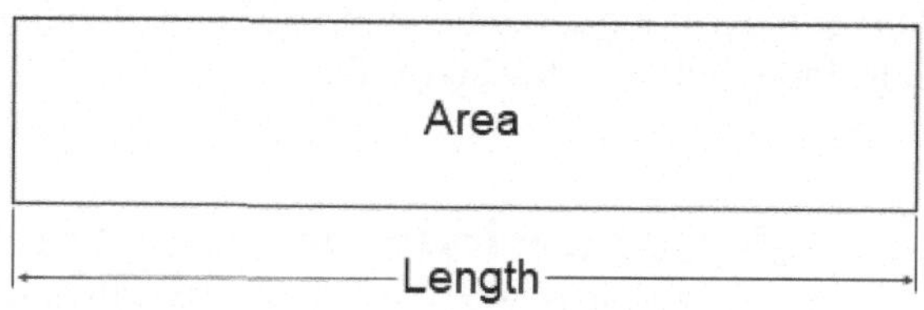

Note: The value entered inside the < > symbol in the command prompt is the last defined or default value of the command. For example, in the prompt "`Calculate rectangle dimensions based on [Length Width] <Length>:`", the length entered inside the <> is the default option of the command. If you want to go with the default selected option, you can directly press ENTER; else, specify the new option in the Command Line window and then press ENTER.

Drawing a Rectangle by Specifying Dimensions

You can draw a rectangle by specifying dimensions; length and width by using the **Rectangle** tool. The method is discussed below:

1. Click on the **Rectangle** tool or enter **REC** in the Command Line window. You are prompted to specify the first corner of the rectangle.

```
Specify first corner point or [Chamfer Elevation Fillet Thickness
Width]:
```

2. Click the left mouse button in the drawing area or specify coordinates (X, Y) to specify the first corner of the rectangle. You are prompted to specify the second corner of the rectangle.

```
Specify other corner point or [Area Dimensions Rotation]:
```

3. Enter **D** and then press ENTER. You are prompted to specify the length of the rectangle. Alternatively, you can click on the **Dimensions** option in the command prompt.

```
Specify length for rectangles <100.000>:
```

4. Enter the length value for the rectangle and then press ENTER. You are prompted to specify the width of the rectangle.

```
Specify width for rectangles <2.0000>:
```

5. Enter the width value for the rectangle and then press ENTER. You are prompted to specify the other corner of the rectangle.

```
Specify other corner point or [Area Dimensions Rotation]:
```

6. Click to specify the other corner point of the rectangle. A rectangle with the defined length and width is drawn in the drawing area, see Figure 4.5.

4.5

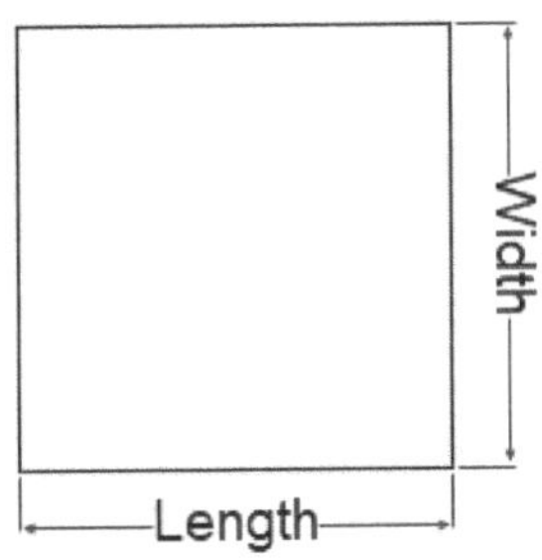

Drawing a Rectangle at an Angle

You can draw a rectangle at an angle by using the **Rectangle** tool. The method is discussed below:

1. Click on the **Rectangle** tool. You are prompted to specify the first corner of the rectangle.

```
Specify first corner point or [Chamfer Elevation Fillet Thickness
Width]:
```

2. Click the left mouse button in the drawing area or enter coordinates (X, Y) to specify the first corner of the rectangle. You are prompted to specify the second corner of the rectangle.

```
Specify other corner point or [Area Dimensions Rotation]:
```

3. Enter **R** and then press ENTER. You are prompted to specify the rotation angle of the rectangle. You can also click on the **Rotation** option in the command prompt to specify the rotational angle of the rectangle.

```
Specify rotation angle or [Pick points] <0.0000>:
```

4. Enter the rotational angle and then press ENTER, see Figure 4.6. You are prompted to specify the other corner of the rectangle.

```
Specify other corner point or [Area Dimensions Rotation]:
```

5. Move the cursor in the drawing area. A preview of the rectangle at the specified angle appears in the drawing area. Next, click the left mouse button in the drawing area to define the second corner of the rectangle, see Figure 4.6. You can also enter coordinates (X, Y) to define the second corner of the rectangle.

4.6

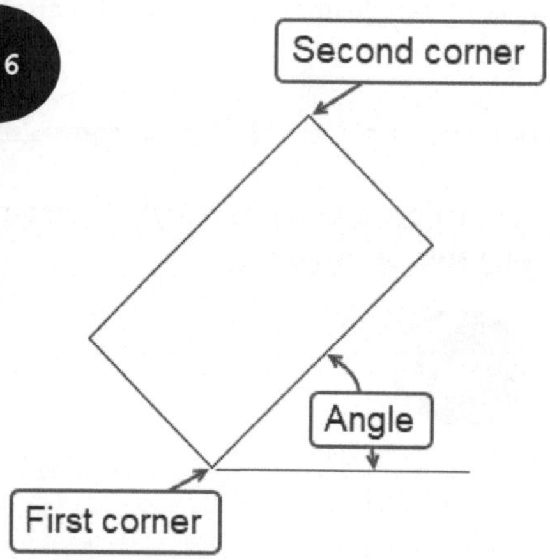

Drawing a Rectangle with Chamfer

In AutoCAD, you can draw a rectangle with chamfers on its corners by using the **Rectangle** tool, see Figure 4.7. The method is discussed below:

4.7

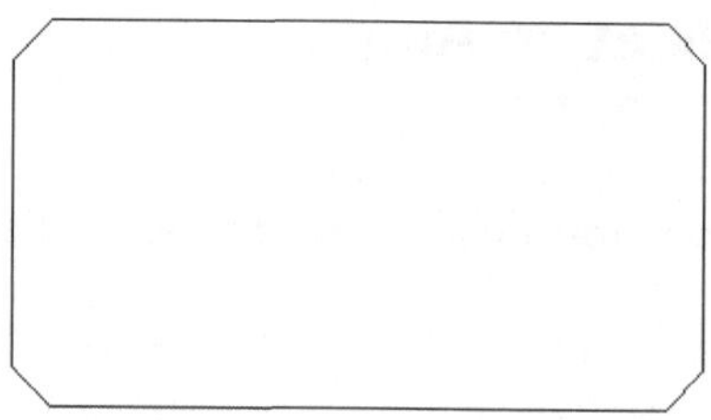

1. Click on the **Rectangle** tool. You are prompted to specify the first corner of the rectangle.

```
Specify first corner point or [Chamfer Elevation Fillet Thickness
Width]:
```

2. Click on the **Chamfer** option in the command prompt or enter C and then press ENTER. You are prompted to specify the first chamfer distance.

```
Specify first chamfer distance for rectangles <0.0000>:
```

3. Enter the first chamfer distance and then press ENTER. You are prompted to specify the second chamfer distance.

```
Specify second chamfer distance for rectangles <0.0000>:
```

4. Enter the second chamfer distance and then press ENTER. You are prompted to specify the first corner of the rectangle.

```
Specify first corner point or [Chamfer Elevation Fillet Thickness
Width]:
```

5. Click the left mouse button in the drawing area or enter coordinates (X, Y) to specify the first corner of the rectangle. You are prompted to specify the second corner of the rectangle.

```
Specify other corner point or [Area Dimensions Rotation]:
```

6. Click the left mouse button in the drawing area or enter coordinates (X, Y) to specify the second corner of the rectangle. A rectangle with chamfers on each of its corners is drawn in the drawing area.

Drawing a Rectangle with Fillets

In AutoCAD, you can draw a rectangle with fillets on its corners by using the **Rectangle** tool, see Figure 4.8. The method is discussed below:

4.8

1. Click on the **Rectangle** tool. You are prompted to specify the first corner of the rectangle.

```
Specify first corner point or [Chamfer Elevation Fillet Thickness
Width]:
```

2. Click on the **Fillet** option in the command prompt or enter **F** and then press ENTER. You are prompted to specify the fillet radius of the rectangle.

```
Specify fillet radius for rectangles <0.0000>:
```

3. Enter the fillet radius of the rectangle and then press ENTER. You are prompted to specify the first corner of the rectangle.

```
Specify first corner point or [Chamfer Elevation Fillet Thickness Width]:
```

4. Click the left mouse button in the drawing area or enter coordinates (X, Y) to specify the first corner of the rectangle. You are prompted to specify the second corner of the rectangle.

```
Specify other corner point or [Area Dimensions Rotation]:
```

5. Click the left mouse button in the drawing area or enter coordinates (X, Y) to specify the second corner of the rectangle. A rectangle with fillets on its corners is drawn in the drawing area.

Drawing a Rectangle with Elevation

You can draw a rectangle at a specified elevation along the Z direction from the origin (0,0,0), see Figure 4.9 by using the **Rectangle** tool. The method is discussed below:

4.9

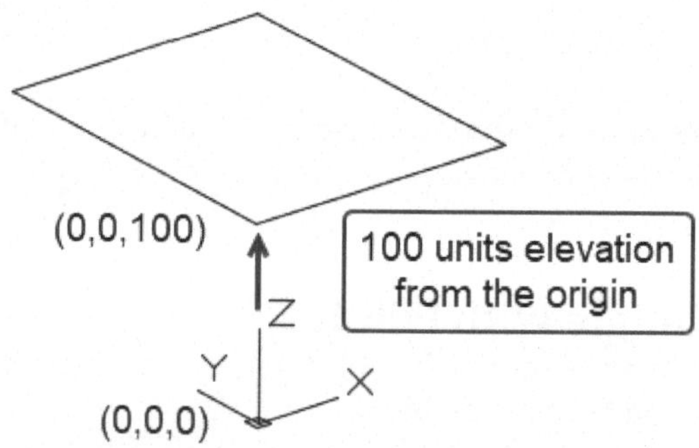

1. Click on the **Rectangle** tool. You are prompted to specify the first corner of the rectangle.

```
Specify first corner point or [Chamfer Elevation Fillet Thickness Width]:
```

2. Click on the **Elevation** option in the command prompt or enter **E** and then press ENTER. You are prompted to specify the elevation of the rectangle.

```
Specify the elevation for rectangles <0.0000>:
```

3. Enter the elevation value along the z-axis from the origin (0,0,0) and then press ENTER. You are prompted to specify the first corner of the rectangle.

```
Specify first corner point or [Chamfer Elevation Fillet Thickness Width]:
```

4. Specify the first corner of the rectangle. You are prompted to specify the second corner of the rectangle.

```
Specify other corner point or [Area Dimensions Rotation]:
```

5. Specify the second corner of the rectangle. A rectangle with the specified elevation is drawn in the drawing area, see Figure 4.9.

Note: You can change the orientation of the rectangle to isometric to view the elevation of the rectangle drawn by clicking on the **Home** button in the **ViewCube**, which is available at the upper right corner of the screen.

Drawing a Rectangle with Thickness

You can draw a rectangle with a specified thickness along the z-axis by using the **Rectangle** tool, see Figure 4.10. The method is discussed below:

4.10

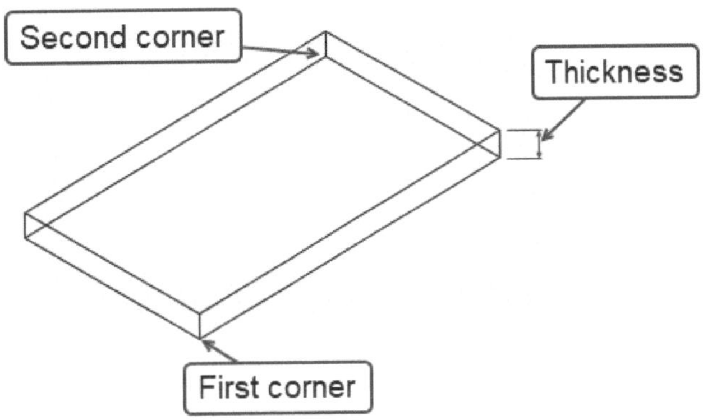

1. Click on the **Rectangle** tool. You are prompted to specify the first corner of the rectangle.

```
Specify first corner point or [Chamfer Elevation Fillet Thickness
Width]:
```

2. Click on the **Thickness** option in the command prompt or enter **T** and then press ENTER. You are prompted to specify the thickness along the z-axis for the rectangle.

```
Specify thickness for rectangles <0.0000>:
```

3. Enter the thickness value along the z-axis from the origin (0,0,0) and then press ENTER. You are prompted to specify the first corner of the rectangle.

```
Specify first corner point or [Chamfer Elevation Fillet Thickness
Width]:
```

4. Specify the first corner of the rectangle. You are prompted to specify the second corner of the rectangle.

```
Specify other corner point or [Area Dimensions Rotation]:
```

5. Specify the second corner of the rectangle. A rectangle with the specified thickness is drawn in the drawing area.

6. Click on the **Home** button in the **ViewCube**, which is available in the upper right corner of the screen. The orientation of the drawing gets changed to isometric, see Figure 4.10.

Drawing a Rectangle with Width

You can draw a rectangle with the specified width by using the **Rectangle** tool, see Figure 4.11. The method is discussed below:

1. Click on the **Rectangle** tool. You are prompted to specify the first corner of the rectangle.

```
Specify first corner point or [Chamfer Elevation Fillet Thickness Width]:
```

2. Click on the **Width** option in the command prompt or enter **W** and then press ENTER. You are prompted to specify the width of the rectangle.

```
Specify line width for rectangles <0.0000>:
```

3. Enter the width value of the rectangle and then press ENTER. You are prompted to specify the first corner of the rectangle.

```
Specify first corner point or [Chamfer Elevation Fillet Thickness Width]:
```

4. Specify the first corner of the rectangle. You are prompted to specify the second corner of the rectangle.

```
Specify other corner point or [Area Dimensions Rotation]:
```

5. Specify the second corner of the rectangle. A rectangle with the specified width is drawn in the drawing area, refer to Figure 4.11.

Drawing a Polygon

AutoCAD allows you to draw polygons with the number of sides ranging from 3 to 1024. A polygon is a closed geometry having equal sides as well as equal angles between the sides. Figure 4.12 shows a polygon having five sides. You can draw a polygon by using the **Polygon** tool of the **Draw** panel (see Figure 4.13) or by entering **POL** in the Command Line window. POL is the shortcut of the POLYGON command.

4.12

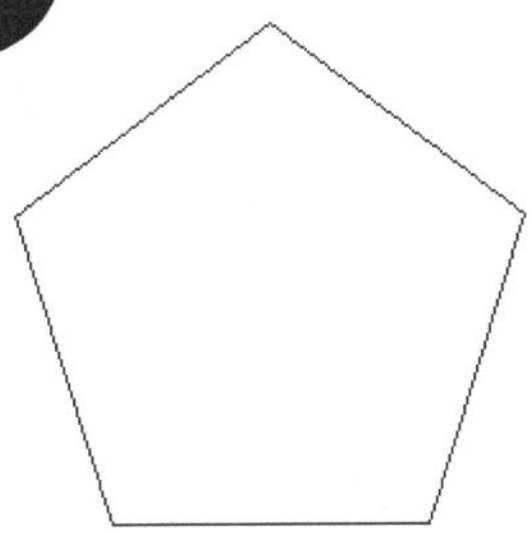

4.13

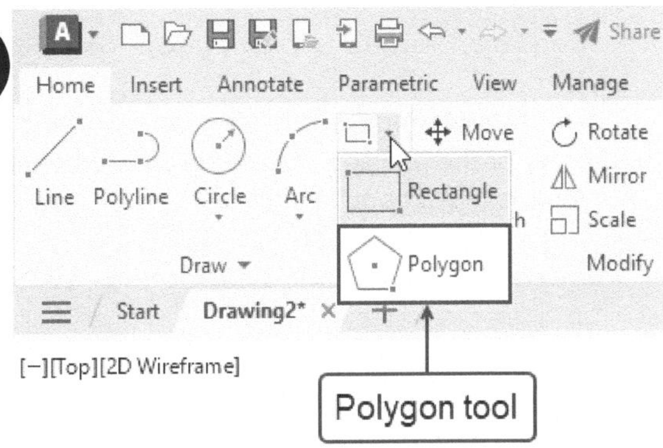

In AutoCAD, you can draw two types of polygons: Inscribed polygon and Circumscribed polygon, by using the **Polygon** tool, see Figures 4.14 and 4.15. Both the types are discussed next.

4.14

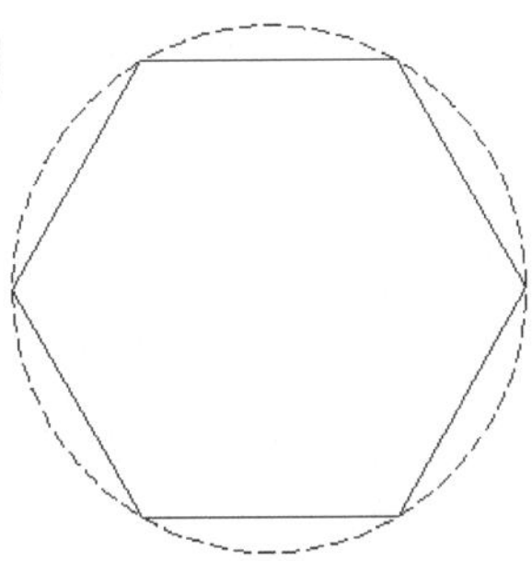

Inscribed polygon

4.15

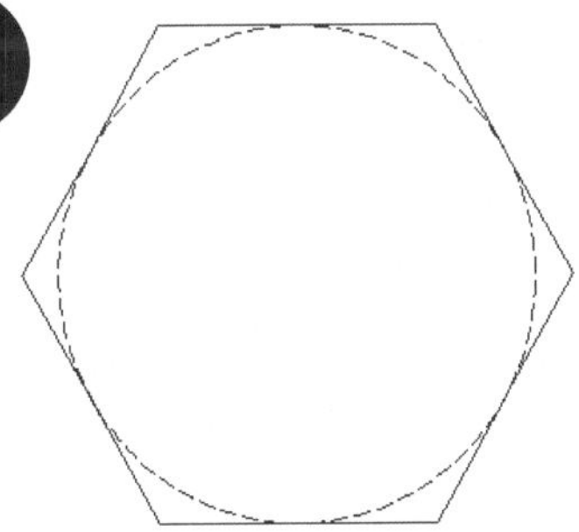

Circumscribed polygon

Inscribed Polygon

An Inscribed polygon is created inside an imaginary circle such that its vertices touch the imaginary circle, see Figure 4.14.

Circumscribed Polygon

A Circumscribed polygon is created outside an imaginary circle such that the midpoints of the polygon sides touch the imaginary circle, see Figure 4.15. The method for drawing a polygon (inscribed or circumscribed) is discussed below:

1. Click on the down arrow in the **Rectangle** tool of the **Draw** panel. A flyout appears, refer to Figure 4.13. In this flyout, click on the **Polygon** tool. The **Polygon** tool is activated, and you are prompted to specify the number of polygon sides. Alternatively, enter **POL** in the Command Line window and then press ENTER to activate the **Polygon** tool.

```
Enter number of sides <4>:
```

2. Enter the number of polygon sides and then press ENTER. You are prompted to specify the center of the polygon.

```
Specify center of polygon or [Edge]:
```

3. Click the left mouse button in the drawing area or enter coordinates (X, Y) to specify the center of the polygon. You are prompted to specify the type of polygon (Inscribed in a circle or Circumscribed about a circle).

```
Enter an option [Inscribed in circle Circumscribed about circle]
<I>:
```

4. Enter **I** or **C** in the Command Line window for drawing Inscribed or circumscribed polygon, respectively. Next, press ENTER. You are prompted to specify the radius of an imaginary circle.

```
Specify radius of circle:
```

5. Enter the radius value of an imaginary circle and then press ENTER. The polygon is drawn depending upon the option selected, i.e. **Inscribed in circle** or **Circumscribed about circle.**

Drawing a Polyline

A Polyline consists of one or more than one line or arc segment and acts as a single object. In AutoCAD, drawing a polyline is similar to drawing a line with the only difference being that the polyline consists of a series of line segments, arc segments, or a combination of line and arc segments and acts as a single object, see Figure 4.16. You can draw a polyline by using the **Polyline** tool of the **Draw** panel or by entering **PL** in the Command Line window. PL is the shortcut for the POLYLINE command. The different methods for drawing a polyline are discussed next.

4.16

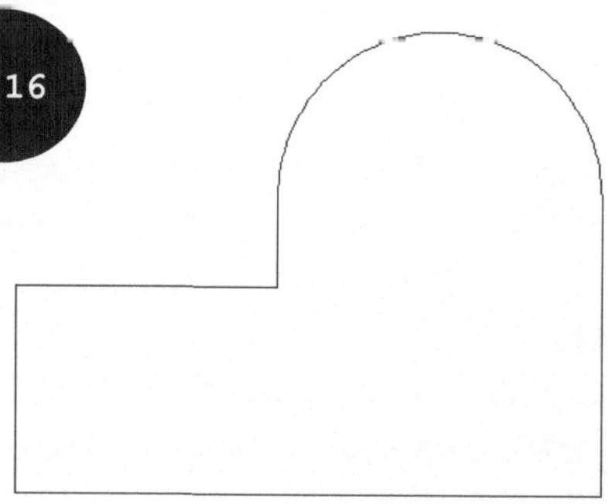

Drawing a Polyline with Line Segments

The method for drawing a polyline with line segments is discussed below:

1. Click on the **Polyline** tool in the **Draw** panel of the **Home** tab or enter **PL** in the Command Line window and then press ENTER. You are prompted to specify the start point of the polyline.

   ```
   Specify start point:
   ```

2. Click the left mouse button in the drawing area or specify coordinates (X, Y) to specify the start point of the polyline. You are prompted to specify the next point of the polyline.

   ```
   Specify next point or [Arc Halfwidth Length Undo Width]:
   ```

3. Specify the next point of the polyline. A line segment is created in the drawing area, and you are prompted to specify the next point of the polyline.

   ```
   Specify next point or [Arc Close Halfwidth Length Undo Width]:
   ```

4. Specify the next point of the polyline. The second line segment of the polyline is drawn in the drawing area, see Figure 4.17. You are prompted to specify the next point of the polyline.

   ```
   Specify next point or [Arc Close Halfwidth Length Undo Width]:
   ```

4.17

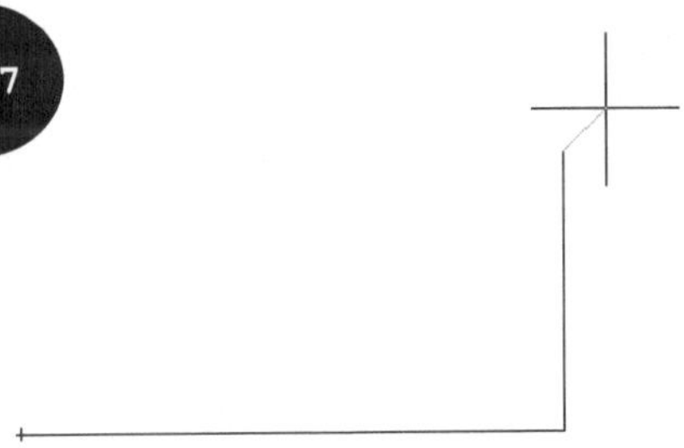

5. Similarly, you can draw a series of continuous line segments of a polyline, one after the other by specifying points in the drawing area.

Drawing a Polyline with Line and Arc Segments

The method for drawing a polyline with line and arc segments is discussed below:

1. Click on the **Polyline** tool in the **Draw** panel or enter **PL** in the Command Line window and then press ENTER. You are prompted to specify the start point of the polyline.

   ```
   Specify start point:
   ```

2. Specify the start point of the polyline. You are prompted to specify the next point of the polyline.

   `Specify next point or [Arc Halfwidth Length Undo Width]:`

3. Specify the next point of the polyline. A line segment is created, and you are prompted to specify the next point of the polyline.

   `Specify next point or [Arc Close Halfwidth Length Undo Width]:`

   You can also draw arc segments in a polyline.

4. Click on the **Arc** option in the command prompt. The Arc mode for drawing the arc segment is activated, and you are prompted to specify the endpoint of the arc. Alternatively, enter **A** in the Command Line window and then press ENTER to activate the Arc mode.

   ```
   Specify endpoint of arc (hold Ctrl to switch direction) or [Angle
   CEnter CLose Direction Halfwidth Line Radius Second pt Undo Width]:
   ```

5. Click to specify the endpoint of the arc. An arc segment is created, see Figure 4.18. Note that the Arc mode is still activated, and you are prompted to specify the endpoint of another arc.

   ```
   Specify endpoint of arc (hold Ctrl to switch direction) or [Angle
   CEnter CLose Direction Halfwidth Line Radius Second pt Undo Width]:
   ```

4.18

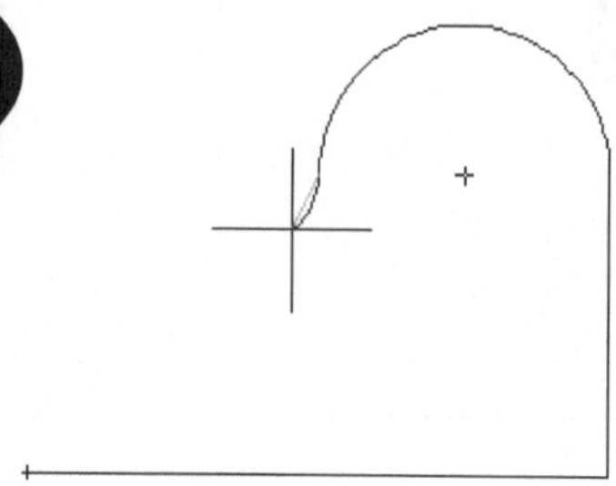

6. To draw the line segment again, enter **L** in the Command Line window and then press ENTER. Alternatively, click on the **Line** option in the command prompt. You are prompted to specify the endpoint of the line segment.

   `Specify next point or [Arc Close Halfwidth Length Undo Width]:`

7. Similarly, you can draw a polyline with a series of line and arc segments. Once you have drawn a polyline, press the ENTER key to exit from the **Polyline** tool.

Tip: While drawing a polyline, when the Arc mode is activated, you are prompted to specify the endpoint of the arc segment also provided with additional options such as angle, center, and direction, in the command prompt for drawing the arc. These options are discussed next.

```
Specify endpoint of arc or [Angle CEnter CLose Direction Halfwidth
Line Radius Second pt Undo Width]:
```

Angle: By clicking on the **Angle** option in the command prompt, you can specify the angle of the arc segment from the start point, see Figure 4.19. A positive angle value creates a counter-clockwise arc segment, and a negative angle value creates a clockwise arc segment.

Center: By clicking on the **Center** option in the command prompt, you can specify the center point of the arc segment to be drawn, see Figure 4.20.

4.19

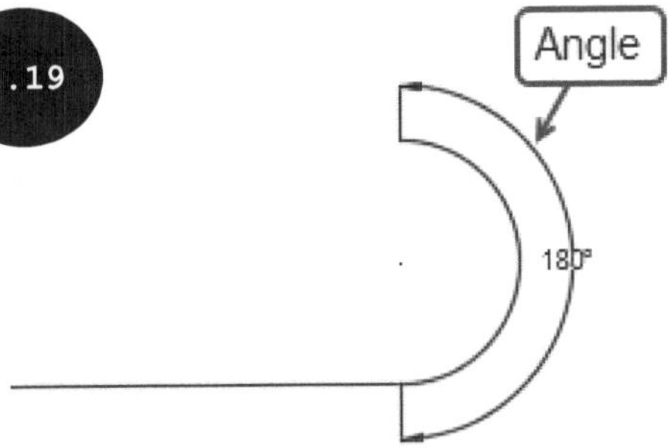

4.20

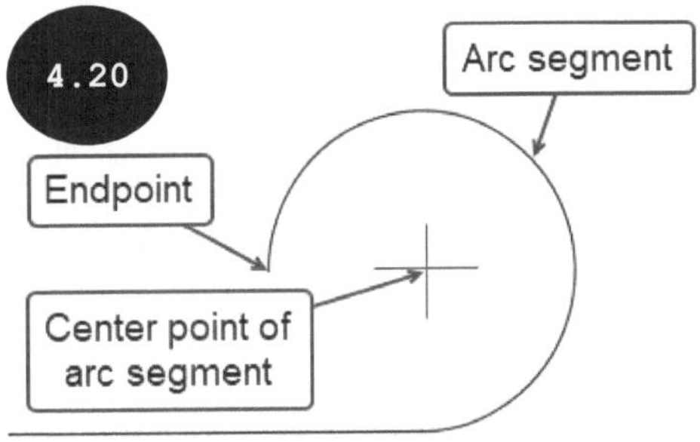

Direction: By clicking on the **Direction** option in the command prompt, you can specify the direction of the tangent for the arc segment, see Figure 4.21.

Radius: By clicking on the **Radius** option in the command prompt, you can specify the radius of the arc segment, see Figure 4.22.

4.21

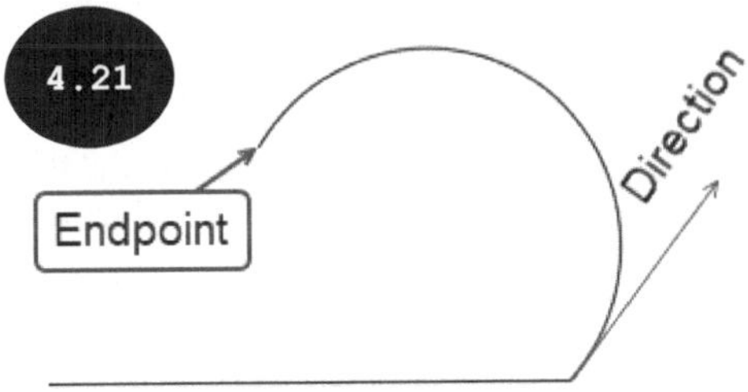

4.22

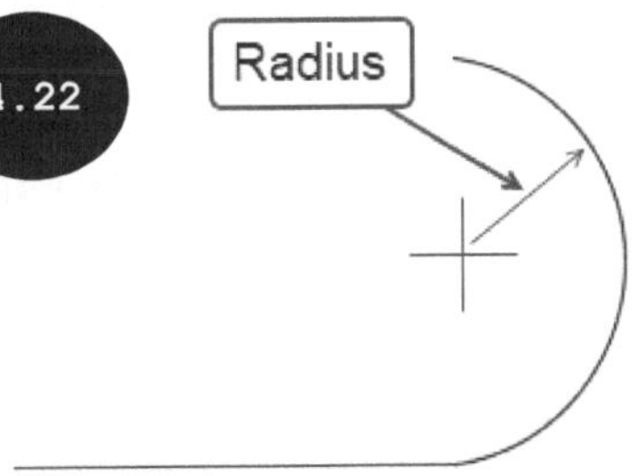

Drawing a Polyline with Width

The method for drawing a polyline by specifying its start and end width is discussed below:

1. Click on the **Polyline** tool in the **Draw** panel of the **Home** tab or enter **PL** in the Command Line window and then press ENTER. You are prompted to specify the start point of the polyline.

   ```
   Specify start point:
   ```
2. Specify the start point of the polyline. You are prompted to specify the next point of the polyline.

   ```
   Specify next point or [Arc Halfwidth Length Undo Width]:
   ```
3. Click on the **Width** option in the command prompt. You are prompted to specify the starting width of the polyline. Alternatively, enter W and then press ENTER.

   ```
   Specify starting width <0.0000>:
   ```
4. Enter the starting width value (see Figure 4.23) and then press ENTER. You are prompted to specify the ending width of the polyline.

   ```
   Specify ending width <0.0000>:
   ```
5. Enter the ending width value (see Figure 4.23) and then press ENTER. You are prompted to specify the next point of the polyline.

   ```
   Specify next point or [Arc Halfwidth Length Undo Width]:
   ```
6. Specify the next point of the polyline. A line segment with a specified width is created, and you are prompted to specify the next point of the polyline. Also, a rubber band line segment with a constant width (defined as the ending width) appears in the drawing area with one end fixed at the last specified point, and the other end attached to the cursor, see Figure 4.23.

   ```
   Specify next point or [Arc Close Halfwidth Length Undo Width]:
   ```
7. Similarly, you can draw a continuous series of line and arc segments in a polyline with a specified width. Once you have drawn the polyline, press the ENTER key to exit the **Polyline** tool.

4.23

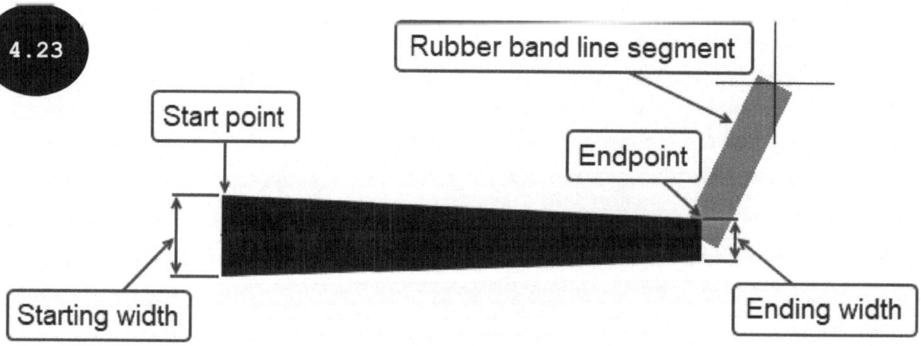

Note: By default, the fill mode for polyline is set to 1. As a result, the polyline segments having width are drawn as solid, see Figure 4.23. However, if you change the fill mode to 0 (zero), the polyline segments having width are drawn as outlines only, see Figure 4.24. To change the fill mode, enter **FILLMODE** in the Command Line window and then press ENTER. Next, enter 1 or 0 in the Command Line window, as required.

The width specified for the endpoint of a polyline segment becomes a uniform width for other polyline segments until changed again.

Tip: Similar to defining the width of a line segment of a polyline, you can specify start width and end width for an arc segment of the polyline, see Figure 4.25.

4.24

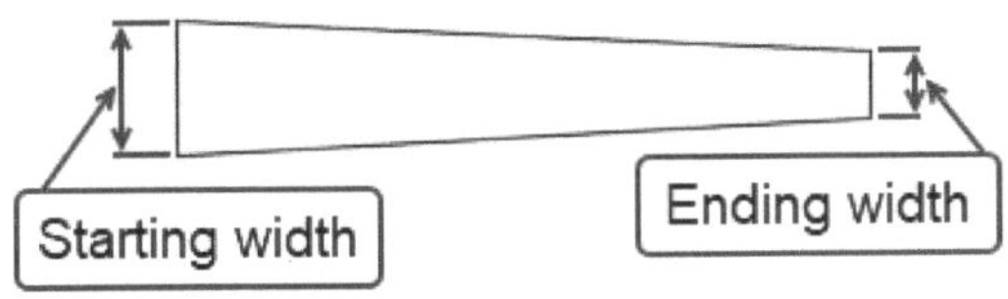

4.25

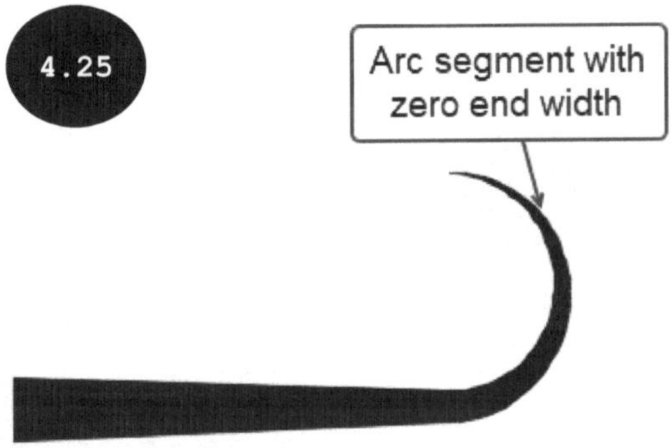

Drawing a Polyline with Halfwidth

The method for drawing a polyline by specifying its half width is discussed below:

1. Invoke the **Polyline** tool.

```
Specify start point:
```

2. Specify the start point of the polyline.

```
Specify next point or [Arc Halfwidth Length Undo Width]:
```

3. Click on the **Halfwidth** option in the command prompt or enter **H** and then press ENTER. You are prompted to specify the starting half-width of the polyline segment.

```
Specify starting half-width <0.0000>:
```

Note: The half-width of a polyline segment is the distance from the center of the polyline segment to one of its side edges, see Figure 4.26.

4. Specify the starting half width of the polyline segment (see Figure 4.26) and then press ENTER. You are prompted to specify the ending half-width of the polyline segment.

```
Specify ending half-width <5.0000>:
```

5. Enter the ending half-width value (see Figure 4.26) and then press ENTER. You are prompted to specify the next point of the polyline.

```
Specify next point or [Arc Halfwidth Length Undo Width]:
```

6. Specify the next point of the polyline segment. A line segment with a specified half-width is drawn, and you are prompted to specify the next point of the polyline. Also, a rubber band line segment with a constant half-width (defined as the ending half width) appears in the drawing area with one end fixed at the last specified point, and the other end attached to the cursor, see Figure 4.26.

```
Specify next point or [Arc Close Halfwidth Length Undo Width]:
```

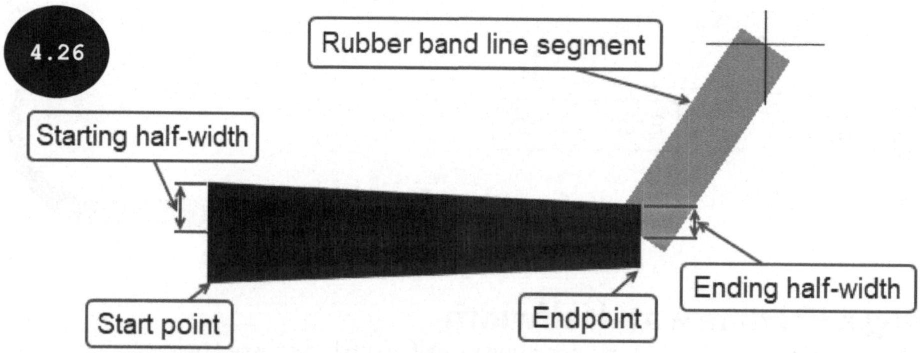

7. Similarly, you can draw a series of line and arc segments in a polyline. Once you have drawn the polyline, press the ENTER key to exit from the tool.

Drawing an Ellipse

An ellipse is created by defining its major axis and the minor axis, see Figure 4.27. In AutoCAD, you can draw an ellipse by using the **Center** and **Axis, End** tools. These tools are available in the **Ellipse** flyout of the **Draw** panel, see Figure 4.28. The methods for creating an ellipse are discussed next.

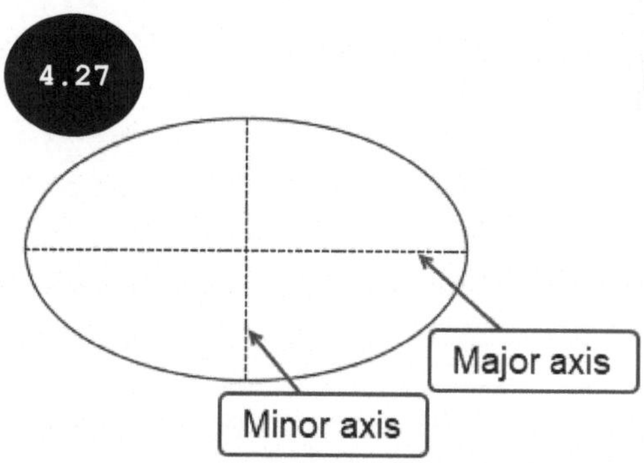

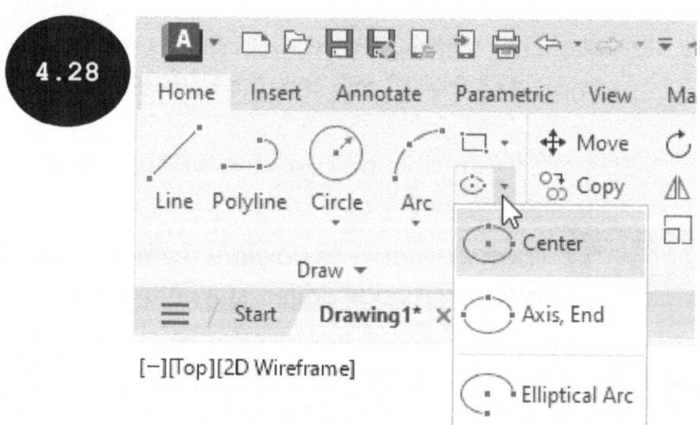

Drawing an Ellipse by Using the Axis, End Tool

The method for drawing an ellipse by using the **Axis, End** tool is discussed below:

1. Invoke the **Ellipse** flyout by clicking on the down arrow next to the ellipse tool in the **Draw** panel, see Figure 4.28.

2. Click on the **Axis, End** tool in the **Ellipse** flyout. The **Axis, End** tool is activated, and you are prompted to specify the first endpoint of the ellipse axis. Alternatively, enter **EL** in the Command Line window and then press ENTER to activate the **Axis, End** tool.

   ```
   Specify axis endpoint of ellipse or [Arc Center]:
   ```

3. Click the left mouse button in the drawing area or enter coordinates (X, Y) to specify the first endpoint of the ellipse axis (P1), see Figure 4.29. You are prompted to specify the second endpoint of the ellipse axis.

   ```
   Specify other endpoint of axis:
   ```

4. Click the left mouse button in the drawing area or enter coordinates (X, Y) or length of the axis to specify the second endpoint (P2), see Figure 4.29. You are prompted to specify the distance of the other ellipse axis.

   ```
   Specify distance to other axis or [Rotation]:
   ```

5. Move the cursor, in a clockwise or anti-clockwise direction to a distance. The preview of an ellipse appears in the drawing area, see Figure 4.30. Next, click the left mouse button or enter a length to specify the distance of the other ellipse axis (P3), see Figure 4.29. An ellipse with specified major and minor axes is created.

4.29

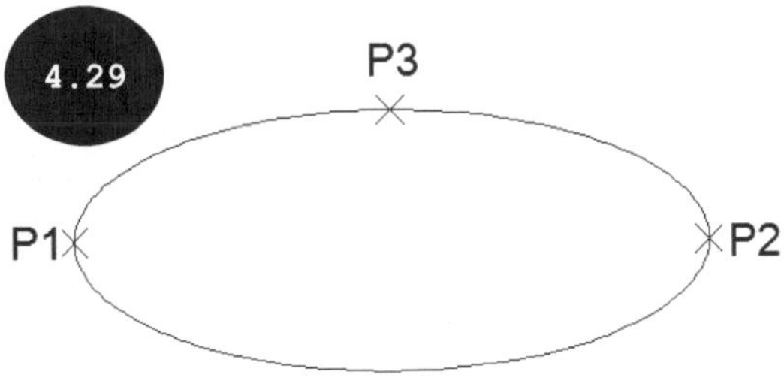

4.30

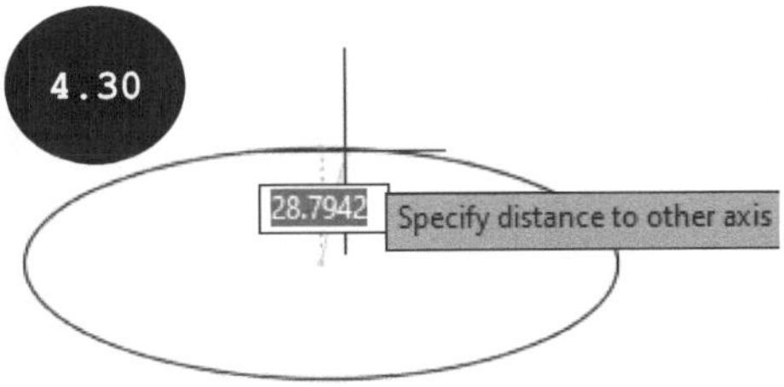

Drawing an Ellipse by Using the Center Tool

The method for drawing an ellipse by using the **Center** tool is discussed below:

1. Invoke the **Ellipse** flyout, see Figure 4.28.

2. Click on the **Center** tool in the **Ellipse** flyout. You are prompted to specify the center point of the ellipse axis. Alternatively, enter **EL** in the Command Line window and then press ENTER. Next, type **C** and then press ENTER to activate the **Center** tool.

   ```
   Specify center of ellipse:
   ```

3. Click the left mouse button in the drawing area or enter coordinates (X, Y) to specify the center point of the ellipse axis (P1), see Figure 4.31. You are prompted to specify the endpoint of the ellipse axis.

```
Specify endpoint of axis:
```

4. Specify the endpoint of the ellipse axis (P2), see Figure 4.31. You are prompted to specify the distance to the other ellipse axis.

```
Specify distance to other axis or [Rotation]:
```

5. Move the cursor, clockwise or anti-clockwise to a distance. The preview of an ellipse appears in the drawing area. Next, enter the length of the ellipse axis and then press ENTER. The ellipse of specified major and minor axes is created in the drawing area.

4.31

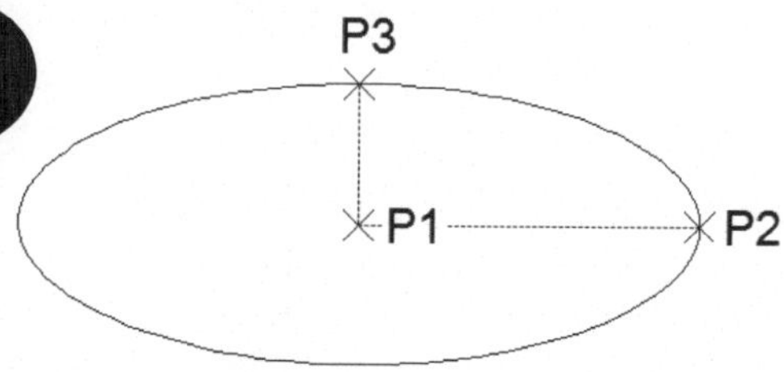

Drawing an Elliptical Arc

In addition to drawing an ellipse, you can also draw an elliptical arc, see Figure 4.32. You can draw an elliptical arc by using the **Elliptical Arc** tool of the **Ellipse** flyout, see Figure 4.33. You can also enter **EL** and then type **A** in the Command Line window to activate this tool. The method for drawing an elliptical arc is discussed below:

4.32

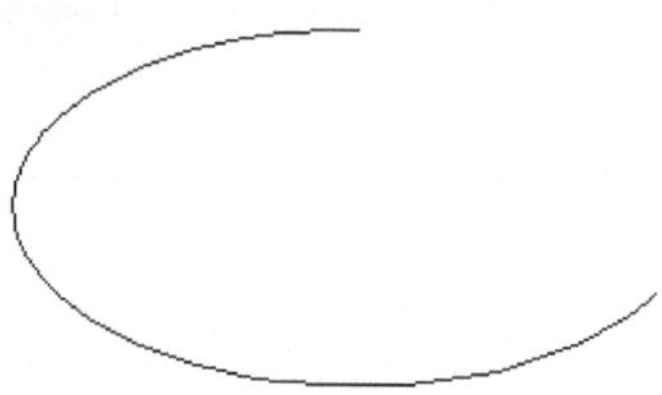

4.33

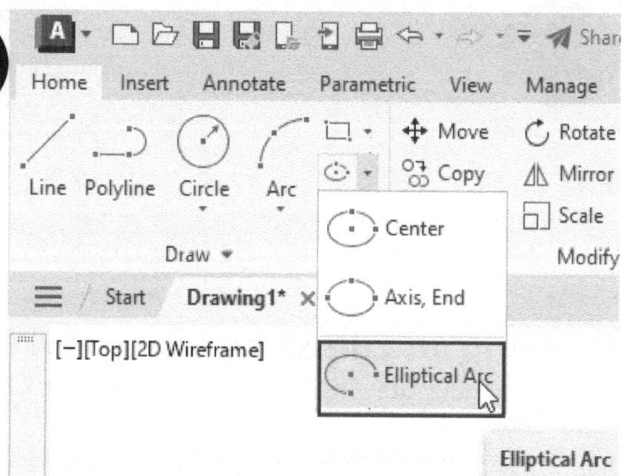

1. Invoke the **Ellipse** flyout and then click on the **Elliptical Arc** tool, see Figure 4.33. Alternatively, enter **EL** in the Command Line window and then press ENTER. Next, enter **A** and then press ENTER to activate the **Elliptical Arc** tool.

```
Specify axis endpoint of elliptical arc or [Center]:
```

2. Specify the start point of the elliptical arc axis (P1), see Figure 4.34. You are prompted to specify the endpoint of the elliptical arc axis.

```
Specify other endpoint of axis:
```

3. Specify the endpoint of the elliptical arc axis (P2), see Figure 4.34. You are prompted to specify the distance to the other axis.

```
Specify distance to other axis or [Rotation]:
```

4. Move the cursor clockwise or counter-clockwise to a distance. The preview of an imaginary ellipse appears in the drawing area. Next, specify a point (P3) to define the length of the other axis, see Figure 4.34. You are prompted to specify the start angle of the elliptical arc.

```
Specify start angle or [Parameter]:
```

5. Move the cursor clockwise or counter-clockwise and then specify the start angle for the elliptical arc, see Figure 4.34. You are prompted to specify the end angle of the elliptical arc.

```
Specify end angle or [Parameter Included angle]:
```

6. Move the cursor clockwise or counter-clockwise and then specify the end angle for the elliptical arc, see Figure 4.34. The elliptical arc is created in the drawing area.

4.34

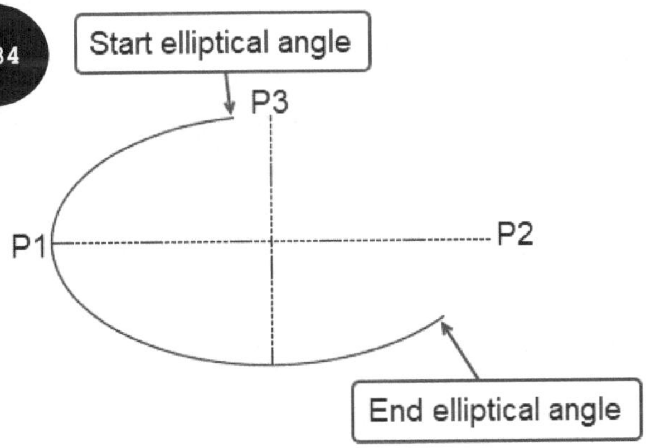

Drawing a Spline

A spline is defined as a smooth curve having a high degree of smoothness and passing through a set of fit points that influence the shape of the curve, see Figure 4.35. You can also create a spline that passes near the control vertices, see Figure 4.36. The smooth curves are technically known as NURBS (non-uniform rational B-splines). However, the curve is referred to as a spline. In AutoCAD, you can draw a spline by using the **Spline Fit** and **Spline CV** tools. Both these tools are discussed next.

4.35

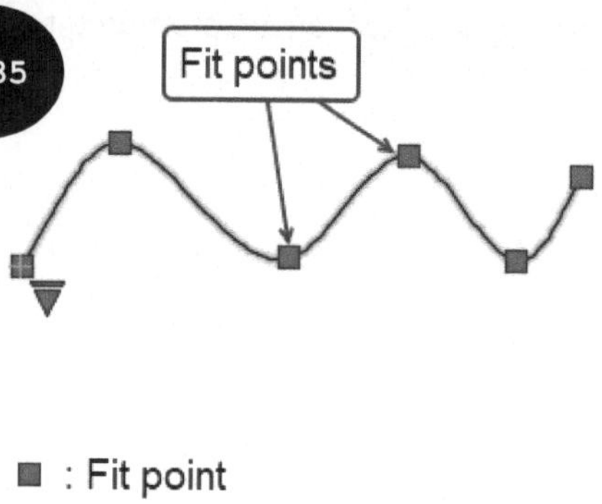

4.36

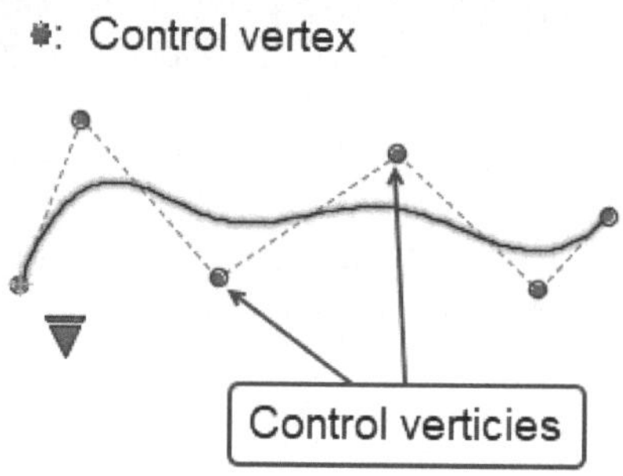

Drawing a Spline by Using the Spline Fit Tool

The **Spline Fit** tool is used for creating a spline such that it passes through a set of fit points that influence the shape of the spline, see Figure 4.35. The method for drawing a spline by using the **Spline Fit** tool is discussed below:

1. Expand the **Draw** panel by clicking on the down arrow in the title bar of the **Draw** panel, see Figure 4.37. Figure 4.38 shows the expanded **Draw** panel.

2. Click on the **Spline Fit** tool in the expanded **Draw** panel, see Figure 4.38. The **Spline Fit** tool gets activated, and you are prompted to specify the first fit point of the spline. Alternatively, enter **SPL** in the Command Line window and then press ENTER to invoke the **Spline Fit** tool.

```
Specify first point or [Method Knots Object]:
```

4.37

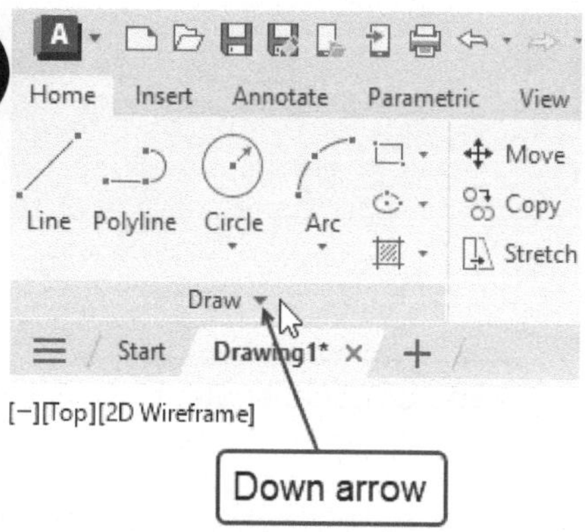

4.38

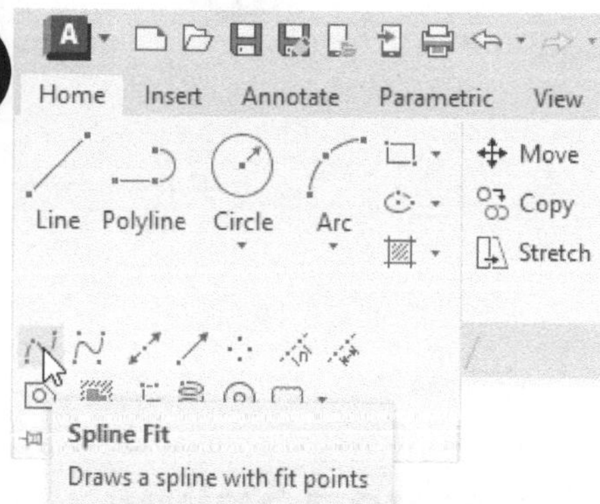

3. Click the left mouse button in the drawing area to specify the first fit point of the spline. You are prompted to specify the next fit point of the spline.

```
Enter next point or [start Tangency toLerance]:
```

Note: Before you specify the second fit point of a spline, you can define its start tangency by entering T in the Command Line window or by clicking on the **start Tangency** option in the command prompt. Figure 4.39 shows a spline with start tangency point.

By default, the tolerance value for a spline is set to 0 (zero). As a result, the resultant spline passes exactly through the specified fit points. On defining a positive tolerance value, the resultant spline deviates from the specified fit points and maintains uniform tolerance distance between the spline and fit points, see Figure 4.40. To define the tolerance for a spline, enter **L** in the Command Line window or click on the **toLerance** option in the command prompt, which appears after specifying the first fit point of a spline. The tolerance value gets applied to all fit points except the start and end fit points, see Figure 4.40.

4.39

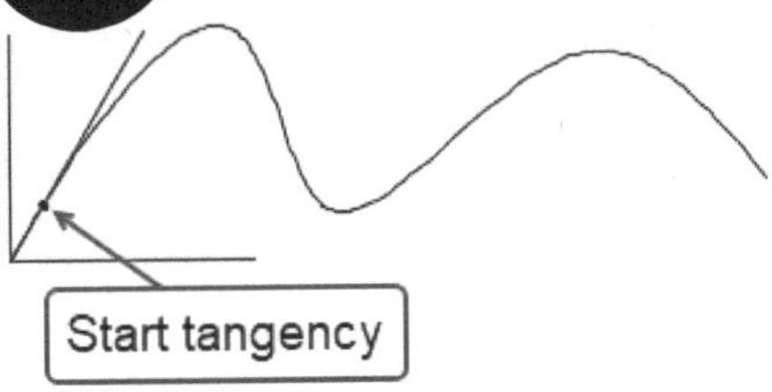

4.40

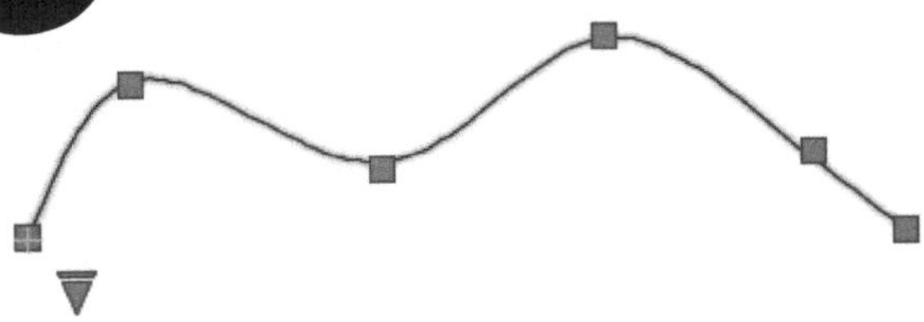

4. Click to specify the second fit point of the spline. You are prompted to specify the next fit point of the spline. Also, a preview of the spline appears such that it passes through the specified fit points.

```
Enter next point or [end Tangency toLerance Undo]:
```

5. Click to specify the third fit point of the spline. You are prompted to specify the next fit point of the spline. Also, a preview of the spline appears such that it passes through the specified fit points.

```
Enter next point or [end Tangency toLerance Undo Close]:
```

6. Similarly, you can continue specifying fit points for creating a spline. Once you have defined all the fit points of the spline, press ENTER to exit the tool.

Note: Before you terminate the creation of spline, you can define its end tangency by entering T in the Command Line window or by clicking on the **end Tangency** option in the command prompt. Figure 4.41 shows a spline with end tangency point.

You can also draw a closed spline. To draw a closed spline whose end fit point joins to the start point, enter **C** in the Command Line window and then press ENTER. Figure 4.42 shows a closed spline. To draw a closed spline, you need to define minimum three fit points.

4.41

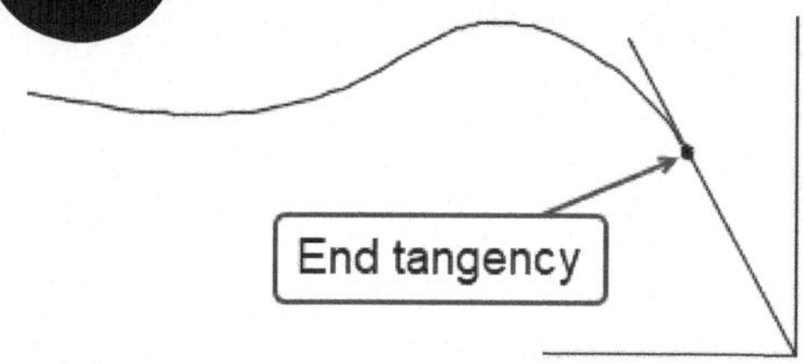

4.42

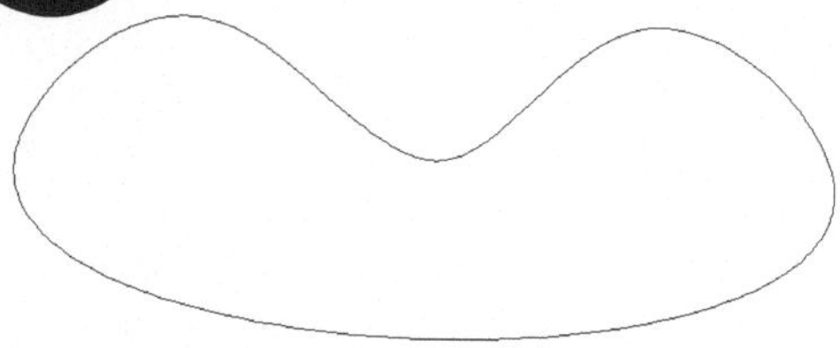

Tip: You can also undo/remove the last specified fit point by entering **U** in the Command Line window and then pressing the ENTER key. You can undo multiple specified last points one after the other by using this command.

Drawing a Spline by Using the Spline CV Tool

The **Spline CV** tool is used for creating a spline such that it passes near a set of control vertices that influence the shape of the spline, see Figure 4.43. The method for drawing a spline by using the **Spline CV** tool is discussed below:

1. Expand the **Draw** panel by clicking on the down arrow available in the title bar of the **Draw** panel and then click on the **Spline CV** tool, see Figure 4.44. The **Spline CV** tool gets activated, and you are prompted to specify the first control point for creating the spline.

```
Specify first point or [Method Degree Object]:
```

4.43

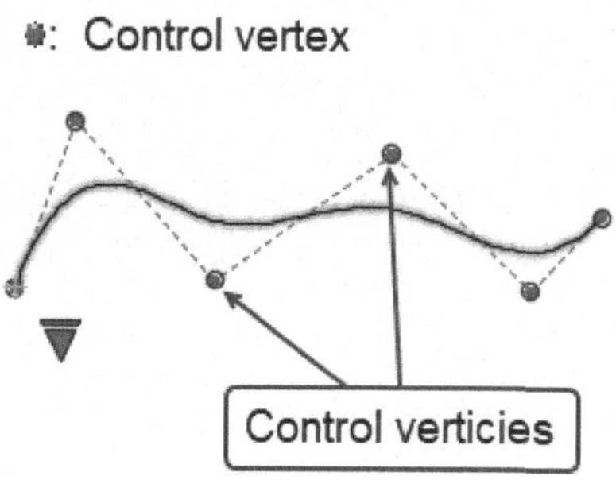

4.44

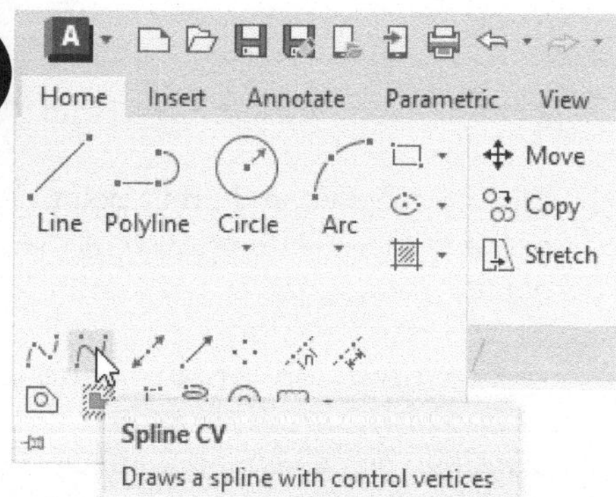

2. Click the left mouse button in the drawing area to specify the first control point of the spline. You are prompted to specify the next control point of the spline.

```
Enter next point:
```

3. Click to specify the second control point of the spline. You are prompted to specify the next control point of the spline. A preview of the spline also appears such that it passes near the specified control points.

```
Enter next point or [Undo]:
```

4. Click to specify the third control point of the spline. You are prompted to specify the next control point of the spline.

```
Enter next point or [Close Undo]:
```

5. Similarly, you can continue specifying control points for creating the spline. Once you have defined all the control points, press the ENTER key. The spline gets created in the drawing area.

Note: You can also draw a closed spline. To draw a closed spline whose end control point joins to the start control point, enter **C** in the Command Line window and then press ENTER.

You can also undo/remove the last specified control point by entering **U** in the Command Line window and then pressing the ENTER key.

Drawing Donuts

A donut is a filled solid ring/circle, which is made up of two end-to-end joined polyarcs with a defined width. The width of the polyarc is defined by specifying the inside and outside diameters, see Figure 4.45. If you specify the inside diameter as 0 (zero), the donut will be drawn as a filled circle, see Figure 4.46. In AutoCAD, you can draw donuts by using the **Donut** tool, which is available in the expanded **Draw** panel. The method for drawing donuts is discussed below:

4.45

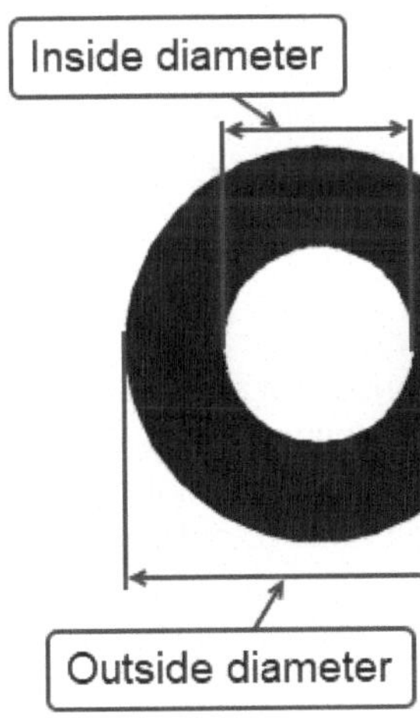

4.46

1. Expand the **Draw** panel of the **Home** tab and then click on the **Donut** tool, see Figure 4.47. You are prompted to specify the inside diameter of the donut. Alternatively, enter **DO** in the Command Line window and then press ENTER to activate the **Donut** tool.

```
Specify inside diameter of donut <0.0000>:
```

4.47

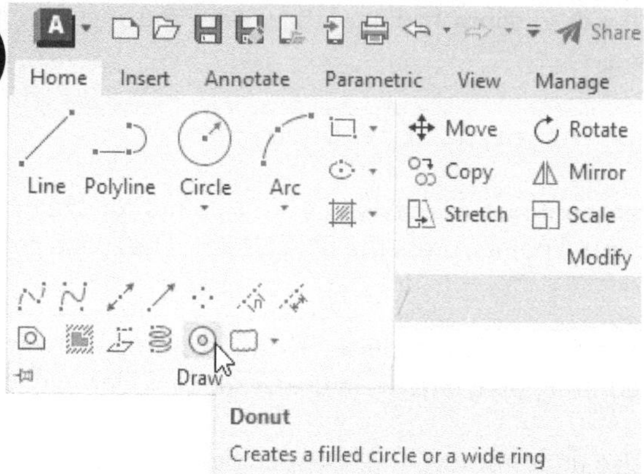

2. Enter the inside diameter value of the donut and then press ENTER. You are prompted to specify the outside diameter of the donut.

```
Specify outside diameter of donut <0.0000>:
```

3. Enter the outside diameter value of the donut and then press ENTER. You are prompted to specify the center of the donut.

```
Specify center of donut or <exit>:
```

4. Click the left mouse button in the drawing area or specify coordinates (X, Y) to define the center of the donut. A donut gets drawn with the specified parameters in the drawing area. Also, another donut of the same parameters is attached to the cursor. This means that you can draw multiple donuts one after another by specifying their centers in the drawing area.

5. Press ENTER to exit creating donuts.

Note: By default, the fill mode is set to 1. As a result, the resultant donut appears as a solid ring/circle. However, if you change the fill mode to 0 (zero), the resultant donut will not be filled and appears similar to the one shown in Figure 4.48. To define the fill mode, enter **FILLMODE** in the Command Line window and then specify the fill value (0 or 1). Next, press ENTER.

4.48

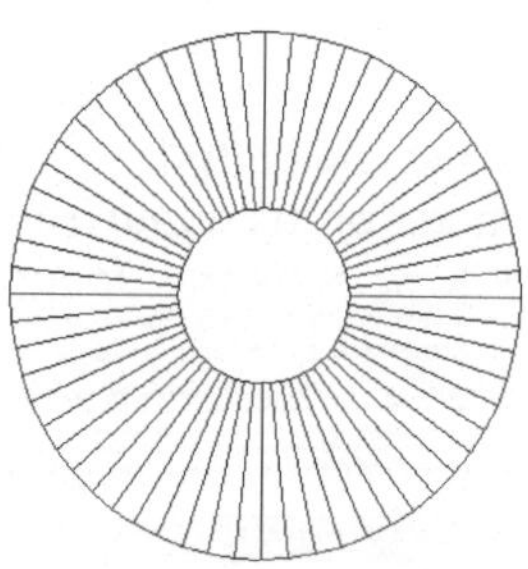

Drawing Construction and Ray lines

Construction lines and ray lines act as reference lines for creating objects. A construction line is also known as XLINE. A construction line is extended to an infinite length in both directions and passes through two specified points, see Figure 4.49. Whereas, a ray line is extended to an infinite length in one direction only from the first specified point, see Figure 4.49. You can create a construction line (XLINE) by using the **Construction Line** tool and a ray line by using the **Ray** tool. Both tools are available in the expanded **Draw** panel of the **Home** tab, see Figure 4.50. The methods for drawing a construction line and a ray line are discussed next.

4.49

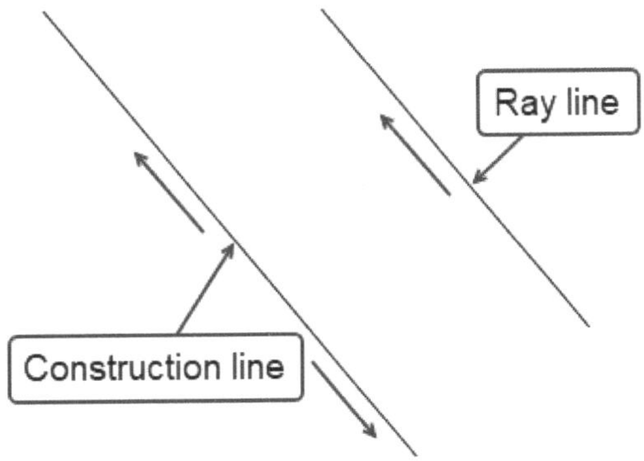

4.50

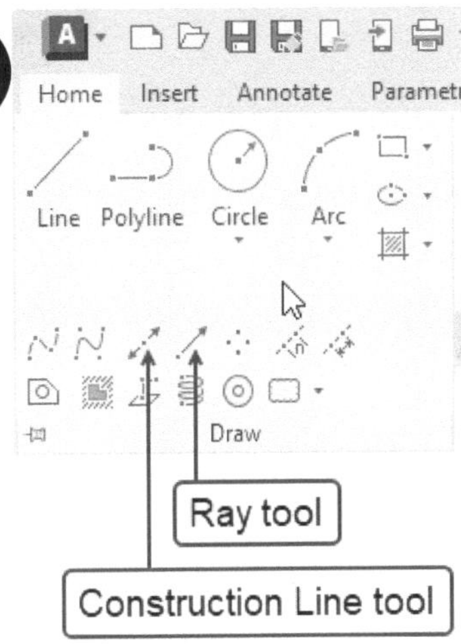

Drawing Construction Lines

The method for drawing construction lines is discussed below:

1. Expand the **Draw** panel of the **Home** tab and then click on the **Construction Line** tool, see Figure 4.50. The **Construction Line** tool gets activated, and you are prompted to specify a point in the drawing area. Alternatively, enter **XLINE** in the Command Line window and then press ENTER to activate the **Construction Line** tool.

   ```
   Specify a point or [Hor Ver Ang Bisect Offset]:
   ```

2. Click to specify a point (P1) in the drawing area, see Figure 4.51. You are prompted to specify a through point.

   ```
   Specify through point:
   ```

3. Click to specify a point (P2) in the drawing area, see Figure 4.51. A construction line of infinite length passing through the specified points (P1 and P2) is drawn in the drawing area. Also, the preview of another construction line appears in the drawing area such that it passes through the first specified point and is attached to the cursor. This means that you can create multiple construction lines one after another by specifying points in the drawing area.

4. Click to specify another point (P3) in the drawing area, see Figure 4.51. Another construction line of infinite length passing through the points (P1 and P3) is drawn in the drawing area. Also, the preview of another construction line appears in the drawing area. Similarly, you can create multiple construction lines passing through a common point.

5. After creating the construction lines, press ENTER to exit the tool. Figure 4.51 shows two construction lines created in the drawing area.

4.51

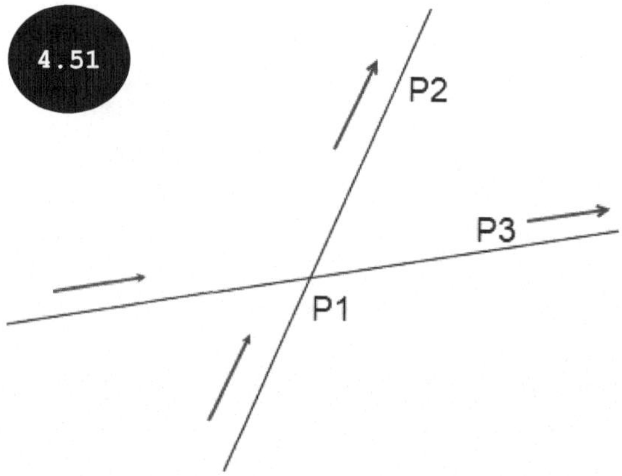

You can also create construction lines that are horizontal, vertical, at an angle, bisecting, and offset by using the **Construction Line** tool. The methods for creating these construction lines are discussed next.

Drawing Horizontal and Vertical Construction Lines

1. Expand the **Draw** panel of the **Home** tab and then click on the **Construction Line** tool. The **Construction Line** tool gets activated, and you are prompted to specify a point in the drawing area. Alternatively, you can enter **XLINE** in the Command Line window and then press ENTER to activate the **Construction Line** tool.

   ```
   Specify a point or [Hor Ver Ang Bisect Offset]:
   ```

2. Enter **H** in the Command Line window and then press ENTER. Alternatively, you can click on the **Hor** option in the command prompt. A horizontal construction line attached to the cursor is displayed, and you are prompted to specify a through point.

   ```
   Specify through point:
   ```

3. Click to specify a point in the drawing area. A horizontal construction line gets created such that it passes through the specified point, see Figure 4.52. Note that another horizontal construction line attached to the cursor is displayed. As a result, you can create multiple horizontal construction lines one after another by specifying points in the drawing area.

4. Once you have created horizontal construction lines, press ENTER.

5. Similarly, you can create vertical construction lines by entering **V** in the Command Line window or by clicking on the **Ver** option in the command prompt, see Figure 4.52.

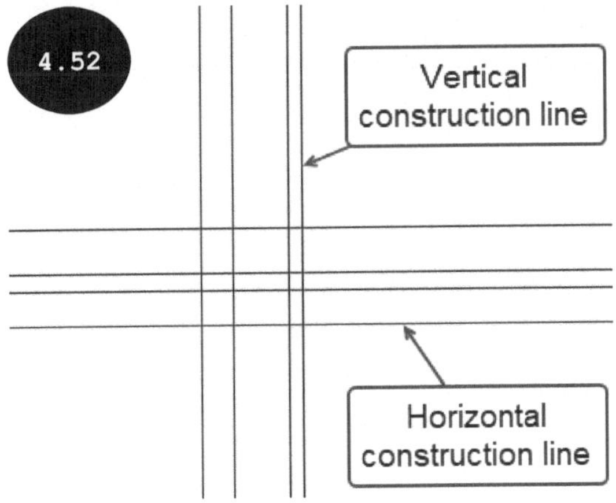

Drawing Construction Lines at an Angle

1. Invoke the **Construction Line** tool. You are prompted to specify a point in the drawing area.

   ```
   Specify a point or [Hor Ver Ang Bisect Offset]:
   ```

2. Enter **A** in the Command Line window and then press ENTER. You are prompted to specify the angle value for the construction line. Alternatively, you can click on the **Ang** option of the command prompt.

   ```
   Enter angle of xline (0) or [Reference]:
   ```

3. Enter the angle value and then press ENTER. A construction line at the specified angle is attached to the cursor. Also, you are prompted to specify a through point.

   ```
   Specify through point:
   ```

4. Click to specify a point in the drawing area. A construction line at the specified angle is created such that it passes through the specified point, see Figure 4.53. Also, another construction line of a specified angle is attached to the cursor. As a result, you can create multiple construction lines one after another by specifying points in the drawing area.

5. After creating the construction lines, press ENTER or right-click to exit.

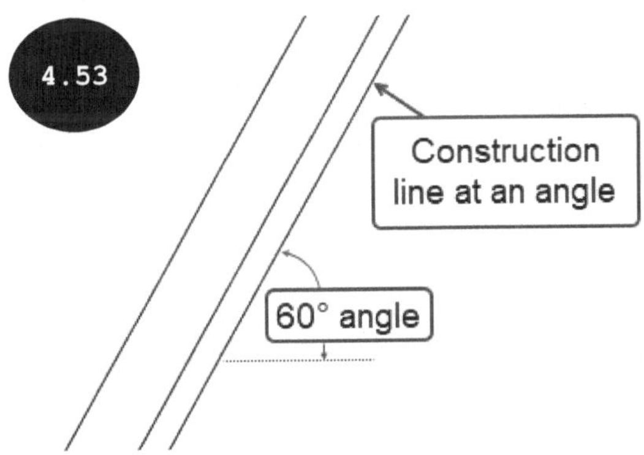

Drawing Bisecting Construction Lines

1. Invoke the **Construction Line** tool. You are prompted to specify a point in the drawing area.

   `Specify a point or [Hor Ver Ang Bisect Offset]:`

2. Enter **B** in the Command Line window and then press ENTER. You are prompted to specify the vertex point. Alternatively, you can click on the **Bisect** option in the command prompt.

   `Specify angle vertex point:`

3. Click to specify the vertex point (P1) in the drawing area, see Figure 4.54. You are prompted to specify the angle start point.

   `Specify angle start point:`

4. Click to specify the angle start point (P2) in the drawing area, see Figure 4.54. You are prompted to specify the angle endpoint.

   `Specify angle end point:`

5. Click to specify the angle endpoint (P3) in the drawing area, see Figure 4.54. A construction line gets created such that it passes through the vertex (P1) and bisects the angle formed by the specified points, see Figure 4.54. Next, press the ENTER key or right-click to exit.

4.54

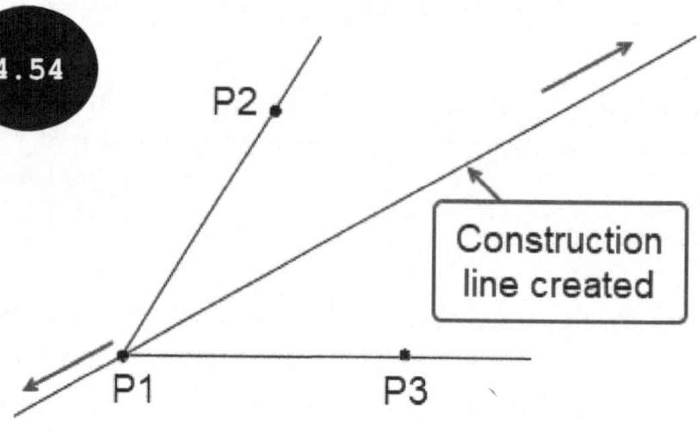

Drawing Construction Lines at an Offset Distance

1. Invoke the **Construction Line** tool. You are prompted to specify a point in the drawing area.

   `Specify a point or [Hor Ver Ang Bisect Offset]:`

2. Enter **O** in the Command Line window and then press ENTER or click on the **Offset** option of the command prompt. You are prompted to specify the offset distance for the construction line.

   `Specify offset distance or [Through] <Through>:`

Note: The **Offset** option is used for creating a construction line at an offset distance from an entity.

3. Enter the offset distance value and then press ENTER. You are prompted to select a line. You can choose a line or a construction line as the reference line for measuring the offset distance.

```
Select a line object:
```

4. Click to select a line or a construction line. You are prompted to specify the side to offset.

```
Specify side to offset:
```

5. Click on either side of the selected line. The construction line gets created at the specified offset distance in the drawing area, see Figure 4.55.

4.55

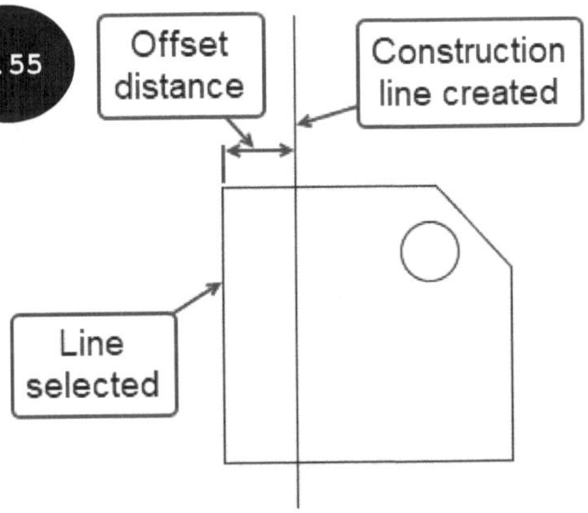

Tip: In addition to defining offset value, you can also specify a point in the drawing area to define the offset distance. For doing so, click on the **Through** option in the command prompt or enter T in the Command Line window when you are prompted to specify the offset distance. Next, click on the line as a reference line and then click in the drawing area to define offset distance. The construction line gets created in the drawing area.

Drawing Ray Lines

A ray line is similar to construction lines (Xlines) with the only difference being that it extends to infinite length in one direction only from the first specified point. The method for drawing a ray line is discussed below:

1. Expand the **Draw** panel of the **Home** tab and then click on the **Ray** tool. Alternatively, enter **RAY** in the Command Line window and then press ENTER. You are prompted to specify the start point.

```
Specify start point:
```

2. Click to specify the start point of the ray line in the drawing area. You are prompted to specify a through point.

```
Specify through point:
```

3. Click to specify a point in the drawing area. A ray line of infinite length in one direction from the start point is created in the drawing area. The preview of another ray line also appears in the drawing area with its origin fixed at the specified start point. You can create multiple ray lines one after another by specifying through points in the drawing area.

4. After creating the ray lines, press ENTER or right-click to exit. Figure 4.56 shows two ray lines sharing the same start point.

4.56

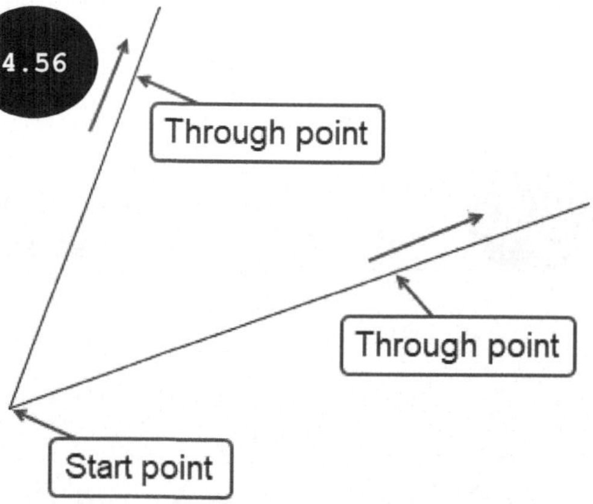

Drawing Points and Defining Point Style/Size

In AutoCAD, a point acts as reference geometry for creating other drawing objects, measuring distance, and so on. You can create points by using the **Multiple Points** tool, which is in the expanded **Draw** panel of the **Home** tab, see Figure 4.57. Alternatively, you can use the **POINT** command to create points. By default, the point style of a point is a simple dot which is relatively small. As the default size of a point is small and it's hard to be visible on the screen, you can make the required changes in the point style and size by using the **Point Style** tool. The methods for drawing reference points, changing point style, and point size are discussed next.

Drawing Reference Points

1. Expand the **Draw** panel of the **Home** tab and then click on the **Multiple Points** tool, see Figure 4.57. The **Multiple Points** tool gets activated, and you are prompted to specify a point in the drawing area.

```
Specify a point:
```

4.57

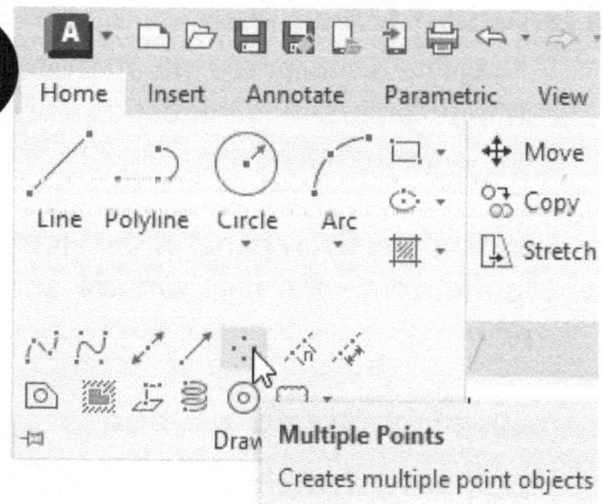

2. Click to specify a point in the drawing area. The point gets created with the default point style (dot). You are prompted to specify another point.

```
Specify a point:
```

Note: The point created with default point style and size may not be visible easily in the drawing area due to its small size. You can change the point style and size by using the **Point Style** tool. The method for changing the point style and size is discussed later in this chapter.

3. You can continue specifying points in the drawing area to create multiple points. Once you have drawn points, press ESC to exit.

Defining the Point Style and Point Size

1. Expand the **Utilities** panel of the **Home** tab and then click on the **Point Style** tool, see Figure 4.58. The **Point Style** dialog box appears, see Figure 4.59. Alternatively, you can enter **DDPTYPE** or **PTYPE** in the Command Line window and then press ENTER to invoke the **Point Style** dialog box.

4.58

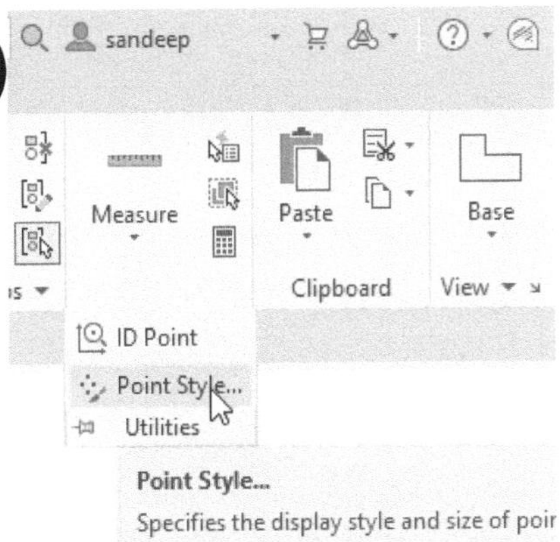

4.59

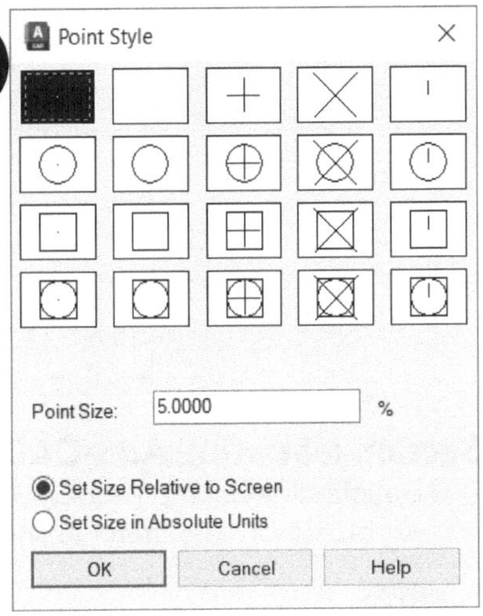

2. Select the required point style in the **Point Style** dialog box.

   After selecting the required point style, you can define the point size by using the **Set Size Relative to Screen** and **Set Size in Absolute Units** radio buttons of the **Point Style** dialog box. By default, the **Set Size Relative to Screen** radio button is selected. As a result, you can specify a percentage relative to the screen for defining the point size in the **Point Size** field of the dialog box. To define the point size in absolute units, click to select the **Set Size in Absolute Units** radio button and then enter the absolute units of the point size in the **Point Size** field of the dialog box, see Figure 4.60.

4.60

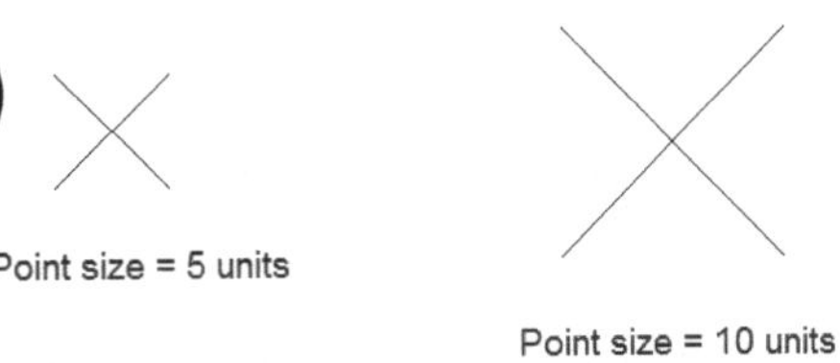

3. Click to select the required radio button: **Set Size Relative to Screen** or **Set Size in Absolute Units** in the **Point Style** dialog box for defining the point size.

4. Specify the point size in terms of percentage relative to the screen or absolute unit in the **Point Size** field of the **Point Style** dialog box, respectively.

5. Click on the **OK** button in the dialog box to accept the changes as well as to exit the dialog box.

Tutorial 1

Create the drawing shown in Figure 4.61. The dimensions shown in the figure are for your reference only.

4.61

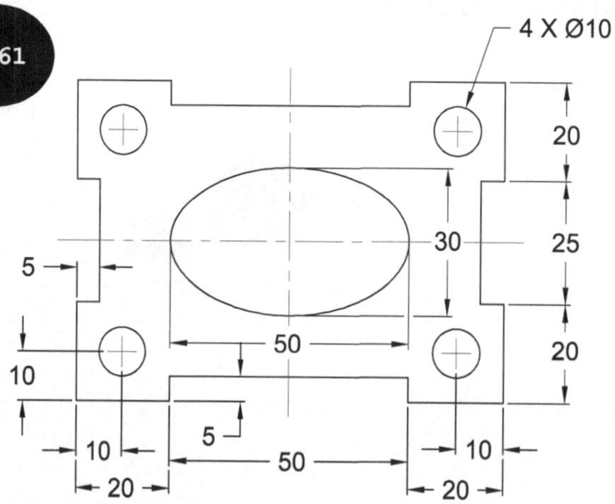

Section 1: Starting AutoCAD

1. Double-click on the AutoCAD icon on your desktop to start AutoCAD. The initial screen of AutoCAD with the **Start** tab appears, see Figure 4.62.

4.62

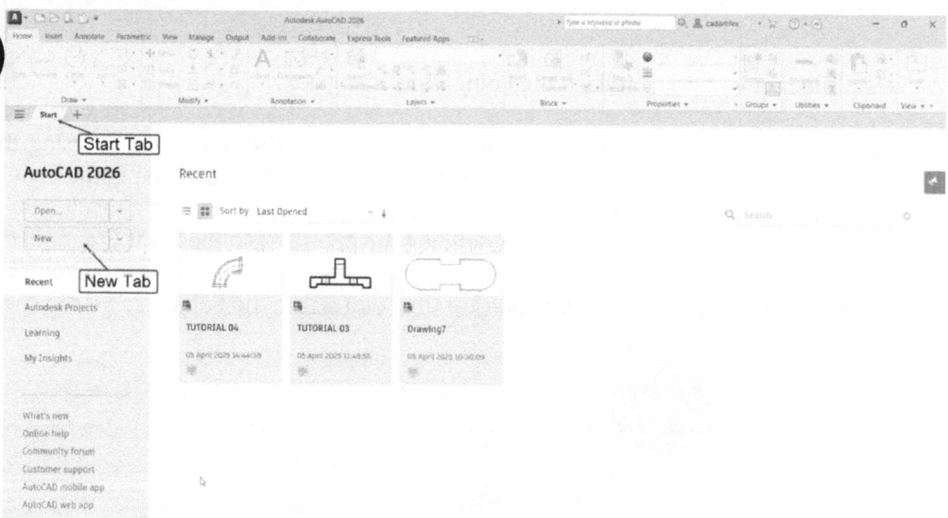

2. Click on the + sign next to the **Start** tab, see Figure 4.62. A new drawing file with the default drawing template gets invoked. Alternatively, click on the **New** tool of the **Start** tab to start a new

drawing file with the default drawing template. You can also start a new drawing file by using the **New** tool from the **Quick Access Toolbar**, which is at the top left corner of AutoCAD.

Section 2: Selecting Workspace for Creating Drawing

1. Click on the **Workspace Switching** button in the Status Bar. A flyout appears, see Figure 4.63.

4.63

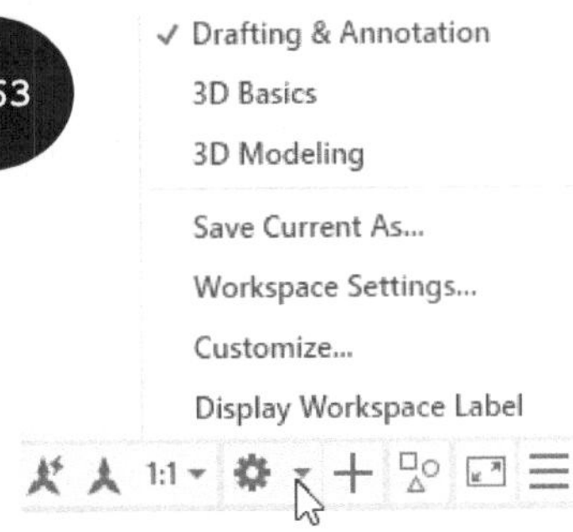

2. In this flyout, ensure that the **Drafting & Annotation** option is tick-marked to create a drawing in the Drafting & Annotation workspace.

Section 3: Defining Drawing Limits

1. Define the drawing limits. You can define the drawing limits based on the overall dimensions of the drawing and keep some extra space for placing dimensions in the drawing area.

Section 4: Drawing Outer Loop of the Drawing

1. Click on the **Line** tool in the **Draw** panel of the **Home** tab. The **Line** tool gets activated, and you are prompted to specify the first point of the line. Alternatively, you can enter **L** in the Command Line window and then press ENTER to activate the **Line** tool.

   `Specify first point:`

2. Click on the **Ortho Mode** button of the Status Bar or press the F8 key to turn on the Ortho mode. Note that this is a toggle button.

3. Ensure that the Dynamic Input mode is activated. You can enable the Dynamic Input mode by clicking on the **Dynamic Input** button in the Status Bar.

4. Follow the command sequence given below for creating the drawing.

   `Specify first point:` *0,0* (***ENTER***).
   `Specify next point or [Undo]:` *Move the cursor horizontally toward right and then enter 20 in the Dynamic Input box* (***ENTER***).
   `Specify next point or [Undo]:` *Move the cursor vertically upward and then enter 5* (***ENTER***).
   `Specify next point or [Close Undo]:` *Move the cursor horizontally toward right and then enter 50* (***ENTER***).
   `Specify next point or [Close Undo]:` *Move the cursor vertically downward and then enter 5* (***ENTER***).

`Specify next point or [Close Undo]:` *Move the cursor horizontally toward right and then enter* **20** (**ENTER**).

`Specify next point or [Close Undo]:` *Move the cursor vertically upward and then enter* **20** (**ENTER**).

`Specify next point or [Close Undo]:` *Move the cursor horizontally toward left and then enter* **5** (**ENTER**).

`Specify next point or [Close Undo]:` *Move the cursor vertically upward and then enter* **25** (**ENTER**).

`Specify next point or [Close Undo]:` *Move the cursor horizontally toward right and then enter* **5** (**ENTER**).

`Specify next point or [Close Undo]:` *Move the cursor vertically upward and then enter* **20** (**ENTER**).

`Specify next point or [Close Undo]:` *Move the cursor horizontally toward left and then enter* **20** (**ENTER**).

`Specify next point or [Close Undo]:` *Move the cursor vertically downward and then enter* **5** (**ENTER**).

`Specify next point or [Close Undo]:` *Move the cursor horizontally toward left and then enter* **50** (**ENTER**).

`Specify next point or [Close Undo]:` *Move the cursor vertically upward and then enter* **5** (**ENTER**).

`Specify next point or [Close Undo]:` *Move the cursor horizontally toward left and then enter* **20** (**ENTER**).

`Specify next point or [Close Undo]:` *Move the cursor vertically downward and then enter* **20** (**ENTER**).

`Specify next point or [Close Undo]:` *Move the cursor horizontally toward right and then enter* **5** (**ENTER**).

`Specify next point or [Close Undo]:` *Move the cursor vertically downward and then enter* **25** (**ENTER**).

`Specify next point or [Close Undo]:` *Move the cursor horizontally toward left and then enter* **5** (**ENTER**).

`Specify next point or [Close Undo]:` **C** *or* **Close** *(See Figure 4.64).*

4.64

Section 5: Drawing Ellipse

1. Invoke the **Ellipse** flyout in the **Draw** panel and then click on the **Center** tool, see Figure 4.65. You are prompted to specify the center of the ellipse. Alternatively, you can enter **EL** in the Command Line window and then press ENTER. Next, enter C and then press ENTER to activate the tool.

```
Specify center of ellipse:
```

2. Move the cursor to the midpoint of the left middle vertical line (P1) (see Figure 4.66) and then move the cursor to the midpoint of the upper middle horizontal line (P2), see Figure 4.66. Next, move the cursor vertically downward. A reference/tracking line appears.

3. Continue moving the cursor vertically downward and then click to specify the center point of the ellipse when the cursor snaps to the intersection of reference/tracking lines, which are passing through the points (P1 and P2), see Figure 4.66.

4.65

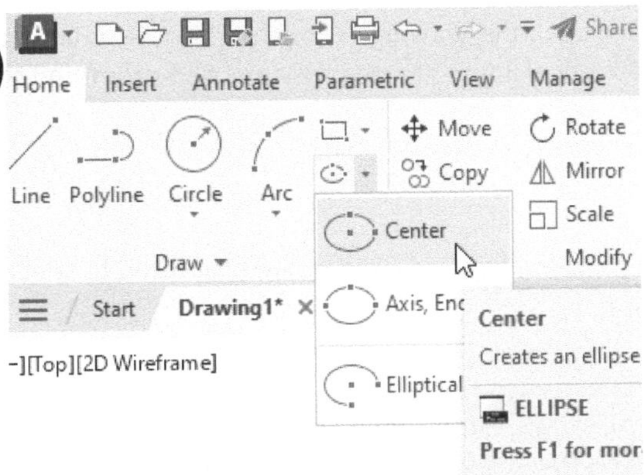

4.66

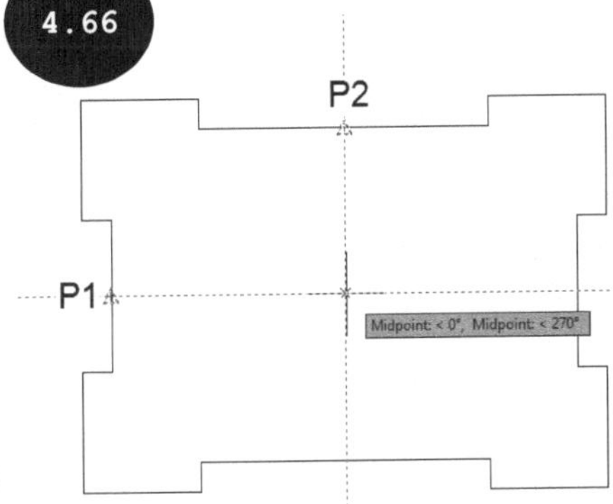

4. Move the cursor horizontally toward the right and then enter **25** in the Dynamic Input box. Next, press ENTER.

5. Move the cursor vertically upward to a distance. Next, enter **15** in the Dynamic Input box and then press ENTER. An ellipse of the major axis measuring 50 units and the minor axis measuring 30 units is created in the drawing area, see Figure 4.67.

4.67

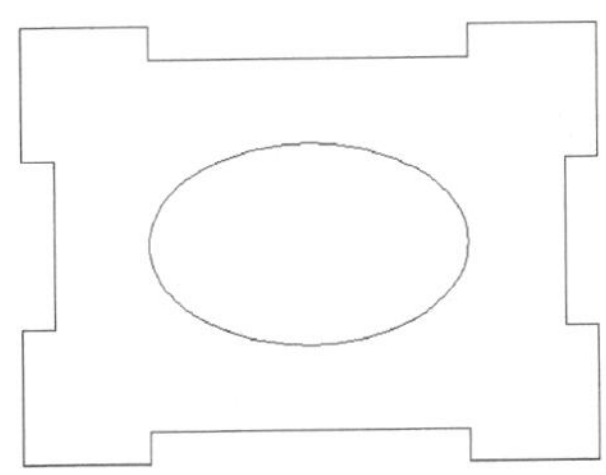

Section 6: Drawing Circles

In this section, you will draw the circles of the drawing with the help of construction lines.

1. Expand the **Draw** panel of the **Home** tab and then click on the **Construction Line** tool. You are prompted to specify the start point of the construction line (xline). Alternatively, you can enter **XLINE** in the Command Line window to activate the **Construction Line** tool.

```
Specify a point or [Hor Ver Ang Bisect Offset]:
```

2. Click on the **Offset** option in the command prompt or enter **O** and then press ENTER. You are prompted to specify offset distance.

```
Specify offset distance or [Through] <Through>:
```

3. Enter **10** as the offset distance value and then press ENTER. You are prompted to select a line object.

```
Select a line object:
```

4. Click on the lower left vertical line (L1), see Figure 4.68. You are prompted to specify the side to offset the construction line (xline).

```
Specify side to offset:
```

5. Click anywhere inside the outer closed loop of the drawing. A construction line (xline) at an offset distance of 10 units from the selected vertical line is created. You are also prompted to choose a line object.

```
Select a line object:
```

6. Click on the lower left horizontal line (L2), see Figure 4.68. You are prompted to specify the side to offset the construction line (xline).

```
Specify side to offset:
```

7. Click anywhere inside the outer closed loop of the drawing. A construction line (xline) at an offset distance of 10 units from the selected horizontal line gets created, see Figure 4.69. You are also prompted to choose a line object.

```
Select a line object:
```

4.68

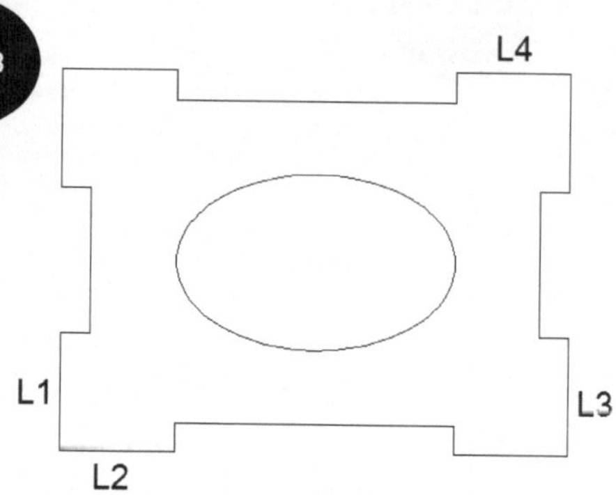

4.69

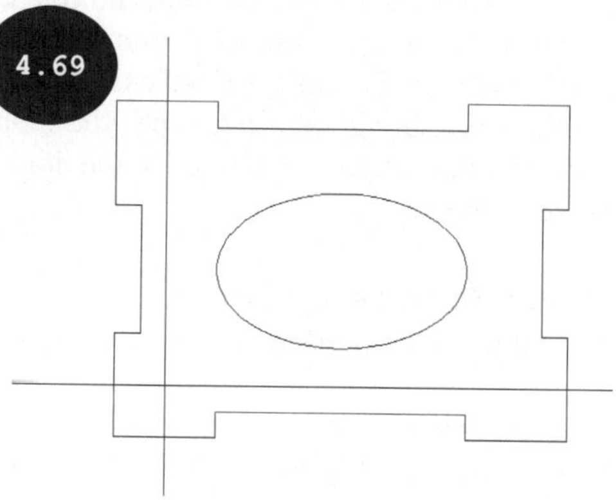

8. Similarly, select the lower right vertical line (L3) and the upper right horizontal line (L4) for creating other construction lines, refer to Figure 4.68. Figure 4.70 shows the drawing after creating all the construction lines.

9. Press ENTER or right-click to exit from the creation of construction lines.

After creating the construction lines (xlines), you can use the intersection of the construction lines to specify the center point of the circles.

10. Enter **C** in the Command Line window and then press ENTER to activate the **Center, Radius** tool. You can also click on the **Center, Radius** tool in the **Draw** panel. You are prompted to specify the center point of the circle.

```
Specify center point for circle or [3P 2P Ttr (tan tan radius)]:
```

11. Move the cursor over the lower left intersection of the construction lines (P1) (see Figure 4.70) and then click to specify the center point of the circle when the cursor snaps to the intersection (P1). You are prompted to specify the radius of the circle.

```
Specify radius of circle or [Diameter] <0.0000>:
```

12. Enter **5** as the radius value of the circle and then press ENTER. A circle of radius 5 units gets created in the drawing area, see Figure 4.71.

4.70

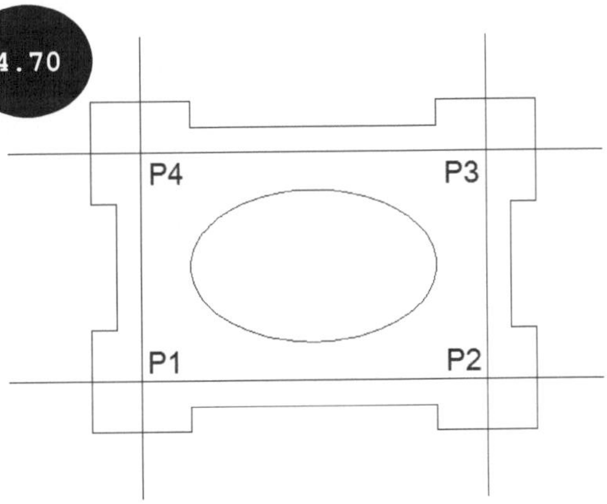

4.71

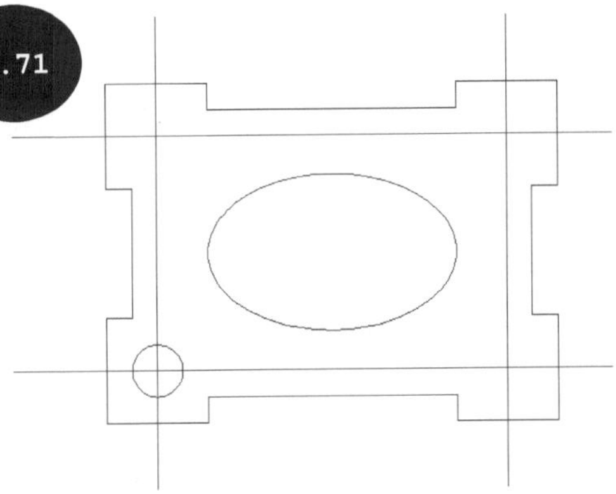

13. Similarly, draw the other three circles of radius 5 units at the intersections (P2, P3, and P4) of construction lines, see Figure 4.72.

14. After drawing all the circles, you can delete the construction lines. However, it is recommended that you create a layer and move all the construction lines to it. Next, hide the layer. Figure 4.73 shows the final drawing after hiding the construction lines.

4.72

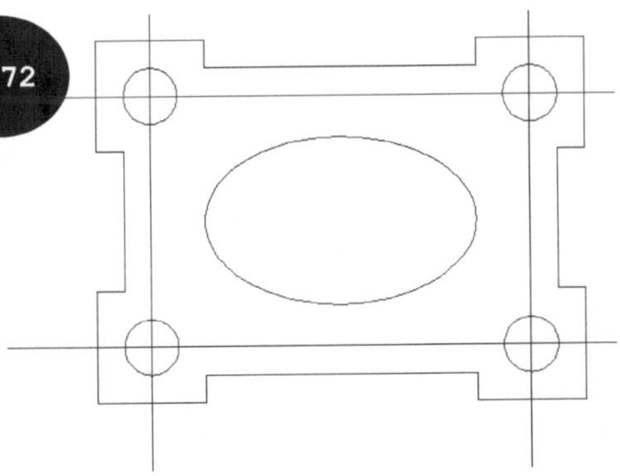

4.73

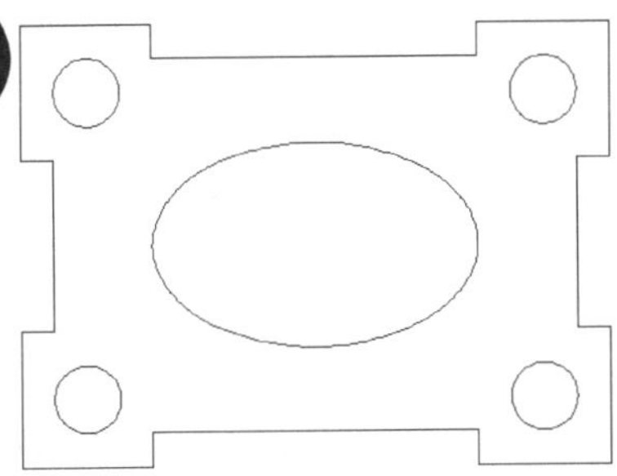

Tip: To move a set of entities to a layer, select the entities to be moved. Next, invoke the **Layer** drop-down list in the **Layers** panel of the **Home** tab and then click on the layer to which you want to move the selected set of entities.

Section 7: Saving the Drawing

After creating the drawing, you need to save it.

1. Click on the **Save** tool in the **Quick Access Toolbar**. The **Save Drawing As** dialog box appears.

2. Browse to the *AutoCAD* folder and then create a folder with the name *Chapter 4* inside the *AutoCAD* folder.

3. Enter **Tutorial 1** in the **File name** field of the dialog box and then click on the **Save** button. The drawing gets saved with the name Tutorial 1 in the *Chapter 4* folder.

Tutorial 2

Create the drawing shown in Figure 4.74. The dimensions shown in the figure are for your reference only.

4.74

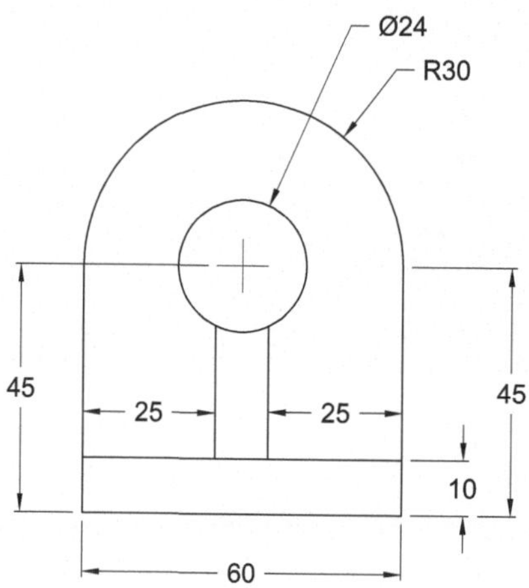

Section 1: Starting AutoCAD

1. Start AutoCAD and click on the **New** tool in the **Quick Access Toolbar**, which is at the top left corner of AutoCAD. The **Select template** dialog box appears.

2. In the **Select template** dialog box, click on the ***acad.dwt*** template and then click on the **Open** button. A new drawing file with the ***acad.dwt*** template gets invoked.

Section 2: Defining Drawing Limits

1. Define the drawing limits. You can define the drawing limits based on the overall dimensions of the drawing and keep some extra space for placing dimensions in the drawing area.

Section 3: Creating Drawing

1. Click on the **Rectangle** tool in the **Draw** panel of the **Home** tab. The **Rectangle** tool gets activated, and you are prompted to specify the first corner of the rectangle. Alternatively, you can enter **REC** in the Command Line window and then press ENTER to activate the **Rectangle** tool.

```
Specify first corner point or [Chamfer Elevation Fillet Thickness
Width]:
```

2. Click in the drawing area to specify the first corner of the rectangle. You are prompted to specify the other corner of the rectangle.

```
Specify other corner point or [Area Dimensions Rotation]:
```

You need to create a rectangle by specifying dimensions (length 60 units and width 10 units).

3. Click on the **Dimensions** option in the command prompt. You are prompted to specify the length of the rectangle. Alternatively, you can enter **D** and then press ENTER.

```
Specify length for rectangles <0.0000>:
```

4. Enter **60** as the length of the rectangle and then press ENTER. You are prompted to specify the width of the rectangle.

```
Specify width for rectangles <0.0000>:
```

5. Enter **10** as the width of the rectangle and then press ENTER. You are prompted to specify another corner of the rectangle.

```
Specify other corner point or [Area Dimensions Rotation]:
```

6. Click to specify the corner point of the rectangle in the drawing area. A rectangle of length 60 units and width 10 units is created in the drawing area, see Figure 4.75.

4.75

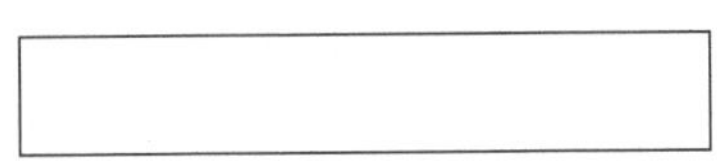

Now, you need to create the line entities of the drawing.

7. Click on the **Line** tool in the **Draw** panel. You are prompted to specify the first point of the line. Alternatively, you can enter **L** in the Command Line window and then press ENTER.

```
Specify first point:
```

8. Move the cursor over the upper left corner of the rectangle and then click to specify the start point of the line when the cursor snaps to it. You are prompted to specify the next point of the line.

```
Specify next point or [Undo]:
```

9. Move the cursor vertically upward and then enter **35** as the length of the line. Next, press ENTER. A line of length 35 units gets created, see Figure 4.76. Ensure that the Ortho mode and the Dynamic Input mode are activated.

10. Right-click and then select the **Enter** option from the shortcut menu that appears to exit from the **Line** tool.

11. Similarly, draw another vertical line of the same length starting from the upper right corner of the rectangle, see Figure 4.77.

4.76

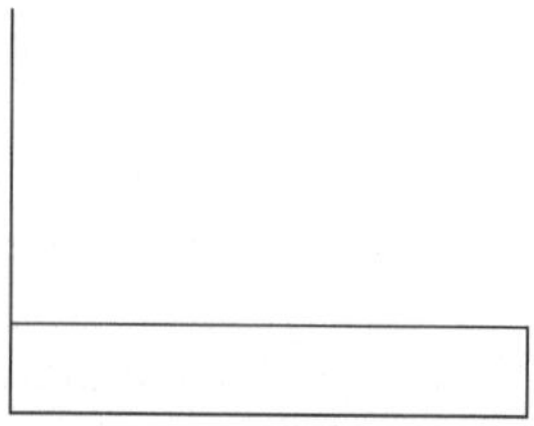

4.77

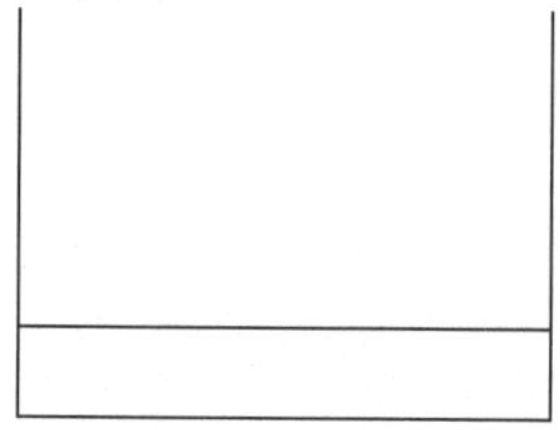

After creating the line entities, you need to create an arc of radius 30 units.

12. Invoke the **Arc** flyout and then click on the **Start, End, Radius** tool. You are prompted to specify the start point of the arc.

```
Specify start point of arc or [Center]:
```

13. Move the cursor over the endpoint of the right vertical line and then click to specify the start point of the arc when the cursor snaps to it. You are prompted to specify the endpoint of the arc.

```
Specify end point of arc:
```

14. Move the cursor over the endpoint of the left vertical line and then click to specify the endpoint of the arc when the cursor snaps to it. You are prompted to specify the radius of the arc.

```
Specify radius of arc (hold Ctrl to switch direction):
```

15. Move the cursor vertically upward and then enter **30** as the radius of the arc. Next, press ENTER. An arc with a radius of 30 units gets created, see Figure 4.78.

4.78

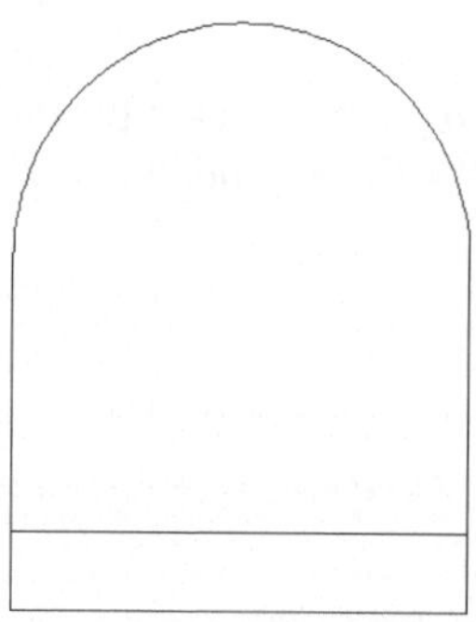

After creating the arc, you need to create a circle such that it is concentric to the arc drawn.

16. Invoke the **Center, Radius** tool in the **Draw** panel. The **Center, Radius** tool gets activated, and you are prompted to specify the center point of the circle. Alternatively, you can enter **C** in the Command Line window and then press ENTER.

```
Specify center point for circle or [3P 2P Ttr (tan tan radius)]:
```

17. Move the cursor over the circumference of the previously drawn arc and then toward its center point. Next, click to specify the center point of the circle when the cursor snaps to the center point of the arc. You are prompted to specify the radius of the circle.

```
Specify radius of circle or [Diameter]:
```

18. Enter **12** as the radius of the circle and then press ENTER. A circle of radius 12 units gets created, see Figure 4.79.

4.79

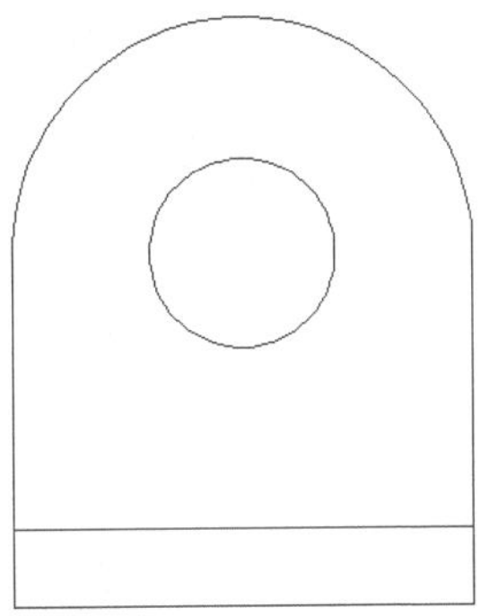

Now, you need to draw two inner vertical lines in the drawing with the help of construction lines (xlines).

19. Expand the **Draw** panel of the **Home** tab and then click on the **Construction Line** tool. You are prompted to specify the start point of the construction line (xline). Alternatively, you can enter XLINE in the Command Line window to invoke the tool.

```
Specify a point or [Hor Ver Ang Bisect Offset]:
```

20. Click on the **Offset** option of the command prompt or enter **O** and then press ENTER. You are prompted to specify the offset distance.

```
Specify offset distance or [Through] <Through>:
```

21. Enter **25** as the offset distance and then press ENTER. You are prompted to select a line object.

```
Select a line object:
```

22. Click on the left vertical line. You are prompted to specify a side to offset the construction line.

```
Specify side to offset:
```

23. Click anywhere on the right side of the selected line. A construction line (xline) at an offset distance of 25 units from the left vertical line gets created, see Figure 4.80. Also, you are prompted to select a line object.

```
Select a line object:
```

24. Click on the right vertical line. You are prompted to specify a side to offset the construction line.

```
Specify side to offset:
```

25. Click anywhere on the left side of the selected line. A construction line (xline) at an offset distance of 25 units from the right vertical line gets created, see Figure 4.81. Next, right-click to exit the tool.

4.80

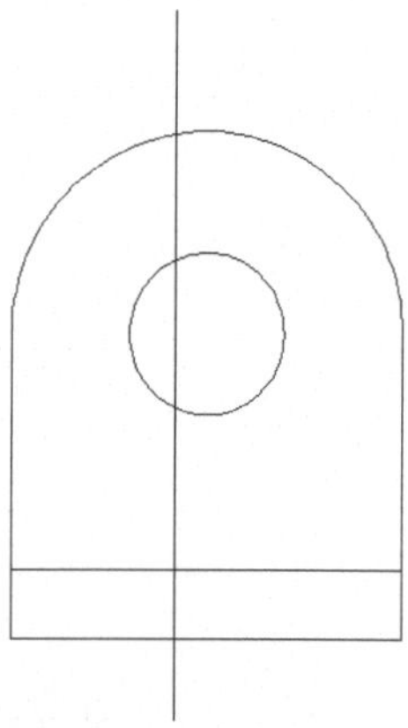

4.81

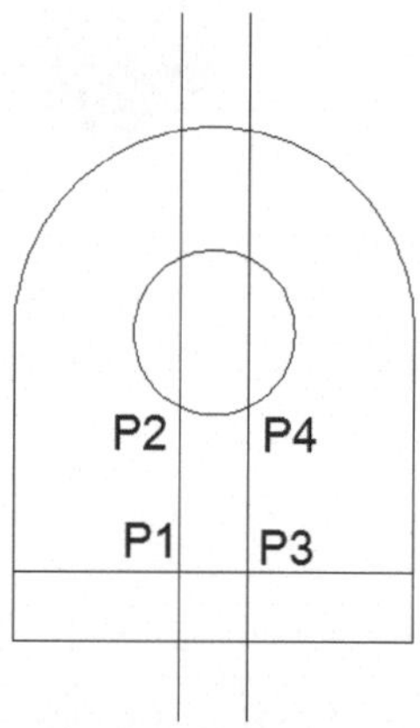

After creating the construction lines (xlines), you can use them to create vertical lines in the drawing.

26. Invoke the **Line** tool and then create a vertical line whose start point is at the intersection P1 and endpoint is at the intersection P2, refer to Figure 4.81.

27. Similarly, create another vertical line whose start point is at intersection P3 and endpoint is at intersection P4, refer to Figure 4.81.

28. After creating all the drawing entities, you can delete the construction lines. However, it is recommended that you create a layer named Construction, and then move the construction lines to this layer. Next, hide the Construction layer. Figure 4.82 shows the final drawing after hiding the construction lines.

4.82

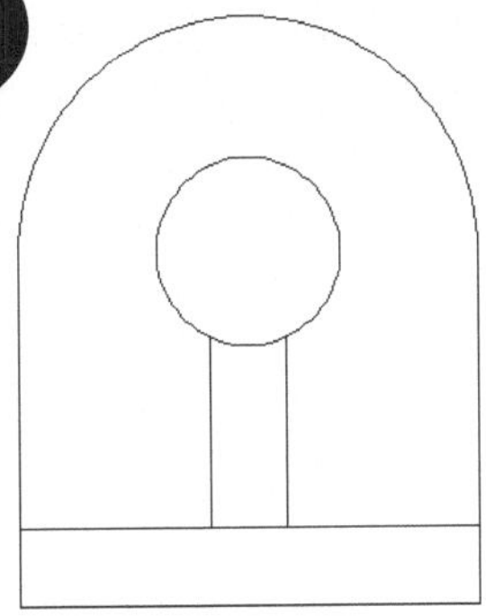

Section 4: Saving the Drawing

After creating the drawing, you need to save it.

1. Click on the **Save** tool in the **Quick Access Toolbar**. The **Save Drawing As** dialog box appears.

2. Browse to the *Chapter 4 folder* inside the *AutoCAD* folder. If the *Chapter 4 folder is* not created in Tutorial 1 of this chapter, then you first need to create this folder.

3. Enter **Tutorial 2** in the **File name** field of the dialog box and then click on the **Save** button. The drawing gets saved with the name Tutorial 2 in the *Chapter 4* folder.

Tutorial 3

Create the drawing shown in Figure 4.83. You need to create the drawing by using polylines and donut. The dimensions shown in the figure are for your reference only.

4.83

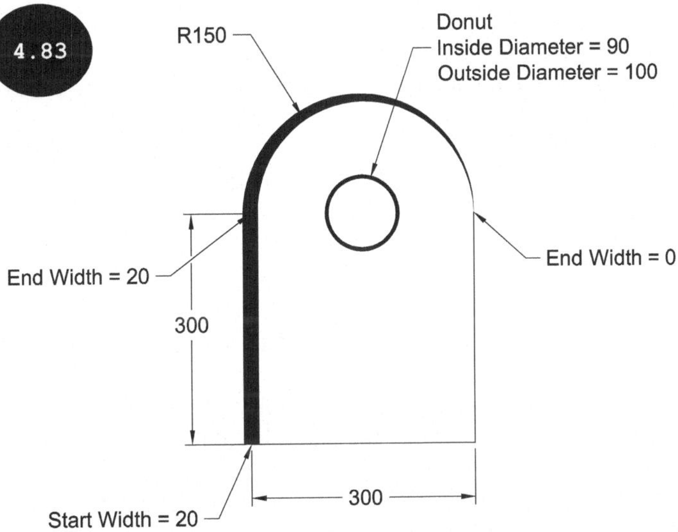

Section 1: Starting AutoCAD

1. Start a new drawing file in AutoCAD. Ensure that the Drafting & Annotation workspace is activated.

2. Define the drawing limits.

Section 2: Creating a Drawing

1. Click on the **Polyline** tool in the **Draw** panel. You are prompted to specify the start point of the polyline. Alternatively, you can enter **PL** in the Command Line window.

   ```
   Specify start point:
   ```

2. Click in the drawing area to specify the start point of the polyline. You are prompted to specify the next point of the polyline.

   ```
   Specify next point or [Arc Halfwidth Length Undo Width]:
   ```

3. Click on the **Width** option in the command prompt or enter **W** and then press ENTER. You are prompted to specify the starting width of the polyline.

   ```
   Specify starting width <0.0000>:
   ```

4. Enter **20** as the starting width of the polyline and then press ENTER. You are prompted to specify the end width of the polyline.

   ```
   Specify ending width <20.0000>:
   ```

5. Enter **20** as the end width of the polyline and then press ENTER. You are prompted to specify the next point of the polyline.

   ```
   Specify next point or [Arc Halfwidth Length Undo Width]:
   ```

6. Ensure that the Ortho mode is activated. Next, move the cursor vertically upward to a distance in the drawing area.

7. Enter **300** as the length of the polyline and then press ENTER. You are prompted to specify the next point of the polyline.

   ```
   Specify next point or [Arc Close Halfwidth Length Undo Width]:
   ```

   Now, you need to create a polyarc having starting width of 20 units and end width as 0.

8. Click on the **Arc** option in the command prompt or enter **A** in the Command Line window and then press ENTER. You are prompted to specify the endpoint of the arc.

   ```
   Specify endpoint of arc (hold Ctrl to switch direction) or [Angle
   CEnter Close Direction Halfwidth Line Radius Second pt Undo Width]:
   ```

9. Click on the **Width** option in the command prompt or enter W in the Command Line window and then press ENTER. You are prompted to specify the starting width of the arc.

   ```
   Specify starting width <20.0000>:
   ```

10. Enter **20** as the starting width of the arc and then press ENTER. You are prompted to specify the end width of the arc.

    ```
    Specify ending width <20.0000>:
    ```

11. Enter **0** (Zero) as the end width of the polyline and then press ENTER. You are prompted to specify the endpoint of the arc.

    ```
    Specify endpoint of arc (hold Ctrl to switch direction) or [Angle CEnter Close Direction Halfwidth Line Radius Second pt Undo Width]:
    ```

12. Move the cursor horizontally toward the right and then enter **300**. Next, press ENTER. A polyarc gets created, see Figure 4.84. Also, you are prompted to specify the endpoint of the arc.

    ```
    Specify endpoint of arc (hold Ctrl to switch direction) or [Angle CEnter Close Direction Halfwidth Line Radius Second pt Undo Width]:
    ```

13. Enter **L** and then press ENTER to invoke the Line mode of the polyline. You are prompted to specify the next point of the line.

    ```
    Specify next point or [Arc Close Halfwidth Length Undo Width]:
    ```

14. Move the cursor vertically downward and then enter **300** as the length of the line. Next, press ENTER. You are prompted to specify the next point of the line.

    ```
    Specify next point or [Arc Close Halfwidth Length Undo Width]:
    ```

15. Enter **C** in the Command Line window and then press ENTER or click on the **Close** option in the command prompt to close the polyline, see Figure 4.85.

4.84

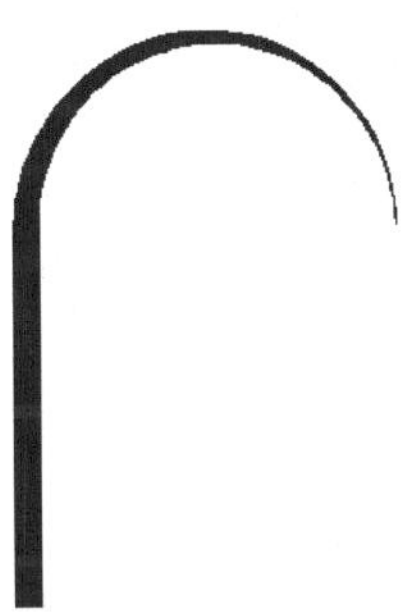

4.85

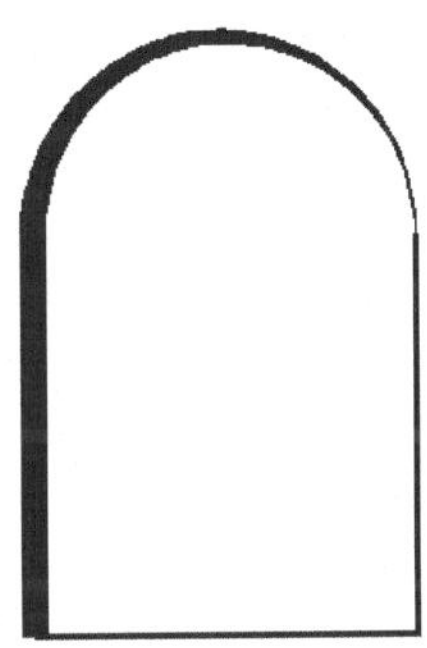

Section 3: Creating a Donut

1. Expand the **Draw** panel of the **Home** tab and then click on the **Donut** tool. You are prompted to specify the inside diameter of the donut. Alternatively, enter **DO** in the Command Line window and then press ENTER.

```
Specify inside diameter of donut <0.0000>:
```

2. Enter **90** as the inside diameter of the donut and then press ENTER. You are prompted to specify the outside diameter of the donut.

```
Specify outside diameter of donut <0.0000>:
```

3. Enter **100** as the outside diameter of the donut and then press ENTER. A donut of the specified parameter gets attached to the cursor. Also, you are prompted to specify the center point of the donut.

```
Specify center of donut or <exit>:
```

4. Ensure that Object Snap mode is activated.

5. Move the cursor over the circumference of the arc and then toward the center point of the arc. Next, click to specify the center point of the donut when the cursor snaps to the center point of the arc. A donut gets created in the drawing area, see Figure 4.86.

6. Press ENTER or right-click to exit from the **Donut** tool. Figure 4.86 shows the final drawing.

4.86

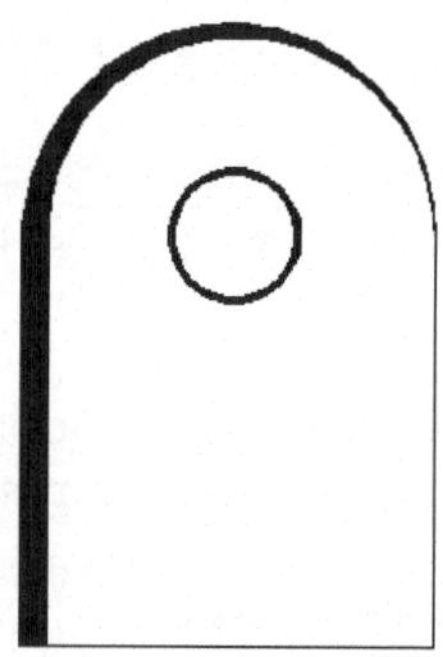

Section 4: Saving the Drawing

After creating the drawing, you need to save it.

1. Click on the **Save** tool in the **Quick Access Toolbar**. The **Save Drawing As** dialog box appears.

2. Browse to the *Chapter 4* folder inside the *AutoCAD* folder.

3. Enter **Tutorial 3** in the **File name** field of the dialog box and then click on the **Save** button. The drawing gets saved with the name Tutorial 3 in the *Chapter 4* folder.

Hands-on Test Drive 1

Create the drawing shown in Figure 4.87. The dimensions shown in the figure are for your reference only. You will learn about applying dimensions in later chapters.

4.87

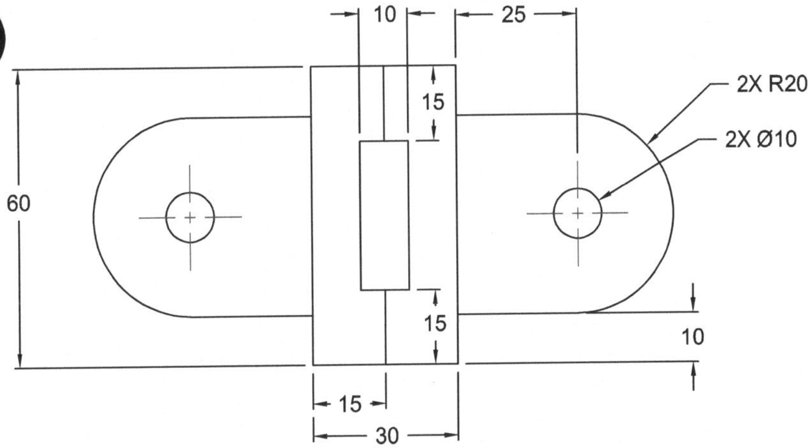

Hands-on Test Drive 2

Create the drawing shown in Figure 4.88. The dimensions shown in the figure are for your reference only.

4.88

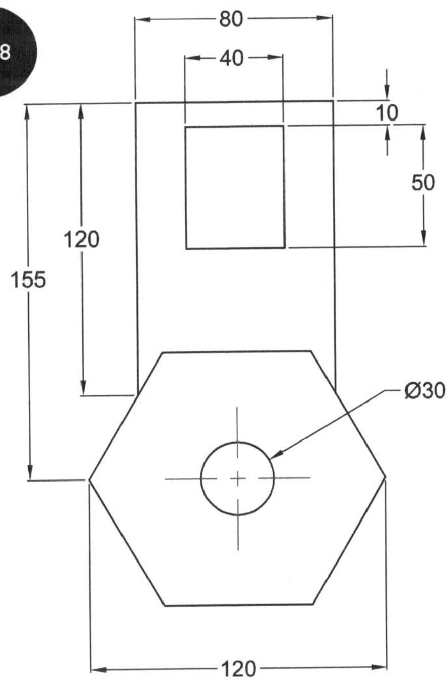

Summary

The chapter introduced methods for creating rectangles, polygons, polylines, ellipses, elliptical arcs, splines, donuts, construction lines, ray lines, and points, in addition to defining point style and size.

Questions

Complete the following sentences:

- The _________ tool is used for drawing rectangles by using different methods.
- The value entered inside the _________ symbol in the command prompt is the last defined or default value of the command.
- AutoCAD allows you to draw polygons of equal sides in the range between _________ to _________.
- In AutoCAD, you can draw two types of polygons; _________ and _________.
- You can draw a polyline by using the _________ tool.
- An ellipse is drawn by defining its _________ and _________ axes.
- You can draw an elliptical arc by using the _________ tool.
- In AutoCAD, you can draw splines by using the _________ and _________ tools.
- The _________ tool is used for creating a spline such that it passes through a set of fit points that influence the shape of the spline.
- A construction line is also known as _________.
- A _________ line is extended to infinite length in both directions and passes through two specified points.
- You can draw donuts by using the _________ tool.

CHAPTER

5

Modifying and Editing Drawings - I

In this chapter, the following topics will be discussed:

- Working with Object Selection Methods
- Invoking a Selection Method within a Command
- Trimming Drawing Entities
- Extending Drawing Entities
- Working with Arrays
- Mirroring Drawing Entities
- Filleting Drawing Entities
- Chamfering Drawing Entities
- Offsetting Drawing Entities
- Moving Drawing Objects
- Copying Drawing Objects
- Rotating Drawing Objects
- Scaling Drawing Objects
- Stretching Drawing Objects
- Lengthening Drawing Objects

Performing editing and modifying operations in a drawing is imperative to complete the drawing as per the requirements. In AutoCAD, you can perform various editing operations such as trimming unwanted entities, extending, mirroring, moving, rotating entities, and creating arrays. The tools for performing various editing and modifying operations are available in the **Modify** panel of the **Home** tab, see Figure 5.1.

5.1

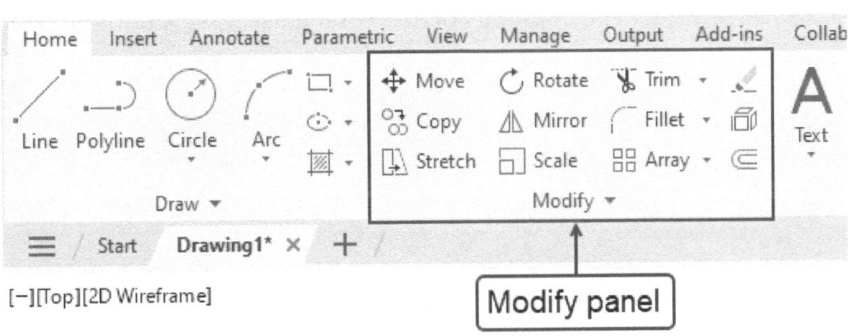

Before you learn about various editing and modifying operations, it is important to understand the different object selection methods available in AutoCAD.

Working with Object Selection Methods

In AutoCAD, you can select drawing objects individually by clicking the left mouse button. However, selecting objects one by one is time-consuming if you have to perform an editing operation on multiple objects of a drawing, for example, moving a group of objects from one location to another. AutoCAD is equipped with various selection methods such as Window selection, Cross Window selection, Crossing Polygon, Fence, and All. Out of all these, the Window selection and Cross Window selection methods are the most widely used methods. The different selection methods are discussed next.

Window Selection Method

The Window selection method is used for selecting a group of objects together by creating a rectangular window from left (P1) to right (P2) around the objects to be selected, see Figure 5.2. Note that only the objects that are completely enclosed within the rectangular window will be selected and the objects that lie partially inside the rectangular window will not be selected. Also, the boundaries of the rectangular window appear as solid outlines.

5.2

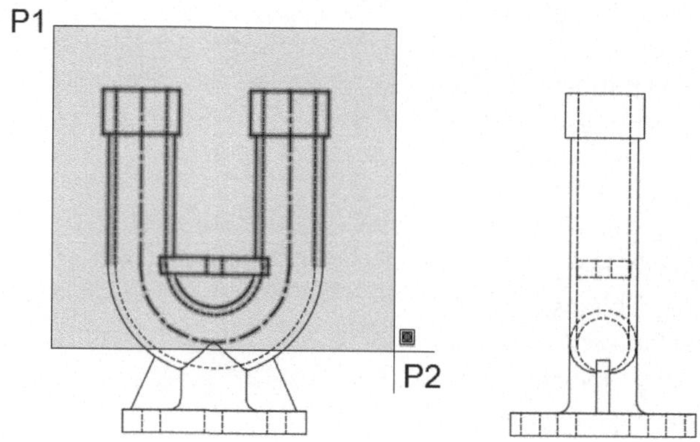

Cross Window Selection Method

The Cross Window selection method is used for selecting a group of objects together by creating a rectangular cross window from right (P1) to left (P2) around the objects to be selected, see Figure 5.3. Note that all objects that are completely enclosed as well as the objects that touch the rectangular cross window will be selected, which means that the objects that lie partially inside the rectangular cross window will also be selected. The boundary of the rectangular cross window appears as dashed outlines.

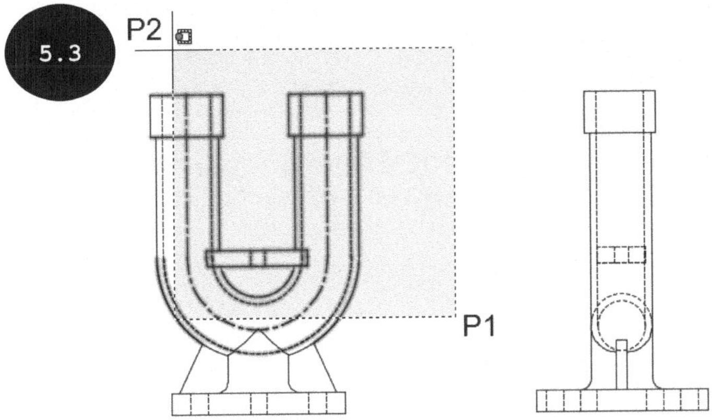

Invoking a Selection Method within a Command

In AutoCAD, you may have noticed that on invoking some of the tools/commands, you are prompted to select objects. When you are prompted to select objects, you can invoke different selection methods, as per your requirement. For example, on invoking the **Move** tool, you are prompted to select objects to be moved. Now, you can select objects by using different selection methods which are discussed next.

```
Tool/Command: M or MOVE (ENTER)
Select objects:
```

Window Selection Method

To invoke the Window selection method, when you are prompted to select objects in the command prompt, enter W in the Command Line window and then press ENTER. The method for selecting objects by using the Window selection method has been discussed earlier.

For example,

```
Tool/Command: M or MOVE (ENTER)
Select objects: W (ENTER)
Specify first corner:
Specify opposite corner:
```

Note: M is the short form of the MOVE command. This command is used for moving drawing objects from one location to another. You will learn more about the MOVE command later in this chapter.

Cross Window Selection Method

To invoke the Cross Window selection method, when you are prompted to select objects in the command prompt, enter C in the Command Line window and then press ENTER. The method for selecting objects by using the Cross Window selection method has been discussed earlier.

```
Tool/Command: M or MOVE (ENTER)
Select objects: C (ENTER)
```

```
Specify first corner:
Specify opposite corner:
```

All Selection Method

The All selection method is used for selecting all drawing objects except the objects assigned to the frozen or locked layers. To invoke the All selection method, enter **ALL** in the Command Line window and then press ENTER when you are prompted to select objects in the command prompt.

For example,

Tool/Command: *M or MOVE* (***ENTER***)
Select objects: *ALL* (***ENTER***)

Cross Polygon Selection Method

The Cross Polygon selection method is used for selecting a group of objects by drawing a cross polygon boundary around the objects to be selected, see Figure 5.4. Note that all the objects that are completely enclosed as well as the objects that touch the cross polygon boundary will be selected. Also, the cross polygon boundary appears as a dashed outline.

To invoke this selection method, enter **CP** in the Command Line window and then press ENTER when you are prompted to select objects in the command prompt. After invoking the Cross Polygon selection method, click in the drawing area to specify the first polygon point (P1) followed by the endpoints of the polygon lines, as required, see Figure 5.4. After drawing a cross polygon boundary around the objects to be selected, press ENTER to exit. All the objects that are completely enclosed or touch the cross polygon boundary are selected.

5.4

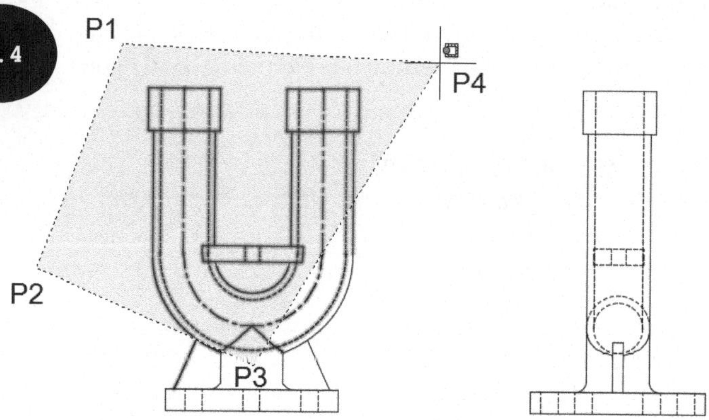

Window Polygon Selection Method

The Window Polygon selection method is used for selecting a group of objects by drawing a polygon boundary around the objects to be selected, see Figure 5.5. Note that, only the objects that are completely enclosed within the polygon boundary will be selected. The polygon boundary appears as a solid outline.

5.5

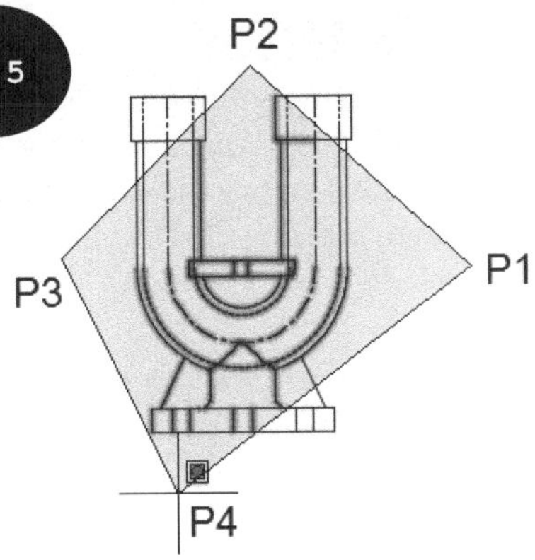

To invoke this selection method, enter **WP** in the Command Line window and then press ENTER when you are prompted to select objects in the command prompt. Next, you can click in the drawing area to specify the first polygon point (P1) followed by the endpoints of the polygon lines, as required, see Figure 5.5. After drawing a polygon boundary around the objects to be selected, press ENTER to exit. All the objects completely enclosed within the polygon boundary are selected.

Fence Selection Method

The Fence selection method is used for selecting a group of objects by drawing a series of continuous lines over the objects to be selected, see Figure 5.6. Note that the objects which come across the lines drawn will be selected.

To invoke this selection method, enter **F** in the Command Line window and then press ENTER when you are prompted to select objects in the command prompt. Next, you can click in the drawing area to specify the first point (P1) of the fence line followed by the continuous endpoints one after another, as required, see Figure 5.6. After drawing a series of continuous lines over the objects to be selected, press ENTER to exit. All the objects which come across the fence line are selected.

5.6

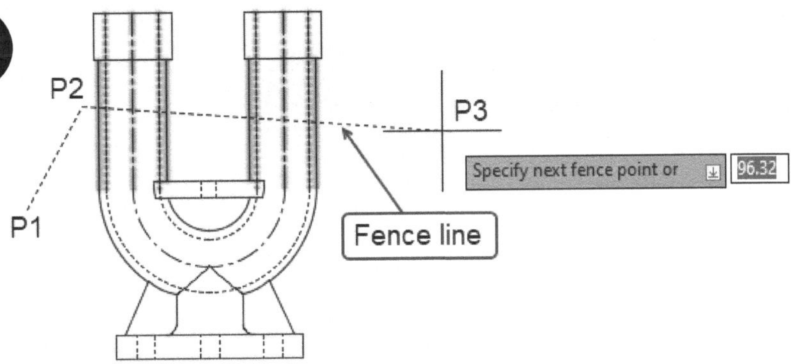

Last Selection Method

The Last selection method is used for selecting the last drawn object in the drawing. To invoke this selection method, enter **L** in the Command Line window and then press ENTER when you are prompted to select objects in the command prompt. The last drawn object gets selected.

Trimming Drawing Entities

In AutoCAD, you can trim the unwanted drawing entities of a drawing up to their nearest intersection or an intersection with cutting edges/boundaries. You can trim the entities by using the **Trim** tool of the **Modify** panel, see Figure 5.7. You can also invoke the **Trim** tool for trimming entities by entering **TR** in the Command Line window and then pressing ENTER. The method for trimming the unwanted entities of a drawing is discussed below:

5.7

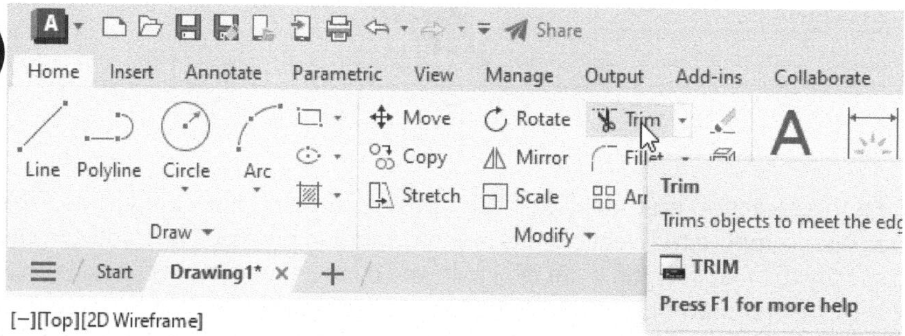

1. Click on the **Trim** tool in the **Modify** panel, see Figure 5.7. You are prompted to select objects to be trimmed to their nearest intersection. Alternatively, enter **TR** in the Command Line window and then press ENTER to invoke the **Trim** tool.

```
Select object to trim or shift-select to extend or
[cuTting edges Crossing mOde Project eRase]:
```

2. Click on the entity to be trimmed, see Figure 5.8. The portion of the selected entity where you click the left mouse button gets trimmed up to the nearest intersection, see Figure 5.9. Also, you are prompted to select another object to be trimmed.

```
Select object to trim or shift-select to extend or
[cuTting edges Crossing mOde Project eRase Undo]:
```

5.8

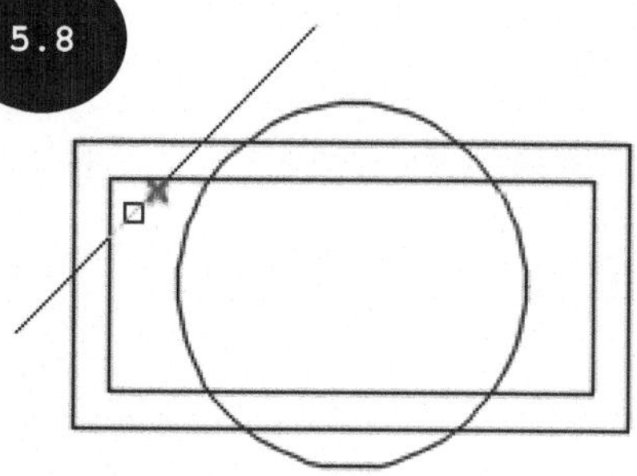

5.9

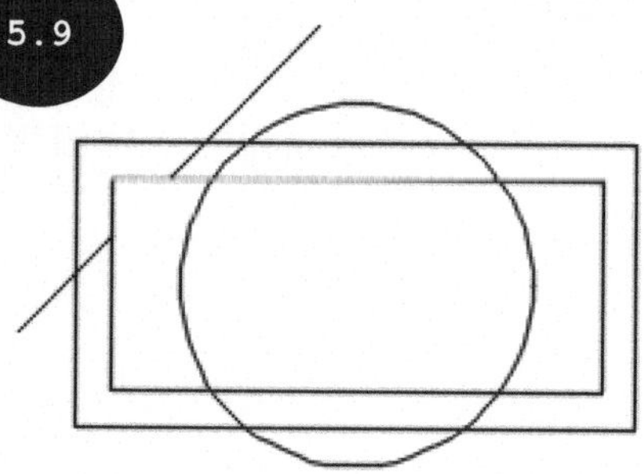

Tip: You can select the objects to be trimmed one by one by clicking the left mouse button or by clicking and dragging the cursor over multiple entities to be trimmed.

Note: Instead of trimming entities to their nearest intersection, you can define a cutting edge so that the selected entities are trimmed up to their intersection with the cutting edges. For doing so, click on the **cuTting edges** option in the command prompt or enter T and then press ENTER. You are prompted to select the cutting edges. Click on the objects/entities to be used as the cutting edges/boundaries to trim entities, see Figure 5.10. You can select rectangles, lines, circles, polylines, or construction lines as the cutting edges to trim entities. Next, press ENTER. You are prompted to select objects to be trimmed. Click on the entity to be trimmed, see Figure 5.10. The portion of the selected entity where you click the left mouse button gets trimmed up to the intersection with the cutting edges, see Figure 5.11.

5.10

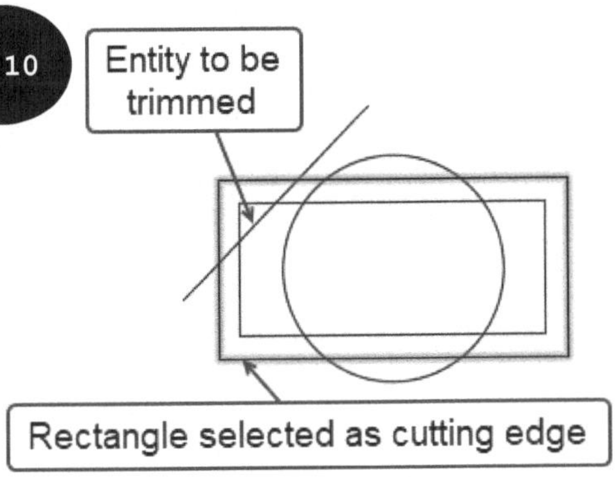

5.11

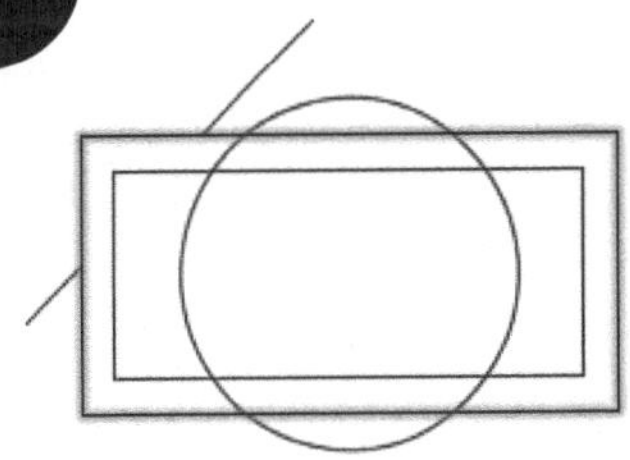

3. Similarly, click on the other entities to be trimmed one by one, see Figure 5.12. The portion of the selected entities is trimmed up to the nearest intersection, see Figure 5.13.

4. Once you have trimmed all the unwanted entities of the drawing, press ENTER to exit.

5.12

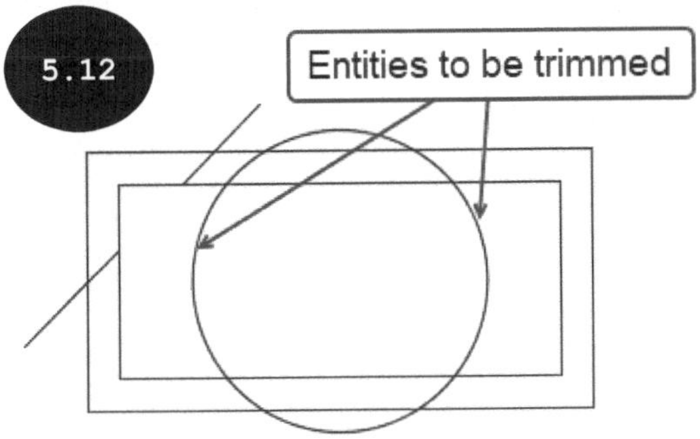

5.13

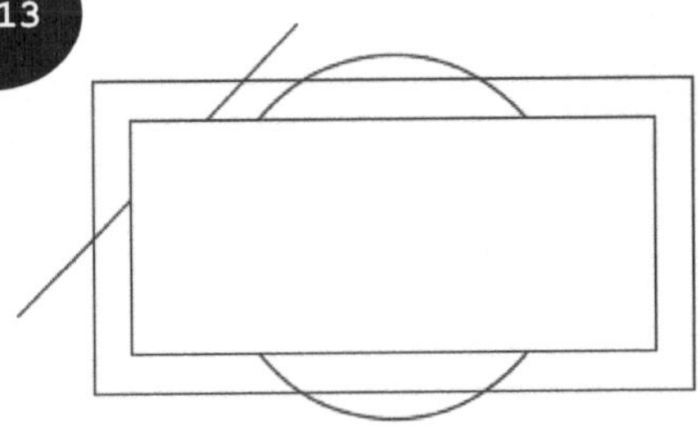

Note: You can also extend the entities up to the nearest intersection or at the intersection with cutting edges/boundaries by using the **Trim** tool. To extend the entities by using the **Trim** tool, press and hold the SHIFT key and then click on the entity to be extended. The selected entity, from the side you have chosen, is extended up to the nearest intersection.

Extending Drawing Entities

You can extend the entities up to their nearest intersection or the intersection with boundaries by using the **Extend** tool of the **Trim** flyout in the **Modify** panel, see Figure 5.14. You can also invoke the **Extend** tool by entering **EX** in the Command Line window and then pressing ENTER. The method for extending drawing entities by using the **Extend** tool is discussed below:

5.14

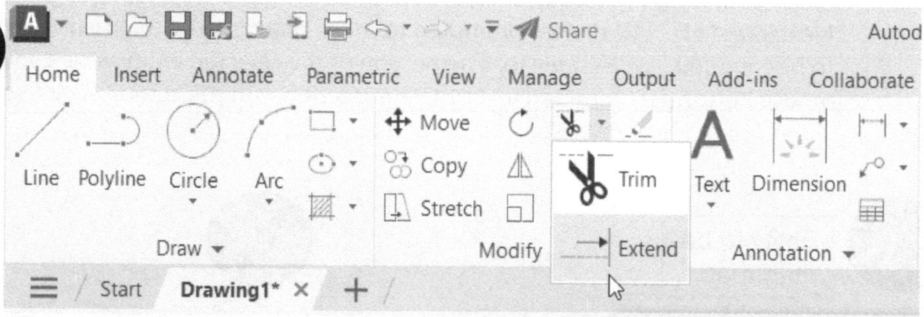

1. Click on the down arrow next to the **Trim** tool in the **Modify** panel. A flyout appears, see Figure 5.14. In this flyout, click on the **Extend** tool. You are prompted to select objects to be extended. Alternatively, enter **EX** in the Command Line window and then press ENTER to invoke the **Extend** tool.

```
Select object to extend or shift-select to trim or
[Boundary edges Crossing mOde Project]:
```

2. Click on the entity to be extended, see Figure 5.15. The portion of the selected entity is extended up to the nearest intersection, see Figure 5.16. Also, you are prompted to select another object to be extended.

```
Select object to extend or shift-select to trim or
[Boundary edges Crossing mOde Project Undo]:
```

5.15

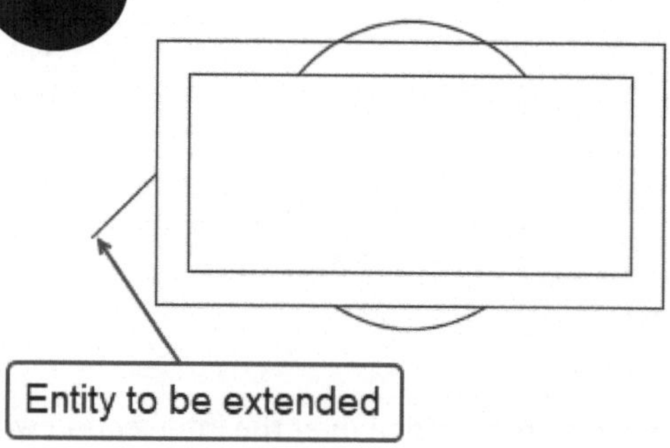

5.16

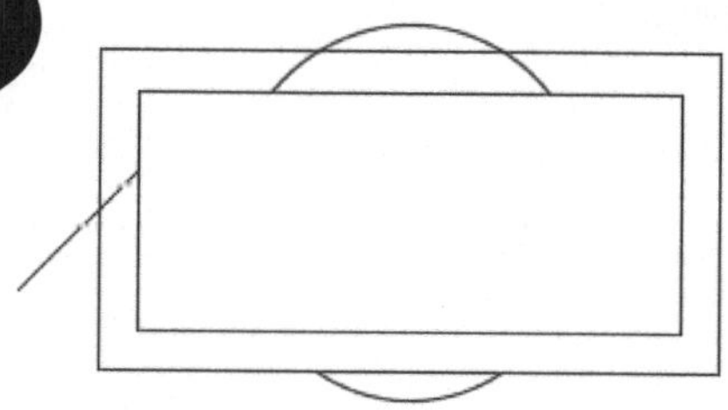

Note: If you want to extend entities up to a boundary edge instead of their nearest intersection, click on the **Boundary edges** option in the command prompt or enter **B** and then press ENTER. You are prompted to select boundary edges. Click on the objects/entities to be used as the boundary edges to extend entities, see Figure 5.17. Next, press ENTER. You are prompted to select objects to be extended. Click on the entity to be extended, see Figure 5.17. The side of the selected entity where you click the left mouse button gets extended up to the intersection with the boundary edges, see Figure 5.18.

5.17

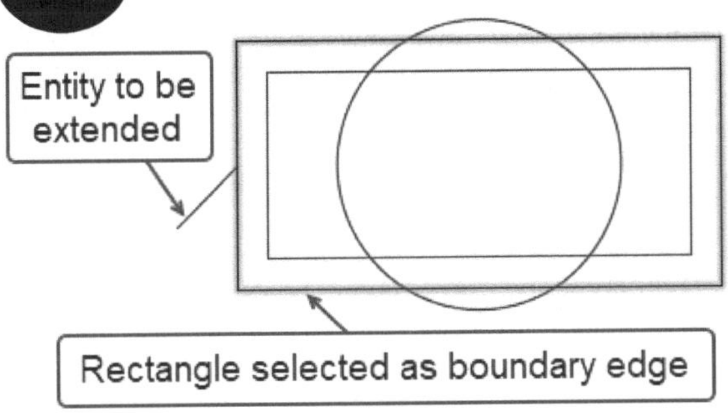

5.18

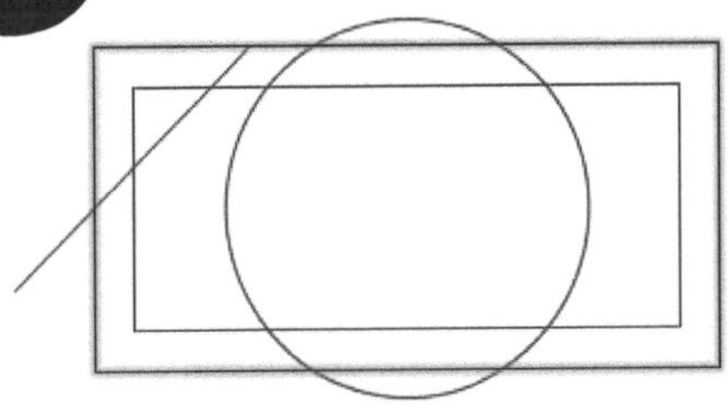

3. Similarly, click on the entities to be extended one by one, see Figure 5.19. The portion of the selected entities gets extended up to the nearest intersection, see Figure 5.20.

Tip: You can select the entities to be extended one by one by clicking the left mouse button or by clicking and dragging the cursor over multiple entities to be extended.

4. Once you have extended the required entities of a drawing, press ENTER or right-click to exit the **Extend** tool.

5.19

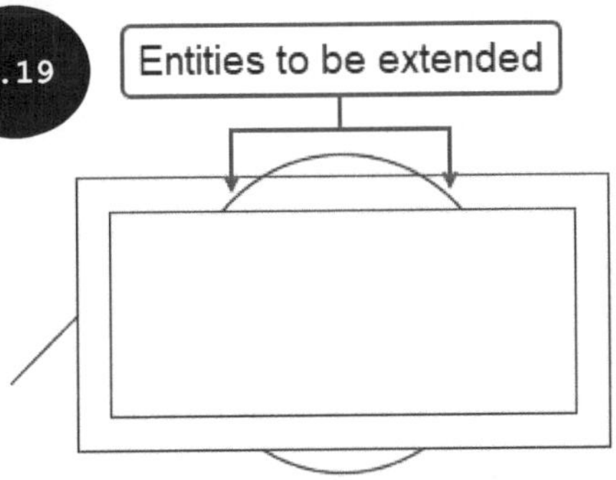

5.20

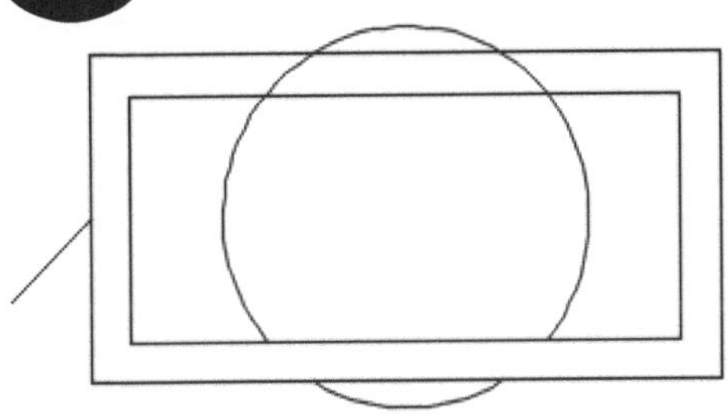

Note: You can also trim entities up to the nearest intersection or at the intersection of boundaries by using the **Extend** tool. To trim the entities by using the **Extend** tool, press and hold the SHIFT key and then click on the entity to be trimmed. The selected entity, is trimmed up to the intersection.

Working with Arrays

The Array is a very powerful feature of AutoCAD for creating multiple instances/duplicate copies of an existing geometry in a rectangular fashion, circular fashion, or along a path, see Figures 5.21 through 5.23.

5.21

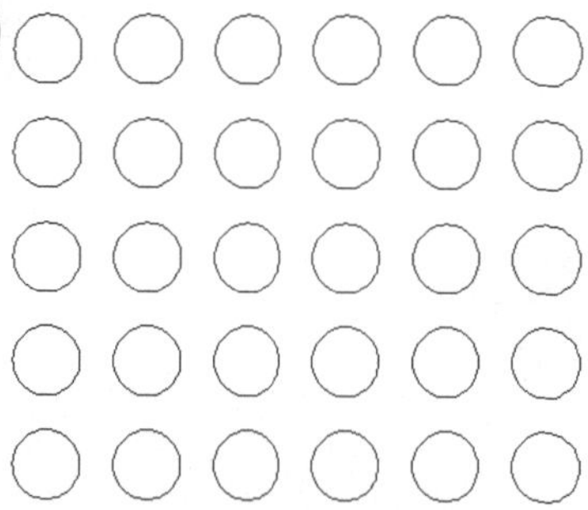

Rectangular array

5.22

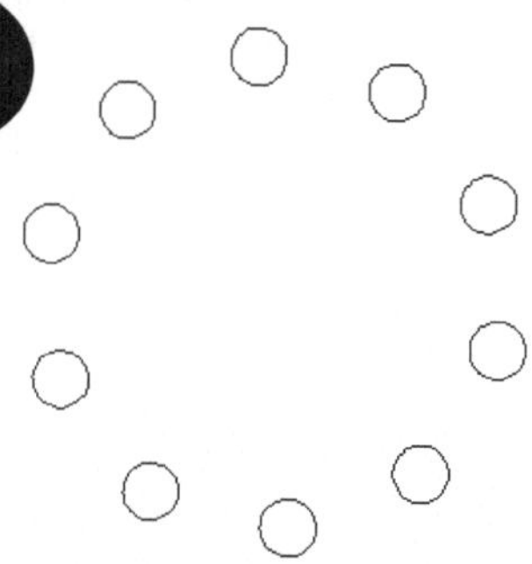

Polar/Circular array

5.23

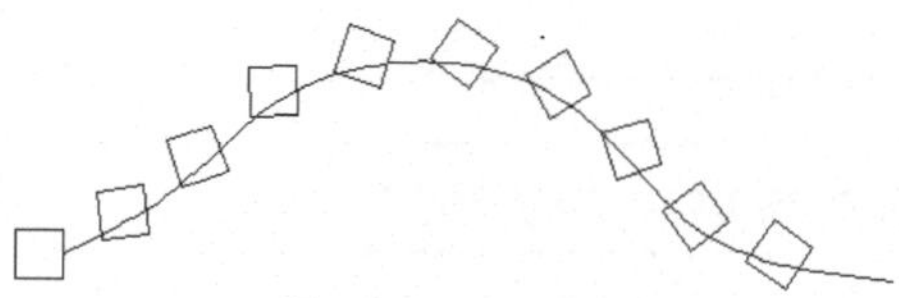

Path array

In AutoCAD, you can create a rectangular array, a polar/circular array, and a path array by using the **Rectangular Array**, **Polar Array**, and **Path Array** tools of the **Array** flyout in the **Modify** panel, see Figure 5.24. The methods for creating various types of arrays are discussed next.

5.24

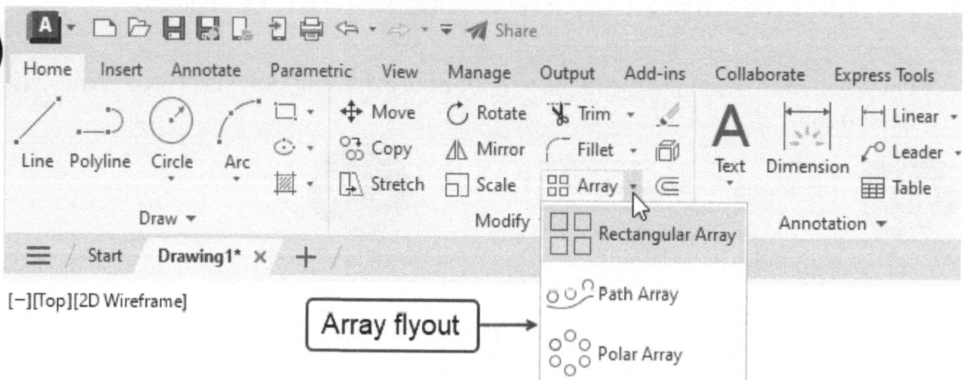

Creating a Rectangular Array

1. Invoke the **Array** flyout in the **Modify** panel (see Figure 5.24) and then click on the **Rectangular Array** tool. You are prompted to select objects. Alternatively, enter **AR** in the Command Line window and then press ENTER to invoke the tool.

```
Select objects:
```

2. Click on one or more objects in the drawing area, see Figure 5.25. Next, press ENTER or right-click. A preview of the rectangular array appears with default parameters, see Figure 5.26. Also, the **Array Creation** tab appears in the **Ribbon** which provides different options for controlling the array parameters, see Figure 5.27.

```
Select grip to edit array or [ASsociative Base point COUnt Spacing
COLumns Rows Levels eXit] <eXit>:
```

5.25

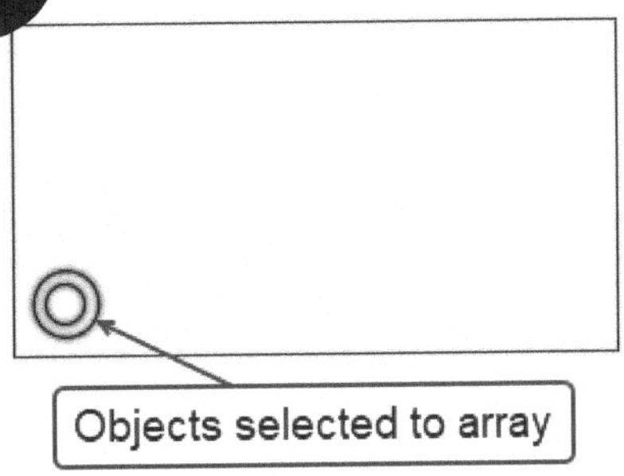

5.26

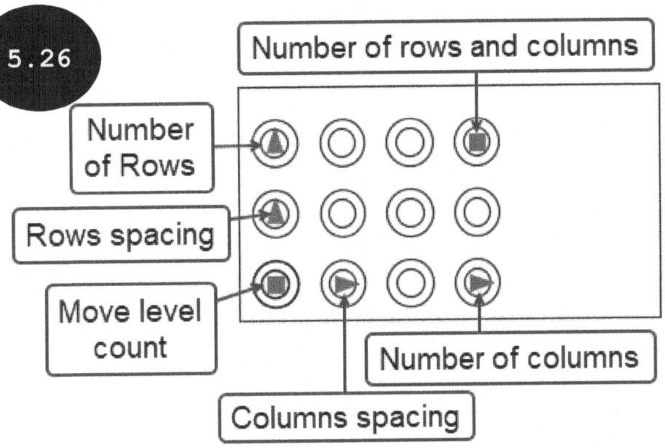

Tip: You can select the objects to be arrayed by clicking the left mouse button or by using a selection method such as Window, Cross Window, or Fence, as discussed earlier.

Note: If you have invoked the array tool by entering **AR** in Command Line window then after selecting the objects to be arrayed, you are prompted to select the type of array "`Enter array type [Rectangular PAth POlar] <Polar>:`". Click on the **Rectangular** option in the command prompt or enter **R** and then press ENTER to create the rectangular array.

3. Specify the column count, row count, column spacing, and row spacing for the rectangular array in the respective fields of the **Columns** and **Rows** panel in the **Array Creation** tab, see Figure 5.27.

5.27

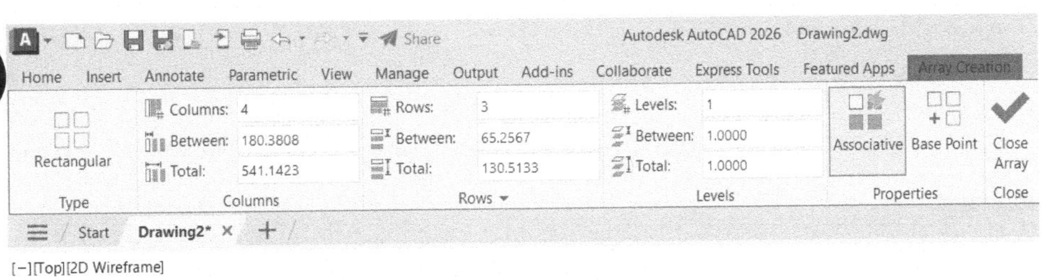

Tip: You can also use the grips that appear in the preview of the rectangular array (refer to Figure 5.26) for specifying array parameters such as columns count, rows count, and column spacing. For example, to increase or decrease the number of array columns, click on the **Number of columns** grip (refer to Figure 5.26) and then move the cursor toward the right or left to change the array columns count and then click to specify the placement point.

4. After editing the array parameters, press ENTER to exit. A rectangular array is created in the drawing area, see Figure 5.28.

5.28

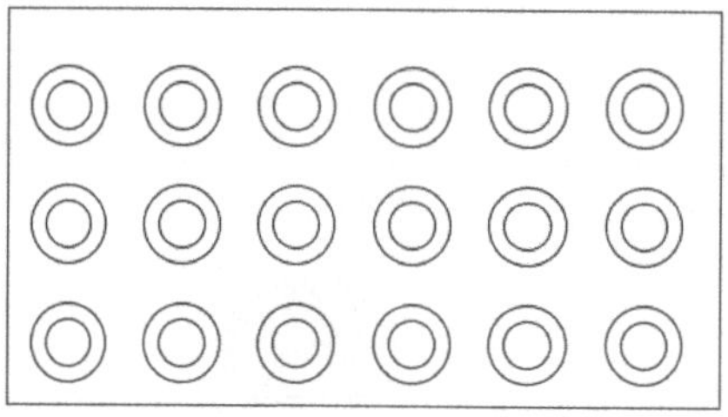

Creating a Polar/Circular Array

1. Invoke the **Array** flyout and then click on the **Polar Array** tool, see Figure 5.29. You are prompted to select objects. Alternatively, enter **AR** in the Command Line window and then press ENTER.

```
Select objects:
```

5.29

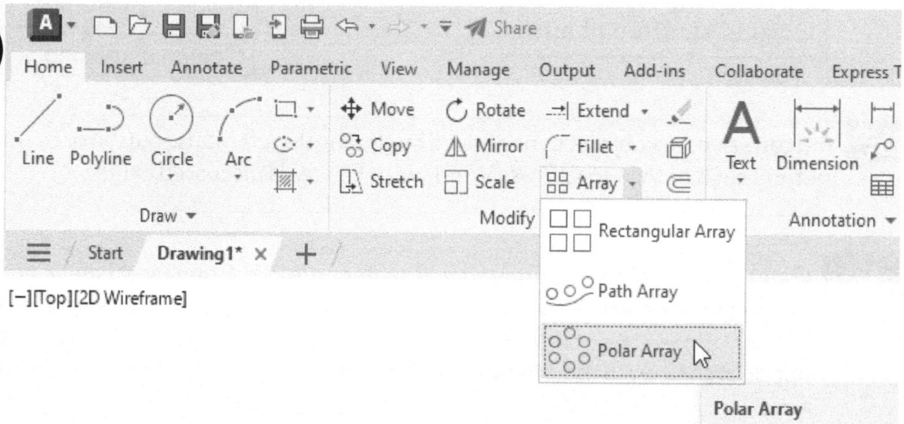

2. Select the objects in the drawing area. The selected objects get highlighted, see Figure 5.30. You can select one or more objects to be arrayed by clicking the left mouse button.

3. After selecting the objects, press ENTER or right-click. You are also prompted to specify the center point of the array.

```
Specify center point of array or [Base point Axis of rotation]:
```

Note: If you have invoked the array tool by entering **AR** in Command Line window then after selecting the objects to be arrayed, you are prompted to select the type of array; "`Enter array type [Rectangular PAth POlar] <Polar>:`". Click on the **Polar** option in the command prompt or enter **PO** in the Command Line window and then press ENTER to create the polar array.

4. Click to specify the center point of the array. The preview of the circular/polar array appears in the drawing area with default parameters, see Figure 5.31. Also, the **Array Creation** tab appears in the **Ribbon** which provides different options for controlling the array parameters. You are also prompted to select array grips to edit the array.

```
Select grip to edit array or [ASsociative Base point Items Angle
between Fill angle ROWs Levels ROTate items eXit] <eXit>:
```

5.30

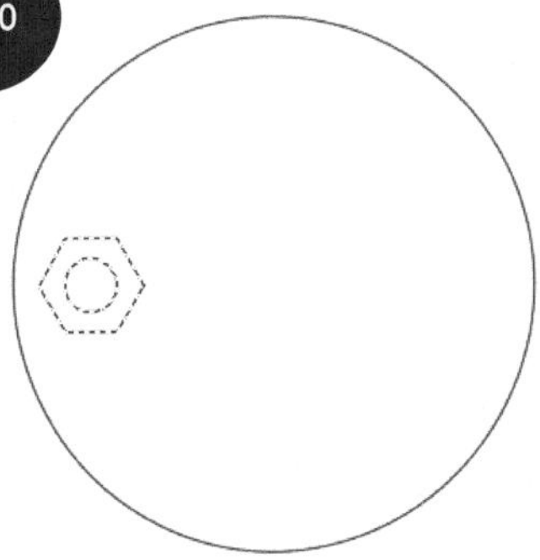

5.31

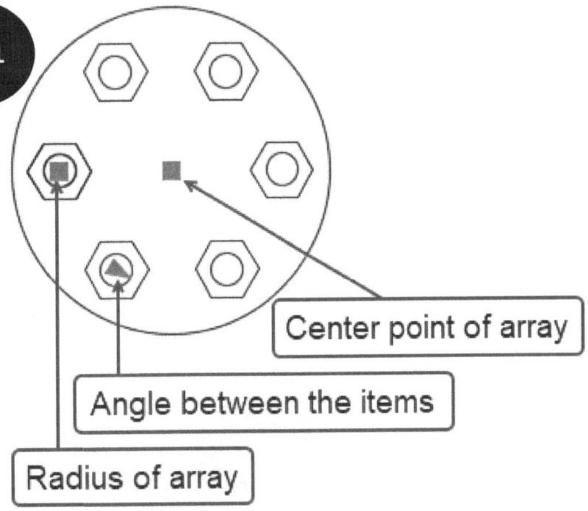

5. Specify the item count and angle between items for the circular array in the respective fields available in the **Items** panel of the **Array Creation** tab. Alternatively, use the grips, which appear in the preview of the array (refer to Figure 5.31) for specifying array parameters.

6. After editing the array parameters, press ENTER to exit. The circular/polar array gets created in the drawing area, see Figure 5.32.

5.32

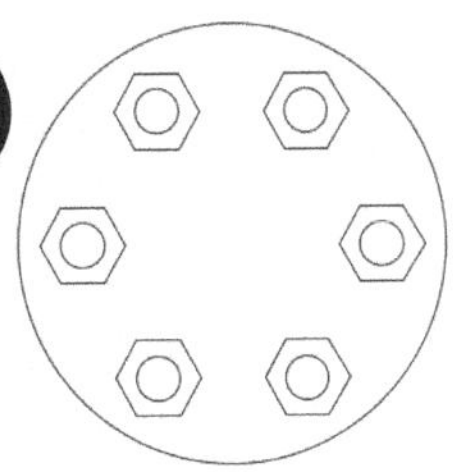

Creating a Path Array

1. Invoke the **Array** flyout and then click on the **Path Array** tool. You are prompted to select objects. Alternatively, enter **AR** in the Command Line window and then press ENTER.

```
Select objects:
```

2. Select the objects in the drawing area. The selected objects get highlighted, see Figure 5.33. For selecting multiple objects, you can use the Window or Cross Window selection method. After selecting the objects to be arrayed, press ENTER or right-click. You are also prompted to select a path curve.

```
Select path curve:
```

3. Click on the path curve along which you want to pattern the selected objects, see Figure 5.33. The preview of the path array appears in the drawing area with default parameters, see Figure 5.34. Also, the **Array Creation** tab appears in the **Ribbon** which provides different options for controlling the array parameters. You are also prompted to select grips to edit the array.

```
Select grip to edit array or [ASsociative Method Base point Tangent
direction Items Rows Levels Align items Z direction eXit] <eXit>:
```

5.33

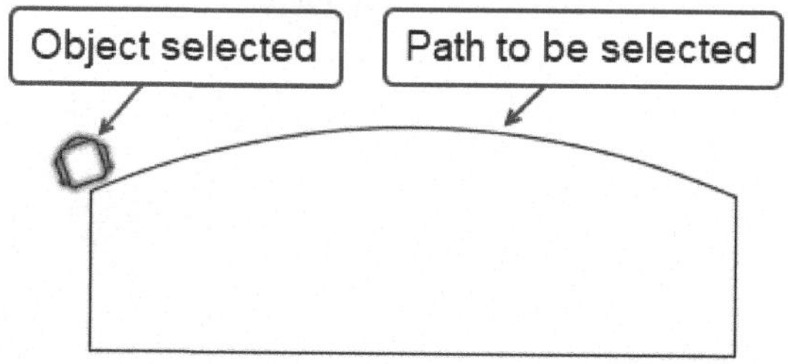

5.34

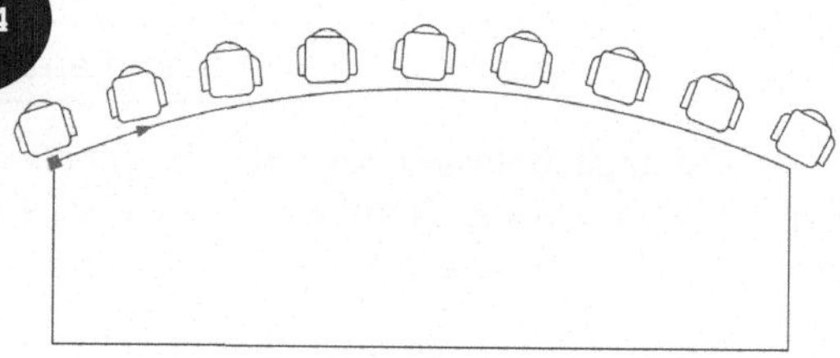

4. Specify the item spacing for the path array in the respective field available in the **Items** panel of the **Array Creation** tab. Alternatively, use the grips that appear in the preview of the path array to specify the spacing between the items.

5. After editing the array parameters, press ENTER. The path array gets created in the drawing area, see Figure 5.35.

5.35

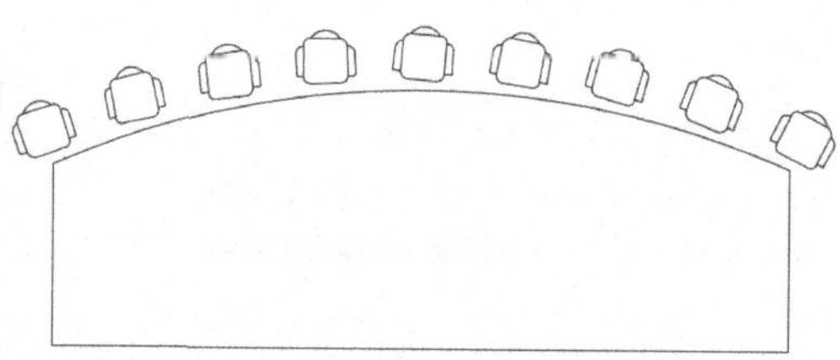

Mirroring Drawing Entities

In AutoCAD, you can create a mirror image of the drawing entities/objects about a mirroring line by using the **Mirror** tool of the **Modify** panel, see Figure 5.36. The method for mirroring drawing objects is discussed below:

5.36

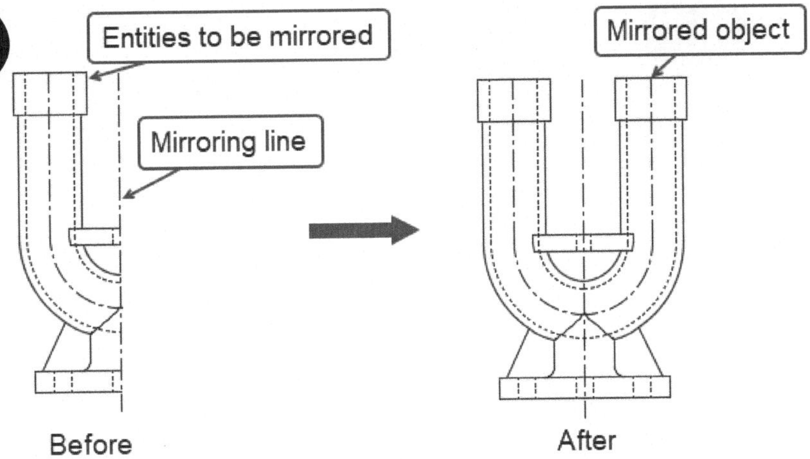

1. Click on the **Mirror** tool in the **Modify** panel. You are prompted to select objects. Alternatively, enter **MI** in the Command Line window and then press ENTER.

```
Select objects:
```

2. Select objects to be mirrored and then press ENTER. You are prompted to select the first point of the mirror line. For selecting multiple objects, you can use the Window or Cross Window selection method.

```
Specify first point of mirror line:
```

3. Click to specify the first point of the mirror line. You are prompted to select the second point of the mirror line.

```
Specify second point of mirror line:
```

4. Click to specify the second point of the mirror line. You are prompted to define whether to erase the source/original objects. By default, the **No** option is selected.

```
Erase source objects? [Yes No] <No>:
```

Note: The mirroring line is an imaginary line which can be defined by specifying two points in the drawing area.

5. Press ENTER to accept the default option (**No**) for keeping the source/original objects in the resultant drawing, see Figure 5.37 (a). The mirror image is created in the drawing area.

Note: If you do not want to keep the source/original objects in the resultant drawing, then enter **Y** in the Command Line window and then press ENTER, see Figure 5.37 (b).

5.37

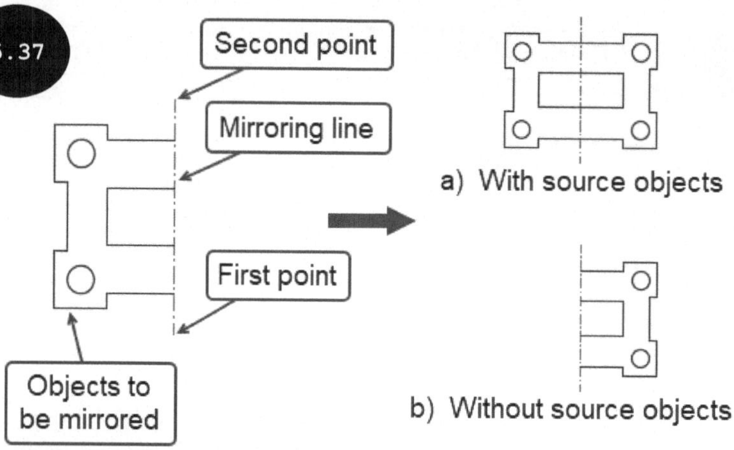

Filleting Drawing Entities

A fillet is a curved edge that is used for removing or eliminating sharp edges of a model that can cause injury while handling. Also, fillets distribute the stress of the model, which makes the model more durable and capable of withstanding larger loads. Figure 5.38 shows a drawing with fillets on its corners.

5.38

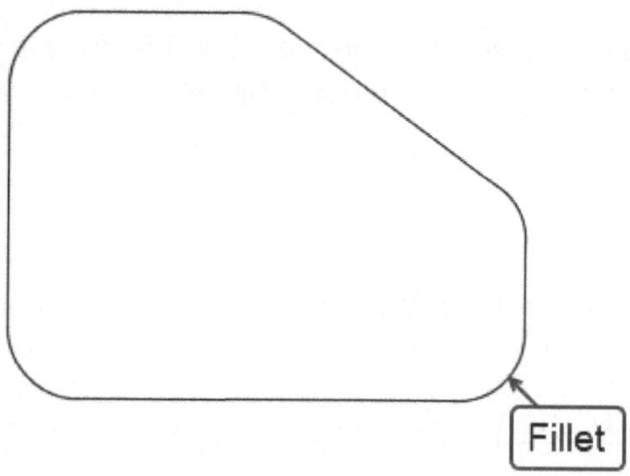

In AutoCAD, you can create a fillet between two intersecting or non-intersecting entities/objects by using the **Fillet** tool of the **Modify** panel, see Figure 5.39. The method for creating a fillet is discussed below:

5.39

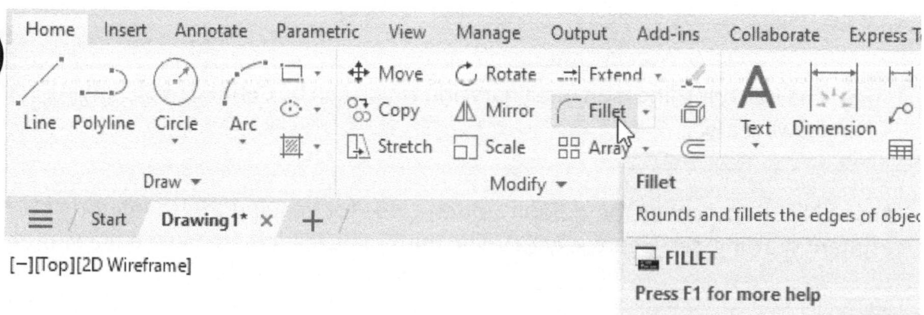

1. Click on the **Fillet** tool in the **Modify** panel, see Figure 5.39. You are prompted to select the first object. Alternatively, enter **F** in the Command Line window and then press ENTER to invoke the **Fillet** tool.

```
Select first object or [Undo Polyline Radius Trim Multiple]:
```

Before you select the first object for the fillet, it is recommended to specify the radius of the fillet. If you do not specify the fillet radius, then the default fillet radius will be applied.

2. Click on the **Radius** option in the command prompt or enter **R** in the Command Line window and then press ENTER. You are prompted to specify the fillet radius.

```
Specify fillet radius <0.0000>:
```

3. Enter the radius value and then press ENTER. You are prompted to select the first object.

```
Select first object or [Undo Polyline Radius Trim Multiple]:
```

4. Click on the first object of the fillet, see Figure 5.40. You are prompted to select the second object.

```
Select second object or shift-select to apply corner or [Radius]:
```

5. Click on the second object of the fillet, see Figure 5.40. A fillet with the specified radius is created, see Figure 5.41.

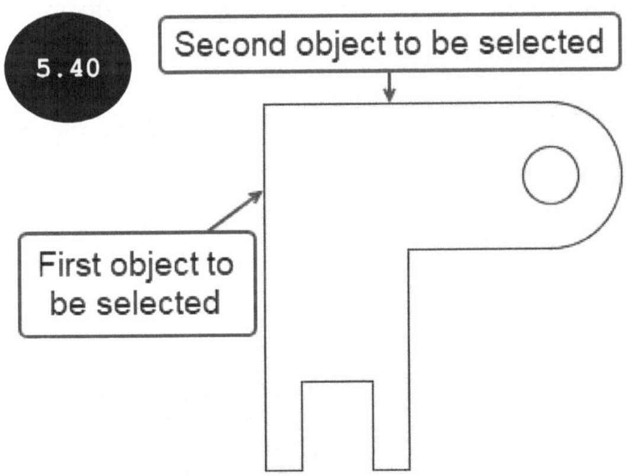

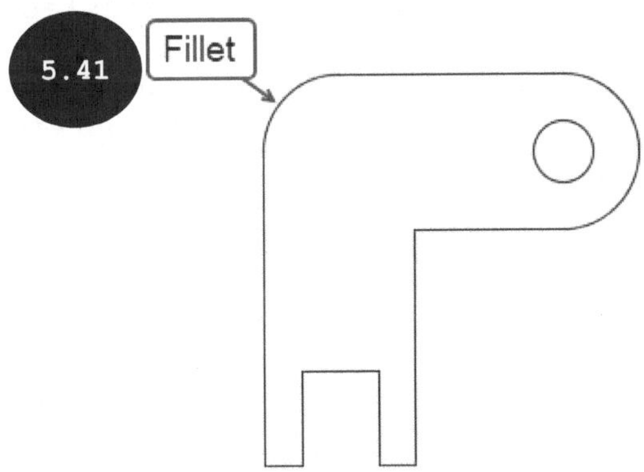

You can also fillet parallel or non-parallel entities, see Figures 5.42 and 5.43.

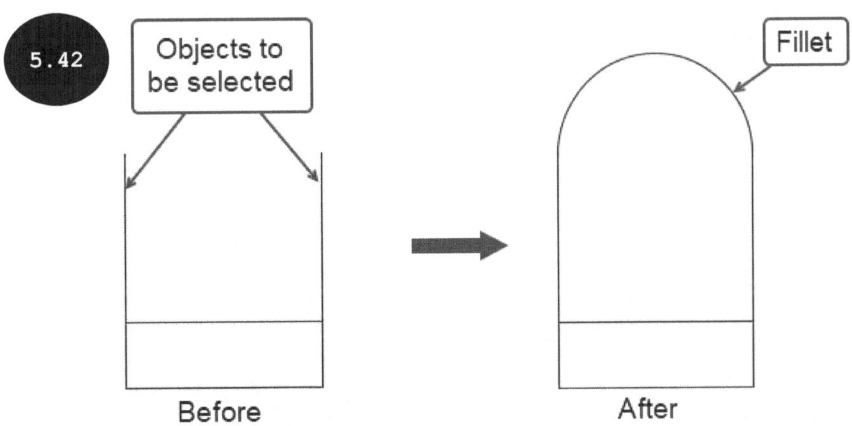

5.43

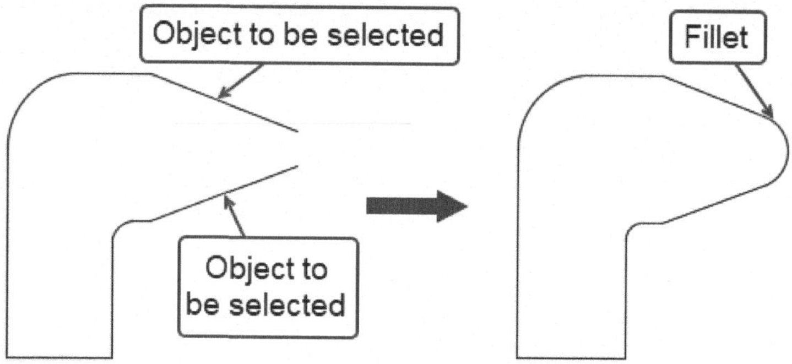

Note: You can fillet all the corners of a polyline object at a time, see Figure 5.44. For doing so, click on the **Polyline** option in the command prompt when you are prompted to select the first object "`Select first object or [Undo Polyline Radius Trim Multiple]:`". Alternatively, enter **P** in the Command Line window and then press ENTER. Next, select the polyline object whose all corners are to be filleted.

By default, when you create a fillet at a corner, an arc is created by trimming the selected objects since the trim mode is set to **Trim**, see Figure 5.45 (a). To set the trim mode to **No Trim**, click on the **Trim** option in the command prompt when you are prompted to select first object "`Select first object or [Undo Polyline Radius Trim Multiple]:`". Next, enter **N** in the Command Line window and then press ENTER. Now, on creating a fillet at a corner, an arc is created without trimming the selected objects, see Figure 5.45 (b).

5.44

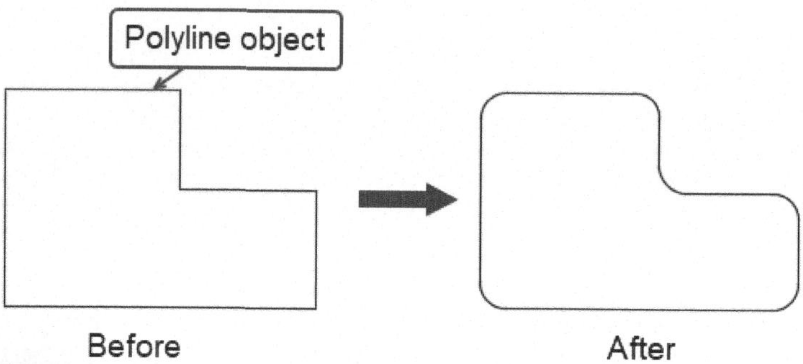

5.45

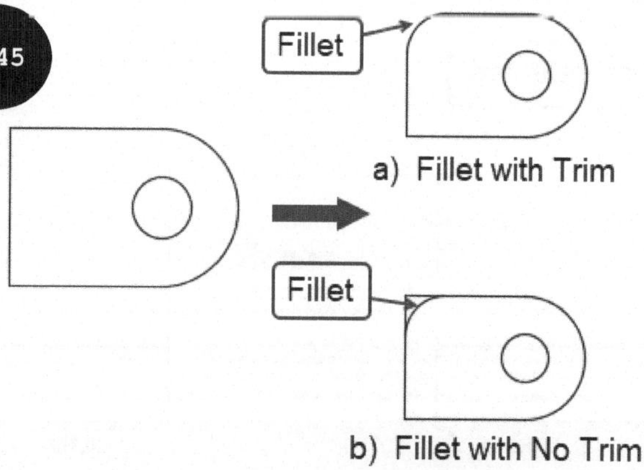

Chamfering Drawing Entities

A chamfer is a bevel edge that is non-perpendicular to its adjacent edges. In AutoCAD, you can create a chamfer by using the **Chamfer** tool of the **Modify** panel, see Figure 5.46. Figure 5.47 shows a drawing with a chamfer in its upper left corner.

5.46

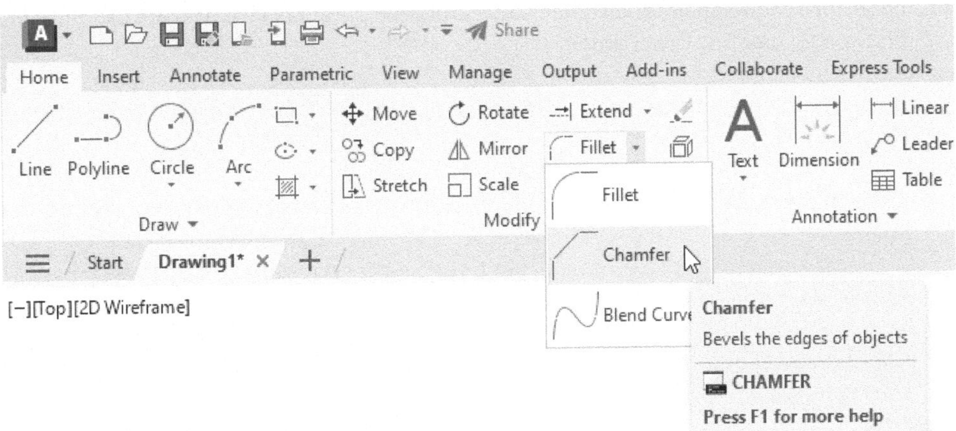

5.47

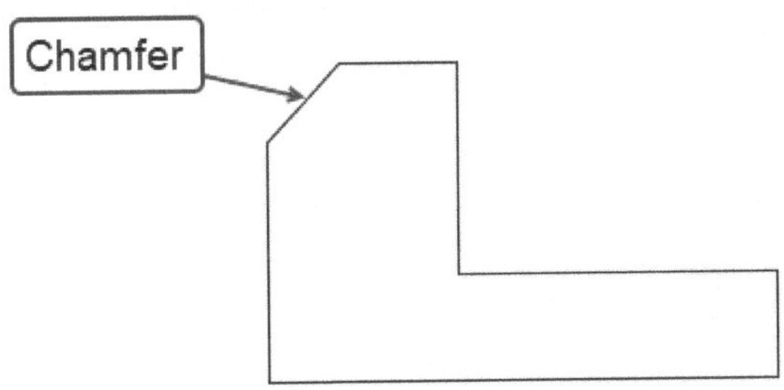

In AutoCAD, you can create a chamfer by using two methods: **Distance distance** method and **Angle distance** method. Both these methods are discussed next.

Creating a Chamfer Using the Distance Distance Method

1. Click on the down arrow next to the **Fillet** tool in the **Modify** panel. A flyout appears. In this flyout, click on the **Chamfer** tool, see Figure 5.46. Alternatively, enter **CHA** in the Command Line window and then press ENTER. You are prompted to select the first line for creating a chamfer.

```
Select first line or [Undo Polyline Distance Angle Trim mEthod
Multiple]:
```

   Before you select the first line for the chamfer, it is recommended to define the type of method for creating the chamfer.

2. Click on the **Distance** option in the command prompt or enter **D** and then press ENTER to invoke the **Distance Distance** method. You are prompted to specify the first chamfer distance.

```
Specify first chamfer distance <0.0000>:
```

3. Enter the first chamfer distance value and then press ENTER. You are prompted to specify the second chamfer distance.

```
Specify second chamfer distance <0.0000>:
```

4. Enter the second chamfer distance value and then press ENTER. You are prompted to select the first line for creating the chamfer.

```
Select first line or [Undo Polyline Distance Angle Trim mEthod Multiple]:
```

5. Click on the first chamfer line, see Figure 5.48. You are prompted to select second chamfer line.

```
Select second line or shift-select to apply corner or [Distance Angle Method]:
```

6. Click on the second chamfer line, see Figure 5.48. A chamfer with the specified distance is created, see Figure 5.49.

5.48

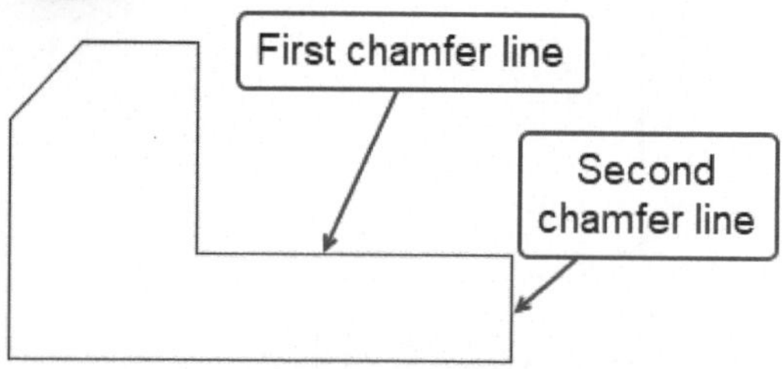

5.49

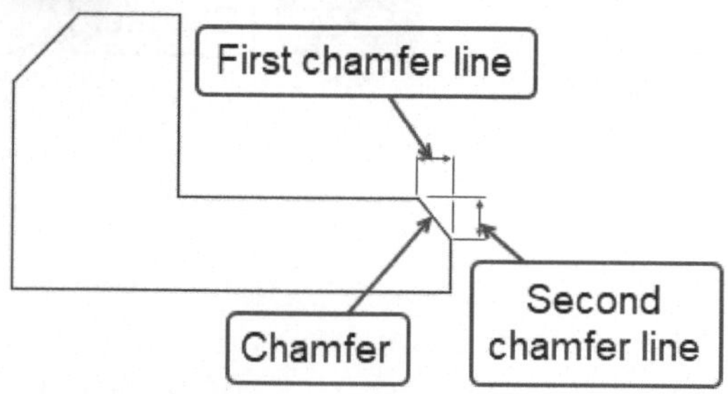

Creating a Chamfer Using the Angle Distance Method

1. Click on the down arrow next to the **Fillet** tool in the **Modify** panel. A flyout appears. In this flyout, click on the **Chamfer** tool. Alternatively, enter **CHA** in the Command Line window and then press ENTER. You are prompted to select the first line for creating a chamfer.

```
Select first line or [Undo Polyline Distance Angle Trim mEthod Multiple]:
```

2. Click on the **Angle** option in the command prompt or enter **A** and then press ENTER to invoke the **Angle Distance** method. You are prompted to specify the chamfer length on the first line.

```
Specify chamfer length on the first line <0.0000>:
```

3. Enter the chamfer length value and then press ENTER. You are prompted to specify the chamfer angle.

```
Specify chamfer angle from the first line <0>:
```

4. Enter the chamfer angle value and then press ENTER. You are prompted to select the chamfer first line.

```
Select first line or [Undo Polyline Distance Angle Trim mEthod
Multiple]:
```

5. Click on the first chamfer line, see Figure 5.50. You are prompted to select the second line.

```
Select second line or shift-select to apply corner or [Distance
Angle Method]:
```

6. Click on the second chamfer line, see Figure 5.50. A chamfer with the specified angle and distance is created, see Figure 5.51.

5.50

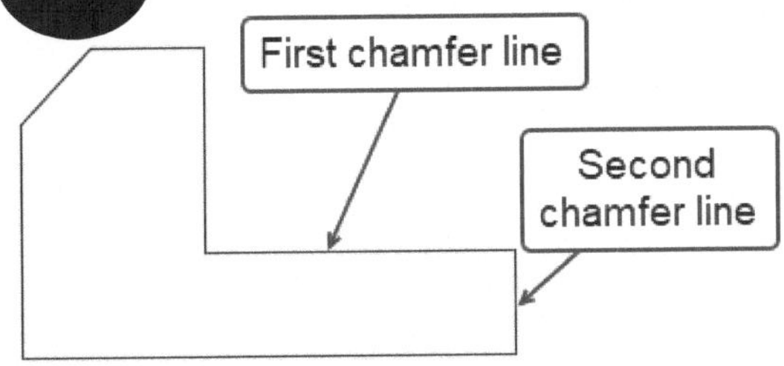

5.51

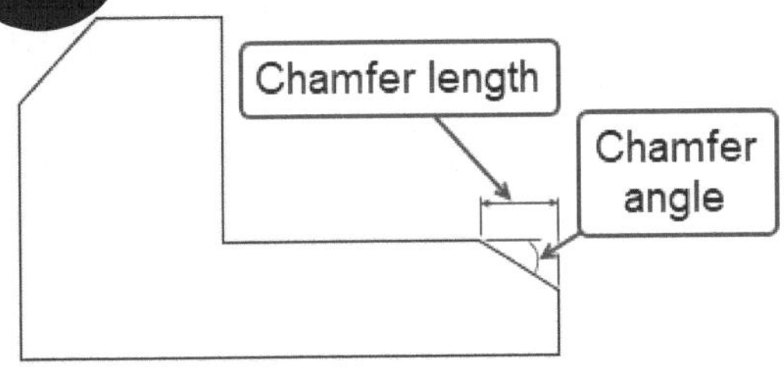

Offsetting Drawing Entities

In AutoCAD, you can offset an existing object/entity at a specified offset distance and create a new object, see Figure 5.52. Note that the shape of the newly created object is the same and parallel to the existing object. You can offset one or more existing entities by using the **Offset** tool of the **Modify** panel, see Figure 5.53. The method for creating objects by offsetting existing entities is discussed below:

5.52

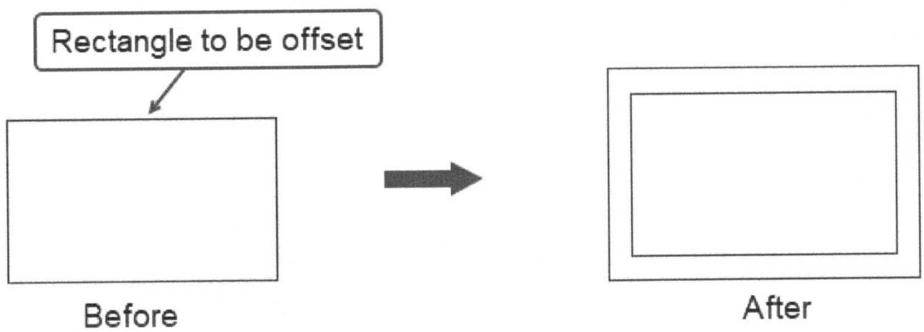

5.53

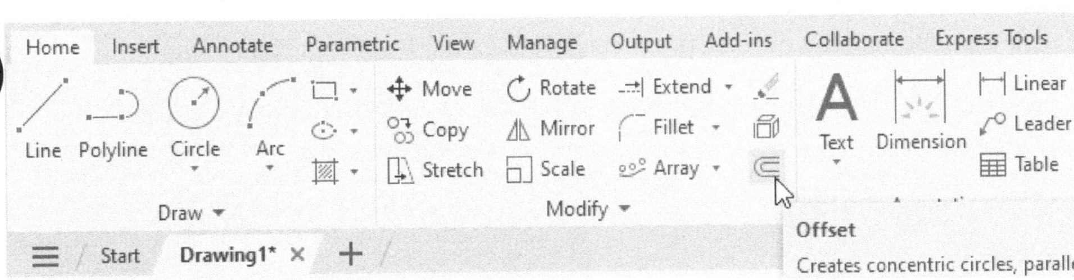

1. Click on the **Offset** tool in the **Modify** panel. You are prompted to specify offset distance. Alternatively, enter O in the Command Line window and then press ENTER.

```
Specify offset distance or [Through Erase Layer] <Through>:
```

2. Enter the offset distance value and then press ENTER. You are prompted to select an object to offset.

```
Select object to offset or [Exit Undo] <Exit>:
```

Note: In addition to specifying the offset distance value, you can specify two points in the drawing area by clicking the left mouse button for defining the offset distance.

3. Click on the object to be offset, see Figure 5.54. A preview of the offset entity appears attached to the cursor, see Figure 5.54. You are prompted to specify a point for defining the offset side.

```
Specify point on side to offset or [Exit Multiple Undo] <Exit>:
```

4. Click on either side of the selected entity to define the offset side. The offset object is created, see Figure 5.55. Also, you are again prompted to select an object to offset.

```
Select object to offset or [Exit Undo] <Exit>:
```

5.54

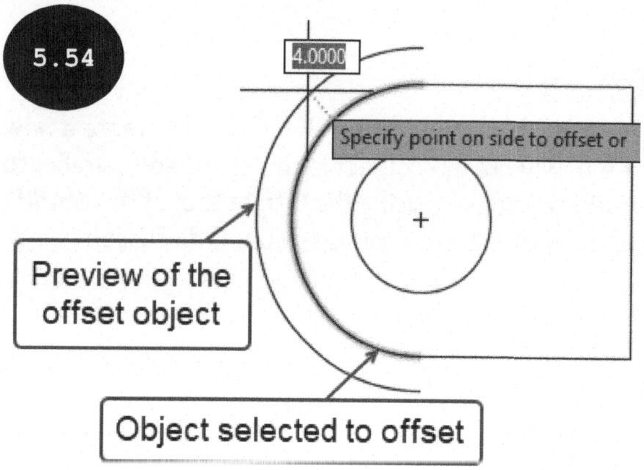

5.55

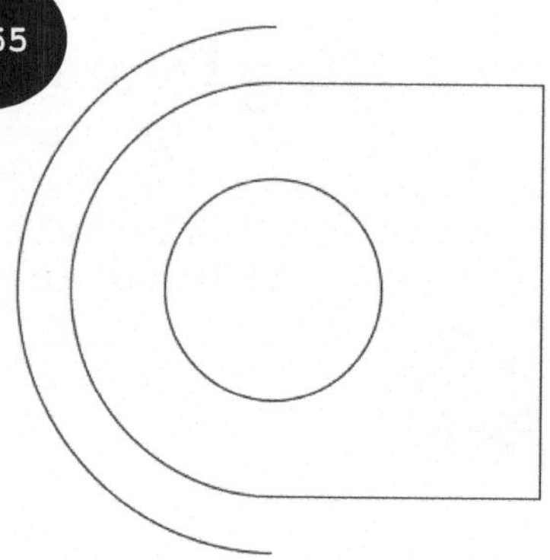

5. Similarly, you can select the other objects one by one to offset, see Figure 5.56.

6. After offsetting the objects, press ENTER to exit.

5.56

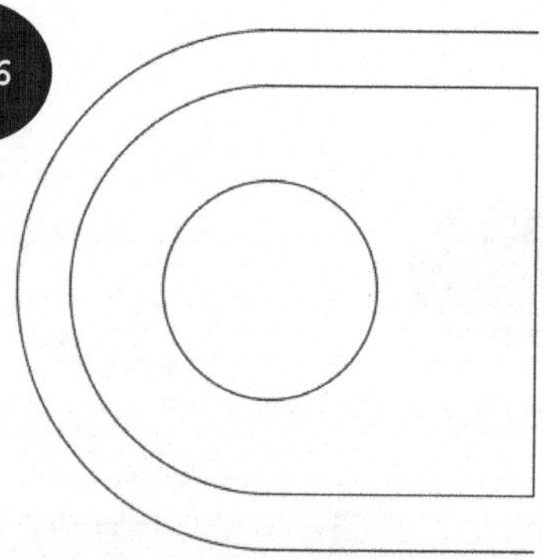

Note: By default, when you offset an entity, the original/parent selected entity remains available in the drawing area, and a new offset entity gets created. This is because the erase mode is turned off, by default. To activate the erase mode, click on the **Erase** option in the command prompt when you are prompted to select the first object "`Specify offset distance or [Through Erase Layer] <0.0000>:`". Next, enter **Y** and then press ENTER. Now, on offsetting an object, the original/parent object gets erased from the drawing area and a new offset object is created.

Moving Drawing Objects

While creating a drawing in AutoCAD, sometimes you may need to move the drawing objects from their current location to a new location in the drawing area. In AutoCAD, you can move the drawing objects from one place to another by using the **Move** tool of the **Modify** panel, see Figure 5.57. The method for moving the drawing objects is discussed below:

5.57

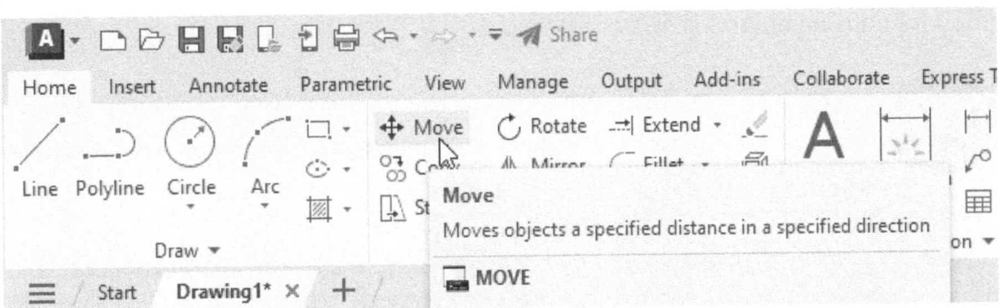

1. Click on the **Move** tool in the **Modify** panel (refer to Figure 5.57) or enter **M** in the Command Line window and then press ENTER. You are prompted to select objects to be moved.

```
Select objects:
```

2. Click on the object to be moved in the drawing area, see Figure 5.58 (a). You can select one or more objects to move. For selecting multiple objects, you can use the Window or Cross Window selection method.

3. After selecting the objects, press ENTER. You are prompted to specify a base point. Note that the base point acts as a reference point for moving the selected objects.

```
Specify base point or [Displacement] <Displacement>:
```

4. Click to specify the base point in the drawing area, see Figure 5.58 (a). You are prompted to specify the second/placement point for the selected objects. Also, a preview of the selected objects is attached to the cursor.

```
Specify second point or <use first point as displacement>:
```

5. Click to specify the second point in the drawing area as the placement point, see Figure 5.58 (a). The selected objects are moved to the specified location, see Figure 5.58 (b).

5.58

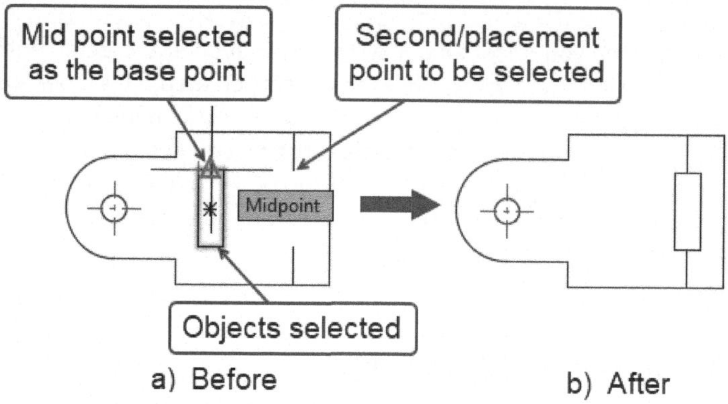

Copying Drawing Objects

While creating a drawing in AutoCAD, you may need to create duplicate copies of an object. You can create multiple copies of an object by using the **Copy** tool of the **Modify** panel, see Figure 5.59. The method for copying objects is discussed below:

5.59

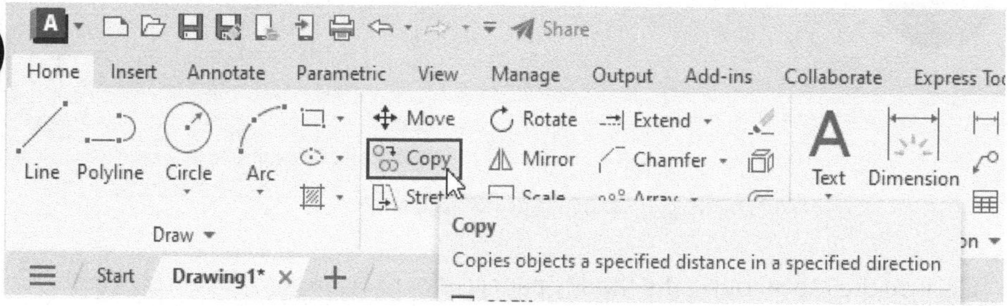

1. Click on the **Copy** tool in the **Modify** panel (refer to Figure 5.59) or enter **CO** in the Command Line window and then press ENTER. You are prompted to select objects to be copied.

```
Select objects:
```

2. Click on the object to be copied, see Figure 5.60 (a). You can select one or multiple objects to be copied. For selecting multiple objects, you can use the Window or Cross Window selection method.

3. After selecting objects, press ENTER. You are prompted to specify a base point. Note that the base point acts as a reference point for copying the selected objects.

```
Specify base point or [Displacement mOde] <Displacement>:
```

4. Click to specify the base point in the drawing area, see Figure 5.60 (a). You are prompted to specify the second point for the selected objects. Also, a preview of selected objects is attached to the cursor.

```
Specify second point or [Array] <use first point as displacement>:
```

5. Click to specify the second/placement point for the selected objects in the drawing area, see Figure 5.60 (a). The selected objects are copied to the specified location, see Figure 5.60 (b). Also, you are still prompted to specify the second point. You can create multiple copies of the selected objects similarly by specifying the placement points one after the other.

5.60

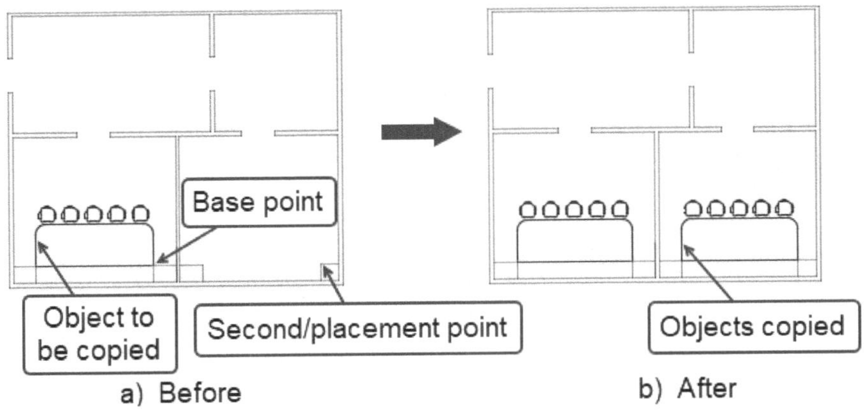

6. After copying the selected objects, press the ENTER key to exit.

Rotating Drawing Objects

While creating a drawing in AutoCAD, you may need to rotate objects at an angle around a point. You can rotate an object or a set of objects at an angle by using the **Rotate** tool of the **Modify** panel, see Figure 5.61. The method for rotating objects is discussed below:

5.61

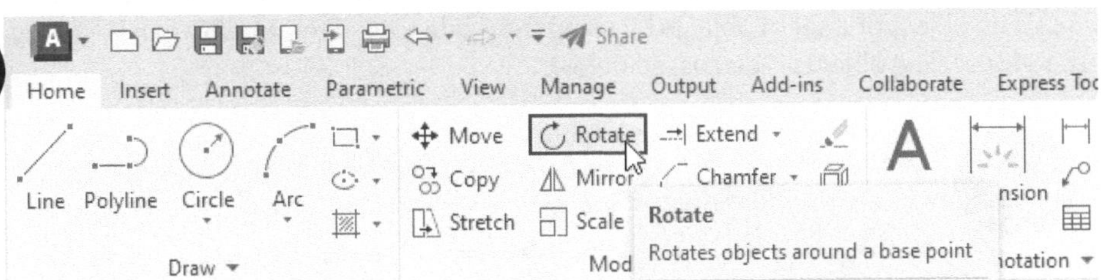

1. Click on the **Rotate** tool in the **Modify** panel, (refer to Figure 5.61) or enter **RO** in the Command Line window and then press ENTER. You are prompted to select objects.

```
Select objects:
```

2. Click on the object to be rotated, see Figure 5.62 (a). You can select one or multiple objects to be rotated. For selecting multiple objects, you can use the Window or Cross Window selection method.

3. After selecting the objects, press ENTER. You are prompted to specify a base point. Note that the base point acts as a reference point for rotating the selected objects.

```
Specify base point:
```

4. Click to specify the base point in the drawing area, see Figure 5.62 (a). You are prompted to specify the rotational angle. Also, a preview of the selected objects is attached to the cursor.

```
Specify rotation angle or [Copy Reference] <0>:
```

5. Enter the rotational angle value and then press ENTER. The selected objects are rotated at the specified angle, see Figure 5.62 (b). Note that you can also specify the rotational angle by clicking the left mouse button in the drawing area.

5.62

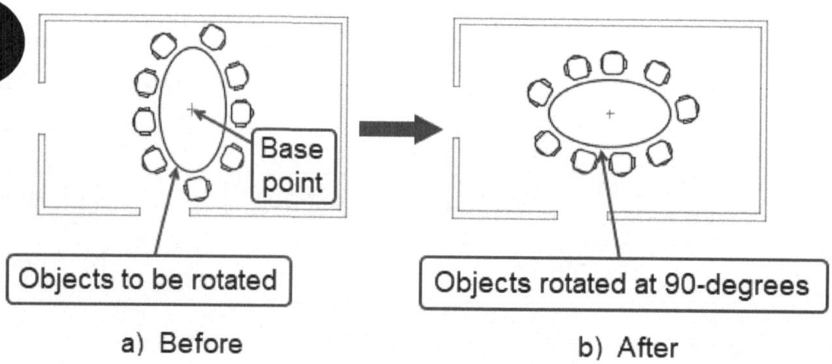

Scaling Drawing Objects

In addition to moving, rotating, and copying drawing objects, you may need to increase or decrease the scale of the objects as well. Note that on increasing/decreasing the scale of a drawing object, the size of the object is enlarged/shrunk, respectively, by maintaining the aspect ratio of the object. You can scale an object or a set of objects by using the **Scale** tool of the **Modify** panel, see Figure 5.63. The method for scaling objects is discussed below:

5.63

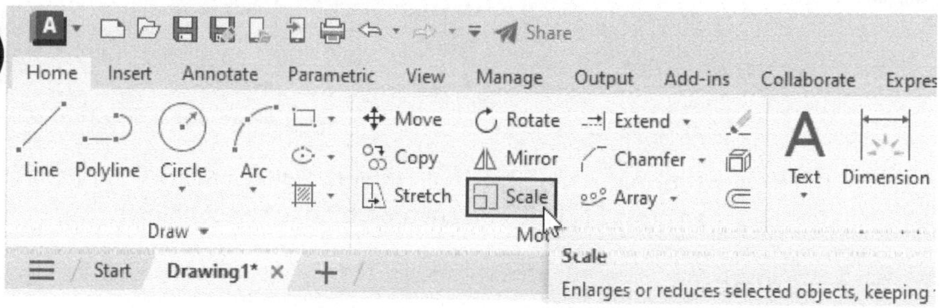

1. Click on the **Scale** tool in the **Modify** panel or enter **SC** in the Command Line window and then press ENTER. You are prompted to select objects.

```
Select objects:
```

2. Click on the object to be scaled, see Figure 5.64 (a). You can select one or multiple objects to be scaled. For selecting multiple objects, you can use the Window or Cross Window selection method.

3. After selecting the objects, press ENTER. You are prompted to specify a base point. Note that the base point acts as a reference point for scaling the selected objects.

```
Specify base point:
```

4. Click to specify a base point in the drawing area, see Figure 5.64 (a). You are prompted to specify a scale factor. Also, a preview of the selected object is attached to the cursor. Note that as you move the cursor, the scale of the objects increases or decreases, accordingly.

```
Specify scale factor or [Copy Reference]:
```

5. Enter the scale factor and then press ENTER. The selected objects are scaled equally by maintaining the aspect ratio of the object to the specified base point, see Figure 5.64 (b). Note that to enlarge the selected object, you need to enter a scale factor greater than 1, and to shrink the selected object, you need to enter a scale factor lesser than 1.

5.64

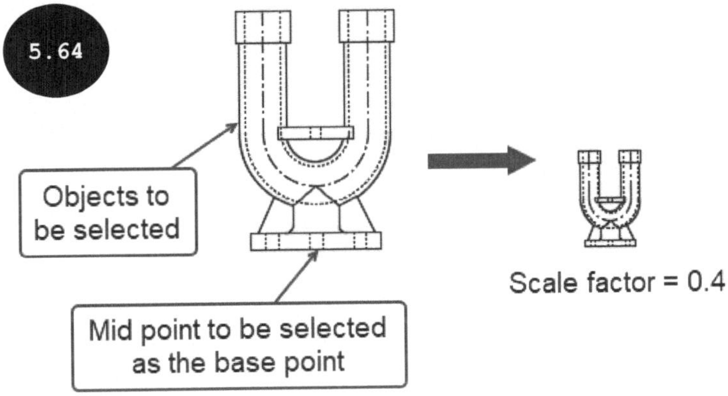

a) Before b) After

Note: You can also scale an object by specifying the current length and the new length of the object instead of specifying the scale factor. If you do so, the object gets scaled relative to the new specified length. To scale an object by specifying the current length and the new length, click on the **Reference** option in the command prompt when you are prompted to specify scale factor "`Specify scale factor or [Copy Reference]:`". Next, specify the current length value of the object and then press ENTER. You can also pick two points in the drawing area to specify the current length of the object. After specifying the current length, enter the new length of the object and then press ENTER. The selected object gets scaled relative to the new length specified. For example, if the current length of the object is 90 units and you want it to be 35 units after scaling it, then you need to enter 90 as the current length and 35 as the new length of the object.

Stretching Drawing Objects

In AutoCAD, you can stretch an object or a group of objects to change its shape and size. You can stretch objects by using the **Stretch** tool, see Figure 5.65. The method for stretching objects is discussed below:

5.65

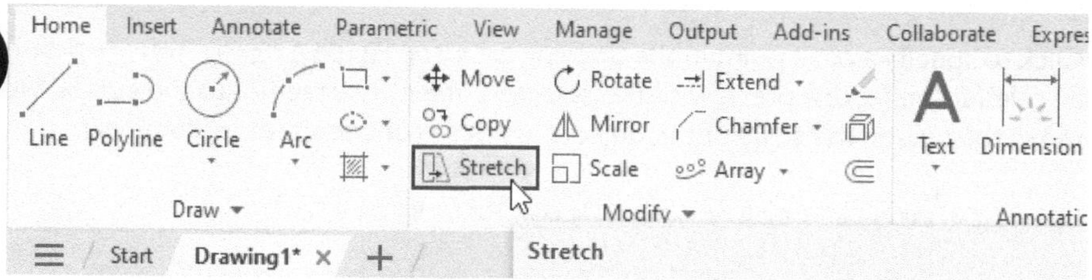

1. Click on the **Stretch** tool in the **Modify** panel (refer to Figure 5.65) or enter **S** in the Command Line window and then press ENTER. You are prompted to select objects to be stretched.

```
Select objects:
```

2. Select objects by drawing a Cross Window around them such that it partially encloses the objects to be stretched, see Figure 5.66 (a). You can select the objects to be stretched by using the Cross Window or Cross Polygon selection method.

Note: You can only stretch objects that are partially enclosed by the boundary of the Cross Window or Cross Polygon window. The objects that are completely enclosed within the boundary will move instead of being stretched.

3. After selecting objects to be stretched, press ENTER. You are prompted to specify a base point.

```
Specify base point or [Displacement] <Displacement>:
```

4 Click to specify the base point for stretching the selected objects in the drawing area, see Figure 5.66 (a). You are prompted to specify the second point.

```
Specify second point or <use first point as displacement>:
```

5. Click to specify the second/placement point. The portion of the objects selected gets stretched by leaving the rest of the portion unchanged, see Figure 5.66 (b).

5.66

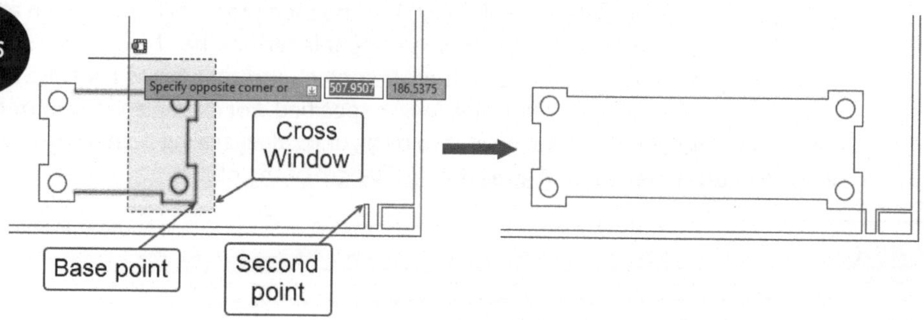

a) Before b) After

Lengthening Drawing Objects

In AutoCAD, you can shorten or extend the line objects by using the **Lengthen** tool of the expanded **Modify** panel, see Figure 5.67. You can expand the **Modify** panel by clicking on the arrow available in the title bar of the **Modify** panel. You can shorten or extend the line object by entering the delta length, percentage, and total length, or by dragging the object. The different methods for lengthening an object are discussed next.

5.67

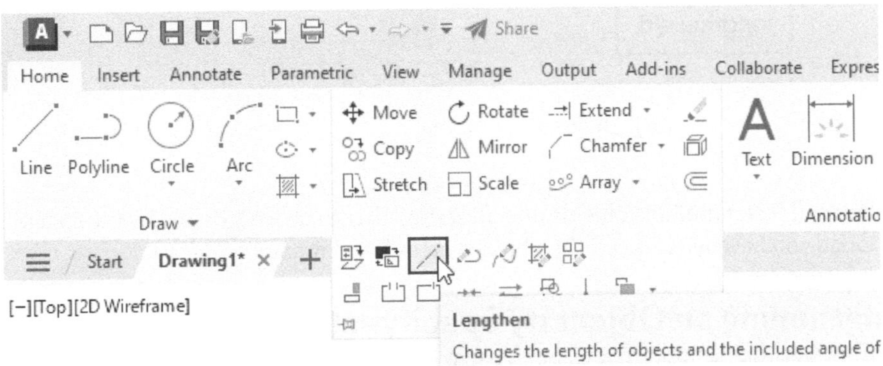

Lengthening an Object by Specifying Delta Value

1. Click on the **Lengthen** tool in the expanded **Modify** panel (see Figure 5.67) or enter **LEN** in the Command Line window and then press ENTER. You are prompted to select an object.

```
Select an object to measure or [DElta Percent Total DYnamic] <Total>:
```

2. Click on the **DElta** option in the command prompt or enter **DE** and then press ENTER. You are prompted to specify the delta length of the object to lengthen.

```
Enter delta length or [Angle]: <0.0000>:
```

Note: The delta length is the length of an object by which the object is to be extended or shortened. On entering a positive delta value, the length of the object is increased (extended) and on entering a negative delta value, the length of the object is decreased (shortened).

3. Enter the delta length and then press ENTER. You are prompted to select an object.

```
Select an object to change or [Undo]:
```

4. Select the object to be lengthened, see Figure 5.68 (a). The length of the object is increased/decreased by the length specified, see Figure 5.68 (b). You are prompted to select the object to be lengthened again.

```
Select an object to change or [Undo]:
```

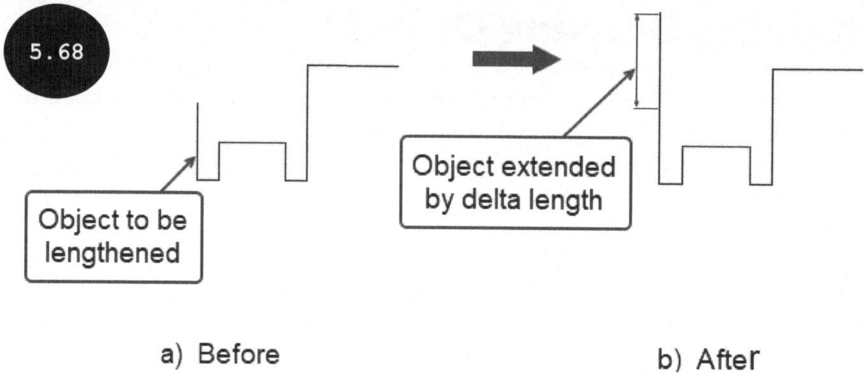

5. You can select multiple objects one after the other to be lengthened by the specified delta length. Once you have lengthened the objects, press ENTER to exit.

Lengthening an Object by Specifying Percentage

1. Click on the **Lengthen** tool in the expanded **Modify** panel or enter **LEN** in the Command Line window and then press ENTER. You are prompted to select an object.

```
Select an object to measure or [DElta Percent Total DYnamic] <Total>:
```

2. Click on the **Percent** option in the command prompt or enter **P** and then press ENTER. You are prompted to specify the percentage length of the object.

```
Enter percentage length <100.0000>:
```

Note: The current length of the object is taken as 100 percent. As a result, on entering a percentage value more than 100, the length of the object is increased, and on entering a percentage value less than 100, the length of the object is decreased. For example, by entering percentage as 200, the length of the object becomes double of the current length.

3. Enter the percentage value for increasing or decreasing the length of the object and then press ENTER. You are prompted to select an object.

```
Select an object to change or [Undo]:
```

4. Select the object to lengthen. The length of the object is increased/decreased by the specified percentage. You are prompted to select the object again.

```
Select an object to change or [Undo]:
```

5. You can select multiple objects one after the other to increase/decrease their length as per the specified percentage value. Once you have lengthened the objects, press ENTER to exit.

Lengthening an Object by Specifying Total Length

1. Click on the **Lengthen** tool in the expanded **Modify** panel or enter **LEN** in the Command Line window and then press ENTER. You are prompted to select an object.

```
Select an object to measure or [DElta Percent Total DYnamic] <Total>:
```

2. Click on the **Total** option in the command prompt or enter **T** and then press ENTER. You are prompted to specify the total length of the object.

```
Specify total length or [Angle] <1.0000>:
```

Note: The total length of an object is its overall length. You can specify the total length as lesser or greater than the current length of the object.

3. Enter the new total length value of the object and then press ENTER. You are prompted to select an object.

```
Select an object to change or [Undo]:
```

4. Select the object. The current length of the object changes to the new specified length. You are prompted to select the object again.

```
Select an object to change or [Undo]:
```

5. You can select objects one after the other to increase or decrease their length. Once you have lengthened the objects, press ENTER to exit.

Lengthening an Object by Dragging

1. Click on the **Lengthen** tool in the expanded **Modify** panel or enter **LEN** in the Command Line window and then press ENTER. You are prompted to select an object.

```
Select an object to measure or [DElta Percent Total DYnamic] <Total>:
```

2. Click on the **DYnamic** option in the command prompt or enter **DY** and then press ENTER. You are prompted to select an object.

```
Select an object to change or [Undo]:
```

3. Select the object. The endpoint of the selected object is attached to the cursor. As you move the cursor, the length of the object is increased or decreased. Also, you are prompted to specify the new endpoint of the object.

```
Specify new end point:
```

4. Click to specify the new endpoint of the object. The length of the object is increased/decreased as per the new endpoint specified. Next, press ENTER to exit.

Tutorial 1

Create the drawing shown in Figure 5.69. The dimensions shown in the figure are for your reference only. You will learn about applying dimensions in later chapters.

5.69

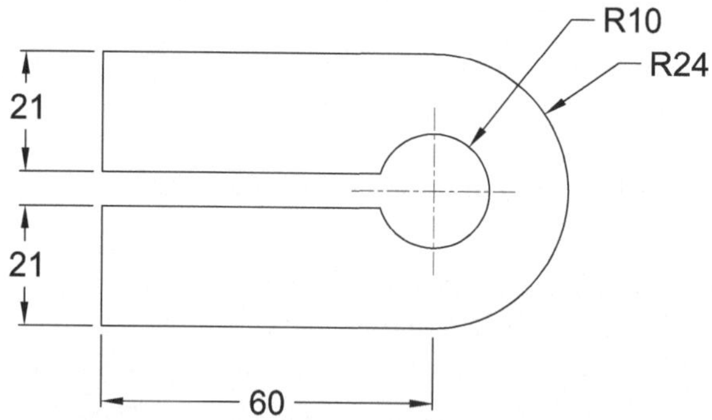

Section 1: Starting AutoCAD

1. Double-click on the AutoCAD icon on your desktop to start AutoCAD. The initial screen of AutoCAD appears with the **Start** tab, see Figure 5.70.

2. Click on the + sign next to the **Start** tab, see Figure 5.70. A new drawing file with the default drawing template gets invoked. Alternatively, click on the **New** tool of the **Start** tab to start a new drawing file with the default drawing template. You can also start a new drawing file by using the **New** tool of the **Quick Access Toolbar**, which is at the top left corner of the AutoCAD screen.

5.70

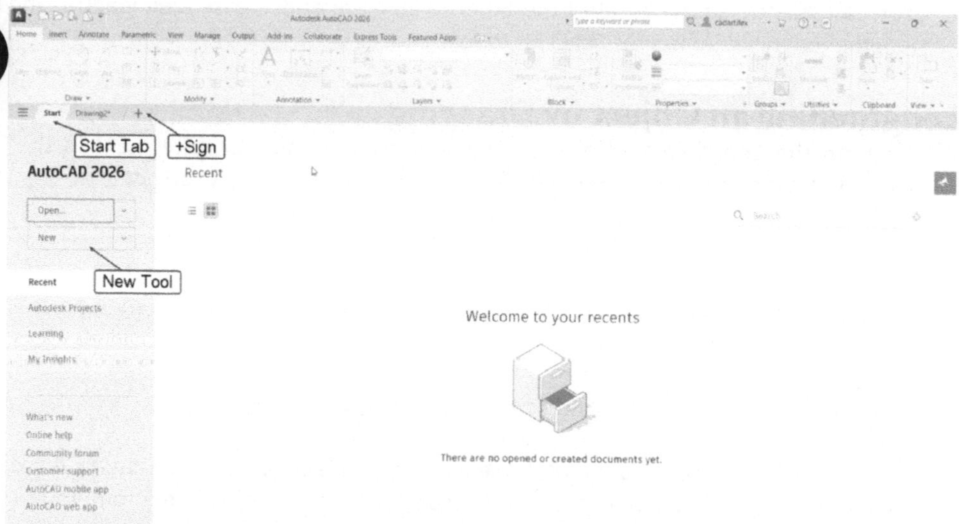

Section 2: Selecting Workspace for Creating a Drawing

1. Ensure that the **Drafting & Annotation** workspace is selected as the workspace for creating the drawing.

Section 3: Defining the Drawing Limits

1. Follow the command sequence given below for defining the drawing limits.

```
Command: LIMITS (ENTER)
Specify lower left corner or [ON/OFF]<0.0000,0.0000>: 0,0 (ENTER)
Specify upper right corner <12.0000,9.0000>: 150,110 (ENTER)
```

Section 4: Creating a Drawing

1. Click on the arrow next to the circle tool in the **Draw** panel. The **Circle** flyout appears. In this flyout, click on the **Center, Radius** tool. Alternatively, enter **C** in the Command Line window and then press ENTER. You are prompted to specify the center point of the circle.

```
Specify center point for circle or [3P 2P Ttr (tan tan radius)]:
```

2. Click in the drawing area to specify the center point of the circle. You are prompted to specify the radius of the circle.

```
Specify radius of circle or [Diameter]:
```

3. Enter **24** and then press ENTER. A circle with a radius of 24 units is created, see Figure 5.71.

4. Invoke the **Center, Radius** tool again. You are prompted to specify the center point of the circle.

```
Specify center point for circle or [3P 2P Ttr (tan tan radius)]:
```

5. Move the cursor toward the center point of the existing circle in the drawing area and then click to specify the center point of the circle when the cursor snaps to it. You are prompted to specify the radius of the circle.

```
Specify radius of circle or [Diameter]:
```

6. Enter **10** and then press ENTER. A circle with a radius of 10 units is created, see Figure 5.72.

5.71

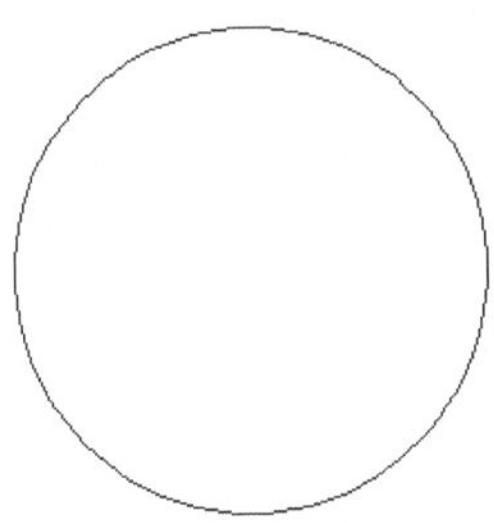

5.72

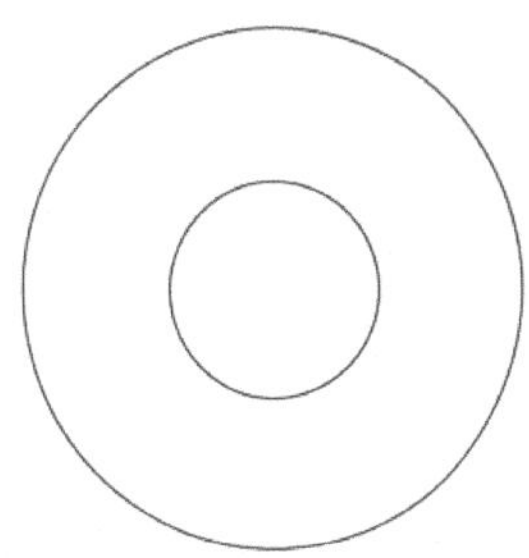

7. Click on the **Line** tool in the **Draw** panel and then move the cursor toward the top quadrant of the first drawn circle, see Figure 5.73.

8. Click to specify the first point of the line when the cursor snaps to the top quadrant of the first drawn circle, see Figure 5.73. You are prompted to specify the second point of the line.

```
Specify next point or [Undo]:
```

9. Ensure that the Ortho mode is turned on. Next, move the cursor horizontally toward the left and then enter **60** as the length of the line, see Figure 5.74. Next, press ENTER. A line with a length of 60 units is drawn. Also, you are prompted to specify next point of the line.

```
Specify next point or [Undo]:
```

5.73

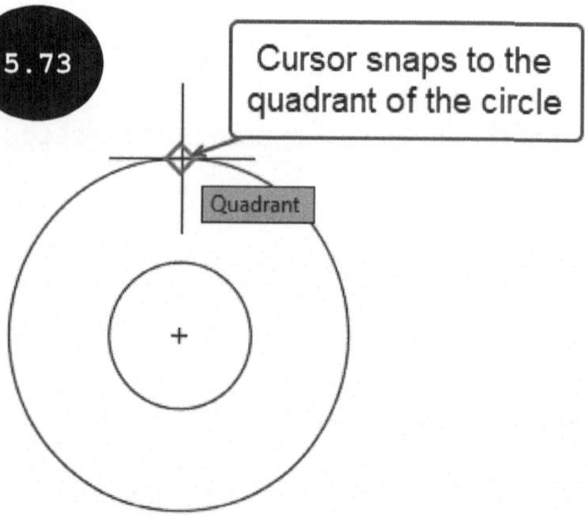

5.74

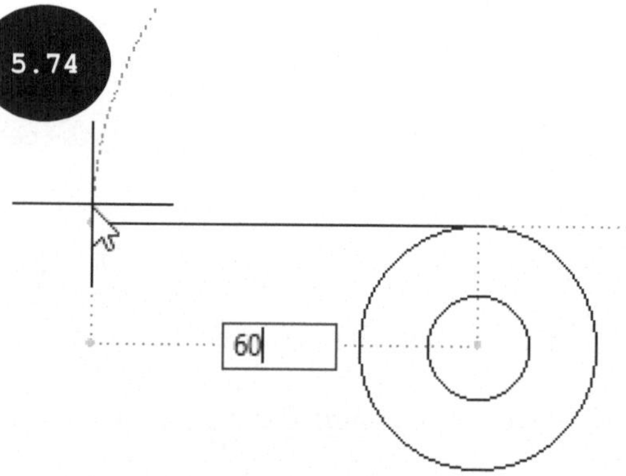

10. Move the cursor vertically downward and then enter **21** as the length of the line. Next, press ENTER. A line with a length of 21 units is drawn, and you are prompted to specify the next point of the line.

```
Specify next point or [Close Undo]:
```

11. Move the cursor horizontally toward the right and then click to specify the endpoint of the line anywhere inside the smaller circle of diameter of 20 units, see Figure 5.75. Next, press ENTER to exit.

12. Similarly, draw the other line entities of the drawing by using the **Line** tool, see Figure 5.76.

5.75

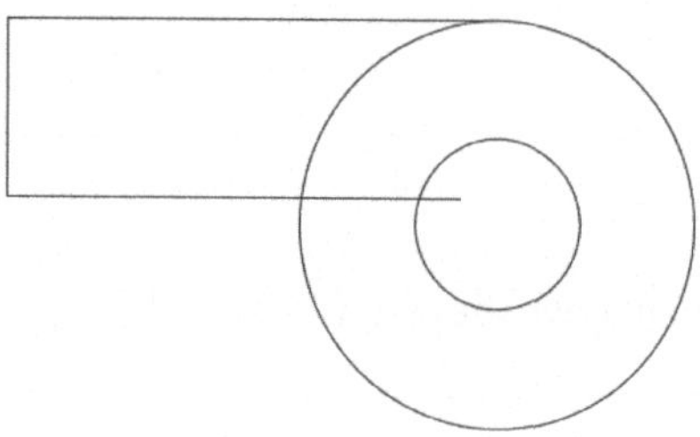

5.76

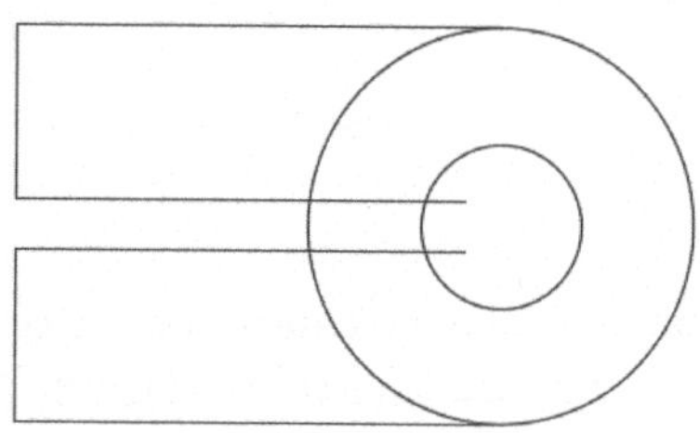

Section 5: Trimming the Drawing Entities

1. Click on the **Trim** tool in the **Modify** panel or enter **TR** in the Command Line window and then press ENTER. You are prompted to select objects to be trimmed.

```
Select object to trim or shift-select to extend or
[cuTting edges Crossing mOde Project eRase]:
```

2. Click on the line entity (1), see Figure 5.77. The selected line entity gets trimmed to its nearest intersection, see Figure 5.78. Also, you are prompted to select objects to trim again.

```
Select object to trim or shift-select to extend or
[cuTting edges Crossing mOde Project eRase Undo]:
```

5.77

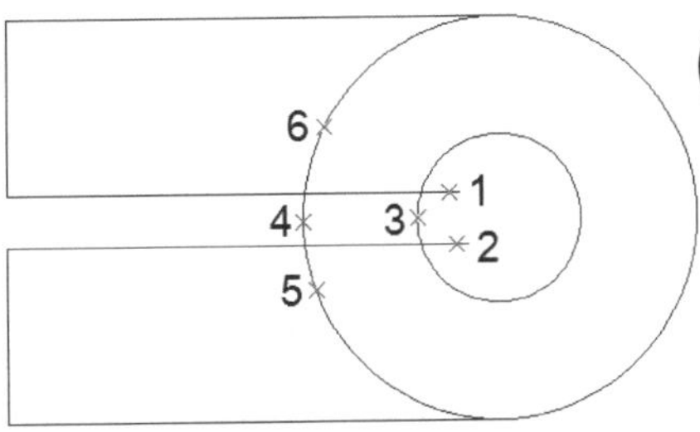

5.78

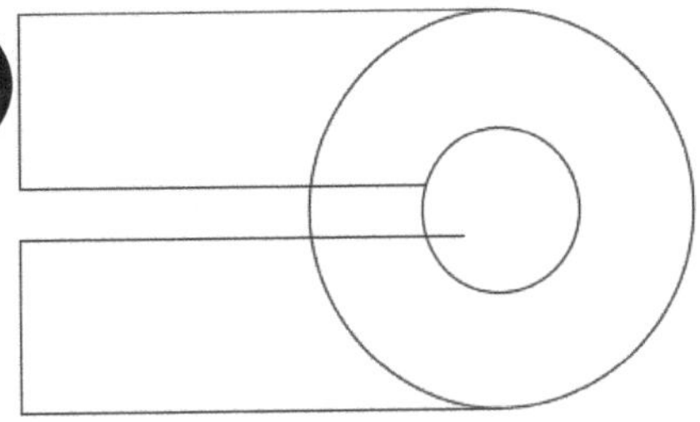

3. Similarly, click on the other entities 2, 3, 4, 5, and 6 (refer to Figure 5.77) to trim them to their nearest intersection. Figure 5.79 shows the drawing after trimming all the unwanted entities.

5.79

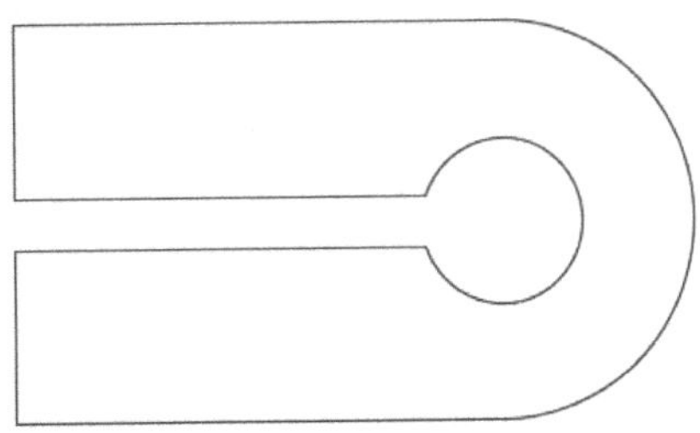

Section 6: Saving the Drawing

After creating the drawing, you need to save it.

1. Click on the **Save** tool in the **Quick Access Toolbar**. The **Save Drawing As** dialog box appears.
2. Browse to the *AutoCAD* folder and then create a folder with the name *Chapter 5* inside the *AutoCAD* folder.
3. Enter **Tutorial 1** in the **File name** field of the dialog box and then click on the **Save** button. The drawing gets saved with the name Tutorial 1 in the *Chapter 5* folder.

Tutorial 2

Create the drawing shown in Figure 5.80. The dimensions shown in the figure are for your reference only. You will learn about applying dimensions in the later chapters.

5.80

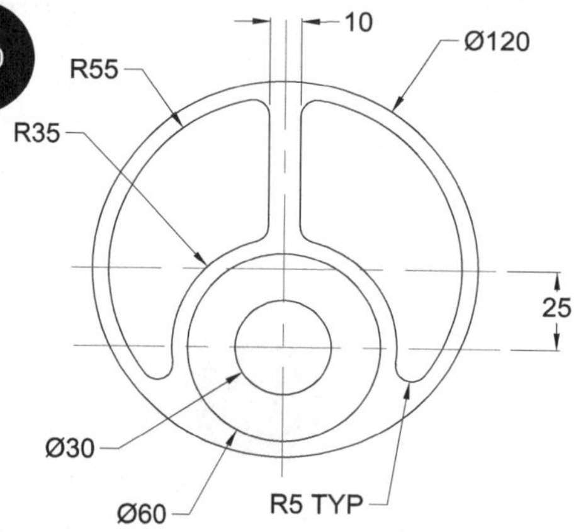

Section 1: Starting AutoCAD

1. Start AutoCAD, if not started already. Next, click on the **New** tool in the **Quick Access Toolbar**, which is at the top left corner of the AutoCAD screen. The **Select template** dialog box appears.

2. In the **Select template** dialog box, click on the ***acad.dwt*** template and then click on the **Open** button. A new drawing file with ***acad.dwt*** template gets invoked.

3. Specify the drawing limits.

Section 2: Creating Construction Lines

1. Click on the **Construction Line** tool in the expanded **Draw** panel of the **Home** tab. You are prompted to specify a point in the drawing area. You can also enter **XLINE** in the Command Line window and then press ENTER to invoke the **Construction Line** tool.

```
Specify a point or [Hor Ver Ang Bisect Offset]:
```

2. Click on the **Hor** option in the command prompt or enter **H** and then press ENTER to create a horizontal construction line. A horizontal construction line is attached to the cursor. Also, you are prompted to specify a through point.

```
Specify through point:
```

3. Click in the drawing area to specify a point in the drawing area. A horizontal construction line gets created such that it passes through the specified point. Also, another horizontal construction line is attached to the cursor.

4. Press ENTER to exit the tool.

Now, you need to create another horizontal construction line at an offset distance of 25 units from the existing horizontal construction line.

5. Invoke the **Construction Line** tool and then click on the **Offset** option of the command prompt or enter O and then press ENTER. You are prompted to specify the offset distance.

```
Specify offset distance or [Through] <Through>:
```

6. Enter **25** and then press ENTER. You are prompted to select a line object.

```
Select a line object:
```

7. Click on the existing horizontal construction line. You are prompted to specify the side to offset.

```
Specify side to offset:
```

8. Click on the bottom side of the existing horizontal construction line. A horizontal construction line at an offset distance of 25 units is created, see Figure 5.81. Next, press ENTER to exit the tool.

9. Similarly, create two vertical construction lines at an offset distance of 5 units from each other by using the **Construction Line** tool, see Figure 5.82.

5.81

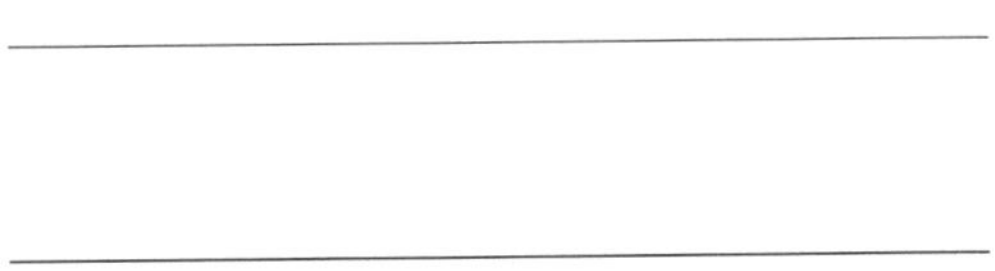

5.82

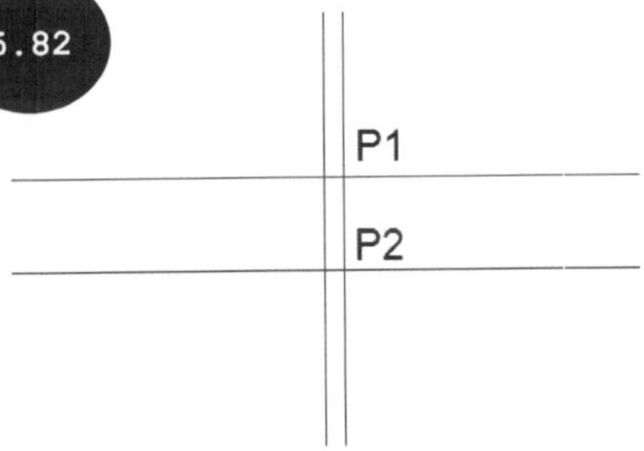

Section 3: Creating a Drawing

1. Invoke the **Circle** flyout of the **Draw** panel and then click on the **Circle, Radius** tool. Alternatively, enter **C** in the Command Line window and then press ENTER. You are prompted to specify the center point of the circle.

```
Specify center point for circle or [3P 2P Ttr (tan tan radius)]:
```

2. Move the cursor toward the intersection point (P1) created between the upper horizontal and right vertical construction lines, refer to Figure 5.82.

3. Click to specify the center point of the circle when the cursor snaps to the intersection point (P1). You are prompted to specify the radius of the circle.

```
Specify radius of circle or [Diameter]:
```

4. Enter **60** as the radius of the circle. A circle of diameter 120 units is created, see Figure 5.83.

5. Similarly, create a circle of radius 55 units whose center point is at the intersection point (P1) and a circle of radius 35 units whose center point is at the intersection point (P2), see Figure 5.84.

5.83

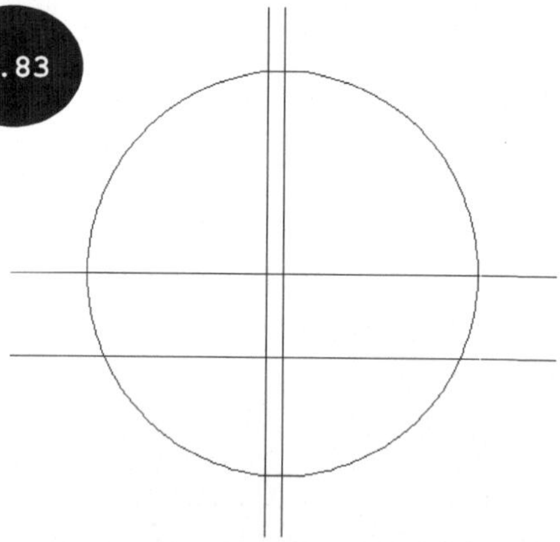

5.84

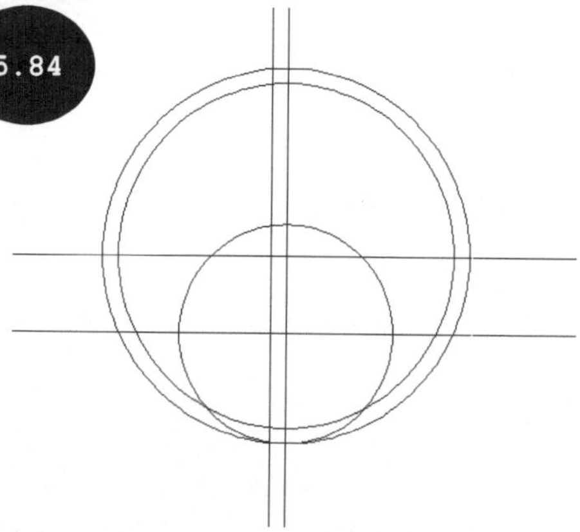

Section 4: Trimming Unwanted Drawing Entities

1. Click on the **Trim** tool in the **Modify** panel or enter **TR** in the Command Line window and then press ENTER. You are prompted to select objects to be trimmed.

```
Select object to trim or shift-select to extend or
[cuTting edges Crossing mOde Project eRase]:
```

2. Click on the entity (1), see Figure 5.85. The selected entity gets trimmed to its next nearest intersection, see Figure 5.86. Also, you are prompted to select objects to be trimmed again.

```
Select object to trim or shift-select to extend or
[cuTting edges Crossing mOde Project eRase Undo]:
```

5.85

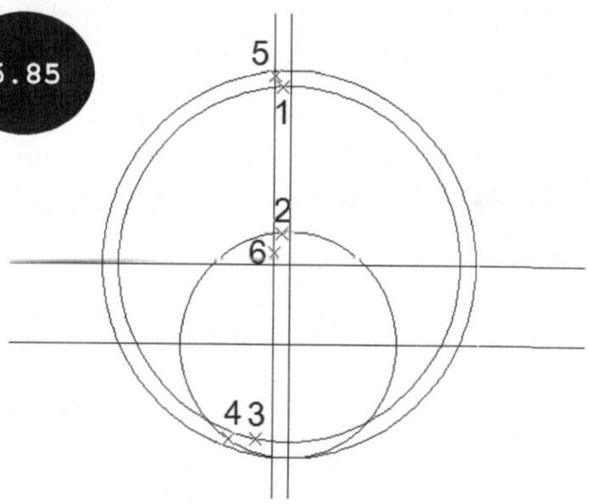

5.86

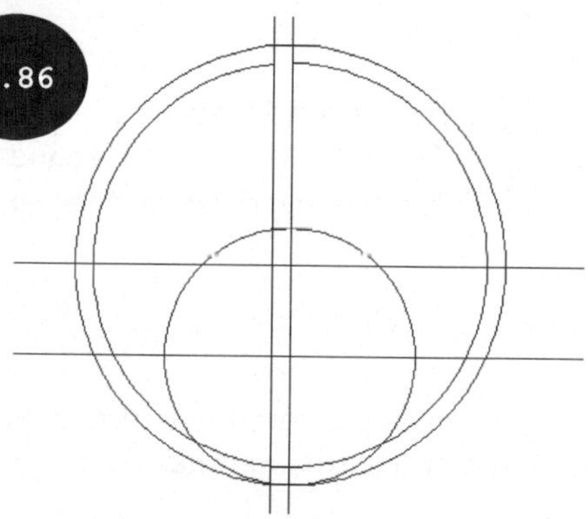

3. Similarly, click on the other entities (2, 3, 4, 5, and 6), see Figure 5.85. Figure 5.87 shows the drawing after trimming all the unwanted entities. Next, press ENTER to exit.

5.87

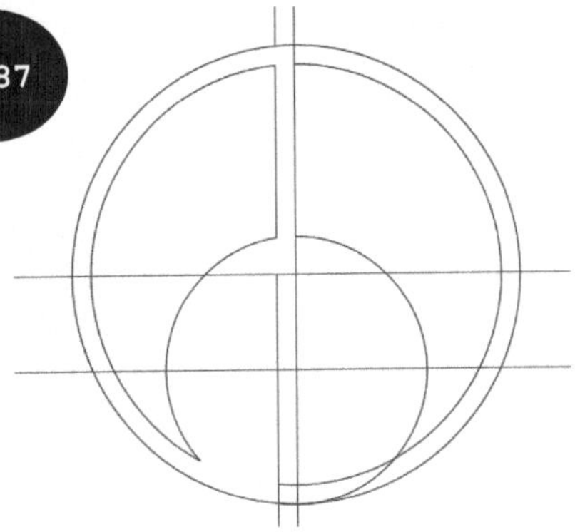

Section 5: Deleting Unwanted Drawing Entities

1. Click on the entities to be deleted (four entities), see Figure 5.88. Next, press the DELETE key. The selected entities of the drawing get deleted, see Figure 5.89.

5.88

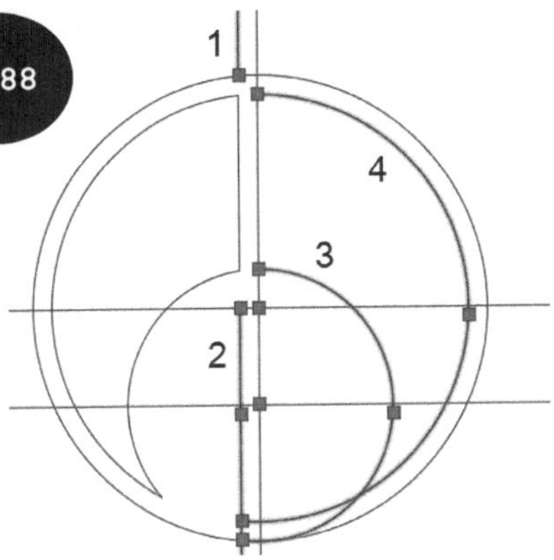

5.89

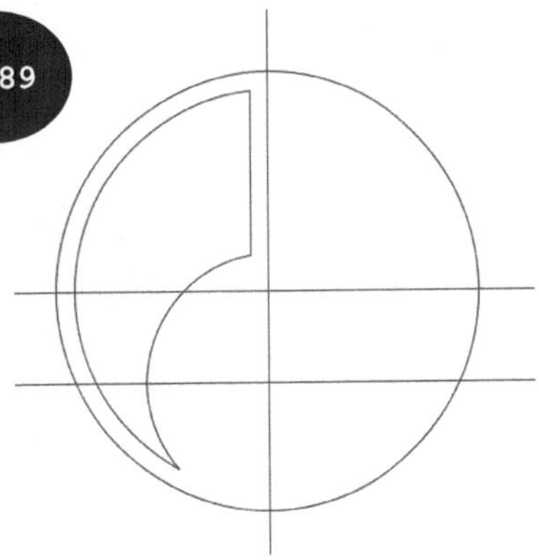

Section 6: Creating Fillets

1. Click on the **Fillet** tool in the **Modify** panel or enter **F** and then press ENTER. You are prompted to select the first object.

```
Select first object or [Undo Polyline Radius Trim Multiple]:
```

2. Click on the **Radius** option of the command prompt or enter **R** and then press ENTER. You are prompted to specify the radius of the fillet.

```
Specify fillet radius <0.0000>:
```

3. Enter **5** as the fillet radius and then press ENTER. You are prompted to select the first object.

```
Select first object or [Undo Polyline Radius Trim Multiple]:
```

4. Click on the first object of the first corner to be filleted, see Figure 5.90. You are prompted to select the second object.

```
Select second object or shift-select to apply corner or [Radius]:
```

5. Click on the second object in the first corner, see Figure 5.90. A fillet of radius 5 units gets created at the first corner of the drawing, see Figure 5.91.

5.90

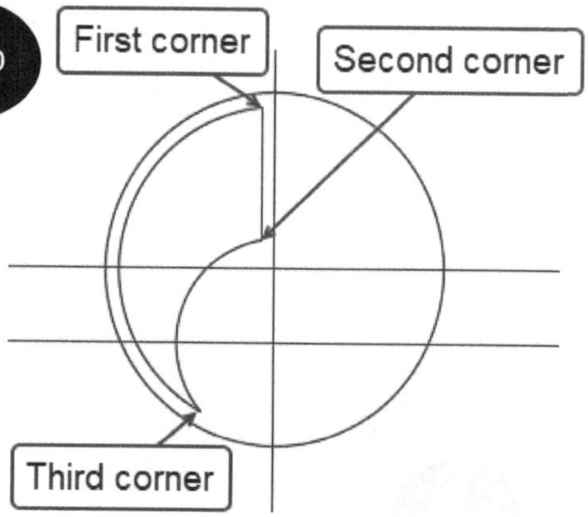

5.91

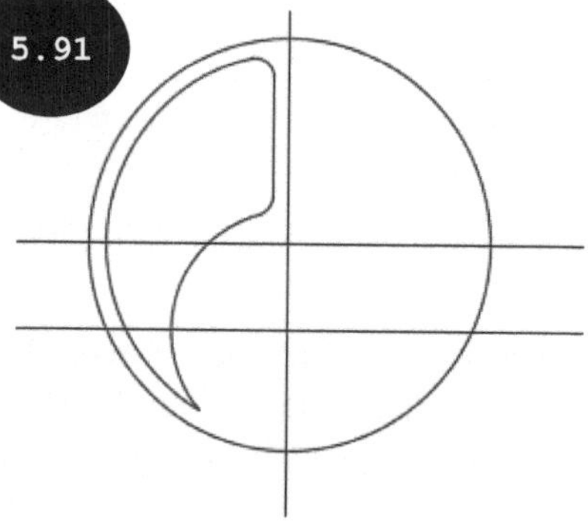

6. Similarly, create fillets of radius 5 units on the second and third corners, see Figure 5.92.

5.92

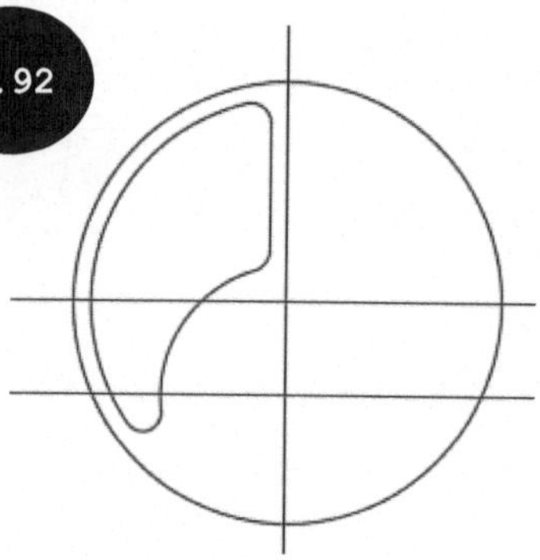

Section 7: Mirroring Drawing Entities

1. Click on the **Mirror** tool in the **Modify** panel or enter **MI** and then press ENTER. You are prompted to select objects.

```
Select objects:
```

2. Click on the entities (six entities) of the drawing, see Figure 5.93. The selected entities get highlighted, see Figure 5.93. Next, press ENTER. You are prompted to specify the first point of the mirror line.

```
Specify first point of mirror line:
```

5.93

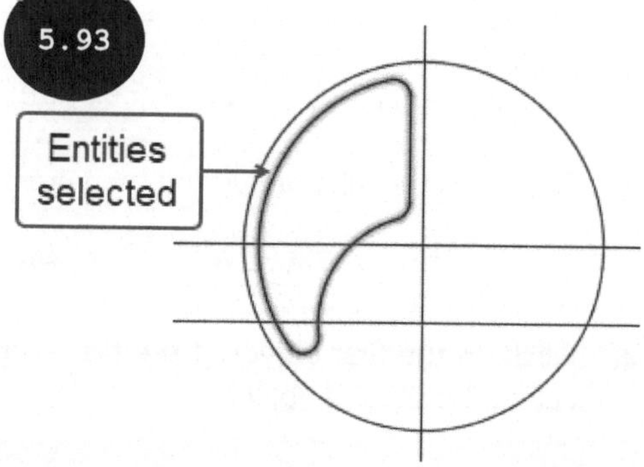

3. Click to specify the first point of the mirroring line anywhere on the vertical construction line. You are prompted to specify the second point of the mirror line.

```
Specify second point of mirror line:
```

4. Move the cursor vertically and then click to specify the second point of the mirror line anywhere on the vertical construction line. You are prompted to specify whether you want to erase source objects.

```
Erase source object? [Yes No] <No>:
```

5. Enter **N** and then press ENTER. The mirror image of the selected entities is created, see Figure 5.94.

5.94

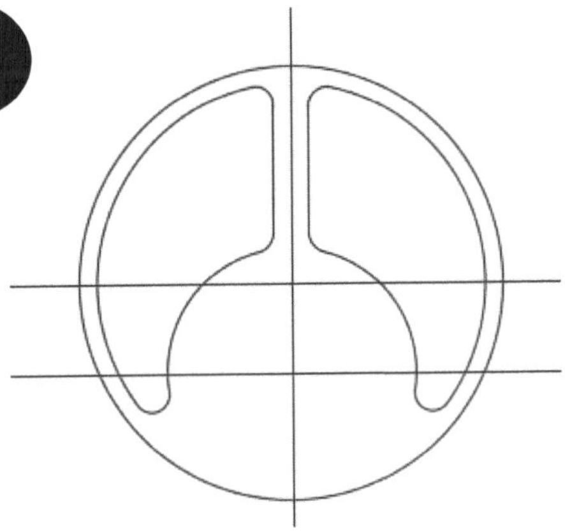

Section 8: Creating Remaining Drawing Entities

1. Create two circles, one of a diameter 60 units and another a of diameter 30 units by using the **Circle, Diameter** tool, see Figure 5.95.

5.95

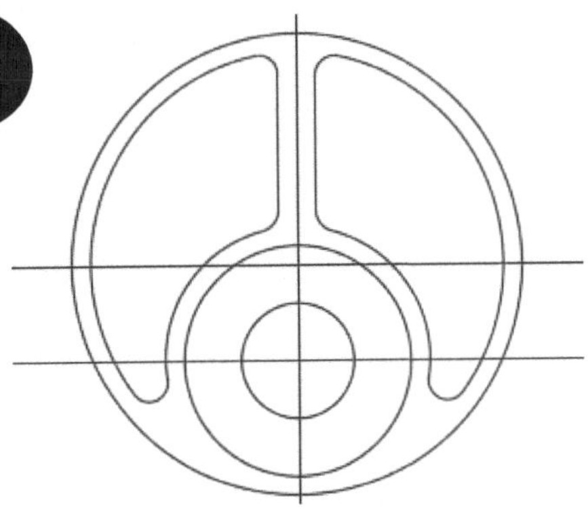

2. Create a layer named as **Construction Line** and then move the construction lines of the drawing to the **Construction Line** layer. Next, hide the **Construction Line** layer. Figure 5.96 shows the final drawing after hiding the construction lines.

Tip: The method for creating layers and assigning objects to them is discussed in Chapter 3.

5.96

Section 9: Saving the Drawing

1. Click on the **Save** tool the **Quick Access Toolbar**. The **Save Drawing As** dialog box appears.
2. Browse to the *Chapter 5* folder inside the *AutoCAD* folder.
3. Enter **Tutorial 2** in the **File name** field of the dialog box and then click on the **Save** button. The drawing gets saved with the name Tutorial 2 in the *Chapter 5* folder.

Tutorial 3

Create the drawing shown in Figure 5.97. The dimensions shown in the figure are for your reference only. You will learn about applying dimensions in later chapters.

5.97

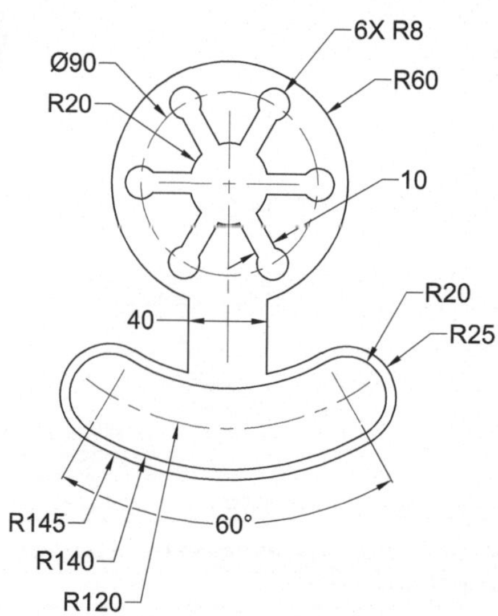

Section 1: Starting AutoCAD

1. Start a new AutoCAD drawing file and then define the drawing limits.

Section 2: Creating Reference Entities

1. Click on the **Construction Line** tool in the expanded **Draw** panel of the **Home** tab. You are prompted to specify a point in the drawing area. You can also enter **XLINE** in the Command Line window and then press ENTER to invoke the **Construction Line** tool.

```
Specify a point or [Hor Ver Ang Bisect Offset]:
```

2. Click on the **Ver** option in the command prompt or enter **V** and then press ENTER. A vertical construction line is attached to the cursor. Also, you are prompted to specify a through point.

```
Specify through point:
```

3. Click in the drawing area to specify the through point. A vertical construction line is created such that it passes through the specified point. Next, press ENTER to exit.

4. Similarly, create a horizontal construction line by using the **Construction Line** tool.

   Now, you need to create construction lines at an angle.

5. Invoke the **Construction Line** tool and then click on the **Ang** option in the command prompt or enter **A** and then press ENTER. You are prompted to specify an angle for the construction line.

```
Enter angle of xline (0) or [Reference]:
```

6. Enter **60** and then press ENTER. A construction line at an angle of 60 degrees, measured from the horizontal X-axis is attached to the cursor. Also, you are prompted to specify a through point.

```
Specify through point:
```

7. Click on the intersection point created between the horizontal and vertical construction lines to specify the through point. A construction line with an angle of 60 degrees is created, see Figure 5.98.

8. Similarly, create another construction line at an angle of 120 degrees from the horizontal X-axis, see Figure 5.99.

5.98

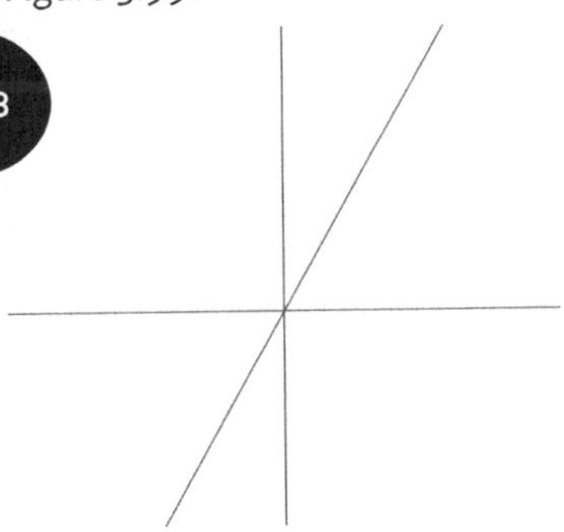

5.99

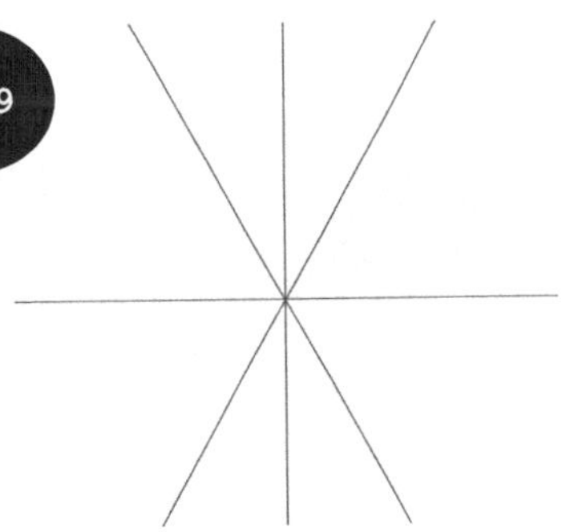

After creating the construction lines, you need to create a reference circle.

9. Invoke the **Circle, Diameter** tool in the **Draw** panel and then create a circle of diameter 90 units whose center point is at the intersection of the construction lines, see Figure 5.100.

5.100

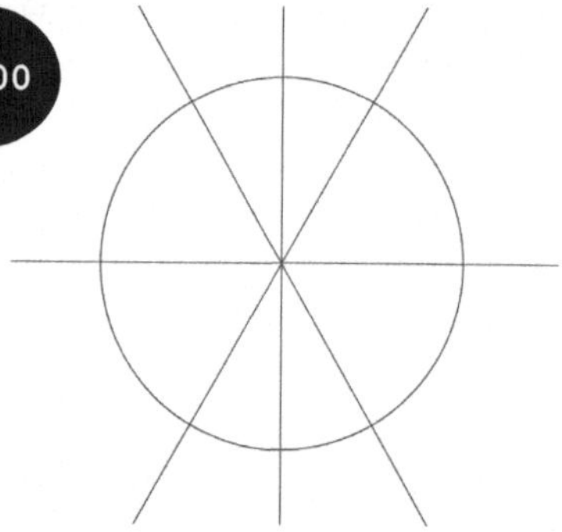

Section 3: Creating a Reference Layer

1. Invoke the **LAYER PROPERTIES MANAGER** by clicking on the **Layer Properties** tool in the **Layers** panel of the **Home** tab. Alternatively, enter **LA** in the Command Line window and then press ENTER to invoke the **LAYER PROPERTIES MANAGER**.

2. Create a layer named as Reference in the **LAYER PROPERTIES MANAGER** and then assign the Red color and Center linetype to it, see Figure 5.101. Next, exit the **LAYER PROPERTIES MANAGER** by clicking on the cross mark ✕.

5.101

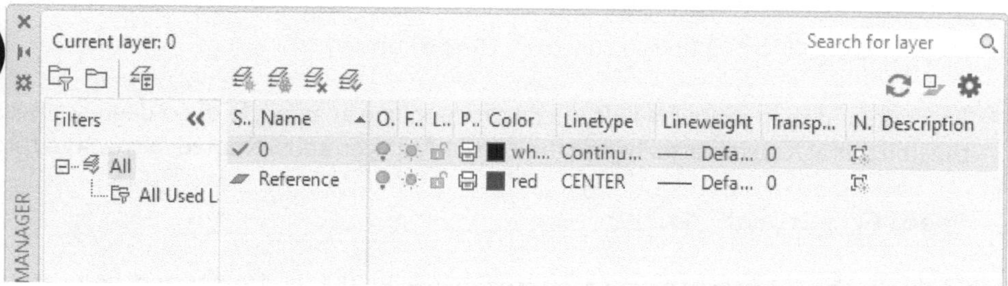

After creating the Reference layer, you need to move construction lines and a circle of diameter 90 units to this Reference layer.

3. Select all construction lines and the circle of diameter 90 units. Next, invoke the **Layer** drop-down list of the **Layer** panel (see Figure 5.102) and then click on the **Reference** layer to assign all the selected objects to it. Figure 5.103 shows the drawing after moving the construction lines and circle to the Reference layer.

5.102

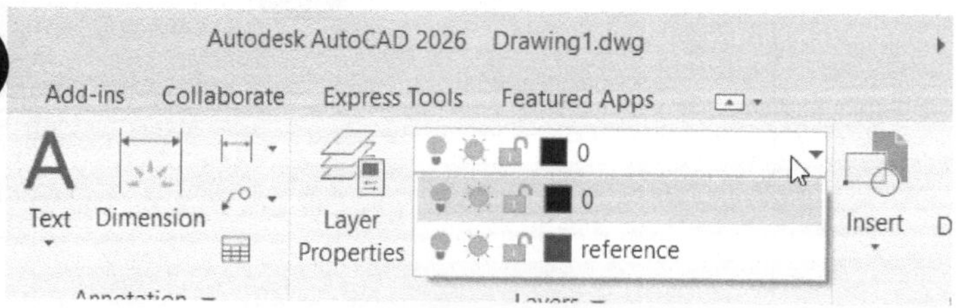

5.103

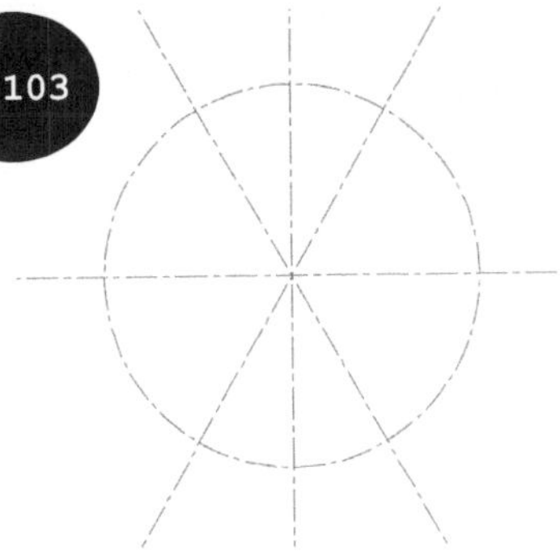

Section 4: Creating Drawing Circles

1. Ensure that the **0** layer is activated and selected in the **Layer** drop-down list of the **Layers** panel in the **Ribbon**.

2. Click on the **Circle, Diameter** tool in the **Circle** flyout in the **Draw** panel or enter **C** in the Command Line window and then press ENTER. You are prompted to specify the center point of the circle.

   ```
   Specify center point for circle or [3P 2P Ttr (tan tan radius)]:
   ```

3. Move the cursor toward the intersection point created between the construction lines and then click to specify the center point of the circle. You are prompted to specify the diameter of the circle.

   ```
   Specify radius of circle or [Diameter]:_d Specify diameter of circle:
   ```

4. Enter **120** as the diameter of the circle. A circle of diameter 120 units is created, see Figure 5.104.

5. Similarly, create a circle of diameter 40 units at the intersection of construction lines and a circle of diameter 16 units whose center point is at the intersection of the horizontal construction line and the reference circle, see Figure 5.105.

5.104

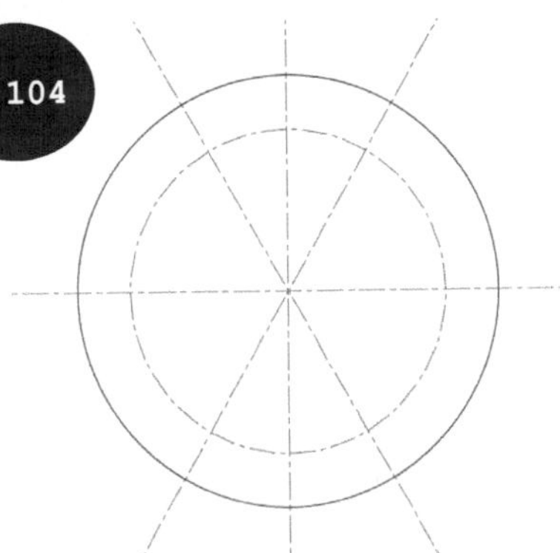

5.105

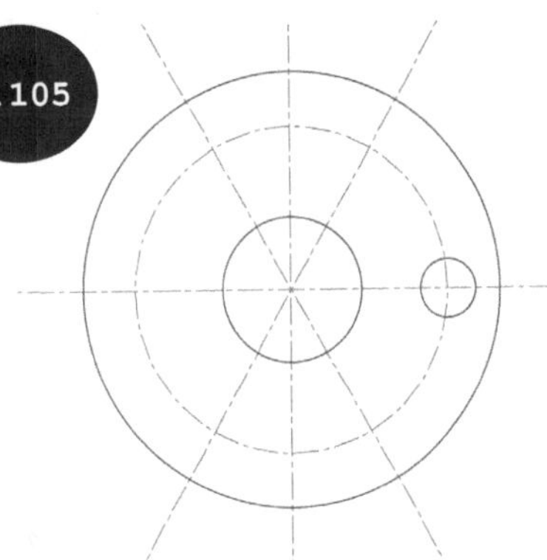

Section 5: Creating Reference Entities

1. Click on the **Offset** tool in the **Modify** panel. Alternatively, enter **O** and then press ENTER. You are prompted to specify the offset distance.

```
Specify offset distance or [Through Erase Layer] <Through>:
```

2. Enter **5** as the offset distance and then press ENTER. You are prompted to select an object to offset.

```
Select object to offset or [Exit Undo] <Exit>:
```

3. Click on the horizontal construction line and then click to specify the placement point on the upper side of the horizontal construction line. A construction line at an offset distance of 5 units from the horizontal construction line is created. Also, you are prompted to select an object to offset.

```
Select object to offset or [Exit Undo] <Exit>:
```

4. Click on the horizontal construction line again and then click to specify the placement point on the lower side of the horizontal construction line. A construction line at an offset distance of 5 units from the horizontal construction line is created, see Figure 5.106.

5.106

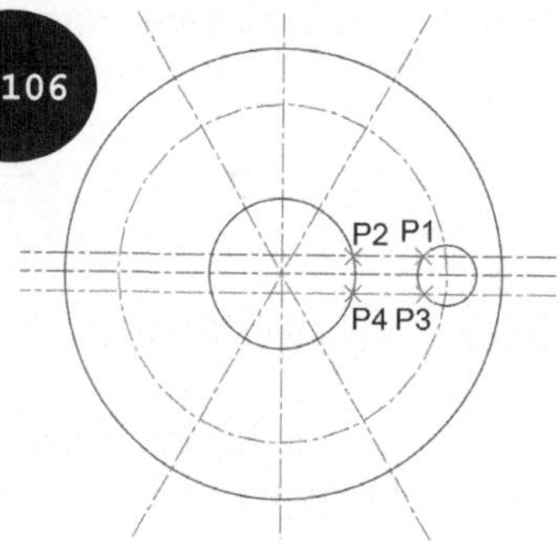

Section 6: Creating Line Entities

1. Click on the **Line** tool in the **Draw** panel. Alternatively, enter **L** and then press ENTER. You are prompted to specify the first point of the line.

```
Specify first point:
```

2. Move the cursor to the intersection point P1, refer to Figure 5.106. Next, click to specify the first point of the line when the cursor snaps to the intersection point P1. You are prompted to specify the next point of the line.

```
Specify next point or [Undo]:
```

3. Move the cursor horizontally toward left and then click to specify the endpoint of the line when the cursor snaps to the intersection point P2, refer to Figure 5.106. Next, press ENTER to exit the **Line** tool.

4. Similarly, create another line from intersection point P3 to intersection point P4, refer to Figure 5.106. Figure 5.107 shows the resultant drawing after creating the line entities.

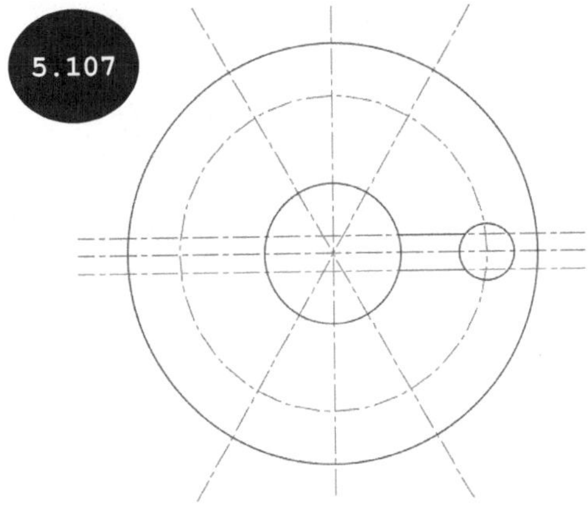

Section 7: Trimming Unwanted Entities

1. Click on the **Trim** tool in the **Modify** panel or enter **TR** in the Command Line window and then press ENTER. You are prompted to select objects to be trimmed.

```
Select object to trim or shift-select to extend or
[cuTting edges Crossing mOde Project eRase]:
```

2. Click on the unwanted entities (four entities) to be trimmed one by one, see Figure 5.108. Figure 5.109 shows the drawing after trimming the unwanted entities.

3. After trimming the unwanted entities, press ENTER to exit the **Trim** tool.

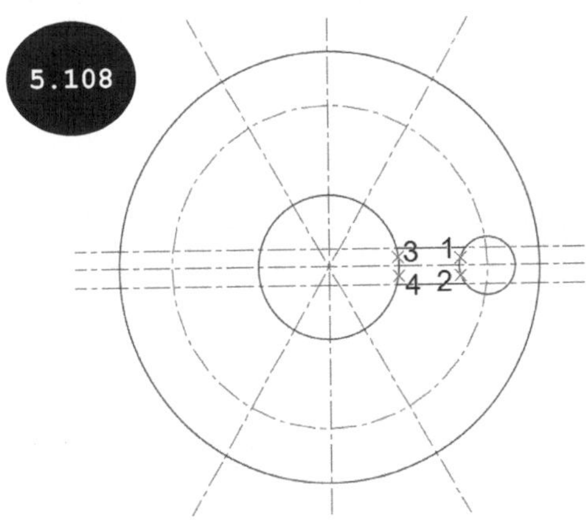

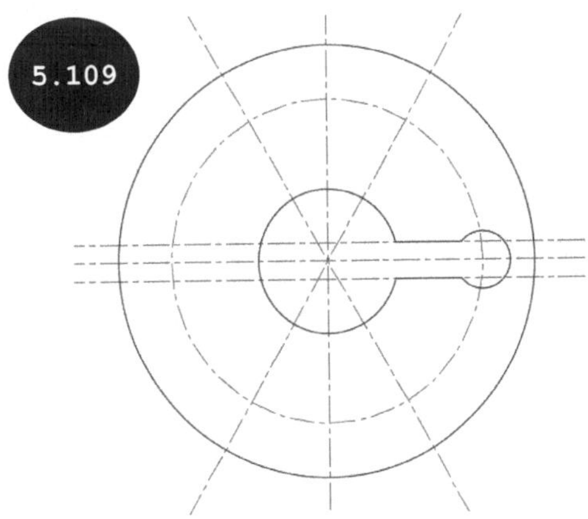

Section 8: Creating Circular/Polar Array

1. Invoke the **Array** flyout of the **Modify** panel and then click on the **Polar Array** tool, see Figure 5.110. You are prompted to select objects.

```
Select objects:
```

5.110

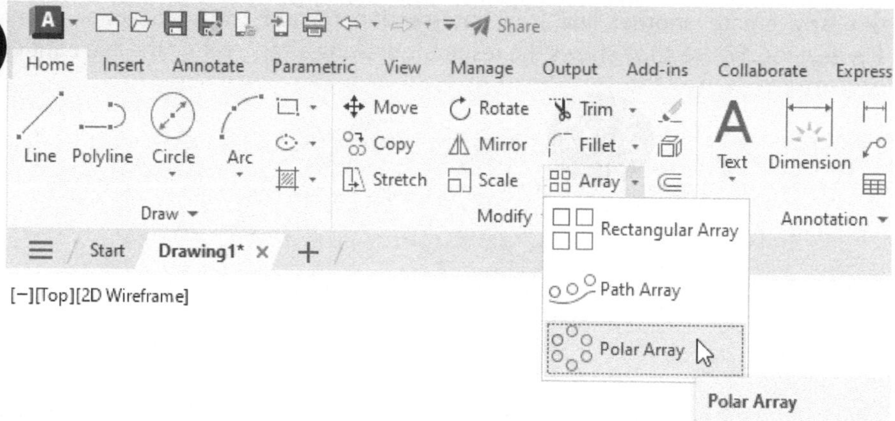

2. Click on the circle of diameter 16 units and two horizontal lines, see Figure 5.111. The selected objects get highlighted.

3. After selecting the objects, press ENTER. You are prompted to specify the center point of the array.

```
Specify center point of array or [Base point Axis of rotation]:
```

4. Click to specify the center point of the array at the intersection of the horizontal and vertical construction lines. A preview of the array with default parameters appears in the drawing area. Also, you are prompted to select the grip to edit the array.

```
Select grip to edit array or [ASsociative Base point Items Angle
between Fill angle ROWs Levels ROTate items eXit] <eXit>:
```

5. Ensure that **6** is entered in the **Items** field and **360** in the **Fill** field of the **Items** panel in the **Array Creation** tab. Next, press ENTER. The circular/polar array is created, see Figure 5.112.

5.111

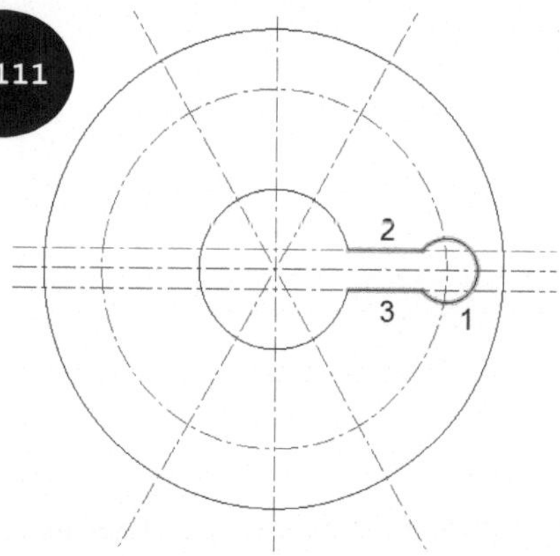

5.112

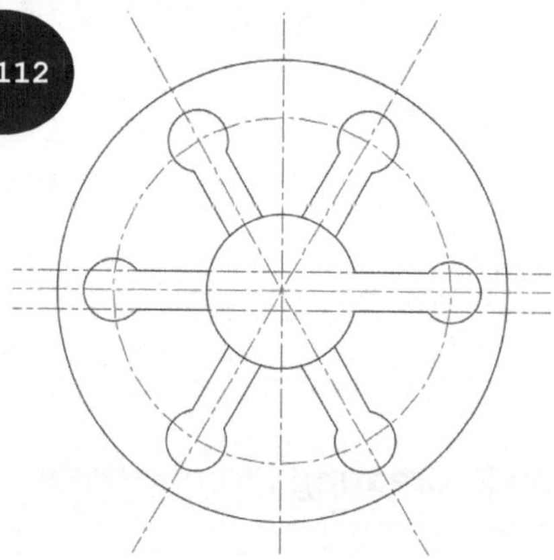

After creating the circular/polar array, you need to trim the remaining unwanted entities of the drawing by using the **Trim** tool.

6. Invoke the **Trim** tool and then trim the unwanted entities of the innermost circle of the drawing. Figure 5.113 shows the entities to be trimmed and Figure 5.114 shows the resultant drawing after trimming the entities.

5.113

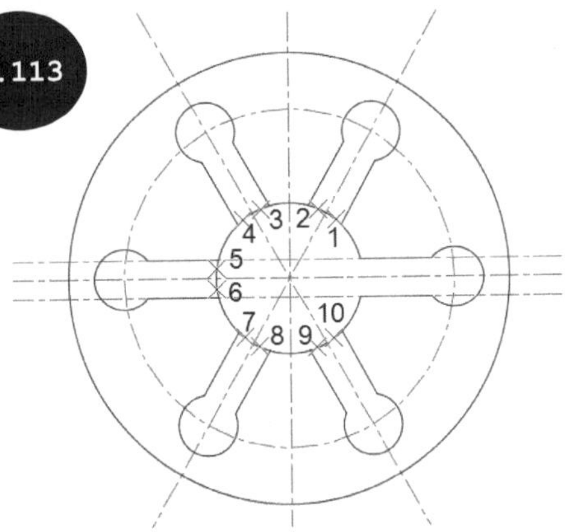

5.114

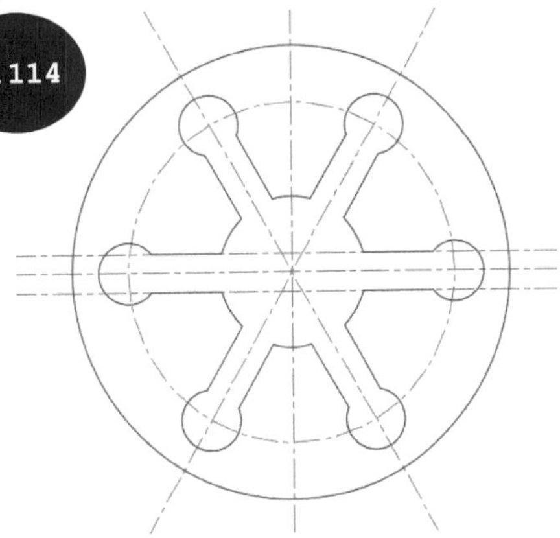

Section 9: Creating the Remaining Drawing Entities

1. Invoke the **Circle, Diameter** tool of the **Circle** flyout in the **Draw** panel and create a circle of diameter 240 units whose center point is at the intersection of the horizontal and vertical construction lines, see Figure 5.115. This circle will be used as the reference circle for creating drawing entities.

2. Assign the newly created circle of diameter 240 units to the Reference layer. To do so, select the circle and then invoke the **Layer** drop-down list in the **Layers** panel. Next, click on the **Reference** layer in the **Layer** drop-down list and then press the ESC key to exit the selection set. Figure 5.116 shows the circle after assigning it to the Reference layer.

5.115

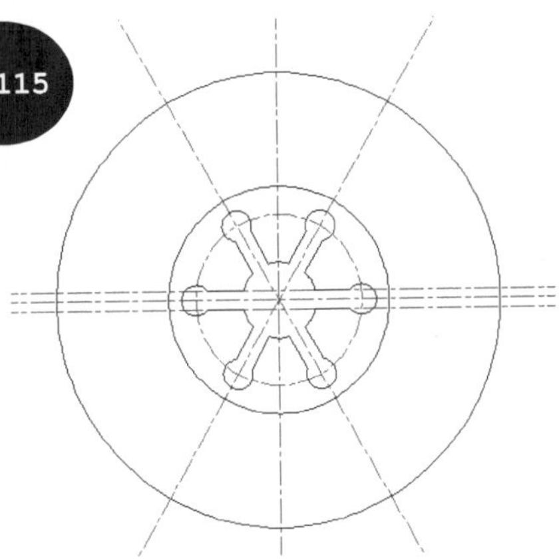

5.116

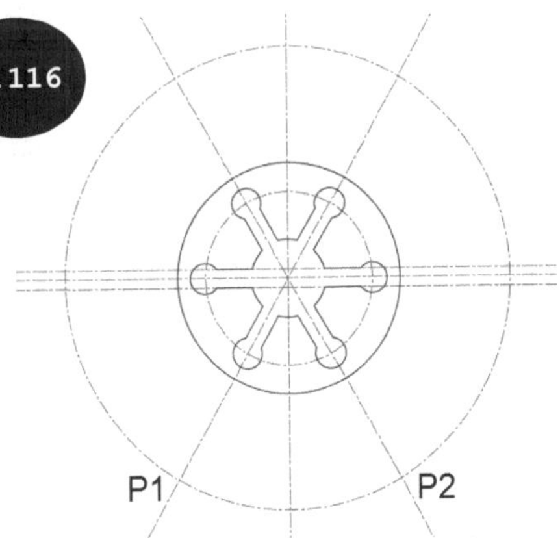

3. Invoke the **Circle, Diameter** tool and then create two circles of diameter 40 units at the intersection points 'P1' and 'P2', refer to Figure 5.116. Figure 5.117 shows the drawing after creating two circles of diameter 40 units.

4. Similarly, create two more circles (one of diameter 200 units and another of diameter 280 units) at the intersection of the horizontal and vertical construction lines, see Figure 5.118.

5.117

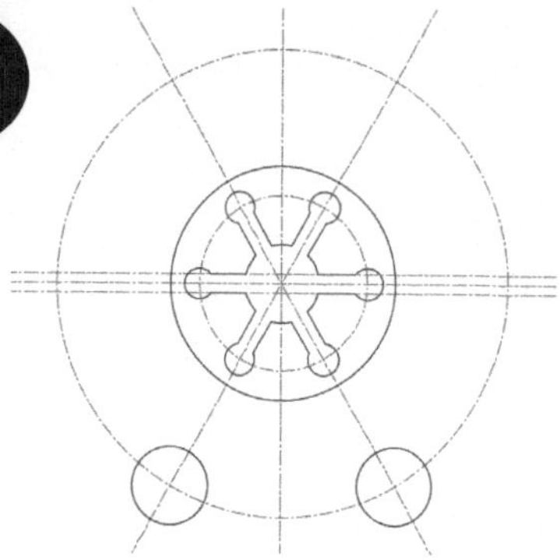

5.118

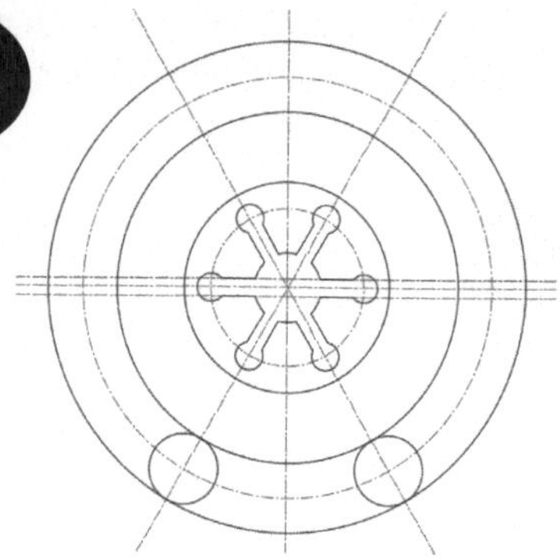

5. Click on the **Trim** tool in the **Modify** panel and then select the unwanted entities to be trimmed. Figure 5.119 shows the entities to be trimmed and Figure 5.120 shows the drawing after trimming the entities. Next, press ENTER to exit the **Trim** tool.

5.119

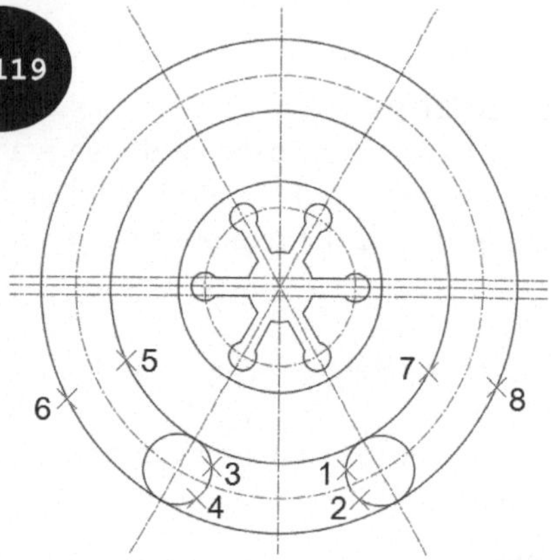

5.120

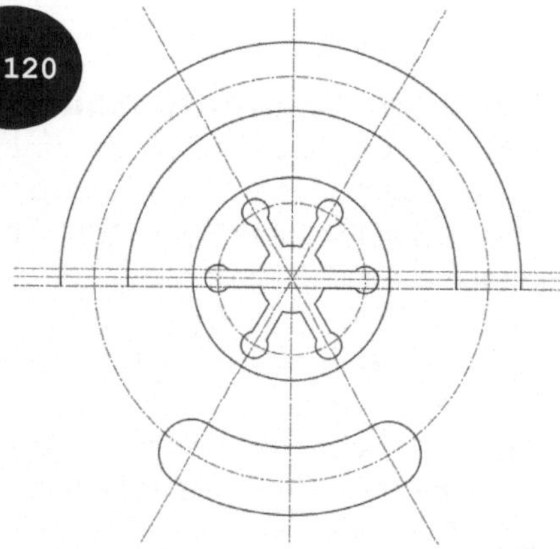

Now, you need to delete the unwanted entities of the drawing.

6. Click on the entities (two entities) to be deleted one by one, see Figure 5.121. Next, press the DELETE key. The selected entities get deleted, see Figure 5.122.

5.121

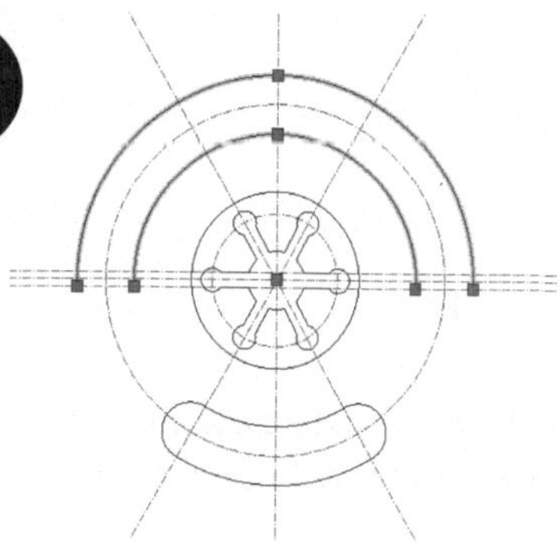

5.122

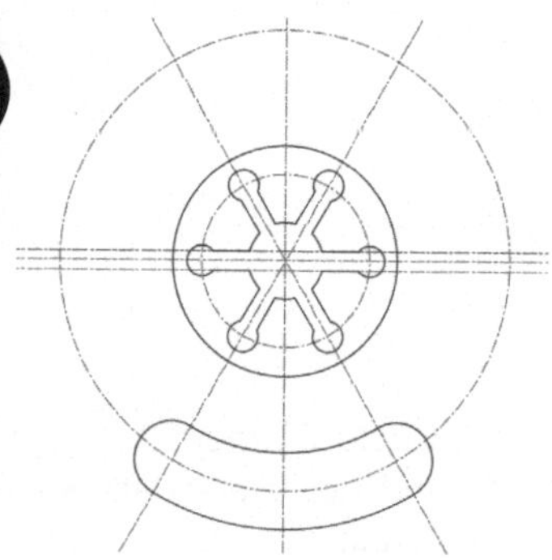

Now, you need to offset the slot entities at an offset distance of 5 units.

7. Click on the **Offset** tool in the **Modify** panel or enter O and then press ENTER. You are prompted to specify the offset distance.

```
Specify offset distance or [Through Erase Layer] <Through>:
```

8. Enter **5** as the offset distance and then press ENTER. You are prompted to select objects.

```
Select object to offset or [Exit Undo] <Exit>:
```

9. Click on the lower larger arc of the slot and then move the cursor outside it, see Figure 5.123. You are prompted to specify the point to define the offset direction.

```
Specify point on side to offset or [Exit Multiple Undo] <Exit>:
```

10. Click outside the slot to specify the position of the offset entity. The offset entity is created, see Figure 5.124. Also, you are prompted to select objects to offset again.

```
Select object to offset or [Exit Undo] <Exit>:
```

5.123

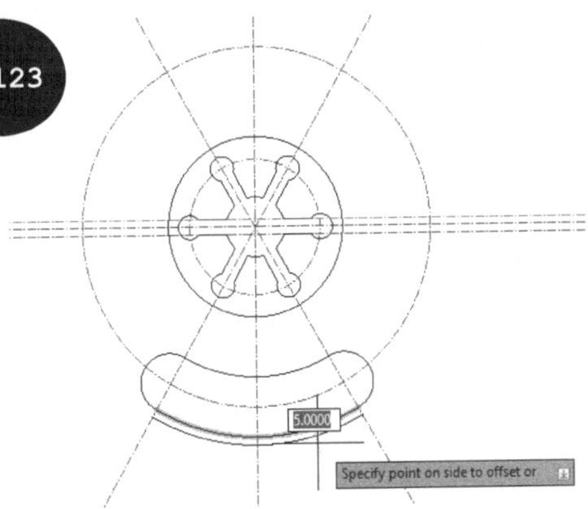

5.124

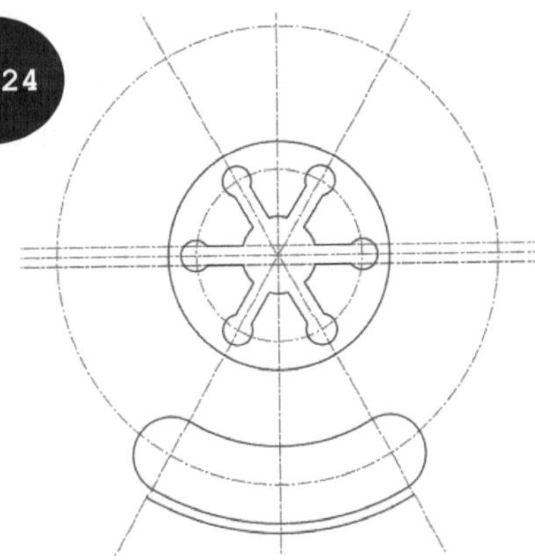

11. Similarly, click on the other entities of the slot one by one and offset them at an offset distance of 5 units, see Figure 5.125. Next, press ENTER to exit the **Offset** tool.

5.125

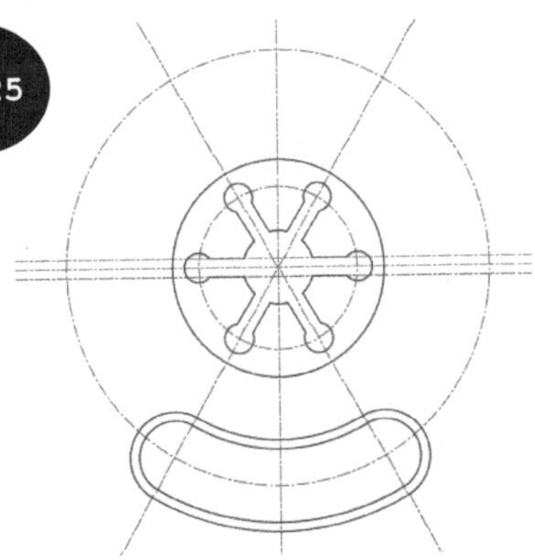

Now, you need to create construction lines which help in creating other entities of the drawing.

12. Click on the **Construction Line** tool in the expanded **Draw** panel or enter **XLINE** and then press ENTER. You are prompted to specify a point in the drawing area for creating a construction line.

```
Specify a point or [Hor Ver Ang Bisect Offset]:
```

13. Click on the **Offset** option in the command prompt or enter **O** and then press ENTER. You are prompted to specify the offset distance.

```
Specify offset distance or [Through] <5.0000>:
```

14. Enter **20** as the offset distance and then press ENTER. You are prompted to select the line object to offset.

```
Select a line object:
```

15. Click on the vertical construction line and then click on its left side to specify the placement point for creating a new vertical construction line. The vertical construction line is created, see Figure 5.126. Also, you are prompted to select the object to offset.

16. Click on the vertical construction line again and then click on its right side. The vertical construction line is created on the right side of the existing construction line, see Figure 5.127. Next, press ENTER to exit the **Construction Line** tool.

5.126

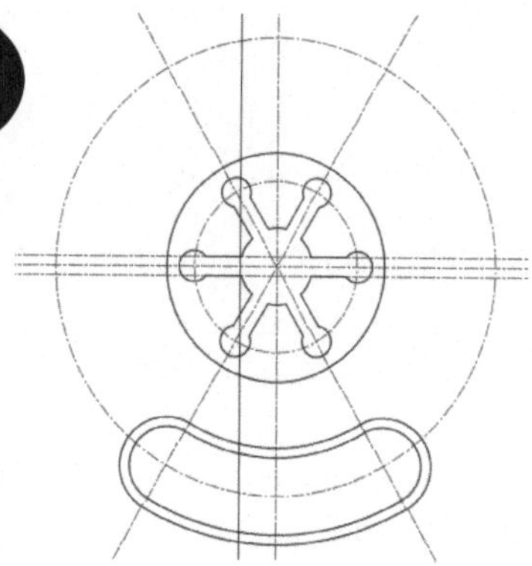

5.127

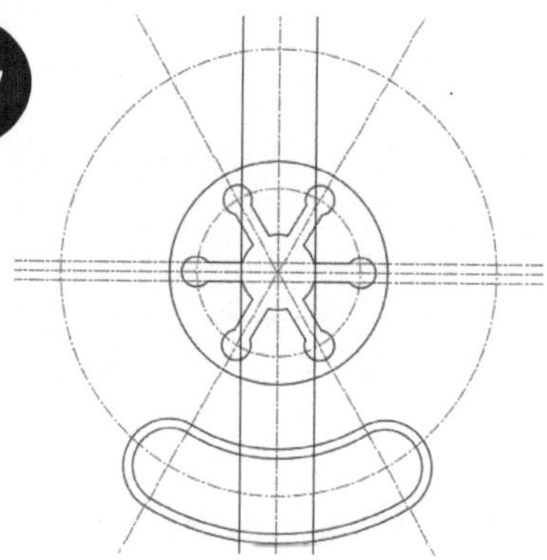

Now, you need to assign the newly created vertical construction lines to the Reference layer.

17. Click on the newly created vertical construction lines and then invoke the **Layer** drop-down list in the **Layers** panel. Next, click on the **Reference** layer in the **Layer** drop-down list and then press ESC. The selected objects are assigned to the Reference layer, see Figure 5.128.

18. Invoke the **Line** tool and then click to specify the start point and endpoint of the line at the intersection points 'P1' and 'P2', respectively, refer to Figure 5.128. Next, press ENTER to exit the tool.

19. Similarly, create a line whose start point and endpoint are at the intersection points 'P3' and 'P4', respectively, refer to Figure 5.128. Figure 5.129 shows the drawing after creating the line entities at the intersection points. Next, press ENTER to exit the tool.

5.128

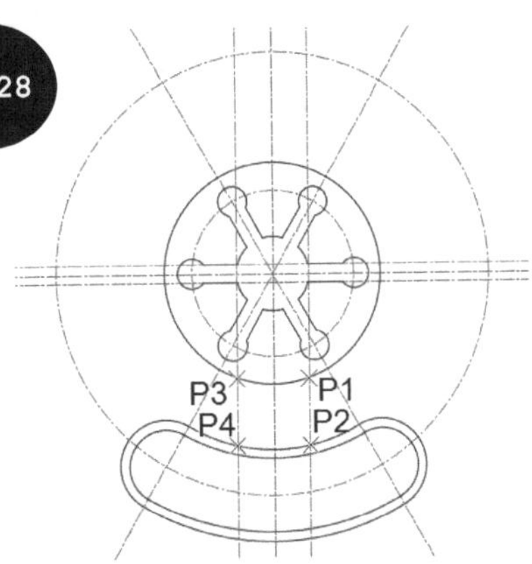

5.129

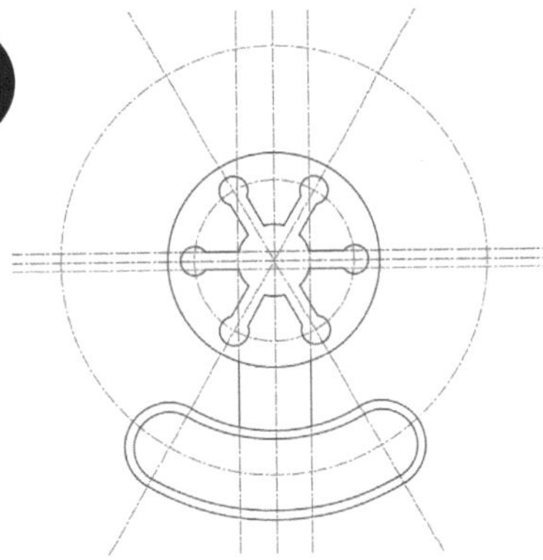

Now, you need to trim the unwanted entities of the drawing.

20. Invoke the **Trim** tool and then trim the entities shown in Figure 5.130. Figure 5.131 shows the drawing after trimming the entities.

5.130

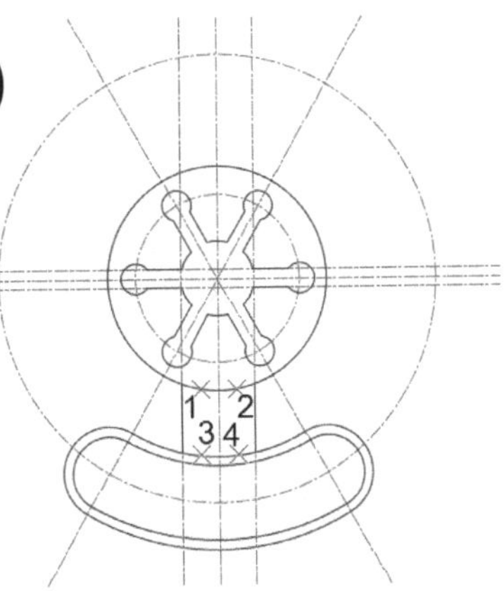

5.131

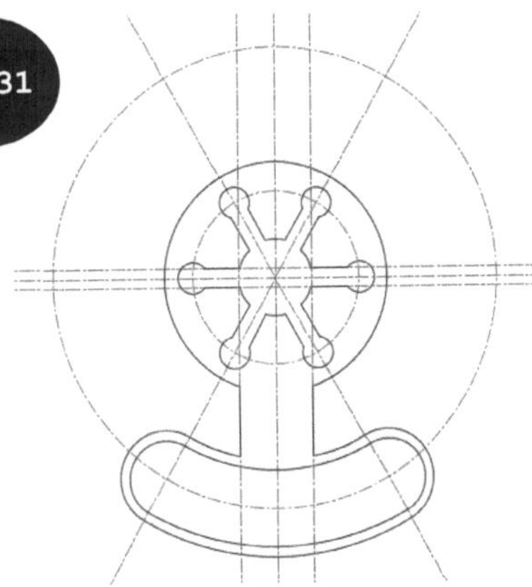

Now, you can hide the Reference layer.

21. Invoke the **Layer** drop-down list of the **Layer** panel, see Figure 5.132. Next, click on the **Turn a layer On or Off** icon of the Reference layer, see Figure 5.132. All the construction lines assigned to the Reference layer get hidden in the drawing area. Figure 5.133 shows the final drawing.

5.132

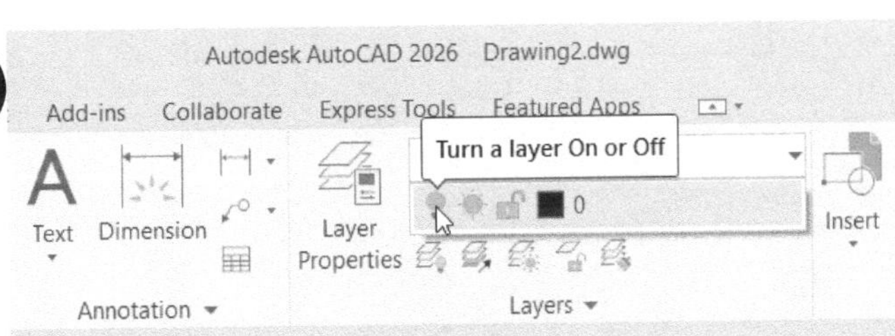

5.133

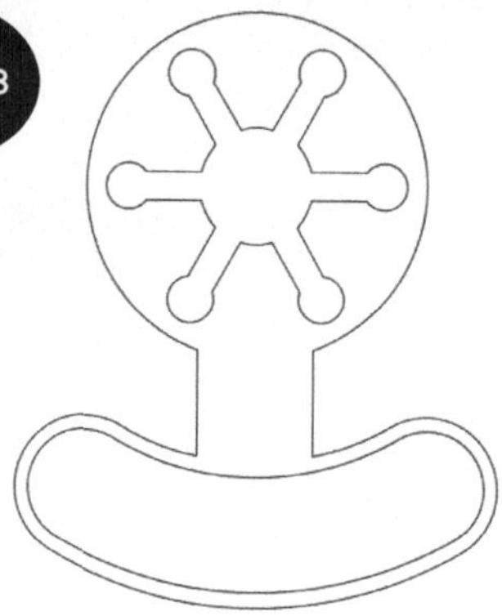

Section 10: Saving the Drawing

After creating the drawing, you need to save it.

1. Click on the **Save** tool in the **Quick Access Toolbar**. The **Save Drawing As** dialog box appears.
2. Browse to the *Chapter 5* folder inside the *AutoCAD* folder.
3. Enter **Tutorial 3** in the **File name** field of the dialog box and then click on the **Save** button. The drawing gets saved with the name Tutorial 3 in the *Chapter 5* folder.

Hands-on Test Drive 1

Create the drawing shown in Figure 5.134. The dimensions shown in the figure are for your reference only. You will learn about applying dimensions in later chapters.

5.134

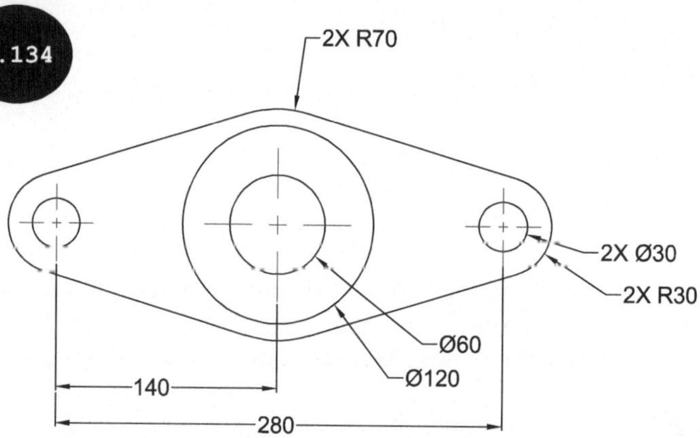

Hands-on Test Drive 2

Create the drawing shown in Figure 5.135.

5.135

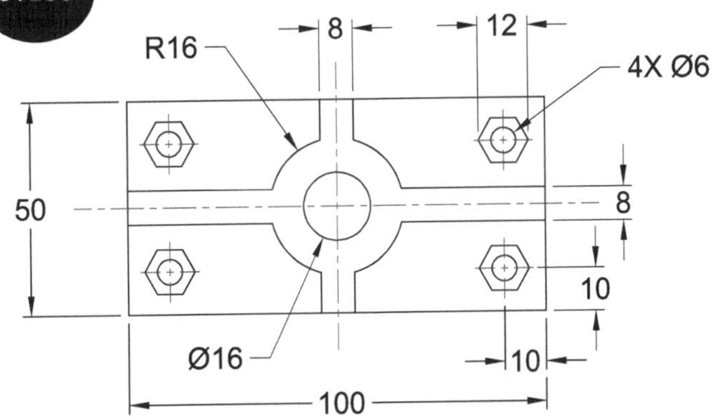

Hands-on Test Drive 3

Create the drawing shown in Figure 5.136.

5.136

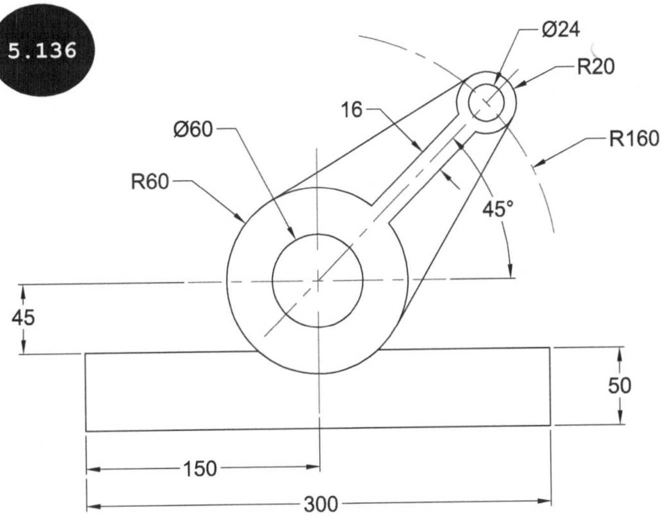

Summary

The chapter introduced various object selection methods and methods for trimming and extending drawing entities. It also described methods for creating arrays, fillets, and chamfer, and methods for mirroring, offsetting, moving, copying, rotating, scaling, stretching, and lengthening drawing entities.

Questions

Complete the following sentences:

- In the _________ selection method, only the objects that are completely enclosed within the rectangular window get selected.
- In the _________ selection method, all objects that are completely enclosed or touch the rectangular window get selected.
- The _________ selection method is used for selecting a group of objects by drawing a series of continuous lines over the objects to be selected.
- In AutoCAD, you can trim the unwanted drawing entities by using the _________ tool.
- In AutoCAD, you can create different types of arrays by using the _________ , _________ , and _________ tools.
- You can create a mirror image of the drawing entities about a mirroring line by using the _________ tool.
- A _________ is a curved edge which is used for removing or eliminating sharp edges of the model that can cause injury while handling the object.
- You can create a chamfer by using the _________ tool.
- You can move drawing objects from one location to another by using the _________ tool.
- You can stretch objects by using the _________ tool.
- You can rotate an object or a set of objects at an angle by using the _________ tool.

CHAPTER

6

Working with Dimensions and Dimension Styles

In this chapter, the following topics will be discussed:

- Working with Components of a Dimension
- Creating a New Dimension Style
- Modifying an Existing Dimension Style
- Overriding a Dimension Style
- Applying Dimensions
- Applying a Linear Dimension
- Applying an Aligned Dimension
- Applying an Angular Dimension
- Applying an Arc Length Dimension
- Applying a Radius Dimension
- Applying a Diameter Dimension
- Applying a Jogged Radius Dimension
- Applying a Jogged Linear Dimension
- Applying an Ordinate Dimension
- Applying Baseline Dimensions
- Applying Continue Dimensions
- Applying Multiple Dimensions

After creating a drawing, it is imperative to assign dimensions to it. A good AutoCAD drawing with all the desired dimensions conveys all the necessary information clearly and accurately. Note that 2D drawings are the only source for manufacturing components. These are not just drawings but a language for engineers and designers to communicate information regarding the manufacture of components. Therefore, it is extremely vital to generate accurate and error-free drawings with all the desired dimensions and annotations for production. Any incorrect or missing information in drawings about a component can lead to faulty production.

AutoCAD is provided with various dimensioning tools in the **Dimension** flyout of the **Annotation** panel in the **Home** tab for applying dimensions quickly and easily, see Figure 6.1.

6.1

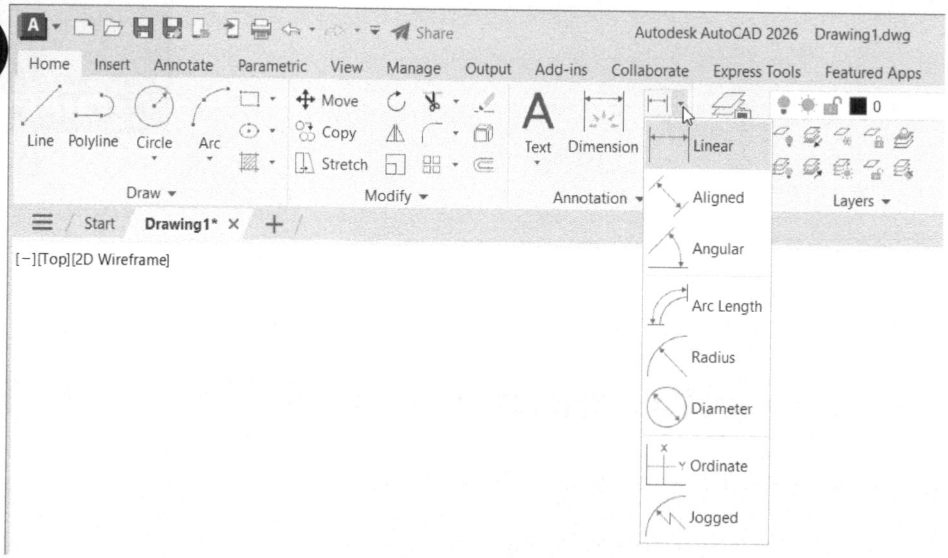

On adding dimensions to a drawing, the dimensions appear as per the default dimension style which is the Standard dimension style. The Standard dimension style is the current dimension style of a drawing which controls the appearance of dimensions such as the size of dimension text and arrows, the length of extension lines, and so on. In most of the drawings, the default dimension style may not meet your requirements. Therefore, AutoCAD allows you to modify the existing dimension style or create new dimension styles as per your requirements. In this chapter, you will learn about various components of dimensions that can be controlled by dimension styles, creating new dimension style, and adding dimensions to a drawing.

Working with Components of a Dimension

In AutoCAD, each dimension has several components such as a dimension line, dimension text, extension line, and so on, see Figure 6.2. You can control these dimension components by using the dimension style. You can modify the existing dimension style or create a new dimension style as required by using the **Dimension Style Manager** dialog box. Note that each industry follows a different dimension style. Therefore, it is important to become familiar with the **Dimension Style Manager** dialog box for creating your industry-specific dimension style.

6.2

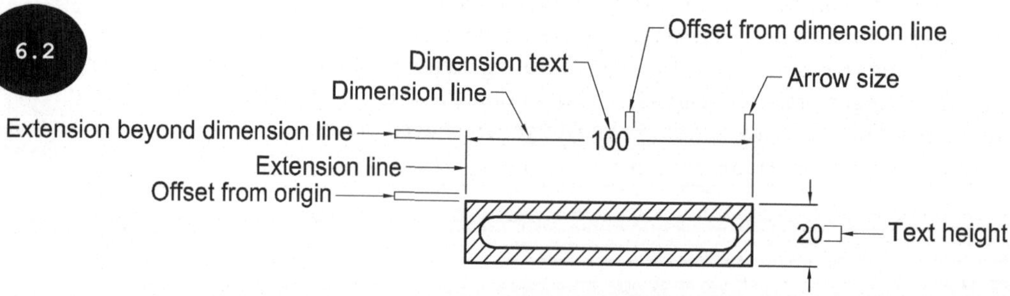

To invoke the **Dimension Style Manager** dialog box, enter **D** in the Command Line window and then press ENTER. Figure 6.3 shows the **Dimension Style Manager** dialog box. You can also invoke this dialog box by clicking on the **Dimension Style** tool in the expanded **Annotation** panel of the **Home** tab, see Figure 6.4. The options of the **Dimension Style Manager** dialog box are discussed next.

6.3

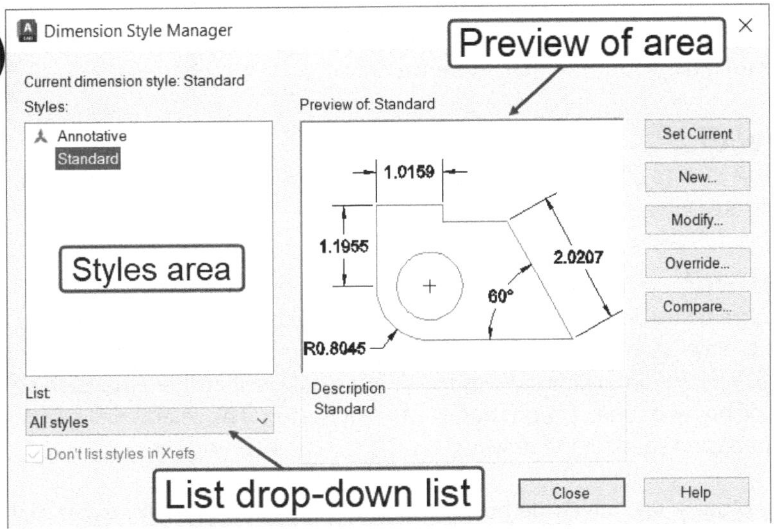

6.4

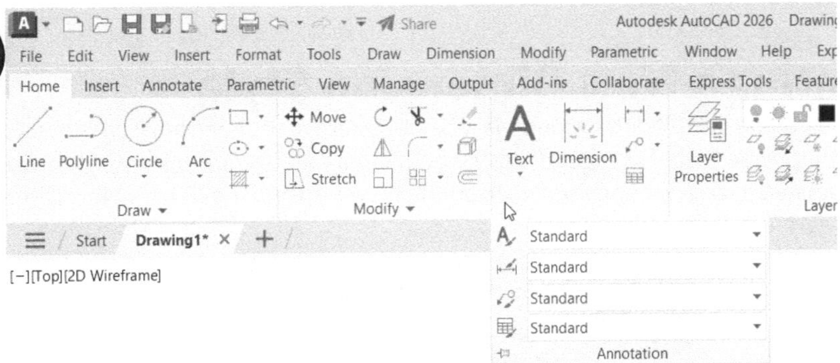

Styles

The **Styles** area is available on the left of the **Dimension Style Manager** dialog box. This area displays the list of all the available dimension styles. Note that the display of dimension styles in this area is controlled by the option selected in the **List** drop-down list of the dialog box. The options of the **List** drop-down list are discussed next.

List

The options in the **List** drop-down list control the display of dimension styles in the **Styles** area of the dialog box. By default, the **All styles** option is selected in this drop-down list. As a result, all the dimension styles available in the drawing are displayed in the **Styles** area of the dialog box. If you select the **Styles in use** option, only the dimension styles that are in use get listed in the **Styles** area of the dialog box.

Don't list styles in Xrefs

On selecting the **Don't list styles in Xrefs** check box, the Xref dimension styles will not be displayed in the **Styles** area of the dialog box. If you uncheck this check box, all the Xref dimension styles get displayed in the **Styles** area of the dialog box. Note that this check box is enabled if an Xref drawing is attached to the current drawing. The Xref is an external reference drawing which is attached to the current drawing as a reference file. You can attach multiple external drawings to the current drawing. You will learn more about external reference drawings in later chapters.

Preview of

The **Preview of** area of the dialog box displays the preview of the currently selected dimension style in the **Style** area.

Set Current

The **Set Current** button of the dialog box is used for making a dimension style as the current dimension style of the drawing. Note that the current dimension style controls the dimensions applied in the drawing. To make a dimension style as the current style, select the dimension style in the **Styles** area of the dialog box and then click on the **Set Current** button. The selected dimension style becomes the current dimension style for the drawing.

The **New**, **Modify**, and **Override** buttons of the **Dimension Style Manager** dialog box are used for creating new dimension style, modifying existing dimension style, and overriding existing dimension style, respectively. All these are discussed next.

Creating a New Dimension Style

In addition to the default dimension style, you can create new dimension styles by using the **New** button of the **Dimension Style Manager** dialog box. To create a new dimension style, invoke the **Dimension Style Manager** dialog box and then click on the **New** button. The **Create New Dimension Style** dialog box appears, see Figure 6.5.

6.5

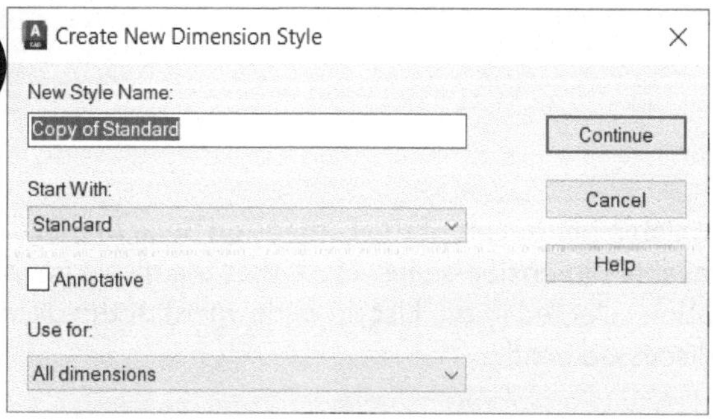

In the **New Style Name** field of the **Create New Dimension Style** dialog box, you can specify a name for the dimension style. Next, select the base dimension style in the **Start With** drop-down list of the dialog box. Next, choose the type of dimension to which you want to apply this dimension style in the **Use for** drop-down list of the dialog box. By default, the **All dimensions** option is selected in this drop-down list. As a result, the new dimension style applies to all dimension types. If you want to apply the new dimension style only to a particular dimension type, then you need to select that dimension type in this drop-down list. For example, if you want to apply the new dimension style only to the radial dimensions then select the **Radius dimensions** option in this drop-down list. To make the annotative dimension style, select the **Annotative** check box. Next, click on the **Continue** button in the dialog box. The **New Dimension Style** dialog box appears, see Figure 6.6. In this dialog box, you can specify dimension parameters as required by using the respective options available under the respective tabs of the dialog box. The different tabs and options of this dialog box are discussed next.

6.6

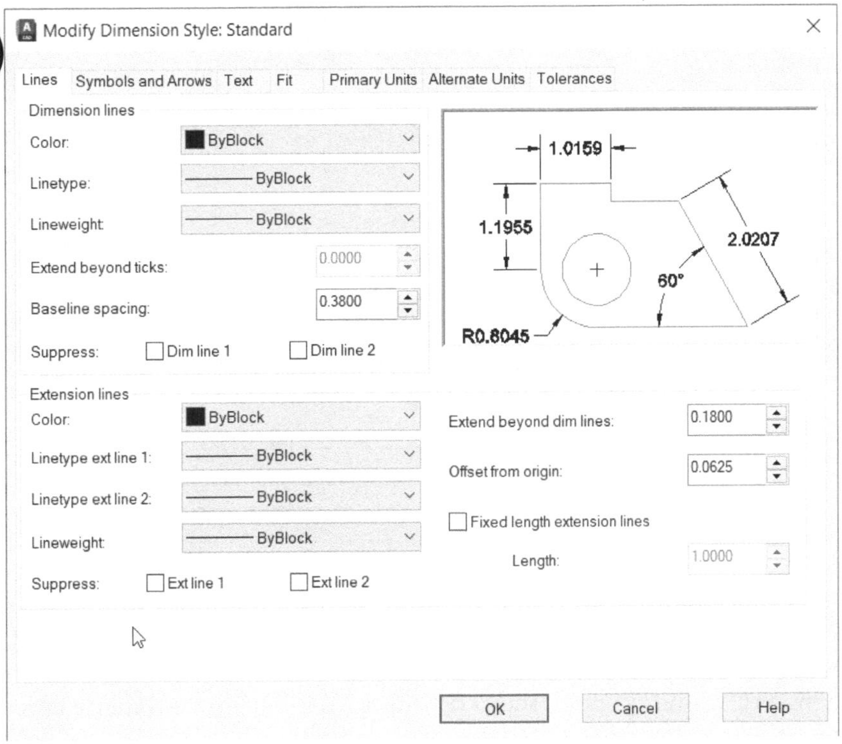

Lines Tab

The options in the **Lines** tab of the dialog box are arranged in two areas: **Dimension lines** and **Extension lines**, refer to Figure 6.6. The options available in both these areas are discussed next.

Dimension lines Area

The options of the **Dimension lines** area are used for controlling the appearance of dimension lines, as discussed next.

Color

The **Color** drop-down list is used for selecting a color for the dimension lines. Figure 6.7 shows dimension lines in red color. Note that the color set for dimension lines also applies to dimension arrowheads.

Linetype

The **Linetype** drop-down list is used for selecting a linetype such as Continuous (solid line), Center, or Hidden for dimension lines. Figure 6.8 shows dimension lines with the DASHED linetype.

6.7

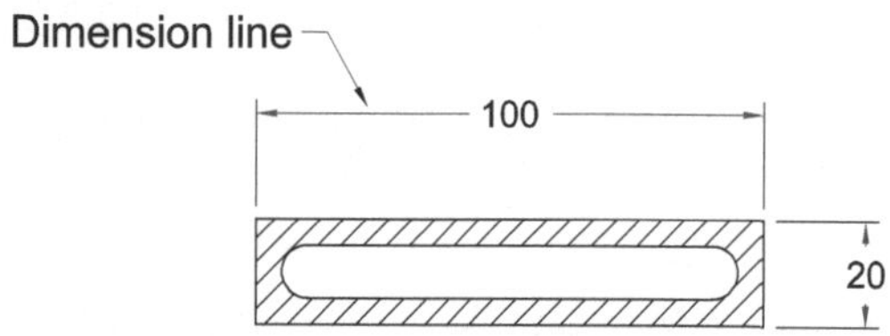

6.8

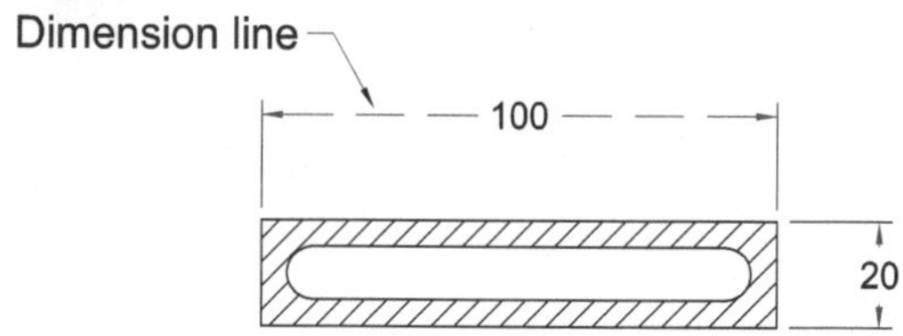

Lineweight

The **Lineweight** drop-down list is used for selecting a lineweight (thickness) for dimension lines. Figure 6.9 shows dimension lines with 0.80 mm lineweight.

6.9

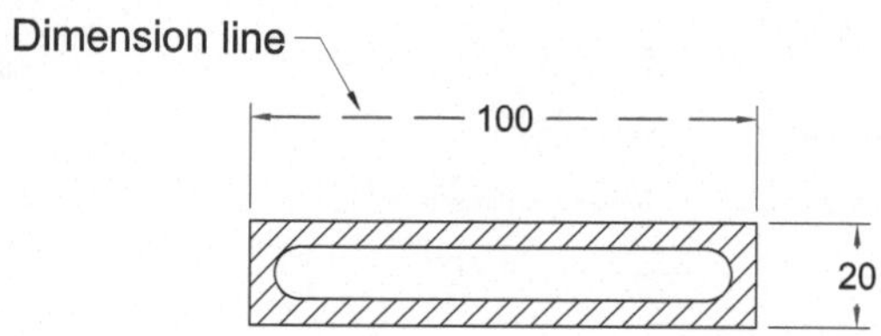

Extend beyond ticks

The **Extend beyond ticks** field is used for specifying the distance for the dimension line to extend beyond the extension lines. Figure 6.10 shows dimension lines with 0 (zero) distance beyond the extension lines and Figure 6.11 shows dimension lines with 3 units distance beyond the extension lines. By default, this field is not enabled in the dialog box. It is activated only when the arrowhead style for dimension lines is set to architectural tick, integral, or similar in the **First** or **Second** drop-down lists of the **Arrowheads** area which is available in the **Symbols and Arrows** tab of the dialog box.

6.10

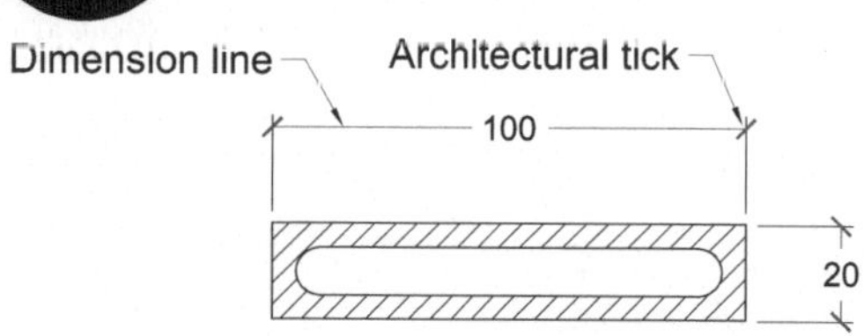

Extend beyond ticks = 0 (Zero)

6.11

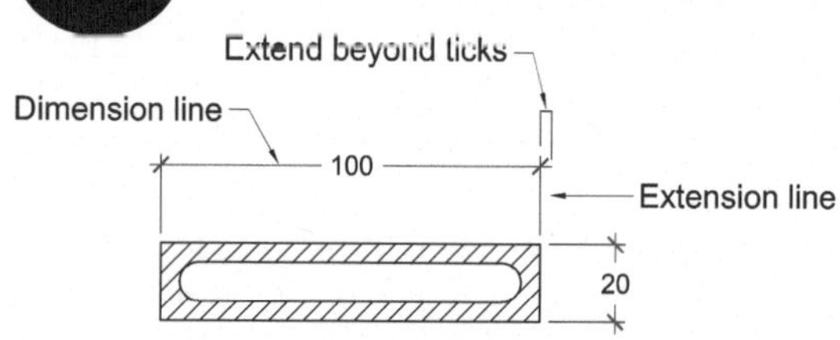

Extend beyond ticks = 3 units

Baseline spacing

The **Baseline spacing** field is used for specifying the spacing between dimension lines of the baseline dimensions, see Figure 6.12. You will learn more about applying baseline dimensions later in this chapter.

6.12

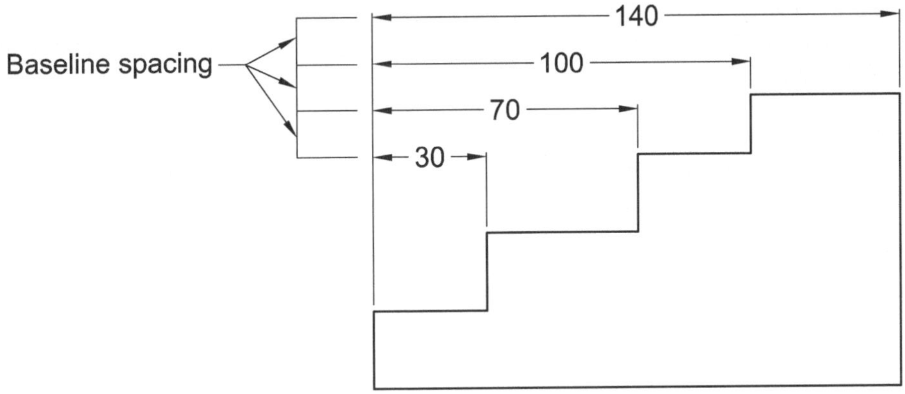

Suppress

The **Dim line 1** and **Dim line 2** check boxes are used for suppressing first and second dimension lines, respectively. Figure 6.13 shows dimensions with the first dimension line suppressed and Figure 6.14 shows dimensions with the second dimension line suppressed. By default, these check boxes are unchecked. As a result, both the dimension lines of the dimension appear in the drawing.

6.13

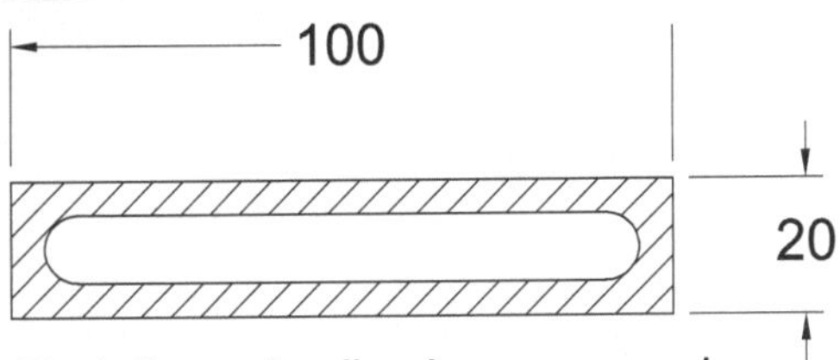

First dimension line is suppressed

6.14

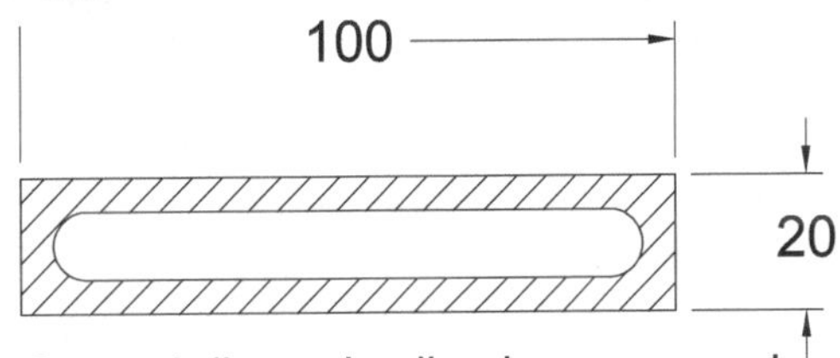

Second dimension line is suppressed

Extension lines Area

The options of the **Extension lines** area are used for controlling the appearance of extension lines of dimensions. The options are discussed next.

Color

The **Color** drop-down list of the **Extension lines** area is used for selecting the color for the extension lines. You can assign a different color to extension lines of dimensions.

Linetype ext line 1

The **Linetype ext line 1** drop-down list of this area is used for selecting a linetype such as Continuous (solid line), Center, or Hidden for the first extension lines of dimensions.

Linetype ext line 2

The **Linetype ext line 2** drop-down list of this area is used for selecting a linetype such as Continuous (solid line), Center, or Hidden for the second extension lines of dimensions.

Lineweight

The **Lineweight** drop-down list of this area is used for selecting a lineweight (thickness) for extension lines.

Extend beyond dim lines

The **Extend beyond dim lines** field is used for specifying a distance value for the extension lines to extend beyond the dimension line, see Figure 6.15.

Offset from origin

The **Offset from origin** field is used for specifying an offset distance for the extension lines from their origin, see Figure 6.16.

6.15

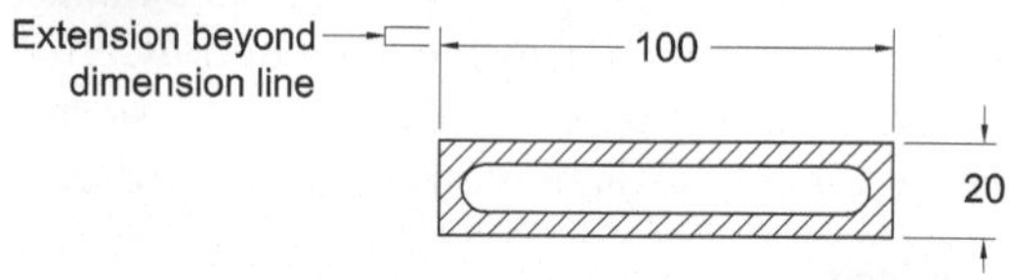

6.16

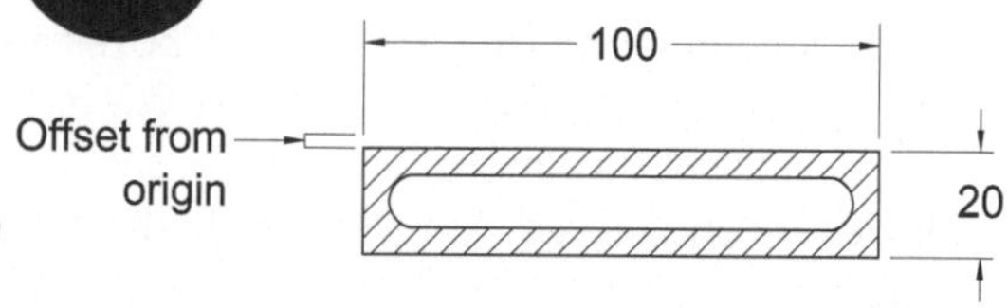

Fixed length extension lines

On selecting the **Fixed length extension lines** check box, the **Length** field which is available below this check box gets enabled. In the **Length** field, you can specify a fixed distance for the extension line, starting from the dimension line, see Figure 6.17. By default, the **Fixed length extension lines** check box is unchecked. As a result, dimensions are applied with full-length extension lines. Figure 6.17 shows dimensions with specified fixed length extension lines and Figure 6.18 shows dimensions with the full-length extension lines.

6.17

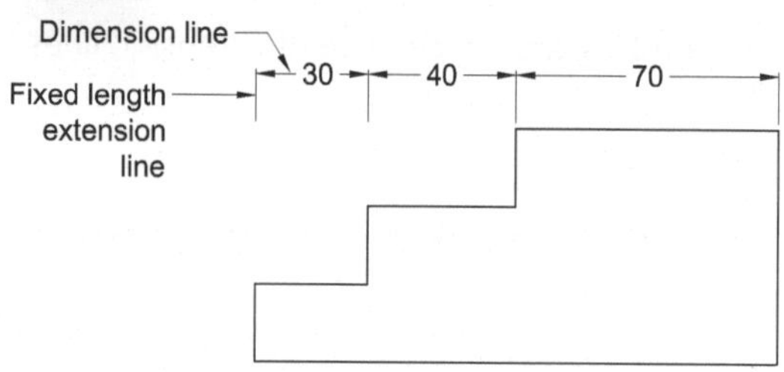

6.18

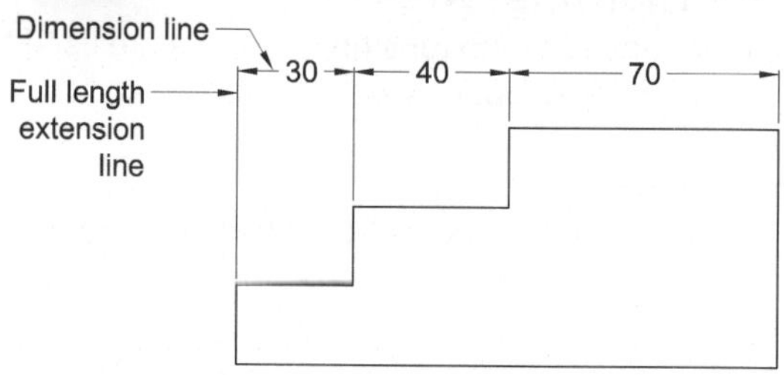

Suppress

The **Ext line 1** and **Ext line 2** check boxes of the **Extension lines** area are used for suppressing the first and second extension lines of dimensions, respectively.

Symbols and Arrows Tab

The options in the **Symbols and Arrows** tab of the dialog box are used for specifying dimension arrowheads, arrow size, center marks, dimension break, and so on, see Figure 6.19. The options in the **Symbols and Arrows** tab are discussed next.

6.19

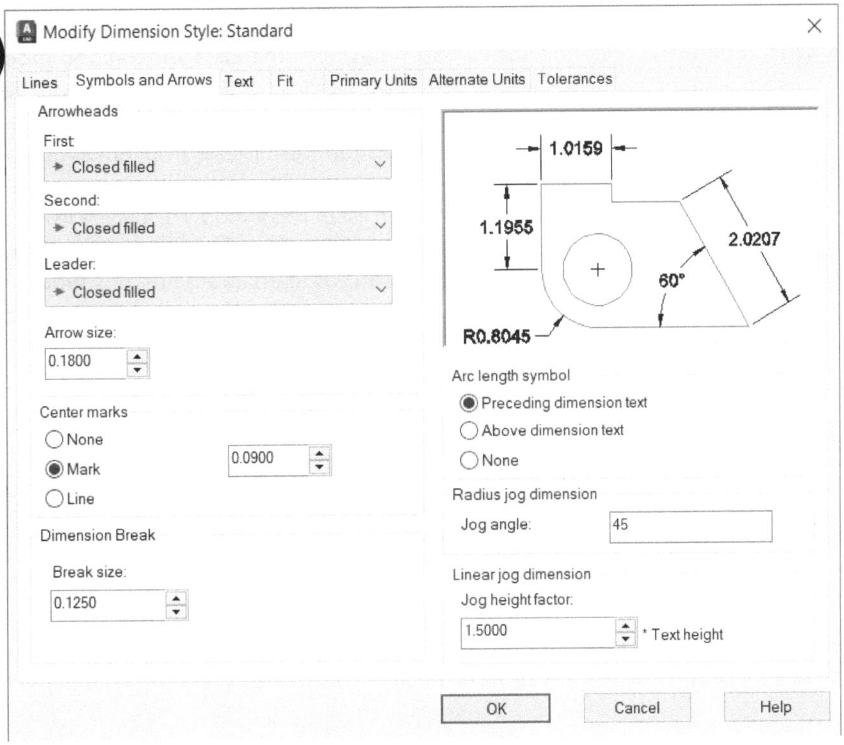

Arrowheads Area

The options in the **Arrowheads** area of the **Symbols and Arrows** tab are used for controlling the styles and parameters for arrowheads. The options are discussed next.

First and Second

The **First** and **Second** drop-down lists are used for specifying the first and second arrowheads for dimension lines, respectively. By default, the same arrowhead style (Closed filled) is applied at both ends (first and second) of the dimension lines. Also, on selecting the first arrowhead style in the **First** drop-down list, the same arrowhead style gets selected automatically in the **Second** drop-down list. To apply a different arrowhead style for the second arrowhead of the dimension lines, select the required arrowhead style in the **Second** drop-down list. Figure 6.20 shows dimensions with the **Closed filled** as the first arrowhead style and the **Architectural tick** as the second arrowhead style.

6.20

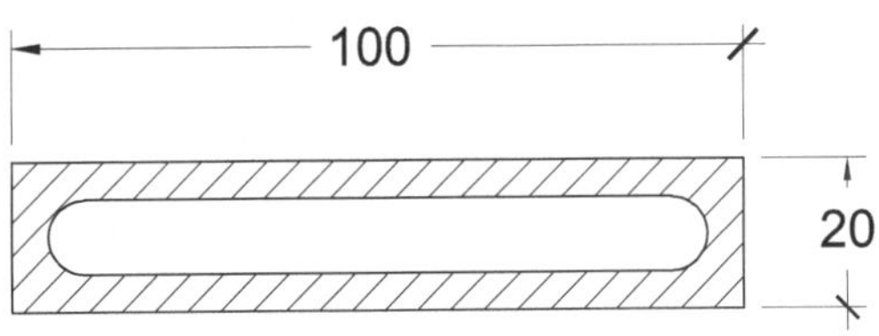

Note: In addition to selecting arrowhead styles from the **First** and **Second** drop-down lists, you can use custom/user-defined arrowhead styles for dimensions, as per your requirement. To define a custom/user-defined arrowhead style, you need to first create it as a block, and then you can select the **User Arrow** option from these drop-down lists. On selecting the **User Arrow** option, the **Select Custom Arrow Block** window appears, see Figure 6.21. The **Select from Drawing Blocks** drop-down list of this window displays a list of all blocks created in the drawing. You can select the required block as the arrowhead style in this drop-down list and then click on the **OK** button. You will learn about creating blocks in later chapters.

6.21

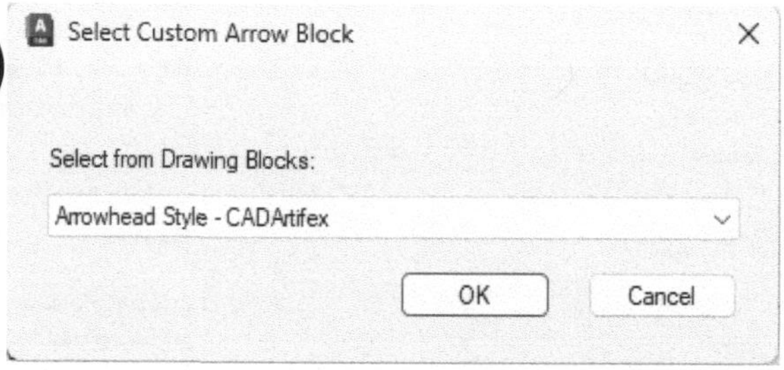

Leader

The **Leader** drop-down list is used for specifying arrowhead style for leader lines.

Arrow size

The **Arrow size** field is used for specifying a size for dimension arrowheads.

Center marks Area

The options in the **Center marks** area are used for controlling the display of the center marks for the radius and diameter dimensions, see Figure 6.22.

6.22

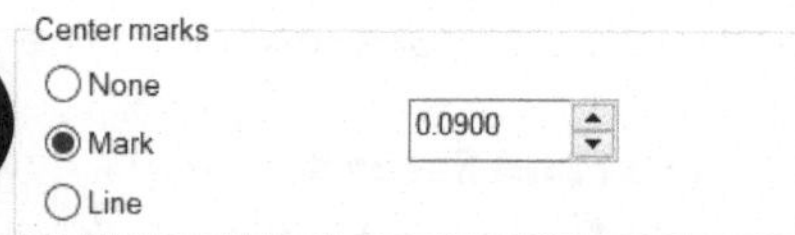

If you select the **None** radio button, no center mark appears at the center of circles or arcs on applying diameter or radius dimensions. If you select the **Mark** radio button, a cross mark appears at the center of circles or arcs on applying diameter or radius dimensions, see Figure 6.23. If you select the **Line** radio button, centerlines appear at the center of circles or arcs on applying diameter or radius dimensions, see Figure 6.24.

6.23

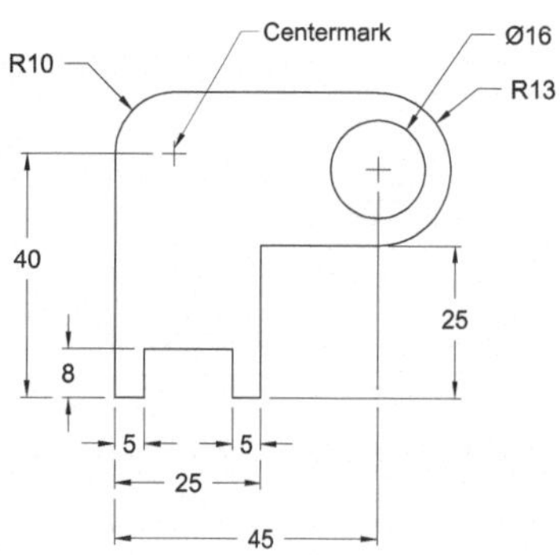

6.24

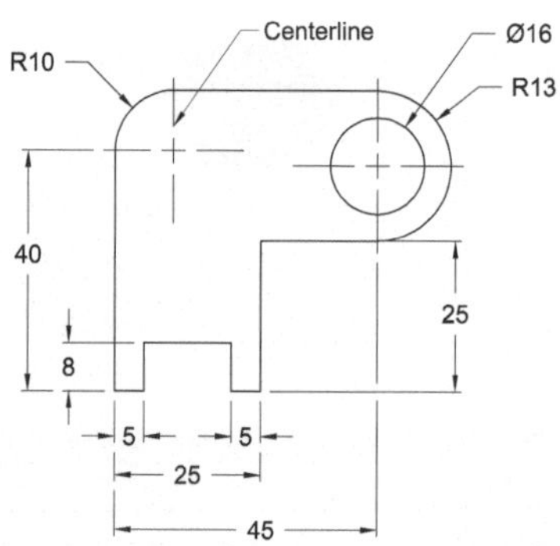

Note that when you select the **Mark** or **Line** radio button, the **Size** field becomes enabled in this area. In this field, you can specify the size of the center mark or centerline to appear at the center of circles or arcs on applying diameter or radius dimensions.

Dimension Break Area

The **Break size** field of the **Dimension Break** area (see Figure 6.25) is used for specifying the default break size for the dimension lines. Note that you can break dimension lines that intersect with each other or with drawing objects to avoid overlapping or confusion by using the DIMBREAK command. When you break dimension lines by using the DIMBREAK command, the break size specified in the **Break size** field will be applied, automatically. Figure 6.26 shows the intersecting dimension lines and Figure 6.27 shows the dimensions after breaking the dimension lines by using the DIMBREAK command.

6.25

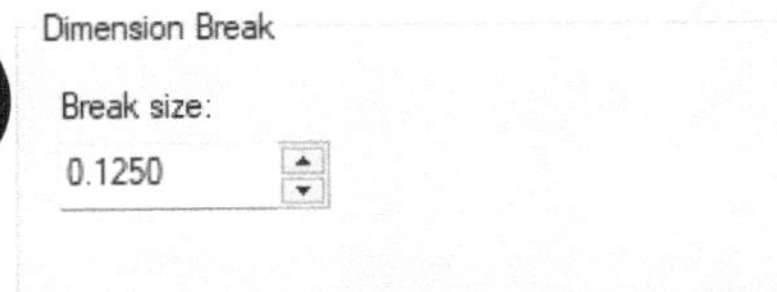

6.26

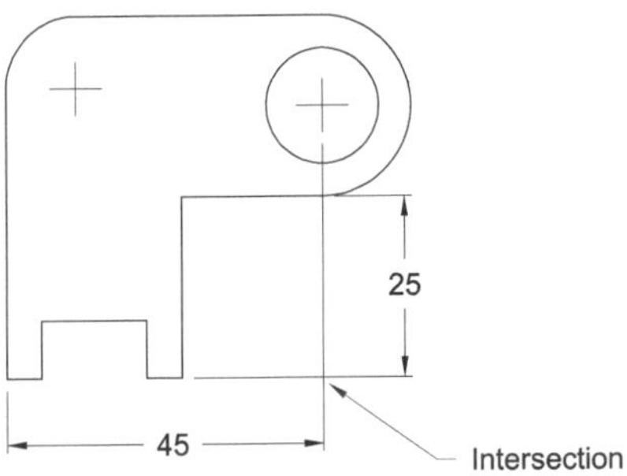

Intersecting dimension lines

6.27

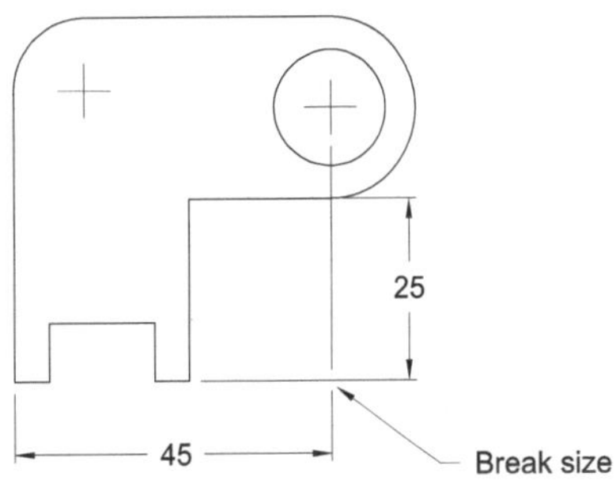

Breaked dimension lines

Tip: To break dimension lines which are intersecting with other dimensions or drawing objects, enter DIMBREAK command and then press ENTER. You are prompted to select the dimension to add/remove break. Click on the dimension to be broken and then click on the object for breaking the selected dimension. The object used for breaking the selected dimension can be a drawing entity or another dimension.

Arc length symbol Area

The options in the **Arc length symbol** area (see Figure 6.28) are used for controlling the position of the arc length dimension symbol. By default, the **Preceding dimension text** radio button is selected in this area. As a result, on applying the arc length dimension, the arc length symbol appears before the dimension text, see Figure 6.29. On selecting the **Above dimension text** radio button, the arc length symbol appears above the dimension text. If you select the **None** radio button, the arc length symbol gets suppressed, and does not appear in the dimension text. You will learn about applying the arc length dimension later in this chapter.

6.28

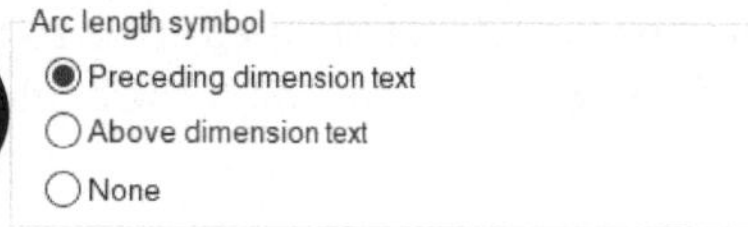

6.29

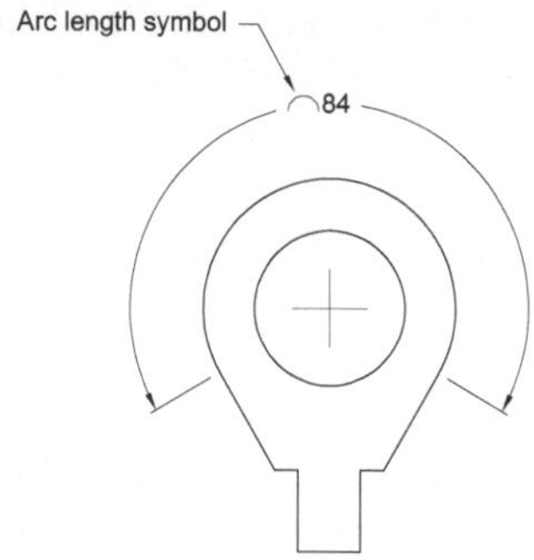

Radius jog dimension Area

The **Jog angle** field in the **Radius jog dimension** area (see Figure 6.30) is used for specifying the jogging angle for the jogged dimension. By default, a 45-degree jog angle is specified in this field. As a result, a jog with a 45-degree angle is applied on applying the radius jog dimension to arcs or circles, see Figure 6.31. You will learn about applying a jogged dimension later in this chapter.

6.30

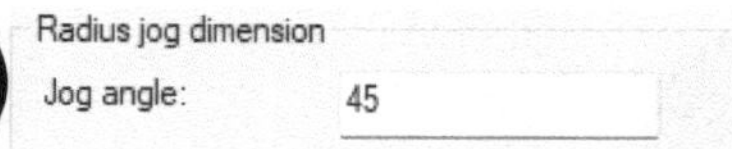

6.31

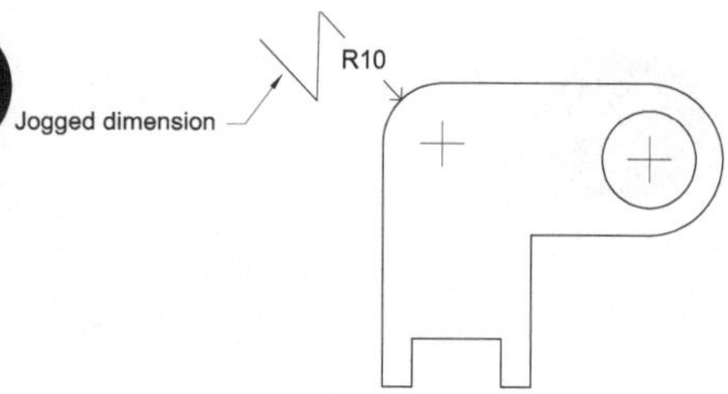

Linear jog dimension Area

The **Jog height factor** field of the **Linear jog dimension** area is used for specifying the jog factor which controls the jog height of the linear jog dimensions. A jog height is the distance between two vertices of the jog angles that make the jog, see Figure 6.32. Note that the value entered as the jog height factor in this field gets multiplied by the text height of the dimension to calculate the jog height. You will learn about applying linear jog dimensions later in this chapter.

6.32

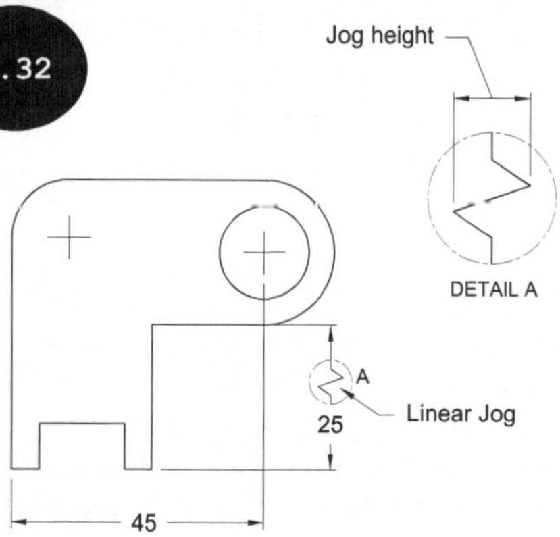

Text Tab

The options in the **Text** tab of the dialog box are used for controlling the dimension text style and format, see Figure 6.33. The options are discussed next.

6.33

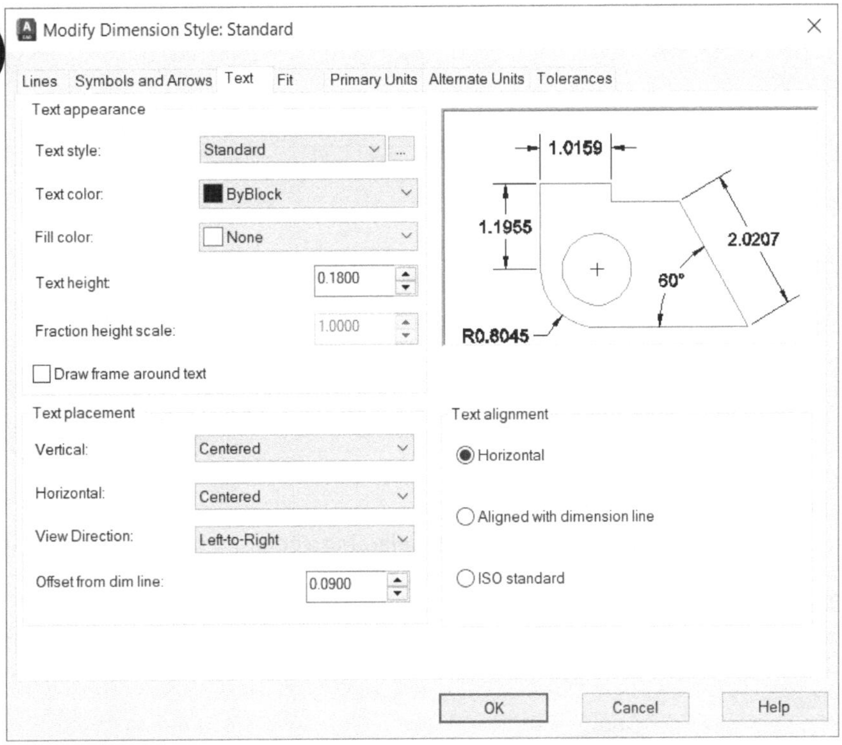

Text appearance Area

The options in the **Text appearance** area are used for controlling the appearance of the dimension text such as text style and color. The options are discussed next.

Text style

The **Text style** drop-down list is used for specifying the predefined text style for dimensions. You can also modify the predefined text style and create a new text style, as required. To edit the existing text style and create a new text style, click on the ... button, which is available in front of the **Text style** drop-down list. The **Text Style** dialog box appears, see Figure 6.34. By using the options in this dialog box, you can modify the existing text style such as text font, font style, and height. Also, you can create a new text style by using the **New** button in this dialog box. To close the dialog box, click on the **Cancel** button.

6.34

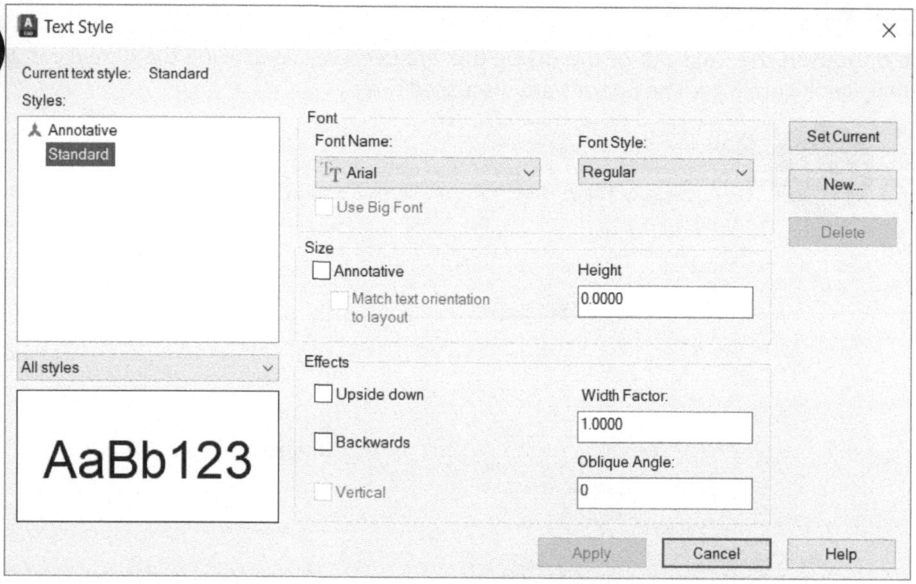

Text color

The **Text color** drop-down list is used for selecting a color for the dimension text.

Fill color

The **Fill color** drop-down list is used for selecting a fill color that appears in the background of the dimension text in a box. Figure 6.35 shows a box around the dimension text which is filled with red color.

6.35

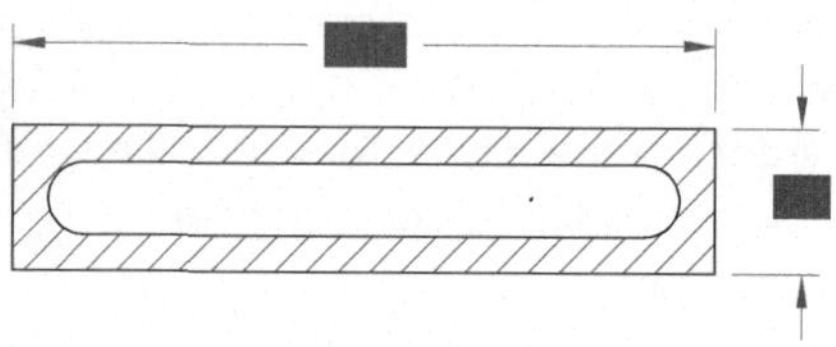

Text height

The **Text height** field is used for specifying the dimension text height.

Fraction height scale

The **Fraction height scale** field is used for specifying the scale for the fraction unit format. The value specified in this field is multiplied by the text height to calculate the height for the fraction dimensions. Note that this field is enabled only when the unit format is set to **Fractional** in the **Primary Units** tab of the dialog box.

Draw frame around text

On selecting the **Draw frame around text** check box, a frame box is drawn around the dimension text. By default, this check box is cleared. As a result, the frame box is not drawn around the dimension text.

Text placement Area

The options in the **Text placement** area of the dialog box are used for controlling the dimension text placement, see Figure 6.36. The options are discussed next.

6.36

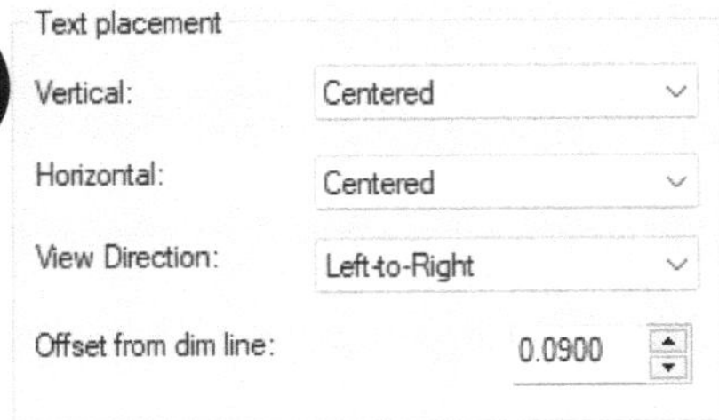

Vertical

The **Vertical** drop-down list of this area is used for controlling the vertical placement of dimension text on the dimension line. On selecting the **Centered** option is selected in this drop-down list. As a result, the dimension text is placed at the center of the dimension line, see Figure 6.37 (a). On selecting the **Above** option, the dimension text is placed above the dimension line, see Figure 6.37 (b). On selecting the **Outside** option, the dimension text is placed on the side of the dimension line, see Figure 6.37 (c). On selecting the **Below** option, the dimension text is placed below the dimension line, see Figure 6.37 (d). On selecting the **JIS** option, the dimension text is set to conform to the JIS (Japanese Industrial Standards) representation.

6.37

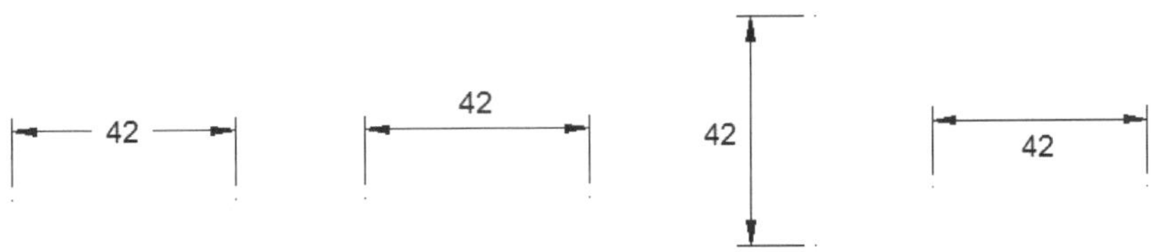

a) Centered b) Above c) Outside d) Below

Horizontal

The **Horizontal** drop-down list is used for controlling the horizontal placement of the dimension text along the dimension line concerning the extension lines. By default, the **Centered** option is selected in this drop-down list. As a result, the dimension text is placed at the center of extension lines along the dimension line, see Figure 6.38 (a). On selecting the **At Ext Line 1** option, the dimension text is placed near the first extension line, see Figure 6.38 (b). On selecting the **At Ext Line 2** option, the dimension text is placed near the second extension line, see Figure 6.38(c). On selecting the **Over Ext Line 1** option, the dimension text is placed over or along the first extension line, see Figure 6.38 (d). On selecting the **Over Ext Line 2** option, the dimension text is placed over or along the second extension line, see Figure 6.38 (e).

6.38

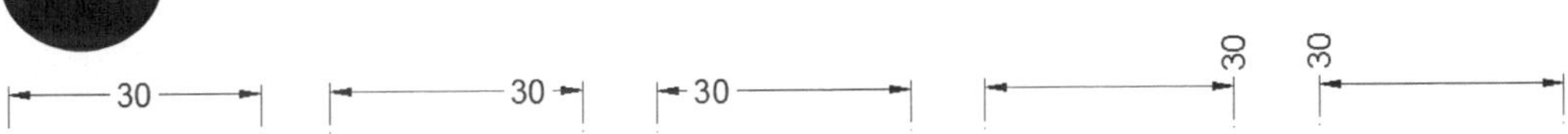

a) Centered b) At Ext Line 1 c) At Ext Line 2 d) Over Ext Line 1 e) Over Ext Line 2

View Direction

The **View Direction** drop-down list is used for controlling the viewing direction of the dimension text from left to right or from right to left by selecting the respective options from this drop-down list.

Offset from dim line

The **Offset from dim line** field is used for specifying the offset distance between the dimension text and the dimension line, see Figure 6.39.

6.39

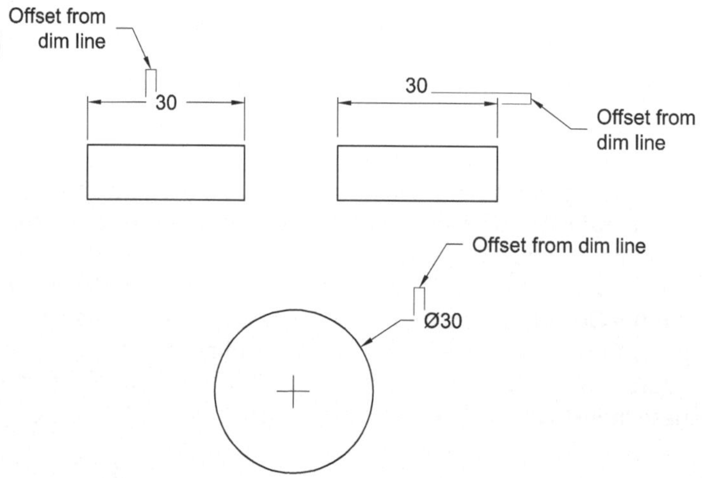

Text alignment Area

The options in the **Text alignment** area are used for controlling the orientation of the dimension text, see Figure 6.40. The options are discussed next.

6.40

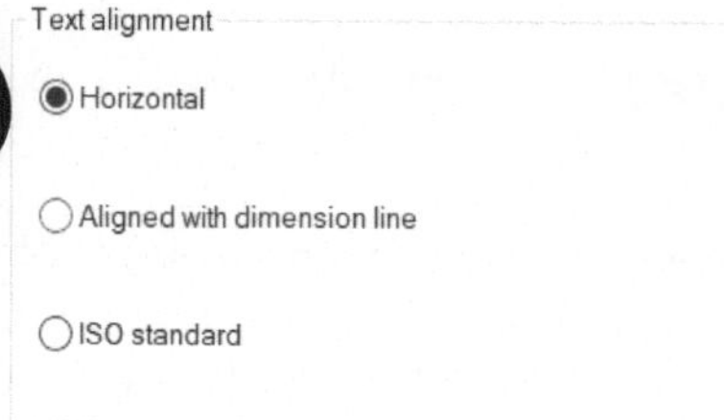

Horizontal

By default, the **Horizontal** radio button is selected in the **Text alignment** area. As a result, the dimension text is placed horizontally to the specified dimension, see Figure 6.41.

Aligned with dimension line

On selecting the **Aligned with dimension line** radio button, the dimension text aligns with the dimension line, see Figure 6.41.

6.41

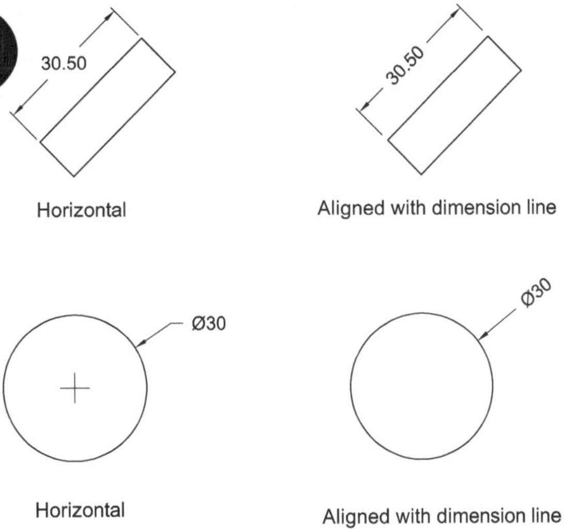

ISO standard

On selecting the **ISO standard** radio button, the dimension text aligns with the dimension line when the dimension text is placed inside the extension lines. If the dimension text is placed outside the extension lines then on selecting this radio button, the dimension text aligns horizontally.

Fit Tab

The options of the **Fit** tab in the dialog box are used for controlling the placement of dimension lines, arrowheads, leader lines, and scale of all dimension components, see Figure 6.42. The options are discussed next.

6.42

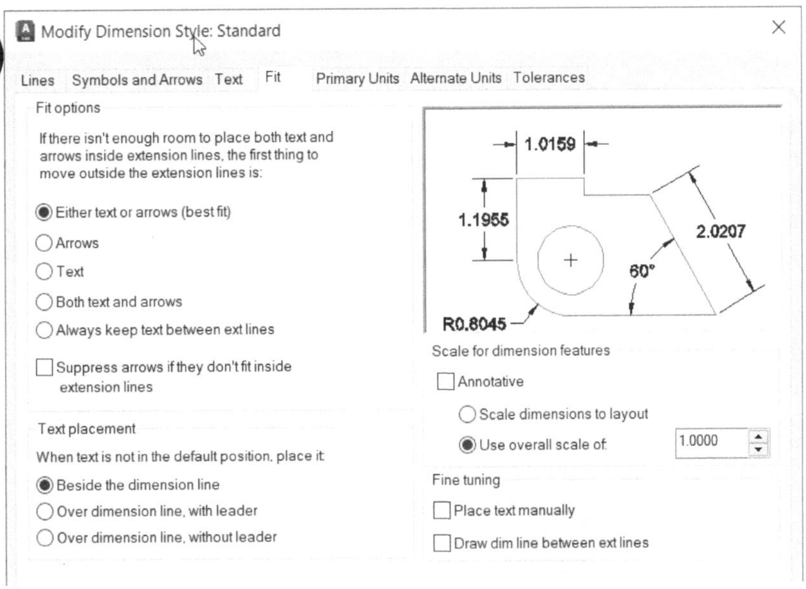

Fit options Area

The options in the **Fit options** area of the dialog box are used for controlling the placement of dimension text and arrowheads depending upon the availability of space between the extension lines. If space is available for the placement, then the text and arrowheads are placed between the extension lines. Whereas, if enough space is not available between the extension lines for the placement of dimension text and arrowheads then the dimension text and arrowheads get placed according to the fit option selected in this area. The options of the **Fit options** area are discussed next.

Either text or arrows (best fit)

By default, this radio button is selected in the **Fit options** area of the dialog box. As a result, either the dimension text or arrowheads move outside the extension lines based on the best fit. Note that if enough space is available between the extension lines, then both text and arrowheads are placed between the extension lines. Otherwise, either the text, the arrowheads, or both move outside the extension lines based on the best fit.

Arrows

On selecting the **Arrows** radio button, the arrowheads move outside the extension lines first and then the dimension text. For example, if the space between the extension lines is available either for text or arrowheads, then the arrowheads move outside the extension lines.

Text

On selecting the **Text** radio button, the dimension text moves outside the extension lines first and then the arrowheads. For example, if the space between the extension lines is available either for text or arrowheads, then the text moves outside the extension lines.

Both text and arrows

On selecting this radio button, the dimension text and arrowheads both move outside the extension lines when enough space is not available between the extension lines.

Always keep text between ext lines

On selecting this radio button, the dimension text is always placed between the extension lines regardless of the space available between them.

Suppress arrows if they don't fit inside extension lines

On selecting this radio button, the arrowheads get suppressed, if enough space is not available to place them inside the extension lines.

Text placement Area

The options in the **Text placement** area of the dialog box are used for controlling the placement of dimension text when it is not in the default position or is moved from the default position, see Figure 6.43. These options are discussed next.

6.43

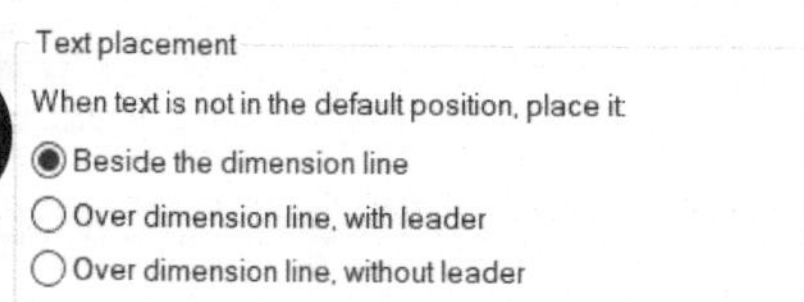

Beside the dimension line

This radio button is selected, by default. As a result, the dimension text is placed beside the dimension line or the dimension line moves whenever dimension text is moved.

Over dimension line, with leader

On selecting this radio button, the dimension line will not move on moving the dimension text. Whereas, on moving the dimension text away from the dimension line, a leader line is added to the dimension text which connects the dimension text to the dimension line, see Figure 6.44. Note that if the dimension text is placed very close to the dimension line, then the leader line cannot be added.

6.44

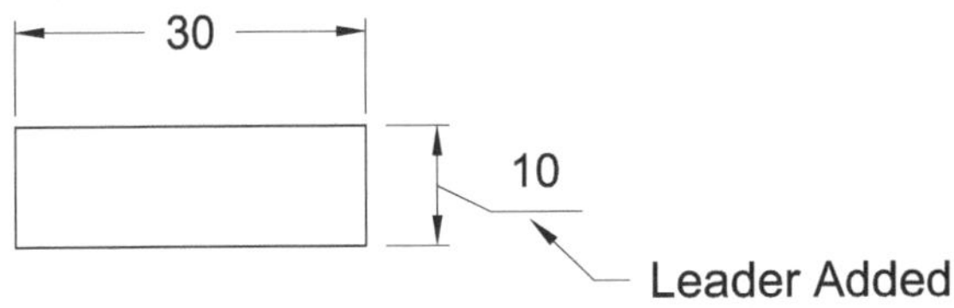

Over dimension line, without leader

On selecting this radio button, the dimension line will not move on moving the dimension text. However, you can move the dimension text freely or independent of the dimension line. Note that the moved dimension text will not be connected to the dimension line through a leader line if this radio button is selected.

Scale for dimension features Area

The options in the **Scale for dimension features** area of the dialog box are used for controlling the overall dimension scale value or the paper space scaling, see Figure 6.45. These options are discussed next.

6.45

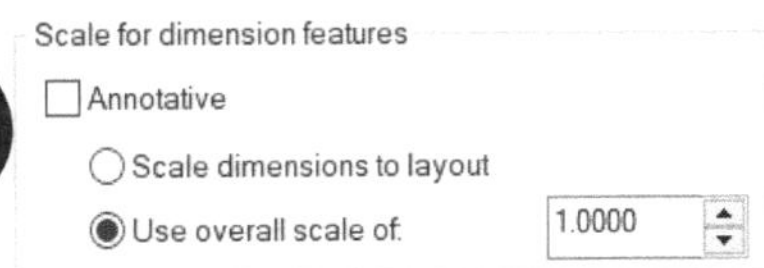

Annotative

The **Annotative** check box is used for defining whether the dimension style is annotative. To make the dimension style annotative, select the **Annotative** check box. You will learn about annotative dimensions later in this chapter.

Scale dimensions to layout

On selecting the **Scale dimensions to layout** radio button, AutoCAD automatically calculates an acceptable scale factor for dimension components such as text height, arrow sizes, and so on based on the scaling between the current model space viewport and the paper space layout. You will learn about layouts in later chapters.

Use overall scale of

On selecting this radio button, the **Scale** field gets enabled in front of it. By default, the scale value is set to 1 (one). As a result, the dimension style such as text height, arrowhead size, and all other settings that specify size, distance, or spacing is plotted on a full scale. You can specify an overall scale for controlling all dimension styles in this field, as required. Note that the scale specified in this field will not change the dimension measurement.

Fine tuning Area

The options in the **Fine tuning** area provide additional options for the placement of dimension text, see Figure 6.46. These options are discussed next.

6.46

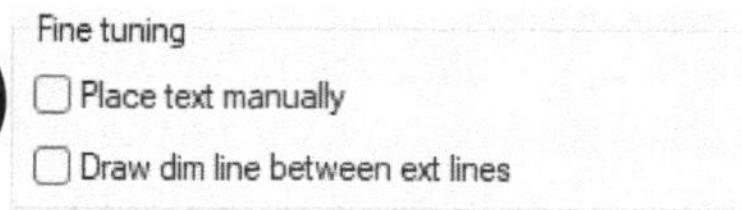

Place text manually

By default, this check box is cleared. As a result, the dimension text is placed at the middle of the dimension line, if enough space is available. However, on selecting this check box, you can position the dimension text anywhere on the dimension line. Also, while positioning the dimension text, it ignores the horizontal justification settings, if specified.

Draw dim line between ext lines

On selecting this check box, the dimension line is drawn between the extension lines even if the dimension text and dimension lines are placed outside the extension lines due to the unavailability of enough space.

Primary Units Tab

The options in the **Primary Units** tab are used for controlling the unit format, dimension precision, fraction format, measurement scale, zero suppression, and so on for linear and angular dimensions, see Figure 6.47. The options are discussed next.

6.47

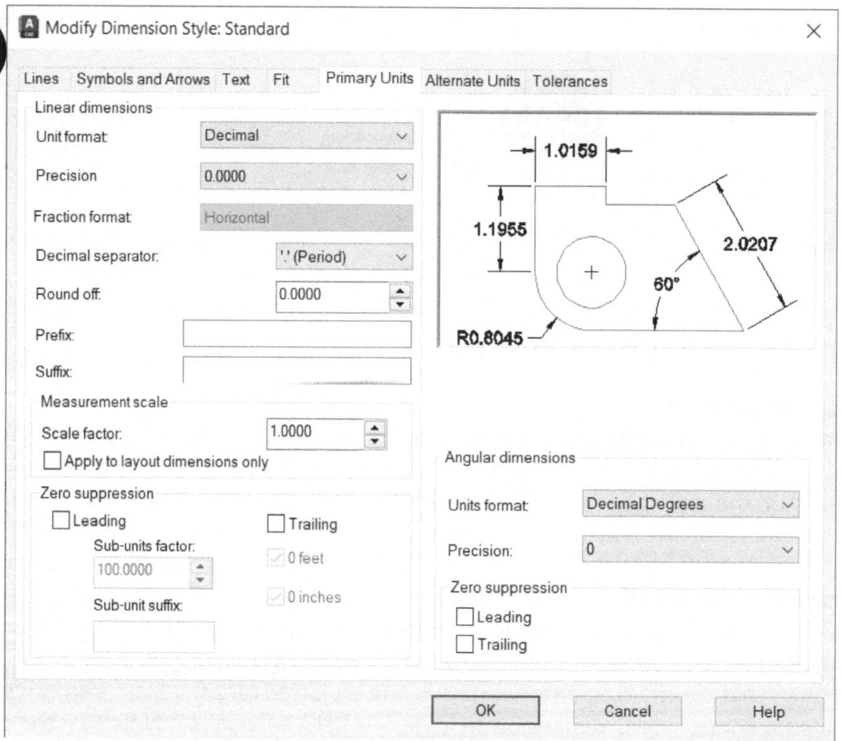

Linear dimensions Area

The options in the **Linear dimensions** area of the dialog box are used for controlling the unit format, precision, and other parameters for linear dimensions. The options for this area are discussed next.

Unit format

The **Unit format** drop-down list is used for selecting the current unit format: Decimal, Scientific, Engineering, Architectural, Fractional, or Windows Desktop for all dimension types except angular dimensions.

Precision

The **Precision** drop-down list is used for specifying the dimension precision (decimal places) for the dimension text of the current/primary dimension units.

Fraction format

The **Fraction format** drop-down list is used for specifying the fraction format: **Horizontal**, **Diagonal**, or **Not Stacked** for the fractional or architectural unit format. Note that this drop-down list is enabled only when the **Fractional** or **Architectural** unit format is selected in the **Unit format** drop-down list of this area.

Decimal separator

The **Decimal separator** drop-down list is used for specifying the separator: **‘.’(Period)**, **‘,’(Comma)**, **‘ ’(Space)** for decimal formats, see Figure 6.48.

6.48

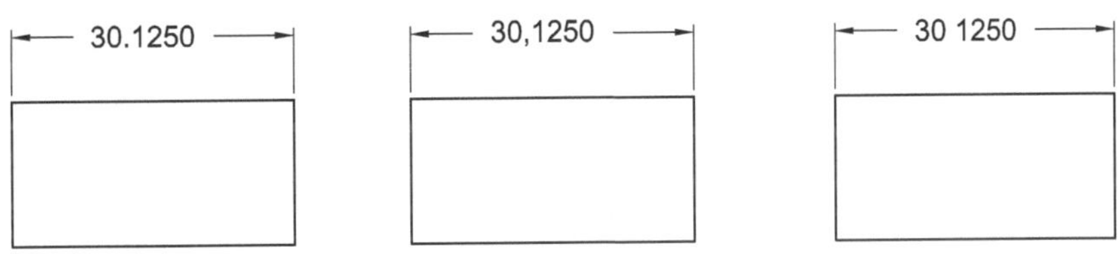

'.'(Period) ','(Comma) ' '(Space)

Round off

The **Round off** field is used for specifying the nearest rounded value for dimension measurements of all dimension types except angular dimensions. For example, if you specify 0.5 in this field then a dimension having a measurement of 30.3 units gets rounded off to 30.5 units, and 30.8 units gets rounded off to 31.0 units. Note that the display of the number of digits after the decimal point depends on the precision setting.

Prefix

The **Prefix** field is used for specifying a prefix for the dimension measurement. The prefix specified in this field is placed in front of the dimension text. You can enter text or any control code as the prefix for the dimension measurement. For example, on entering the text "Cad" as the prefix in this field, "Cad" gets placed in front of the dimension text. Also, if you enter the control code "%%c" as the prefix in this field, the diameter symbol gets placed in front of the dimension text.

Suffix

Similar to specifying the prefix, you can specify the suffix for the dimension measurement. The suffix specified is placed after the dimension text. You can enter text or any control code as the suffix for the dimension measurement. For example, on entering the text "mm" as the suffix, "mm" gets placed after the dimension text. Also, if you enter the control code "%%d" as the suffix, then the symbol of degree gets placed after the dimension text.

Measurement scale Area

The **Scale factor** field of this **Measurement scale** area (see Figure 6.49) is used for specifying a scale factor for linear dimension measurements which also includes radii, diameters, and coordinates measurements. By default, the scale factor is defined as 1 (one) in this field. As a result, the two unit segments are dimensioned as 2 units (2 X 1) only. However, if you specify 2 (two) as the scale factor in this field, then the two unit segments are dimensioned as 4 units (2 X 2). Note that this scale factor does not apply to angular dimensions, round off values, or to the plus or minus tolerance values.

On selecting the **Apply to layout dimension only** check box of this area (see Figure 6.49), the specified measurement scale factor applies only to the dimensions created in the layout viewports.

Zero suppression Area

The options in the **Zero suppression** area of the dialog box are used for suppressing or unsuppressing the leading and trailing zeros in the dimension values, see Figure 6.50.

6.49

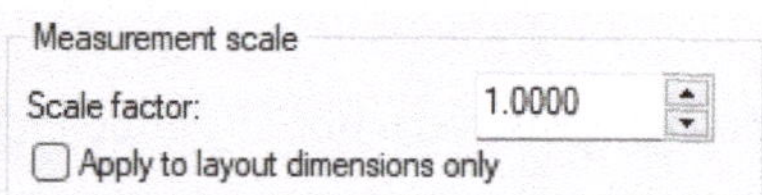

6.50

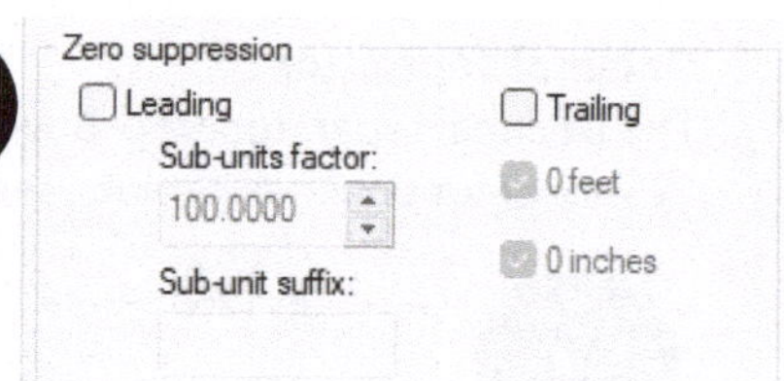

On selecting the **Leading** check box of this area, the leading zeros in all decimal dimensions get suppressed. For example, if the dimension is 0.800 units then by selecting this check box it becomes .800. Similarly, on selecting the **Trailing** check box, the trailing zeros in all decimal dimensions get suppressed. For example, if the dimension is 15.500 units then by selecting this check box it becomes 15.5 and 15.000 units become 15.

By default, the **0 feet** and **0 inches** check boxes are not enabled in this area. These check boxes get enabled when the **Engineering** or **Architectural** format is selected in the **Unit format** drop-down list. If the feet and inches dimensions are less than one, then on selecting the **0 feet** check box, the leading zero (feet portion) of the dimensions gets suppressed. For example, if the **0 feet** check box is selected then the 0'-5 1/2" dimension becomes 5 1/2". Similarly, on selecting the **0 inches** check box, the trailing zeros (inches portion) of the feet and inches dimensions get suppressed. For example, if the **0 inches** check box is selected, the 5'-0" dimension becomes 5'.

The **Sub-units factor** field of this area is used for specifying the sub-unit factor for dimensions. For example, if the current dimension is in meters (2 meters) then on entering 100 as the sub-unit factor, the dimension gets converted to centimeters (2 X 100 = 200 cm). You can also enter the suffix (cm) for the sub-unit in the **Sub-unit suffix** field of this area.

Angular dimensions Area

Similar to specifying the unit format, precision, and zero suppression for the linear dimensions, you can also specify the unit format, precision, and zero suppression for the angular dimensions by using the options in the **Angular dimensions** area of the dialog box, see Figure 6.51.

6.51

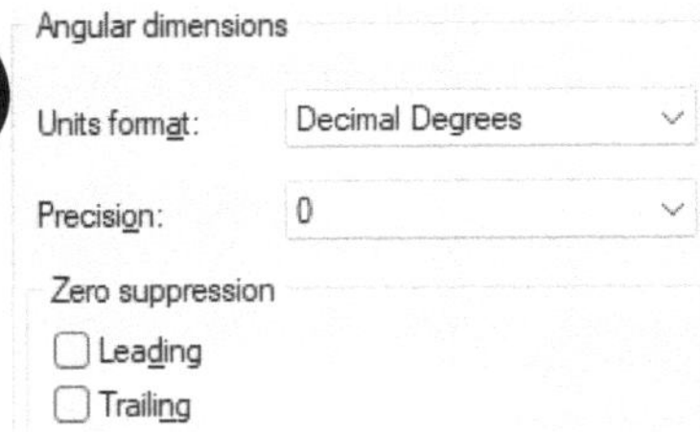

Alternate Units Tab

The options in the **Alternate Units** tab are used for displaying alternate units for the dimension measurements and controlling the format and precision of the alternate unit, see Figure 6.52. The options of the **Alternate Units** tab are discussed next.

6.52

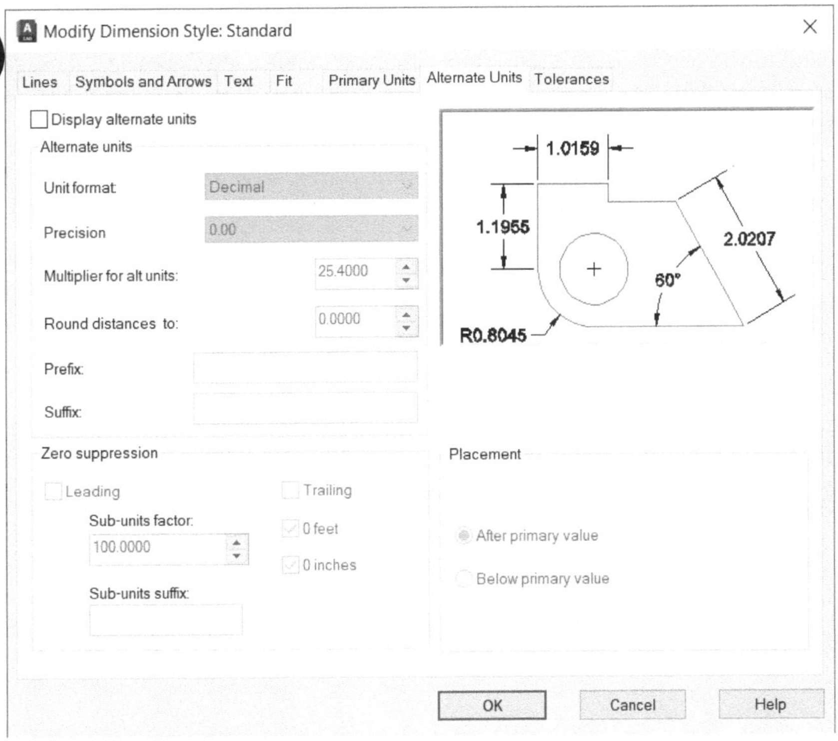

Display alternate units Check Box

By default, the **Display alternate units** check box is unchecked. As a result, the dimensions are displayed only in the primary unit. To display dimensions in the alternate units as well, select the **Display alternate units** check box. When you select this check box, the preview area of the dialog box shows the alternate units in brackets [ ] for all dimensions in addition to the primary units. Also, the other options of the dialog box are enabled to define the format and precision of the alternate units. The options are discussed next.

Alternate units Area

The options in the **Alternate units** area are used for specifying the format and precision for the alternate units. All these options are the same as those discussed in the **Primary Units** tab except the **Multiplier for alt units** field. This is used for specifying the multiplier as the conversion factor for the alternate unit. For example, if the inches unit is specified as the primary unit for the dimensions and you want to add millimeters as the alternate unit for the measurements, in such case, you can enter 25.4 as the conversion factor in this **Multiplier for alt units** field. In doing so, the dimensions for measurement are displayed in inches as well as millimeters, see Figure 6.53. Note that the alternate units are not applied to the angular dimensions, round off values, or the plus or minus tolerance values.

6.53

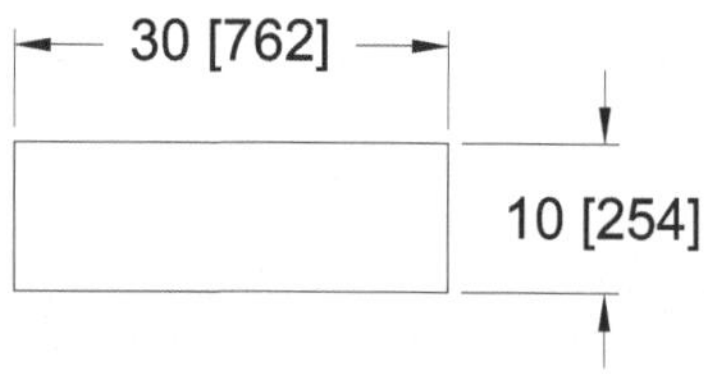

Zero suppression Area

The options in the **Zero suppression** area of the dialog box are used for suppressing or unsuppressing the leading and trailing zeros in the alternate dimension values, see Figure 6.54. These options are same as those discussed in the **Primary Units** tab with the only difference being that these options affect the alternate dimension values.

6.54

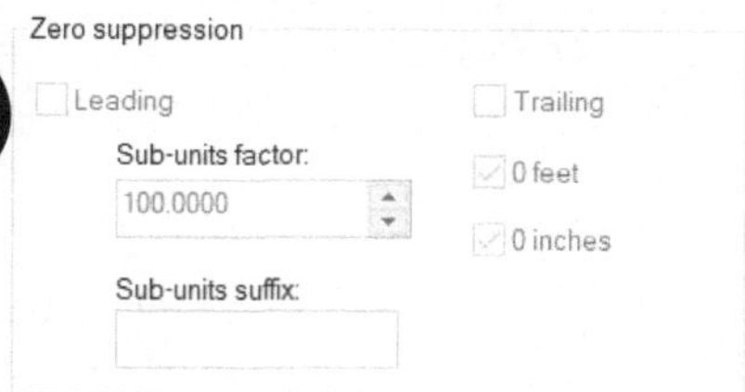

Placement Area

The options in the **Placement** area of the dialog box are used for defining the placement for the alternate unit, see Figure 6.55.

6.55

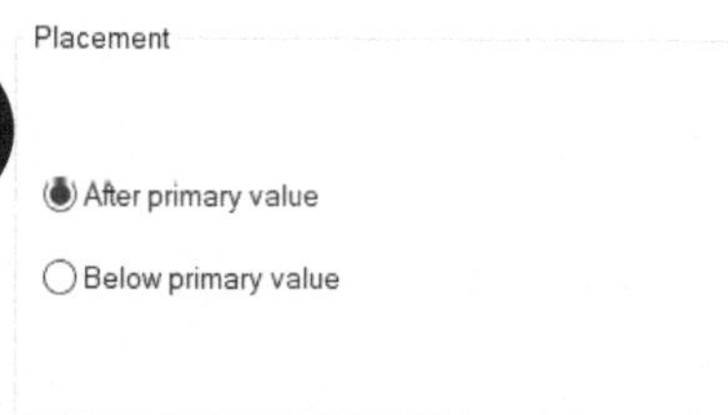

By default, the **After primary value** radio button is selected in the **Placement** area. As a result, the alternate unit is placed after the primary unit, refer to Figure 6.53. If you select the **Below primary value** radio button, then the alternate unit is positioned below the primary unit.

Tolerances Tab

The options in the **Tolerances** tab of the dialog box are used for specifying the parameters that control the format and display of the tolerance in the dimension text, see Figure 6.56. The options are discussed next.

6.56

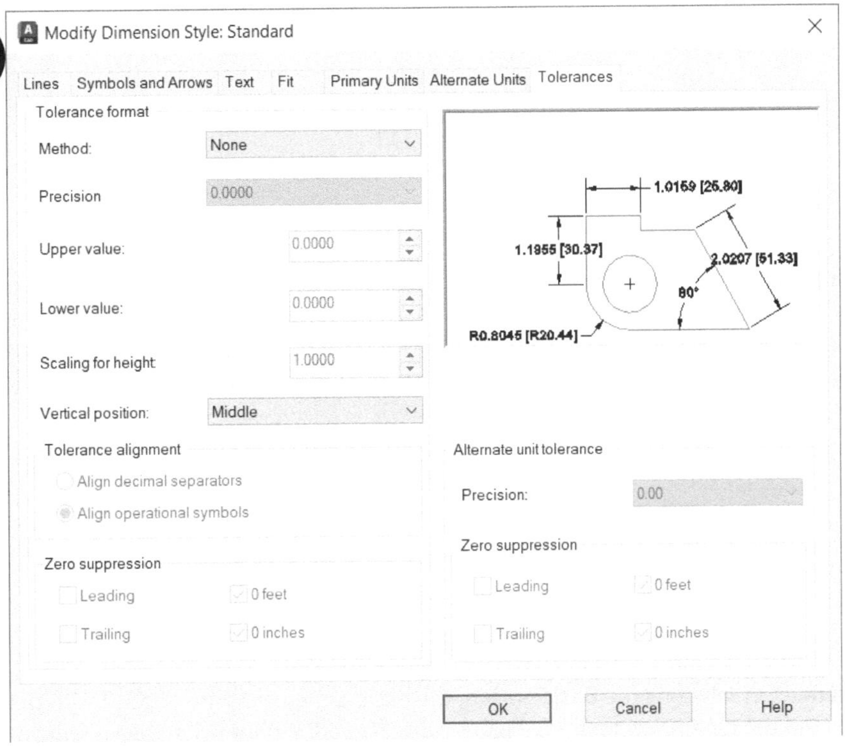

Tolerance format Area

The options in the **Tolerance format** area are used for controlling the tolerance format such as tolerance method, tolerance precision, scaling for height, position, and so on. The options are discussed next.

Method

The **Method** drop-down list is used for selecting the type of tolerance: Symmetrical, Deviation, Limits, or Basic. By default, the **None** option is selected in this drop-down list. As a result, the tolerance values are not added to the dimension text. The other options of this drop-down list are discussed next.

Symmetrical: On selecting the **Symmetrical** option, the symmetrical tolerances get added to the dimension texts with plus (+) and minus (-) expressions to the symmetric tolerance values, see Figure 6.57. As soon as you select this tolerance type, the other respective options of the **Tolerance format** area are enabled. You can specify the precision and tolerance values for the symmetrical tolerance in the **Precision** drop-down list and **Upper value** field of this area, respectively.

Deviation: On selecting the **Deviation** option, the deviation tolerances get added to the dimension texts with the plus (+) and minus (-) expressions to the deviation tolerance values, see Figure 6.58.

You can specify the plus (+) tolerance value in the **Upper value** field and the minus (-) tolerance value in the **Lower value** field of this area.

6.57

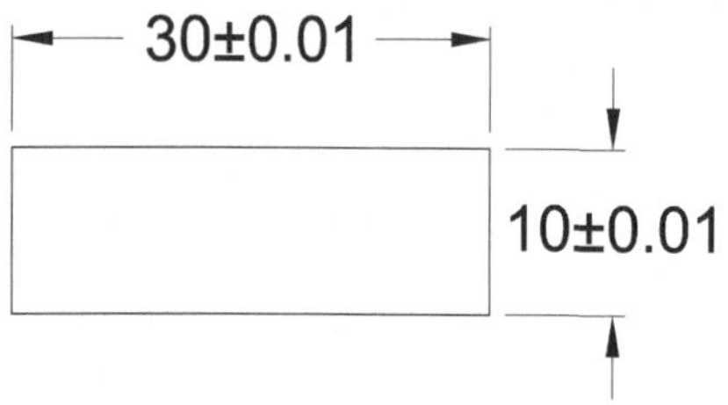

6.58

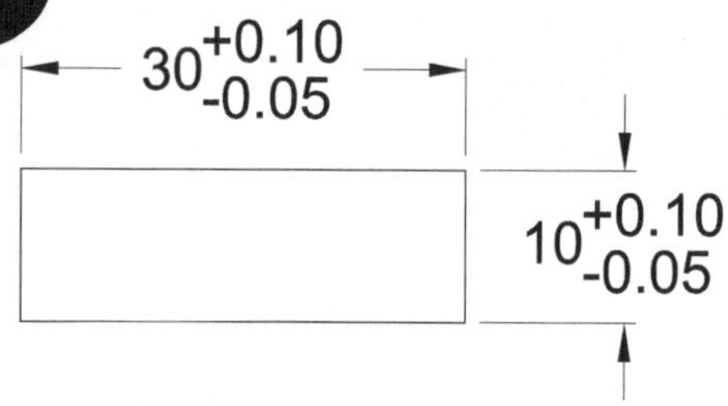

Limits: On selecting the **Limits** option, the maximum and minimum limit dimensions are applied by adding the upper limit value to and subtracting the lower limit value from the actual dimension, respectively, see Figure 6.59. The maximum and minimum limit dimensions appear one above the other in the drawing area. In Figure 6.59, the maximum limit dimension is 30.10 (30 + 0.1) and the minimum limit dimension is 29.95 (30 - 0.05).

6.59

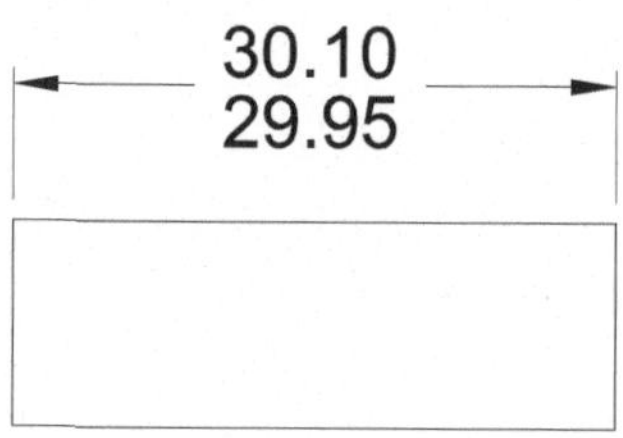

Basic: On selecting the **Basic** option, the basic dimensions are applied with the display of a box around the dimension text, see Figure 6.60. The basic dimension is also known as the reference dimension.

6.60

Precision, Upper value, and Lower value

The **Precision** drop-down list, **Upper value** field, and **Lower value** field are used for specifying the precision, upper value, and lower value for the tolerance dimension values, respectively.

Scaling for height

The **Scaling for height** field is used for specifying the scale factor for the tolerance text height concerning the current height of the dimension text. By default, the scale factor for the tolerance text height is set to 1 (one). As a result, the height of the tolerance dimension is the same as that of the current dimension text height. If you want to set the tolerance dimension height as half of the current dimension text height, then you need to enter 0.5 in this field.

Vertical position
The **Vertical position** drop-down list is used for specifying the position/text justification for the symmetrical and deviation tolerance dimension values. By default, the **Middle** option is selected in this drop-down list. As a result, the tolerance text value is aligned to the middle of the dimension text, see Figure 6.61 (a). On selecting the **Top** option, the tolerance text value gets aligned to the top of the dimension text, see Figure 6.61 (b). On selecting the **Bottom** option, the tolerance text value gets aligned to the bottom of the dimension text, see Figure 6.61 (c).

6.61

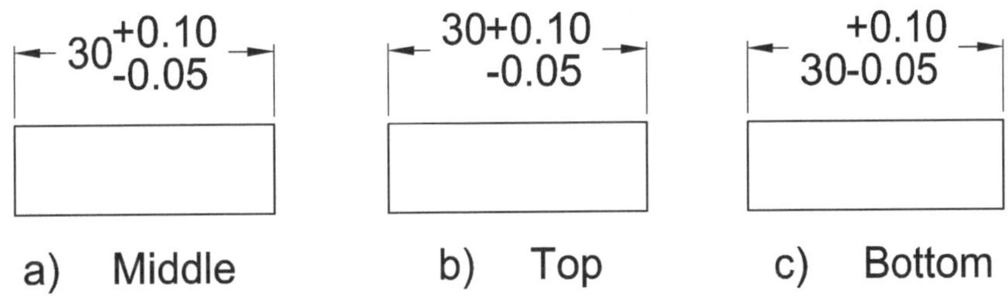

Tolerance alignment Area
The options in the **Tolerance alignment** area are used for controlling the alignment of upper and lower tolerance values when they are stacked. These options are available only when the **Deviation** or **Limits** tolerance type is selected. On selecting the **Align decimal separators** radio button of this area, the tolerance values get aligned vertically to the decimal separators (.), see Figure 6.62 (a). However, on selecting the **Align operational symbols**, the tolerance values get aligned to the operational symbols [plus (+) and minus (-)], see Figure 6.62 (b).

6.62

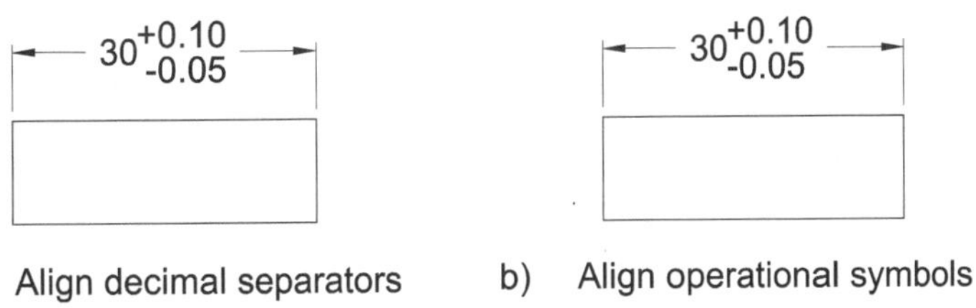

Zero suppression Area
The options in the **Zero suppression** area are used for suppressing or unsuppressing the leading and trailing zeros in the tolerance values, as discussed earlier.

Alternate unit tolerance Area
The options in the **Alternate unit tolerance** area are used for specifying formats such as precision and zero suppression for the alternate tolerance units. Note that these options are enabled only when the display of alternate dimension units along with the primary dimension units are turned on.

Once you have specified all settings for creating the new dimension style, click on the **OK** button of the dialog box to accept the settings and exit the **New Dimension Style** dialog box.

Modifying an Existing Dimension Style
In AutoCAD, you can also modify existing dimension styles, as required by using the **Modify** button of the **Dimension Style Manager** dialog box. To do so, invoke the **Dimension Style Manager** dialog box by entering **D** in the Command Line window and then pressing the ENTER key. Next, select the

dimension style to be modified from the **Styles** area of the dialog box (see Figure 6.63) and then click on the **Modify** button. The **Modify Dimension Style** dialog box appears, see Figure 6.64.

6.63

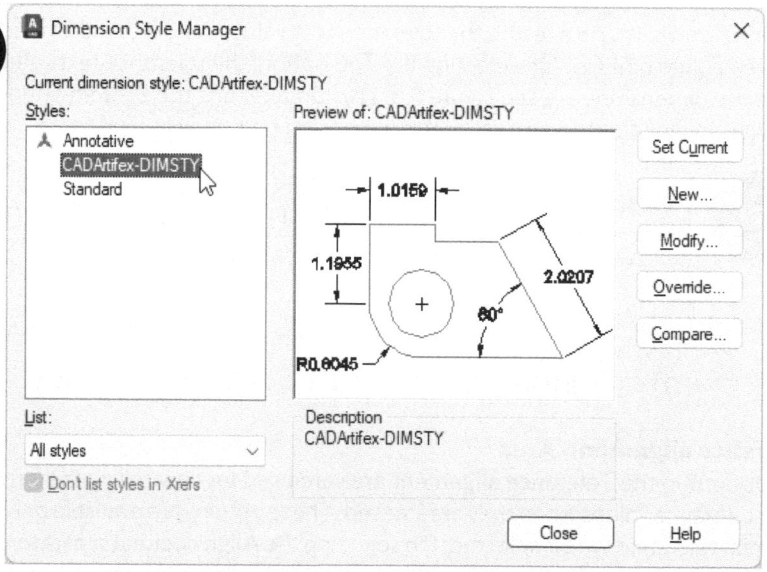

6.64

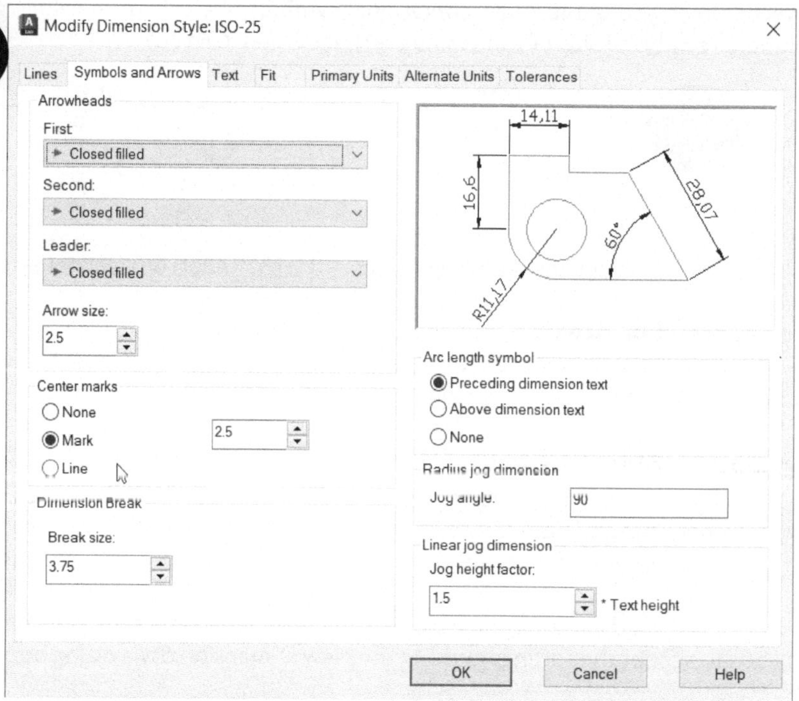

The options available in the **Modify Dimension Style** dialog box for modifying the selected dimension style are the same as those discussed earlier while creating a new dimension style. By using these options, edit the dimension style settings and then click on the **OK** button to accept the modifications and exit the dialog box. Next, click on the **Close** button in the **Dimension Style Manager** dialog box to close it.

Overriding a Dimension Style

In addition to creating new dimension styles and modifying existing dimension styles, you can also define overrides or change specific parameters of an existing dimension style. Most of the time the same dimension style is used throughout a drawing. However, sometimes you may need to make small changes in some of the dimension parameters/settings without altering the entire dimension style. In such a case, you can use dimension style overrides. For example, you can assign a different color to the extension line by overriding the color assigned to the parent dimension style. On creating a dimension style override, a sub-dimension style gets created that varies from its parent/original dimension style. When you create an override for any of the dimension parameters, the original/parent dimension style will remain unchanged, and the new value for color gets stored in the DIMCLRE system variable. Note that all dimensions you apply include the overrides until you delete the overrides or set another style as the current dimension style.

To create a dimension override, invoke the **Dimension Style Manager** dialog box by entering **D** in the Command Line window and then pressing the ENTER key. Once the **Dimension Style Manager** dialog box is invoked, select the dimension style to be overridden from the **Styles** area of the dialog box and then click on the **Override** button. The **Override Current Style** dialog box appears, see Figure 6.65. In this dialog box, you can define overrides for the required dimension style parameters/settings.

6.65

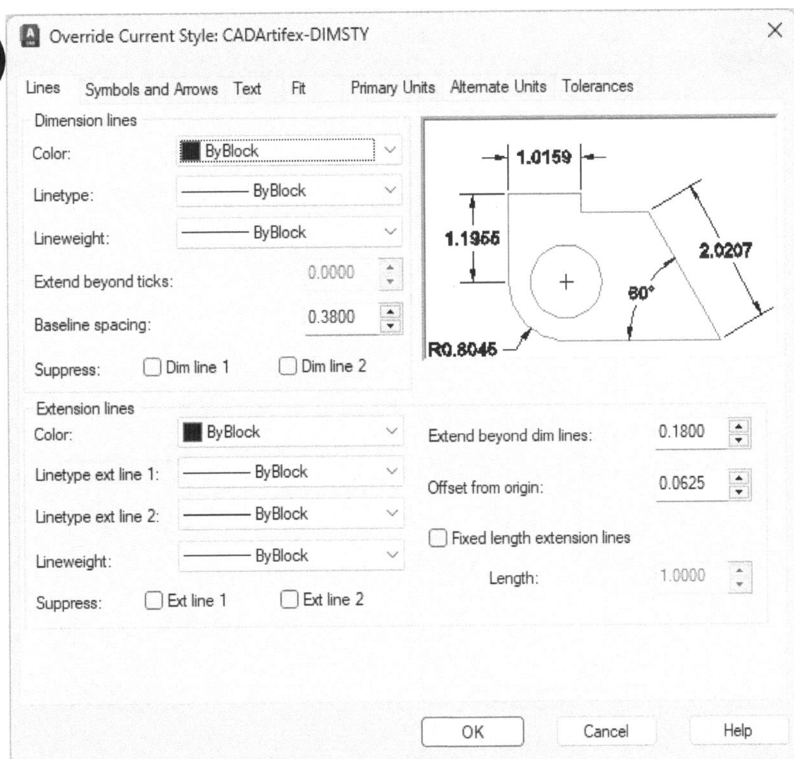

The options of the **Override Current Style** dialog box are the same as those discussed earlier while creating a new dimension style. Once you have defined overrides, click on the **OK** button. The **Override Current Style** dialog box gets closed, and a sub-dimension style *<style overrides>* is created and appears under the parent dimension style in the **Styles** area of the dialog box, see Figure 6.66.

6.66

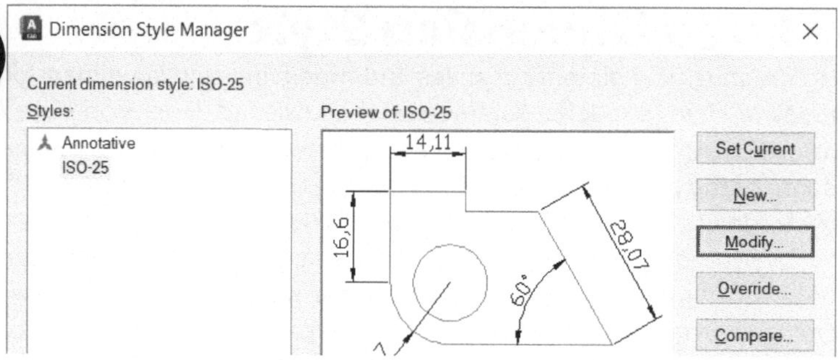

After learning about various dimension components, making a dimension style current, creating a new dimension style, modifying an existing dimension style, and overriding a dimension style, you will now learn about applying the various types of dimensions in a drawing.

Applying Dimensions

As discussed earlier, a good AutoCAD drawing has all the dimensions that convey complete information about the drawing clearly and accurately, see Figure 6.67.

6.67

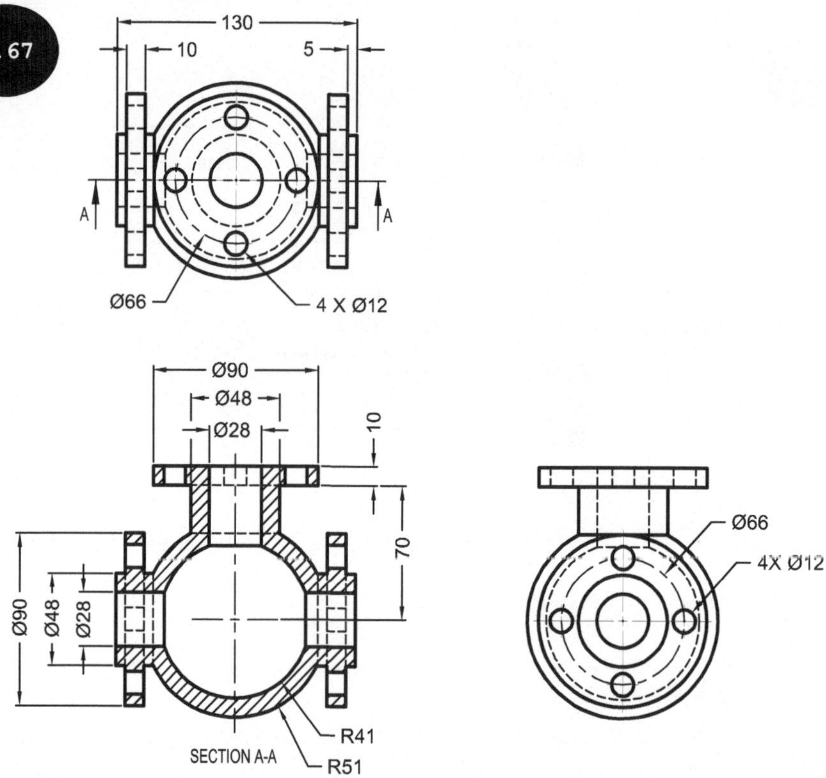

Note: When you apply dimensions, a new layer named as "Defpoints" is created automatically. This "Defpoints" layer stores the dimension properties and cannot be deleted.

AutoCAD is provided with various dimensioning tools in the **Dimension** flyout of the **Annotation** panel in the **Home** tab which helps you to quickly and easily dimension a drawing, see Figure 6.68.

6.68

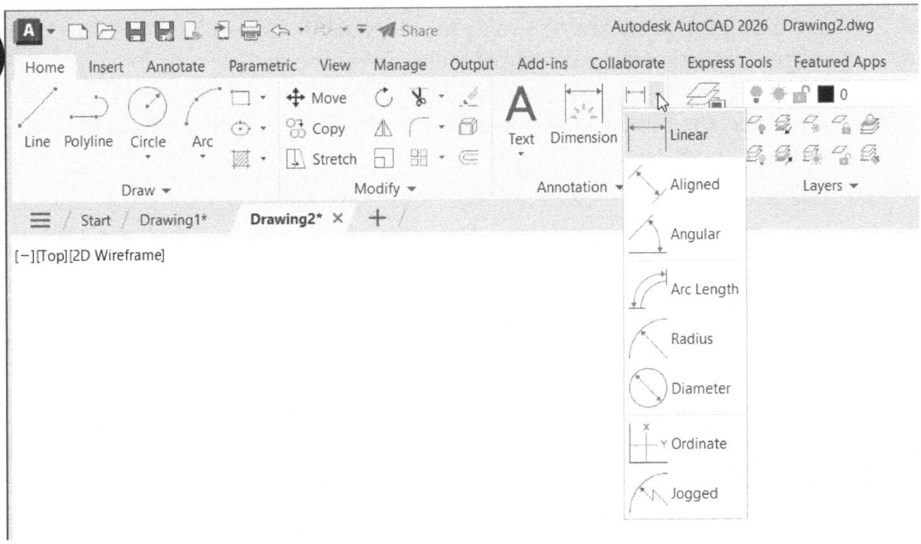

Additionally, you can access dimensioning tools from the **Dimensions** panel of the **Annotate** tab (see Figure 6.69), **Dimension** toolbar (see Figure 6.70), **Dimension** Menu Bar (see Figure 6.71), and by using the DIM command.

6.69

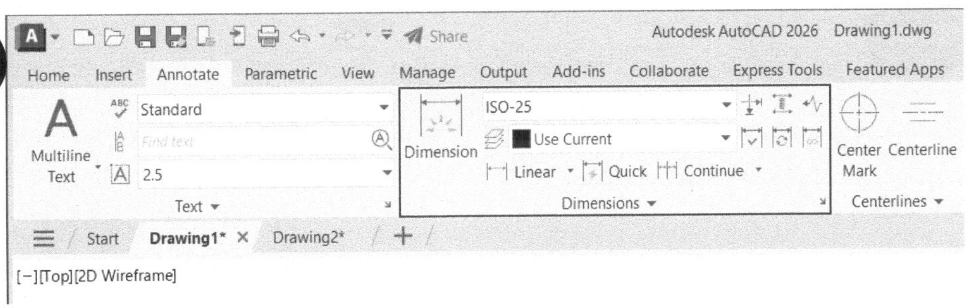

6.70

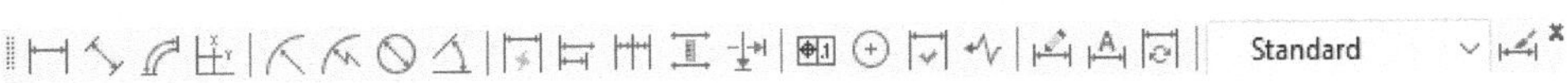

6.71

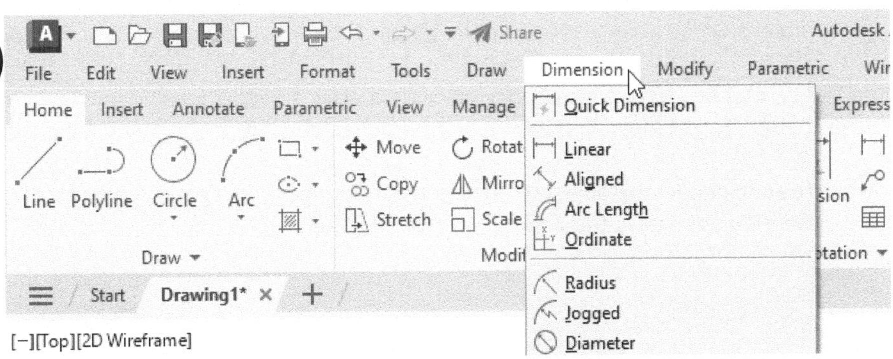

Note: By default, the display of the Menu Bar and **Dimension** toolbar are turned off. To display the Menu Bar, enter **MENUBAR** in the Command Line window and then press ENTER. You are prompted to enter a new value for MENUBAR. Enter **1** (one) to turn on the display and **0** (zero) to turn off the display of Menu Bar, respectively.

To display the **Dimension** toolbar, click on the **Tools > Toolbars > AUTOCAD > Dimension** in the Menu Bar.

You can apply different types of dimensions such as linear, aligned, angular, radius, diameter, arc length, and ordinate by using the respective tools. Moreover, you can apply different types of dimensions by using the **Dimension** tool of the **Annotation** panel in the **Home** tab. The **Dimension** tool is a smart tool, which applies dimension depending on the selected entity. For example, if you select a horizontal entity, the horizontal dimension is applied, and if you select a vertical entity, the vertical dimension is applied. The methods for applying different types of dimensions are discussed next.

Applying a Linear Dimension

A linear dimension is the most widely used dimension type which measures the length and width of an object. You can apply horizontal or vertical linear dimensions to horizontal, vertical, or aligned objects, by using the **Linear** tool or **Dimension** tool, see Figure 6.72. You can either select an object or two points to apply dimension. The method for applying a linear dimension is discussed below:

6.72

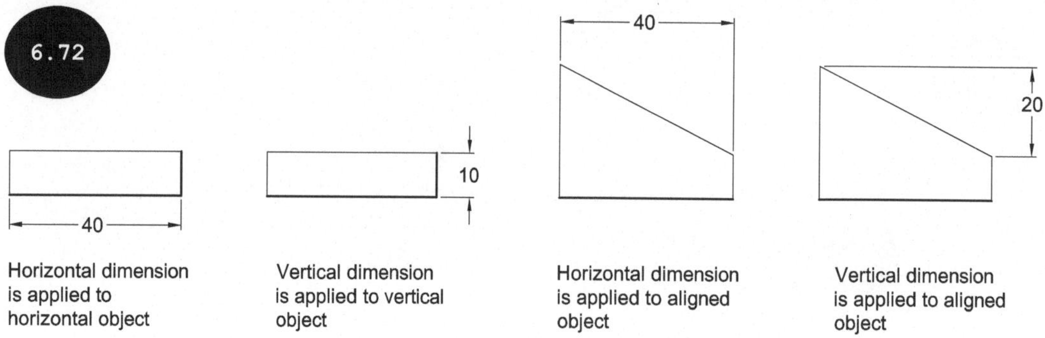

1. Click on the **Dimension** tool in the **Annotation** panel in the **Home** tab. You are prompted to select objects to be dimensioned or specify the origin for the first extension line. Alternatively, invoke the **Dimension** flyout in the **Annotation** panel and then click on the **Linear** tool for applying the linear dimension. You can also invoke the **Linear** tool by using the DIMLINEAR command.

```
Select objects or specify first extension line origin or [Angular
Baseline Continue Ordinate aliGn Distribute Layer Undo]:
```

2. Move the cursor over the object to be dimensioned. The object gets highlighted, and a preview of the dimension appears in the drawing area, see Figure 6.73.

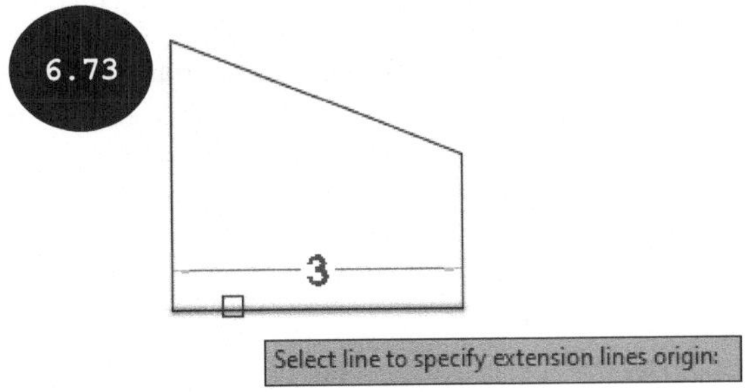

3. Click on the object to be dimensioned. The extension lines of the dimension are attached to the object, and the dimension line is attached to the cursor. Also, you are prompted to specify the location of the dimension line.

```
Specify dimension line location or second line for angle [Mtext
Text text aNgle Undo]:
```

4. Click in the drawing area to specify the location of the dimension line.

Note: In addition to selecting the object to be dimensioned, you can specify the origin for the first and second extension lines of the dimension by clicking the left mouse button on the end points (P1 and P2) one by one, see Figure 6.74. To select the end points of the object, ensure that the **Object Snap** mode is turned on.

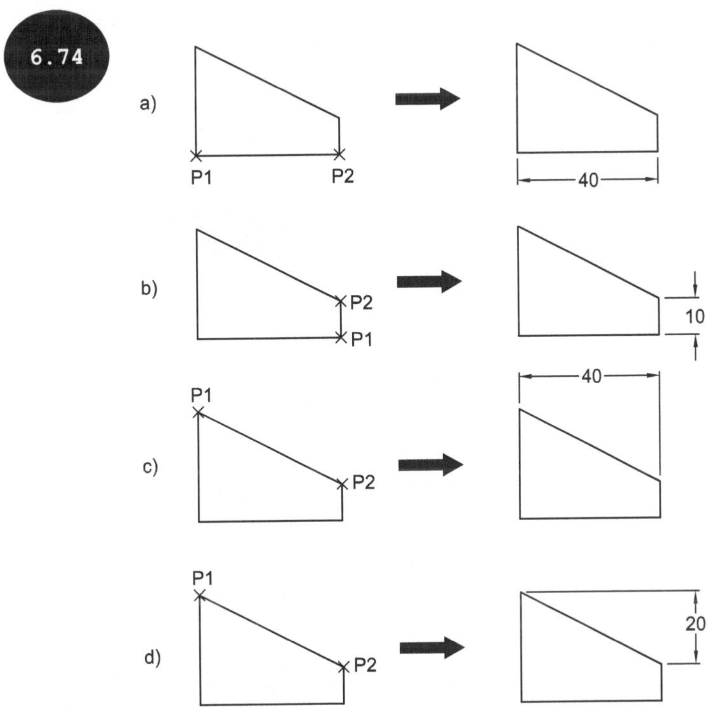

Note: If you invoke the **Linear** tool or the DIMLINEAR command for applying the linear dimension, you will be prompted to specify the origin of the first extension line "`Specify first extension line origin or <select object>:`". Click on the end points (P1 and P2) of the object to be dimensioned one by one (refer to Figure 6.74) as the origin of the first and second extension lines of the dimension and then specify the placement point for the dimension line. You can also select the object to be dimensioned instead of specifying the origin of the extension lines. For doing so, press the ENTER key when you are prompted to specify the origin of the first extension line.

The dimension parameters such as dimension text, text height, text font, arrow height, and arrow style are displayed in the drawing area based on the current dimension style.

Applying an Aligned Dimension

An aligned dimension is used for measuring the true distance of an inclined object, see Figure 6.75. You can apply an aligned dimension by using the **Dimension** tool, **Aligned** tool, or DIMALIGNED command. To apply the aligned dimension, you can select the object or the endpoints of the object to be dimensioned. The method for applying an aligned dimension is discussed below:

1. Click on the **Dimension** tool in the **Annotation** panel in the **Home** tab. You are prompted to select objects to be dimensioned or specify the origin for the first extension line. Alternatively, invoke the **Dimension** flyout in the **Annotation** panel and then click on the **Aligned** tool to apply the aligned dimension. You can also invoke the **Aligned** tool by using the DIMALIGNED command.

```
Select objects or specify first extension line origin or [Angular
Baseline Continue Ordinate aliGn Distribute Layer Undo]:
```

2. Move the cursor over the aligned object to be dimensioned. The object gets highlighted, and a preview of the aligned dimension appears in the drawing area, see Figure 6.76.

6.75

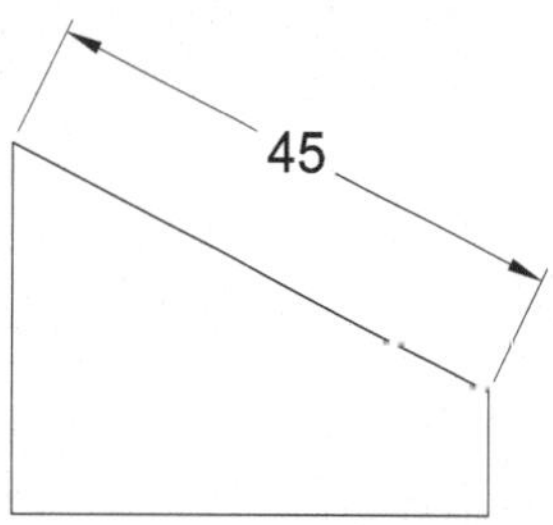

6.76

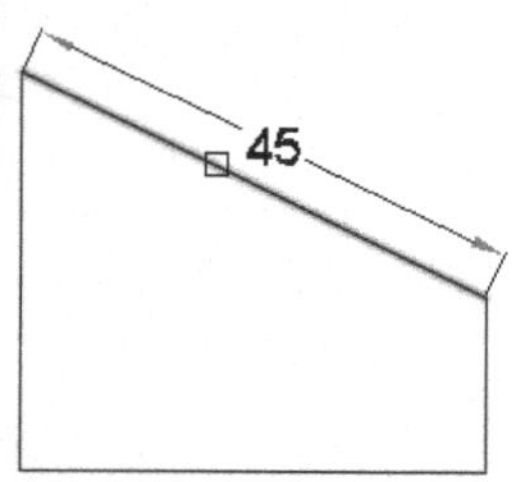

3. Click on the object to be dimensioned. The extension lines of the dimension are attached to the endpoints of the object, and the dimension line is attached to the cursor. Also, you are prompted to specify the location of the dimension line.

```
Specify dimension line location or second line for angle [Mtext
Text text aNgle Undo]:
```

4. Move the cursor perpendicular to the selected object. The aligned dimension appears attached to the cursor.

5. Click in the drawing area to specify the location of the dimension line. The aligned dimension is applied.

Note: In addition to selecting the object to be dimensioned, you can specify the origin for the first and second extension lines of the dimension by clicking the left mouse button on the end points (P1 and P2) of the object one by one, see Figure 6.77. To select the end points of the object, ensure that the **Object Snap** mode is turned on.

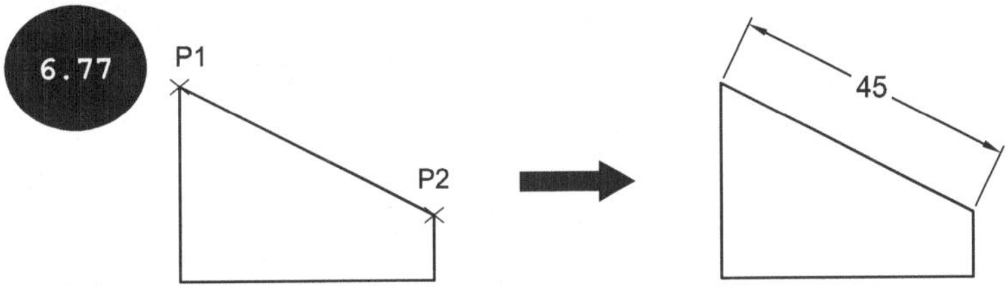

Note: If you invoke the **Aligned** tool or the DIMALIGNED command for applying the aligned dimension, you will be prompted to specify the origin of the first extension line "`Specify first extension line origin or <select object>:`". Click on the end points (P1 and P2) of the aligned object to be dimensioned one by one (refer to Figure 6.77) as the origin of the first and second extension lines of the dimension and then specify the placement point for the dimension line. You can also select the object to be dimensioned instead of specifying the origin of the extension lines. For doing so, press the ENTER key when you are prompted to specify the origin of the first extension line.

The dimension parameters such as dimension text, text height, text font, arrow height, and arrow style are displayed in the drawing area based on the current dimension style.

Applying an Angular Dimension

An angular dimension is used for measuring the angle between two non-parallel line objects, see Figure 6.78. In addition to measuring the angle between two non-parallel line objects, you can also apply angular dimensioning to an arc or a circle, see Figure 6.79. In AutoCAD, you can apply angular dimension by using the **Angular** tool. The methods for applying an angular dimension to different objects are discussed next.

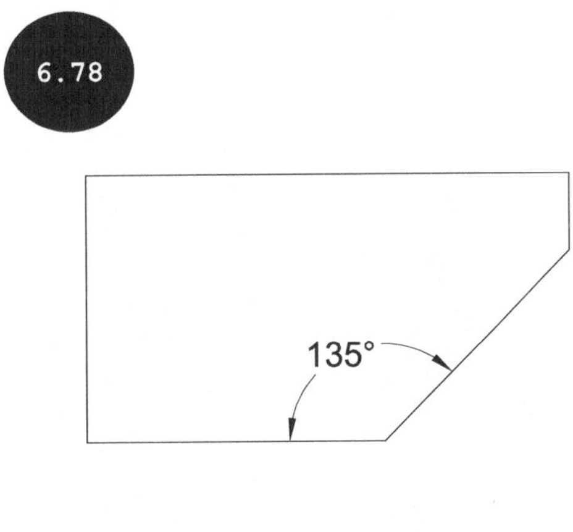

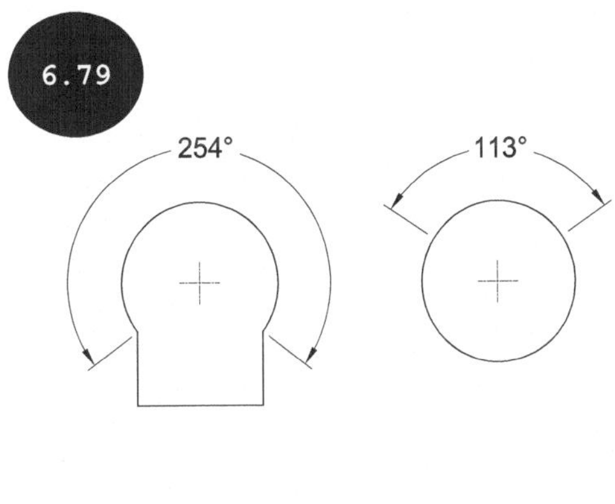

Applying an Angular Dimension between Line Objects

The method for applying an angular dimension between line objects is discussed below:

1. Invoke the **Dimension** flyout in the **Annotation** panel and then click on the **Angular** tool. You are prompted to select an arc, a circle, or a line. You can also invoke the **Angular** tool by using the DIMANGULAR command.

   ```
   Select arc, circle, line, or <specify vertex>:
   ```

2. Click on the first line object. You are prompted to select the second line object.

   ```
   Select second line:
   ```

3. Click on the second line object. The angular dimension is attached to the cursor and you are prompted to specify the location of the dimension in the drawing area.

   ```
   Specify dimension arc line location or [Mtext Text Angle Quadrant]:
   ```

4. Click in the drawing area to specify the location of the angular dimension. The angular dimension is applied.

Applying an Angular Dimension to an Arc

The method for applying an angular dimension to an arc is discussed below:

1. Click on the **Angular** tool in the **Dimension** flyout of the **Annotation** panel. You are prompted to select an arc, circle, or line. Alternatively, enter **DIMANGULAR** in the Command Line window and then press ENTER to invoke the **Angular** tool.

   ```
   Select arc, circle, line, or <specify vertex>:
   ```

2. Click on the arc to be dimensioned (P1), see Figure 6.80. The angular dimension is attached to the cursor, and you are prompted to specify the location of the dimension in the drawing area.

   ```
   Specify dimension arc line location or [Mtext Text Angle Quadrant]:
   ```

3. Click to specify the location for the angular dimension in the drawing area (P2), see Figure 6.80. The angular dimension is applied to the arc and placed at the specified location (P2).

6.80

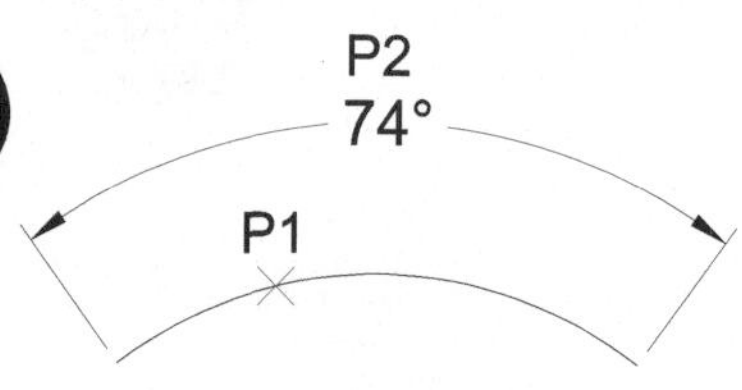

Arc

Applying an Angular Dimension to a Circle

The method for applying the angular dimension to a circle is discussed below:

1. Invoke the **Angular** tool. You are prompted to select an arc, circle, or line.

   ```
   Select arc, circle, line, or <specify vertex>:
   ```

2. Click on the circumference of the circle to be dimensioned (P1), see Figure 6.81. The specified point (P1) on the circle is used as the origin for the first extension line of the angular dimension. Also, you are prompted to specify the second angle endpoint (origin for the second extension line).

   ```
   Specify second angle endpoint:
   ```

3. Click to specify a point (P2) on the circumference of the circle as the origin for the second extension line, see Figure 6.81. The angular dimension is attached to the cursor, and you are prompted to specify the location of the dimension in the drawing area.

   ```
   Specify dimension arc line location or [Mtext Text Angle Quadrant]
   ```

4. Click to specify the location for the angular dimension (P3) in the drawing area, see Figure 6.81.

6.81

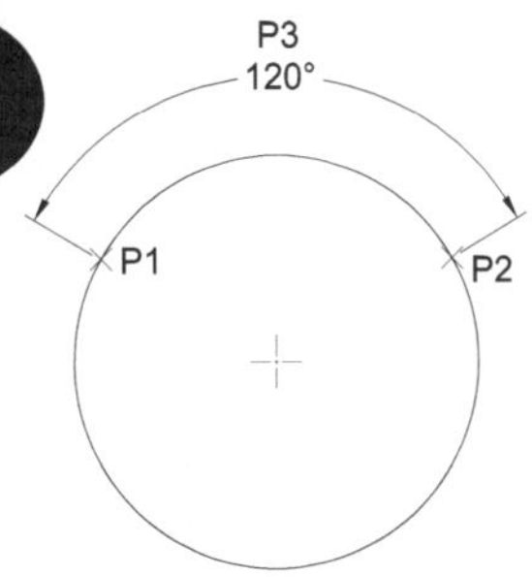

Circle

Applying an Angular Dimension by using Three Points

The method for applying an angular dimension by using three points is discussed below:

1. Invoke the **Angular** tool. You are prompted to select an arc, circle, or line.

   ```
   Select arc, circle, line, or <specify vertex>:
   ```

2. Press the ENTER key to apply the angular dimension by using three points. You are prompted to specify the angle vertex (first point).

   ```
   Specify angle vertex:
   ```

3. Click to specify the angle vertex (V1), see Figure 6.82. You are prompted to specify the first angle endpoint.

```
Specify first angle endpoint:
```

4. Click to specify the first angle endpoint (P1), see Figure 6.82. You are prompted to specify the second angle endpoint.

```
Specify second angle endpoint:
```

5. Click to specify the second angle endpoint (P2), see Figure 6.82. The angular dimension is attached to the cursor and you are prompted to specify the location of the dimension in the drawing area.

```
Specify dimension arc line location or [Mtext Text Angle Quadrant]:
```

6. Click to specify the location for the angular dimension in the drawing area, see Figure 6.82.

6.82

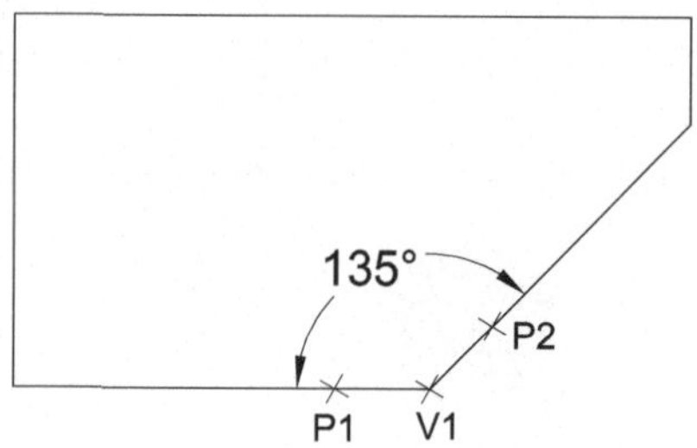

Applying an Arc Length Dimension

An arc length dimension is used for measuring the length of an arc or polyline arc segment, see Figure 6.83. You can apply arc length dimension by using the **Arc Length** tool of the **Dimension** flyout. The method for applying an arc length dimension is discussed below:

6.83

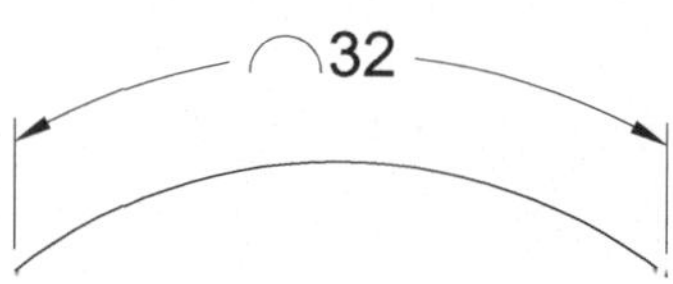

1. Invoke the **Dimension** flyout in the **Annotation** panel and then click on the **Arc Length** tool. You are prompted to select arc or polyline arc segment. You can also invoke this tool by using the DIMARC command.

```
Select arc or polyline arc segment:
```

2. Click on an arc or a polyline to be dimensioned. The arc length dimension is attached to the cursor. Also, you are prompted to specify the location of the dimension in the drawing area.

```
Specify arc length dimension location, or [Mtext Text Angle Partial]:
```

3. Click to specify the location of the arc length dimension in the drawing area.

Applying a Radius Dimension

A radius dimension is used for measuring the distance from the center to a point on the circumference of a circle/arc, see Figure 6.84. You can apply a radius dimension to an arc or a circle by using the **Radius** tool of the **Dimension** flyout. The method for applying a radius dimension is discussed below:

6.84

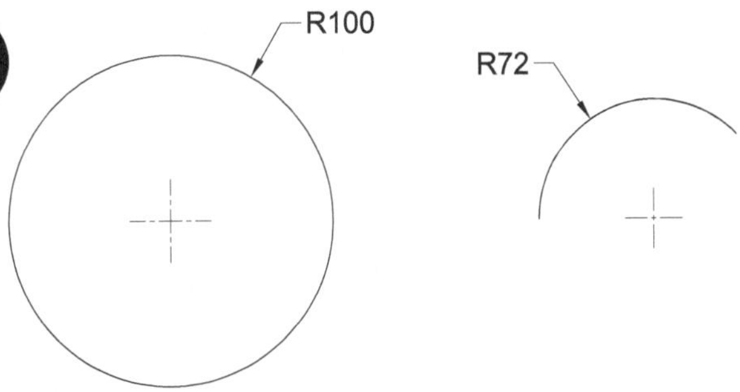

1. Invoke the **Dimension** flyout and then click on the **Radius** tool. You are prompted to select an arc or a circle. You can also invoke this tool by using the DIMRAD command.

```
Select arc or circle:
```

2. Click on an arc or a circle to apply the radius dimension. The radius dimension is attached to the cursor. Also, you are prompted to specify the location for the radius dimension in the drawing area.

```
Specify dimension line location or [Mtext Text Angle]:
```

3. Click to specify the location for the radius dimension in the drawing area.

Applying a Diameter Dimension

A diameter dimension is used for measuring the distance from one point to another (diametrically opposite) on the circumference of a circle or an arc that passes through the center, see Figure 6.85. You can apply the diameter dimension to an arc or a circle by using the **Diameter** tool. The method for applying a diameter dimension is discussed below:

6.85

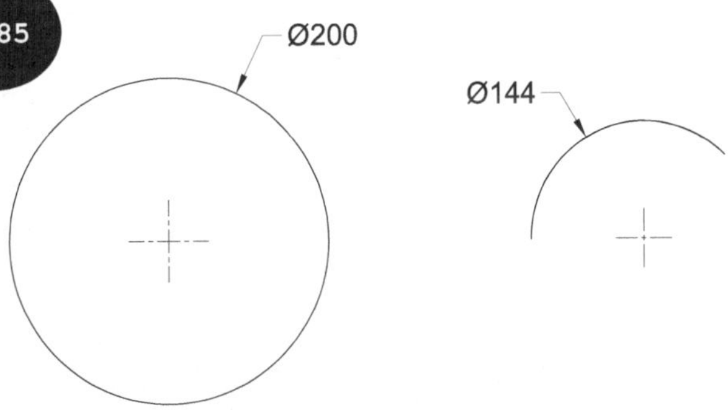

1. Invoke the **Dimension** flyout and then click on the **Diameter** tool. You are prompted to select an arc or a circle. You can also invoke this tool by using the DIMDIA command.

```
Select arc or circle:
```

2. Click on an arc or a circle to apply the diameter dimension. The diameter dimension is attached to the cursor. Also, you are prompted to specify the location for the diameter dimension in the drawing area.

```
Specify dimension line location or [Mtext Text Angle]:
```

3. Click to specify the location for the diameter dimension in the drawing area.

Applying a Jogged Radius Dimension

A jogged dimension is used for applying a jogged radius dimension to a circle or an arc whose center is not displayed in the drawing area or the current viewport, see Figure 6.86. You can apply a jogged radius dimension to an arc or a circle by using the **Jogged** tool. The method for applying jogged radius dimension is discussed below:

6.86

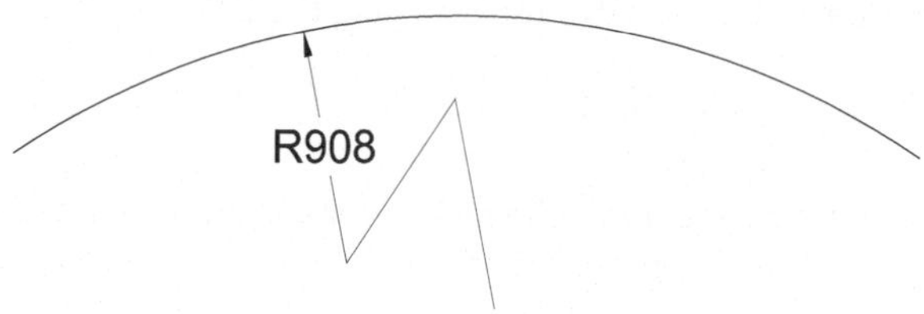

1. Invoke the **Dimension** flyout and then click on the **Jogged** tool. You are prompted to select an arc or a circle. You can also invoke this tool by using the DIMJOGGED command.

```
Select arc or circle:
```

2. Click on an arc or a circle to apply the jogged radius dimension (P1), see Figure 6.87. You are prompted to specify the override center location.

```
Specify center location override:
```

3. Click to specify the override center location (P2) for the selected object (arc or circle), see Figure 6.87. A preview of the jogged dimension is attached to the cursor and you are prompted to specify the dimension line location.

```
Specify dimension line location or [Mtext Text Angle]:
```

4. Click to specify the dimension line location (P3), see Figure 6.87. You are prompted to specify the jog location.

```
Specify jog location:
```

5. Click to specify the jog location (P4), see Figure 6.87. The jogged radius dimension is applied, see Figure 6.87.

6.87

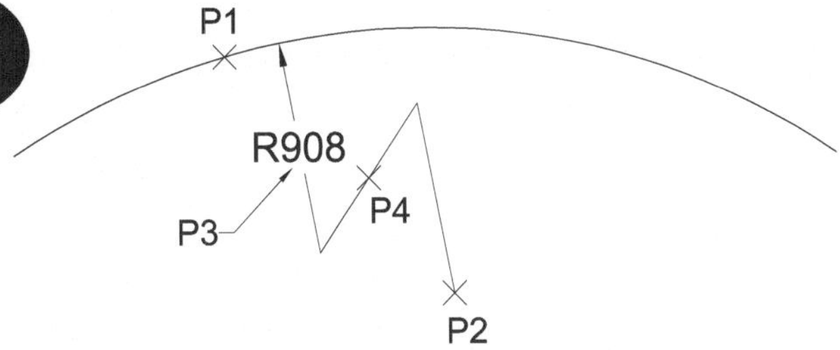

Applying a Jogged Linear Dimension

A linear jogged dimension is applied to an object having a high length-to-width ratio, see Figure 6.88. You can apply linear jogged dimensions by using the **Jogged Linear** tool. The method for applying a jogged linear dimension is discussed below:

6.88

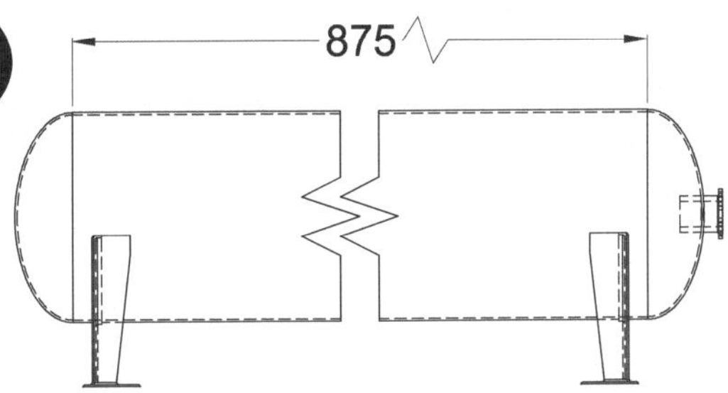

1. Invoke the **Jogged Linear** tool by clicking on the **Dimension > Jogged Linear** in the Menu Bar. You can also invoke this tool by using the DIMJOGLINE command. You are prompted to select the dimension to add a jog.

   ```
   Select dimension to add jog or [Remove]:
   ```

2. Click on a linear dimension to add jog, see Figure 6.89. You are prompted to specify the jog location.

   ```
   Specify jog location (or press ENTER):
   ```

3. Click to specify a location for adding a jog in the selected linear dimension, see Figure 6.89. The jog gets added to the linear dimension at the specified location, see Figure 6.89.

6.89

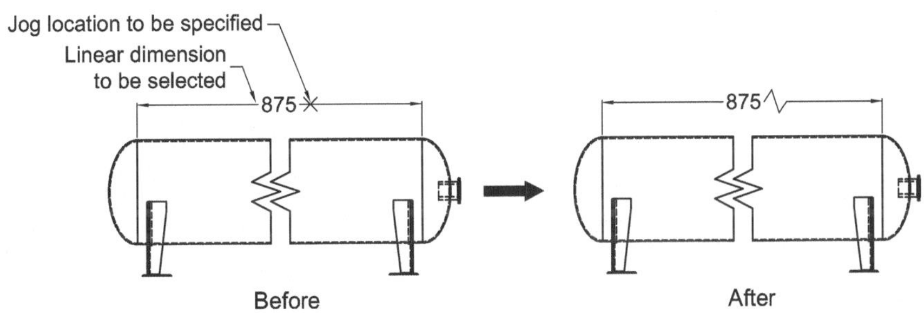

Note: Instead of specifying the jog location, you can press ENTER to add jog in the default location of the linear dimension, automatically.

Applying an Ordinate Dimension

Ordinate dimensions are used for assigning dimensions to machine parts to maintain accuracy. Ordinate dimensions measure the perpendicular distance from the specified origin and are described as X and Y ordinate dimensions, see Figure 6.90. Note that the X ordinate dimensions measure the distance from the origin along the X axis and Y ordinate dimensions measure the distance from the origin along the Y axis, see Figure 6.90. The method for applying ordinate dimension is discussed below:

6.90

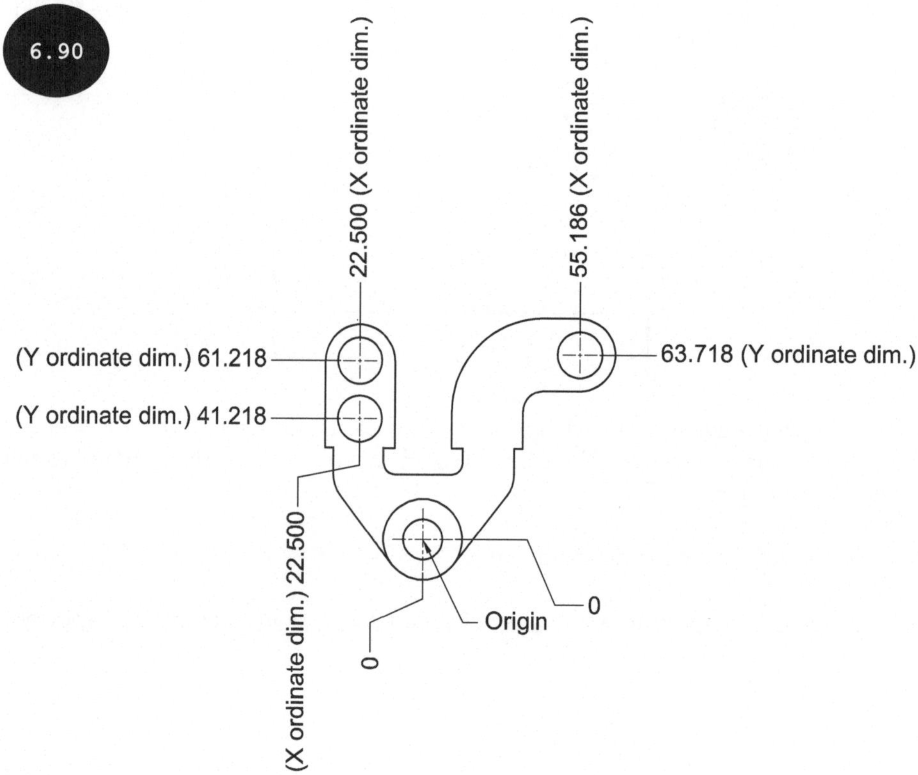

Before you start applying ordinate dimensions, it is important to define the origin for measuring the dimensions.

1. Enter **UCS** in the Command Line window and then press ENTER. You are prompted to specify the origin of the UCS.

```
Specify origin of UCS or [Face NAmed OBject Previous View World X
Y Z ZAxis] <World>:
```

2. Click on the required location to specify the origin (P1), see Figure 6.91. You can also enter coordinates (X, Y) for specifying the origin location. As soon as you specify the origin of the UCS, you are prompted to specify a point on X-axis.

```
Specify point on X-axis or <accept>:
```

3. Click to specify a point for defining the X-axis of the UCS. Similarly, define the Y-axis of the UCS. Note that to specify the X-axis and Y-axis directions of the UCS, it is recommended to turn on the Object snap mode. A UCS is created at the specified origin in the drawing area.

   After specifying the origin location by using the UCS, you can apply the ordinate dimensions.

4. Invoke the **Dimension** flyout of the **Annotation** panel in the **Home** tab and then click on the **Ordinate** tool. You can also use the DIMORD command to invoke this tool. You are prompted to specify the feature location.

```
Specify feature location:
```

5. Click on a point/feature (P2) for applying the X ordinate dimension, see Figure 6.91. You are prompted to specify the leader endpoint location.

```
Specify leader endpoint or [Xdatum Ydatum Mtext Text Angle]:
```

6. Move the cursor vertically upward and then click to specify the leader endpoint location for the X ordinate dimension in the drawing area. The X ordinate dimension is applied.

7. Similarly, invoke the **Ordinate** tool again from the **Dimension** flyout and then click on the point/feature (P2) for applying the Y ordinate dimension, see Figure 6.91.

8. Move the cursor horizontally toward the right and then click to specify the leader endpoint location for the Y ordinate dimension. The Y ordinate dimension is applied.

9. Similarly, invoke the **Ordinate** tool again and apply the remaining ordinate dimensions concerning the specified origin (P1), see Figure 6.91.

6.91

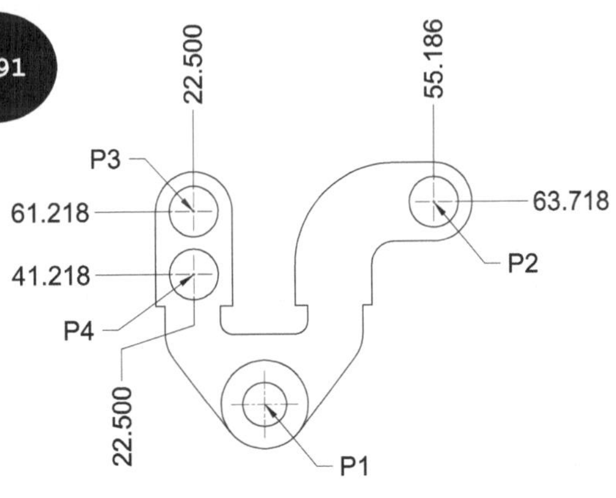

Applying Baseline Dimensions

Baseline dimensions are a series of parallel linear dimensions that share the same base point, see Figure 6.92. The baseline dimensions are used for eliminating cumulative errors that can occur due to the rounded dimension values between consecutive adjacent dimensions or due to the upper and lower dimension limits. In AutoCAD, you can apply baseline dimensions by using the **Baseline** tool or by using the DIMBASE command. The method for applying baseline dimensions is discussed below:

6.92

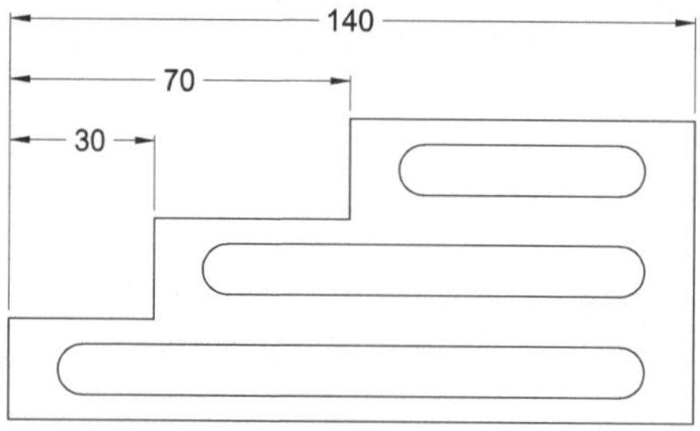

Before you start applying the baseline dimensions, you need to apply a linear/angular dimension which is used as the base dimension.

1. Apply a linear dimension in the drawing as the base dimension by using the **Linear** tool, see Figure 6.93.

6.93

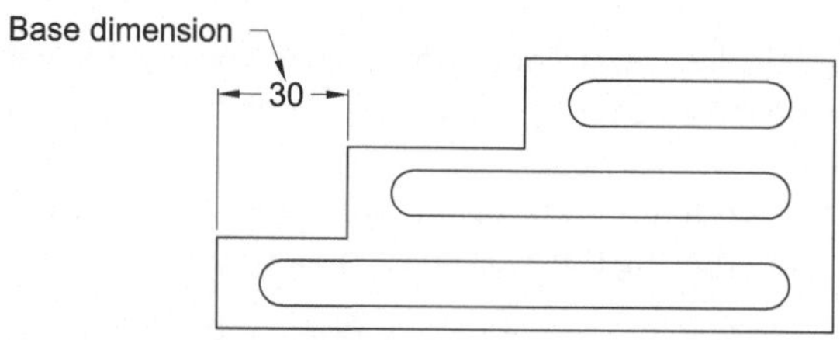

After applying the base dimension, you can apply the baseline dimensions by using the **Baseline** tool.

2. Click on **Dimension** > **Baseline** in the Menu Bar. A preview of the baseline dimension appears whose origin of the first extension line is fixed at the first extension line of the base dimension and you are prompted to specify the origin of the second extension line. You can also invoke this tool by using the DIMBASE command.

```
Specify second extension line origin or [Select Undo] <Select>:
```

Note: If the linear, angular, or ordinate dimensions are present in the current drawing, then the last applied dimension will be selected as the base dimension, automatically. Also, you are prompted to specify the origin of the second extension line. If you want to skip the automatic selection of base dimension, then press the ENTER key. On doing so, you will be prompted to select the base dimension.

3. Move the cursor toward a point (P1) of the drawing which is to be selected as the origin of the second extension line, see Figure 6.94.

4. Click to specify the origin of the second extension line when the cursor snaps to the point in the drawing area. The baseline dimension is placed by maintaining the default baseline spacing, which is specified in the current dimension style. Also, a preview of another baseline dimension is attached to the cursor whose origin of the first extension line is fixed at the first extension line of the base dimension and you are prompted to specify the origin of the second extension line.

```
Specify second extension line origin or [Select Undo] <Select>:
```

Note: The default spacing between the baseline dimensions is controlled by the current dimension style parameters. You can modify the spacing between the baseline dimensions by entering the new value in the **Baseline spacing** field of the **Lines** tab in the **Modify Dimension Style** dialog box, as discussed earlier in this chapter.

5. Move the cursor toward a point (P2) in the drawing which is to be selected as the origin of the second extension line, see Figure 6.94.

6. Click to specify the origin of the second extension line when the cursor snaps to the point. The second baseline dimension is applied (see Figure 6.94), and the preview of another baseline dimension is attached to the cursor, and you are prompted to specify the origin of the second extension line.

```
Specify second extension line origin or [Select Undo] <Select>:
```

6.94

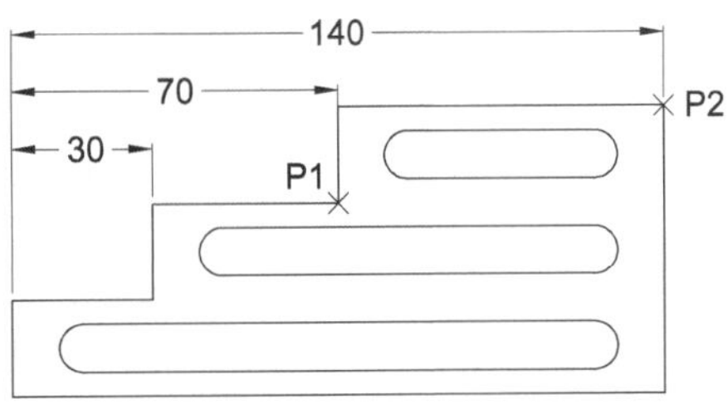

7. Similarly, you can continue to specify the origin of the second extension line and apply multiple baseline dimensions. After applying the baseline dimensions, press the ENTER key twice to exit the tool.

Applying Continue Dimensions

Similar to applying baseline dimensions, you can apply continue dimensions in a drawing, see Figure 6.95. Continue dimensions are a chain of linear dimensions which are placed end to end (second extension line of the first linear dimension is used as the first extension line for the next linear dimension). In AutoCAD, you can apply continue dimensions by using the **Continue** tool or by using the DIMCONT command. The method for applying continue dimensions is discussed below:

6.95

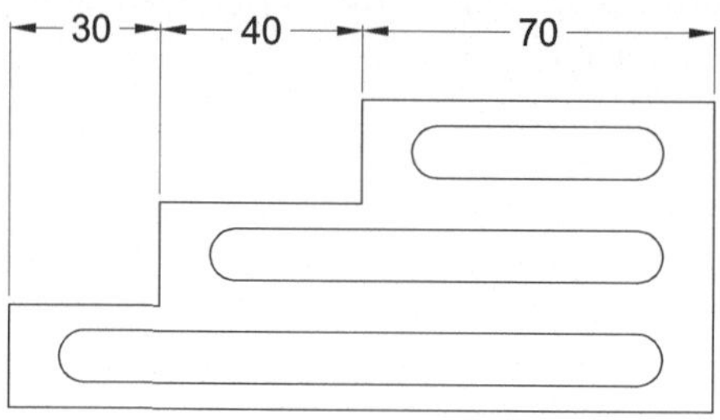

Before you start applying the continue dimensions, you need to apply a linear/angular dimension as the base dimension.

1. Apply a linear dimension in the drawing as the base dimension by using the **Linear** tool, see Figure 6.96.

6.96

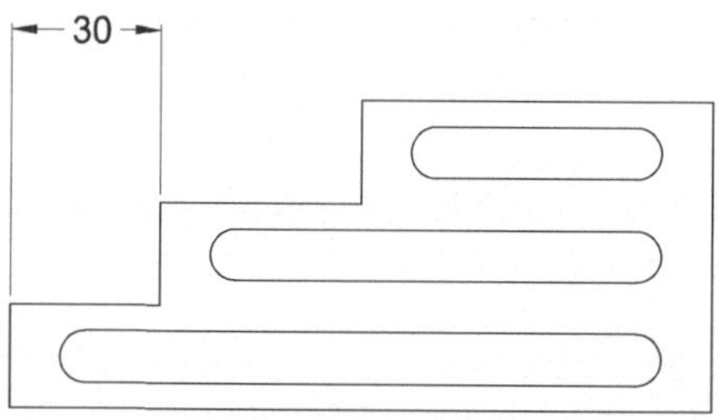

Now, you can apply the continue dimensions by using the **Continue** tool.

2. Click on **Dimension** > **Continue** in the Menu Bar. A preview of the continue dimension is attached to the cursor whose first extension line is fixed at the second extension line of the base dimension and you are prompted to specify the origin of the second extension line. You can also invoke this tool by using the DIMCONT command.

```
Specify second extension line origin or [Select Undo] <Select>:
```

Note: If the linear, angular, or ordinate dimensions are present in the current drawing, then the last applied dimension is selected as the base dimension, automatically. Also, you are prompted to specify the origin of the second extension line. If you want to skip the automatic selection of base dimension, then press the ENTER key. On doing so, you are prompted to select the base dimension.

3. Move the cursor toward a point (P1) which is to be selected as the origin of the second extension line, see Figure 6.97.

4. Click to specify the origin of the second extension line when the cursor snaps to the point in the drawing area. The continue linear dimension is placed in the drawing area and the preview of another linear dimension is attached to the cursor.

5. Move the cursor toward a point (P2) which is to be selected as the origin of the second extension line, see Figure 6.97.

6. Click to specify the origin of the second extension line when the cursor snaps to the point. The second linear dimension is applied, and the preview of another linear dimension is attached to the cursor.

```
Specify second extension line origin or [Select Undo] <Select>:
```

6.97

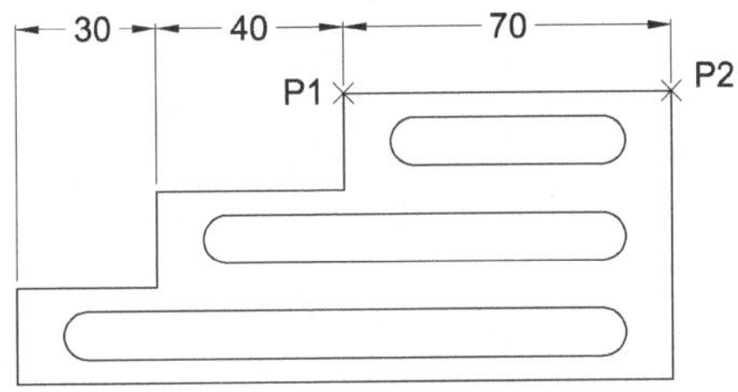

7. Similarly, you can continue to specify the origin of the second extension line and apply multiple continue linear dimensions. After applying all the required continue dimensions, press the ENTER key twice to exit the tool.

Applying Multiple Dimensions

In addition to applying individual dimensions one by one, as discussed, AutoCAD allows you to apply multiple dimensions at a time by using the **Quick Dimension** tool or QDIM command. You can apply multiple dimensions at a time such as radius, diameter, baseline, or continue. The method for applying multiple dimensions is discussed below:

1. Click on **Dimension > Quick Dimension** in the Menu Bar. Alternatively, enter **QDIM** in the Command Line window and then press ENTER. You are prompted to select a geometry.

```
Select geometry to dimension:
```

2. Select the geometries to be dimensioned by using the Window or Cross Window selection method, see Figure 6.98.

6.98

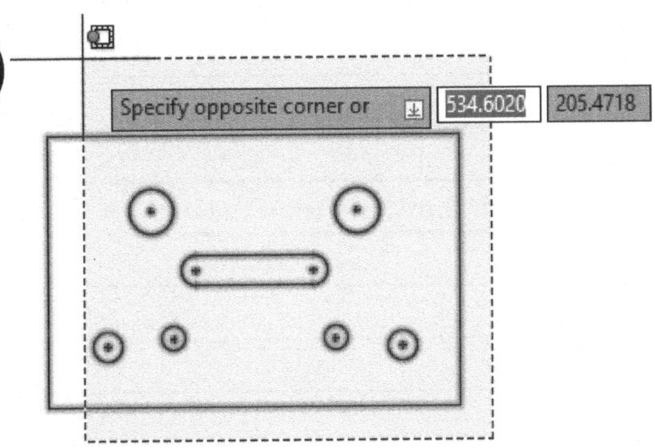

3. After selecting geometries, press ENTER. A preview of continue dimensions gets attached to the cursor and you are prompted to specify the position in the drawing area.

```
Specify dimension line position, or [Continuous Staggered Baseline
Ordinate Radius Diameter datumPoint Edit SeTtings] <Continuous>:
```

Note: By default, the continue dimension is applied to the selected geometries. To apply baseline dimensions, click on the **Baseline** option in the command prompt or enter **B**. Similarly, to apply radius or diameter dimensions, click on the **Radius** or **Diameter** option in the command prompt or enter **R** or **D** in the Command Line window.

4. Select the required type of dimensions to be applied by using the options available in the command prompt. For example, to apply multiple diameter dimensions, click on the **Diameter** option in the command prompt or enter **D**.

5. After specifying the type of dimensions to be applied, click to define the placement point in the drawing area. The selected type of dimensions are applied to the geometries. Figure 6.99 shows a drawing in which multiple diameter dimensions are applied.

6.99

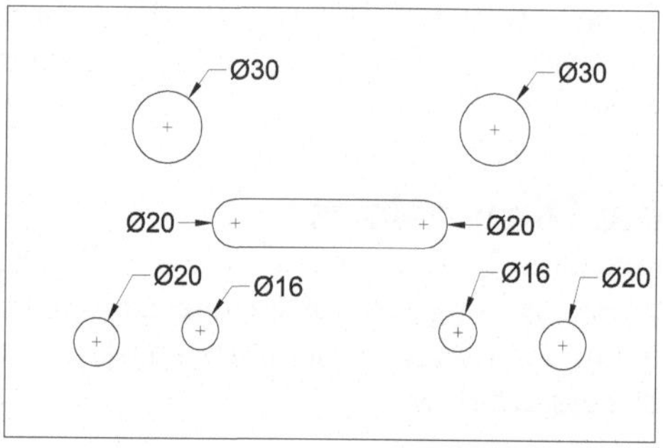

Tutorial 1

Create the drawing and apply dimensions as shown in Figure 6.100. You need to apply dimensions as per the new dimension style having the following dimension parameters.

New Dimension Style Parameters	
Text font	Arial
Text font style	Regular
Text height	4.75
Text placement - Offset from dimension line	2.5
Arrowheads style	Closed filled
Arrow size	4.5
Center marks	Mark - 1
Dimension break size	3.5
Extension lines - Extend beyond dimension lines	2
Extension lines - Offset from origin	1.75
Linear dimensions - Precision	0
Angular dimensions - Precision	0

6.100

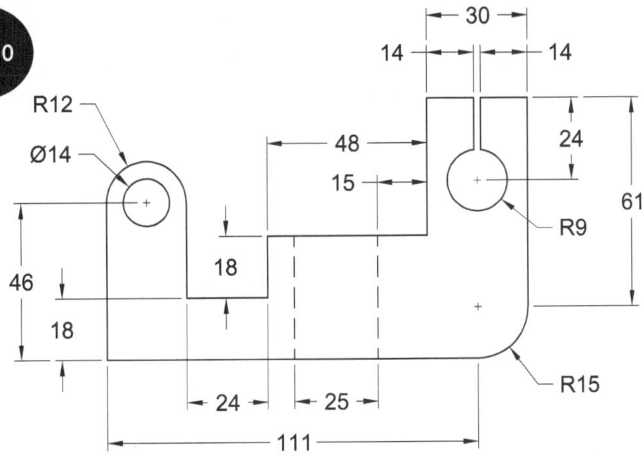

Section 1: Starting a new AutoCAD Drawing

1. Start AutoCAD and then open a new drawing file. Next, set the drawing limits.

Section 2: Creating a Drawing

1. Click on the **Line** tool in the **Draw** panel of the **Home** tab. You are prompted to specify the first point of the line. Alternatively, enter **L** in the Command Line window and then press ENTER to invoke the **Line** tool.

   `Specify first point:`

2. Click to specify the start point of the line in the drawing area. You are prompted to specify the next point of the line.

3. Ensure that the Dynamic Input mode and the Ortho mode are turned on.

4. Follow the command sequence given below for creating the drawing.

   `Specify next point or [Undo]:` *Move the cursor horizontally toward right and then enter **126** in the Dynamic Input box* (***ENTER***).
   `Specify next point or [Undo]:` *Move the cursor vertically upward and then enter **76*** (***ENTER***).
   `Specify next point or [Close Undo]:` *Move the cursor horizontally toward left and then enter **14*** (***ENTER***).
   `Specify next point or [Close Undo]:` *Move the cursor vertically downward and enter **24*** (***ENTER***).
   `Specify next point or [Close Undo]:` *Move the cursor horizontally toward left and then enter **2*** (***ENTER***).
   `Specify next point or [Close Undo]:` *Move the cursor vertically upward and then enter **24*** (***ENTER***).
   `Specify next point or [Close Undo]:` *Move the cursor horizontally toward left and then enter **14*** (***ENTER***).
   `Specify next point or [Close Undo]:` *Move the cursor vertically downward and then enter **40*** (***ENTER***).

`Specify next point or [Close Undo]:` *Move the cursor horizontally toward left and then enter 48* (**ENTER**).
`Specify next point or [Close Undo]:` *Move the cursor vertically downward and then enter 18* (**ENTER**).
`Specify next point or [Close Undo]:` *Move the cursor horizontally toward left and then enter 24* (**ENTER**).
`Specify next point or [Close Undo]:` *Move the cursor vertically upward and then enter 28* (**ENTER**).
`Specify next point or [Close Undo]:` *Move the cursor horizontally toward left and then enter 24* (**ENTER**).
`Specify next point or [Close Undo]:` *C or Close* (**ENTER**) *(See Figure 6.101).*

6.101

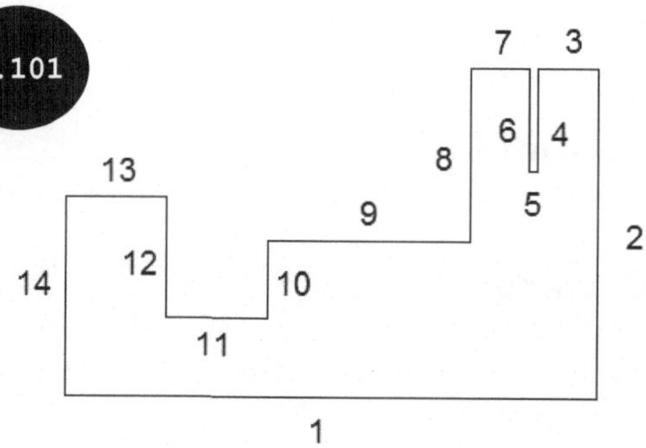

Note: In Figure 6.101, the entities are numbered for your reference to create other entities of the drawing.

After creating the line entities of the drawing, you need to create circle entities.

5. Click on the **Circle, Radius** tool in the **Circle** flyout of the **Draw** panel or enter **C** in the Command Line window and then press ENTER. You are prompted to specify the center point of the circle.

   `Specify center point for circle or [3P 2P Ttr (tan tan radius)]:`

6. Move the cursor toward the midpoint of the horizontal line (13), refer to Figure 6.101.

7. Click to specify the center point of the circle when the cursor snaps to the midpoint of the horizontal line (13), see Figure 6.102. You are prompted to specify the radius of the circle.

   `Specify radius of circle or [Diameter]:`

8. Enter **12** as the radius of the circle and then press ENTER. A circle of radius 12 units is created in the drawing area, see Figure 6.103.

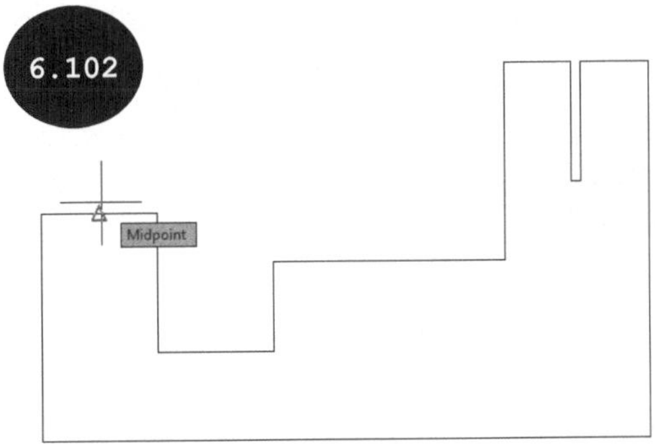

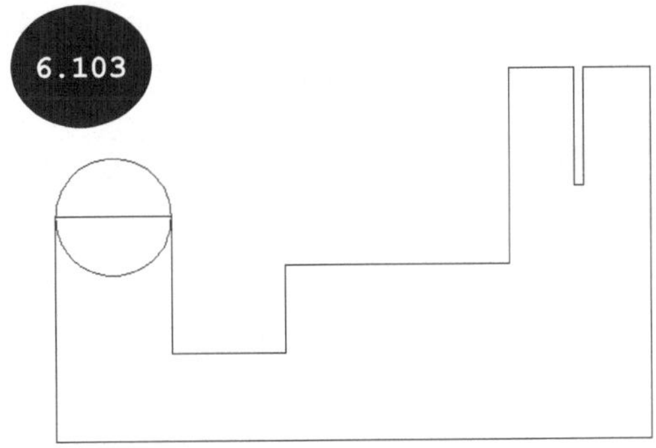

9. Similarly, create another two circles of radius 9 units and 7 units, see Figure 6.104. The center point of the circle having radius of 9 units is at the midpoint of line (5), and the center point of the circle having a radius of 7 units is at the midpoint of line (13), see Figure 6.104.

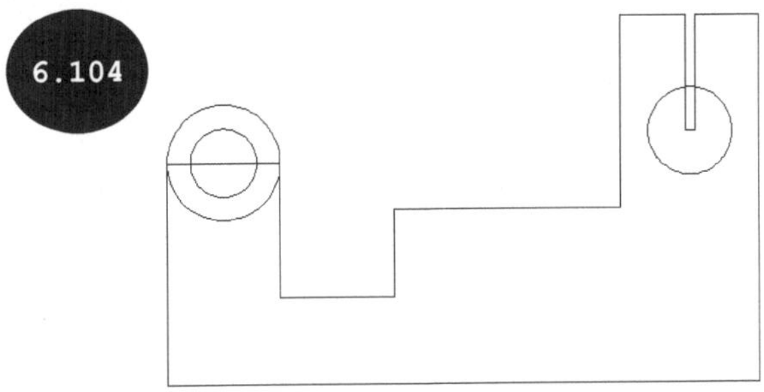

Now, you need to create a vertical line at an offset distance of 45 units from the vertical line (2).

10. Click on the **Offset** tool in the **Modify** panel of the **Home** tab or enter **O** in the Command Line window and then press ENTER. You are prompted to specify the offset distance.

```
Specify offset distance or [Through Erase Layer] <Through>:
```

11. Enter **45** as the offset distance and then press ENTER. You are prompted to select an object to offset.

```
Select object to offset or [Exit Undo] <Exit>:
```

12. Click on the vertical line (2) as the object to offset, refer to Figure 6.101. You are prompted to specify a point on the side to offset.

```
Specify point on side to offset or [Exit Multiple Undo] <Exit>:
```

13. Move the cursor toward left and then click to specify a point on the left side of the selected vertical line (2). A vertical line at an offset distance of 45 units is created, see Figure 6.105.

14. Press ENTER to exit the tool.

15. Similarly, create another vertical line at an offset distance of 25 units from the newly created vertical line, see Figure 6.106.

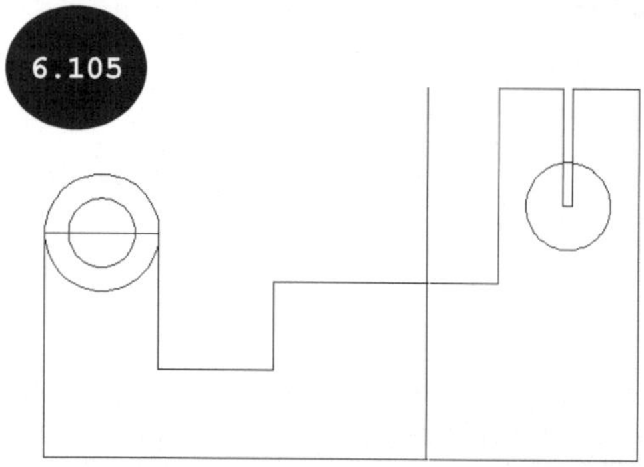
6.105

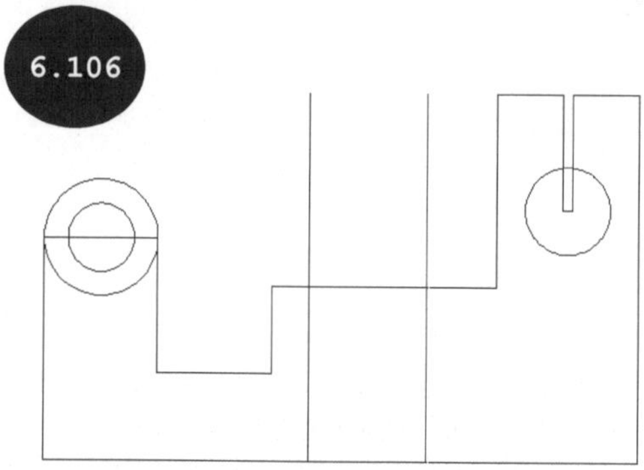
6.106

Now, you need to trim the unwanted portions of the entities.

Section 3: Trimming the Drawing Entities

1. Click on the **Trim** tool in the **Modify** panel or enter **TR** in the Command Line window and then press ENTER. You are prompted to select an object to trim.

```
Select object to trim or shift-select to extend or
[cuTting edges Crossing mOde Project eRase]:
```

2. Click on the unwanted entity (1) to be trimmed, see Figure 6.107. The selected entity is trimmed to its nearest intersection, see Figure 6.108. Also, you are prompted to select an object to trim.

```
Select object to trim or shift-select to extend or
[cuTting edges Crossing mOde Project eRase Undo]:
```

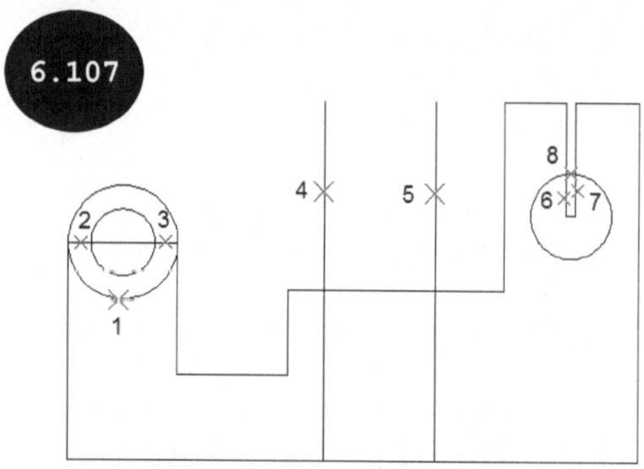

6.107

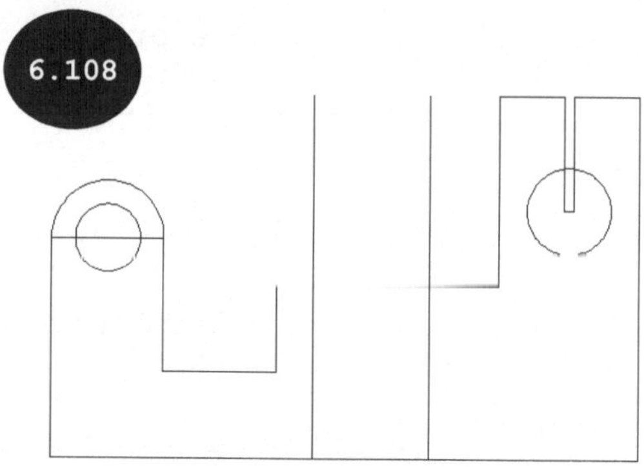
6.108

3. Similarly, click on the other unwanted entities (2, 3, 4, 5, 6, 7, and 8), refer to Figure 6.107. Figure 6.109 shows the drawing after trimming all the unwanted entities.

6.109

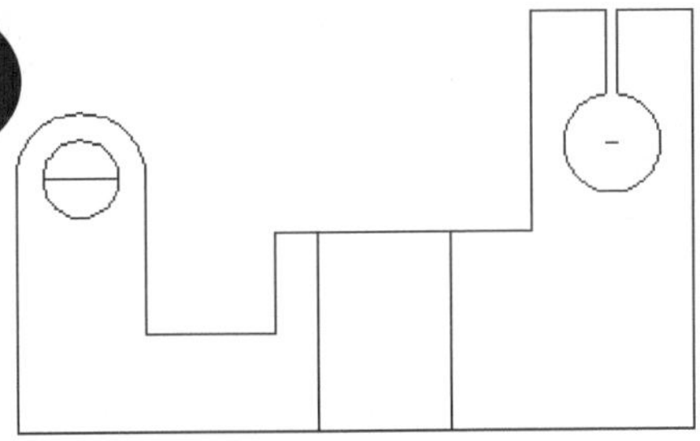

4. After trimming the entities, press the ENTER key to exit the tool.

Section 4: Deleting the Unwanted Entities

1. Click on the horizontal entities inside the circles of radius 7 units and 9 units as the objects to be deleted from the drawing area, see Figure 6.110.

2. Press the DELETE key. The selected entities get removed from the drawing, see Figure 6.111.

6.110

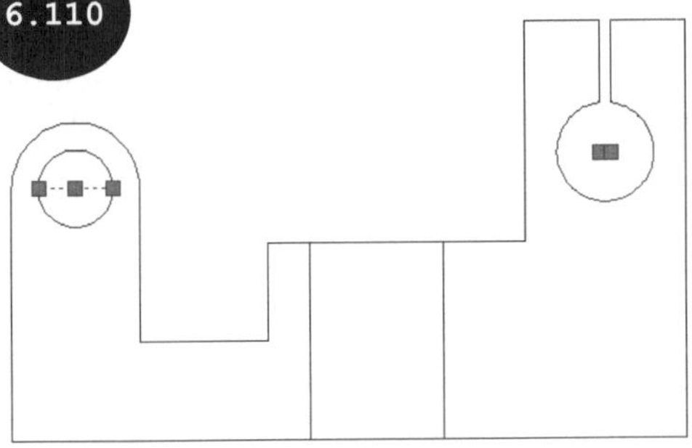

6.111

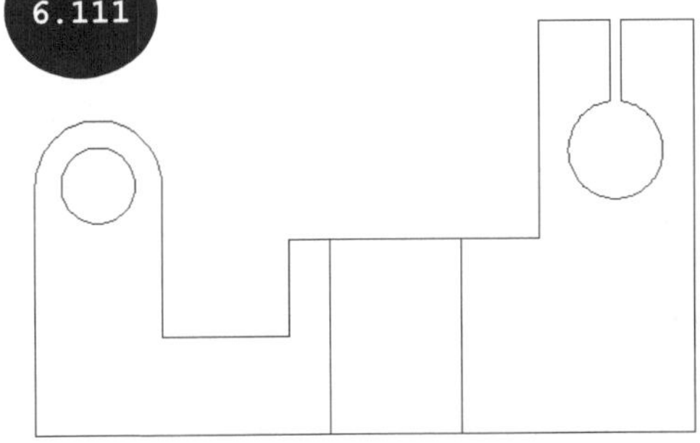

Section 5: Creating a Fillet

1. Click on the **Fillet** tool in the **Modify** panel or enter **F** in the Command Line window and then press ENTER. You are prompted to select the first object of the fillet.

```
Select first object or [Undo Polyline Radius Trim Multiple]:
```

2. Click on the **Radius** option in the command prompt or enter **R** and then press ENTER. You are prompted to specify the fillet radius.

```
Specify fillet radius <0.0000>:
```

3. Enter **15** as the fillet radius and then press ENTER. You are prompted to select the first object.

```
Select first object or [Undo Polyline Radius Trim Multiple]:
```

4. Click on the right-most vertical line of the drawing as the first object of the fillet. You are prompted to select the second object of the fillet.

```
Select second object or shift-select to apply corner or [Radius]:
```

5. Click on the bottom horizontal line as the second object of the fillet. A fillet of radius 15 is created, see Figure 6.112.

6.112

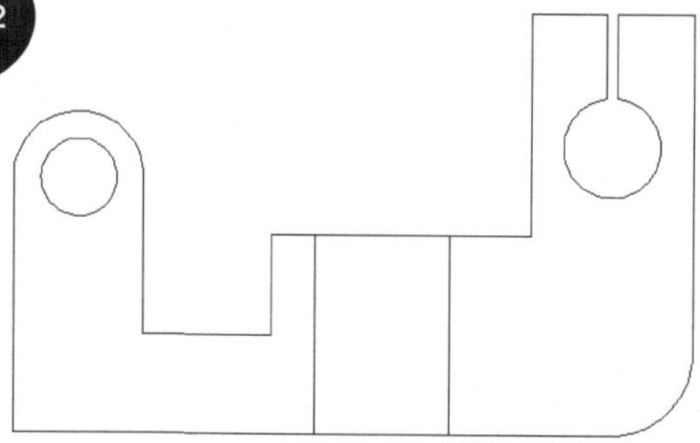

Section 6: Creating Layers

Now, you need to create layers: Object, Hidden, and Dimension. After creating the layers, assign different drawing objects to the respective layers such as hidden objects to the Hidden layer.

1. Click on the **Layer Properties** tool in the **Layers** panel of the **Home** tab or enter **LA** in the Command Line window and then press ENTER. The **LAYER PROPERTIES MANAGER** appears, see Figure 6.113.

6.113

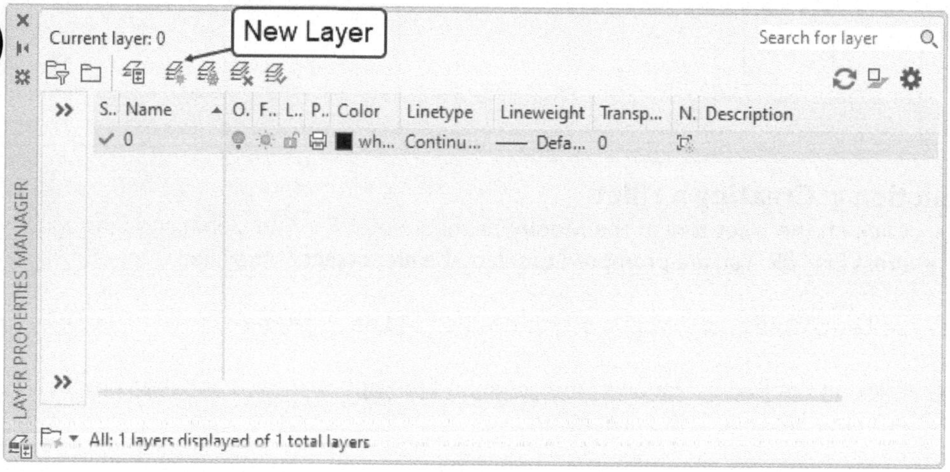

2. Click on the **New Layer** button in the **LAYER PROPERTIES MANAGER** or press ALT + N key. A new layer with the default name "**Layer 1**" is created.

3. Enter **Object** as the name of the newly created layer in the **LAYER PROPERTIES MANAGER**. Accept the default parameters for the newly created Object layer.

4. Similarly, create two more layers: Hidden and Dimension. Also, assign the HIDDEN linetype to the Hidden layer and accept the default parameters for the Dimension layer, see Figure 6.114.

6.114

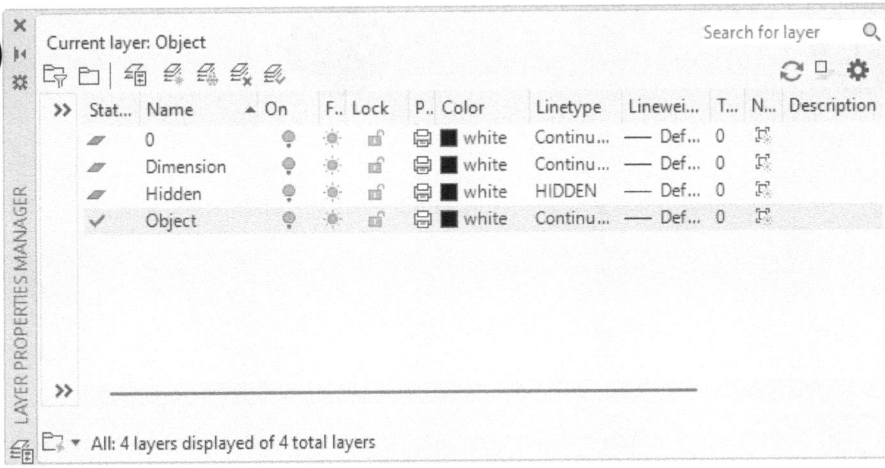

5. After creating all the layers, close the LAYER PROPERTIES MANAGER.

Section 7: Assigning Drawing Objects to the Layers

1. Select all the drawing objects except two vertical lines (hidden lines), see Figure 6.115.

2. Invoke the **Layer** drop-down list in the **Layers** panel of the **Home** tab, see Figure 6.116.

6.115

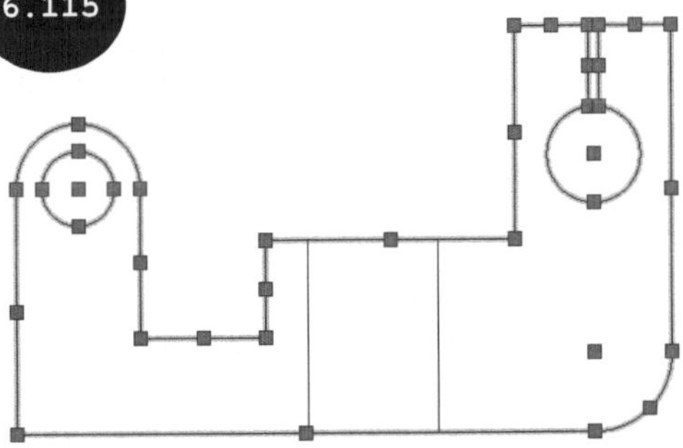

6.116

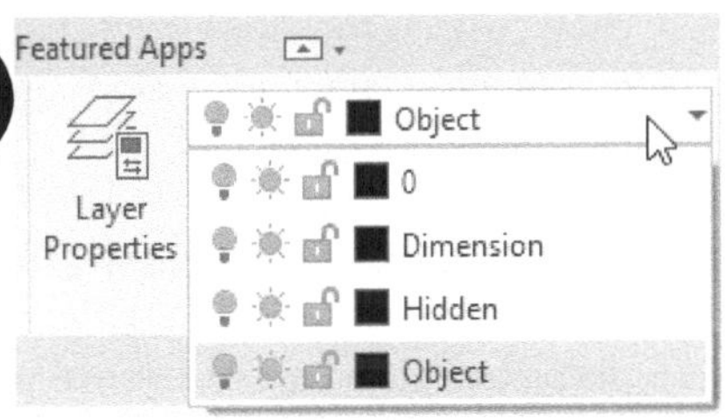

3. Move the cursor over the **Object** layer in the **Layer** drop-down list and then click on it to assign the selected objects to the **Object** layer. Next, press the ESC key to exit the selection.

4. Select two vertical lines to assign them to the Hidden layer, see Figure 6.117.

5. Invoke the **Layer** drop-down list, refer to Figure 6.116, and then click on the **Hidden** layer. The selected vertical lines are assigned to the **Hidden** layer, see Figure 6.118. Next, press the ESC key to exit the selection.

6.117

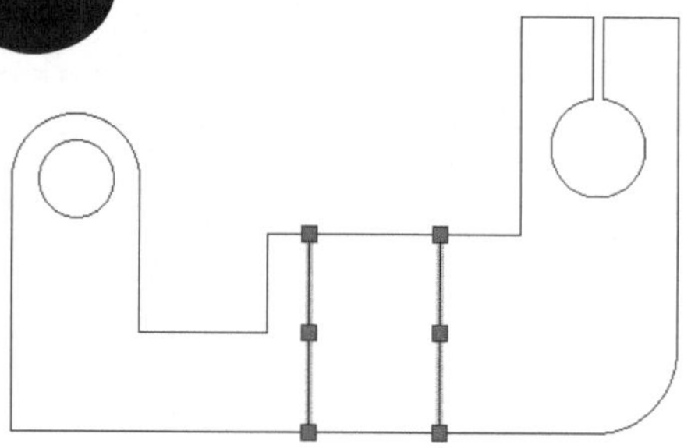

6.118

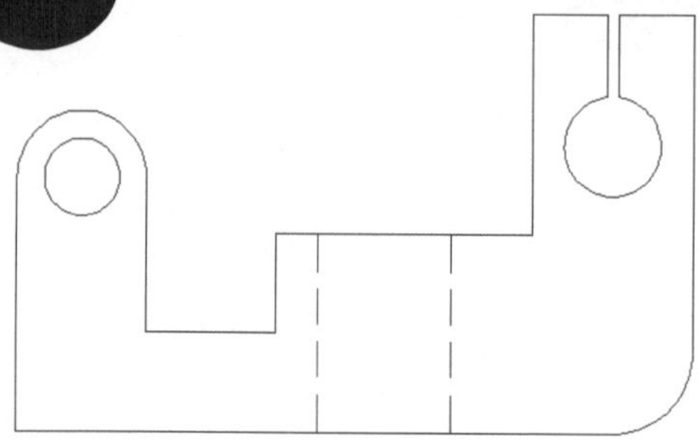

Note: If the entities of the Hidden layer appear as continuous linetype in the drawing area, then you may need to increase or decrease its linetype scale by using the **Properties** panel. To increase or decrease the linetype scale, enter **PR** in the Command Line window and then press ENTER. The **Properties** panel appears to the left of the drawing area. Next, select the entities of the Hidden layer in the drawing area whose linetype scale has to be changed and then enter the scale value in the **Linetype scale** field of the **Properties** panel. You can try any value as the linetype scale to match the display of the hidden line, as required.

After creating the drawing, you need to apply dimensions. As mentioned in the tutorial description, you need to apply dimensions as per the new dimension style. Therefore, you need to create a new dimension style first.

Section 8: Creating a New Dimension Style

1. Enter **D** in the Command Line window and then press ENTER. The **Dimension Style Manager** dialog box appears, see Figure 6.119.

6.119

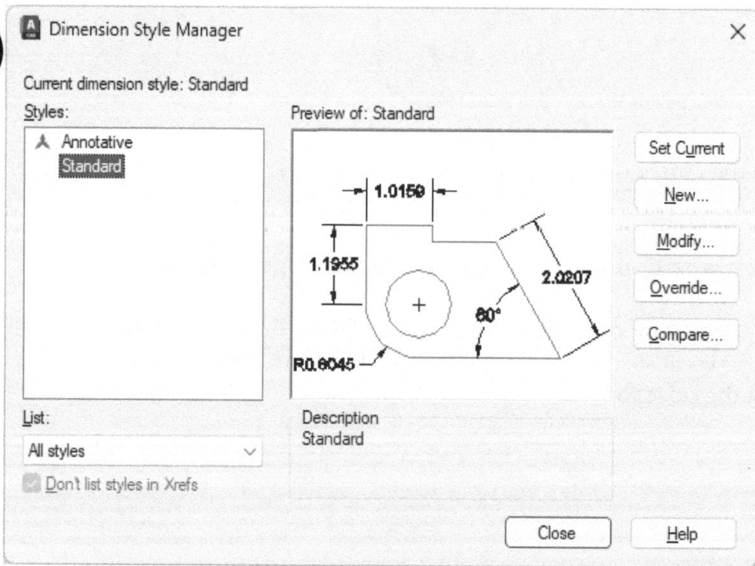

2. Click on the **Standard** dimension style in the **Styles** area of the dialog box as the base dimension style for creating the new dimension style.

3. Click on the **New** button in the **Dimension Style Manager** dialog box. The **Create New Dimension Style** dialog box appears.

4. Enter **C06_TUT** as the name of the new dimension style in the **New Style Name** field of the dialog box.

5. Click on the **Continue** button of the **Create New Dimension Style** dialog box. The **New Dimension Style** dialog box appears, see Figure 6.120.

6. Ensure that the **Text** tab is activated in this dialog box, see Figure 6.120.

7. Ensure that the **Standard** option is selected in the **Text style** drop-down list in the **Text** tab of the dialog box, see Figure 6.120.

6.120

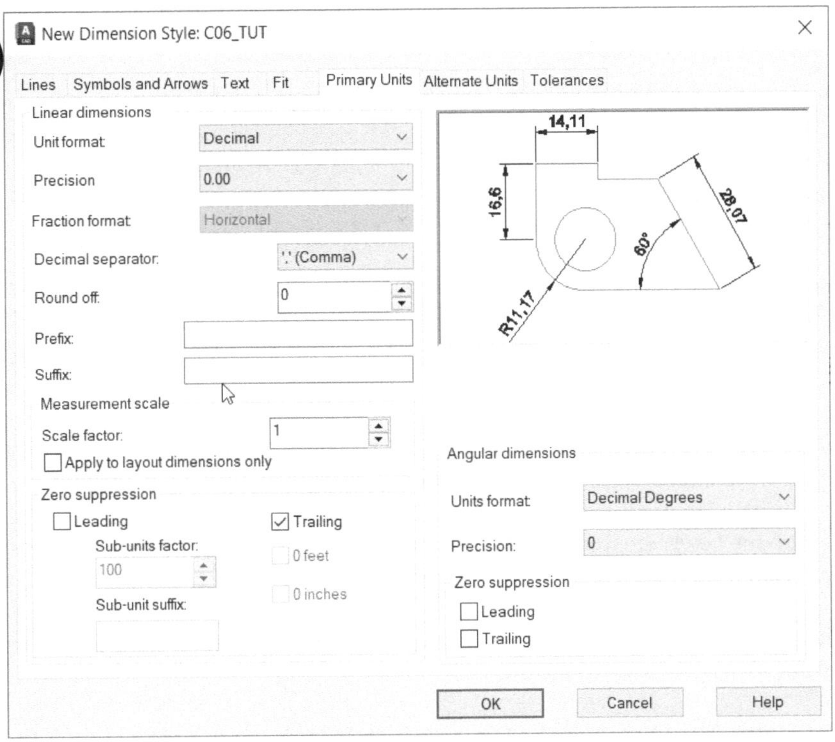

8. Click on the ⋯ button available next to the **Text style** drop-down list. The **Text Style** dialog box appears.

9. Ensure that the **Arial** option is selected in the **Font Name** drop-down list, and the **Regular** option is selected in the **Font Style** drop-down list in this **Text Style** dialog box.
10. Click on the **Cancel** button to exit the **Text Style** dialog box.

11. Enter **4.75** in the **Text height** field of the **Text appearance** area in the **Text** tab of the dialog box.
12. Enter **2.5** in the **Offset from dim line** field of the **Text placement** area in the **Text** tab.
13. Click on the **Symbols and Arrows** tab in the **New Dimension Style** dialog box.
14. Ensure that the **Closed filled** option is selected in the **First**, **Second**, and **Leader** drop-down lists of the **Arrowheads** area in the **Symbols and Arrows** tab.
15. Enter **4.5** in the **Arrow size** field of the **Arrowheads** area.
16. Ensure that the **Mark** radio button is selected in the **Center marks** area.
17. Enter **1** in the field available in front of **Mark** radio button of the **Center marks** area.
18. Enter **3.5** in the **Break size** field of the **Dimension Break** area of the dialog box.
19. Click on the **Lines** tab in the **New Dimension Style** dialog box.
20. Enter **2** in the **Extend beyond dim lines** field of the **Extension lines** area in the **Lines** tab.
21. Enter **1.75** in the **Offset from origin** field of the **Extension lines** area in the **Lines** tab.
22. Click on the **Primary Units** tab in the dialog box.
23. Select the **0** option in the **Precision** drop-down list of the **Linear dimensions** area.
24. Select the **0** option in the **Precision** drop-down list of the **Angular dimensions** area.
25. Accept the remaining default settings and then click on the **OK** button in the **New Dimension Style** dialog box. The new dimension style named C06_TUT is created and listed in the **Styles** area of the **Dimension Style Manager** dialog box.
26. Click on the newly created dimension style "C06_TUT" in the **Styles** area of the **Dimension Style Manager** dialog box.
27. Click on the **Set Current** button in the dialog box to make the newly created dimension style the current dimension style of the drawing.
28. Click on the **Close** button in the **Dimension Style Manager** dialog box to exit the dialog box.

    After creating the dimension style and making it the current style of the drawing, you need to apply dimensions to the drawing.

Section 9: Applying Dimensions

1. Click on the **Linear** tool in the **Dimension** flyout of the **Annotation** panel in the **Home** tab or enter **DIMLIN** in the Command Line window and then press ENTER. You are prompted to specify the origin for the first extension line.

```
Specify first extension line origin or <select object>:
```

2. Press ENTER to select the object to be dimensioned directly. You are prompted to select the object to be dimensioned.

```
Select object to dimension:
```

3. Click on the bottom horizontal line of the drawing. The linear dimension of the selected line is attached to the cursor. Also, you are prompted to specify the dimension line location.

```
Specify dimension line location or
[Mtext Text Angle Horizontal Vertical Rotated]:
```

4. Move the cursor vertically downward to a small distance and then click to specify the location for the attached dimension, see Figure 6.121.

6.121

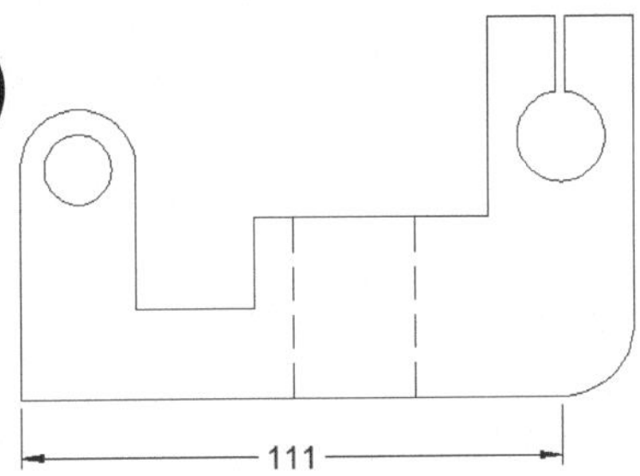

5. Click on the **Linear** tool in the **Dimension** flyout again. You are prompted to specify the origin for the first extension line.

```
Specify first extension line origin or <select object>:
```

6. Move the cursor toward the upper right corner of the drawing (P1), see Figure 6.122. Next, click on it to specify the origin of the first extension line when the cursor snaps to the point (P1). You are prompted to specify the origin of the second extension line.

```
Specify second extension line origin:
```

7. Move the cursor toward the center point of the right circle (P2), see Figure 6.122. Next, click to specify the origin of the second extension line when the cursor snaps to it. The linear dimension between the selected points (P1 and P2) is attached to the cursor. Also, you are prompted to specify the dimension location.

```
Specify dimension line location or
[Mtext Text Angle Horizontal Vertical Rotated]:
```

8. Move the cursor horizontally toward right to a small distance and then click to specify the location for the attached dimension, see Figure 6.122.

6.122

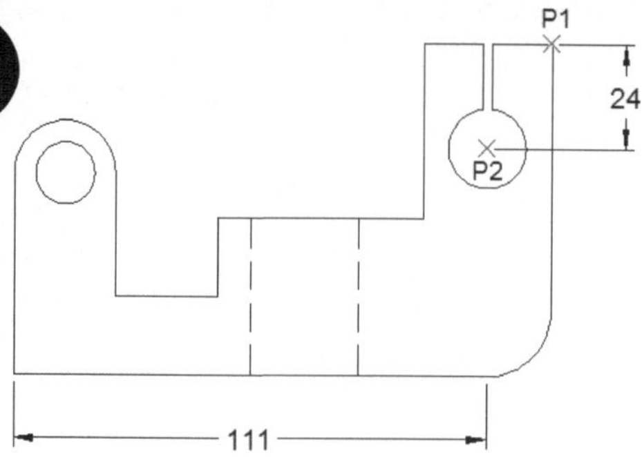

9. Similarly, apply the remaining linear (horizontal and vertical) dimensions to other entities of the drawing, see Figure 6.123. You can apply dimensions by selecting the object to be dimensioned or by selecting points. Ensure that the Object snap mode is turned on for selecting points. Figure 6.123 shows the drawing after applying all the linear dimensions.

   After applying the linear dimensions, you need to apply radius dimensions to the arc entities.

10. Click on the **Dimension** tool in the **Annotation** panel. You are prompted to select the object to be dimensioned. Alternatively, click on the **Radius** tool in the **Dimension** flyout of the **Annotation** panel or enter DIMRAD in the Command Line window and then press ENTER.

```
Select objects or specify first extension line origin or [Angular
Baseline Continue Ordinate aliGn Distribute Layer Undo]:
```

11. Move the cursor toward the upper left arc (A1) (see Figure 6.124) and then click on it. The radius dimension is attached to the cursor, and you are prompted to specify the dimension location.

```
Specify radius dimension location or [Diameter Angular Mtext Text
text aNgle Undo]:
```

12. Click to specify the dimension location on the upper left side of the selected arc (A1). A radius of 12 units is applied to the arc, see Figure 6.124.

13. Similarly, apply the radius dimension to the arc (A2), see Figure 6.124. Note that the **Dimension** tool is still activated.

    After applying the radius dimension, you need to apply the diameter dimension to the circle.

14. Move the cursor toward the circle (C1) (see Figure 6.125) and then click on it. The diameter dimension gets attached to the cursor, and you are prompted to specify the dimension location.

Note: You can also apply diameter dimensions to circles by using the **Diameter** tool of the **Dimension** flyout or by using the DIMDIA command.

6.123

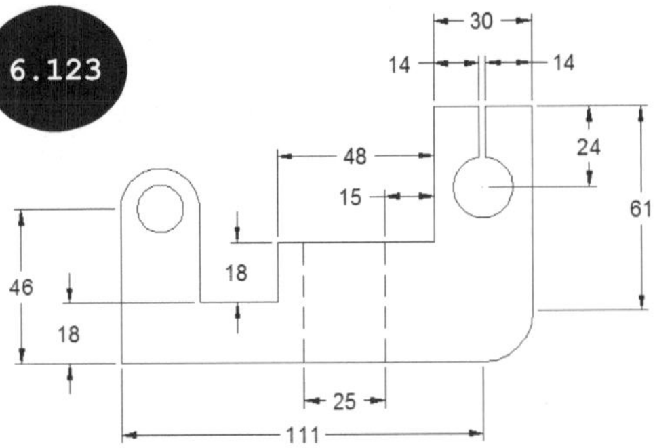

6.124

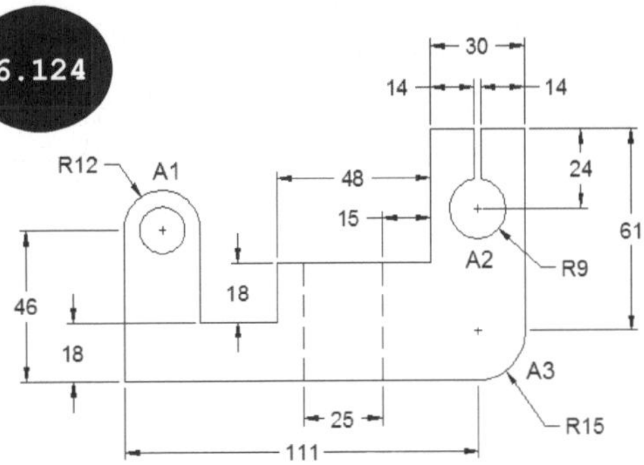

15. Click to specify the dimension location above the selected circle (C1). The diameter dimension is applied, see Figure 6.125.

6.125

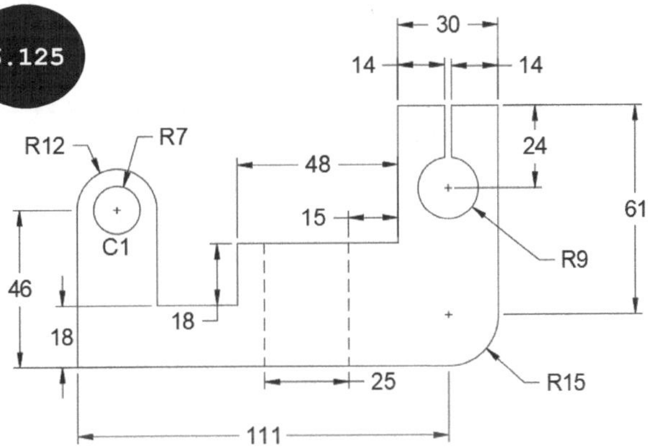

After applying all the dimensions to the drawing entities, you need to move them to the Dimension layer.

16. Select all the dimensions and then invoke the **Layer** drop-down list of the **Layers** panel in the **Home** tab. Next, click on the **Dimension** layer to assign all the selected dimensions to it.

Section 10: Saving the Drawing

After creating the drawing, you need to save it.

1. Click on the **Save** tool in the **Quick Access Toolbar**. The **Save Drawing As** dialog box appears.

2. Browse to the *AutoCAD* folder and then create a folder with the name *Chapter 6* inside the *AutoCAD* folder.

3. Enter **Tutorial 1** in the **File name** field of the dialog box and then click on the **Save** button. The drawing gets saved with the name Tutorial 1 in the *Chapter 6* folder.

Hands-on Test Drive 1

Create the drawing and apply dimensions as shown in Figure 6.126. You need to modify the default dimension style "Standard" for applying the dimensions. Below are the dimension parameters to be modified in the Standard dimension style.

Dimension Style Parameters	
Text font	Arial
Text font style	Regular
Text height	4.5
Text placement - Offset from dimension line	1.75
Arrowheads style	Closed filled
Arrow size	4.25
Dimension break size	3
Extension lines - Extend beyond dimension lines	1.25
Extension lines - Offset from origin	1
Linear dimensions - Precision	0
Angular dimensions - Precision	0

6.126

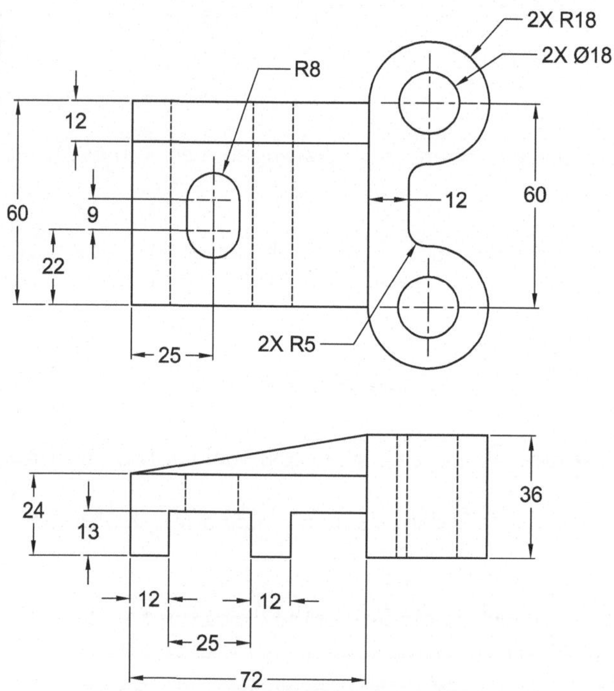

Hands-on Test Drive 2

Create the drawing and apply dimensions as shown in Figure 6.127. You need to modify the default dimension style "Standard" for applying the dimensions. The dimension parameters to be modified in the Standard dimension style are the same as mentioned in the Hands-on Test Drive 1 description.

6.127

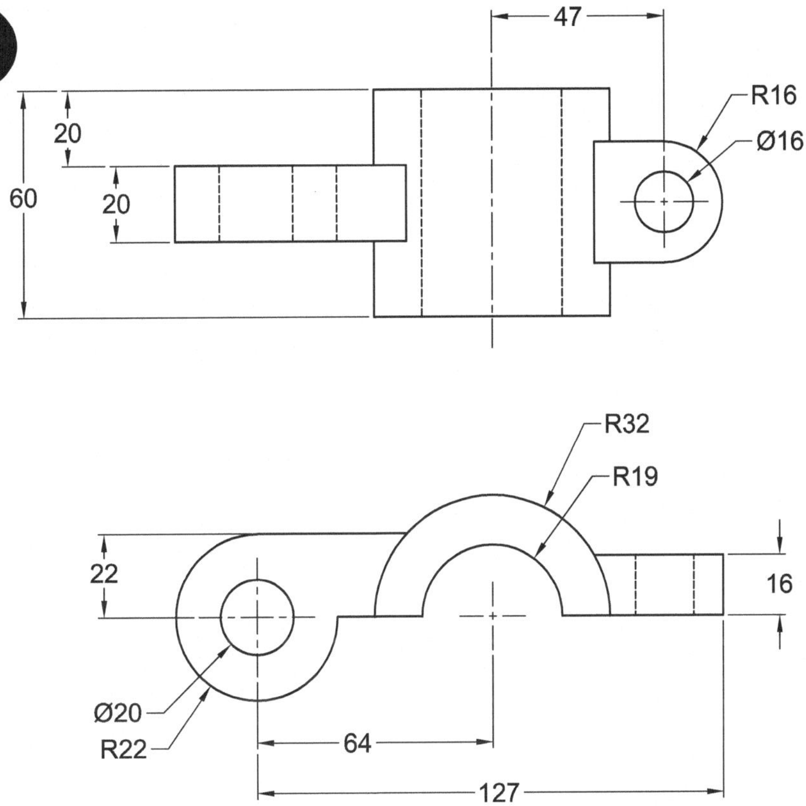

Hands-on Test Drive 3

Create the drawing and apply dimensions as shown in Figure 6.128. You need to create a new dimension style for applying the dimensions. The dimension parameters for creating the new dimension style are discussed next.

New Dimension Style Parameters	
Text font	Arial
Text font style	Regular
Text height	2.75
Text placement - Offset from dimension line	1.5
Arrowheads style	Closed filled
Arrow size	2.5
Dimension break size	3.5
Extension lines - Extend beyond dimension lines	1.25
Extension lines - Offset from origin	1
Linear dimensions - Precision	0.0
Angular dimensions - Precision	0

6.128

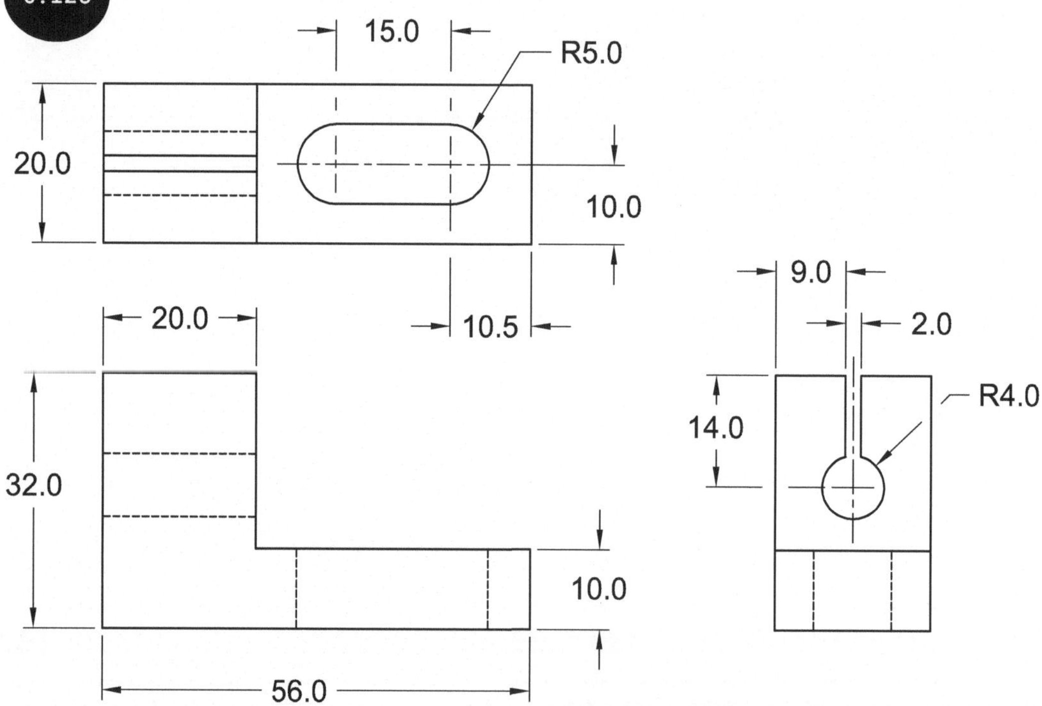

Hands-on Test Drive 4

Create the drawing and apply dimensions as shown in Figure 6.129. You need to modify the default dimension style "Standard" for applying the dimensions. The dimension parameters to be modified in the Standard dimension style are the same as mentioned in the Hands-on Test Drive 3 description.

6.129

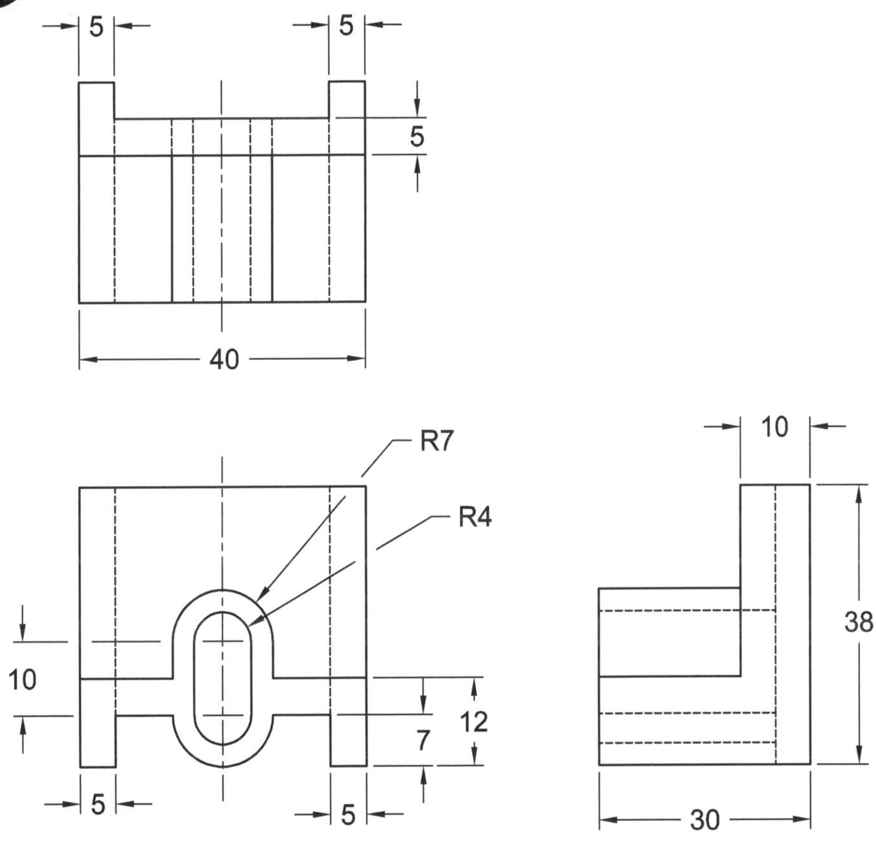

Summary

The chapter introduced various components of a dimension and methods for creating a new dimension style, modifying the existing dimension style, and overriding dimension style. It also explained how to apply various types of dimensions such as linear dimension, aligned dimension, angular dimension, diameter dimension, radius dimension, jogged dimension, ordinate dimension, and baseline dimension.

Questions

Complete the following sentences:

- You can create a new dimension style by using the _________ dialog box.
- You can break dimension lines that intersect with another dimension or drawing object by using the _________ command.
- You can invoke the **Dimension Style Manager** dialog box by entering _________ in the Command Line window and then pressing the ENTER key.
- When you apply a dimension, a new layer named _________ gets created, automatically.
- A _________ dimension is used for measuring the angle between two non-parallel objects.
- A _________ dimension is used for measuring the length of an arc or a polyline arc segment.
- The _________ tool is used for applying a jogged radius dimension to a circle or an arc whose center is not displayed in the drawing area.
- The _________ tool is used for applying a linear dimension to an object having a high length-to-width ratio.
- The _________ dimensions are a series of parallel linear dimensions that share the same base point.
- AutoCAD allows you to apply multiple dimensions at a time by using the _________ tool or _________ command.

CHAPTER

7

Editing Dimensions and Adding Text

In this chapter, the following topics will be discussed:

- Editing Dimensions by using DIMEDIT Command
- Editing Dimensions by using DIMTEDIT Command
- Editing Dimensions by using DDEDIT Command
- Editing Dimensions by using Dimension Grips
- Editing Dimensions by using PROPERTIES Palette
- Editing Dimensions by using Editing Tools
- Adding Text/Notes
- Creating and Modifying a Text Style
- Adding Text by using the Single Line Tool
- Adding Text by using the Multiline Text Tool
- Editing Single Line and Multiline Text
- Converting Single line Text to Multiline Text

In this chapter, you will learn about editing and modifying dimensions. As the drawing process involves several design revisions, editing, and modifying dimensions becomes imperative. AutoCAD is provided with various tools/commands which make the editing and modification process faster and easier. You can edit the dimension text/value, add a prefix or suffix to the dimension value, modify dimension text format, dimension position, dimension text justification, and so on by using the DIMEDIT, DIMTEDIT, and DDEDIT commands, Dimension grips, or by using the Properties palette. Moreover, you can edit the dimensions by using editing tools such as **Trim**, **Extend**, and **Stretch**. In addition to editing dimensions by using various tools/commands, in this chapter, you will also learn about annotating drawings.

Editing Dimensions by using DIMEDIT Command

The DIMEDIT command is used for editing dimension text/value such that you can rotate, modify, restore, and specify new dimension text/value. Moreover, you can change the oblique angle of extension lines by using this command. The methods for specifying new dimension text/value, rotating and restoring dimension text, and changing the oblique angle of dimension text are discussed next.

Specifying the New Dimension Text/Value

1. Enter **DIMEDIT** in the Command Line window and then press ENTER. You are prompted to enter the editing type.

```
Enter type of dimension editing [Home New Rotate Oblique] <Home>:
```

2. Click on the **New** option in the command prompt or enter **N** and then press ENTER. An edit field appears in the drawing area.

3. Enter new dimension text/value in the edit field and then click the left mouse button anywhere in the drawing area. You are prompted to select objects. You can also add a prefix or suffix to the dimension text/value.

```
Select objects:
```

4. Click on the dimension to specify the new dimension text/value. Next, press ENTER. The dimension text/value of the selected dimension is changed.

Note: The newly specified dimension text/value is an override dimension value and it does not affect the original size of the object.

Rotating the Dimension Text

1. Enter **DIMEDIT** in the Command Line window and then press ENTER. You are prompted to enter the editing type.

```
Enter type of dimension editing [Home New Rotate Oblique] <Home>:
```

2. Click on the **Rotate** option in the command prompt or enter **R** and then press ENTER. You are prompted to specify the rotational angle for dimension text.

```
Specify angle for dimension text:
```

3. Enter a rotational angle for dimension text and then press ENTER. You are prompted to select objects to rotate.

```
Select objects:
```

4. Click on the dimension whose dimension text is to be rotated and then press ENTER. The dimension text of the selected dimension gets rotated to the specified angle, see Figure 7.1.

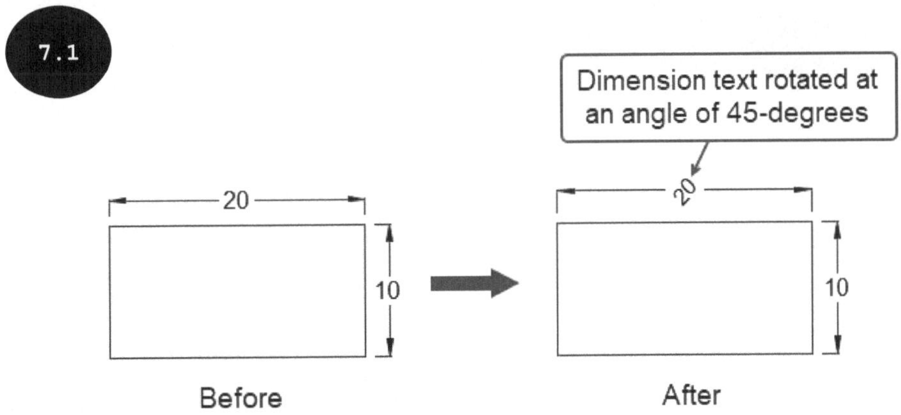

Restoring the Dimension Text to the Original Position

1. Enter **DIMEDIT** in the Command Line window and then press ENTER.

```
Enter type of dimension editing [Home New Rotate Oblique] <Home>:
```

2. Click on the **Home** option in the command prompt or enter **H** and then press ENTER. You are prompted to select objects.

```
Select objects:
```

3. Click on the dimension whose dimension text is to be restored to its original position and then press ENTER. The dimension text of the selected dimension is restored to its original position.

Changing the Oblique Angle of Extension Lines

1. Enter **DIMEDIT** in the Command Line window and then press ENTER.

```
Enter type of dimension editing [Home New Rotate Oblique] <Home>:
```

2. Click on the **Oblique** option in the command prompt or enter **O** and then press ENTER. You are prompted to select objects.

```
Select objects:
```

3. Click on dimensions whose oblique angle of extension lines is to be changed and then press ENTER. You are prompted to enter an oblique angle.

```
Enter obliquing angle (press ENTER for none):
```

4. Enter the oblique angle and then press ENTER. The oblique angle of extension lines is changed, see Figure 7.2.

7.2

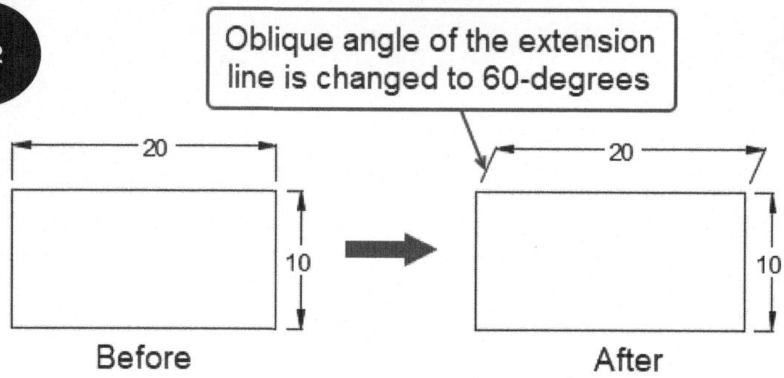

Editing Dimensions by using DIMTEDIT Command

The DIMTEDIT command is used for changing the dimension text justification and angle, the method for which is discussed below:

Changing the Dimension Text Justification and Angle

1. Enter **DIMTEDIT** in the Command Line window and then press ENTER. You are prompted to select a dimension.

```
Select dimension:
```

2. Click on the dimension to be edited. The dimension text is attached to the cursor and you are prompted to specify a new location for the dimension text.

```
Specify new location for dimension text or [Left Right Center Home
Angle]:
```

3. Click on the **Left**, **Right**, or **Center** option in the command prompt for left, right, or center justification of the dimension text, respectively. Alternatively, enter **L**, **R**, or **C** in the Command Line window and then press ENTER. The dimension text is placed in the drawing area as per the option selected, see Figure 7.3.

7.3

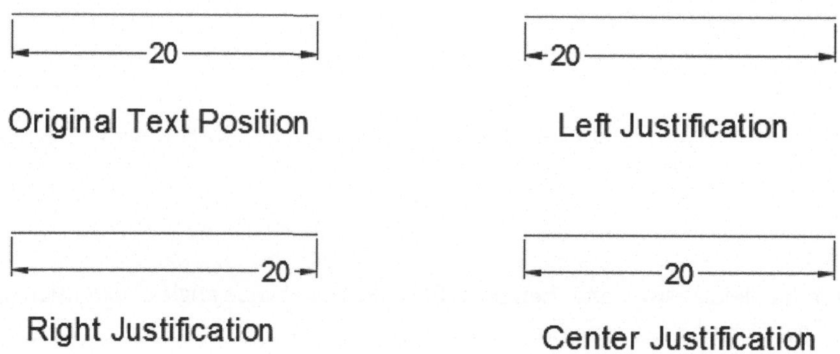

Note: By using the **Angle** option of the command prompt, you can change the angle/orientation of the dimension text. Also, you can restore the dimension text to the previous position or orientation by using the **Home** option of the command prompt.

Editing Dimensions by using DDEDIT Command

The DDEDIT command is used for adding a prefix or suffix to the dimension text/value or specifying a new dimension value. You can also edit the single and multiline annotations of a drawing by using the DDEDIT command. You will learn about adding annotations later in this chapter. The method for editing dimension text/value by using the DDEDIT command is discussed below:

Editing the Dimension text/Value

1. Enter **DDEDIT** in the Command Line window and then press ENTER. You are prompted to select an annotation object to be edited.

   ```
   Select an annotation object or [Undo Mode]:
   ```

2. Click on the dimension text or annotation to be edited. The selected dimension text or annotation appears in an edit box, see Figure 7.4. You will learn about adding annotations later in this chapter.

3. Enter a new dimension text/value in the edit box. You can also add a prefix or suffix to the dimension text/value, see Figure 7.5. For example, to add a diameter symbol to a linear diameter dimension, enter '%%c' followed by the diameter value.

4. Click anywhere in the drawing area. The dimension text/value of the selected dimension is changed or overridden by the new dimension text/value.

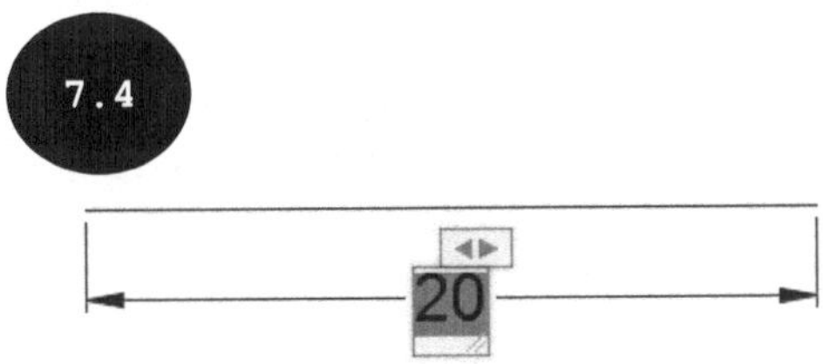

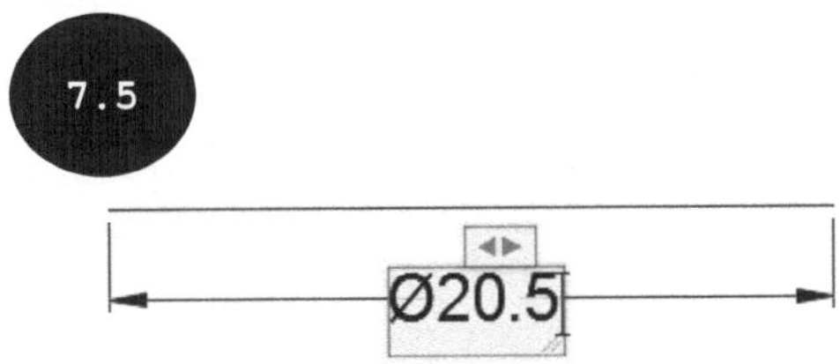

Editing Dimensions by using Dimension Grips

You can also edit dimensions by using dimension grips. Grips of a dimension appear in the drawing area when you select it, see Figure 7.6. By using grips, you can change the position of the dimension text, the spacing between the dimension line and the object, and the position of extension lines. The methods for the same are discussed next.

7.6

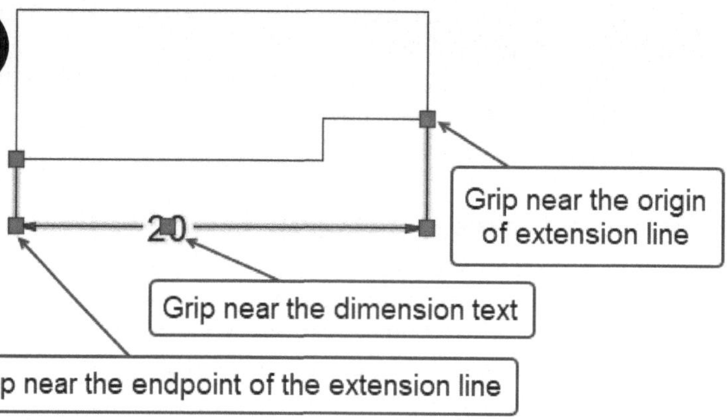

Changing the Position of Dimension Text

The method for changing the position of dimension text is discussed below:

1. Click on the dimension to be edited in the drawing area. The grips of the selected dimension appear in the drawing area, see Figure 7.6.

2. Click on the grip near the dimension text. The dimension text with the dimension line gets attached to the cursor. Now, as you move the cursor, the dimension text along with the dimension line moves in the drawing area, accordingly. Move the cursor and then click the left mouse button anywhere in the drawing area to position the dimension text.

Note: When you click on the grip near the dimension text, the dimension text with the dimension line gets attached to the cursor, since the default option for the movement of dimension text is set to the **Move with Dim Line** option. To change the default option or access other options for editing the dimension text, move the cursor over the grip near the dimension text. A menu appears, see Figure 7.7. In this menu, click on the **Move Text Only** option to move only the dimension text. Now, on moving the cursor, only the dimension text moves in the drawing area. Next, click in the drawing area to specify the new position for the dimension text. You can specify the position of the dimension text along the dimension line or anywhere in the drawing area, as required. To move the dimension text with leader, click on the **Move with Leader** option in the menu. As soon as you click on the **Move with Leader** option, the dimension text gets attached to the cursor such that it is connected to the dimension line with a leader. Now, click to specify the position of the dimension text. The dimension text is placed in the specified position with a leader, which is connected to the dimension line, see Figure 7.8.

To place the dimension text above the dimension line, click on the **Above Dim Line** option in the menu that appears. To move the dimension text to the center of the dimension line, click on the **Center Vertically** option of the menu. To reset the text position, click on the **Reset Text Position** option.

7.7

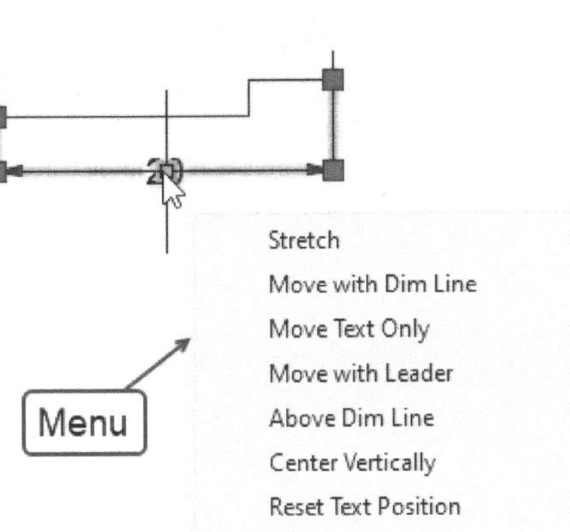

7.8

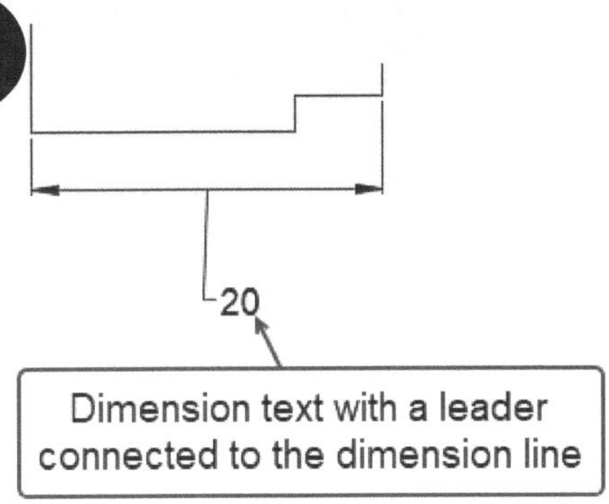

Changing the Space between the Dimension Line and the Object

The method for changing the space between the dimension line and the object is discussed below:

1. Click on the dimension to be edited in the drawing area. The grips of the selected dimension appear in the drawing area, refer to Figure 7.6.

2. Click on the grip near the endpoint of an extension line, refer to Figure 7.6. The dimension line is attached to the cursor. Next, move the cursor away from or near the object, perpendicularly. On moving the cursor, the distance between the dimension line and the object changes. Next, click on the left mouse button in the drawing area to define the new position of the dimension line.

Changing the Position of Extension Lines

The method for changing the position of extension lines is discussed below:

1. Click on the dimension to be edited in the drawing area. The grips of the selected dimension appear in the drawing area, see Figure 7.9.

2. Click on the grip near the origin of the extension line to be edited, refer to Figure 7.6. The respective extension line is attached to the cursor. Now, as you move the cursor, the extension line moves in the drawing area, and the dimension text/value gets modified, accordingly. Next, click to specify the new position for the extension line. The position of the extension line is defined and the dimension text/value also gets modified, see Figure 7.9.

7.9

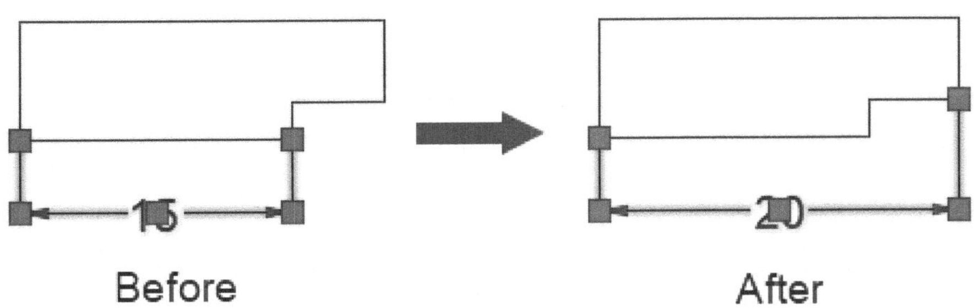

Editing Dimensions by using PROPERTIES Palette

You can also edit dimension properties such as dimension text size, arrowhead size, linetype, lineweight, and so on by using the **PROPERTIES** palette. To invoke the **PROPERTIES** palette, click on the **View** tab in the **Ribbon**. The tools of the **View** tab appear, see Figure 7.10. Next, click on the **Properties** tool in the **Palettes** panel of the **View** tab. The **PROPERTIES** palette appears to the left of the drawing area, refer to Figure 7.11.

7.10

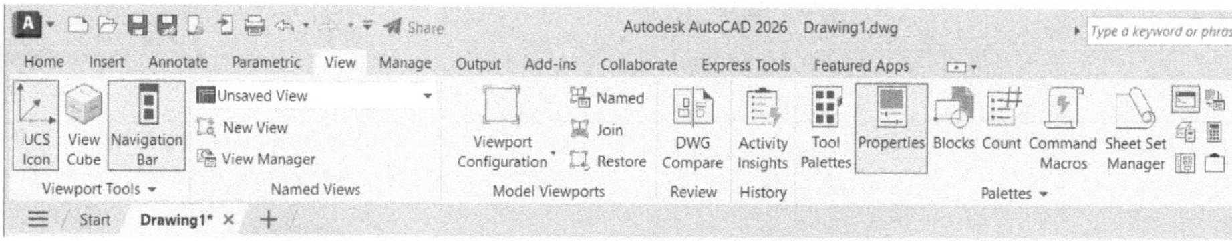

7.11

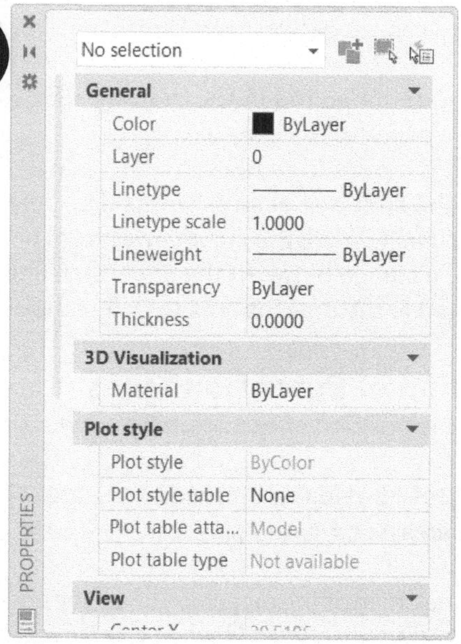

After invoking the **PROPERTIES** palette, click on the dimension to be edited. The properties of the selected dimension appear in the different categories of the **PROPERTIES** palette, see Figure 7.11. You can modify the properties of the selected dimension by using the options from the different categories of the **PROPERTIES** palette. The options are discussed next.

General

The options in the **General** category of the **PROPERTIES** palette are used for editing properties such as color, layer, linetype, linetype scale, lineweight, transparency, and hyperlink of the selected dimension. You can modify these properties by using the options available in the **General** category.

Misc

The options in the **Misc** category are used for changing the dimension style and the annotative property of the selected dimension. You can modify the dimension style and the annotative property by using the options available in this category.

Lines & Arrows

The options in the **Lines & Arrows** category are used for editing the arrowheads style, arrow size, dimension line lineweight, extension line lineweight, dimension line color, and so on. You can modify these parameters by using the options available in this category.

Text

The options in the **Text** category are used for editing the dimension text properties such as dimension text color, text height, text offset, text style, text horizontal position, text vertical position, text rotation, text override, and so on. You can edit these parameters by using the options available in this category.

Fit

The options in the **Fit** category are used for editing the fit parameters of the selected dimension such as the position of the dimension text inside the extension line on/off, text movement, overall dimension scale, and so on. You can edit the fit parameters by using the options available in this category.

Primary Units

The options in the **Primary Units** category are used for editing the unit format, dimension precision, dimension prefix/suffix, dimension scale factor, zero suppression, and so on for the selected dimension.

Alternate Units

The options in the **Alternate Units** category are used to edit the unit format, unit precision, prefix/suffix, unit scale factor, and so on of the alternate unit. Note that by default, the options of this category are not enabled. To enable the options of this category, select the **On** option in the **Alt enabled** drop-down list of this category.

Tolerances

The options in the **Tolerances** category are used for editing parameters that control the format and display of the tolerance in the dimension text.

Editing Dimensions by using Editing Tools

You can also edit the dimensions by using editing tools such as **Trim**, **Extend**, and **Stretch**, the methods for which are discussed next.

Editing Dimensions by using the Trim Tool

The method for editing dimensions by using the **Trim** tool is discussed below:

1. Click on the **Trim** tool in the **Modify** panel of the **Home** tab. You are prompted to select objects to be trimmed.

```
Select object to trim or shift-select to extend or
[cuTting edges Crossing mOde Project eRase]:
```

2. Click on the **cuTting edges** option in the command prompt or enter T and then press ENTER. You are prompted to select cutting objects.

```
Select objects or <select all>:
```

3. Click on an object as the cutting edge to trim the dimension, see Figure 7.12. Next, press ENTER. You are prompted to select objects to be trimmed.

```
Select object to trim or shift-select to extend or
[cuTting edges Crossing mOde Project eRase]:
```

4. Select the dimension by clicking on either side of its dimension value. see Figure 7.12. The selected portion of the dimension is trimmed and the dimension value gets modified accordingly, see Figure 7.13.

5. Press ENTER to exit the tool.

7.12

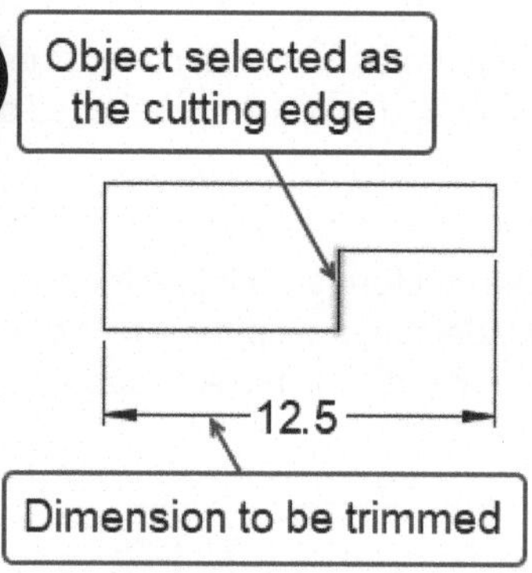

7.13

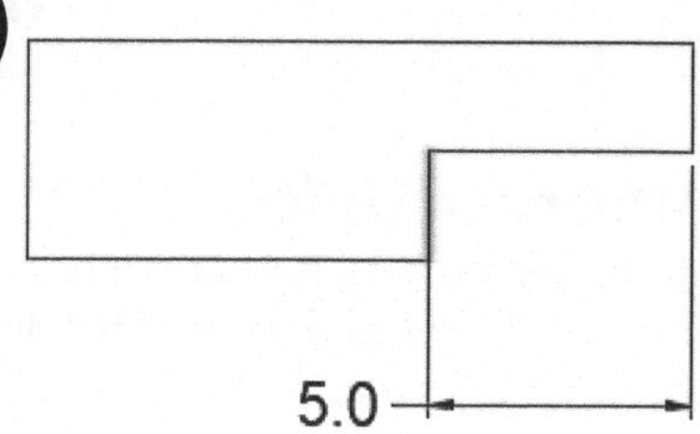

Editing Dimensions by using the Extend Tool

The method for editing dimensions by using the **Extend** tool is discussed below:

1. Click on the down arrow next to the **Trim** tool in the **Modify** panel. A flyout appears. In this flyout, click on the **Extend** tool. You are prompted to select objects to be extended. Alternatively, enter **EX** in the Command Line window and then press ENTER to invoke the **Extend** tool.

```
Select object to extend or shift-select to trim or
[Boundary edges Fence Crossing mOde Project Edge]:
```

2. Click on the **Boundary edges** option in the command prompt or enter **B** and then press ENTER. You are prompted to select boundary edges.

```
Select objects or <select all>:
```

3. Click on the object as the boundary edge for extending dimension, see Figure 7.14. Next, press ENTER. You are prompted to select objects to be extended.

```
Select object to extend or shift-select to trim or
[Boundary edges Crossing mOde Project]:
```

4. Click on the dimension to be extended, see Figure 7.14. Next, press ENTER. The selected dimension is extended up to the boundary edge and the dimension value of the dimension is modified, see Figure 7.15.

7.14

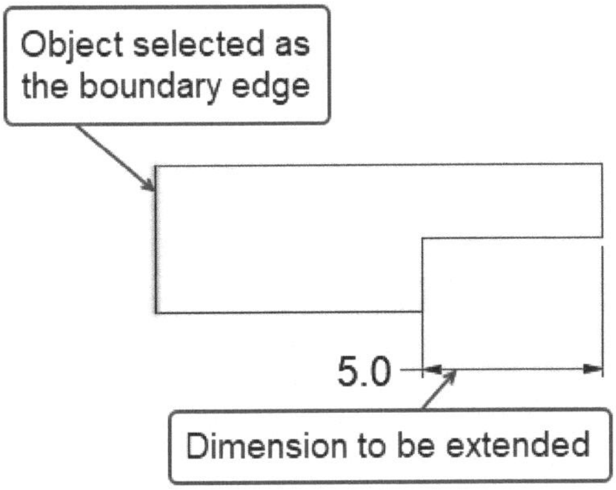

7.15

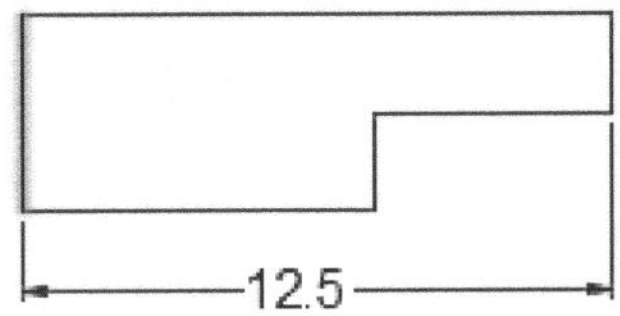

Editing Dimensions by using the Stretch Tool

The method for editing dimensions by using the **Stretch** tool is discussed below:

1. Click on the **Stretch** tool in the **Modify** panel or enter **S** in the Command Line window and then press ENTER. You are prompted to select objects to be stretched.

```
Select objects:
```

2. Draw a cross window by defining first and second corner points around the objects to be stretched such that the boundary of the cross window encloses the objects partially, see Figure 7.16. You can select the objects to be stretched by using the Cross Window or Cross Polygon selection method.

7.16

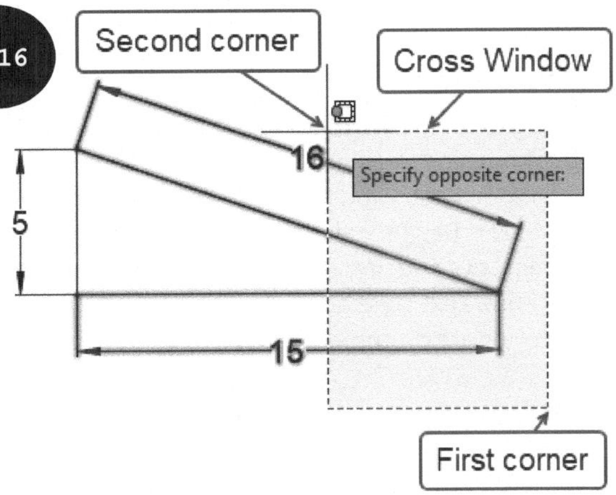

3. Press ENTER. You are prompted to specify the base point for stretching the objects.

```
Specify base point or [Displacement] <Displacement>:
```

4. Click to specify the base point in the drawing area, see Figure 7.17. Next, move the cursor to the drawing area. The selected objects get stretched, dynamically. Also, the dimension values get modified, dynamically. You are prompted to specify the second point.

```
Specify second point or <use first point as displacement>:
```

7.17

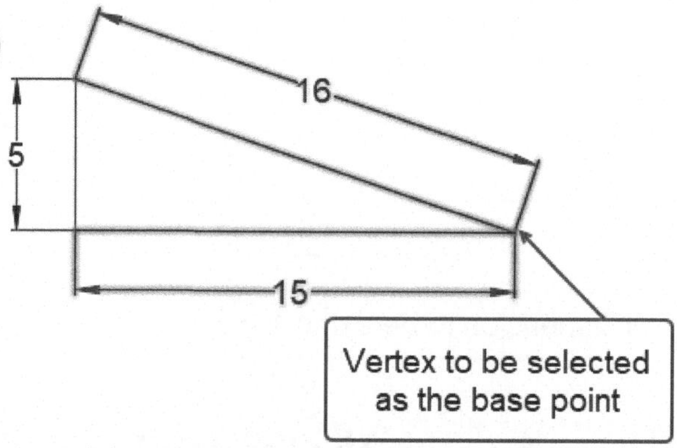

5. Click to specify the second point in the drawing area as the placement point for the objects. The objects get stretched, and dimensions are modified, see Figure 7.18.

7.18

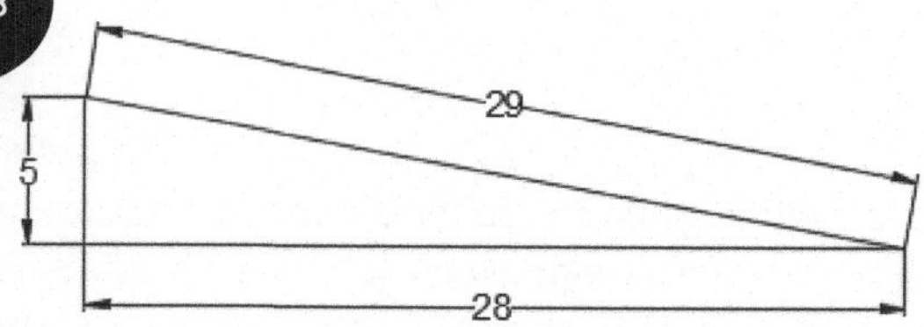

Adding Text/Notes

Text/notes are used in drawings to convey additional information that is not available in the drawings. In AutoCAD, you can add text by using the **Single Line** and **Multiline Text** tools. Before you learn about adding text in drawings, it is important to understand how to set a text style. A text style stores all the information about text such as text height and font. When you open a new AutoCAD drawing file with the default template, the Annotative and Standard text styles are available, by default. You can edit the default text styles or create a new text style as per the requirement. Methods for creating a new text style and adding text to a drawing are discussed next.

Creating and Modifying a Text Style

To create a new text style, enter **ST** in the Command Line window and then press ENTER. The **Text Style** dialog box appears, see Figure 7.19. Alternatively, expand the **Annotation** panel of the **Home** tab and then click on the **Text Style** tool to invoke the **Text Style** dialog box, see Figure 7.20.

7.19

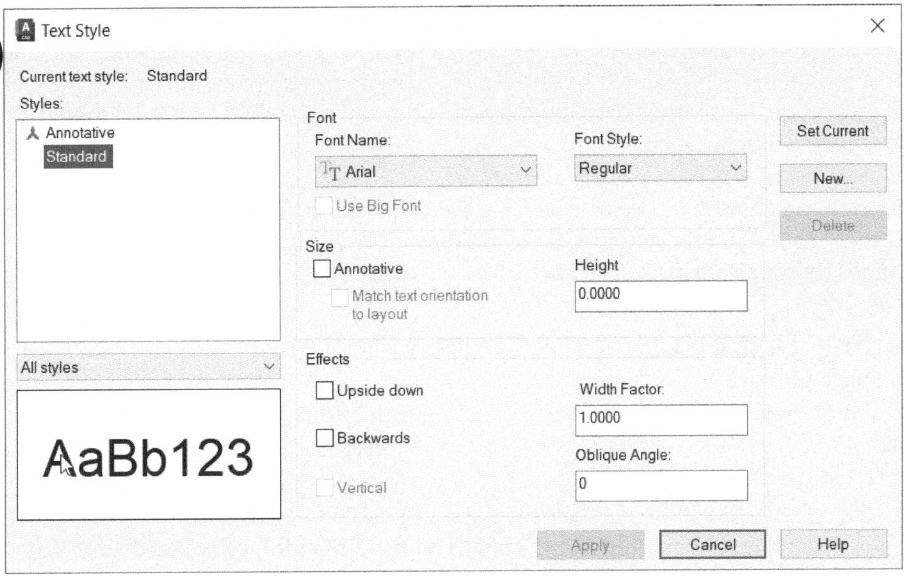

7.20

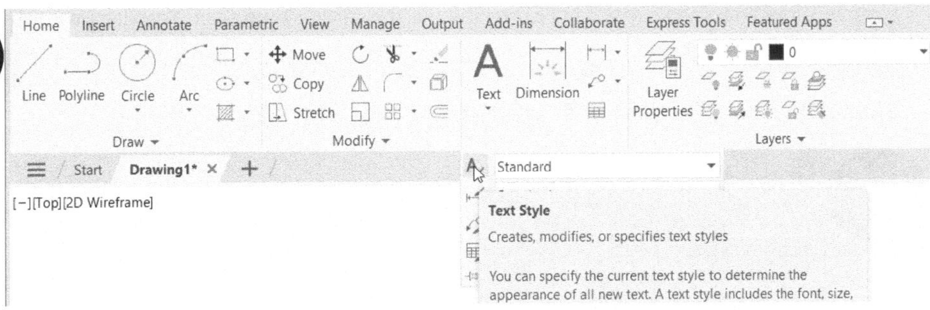

In the **Text Style** dialog box, click on the **New** button. The **New Text Style** window appears, see Figure 7.21.

7.21

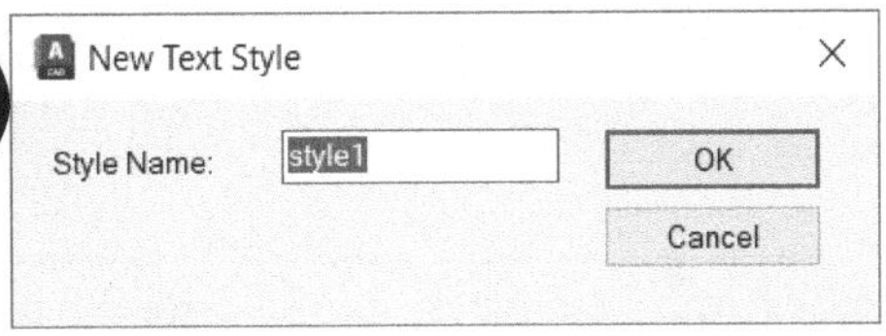

In this window, enter the name of the text style to be created and then click on the **OK** button. A new style gets created, and its name gets listed in the **Styles** area of the **Text Style** dialog box. Ensure that the newly created text style is selected in the **Styles** area of the dialog box. Next, specify the text font in the **Font Name** drop-down list, font style in the **Font Style** drop-down list, text height in the **Height** field, and so on for the text style. After specifying the properties for the text style, click on the **Apply** button and then click on the **Set Current** button in the dialog box to make the newly added text style as the current text style for the drawing. Next, click on the **Close** button to exit the dialog box.

Similar to creating a new text style, you can modify the existing text style parameters as per the requirement. To modify the existing text style, invoke the **Text Style** dialog box by using the **ST** command.

Next, select the text style to be modified in the **Styles** area of the **Text Style** dialog box. The parameters of the selected text style appear to the right of the dialog box. You can modify the parameters such as text font, font style, and text height of the text style by using the options of the dialog box. Once you have made the changes, click on the **Apply** button in the dialog box and then click on the **Close** button to exit the dialog box.

After creating a new text style or modifying the existing text style, you can start by adding text/note in the drawing area. You can add text/notes in a drawing by using the **Single Line** and **Multiline Text** tools, methods for which are discussed next.

Adding Text by using the Single Line Tool

The **Single Line** tool is used for adding single line text such as labels and notes in a drawing. You can add one or more lines of text by using the **Single Line** tool, where each text line is an independent object which can be moved, formatted, or modified individually. The method for adding a single line text is discussed below:

1. Invoke the **Text** flyout in the **Annotation** panel of the **Home** tab, see Figure 7.22. Next, click on the **Single Line** tool in the **Text** flyout, see Figure 7.22. Alternatively, enter **TEXT** in the Command Line window and then press ENTER to invoke the **Single Line** tool. You are prompted to specify the start point of the text.

```
Specify start point of text or [Justify Style]:
```

7.22

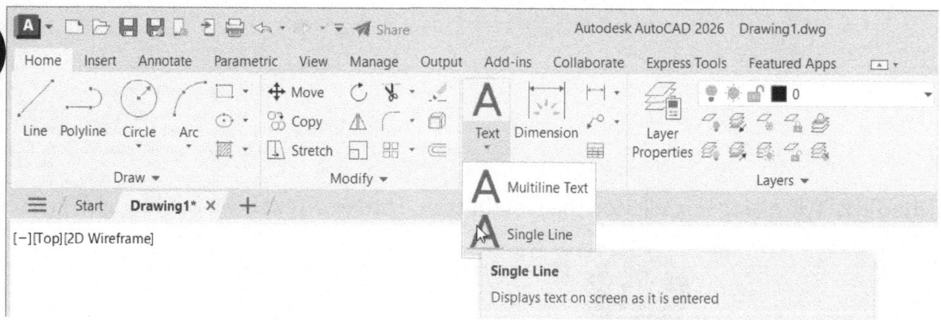

Note: You can also specify the justification and style for the text to be added in the drawing area. To specify the text justification, click on the **Justify** option in the command prompt when you are prompted to '`Specify start point of text or [Justify Style]:`'. Next, select the required text justification such as left, center, right, or middle in the command prompt. Similarly, to specify the text style, click on the **Style** option in the command prompt and then enter the name of the style in the Command Line window and then press ENTER.

2. Click in the drawing area to specify the start point of the text, see Figure 7.23. You are prompted to specify text height.

```
Specify height <0.2000>:
```

Note: If you have specified the text height in the text style by using the **Text Style** dialog box, then you will not be prompted to specify the text height. In such a case, the text height defined in the text style will be used for the text, and you will be directly prompted to specify the rotation angle of the text.

3. Enter a value for the text height (see Figure 7.23) and then press ENTER. Alternatively, click in the drawing area to specify the text height. You are prompted to specify the rotation angle of the text.

```
Specify rotation angle of text <0>:
```

4. Enter a rotation angle for the text (see Figure 7.23) and then press ENTER. A blinking cursor appears in a text window, and you are prompted to enter the text in the drawing area.

7.23

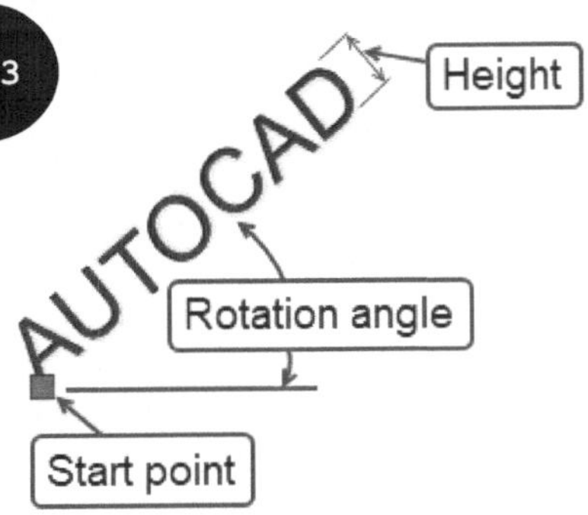

5. Enter a text in the text window, as required. For entering multiple text lines, press ENTER at the end of each line. Figure 7.24 shows a text window with multiple text lines entered. After entering the text, click anywhere in the drawing area and then press the ESC key to exit the tool.

7.24

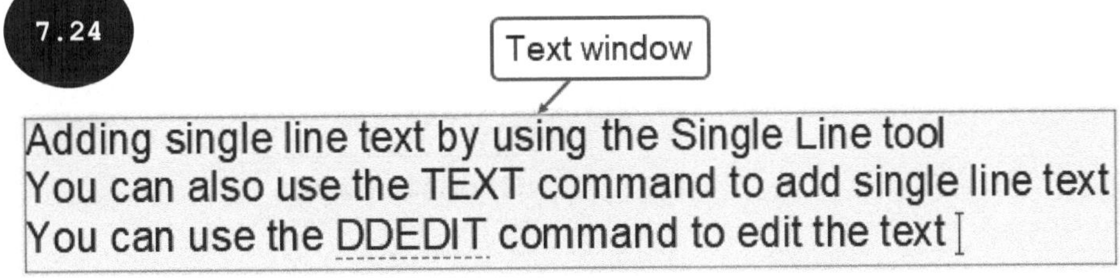

Note: The multiple text lines written by using the **Single Line** tool/TEXT command act as independent objects that can be selected, moved, formatted, or edited individually.

Adding Text by using the Multiline Text Tool

The **Multiline Text** tool is used for entering multiline text such as a paragraph of information, a block of text, and longer notes in a paragraph form in a drawing. In AutoCAD, entering multiline text is similar to writing text in a Word document, where you can select words and change their properties such as height, color, and font. The method for adding multiline text is discussed below:

1. Invoke the **Text** flyout in the **Annotation** panel of the **Home** tab, refer to Figure 7.22. Next, click on the **Multiline Text** tool. Alternatively, enter **MTEXT** in the Command Line window and then press ENTER to invoke the **Multiline Text** tool. You are prompted to specify the first corner of the text window.

```
Specify first corner:
```

2. Click to specify the first corner of the text window in the drawing area, see Figure 7.25. You are prompted to specify the opposite corner of the text window.

```
Specify opposite corner or [Height Justify Line spacing Rotation
Style Width Columns]:
```

Note: You can change the default text height by using the **Height** option of the command prompt, the default text justification by using the **Justify** option, the default text style by using the **Style** options of the command prompt, and so on. For example, to change the default text height, click on the **Height** option in the command prompt when you are prompted to specify the opposite corner. You can also enter **H** in the Command Line window and then press ENTER to change the default text height. Next, enter the new text height and then press ENTER.

3. Click to specify the opposite corner of the text window in the drawing area, see Figure 7.25. The **Text Editor** tab appears in the **Ribbon**, see Figure 7.26. Also, the **In-Place Text Editor** window appears with the tab and indent ruler in the drawing area for entering the text, see Figure 7.27.

7.25

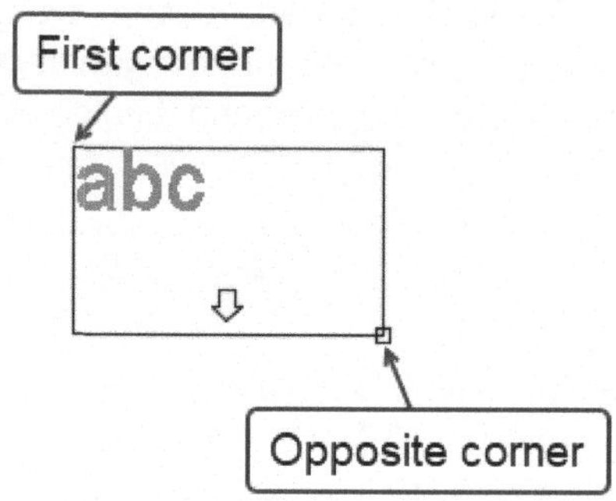

7.26

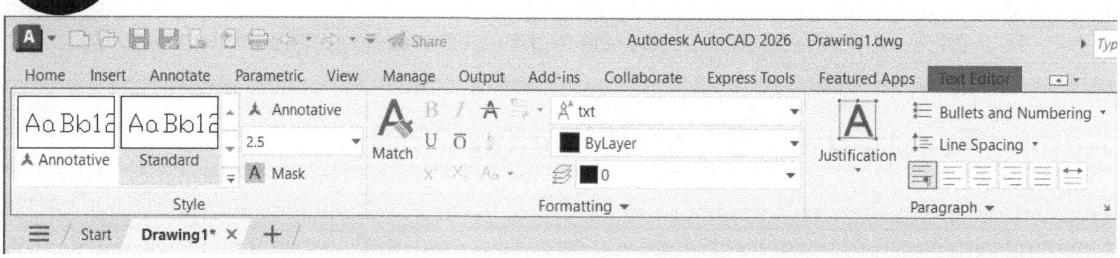

Note: The options in the **Text Editor** tab are used for controlling the text parameters such as text style, text height, text font, layer, bold, italic, underline, text justification, bullets and numbering, columns, symbol, and so on. The **Text Editor** allows you to control the text parameters similar to a word document.

4. Enter text in the text window, as required, see Figure 7.27. Next, click anywhere in the drawing area. The text appears in the area defined by specifying the corners of the text window.

7.27

Note: You can change the width and height of the **In-Place Text Editor** window. To change the width of the window, move the cursor either over the right end of the text frame or the ruler until the cursor changes to a double arrow, see Figure 7.28. Next, drag the cursor to adjust the width. Similarly, to change the height, move the cursor over the bottom of the text frame and then drag the cursor to set the height of the window.

7.28

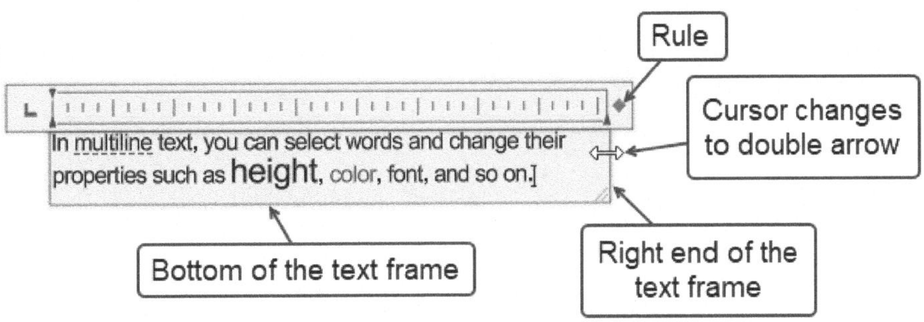

Editing Single Line and Multiline Text

You can edit the single line and multiline text by using the DDEDIT command. To do so, enter DDEDIT in the Command Line window and then press ENTER. Alternatively, double-click on the text to be edited in the drawing area. You are prompted to select an annotation object to be edited.

```
Select an annotation object or [Undo Mode]:
```

Next, click on the text/annotation in the drawing area. The **In-Place Text Editor** window appears. Now, you can edit the text, as required. Once you have made the necessary modifications, click anywhere in the drawing area to exit the command.

Converting Single line Text to Multiline Text

In a drawing, you may need to combine several individual single line text objects into a single multiline text object. You can convert one or more single line text objects to a multiline text object by using the TXT2MTXT command. To do so, enter **TXT2MTXT** in the Command Line window and then press ENTER. You are prompted to select objects to be converted into the multiline text object. Alternatively, click on the **Convert to Mtext** tool in the **Text** panel of the **Express Tools** tab of the **Ribbon**.

```
Select objects or [SEttings]:
```

Click on the single line text objects to be converted into multiline text one by one. Next, press ENTER. All the selected single line text objects get converted into single multiline text objects.

Tutorial 1

Create the drawing and apply dimensions as illustrated in Figure 7.29. You need to edit the linear diameter dimensions of the drawing to add diameter symbols as a prefix to them, see Figure 7.29.

7.29

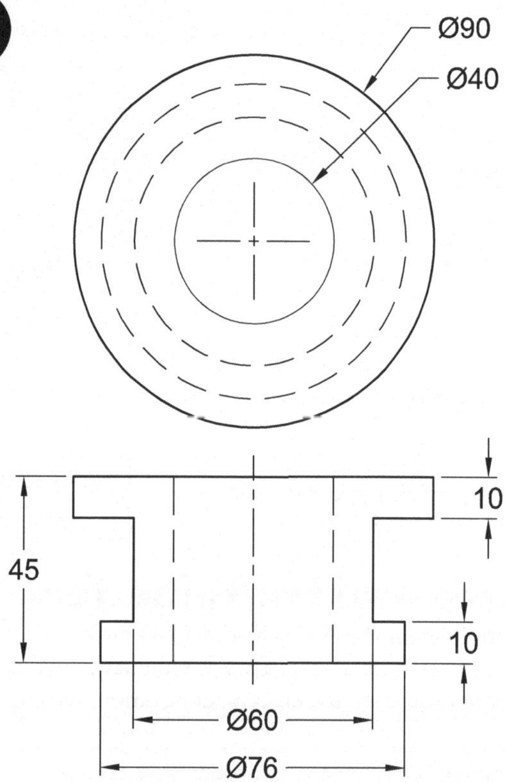

Section 1: Starting AutoCAD

1. Start AutoCAD and then open a new drawing file. Next, set the drawing limits.

Section 2: Creating the Front View

1. Click on the **Line** tool in the **Draw** panel of the **Home** tab. You are prompted to specify the first point of the line. Alternatively, enter **L** in the Command Line window and then press ENTER.

   `Specify first point:`

2. Click to specify the first point of the line in the drawing area. You are prompted to specify the next point of the line.

3. Ensure that the Dynamic Input mode and the Ortho mode are turned on.

4. Follow the command sequence given below for creating the drawing.

   `Specify next point or [Undo]:` *Move the cursor horizontally toward the right and then enter* **76** *in the Dynamic Input box* (***ENTER***).
   `Specify next point or [Undo]:` *Move the cursor vertically upward and then enter* **10** (***ENTER***).
   `Specify next point or [Close Undo]:` *Move the cursor horizontally toward left and then enter* **8** (***ENTER***).
   `Specify next point or [Close Undo]:` *Move the cursor vertically upward and then enter* **25** (***ENTER***).
   `Specify next point or [Close Undo]:` *Move the cursor horizontally toward right and then enter* **15** (***ENTER***).
   `Specify next point or [Close Undo]:` *Move the cursor vertically upward and then enter* **10** (***ENTER***).
   `Specify next point or [Close Undo]:` *Move the cursor horizontally toward left and then enter* **90** (***ENTER***).
   `Specify next point or [Close Undo]:` *Move the cursor vertically downward and then enter* **10** (***ENTER***).
   `Specify next point or [Close Undo]:` *Move the cursor horizontally toward right and then enter* **15** (***ENTER***).
   `Specify next point or [Close Undo]:` *Move the cursor vertically downward and then enter* **25** (***ENTER***).
   `Specify next point or [Close Undo]:` *Move the cursor horizontally toward left and then enter* **8** (***ENTER***).
   `Specify next point or [Close Undo]:` *C or Close* (***ENTER***) *(See Figure 7.30).*

7.30

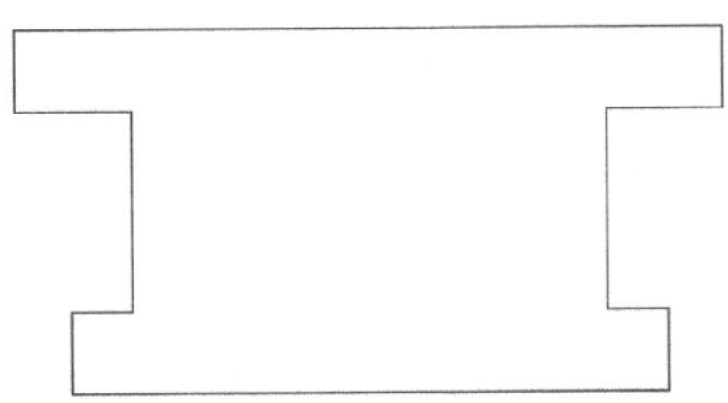

After creating the line entities of the drawing, you need to create hidden and centerline entities.

5. Click on the **Offset** tool in the **Modify** panel. You are prompted to specify the offset distance. Alternatively, enter **O** in the Command Line window and then press ENTER.

```
Specify offset distance or [Through Erase Layer] <Through>:
```

6. Enter **10** as the offset distance and then press ENTER. You are prompted to select an object to offset.

```
Select object to offset or [Exit Undo] <Exit>:
```

7. Click on the left middle vertical line as the object to offset, see Figure 7.31. You are prompted to specify a point on the side to offset.

```
Specify point on side to offset or [Exit Multiple Undo] <Exit>:
```

8. Click the left mouse button on the right of the vertical line selected. The offset entity is created, see Figure 7.31. You are prompted to select an object to offset again.

```
Select object to offset or [Exit Undo] <Exit>:
```

7.31

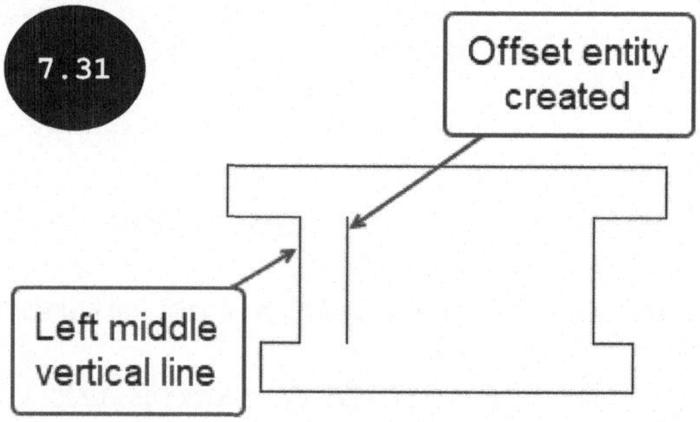

9. Click on the right middle vertical line as the object to offset, see Figure 7.32. Next, click on the left side of the vertical line selected. The offset entity is created, see Figure 7.32.

7.32

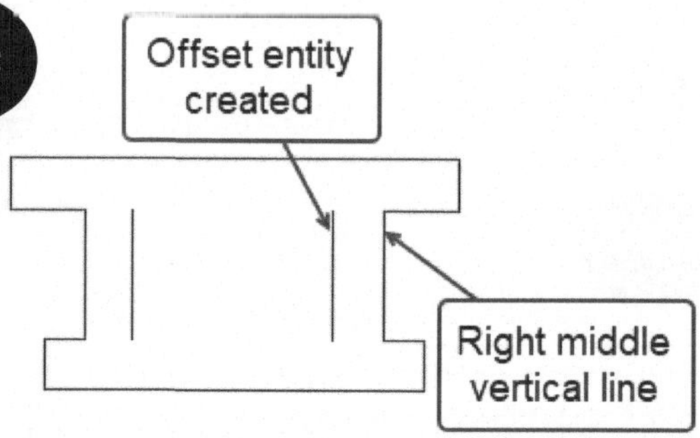

10. Press ENTER to exit the **Offset** tool.

    Now, you need to extend the offset entities up to their next intersection.

11. Enter **EX** in the Command Line window and then press ENTER. The **Extend** tool gets invoked, and you are prompted to select objects to be extended. Alternatively, click on the **Extend** tool in the **Modify** panel of the **Home** tab to invoke the tool.

```
Select object to extend or shift-select to trim or
[Boundary edges Crossing mOde Project]:
```

12. Click on the upper side of the left offset entity in the drawing area. The top portion of the offset entity gets extended up to the next intersection, see Figure 7.33. Next, click on the lower side of the left offset entity. The bottom portion of the entity gets extended, see Figure 7.34.

7.33

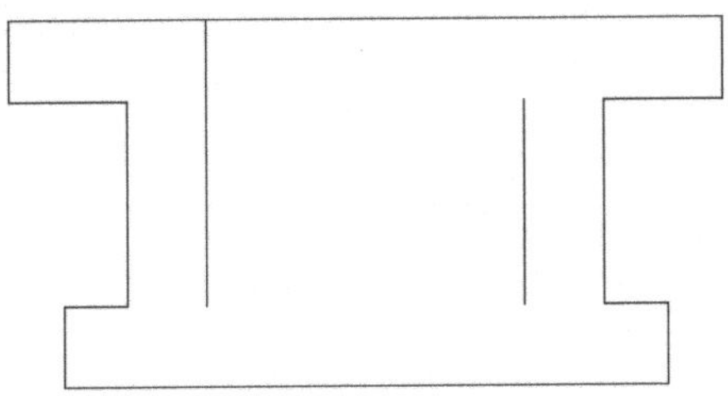

7.34

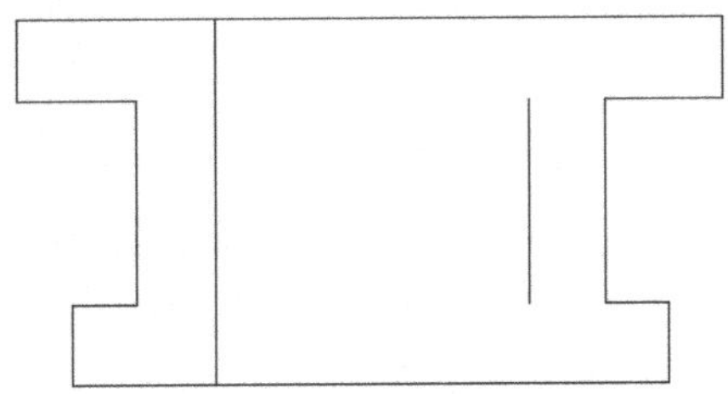

13. Similarly, click on both sides of the right offset entity to extend one by one. Figure 7.35 shows the drawing after extending the entities. Next, press ENTER to exit the **Extend** tool.

7.35

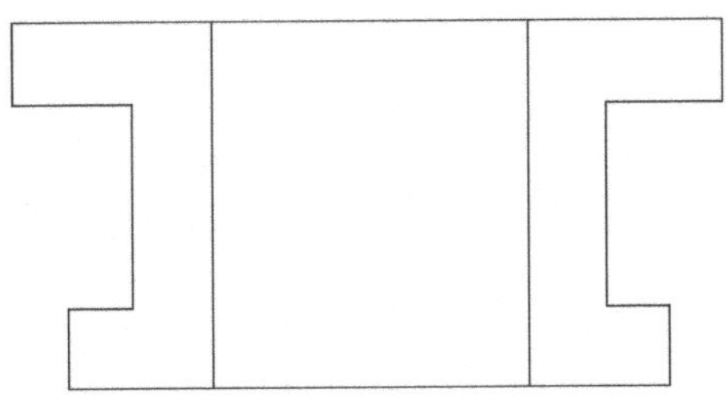

    Now, you need to draw the centerline of the drawing.

14. Click on the **Line** tool in the **Draw** panel or enter **L** and then press ENTER. The **Line** tool gets invoked and you are prompted to specify the first point of the line.

```
Specify first point:
```

15. Ensure that the Object Snap mode is activated.

16. Move the cursor to the midpoint of the upper horizontal line and pause when the cursor snaps to it, see Figure 7.36, move the cursor vertically upward to a small distance. Next, click the left mouse button to specify the first point of the line. You are prompted to specify the next point of the line.

```
Specify next point or [Undo]:
```

17. Move the cursor vertically downward and click to specify the endpoint of the line outside the bottom horizontal line of the drawing. The line is created, see Figure 7.37. Next, press ENTER to exit the **Line** tool.

7.36

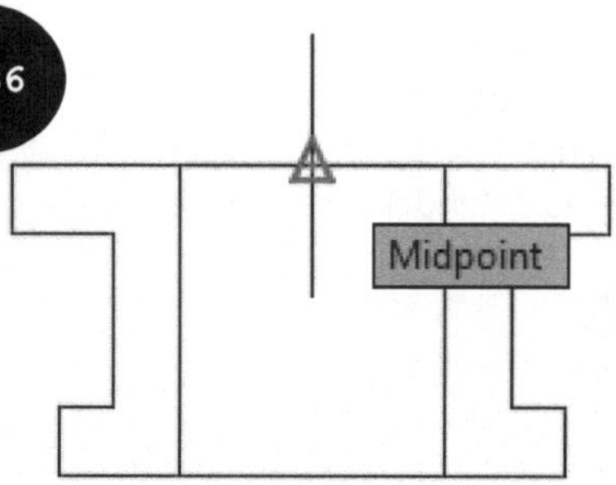

7.37

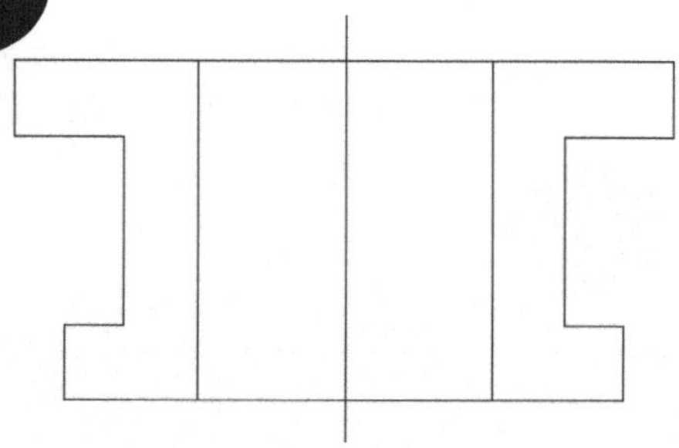

Section 3: Creating Layers and Assigning Objects to Layers

1. Click on the **Layer Properties** tool in the **Layers** panel of the **Home** tab. The **LAYER PROPERTIES MANAGER** appears.

2. Create four layers with the names Object, Hidden, Center, and Dimension in the **LAYER PROPERTIES MANAGER**, see Figure 7.38. Note that you need to assign the HIDDEN linetype to the Hidden layer, the CENTER linetype to the Center layer, and accept the remaining default properties of the layers, see Figure 7.38. Next, exit the **LAYER PROPERTIES MANAGER.**

7.38

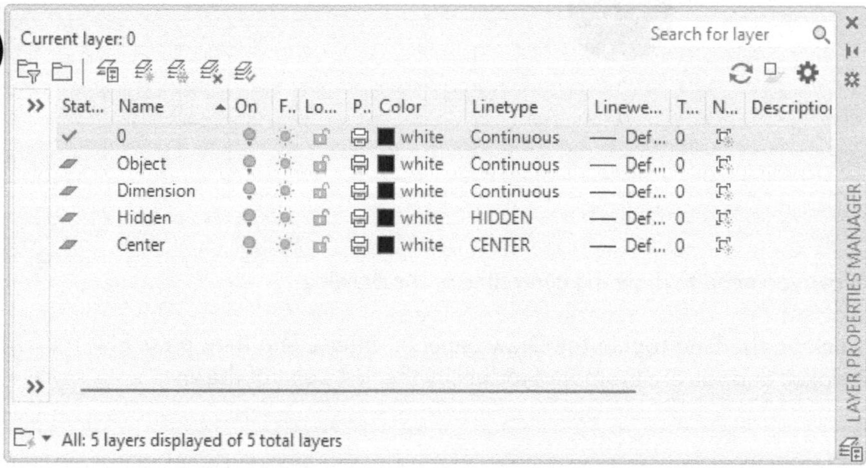

3. After creating the layers, assign the hidden line entities (2 line entities) of the drawing to the Hidden layer, the centerline entity (1 line entity) to the Center layer, and the remaining line

entities of the drawing to the Object layer. Figure 7.39 shows the drawing after assigning the drawing entities to the respective layers.

7.39

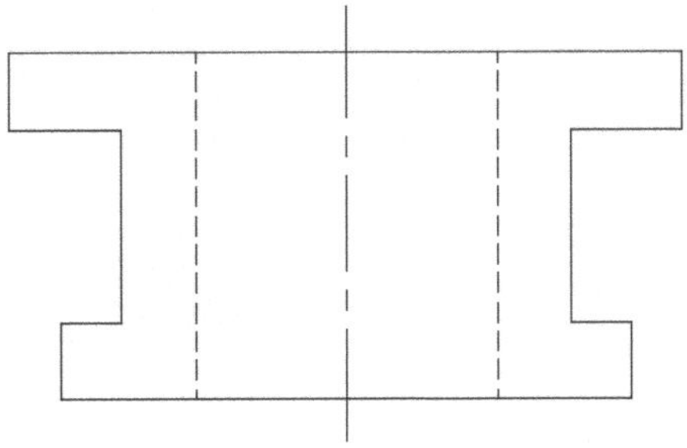

Note: If the hidden lines and the centerline of the drawing appear as continuous/solid lines in the drawing area, then you need to change the linetype scale of the entities. To do so, enter **PR** in the Command Line window and then press ENTER. The **PROPERTIES** palette appears. Alternatively, click on the **Properties** tool in the **Palettes** panel of the **View** tab to invoke the **PROPERTIES** palette. Next, select the entity whose scale has to be changed. The current properties of the selected entity appear in the **PROPERTIES** palette. Next, enter a new linetype scale value for the selected entity in the **Linetype** field of the palette. You can try different scale values to match your requirements.

Section 4: Creating the Top View

1. Create a vertical construction line passing through the center of the Front view by using the **Construction Line** tool or the XL command, see Figure 7.40.

2. Create a circle of diameter of 40 units whose center point is on the newly created vertical construction line, anywhere above the Front view, see Figure 7.40.

7.40

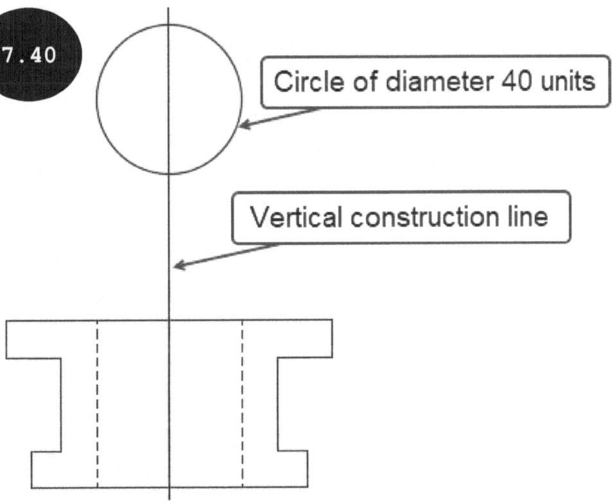

3. Similarly, create the remaining circles of diameter 60, 76, and 90 units, see Figure 7.41.

4. Assign two circles of diameter 60 and 76 units to the Hidden layer and two circles of diameter 40 and 90 units to the Object layer. Next, delete the construction line, see Figure 7.42. Note that if the circles that are assigned to the Hidden layer appear as continuous/solid lines in the drawing area, then you need to change their linetype scale.

7.41

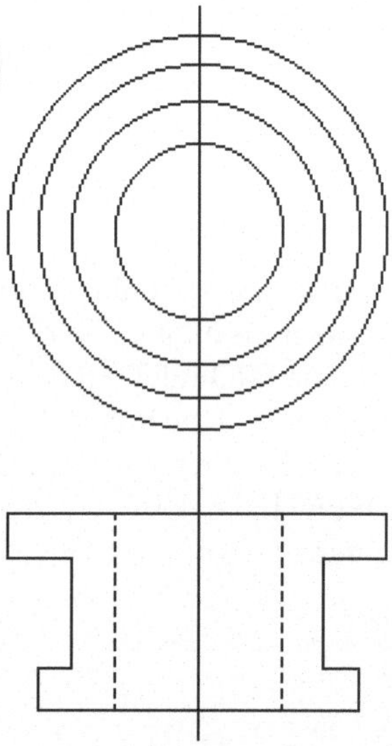

7.42

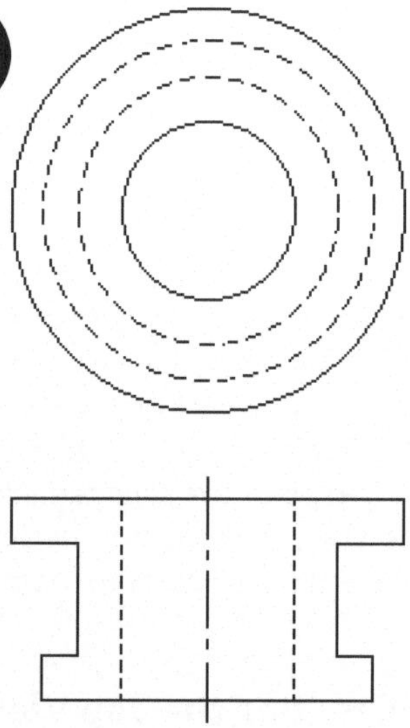

Section 5: Applying Dimensions

1. Apply dimensions to the drawing by using the **Dimension** tool, see Figure 7.43.

7.43

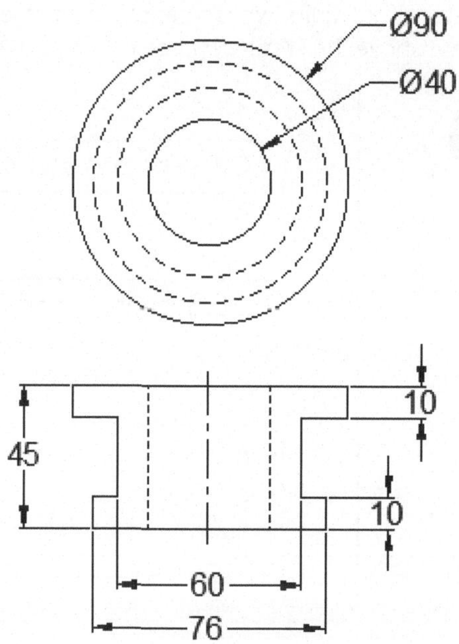

Note: By default, dimensions appear as per the default dimension style properties, which may not fit the requirement and dimensions may appear either very small or large in the drawing. In such a case, you may need to create a new dimension style or edit the existing dimension style to match the dimension properties as per the requirement. You can create a new dimension style or modify an existing dimension style by using the **Dimension Style Manager** dialog box. You can invoke this dialog box by using the **D** command.

2. Select all the dimensions and assign them to the Dimension layer.

Section 6: Editing Dimensions

Now, you need to edit the linear diameter dimensions of the drawing to add diameter symbols.

1. Enter **DDEDIT** in the Command Line window and then press ENTER. You are prompted to select an annotation object to be edited. Alternatively, double-click on the dimension to be edited. You can also use the DIMEDIT command to edit a dimension text.

```
Select an annotation object or [Undo Mode]:
```

2. Click on the dimension measuring 76 units in the drawing area. The dimension text of the selected dimension appears in an edit box, see Figure 7.44.

3. Enter '%%c' as a prefix to the dimension text '76 units' in the edit box. Next, click anywhere in the drawing area. The diameter symbol is added to the selected dimension, see Figure 7.45.

7.44

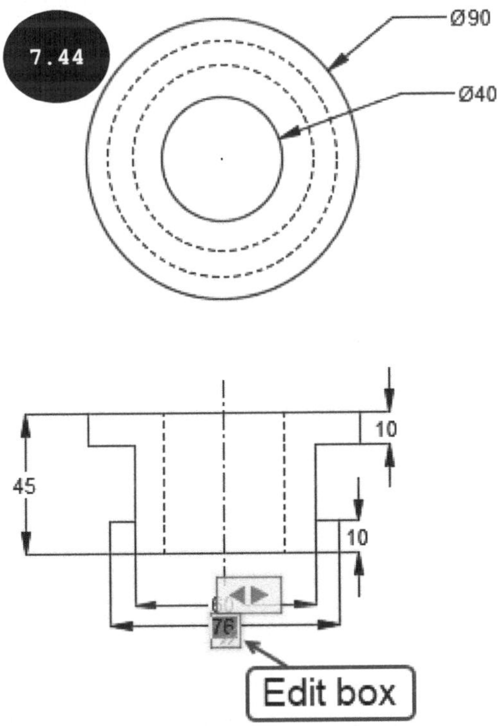

7.45

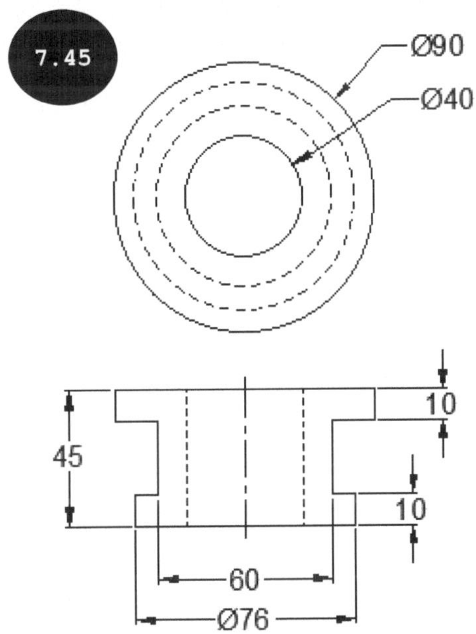

4. Similarly, add the diameter symbol to the dimension measuring 60 units in the drawing. Figure 7.46 shows the final drawing.

7.46

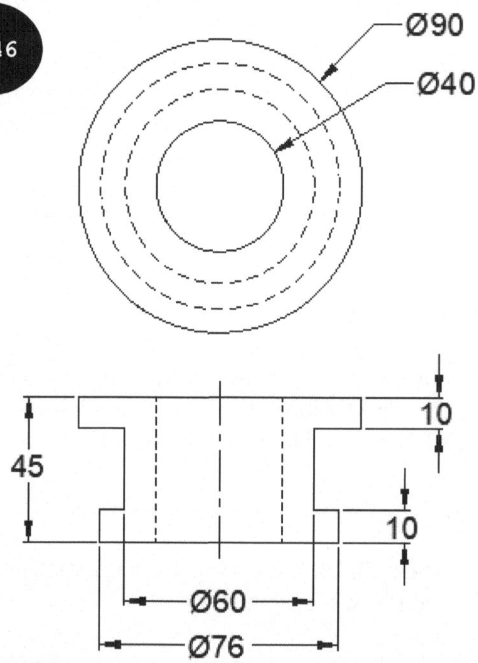

Section 7: Saving the Drawing

After creating the drawing, you need to save it.

1. Click on the **Save** tool in the **Quick Access Toolbar**. The **Save Drawing As** dialog box appears.

2. Browse to the *AutoCAD* folder and then create a folder with the name *Chapter 7* inside the *AutoCAD* folder.

3. Enter **Tutorial 1** in the **File name** field of the dialog box and then click on the **Save** button. The drawing gets saved with the name Tutorial 1 in the *Chapter 7* folder.

Tutorial 2

Create the drawing and apply dimensions as illustrated in Figure 7.47. Also, you need to add labels in different areas of the drawing, see Figure 7.47.

7.47

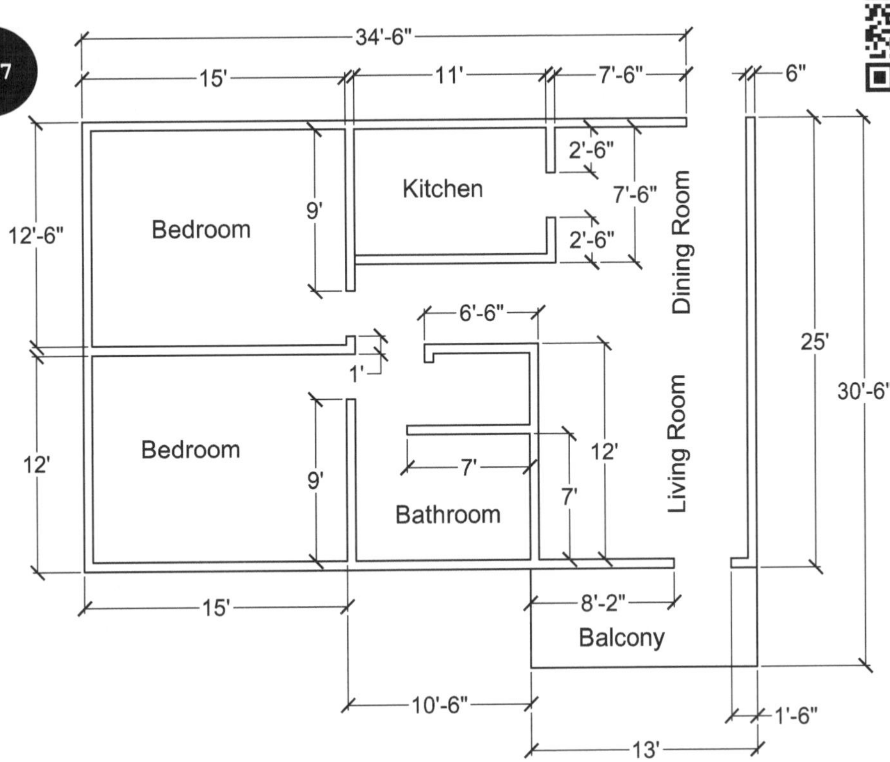

Section 1: Starting AutoCAD

1. Start AutoCAD and then open a new drawing file. Next, set the drawing limits.

Section 2: Specifying Unit System

You need to change the default unit system to the Architectural unit system.

1. Enter **UN** in the Command Line window and then press ENTER. The **Drawing Units** dialog box appears.

2. Select the **Architectural** unit system in the **Type** drop-down list of the **Length** area in the **Drawing Units** dialog box.

3. Ensure that the **0'-0 1/16"** option is selected in the **Precision** drop-down list of the **Length** area in the dialog box.

4. Click on the **OK** button to accept the change and exit the dialog box. The Architectural unit system is set for the current drawing.

Section 3: Creating the Drawing

1. Create the drawing as shown in Figure 7.48. To create the drawing, you can use various drawing tools such as **Line**, **Offset**, **Trim**, and **Extend**. For dimensions, refer to Figure 7.47.

Note: To enter dimension values in feet, use single quote (') and to enter values in inches, use double quotes (") as suffix to the dimension values. You can specify the inches values with or without double quotes ("). For example, 15 feet can be defined as 15' and 10 feet 6 inches can be defined either as 10'6" or 10'6.

7.48

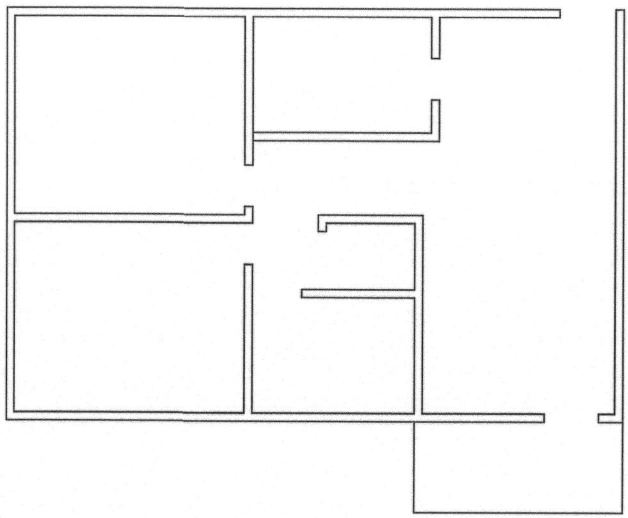

Section 4: Editing Dimension Style and Applying Dimensions

Now, you need to edit the dimension style of the drawing.

1. Enter **D** in the Command Line window and then press ENTER. The **Dimension Style Manager** dialog box appears.

2. Select the **Standard** dimension style in the **Styles** area of the dialog box and then click on the **Modify** button. The **Modify Dimension Style** dialog box appears.

3. Click on the **Symbols and Arrows** tab in the dialog box. Next, select the **Architectural tick** option in the **First** and **Second** drop-down lists of the **Arrowheads** area in the dialog box.

4. Click on the **Primary Units** tab of the dialog box and then select the **Architectural** option in the **Unit format** drop-down list of the **Linear dimensions** area in the dialog box.

5. Similarly, specify the other properties such as arrow size, text height, offset from dimension line, extension beyond dimension lines, and offset from the origin in the respective fields, as required.

6. Click on the **OK** button to accept the change and to exit the **Modify Dimension Style** dialog box. Next, click on the **Close** button in the **Dimension Style Manager** dialog box.

After modifying the dimension style, you can apply dimensions in the drawing area.

7. Apply dimensions to the drawing by using the **Linear** tool, see Figure 7.49.

7.49

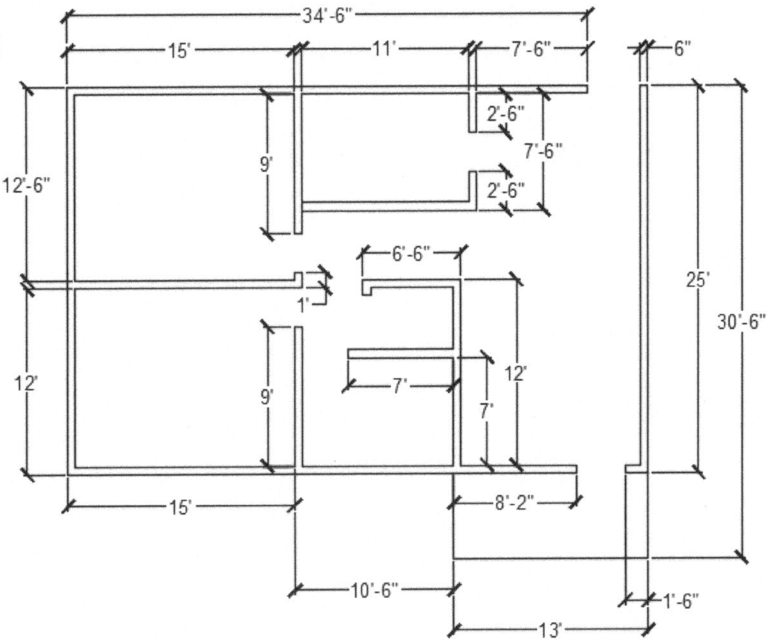

Section 5: Adding the Annotation/Text

1. Enter **TEXT** in the Command Line window and then press ENTER. The **Single Line** text tool gets invoked, and you are prompted to specify the start point of the text. Alternatively, click on the **Single Line** tool in the **Text** flyout of the **Annotation** panel in the **Home** tab.

```
Specify start point of text or [Justify Style]:
```

2. Click in the kitchen area of the drawing to specify the start point of the text. You are prompted to specify the height of the text.

```
Specify height <1'-0">:
```

3. Enter **1'** as the height of the text and then press ENTER.

```
Specify rotation angle of text <0>:
```

4. Enter **0** as the rotation angle of the text and then press ENTER. A blinking cursor appears in a text window, and you are prompted to enter text in the drawing area.

5. Enter **Kitchen** in the text window and then click anywhere in the drawing area. Next, press the ESC key. The Kitchen label is added to the kitchen area of the drawing, see Figure 7.50.

7.50

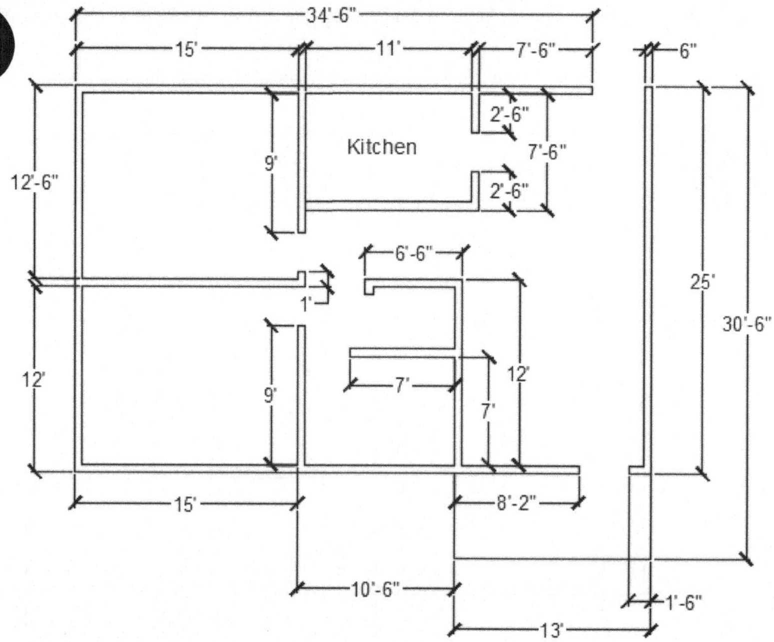

6. Similarly, add labels to other areas of the drawing. Figure 7.51 shows the final drawing after adding all the labels/text to the drawing.

7.51

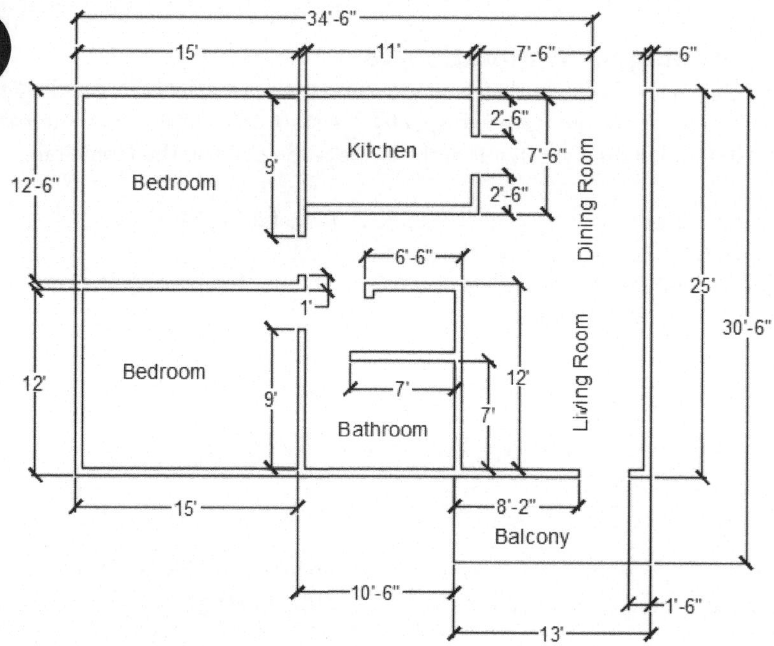

Section 6: Saving the Drawing

1. Save the drawing with the name Tutorial 2 inside the *Chapter 7* folder.

Hands-on Test Drive 1

Create the drawing shown in Figure 7.52 and add multiline text to the drawing.

7.52

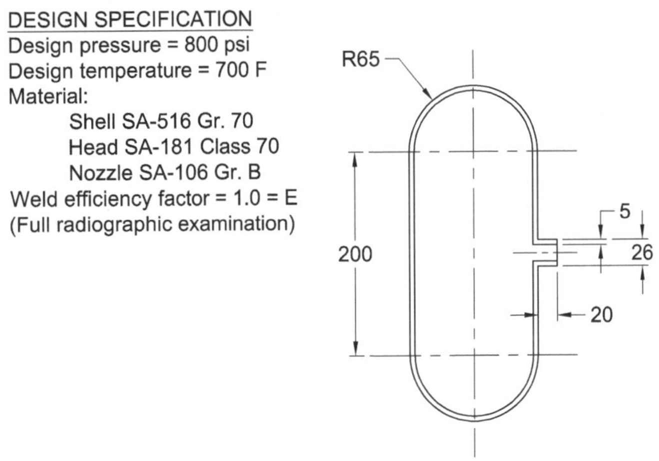

Summary

The chapter introduced methods for modifying dimensions by using the DIMEDIT command, DIMTEDIT command, DDEDIT command, dimension grips, Properties palette, and editing tools such as Trim, Extend, and Stretch. The chapter also described methods for adding text/notes to drawings, creating and modifying text style, adding text, editing single line and multiline texts, and converting a single line text to multiline text.

Questions

Complete the following sentences:

- The _________ command is used for editing the dimension text/value such that you can rotate, modify, restore, and specify a new dimension text/value.
- The _________ command is used for changing the dimension text justification and angle.
- The _________ command is used for adding a prefix or suffix to the dimension text/value for specifying a new dimension value.
- By using the _________ of a dimension, you can change the position of the dimension text, the spacing between the dimension line and the object, and the position of extension lines.
- In AutoCAD, you can add text by using the _________ and _________ tools.

- The ________ command is used for invoking the **Text Style** dialog box.
- The ________ tool is used for entering single line text such as labels and notes in a drawing.
- The ________ tool is used for entering multiline text such as a paragraph of information or a block of text.
- You can convert one or more single line text objects to a multiline text object by using the ________ command.

CHAPTER
8

Modifying and Editing Drawings - II

In this chapter, the following topics will be discussed:

- Editing Objects by using Grips
- Editing Objects by using PROPERTIES Palette
- Matching Properties of an Object
- Identifying Coordinates of a Point

In Chapter 5, you have learned about various editing operations such as trim, extend, mirror, array, move, and rotate. In this chapter, you will learn about some advanced editing operations such as editing objects by using grips, editing object properties, matching object properties, and so on.

Editing Objects by using Grips

In AutoCAD, all objects have grips, which appear when you select them in the drawing area, see Figure 8.1. A grip is a small square blue symbol. The number of grips varies from object to object. For example, a line object has three grips, an arc object has four grips, and a circle object has five grips, see Figure 8.1. By using these grips, you can perform various editing operations such as stretch, move, rotate, scale, and mirror. The methods for editing objects by using the grips are discussed next.

8.1

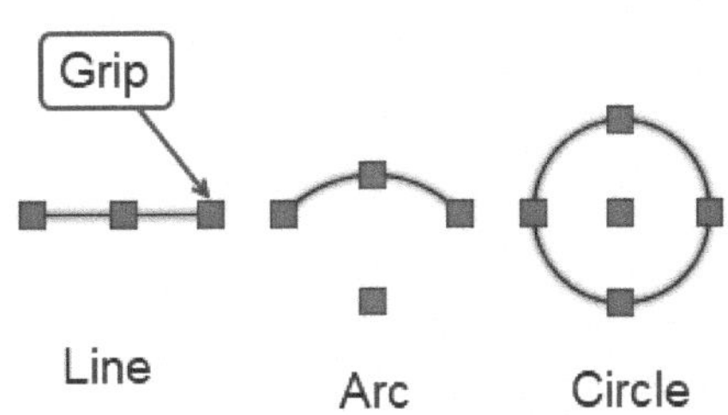

Stretching Objects by using Grips

To stretch objects by using grips, select them. The grips of the selected objects appear in the drawing area, see Figure 8.2. In this figure, the horizontal and inclined lines of the drawing are selected. Next, click on a grip as the base point to stretch objects, see Figure 8.2. As soon as you click on a grip, the **Stretch** command gets activated, automatically. Next, move the cursor to the required distance in the drawing area. As you move the cursor, the objects stretch, dynamically in the drawing area. Next, click to specify the placement point for the objects in the drawing area. The objects get stretched, see Figure 8.3.

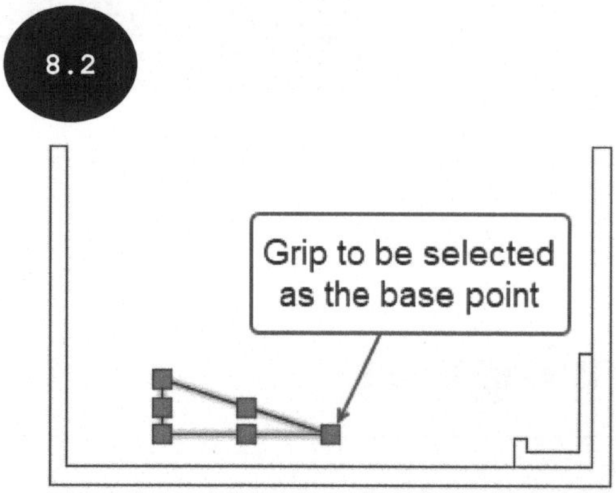

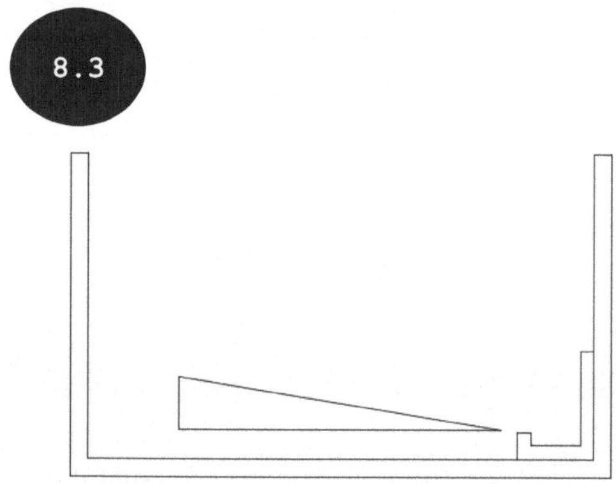

You can select one or more grips to stretch multiple objects, simultaneously. To select multiple grips, press the SHIFT key and then click on the grips one by one. After selecting the grips, release the SHIFT key and then click on a grip as the base point to stretch objects, simultaneously. Next, move the cursor to the required distance and then click to specify the placement point. The selected objects get stretched. Figure 8.4 shows seven objects and four grips selected to stretch. Figure 8.5 shows the resultant drawing after stretching the objects.

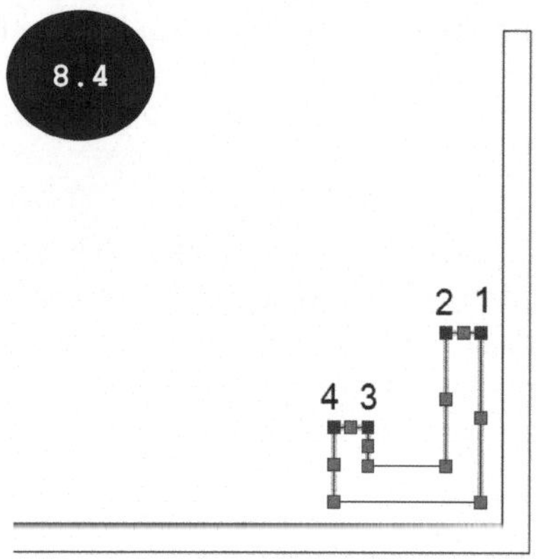

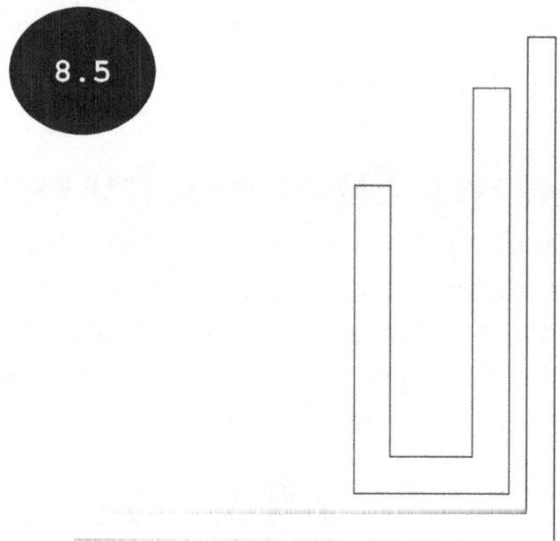

Moving Objects by using Grips

To move objects by using grips, first select the objects to be moved. The grips of the selected objects appear in the drawing area, see Figure 8.6. Next, click on a grip as the base point to move objects, see Figure 8.6. The **Stretch** command gets activated, by default. Next, press ENTER or SPACEBAR to activate the **Move** command. Alternatively, right-click to invoke a shortcut menu and then click on the **Move** option to invoke the **Move** command. Next, move the cursor in the drawing area. As you move the cursor, the objects move, dynamically. Next, click to specify a placement point in the drawing area, see Figure 8.6. The objects are moved to the new specified location, see Figure 8.7. Next, press the ESC key to exit the selection of objects.

8.6

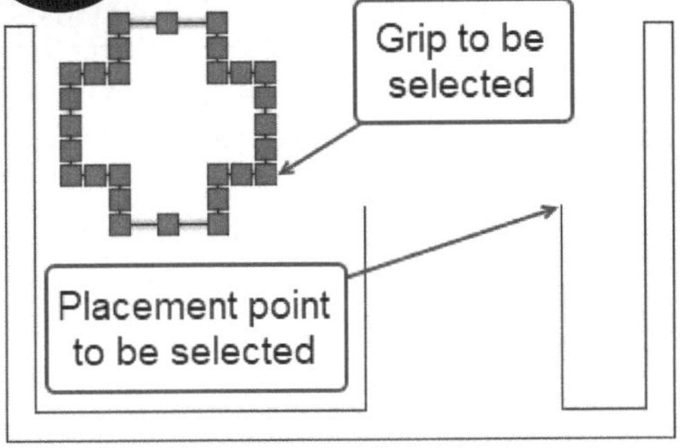

8.7

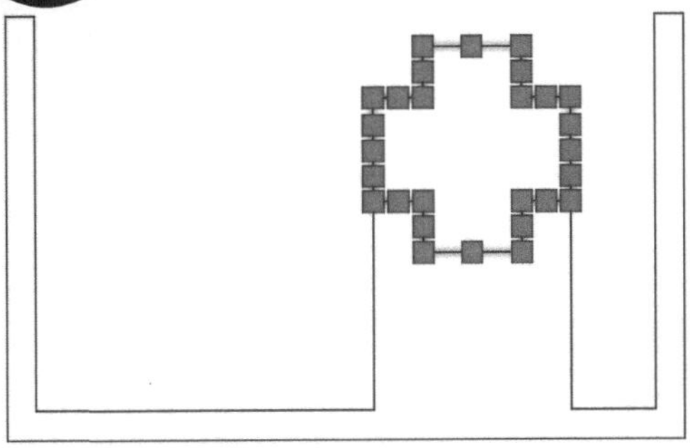

Note: By pressing the ENTER or SPACEBAR key after selecting a grip, you can cycle through the **Stretch**, **Move**, **Rotate**, **Scale**, and **Mirror** commands.

Tip: If you press and hold the CTRL key and then specify the placement point, a copy of the selected objects will be created in the new specified location.

Rotating Objects by using Grips

To rotate objects by using grips, first select the objects to be rotated. The grips of the selected objects appear in the drawing area, see Figure 8.8. Next, click on a grip as the base point to rotate objects, see Figure 8.8. The **Stretch** command gets activated, by default. Press the ENTER or SPACEBAR key twice to activate the **Rotate** command. You can cycle through the **Stretch**, **Move**, **Rotate**, **Scale**, and **Mirror** commands by pressing the ENTER key. Alternatively, right-click to invoke a shortcut menu and then click on the **Rotate** option to invoke the **Rotate** command. Next, enter the value of the rotation angle and then press ENTER. You can also click in the drawing area to specify the rotation angle. The selected objects are rotated around the base point at the specified rotation angle, see Figure 8.9. Next, press the ESC key to exit the selection of objects.

8.8

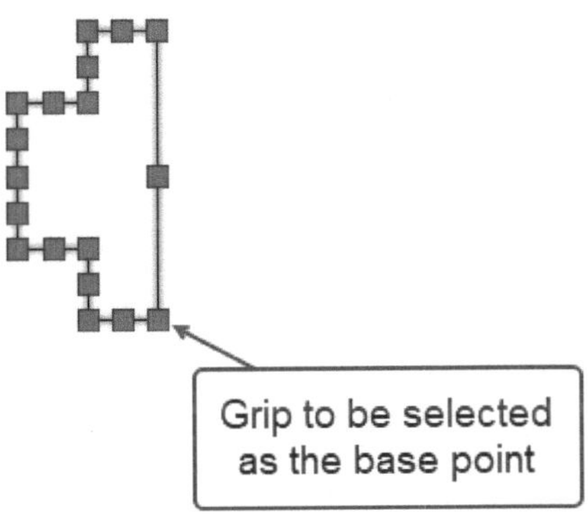

8.9

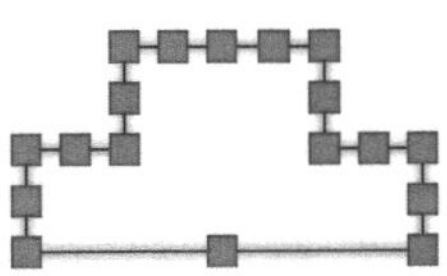

Scaling Objects by using Grips

To scale objects by using grips, first select the objects to be scaled. The grips of the selected objects appear in the drawing area, see Figure 8.10. Next, click on a grip as the base point to scale objects, see Figure 8.10. The **Stretch** command gets activated, by default. Press the ENTER key until the **Scale** command gets activated. Next, enter the scale factor and then press ENTER. The selected objects get scaled, see Figure 8.11. Note that to enlarge the selected objects, you need to enter a scale factor greater than 1 and to shrink them, you need to enter a scale factor lesser than 1. Next, press the ESC key to exit the selection of objects.

8.10

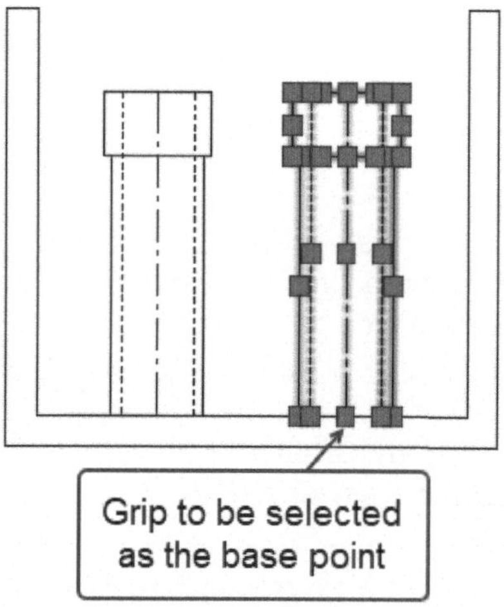

8.11

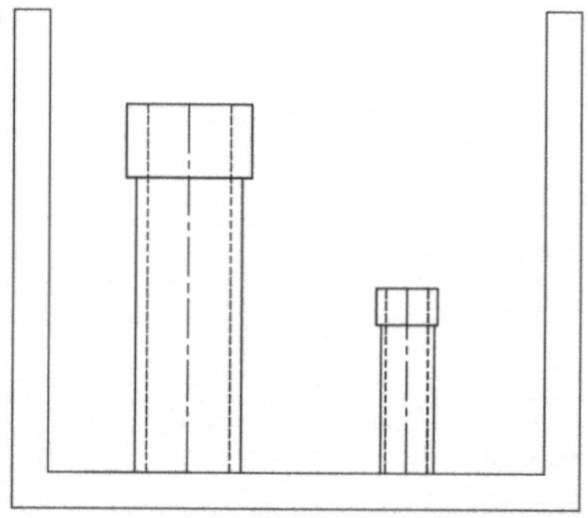

Mirroring Objects by using Grips

To mirror objects by using grips, first select the objects to be mirrored. The grips of the selected objects appear in the drawing area, see Figure 8.12. Next, click on a grip as the start point of the mirroring line, see Figure 8.12. The **Stretch** command gets activated, by default. Press the ENTER key until the **Mirror** command gets activated, and the command prompt appears "`Specify second point or [Base point Copy Undo eXit]:`". Next, click on the **Copy** option in the command prompt to keep the original or source objects in the resultant drawing. Next, click in the drawing area to specify the second point of the mirroring line. The selected objects get mirrored, and the original or source objects are retained in the drawing area, see Figure 8.13. If you do not want to keep or retain the original or source objects, then you can skip the selection of **Copy** option in the command prompt and directly specify the second point of the mirroring line. After mirroring the objects, press the ESC key to exit the selection.

8.12

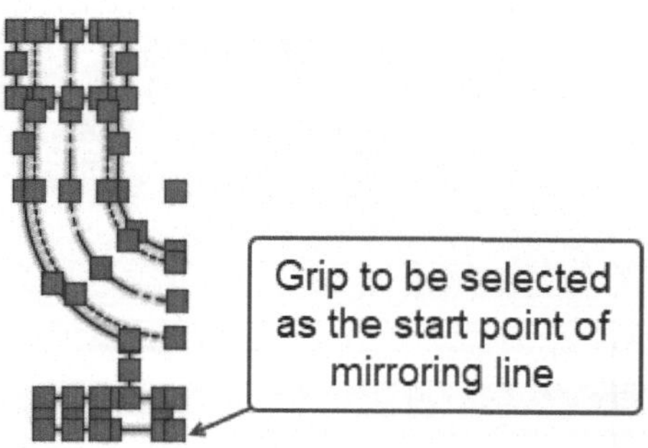

8.13

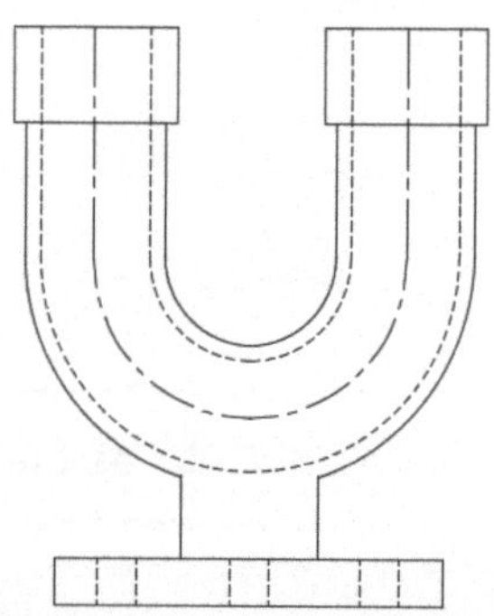

Editing Objects by using PROPERTIES Palette

You can edit object properties such as color, linetype, lineweight, layer, angle, and coordinates by using the **PROPERTIES** palette. To invoke the **PROPERTIES** palette, enter **PR** in the Command Line window and then press ENTER. Alternatively, click on the **Properties** tool in the **Palettes** panel of the **View** tab in the **Ribbon**. The **PROPERTIES** palette appears to the left of the drawing area. Next, select the object whose properties are to be edited. The properties of the selected object appear in the **PROPERTIES** palette, see Figure 8.14. Next, change the properties of the selected object as required by using the respective fields or drop-down lists of the **PROPERTIES** palette. For example, to modify the color of the selected object, click on the **Color** field, see Figure 8.15. Click on the arrow that appears. The **Color** drop-down list appears, see Figure 8.15. In this drop-down list, you can select the required color for the selected object. Similarly, to edit the linetype scale, click on the **Linetype scale** field of the palette and then enter the new linetype scale value in it.

8.14

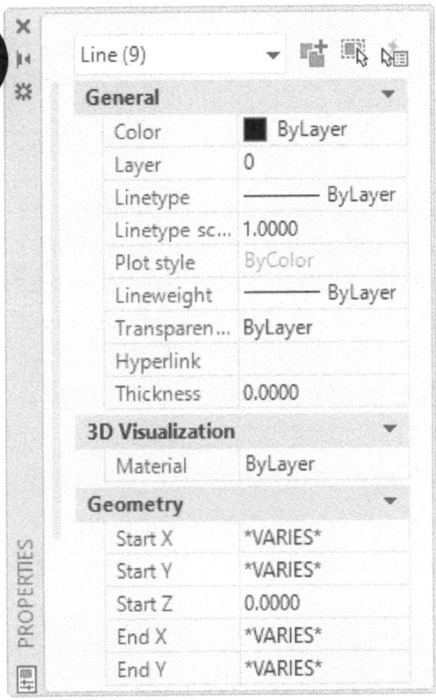

8.15

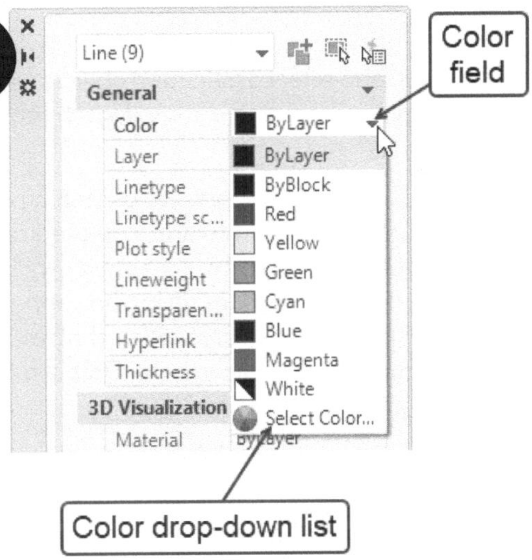

Note: By using the **PROPERTIES** palette, you can also edit the properties of the text/annotation, dimensions, and so on. Also, the availability of options in the **PROPERTIES** palette depends upon the type of object selected.

Matching Properties of an Object

In AutoCAD, you can match or copy properties such as color, linetype, linetype scale, lineweight, and the layer of an object to other objects by using the **Match Properties** tool. For example, if you have assigned a particular set of properties to an object in a drawing then you can transfer the same properties of this object to the other objects in the drawing. You can also control the settings of match properties such that only a particular set of properties of the source object should transfer or copy to other objects. The method for matching properties and controlling the settings of the properties is discussed below:

1. Click on the **Match Properties** tool in the **Properties** panel of the **Home** tab. The **Match Properties** tool gets invoked, and you are prompted to select the source object. Alternatively, enter **MA** in the Command Line window and then press ENTER to invoke the **Match Properties** tool.

   ```
   Select source object:
   ```

2. Click on the source object whose properties are to be transferred to the desired objects in the drawing. You are prompted to select the destination objects.

   ```
   Select destination object(s) or [Settings]:
   ```

3. Click on an object as the destination object to transfer the properties of the source object. The properties of the source object are transferred to the destination object.

4. Similarly, click on other objects as the destination objects to match the properties one by one. You can also select destination objects by using the Window or Cross Window selection method. Next, press ENTER to exit the **Match Properties** tool.

Note: To change the settings of match properties, click on the **Settings** option in the command prompt when you are prompted to select destination objects "`Select destination object(s) or [Settings]:`". Alternatively, enter **S** and then press ENTER. The **Property Settings** dialog box appears, see Figure 8.16. In this dialog box, select the check boxes for the properties that you want to transfer and uncheck the remaining check boxes. Next, click on the **OK** button of the dialog box. The settings of the match properties get changed.

8.16

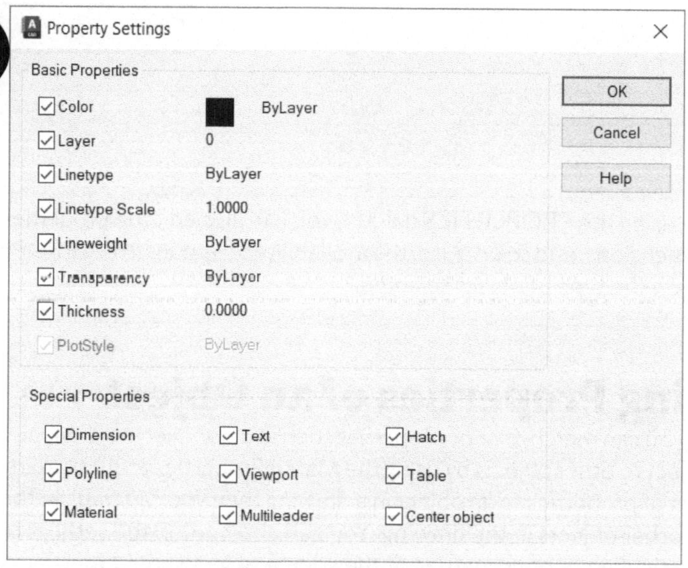

Identifying Coordinates of a Point

In AutoCAD, you can identify the location/coordinates of a point in a drawing by using the **ID Point** tool. To do so, click on the **ID Point** tool in the expanded **Utilities** panel of the **Home** tab, see Figure 8.17. Alternatively, enter **ID** and then press ENTER to invoke this tool.

8.17

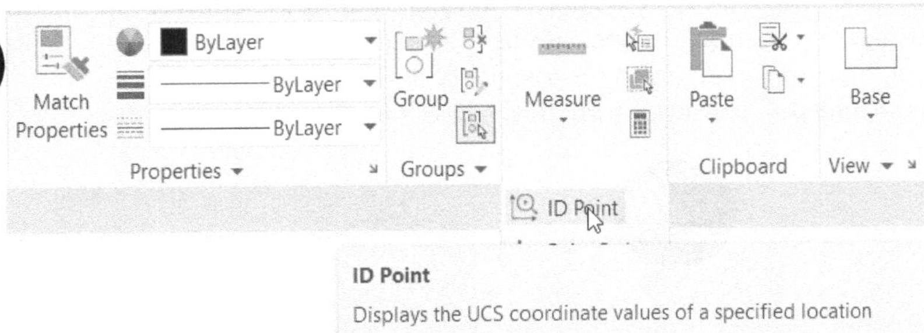

As soon as you invoke the **ID Point** tool, you are prompted to specify a point. Click on the point whose coordinates are to be identified. The coordinates (X, Y, Z) of the specified point appear in the command prompt as well as on the screen, if the Dynamic Input mode is turned on.

Note: The identified coordinates of the point are stored in the LASTPOINT system variable, which can be used as the start point for creating new entities of the drawing by entering @ in the Command Line window and then pressing ENTER. For example, while creating a line by using the **Line** tool when you are prompted to specify the start point of the line, enter @ in the Command Line window and then press ENTER. The start point of the line gets specified to the last identified point in the drawing area.

Tutorial 1

Create the drawing shown in Figure 8.18. In this tutorial, you need to set the dimension properties for a dimension and then use the **Match Properties** tool to transfer the specified properties to other dimensions of the drawing.

8.18

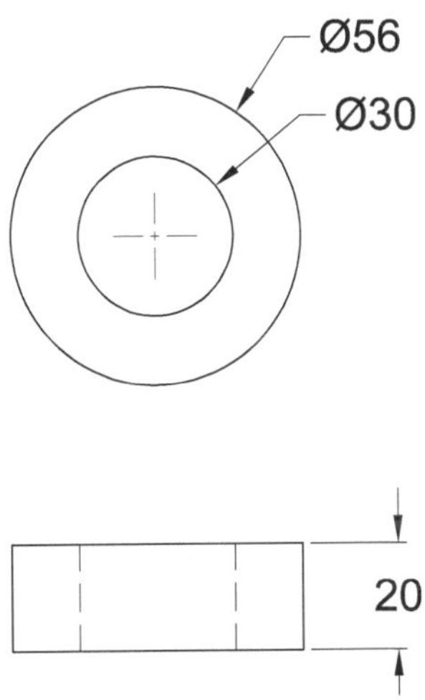

Section 1: Starting AutoCAD

1. Start AutoCAD and then open a new drawing file.

Section 2: Creating the Drawing

1. Create the Front and Top views of the drawing by using the drawing tools, as shown in Figure 8.19. In this figure, construction lines are used for creating the drawing views. Also, the color of the construction lines is changed for the clarity of the image. You can delete the construction lines after creating the drawing or turn off the layer of construction lines.

8.19

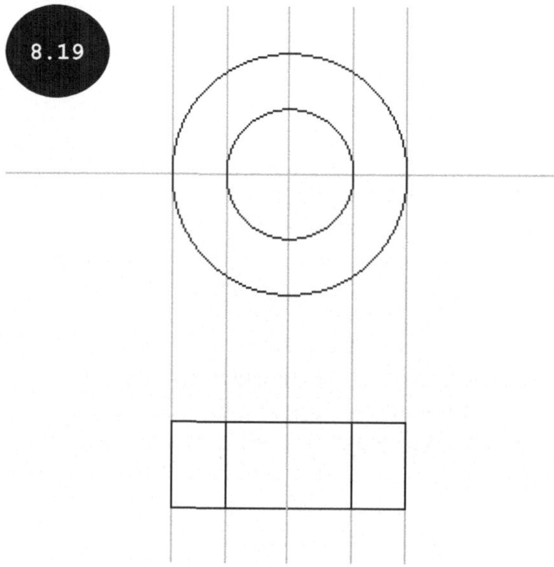

Section 3: Assigning Properties to the Hidden Line

Now, you need to assign the HIDDEN linetype to the hidden lines of the drawing by using the **PROPERTIES** palette. However, you first need to load the HIDDEN linetype in the drawing.

1. Click on the **Layer Properties** tool in the **Layers** panel of the **Home** tab. The **LAYER PROPERTIES MANAGER** window appears, see Figure 8.20.

2. Click on the **Linetype** field of the **0** layer, see Figure 8.20. The **Select Linetype** dialog box appears.

8.20

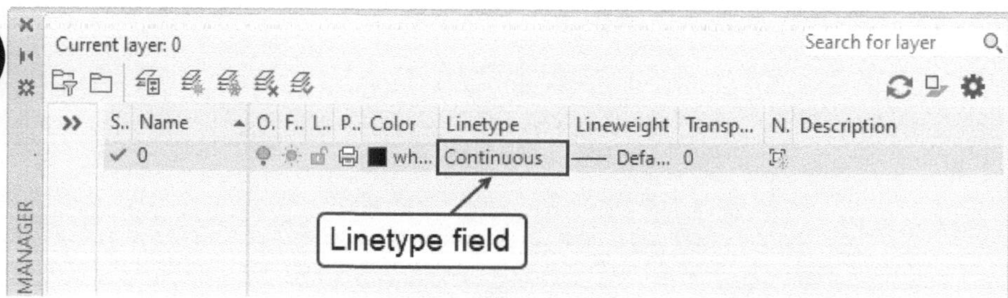

3. In the **Select Linetype** dialog box, click on the **Load** button. The **Load or Reload Linetypes** dialog box appears.

4. Select the HIDDEN linetype in the **Load or Reload Linetypes** dialog box and then click **OK** button. The HIDDEN linetype gets loaded in the dialog box.

5. Click on the **Cancel** button in the **Select Linetype** dialog box and then close the **LAYER PROPERTIES MANAGER** window.

   After loading the HIDDEN linetype in the drawing, you can assign it to the required drawing entities by using the **PROPERTIES** palette.

6. Enter **PR** in the Command Line window and then press ENTER. The **PROPERTIES** palette appears. Alternatively, click on the **Properties** tool in the **Palettes** panel of the **View** tab in the **Ribbon** to invoke the **PROPERTIES** palette.

7. Click on an inner vertical line of the Front view to be converted into the hidden line, see Figure 8.21. The current properties of the selected line appear in the **PROPERTIES** palette.

8. Click on the **Linetype** field of the **PROPERTIES** palette. Click on the arrow that appears. The **Linetype** drop-down list appears, see Figure 8.22.

8.21

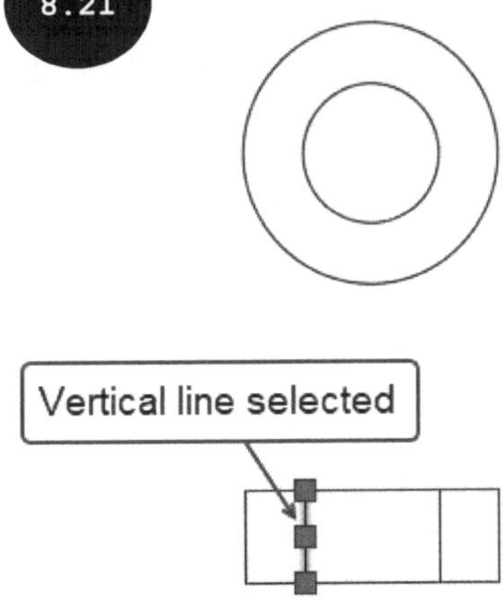

8.22

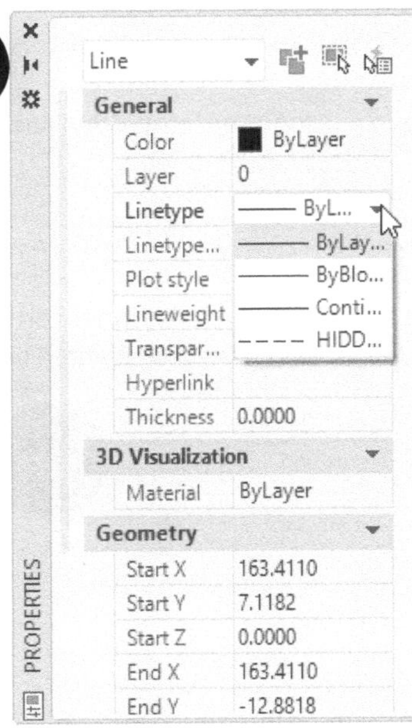

9. Click on the HIDDEN linetype in the **Linetype** drop-down list. The HIDDEN linetype is assigned to the selected line of the drawing.

10. Click on the **Linetype scale** field of the **PROPERTIES** palette and then enter **10** as the linetype scale of the selected line. Next, press the ENTER key. The selected line appears similar to the one shown in Figure 8.23.

8.23

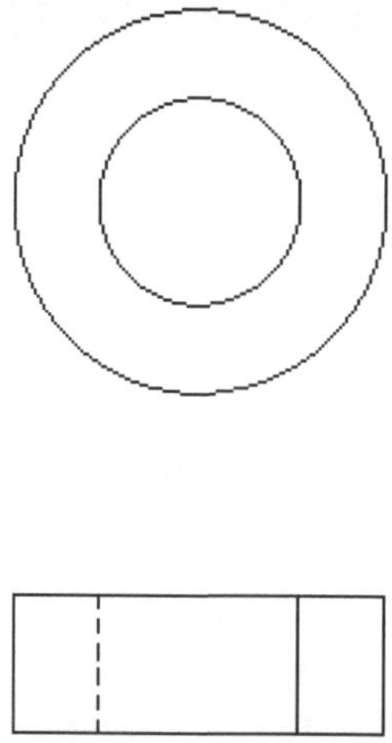

Section 4: Matching the Hidden Line Properties

Now, you need to match the properties of the left hidden line to the right hidden line.

1. Click on the **Match Properties** tool in the **Properties** panel of the **Home** tab. You are prompted to select the source object.

   ```
   Select source object:
   ```

2. Click on the left hidden line of the drawing as the source object. You are prompted to select the destination objects.

   ```
   Select destination object(s) or [Settings]:
   ```

3. Click on the right inner vertical line of the drawing as the destination object, see Figure 8.24. The properties of the selected line are matched with the source object, see Figure 8.24.

8.24

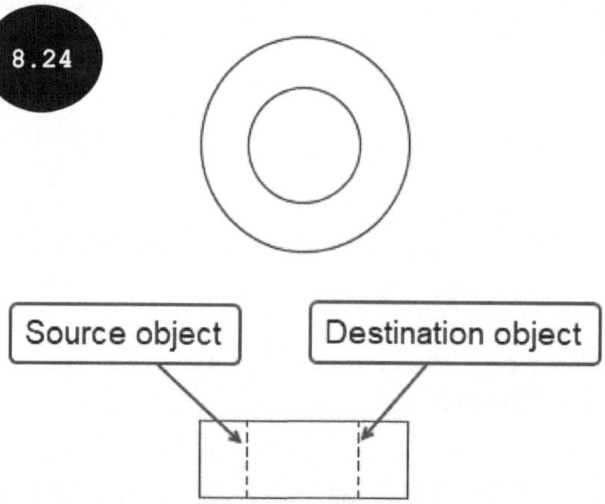

Section 5: Applying Dimensions

Now, you need to apply dimensions in the drawing and then set the dimension properties by using the **PROPERTIES** palette.

1. Click on the **Dimension** tool in the **Annotation** panel of the **Home** tab. You are prompted to select the object to be dimensioned.

```
Select objects or specify first extension line origin or [Angular
Baseline Continue Ordinate aliGn Distribute Layer Undo]:
```

2. Move the cursor over the rightmost vertical line of the Front view and then click on the line when it gets highlighted in the drawing area. The linear dimension is attached to the cursor.

3. Move the cursor horizontally toward right and then click to specify the placement point for the dimension in the drawing area. The linear dimension is applied and placed in the specified location, see Figure 8.25. Note that the dimension text and the arrowheads of the applied dimension may appear very small in size in the drawing area because of the dimension properties of the current dimension style, see Figure 8.25. You will modify the dimension properties later in this tutorial.

8.25

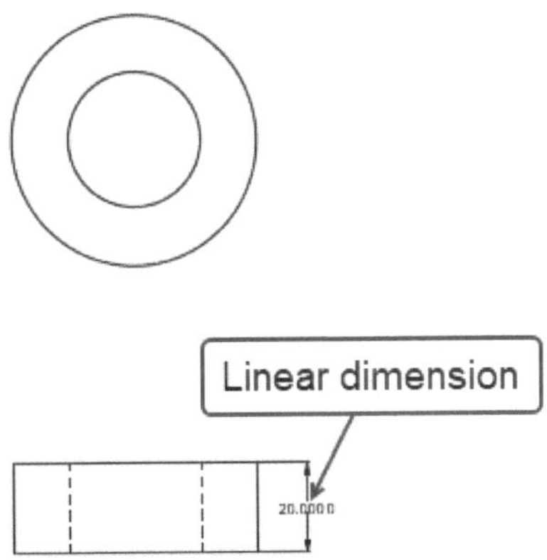

4. Similarly, apply the diameter dimensions in the drawing, see Figure 8.26.

8.26

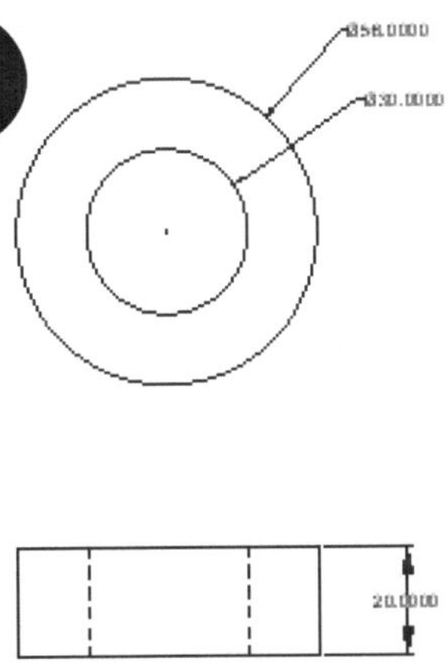

Section 6: Assigning and Matching Dimension Properties

Now, you need to assign the dimension properties to a dimension of the drawing by using the **PROPERTIES** palette and then match these properties to other dimensions of the drawing.

1. Click on the linear dimension of the drawing and then invoke the **PROPERTIES** palette.

2. Click on the **Arrow size** field in the **PROPERTIES** palette and then enter **5** as the arrow size of the dimension.

3. Similarly, enter **5.5** as the text height in the **Text height** field, **1.5** in the **Ext line ext** field, **1.5** in the **Ext line offset** field, and **1.5** in the **Text offset** field of the **PROPERTIES** palette. The selected dimension appears similar to the one shown in Figure 8.27.

8.27

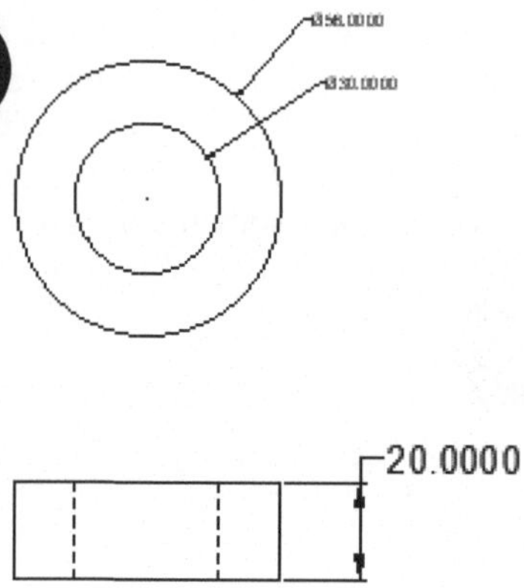

Now, you need to set the precision value of the dimension to 0.

4. In the **Primary Units** category of the **PROPERTIES** palette, click on the **Precision** field. Next, click on the arrow that appears. The **Precision** drop-down list appears. In this drop-down list, select the **0** option as the precision for the selected dimension, see Figure 8.28. Alternatively, right-click on the dimension in the drawing area. A shortcut menu appears. In this shortcut menu, click on **Precision** > **0** to set the precision for the selected dimension. Next, press the ESC key. The dimension properties of the selected dimension are modified, see Figure 8.28.

8.28

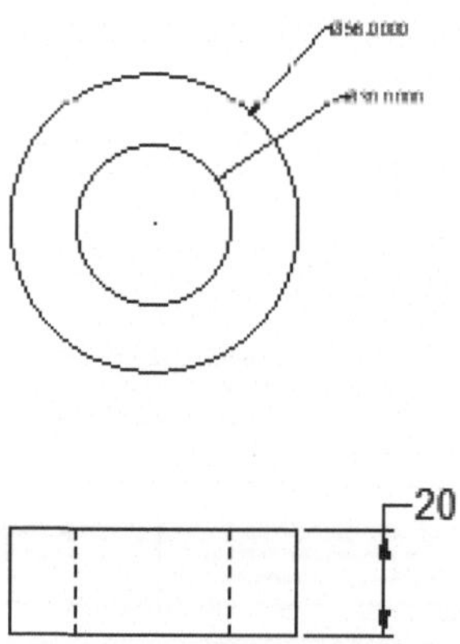

Now, you need to match the properties of this dimension to other dimensions of the drawing.

5. Click on the **Match Properties** tool in the **Properties** panel of the **Home** tab. You are prompted to select the source object.

```
Select source object:
```

6. Click on the linear dimension as the source object. You are prompted to select the destination objects.

```
Select destination object(s) or [Settings]:
```

7. Click on the diameter dimensions of the drawing one by one to match the properties of the source dimension. Figure 8.29 shows the drawing after matching all the dimension properties.

8.29

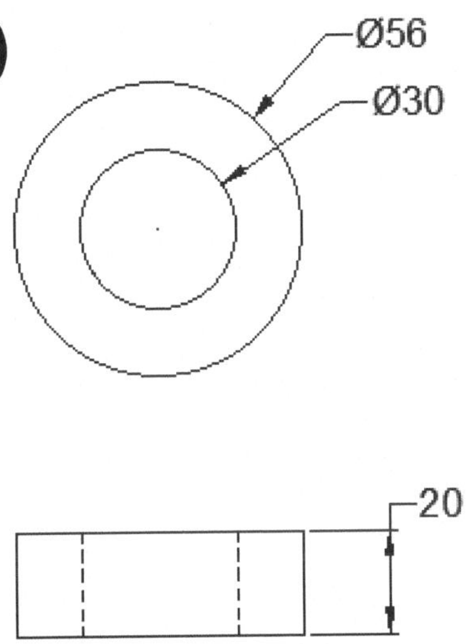

Section 7: Saving the Drawing

After creating the drawing, you need to save it.

1. Click on the **Save** tool in the **Quick Access Toolbar**. The **Save Drawing As** dialog box appears.
2. Browse to the *AutoCAD* folder and then create a folder with the name *Chapter 8* inside the *AutoCAD* folder.
3. Enter **Tutorial 1** in the **File name** field of the dialog box and then click on the **Save** button. The drawing gets saved with the name Tutorial 1 in the *Chapter 8* folder.

Hands-on Test Drive 1

Create the drawing shown in Figure 8.30. Modify dimension properties of the dimension style and then apply dimensions to the drawing. You can arbitrarily assign the values of dimension properties.

8.30

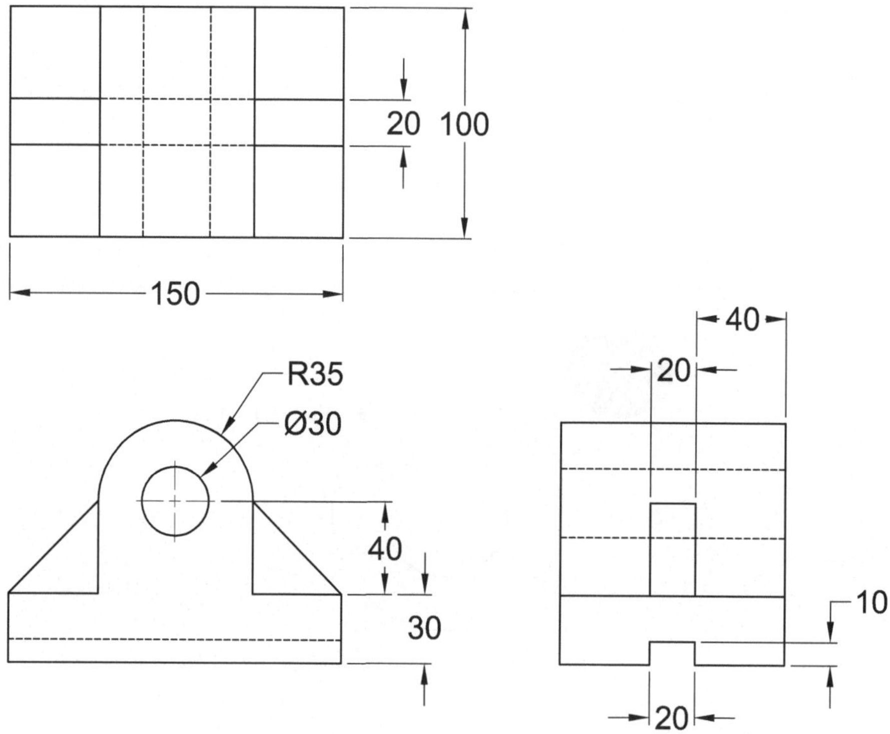

Hands-on Test Drive 2

Create the drawing shown in Figure 8.31. Modify dimension properties of the dimension style and then apply dimensions to the drawing. You can arbitrarily assign the values of dimension properties such as dimension height and arrow size.

8.31

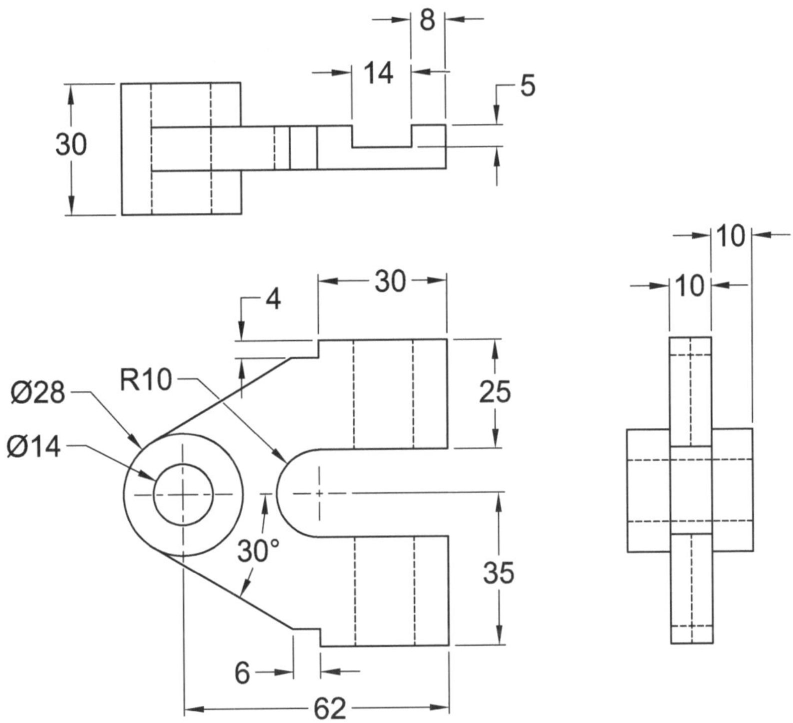

Summary

The chapter introduced methods for editing drawing entities by using the grips and the Properties palette. It also discussed matching the properties of an object with the other drawing objects and identifying the coordinates of a point in a drawing.

Questions

Complete the following sentences:

- A line object has ________ number of grips and an arc object has ________ number of grips.
- After selecting a grip of an object, when you press the ________ or ________ key, you cycle through the **Stretch**, **Move**, **Rotate**, **Scale**, and **Mirror** commands.

- When you click on a grip of an object, the _________ command gets activated, by default.
- Click on a grip of an object and then press the ENTER or SPACEBAR key twice to activate the _________ command.
- You can edit object properties such as color, linetype, lineweight, layer, angle, and coordinates by using the _________ palette.
- To invoke the PROPERTIES palette, enter _________ in the Command Line window and then press ENTER.
- The _________ tool is used for matching or copying the properties of an object such as color, linetype, linetype scale, lineweight, and layer with other objects of the drawing.
- The _________ tool is used for identifying the location/coordinates of a point in the drawing.

CHAPTER

9

Creating Hatches and Gradients

In this chapter, the following topics will be discussed:

- Creating the Hatches
- Creating the Gradients

In mechanical drawings, hatches are used for the representation of the cross-sectional shape and material of components. The cross-sectional shape of a part is created by cutting the component using an imaginary cutting plane and then viewing it from a direction normal to the cutting plane, see Figure 9.1. The view that represents the cross-sectional shape of a component is known as a section view.

9.1

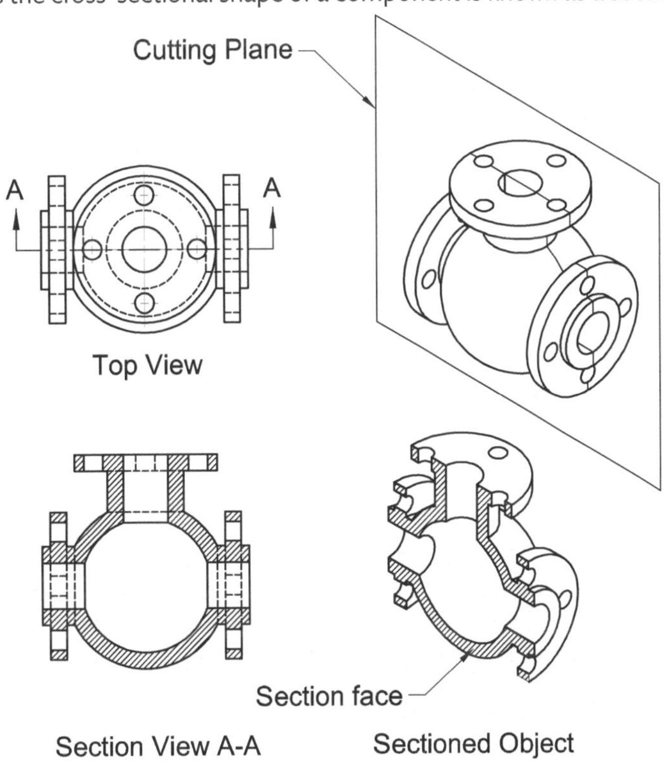

It is evident from the above figure that hatching is created by filling enclosed areas of drawing views with hatch patterns that are composed of hatch lines or solid fill. AutoCAD is provided with various hatch patterns that can be used for representing the cross-sectional shape and material of components. In architectural drawings, the hatches are used for describing the type of material of the object such as brick, stone, wood, and sand. Figure 9.2 shows some of the hatch patterns available in AutoCAD.

9.2

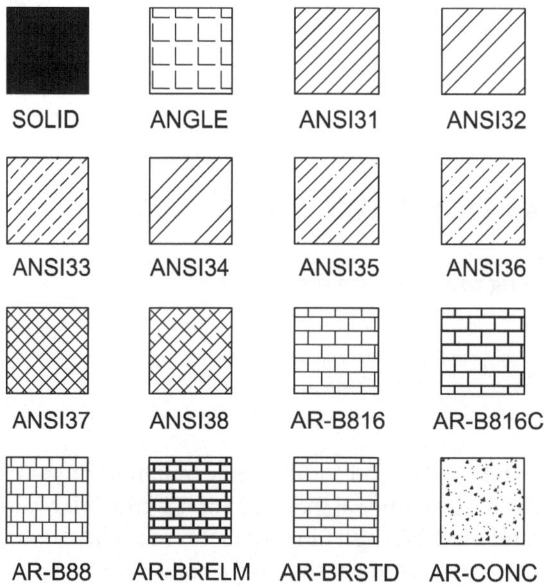

Creating a Hatch within an Enclosed Boundary

You can create hatching in an enclosed area of a drawing view by using the **Hatch** tool or HATCH command. To create a hatch, click on the **Hatch** tool in the **Draw** panel of the **Home** tab. The **Hatch Creation** tab appears in **Ribbon**, see Figure 9.3. Also, you are prompted to pick an internal point. Alternatively, enter **H** in the Command Line window and then press ENTER to invoke this tool.

```
Pick internal point or [Select objects Draw Undo seTtings]:
```

9.3

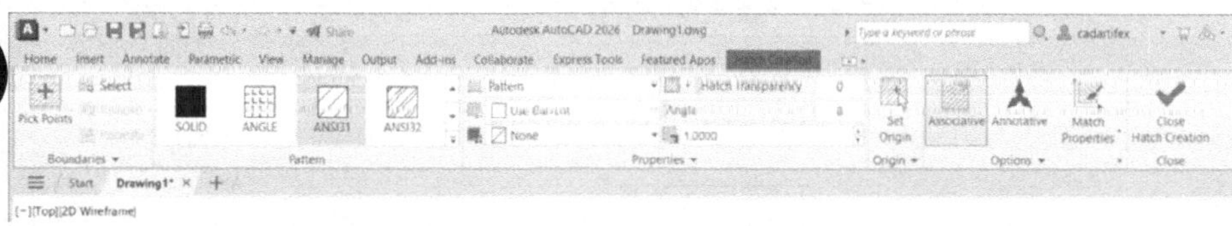

Note: On invoking the **Hatch** tool, if you are prompted to specify a start point of the hatch in the command prompt "`Specify start point or [picK internal Point Select objects Rectangle Circle ALignment Width Mode seTtings]:`", then click on the **pick internal point** option to create a hatch within an enclosed area.

In the **Hatch Creation** tab, you can specify the pattern type and properties such as pattern angle, scale, and transparency. Click on the pattern to be created in the **Pattern** panel and then specify the pattern properties in the respective fields of the **Properties** panel of the **Hatch Creation** tab. Next, click on an enclosed area of the drawing view to create the hatch pattern. The hatch pattern gets created in the specified enclosed area of the drawing view, see Figure 9.4. Next, press the ESC key to exit the creation of the hatch pattern. The options of the **Hatch Creation** tab are discussed next.

9.4

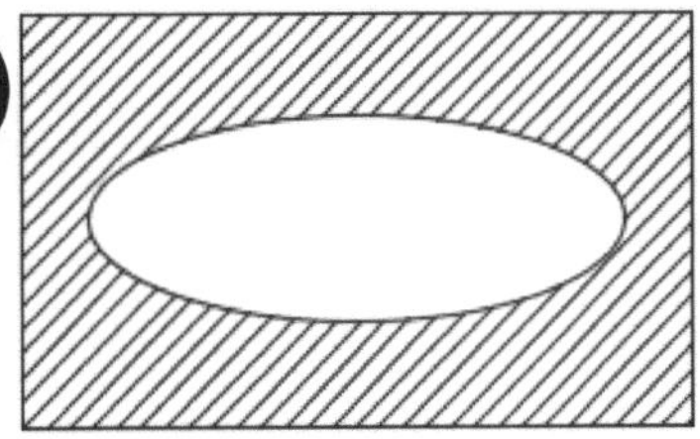

Boundaries Panel

The options in the **Boundaries** panel of the **Hatch Creation** tab are used for defining enclosed areas of drawing views to create hatch patterns, see Figure 9.5. The options are discussed next.

9.5

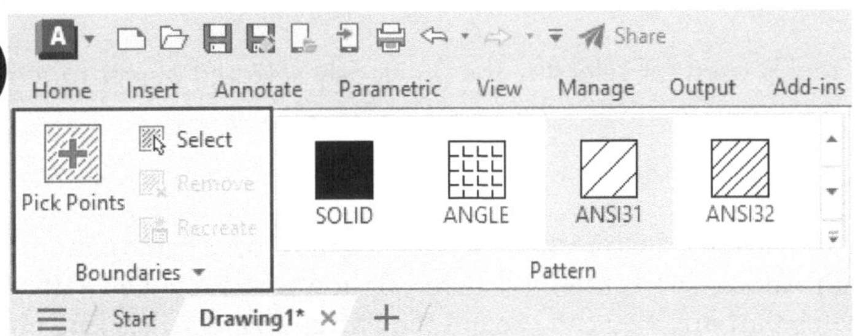

Pick Points

The **Pick Points** tool is used for selecting a pick point in an enclosed area of a drawing view to create the hatch pattern. By default, this tool is activated in the **Boundaries** panel. As a result, you are prompted to specify a pick point. Click to specify a pick point in an enclosed area of a drawing view. The hatch pattern is created in the enclosed area, which is defined by the pick point, see Figure 9.6. You can specify multiple pick points in a drawing to create hatch patterns.

9.6

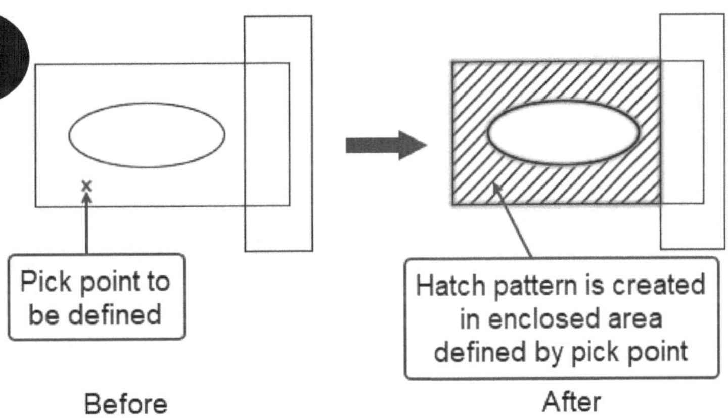

Select

The **Select** tool of the **Boundaries** panel is used for choosing an object for creating the hatch pattern. When you click on the **Select** tool in the **Boundaries** panel, you are prompted to select objects for creating the hatch pattern. Click on an enclosed object of a drawing. The enclosed area of the selected object gets filled with a hatch pattern, see Figure 9.7. You can select multiple enclosed objects in the drawing to create a hatch pattern.

9.7

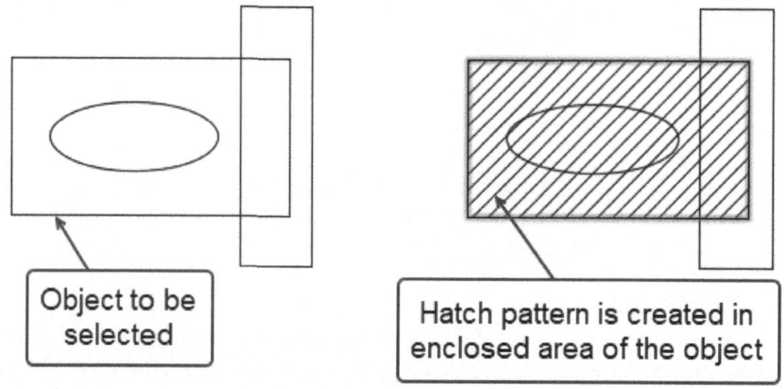

Remove

The **Remove** tool is used for selecting the previously selected object to remove the hatch pattern created in it.

Pattern Panel

The options in the **Pattern** panel are used for selecting the type of hatch pattern to be created. AutoCAD is provided with various hatch patterns. Figure 9.8 shows the expanded **Pattern** panel with the display of different hatch patterns. You can expand the **Pattern** panel by clicking on the down arrow in the lower right corner of the panel.

9.8

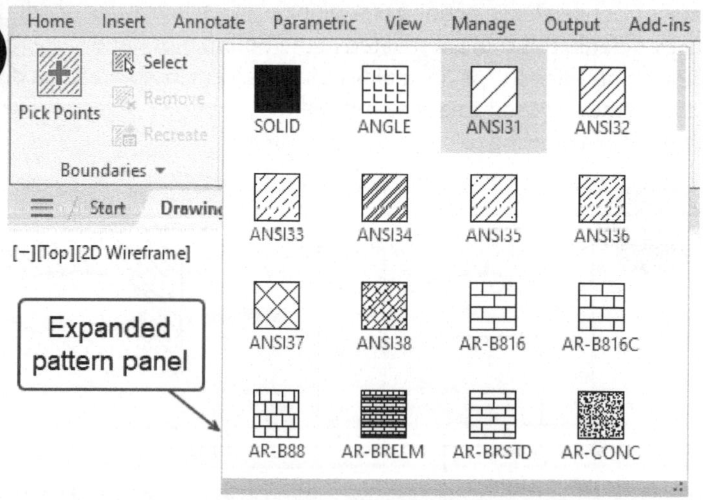

Properties Panel

The **Properties** panel is used for specifying the hatch pattern properties such as hatch pattern color, hatch background color, hatch transparency, hatch angle, and hatch scale in the respective fields of the panel, see Figure 9.9.

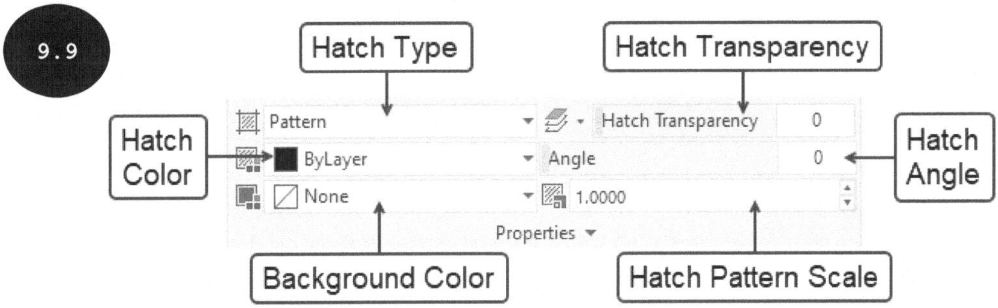

Options Panel

The **Associative** tool of the **Options** panel is used for making the hatch pattern associative to the object selected. An associative hatch pattern is updated automatically on modifying the object. To create an associative hatch pattern, click on the **Associative** tool in the **Options** panel to activate it and then create hatch patterns on enclosed objects.

The **Annotative** tool is used for making the hatch pattern annotative such that the scale of the hatch pattern adjusts automatically to the scale of the viewport.

After specifying the hatch pattern properties, click to specify an enclosed area or object to create the hatch pattern. The hatch pattern is created in the enclosed area selected.

Creating a Hatch by Specifying Points

In AutoCAD 2026, you can also create a hatch by specifying points directly in the drawing area in a similar manner to drawing a polyline. This method allows you to create a hatch without needing pre-defined closed areas.

To create a hatch by specifying points, enter **H** in the Command Line window or select the **Hatch** tool in the **Draw** panel of the **Home** tab. You will be prompted to specify the start point of the hatch.

```
Specify start point or [picK internal Point Select objects Rectangle
Circle ALignment Width Mode seTtings]:
```

Note: On invoking the **Hatch** tool, if you are prompted to pick an internal point in the command prompt "`Pick internal point or [Select objects Draw Undo seTtings]:`", then click on the **Draw** option to create a hatch by specifying points in the drawing area.

Click to specify points in the drawing area one after another to draw a hatch of specified parameters, see Figure 9.10. In this figure, 4 points are specified. These points define the path of the hatch.

9.10

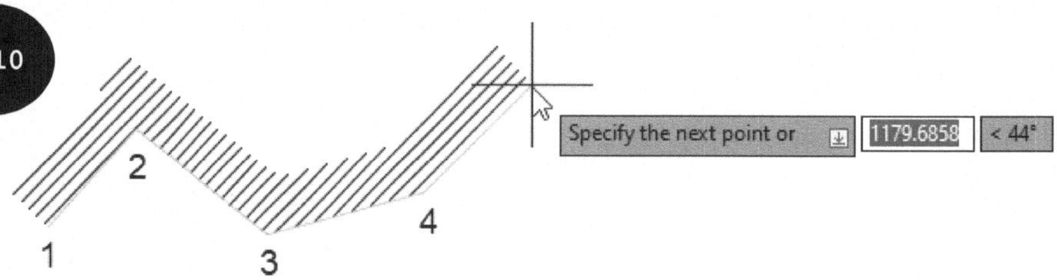

Note that while specifying points, you can also define the width and alignment (inside/center/outside) for the hatch using the **Width** and **Alignment** options in the command prompt, refer to Figures 9.11. These options allow to achieve the desired appearance for the hatch pattern.

9.11

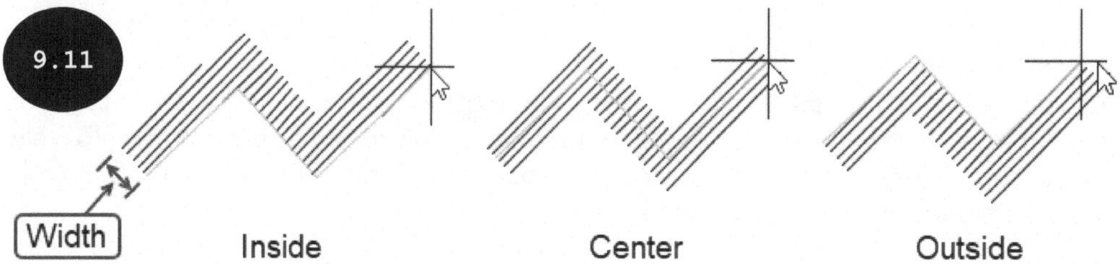

Creating the Gradients

Similar to creating hatches by filling the boundary or enclosed area of a drawing view with a hatch pattern, you can also fill boundaries or enclosed areas with gradients having one or more gradient colors, see Figure 9.12. Applying gradients is very useful in making the drawing presentable and gives a realistic appearance to the drawing views. Gradients are also used for representing the section area and distinguishing between two or more objects or enclosed areas in the drawing views.

9.12

To apply a gradient to an enclosed area of a drawing view, click on the down arrow next to the **Hatch** tool in the **Draw** panel. A flyout appears, see Figure 9.13. In this flyout, click on the **Gradient** tool. The **Hatch Creation** tab appears, see Figure 9.14. Also, you are prompted to pick an internal point.

```
Pick internal point or [Select objects Draw Undo seTtings]:
```

Note: On invoking the **Gradient** tool, if you are prompted to specify a start point of the gradient in the command prompt "`Specify start point or [picK internal Point Select objects Rectangle Circle ALignment Width Mode seTtings]:`", then click on the **pick internal point** option to create a gradient within an enclosed area.

9.13

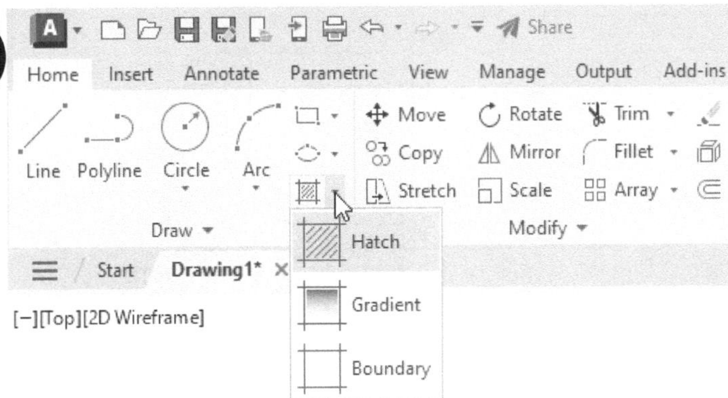

9.14

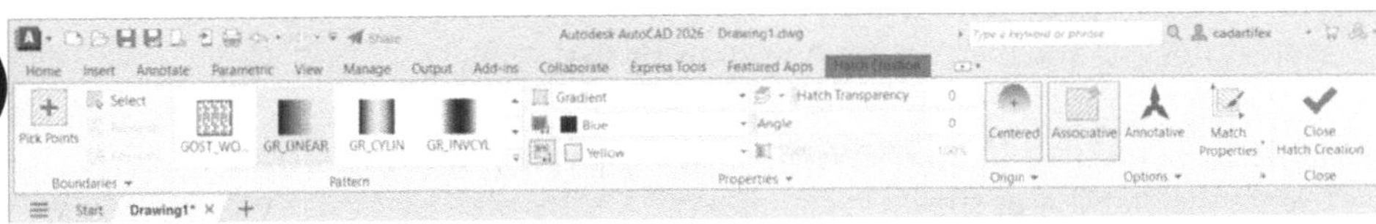

The options in the **Hatch Creation** tab are used for specifying a gradient pattern and its properties. All these options are same as those discussed earlier while creating the hatch patterns. Select a gradient pattern to create in the **Pattern** panel and then specify its properties such as gradient color 1 and gradient color 2 in the respective fields of the **Properties** panel of the **Hatch Creation** tab. Next, click on an enclosed area of the drawing view to create the gradient pattern. The gradient pattern is created in the specified enclosed area of the drawing view, see Figure 9.15. You can specify multiple enclosed areas one by one to create gradient patterns. Next, press the ESC key to exit the creation of a gradient pattern.

9.15

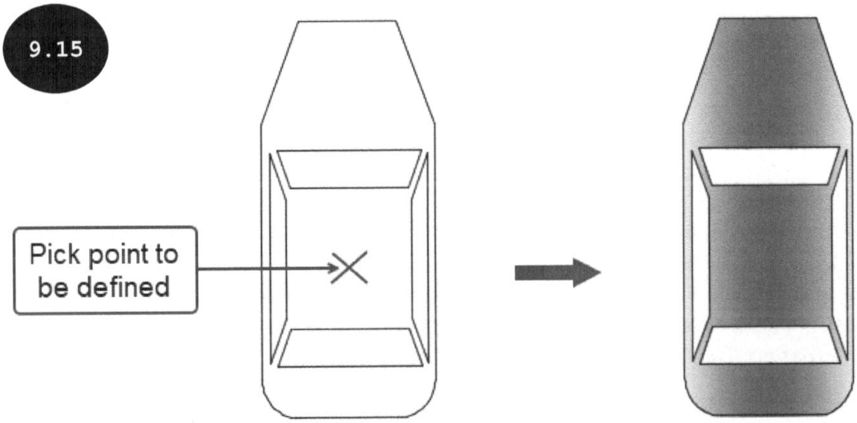

Tutorial 1

Create the drawing shown in the Figure 9.16. You need to apply the ANSI31 hatch pattern to the drawing at different hatch angles.

9.16

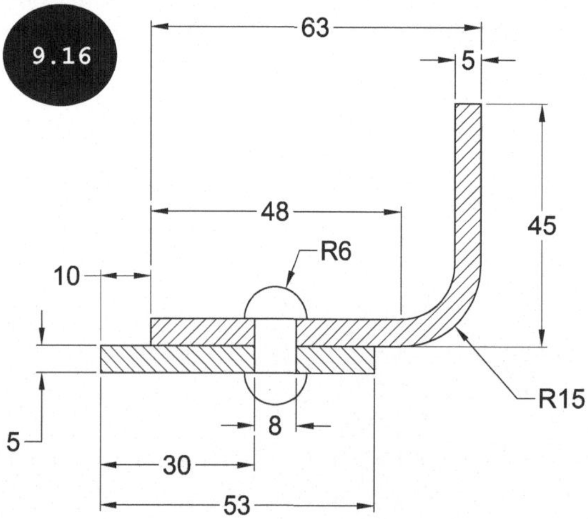

Section 1: Starting AutoCAD

1. Start AutoCAD and then open a new drawing file.

Section 2: Creating the Drawing and Applying Dimensions

1. Create the drawing, as shown in Figure 9.17.

9.17

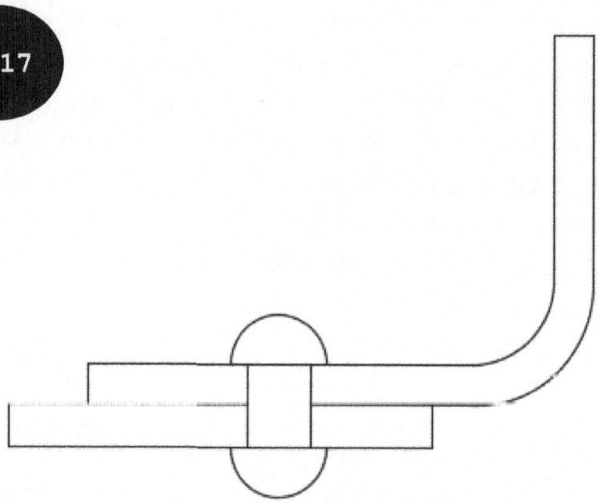

2. Invoke the **Modify Dimension Style** dialog box and then modify the Standard dimension style: Text height = 3.5, Offset from dim line = 1, Arrow size = 3.25, Extend beyond dim lines = 1, Offset from origin = 1, and Precision = 0. To invoke this dialog box, enter **D** in the Command Line window and then press ENTER. Next, select the **Standard** dimension style in the **Dimension Style Manager** dialog box that appears and then click on the **Modify** button.

3. Apply dimensions to the drawing by using the dimension tools, see Figure 9.18.

9.18

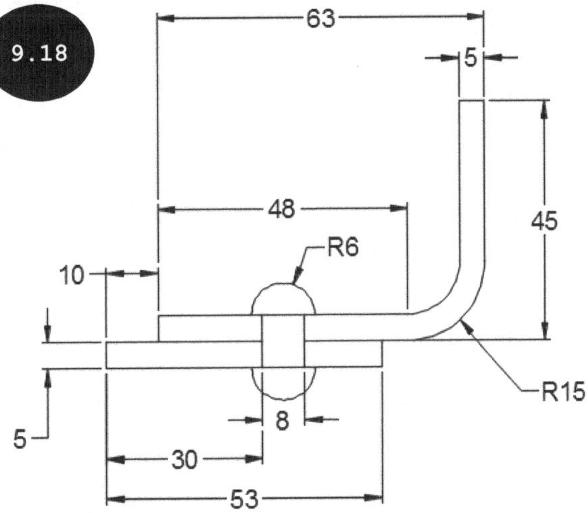

Section 3: Creating Hatches

1. Click on the **Hatch** tool in the **Draw** panel of the **Home** tab, see Figure 9.19. The **Hatch Creation** tab appears in the **Ribbon**. Also, you are prompted to pick an internal point. Alternatively, enter **H** in the Command Line window and then press ENTER.

```
Pick internal point or [Select objects Draw Undo seTtings]:
```

2. Click on the upper left enclosed area of the drawing, see Figure 9.18. The hatching gets created in the selected enclosed area, see Figure 9.20.

9.19

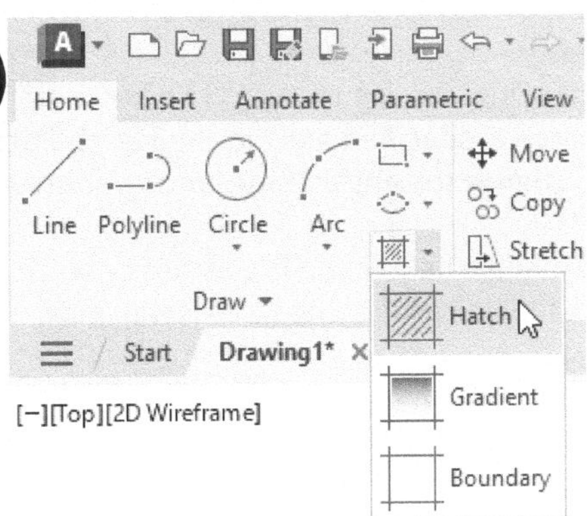

9.20

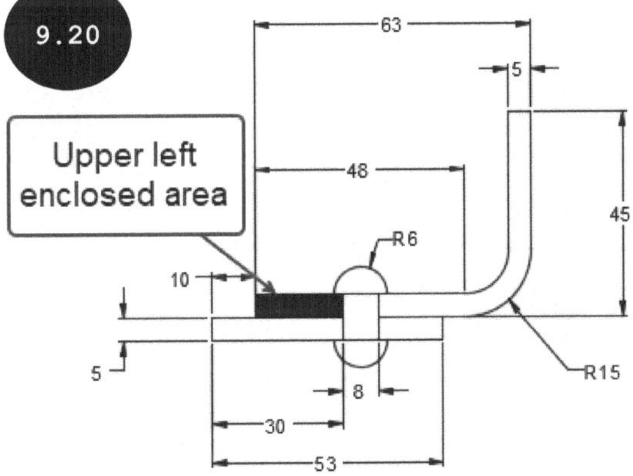

3. Ensure that the ANSI31 is selected as the hatch pattern in the **Pattern** panel of the **Hatch Creation** tab in the **Ribbon**.

   It is evident from Figure 9.20 that the scale of the hatch pattern is minuscule, therefore you need to change it.

4. Enter **12** in the **Hatch Pattern Scale** field of the **Properties** panel of the **Hatch Creation** tab and then press ENTER. The scale of the hatch pattern changes, see Figure 9.21.

5. Click on the right enclosed area of the upper part of the drawing. The hatch gets created, see Figure 9.22.

9.21

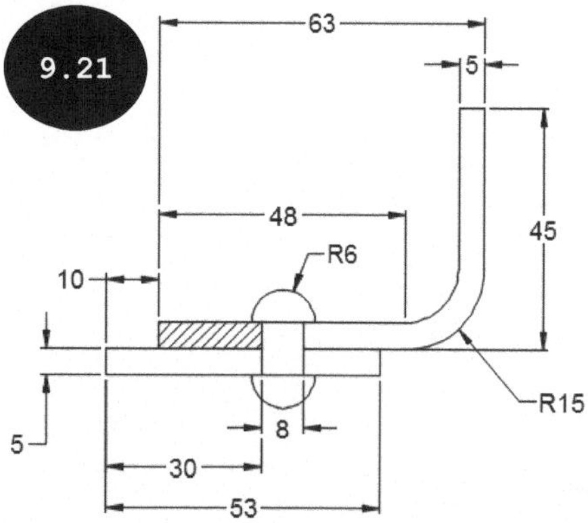

9.22

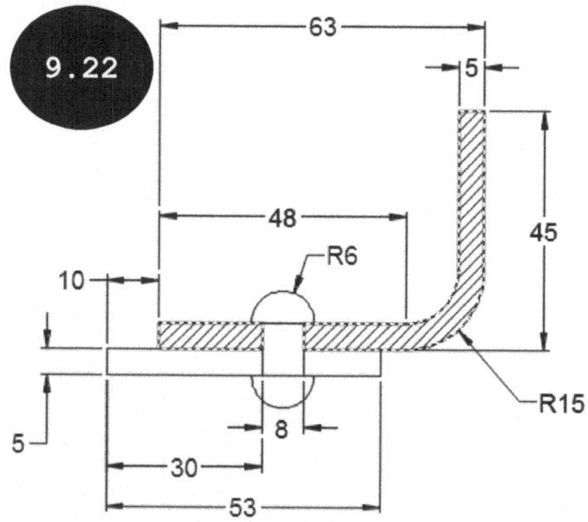

6. Press ENTER to exit the creation of the Hatch. The hatch is created on the upper part of the drawing.

   Now, you need to create the hatch on the lower part of the drawing.

7. Click on the **Hatch** tool in the **Draw** panel of the **Home** tab again. The **Hatch Creation** tab appears. Also, you are prompted to pick an internal point. Alternatively, enter **H** in the Command Line window and then press ENTER.

```
Pick internal point or [Select objects Draw Undo seTtings]:
```

8. Click on the lower left enclosed area of the drawing, see Figure 9.23. The hatching is created, see Figure 9.23. Ensure that the scale of the hatch is specified as 12 in the **Hatch Pattern Scale** field of the **Properties** panel. Now, you need to change the angle of the hatch pattern.

9. Enter **90** as the angle of the hatch pattern in the **Angle** field of the **Properties** panel of the **Hatch Creation** tab. The angle of the hatch pattern is changed as specified, see Figure 9.24.

9.23

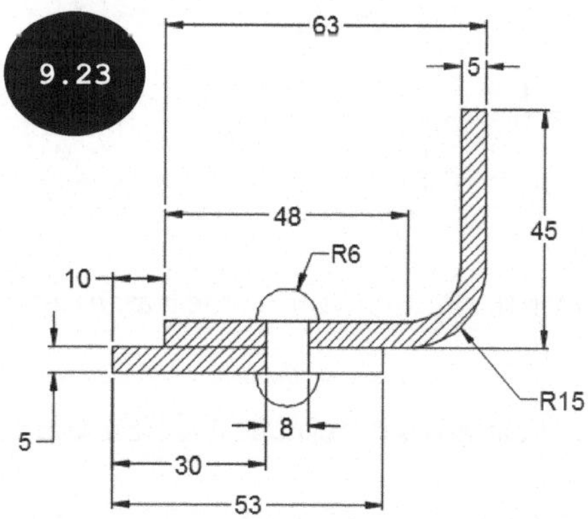

9.24

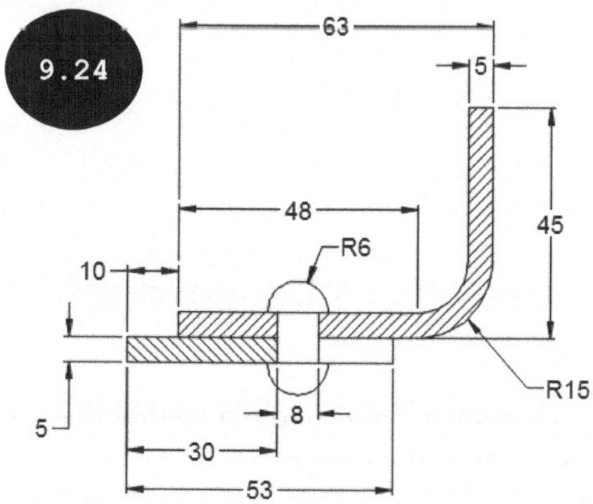

10. Click on the right enclosed area of the lower part of the drawing. The hatch pattern is created, see Figure 9.25. Next, press ENTER. Figure 9.25 shows the final drawing after creating the hatch patterns.

9.25

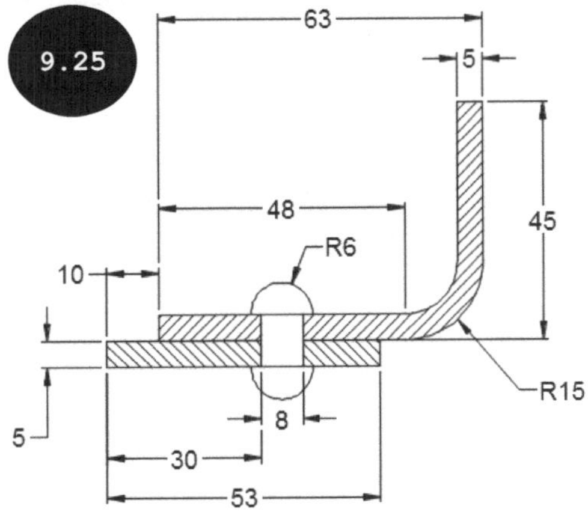

Section 4: Saving the Drawing

1. Click on the **Save** tool in the **Quick Access Toolbar**. The **Save Drawing As** dialog box appears.
2. Browse to the *AutoCAD* folder and then create a folder with the name *Chapter 9* inside the *AutoCAD* folder. Next, enter **Tutorial 1** in the **File name** field of the dialog box.
3. Click on the **Save** button. The drawing is saved with the name Tutorial 1 in the *Chapter 9* folder.

Hands-on Test Drive 1

Create the drawing shown in Figure 9.26. You need to apply ANSI31 hatch patterns to the drawing at different hatch angles as shown in Figure 9.26.

9.26

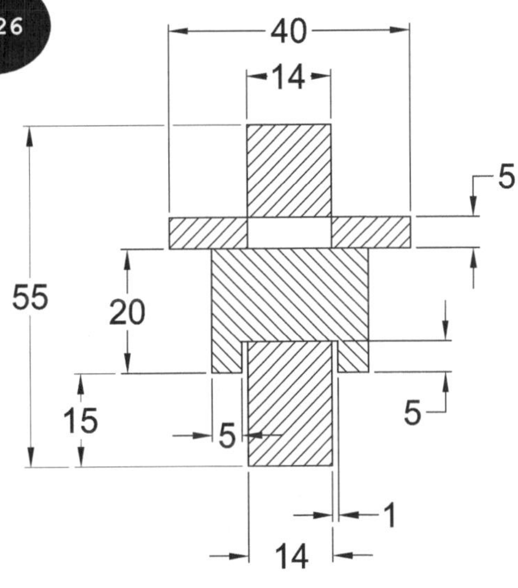

Hands-on Test Drive 2

Create the drawing shown in Figure 9.27. You need to apply ANSI35 hatch patterns to the drawing at different hatch angles as shown in Figure 9.27.

9.27

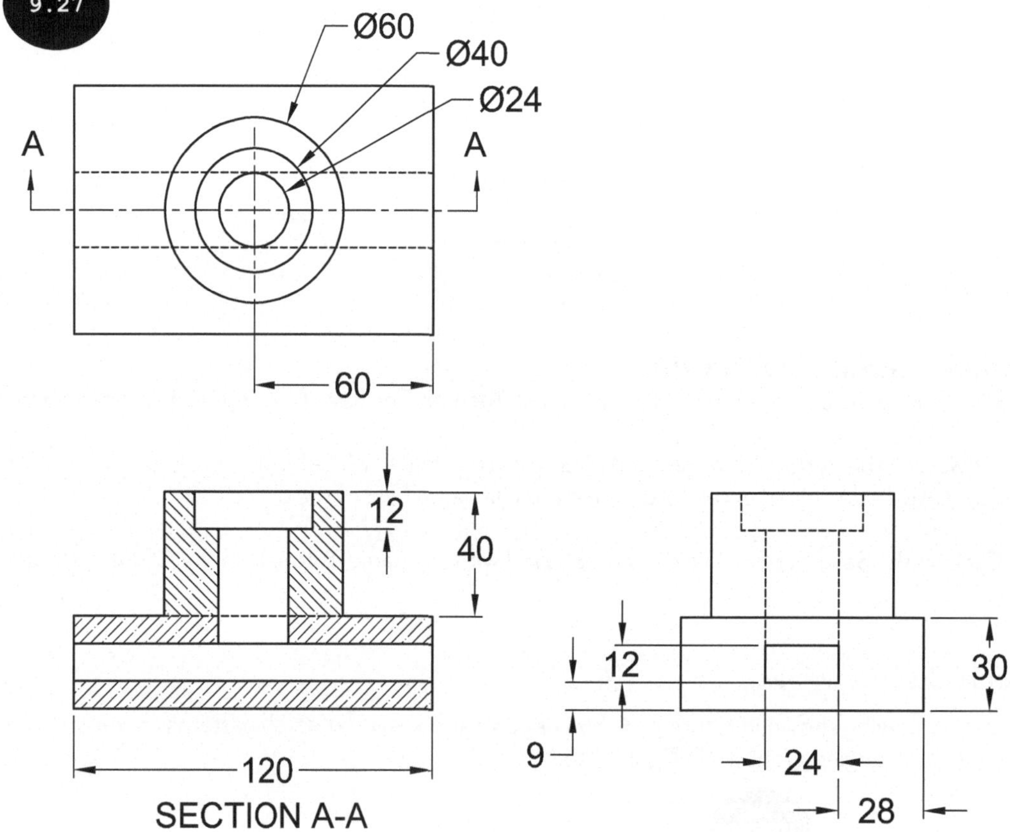

Hands-on Test Drive 3

Create the drawing shown in Figure 9.28. You need to apply ANSI31 hatch patterns to the drawing as shown in Figure 9.28.

9.28

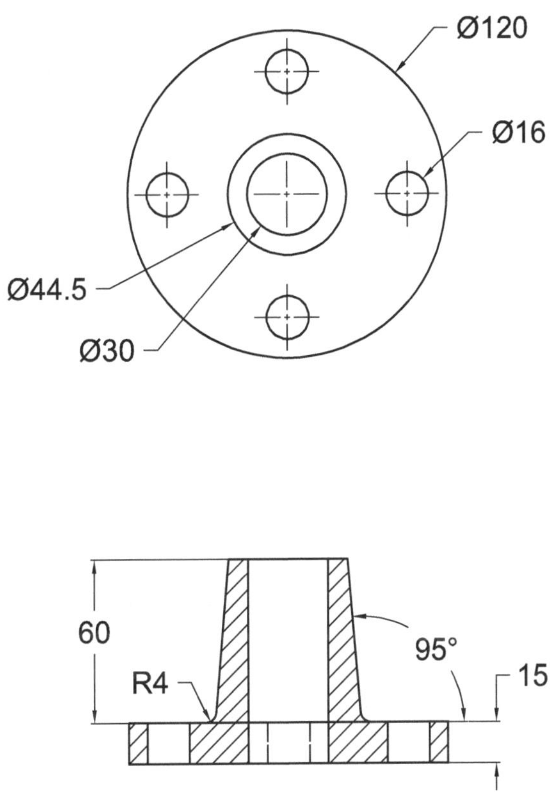

Summary

The chapter introduced methods for creating different types of hatch patterns and gradients in enclosed areas of a drawing.

Questions

Complete the following sentences:

- A drawing view which represents the cross-section of a part is known as _________.
- You can create hatching in an enclosed area of a drawing view by using the _________ tool or the _________ command.

- The _________ tool is used for selecting a pick point in an enclosed area of a drawing view to create a hatch pattern.
- The _________ tool is used for selecting the previously selected object for removing the hatch pattern created in it.
- The _________ tool is used for making the hatch pattern associative with the object selected.
- The _________ tool is used for creating a gradient in an enclosed area of a drawing view.

CHAPTER

10

Working with Blocks and Xrefs

In this chapter, the following topics will be discussed:

- Creating a Block
- Inserting a Block into a Drawing
- Creating a WBlock
- Inserting a WBlock into a Drawing
- Editing a Block
- Making a Dynamic Block
- Working with External References (Xrefs)

Block is a very powerful feature of AutoCAD, which helps designers speed up the creation of design, increases efficiency, and saves time. For example, in a drawing, you often find some repetitive objects such as symbols and fasteners. Instead of creating the same object, again and again, you can create its block and use it several times in a drawing. A block is a collection of objects that are combined and act as a single object. Figure 10.1 shows a geometry having multiple objects and Figure 10.2 shows the same geometry after converting it into a block, in which all its objects are treated as a single object.

10.1

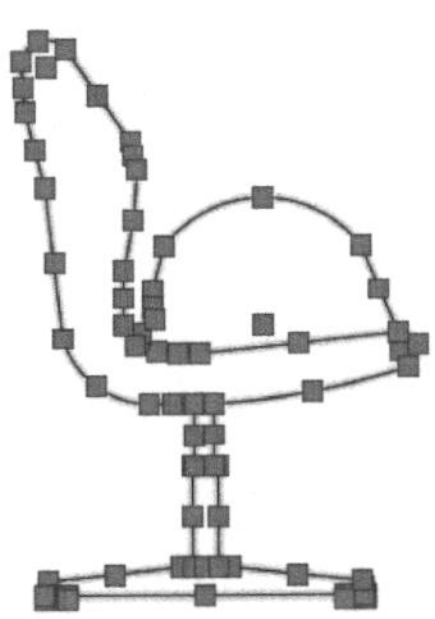

Individual entities/objects

10.2

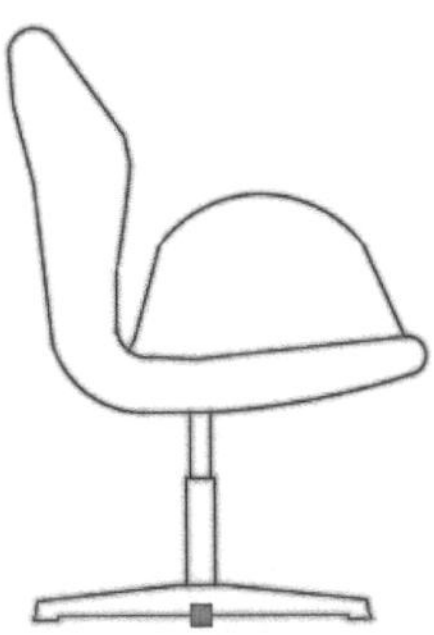

Block (single object)

In AutoCAD, you can create two types of blocks: internal block (Block) and external block (WBlock). An internal block is a group of objects that is saved internally in a drawing and can be used several times within the drawing. It is created by using the BLOCK command and is known as Block. An external block is a group of objects or an entire drawing that is saved as an external file and can be used several times in any drawing. It is created by using the WBLOCK command and is known as WBlock.

Creating a Block

In AutoCAD, you can create a block either by using the **Create Block** tool or the BLOCK command. To create a block, click on the **Create Block** tool in the **Block Definition** panel of the **Insert** tab in the **Ribbon**, see Figure 10.3. The **Block Definition** dialog box appears, see Figure 10.4. Alternatively, enter **B** (shortcut for BLOCK command) in the Command Line window and then press ENTER. The options in the **Block Definition** dialog box are used for specifying the block definition such as block name, insertion point, and objects to be converted into the block. The options are discussed next.

10.3

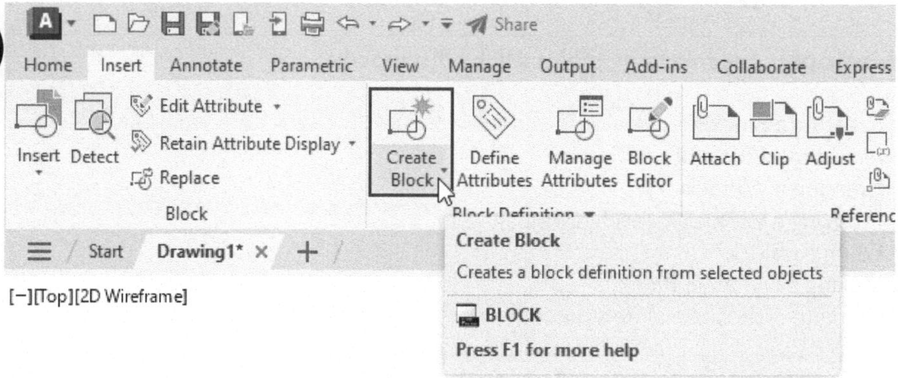

10.4

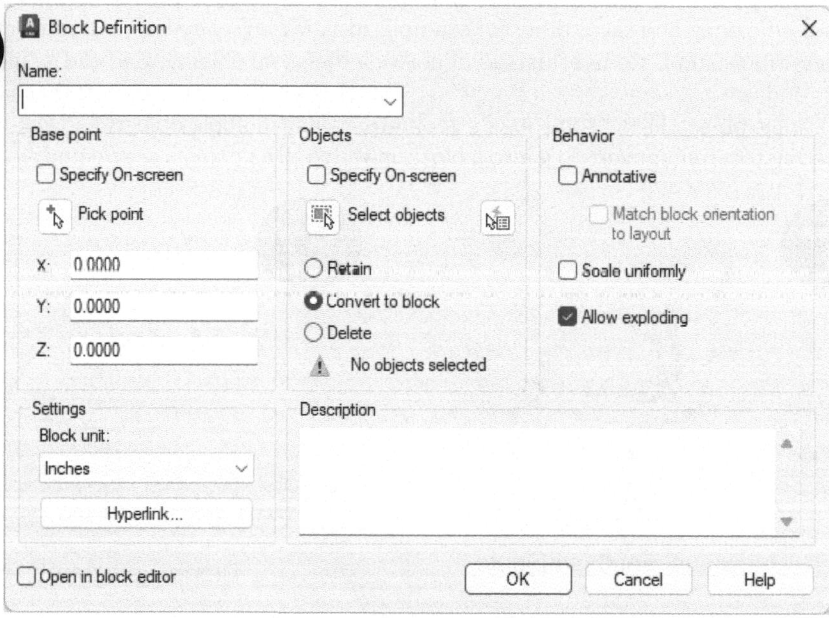

Name

The **Name** field of the dialog box is used for specifying the name of the block. You can write up to 255 characters in a block name, which includes letters, numbers, blank spaces, and any special characters. Note that all the existing blocks created in the current drawing are listed in the **Name** drop-down list of this dialog box. To display the **Name** drop-down list, click on the arrow in the **Name** field of the dialog box, see Figure 10.5.

10.5

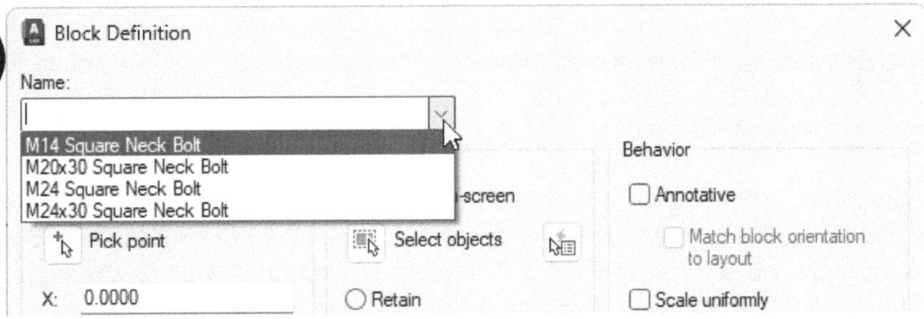

Base Point

The **Base point** area of the dialog box is used for specifying a base/insertion point of the block. A base point of the block is used as a reference point while inserting it into a drawing. You can define a base point by specifying a point in the drawing area or by entering the coordinates (X, Y, Z). To define a base point by specifying a point in the drawing area, click on the **Pick point** button in the **Base point** area. The **Block Definition** dialog box gets closed, and you are prompted to specify the insertion base point.

```
BLOCK Specify insertion base point:
```

Click to specify a point in the drawing area as the base/insertion point of the block, see Figure 10.6. Generally, a corner point or a center point of the geometry is specified as the base point. As soon as you define the base point of the block, the **Block Definition** dialog box appears again, and the coordinates (X, Y, Z) of the selected base point are displayed automatically in the **X**, **Y**, and **Z** fields of the **Base point** area in the dialog box, respectively. Alternatively, you can enter the X, Y, and Z coordinates of the base point in the respective fields of the **Base point** area of the dialog box.

10.6

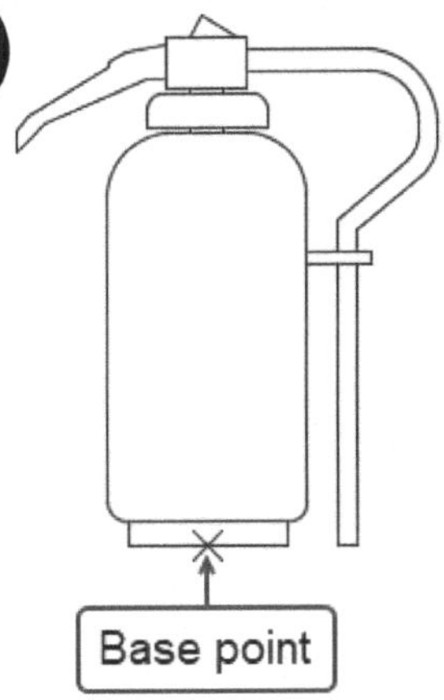

Note: If you do not specify the base point for the block, then the origin point (0,0,0) is used as the base/insertion point of the block, by default.

Objects

The **Objects** area of the dialog box is used for selecting the objects of the drawing to be converted into a block. To select objects, click on the **Select Objects** button in the **Objects** area. The **Block Definition** dialog box gets closed, and you are prompted to select objects to be converted into the block.

```
Select objects:
```

Select objects of the drawing to be converted into a block, see Figure 10.7. You can select the objects by clicking the left mouse button or by using the Window selection or Cross Window selection method. After selecting the objects, press ENTER. The **Block Definition** dialog box appears again and displays information about the number of objects selected at the bottom of the **Objects** area in the dialog box, see Figure 10.8. The remaining options of the **Objects** area of the dialog box are discussed next.

10.7

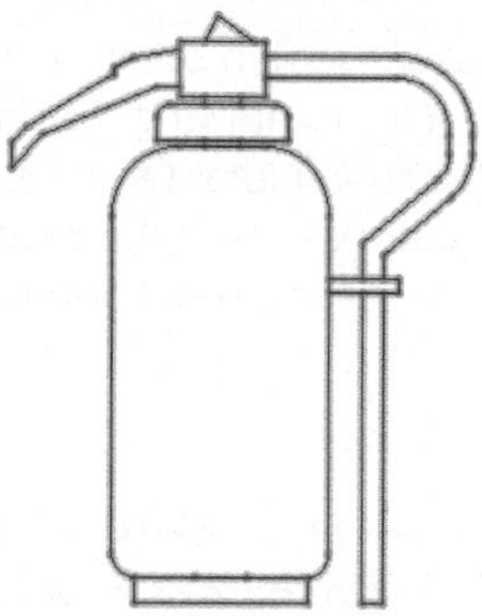

10.8

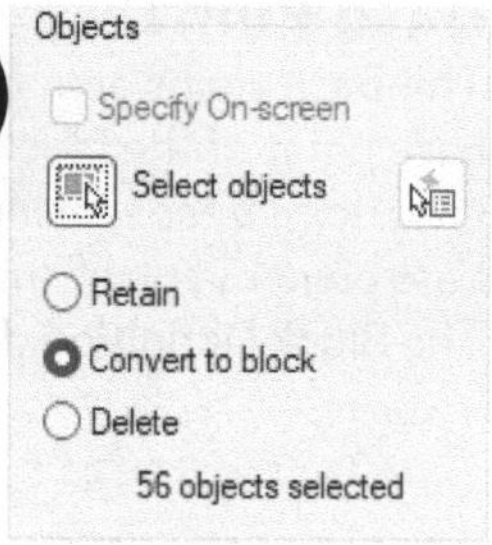

Retain

On selecting the **Retain** radio button in the **Objects** area, the objects that are selected for converting into a block are retained in the drawing area as individual entities and a new block is created, which gets saved internally in the drawing, automatically.

Convert to block

By default, the **Convert to block** radio button is selected in the dialog box. As a result, the selected objects are converted into a block in the drawing area and treated as a single object. Also, a copy of the block gets saved internally in the drawing.

Delete

On selecting the **Delete** radio button, the objects selected for converting into a block get removed from the drawing area, and the block is created, which gets saved internally in the drawing.

Behavior

The options in the **Behavior** area of the dialog box are used for defining the behavior of the block, see Figure 10.9. The options are discussed next.

Annotative

On selecting the **Annotative** check box, the selected objects get converted into an annotative block. An annotative block can be used several times with different scales in a drawing. Also, the size/scale of an annotative block gets adjusted to the appropriate scale of the viewport.

Match block orientation to layout

The **Match block orientation to layout** check box is enabled, if the **Annotative** check box is selected in the **Behavior** area of the dialog box. On selecting this check box, the orientation of the block in the paper space viewports matches the orientation of the layout.

Scale uniformly

On selecting the **Scale uniformly** check box, the block maintains a uniform scale such that it can stretch in all directions evenly. When this check box is unchecked, the block can stretch with different scales in different directions.

Allow exploding

By default, the **Allow exploding** check box is selected in this area. As a result, you can explode the block objects into individual objects.

Settings

The options in the **Settings** area of the dialog box are used for specifying settings for the block, see Figure 10.10. The options are discussed next.

10.9

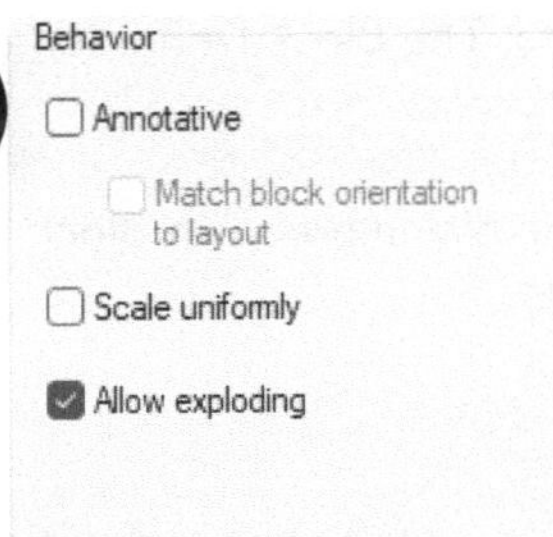

10.10

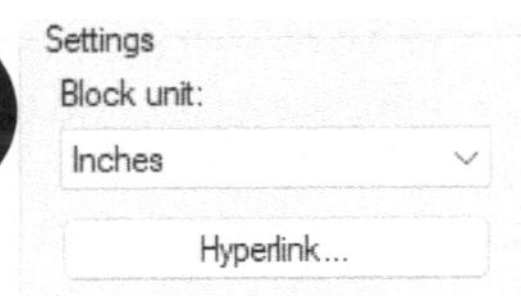

Block unit

The **Block unit** drop-down list is used for specifying the insertion unit for the block. When you insert a block in a drawing, the block will scale as per the insertion unit defined in this drop-down list. By default, the current unit of the drawing is used as the insertion unit for the block and is selected in this drop-down list.

Hyperlink

The **Hyperlink** button is used for assigning a hyperlink to the block. When you click on the **Hyperlink** button, the **Insert Hyperlink** dialog box appears. In this dialog box, you can select the file or specify a web page address (URL) to hyperlink with the block.

Description

The **Description** area of the dialog box is used for adding a brief description of the block.

Open in block editor

On selecting the **Open in block editor** check box, the block is created as per the specified block definitions and opened in the Block Editor when you click on the **OK** button in the dialog box. The Block Editor is used for editing the block definitions. You will learn about editing blocks by using the Block Editor later in this chapter.

After specifying the block definitions such as block name, insertion/base point, and objects to be converted into the block, click on the **OK** button in the dialog box. The block is created and saved internally in the current drawing for further use in the drawing.

Procedure for Creating a Block

1. Click on the **Create Block** tool in the **Block Definition** panel of the **Insert** tab. The **Block Definition** dialog box appears. Alternatively, enter **B** in the Command Line window and then press ENTER.

2. Click on the **Name** field of the dialog box and then specify the name of the block.

3. Click on the **Pick point** button in the **Base point** area of the dialog box. The **Block Definition** dialog box gets closed, and you are prompted to specify the insertion base point. Note that the **Pick point** button is enabled when the **Specify On-screen** check box is unchecked in the **Base point** area of the dialog box.

   ```
   BLOCK Specify insertion base point:
   ```

4. Click to specify a base point for the block in the drawing area. The **Block Definition** dialog box appears again, and the base point is specified.

5. Click on the **Select objects** button in the **Objects** area of the dialog box. The **Block Definition** dialog box gets closed, and you are prompted to select objects.

   ```
   Select objects:
   ```

6. Select the objects to be converted into the block and then press ENTER. The **Block Definition** dialog box appears again, and the objects are selected.

7. Specify remaining block definitions such as annotative, block unit, and hyperlink by using the options of the dialog box. You can also accept the remaining default definitions and skip this step.

8. Click on the **OK** button. The block is created and saved internally in the current drawing.

Inserting a Block into a Drawing

The blocks created in the current drawing can be inserted into the drawing several times by using the **Insert** tool of the **Block** panel in the **Insert** tab. To insert a block into the drawing, click on the **Insert** tool in the **Block** panel of the **Insert** tab. The **Insert** flyout appears which contains a list of all the blocks created in the current drawing, see Figure 10.11. Next, click on the block to be inserted into the drawing. The selected block gets attached to the cursor with its base/insertion point specified while creating the block. Also, you are prompted to specify the insertion point in the drawing area for placing the attached block.

```
Specify insertion point or [Basepoint Scale X Y Z Rotate Explode
REpeat]:
```

10.11

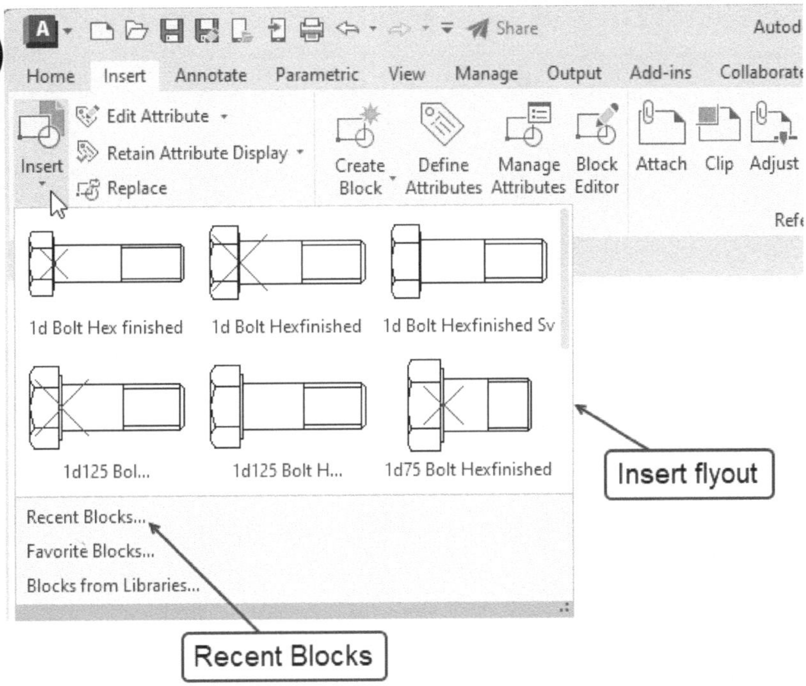

Click in the drawing area to specify the insertion point for the block. The attached block gets inserted at the specified location in the drawing. You can also control the block parameters such as scale and angle of rotation before specifying the insertion point by using the options available in the command prompt or by using the **BLOCKS** palette. The **BLOCKS** palette provides additional options for controlling the block parameters. To invoke the **BLOCKS** palette, click on the **Recent Blocks** option in the **Insert** flyout, refer to Figure 10.11. Alternatively, enter **I** in the Command Line window and press ENTER to invoke the **BLOCKS** palette. Note that the **BLOCKS** palette has four tabs: **Current Drawing**, **Recent**, **Favorites**, and **Libraries**. All these are discussed next.

Recent Tab

By default, the **Recent** tab is activated in the **BLOCKS** palette when you invoke it by clicking on the **Recent Blocks** option in the **Insert** flyout. As a result, all the recently used blocks appear in the **Recent Blocks** area of the **BLOCKS** palette, see Figure 10.12. You can click on a block to be inserted and then specify its insertion point in the drawing area. You can also specify parameters for the block to be inserted such as scale, angle of rotation, and insertion point by using the options available in the **Options** area of the **BLOCKS** palette. The options are discussed next.

Insertion Point

By default, the **Insertion Point** check box is selected in the **Options** area. As a result, when you insert a block, you are prompted to specify an insertion point in the drawing area. If you clear the **Insertion Point** check box, the **X**, **Y**, and **Z** fields appear in front of the **Insertion Point** check box. In these fields, you can specify the X, Y, and Z coordinates of the insertion point.

10.12

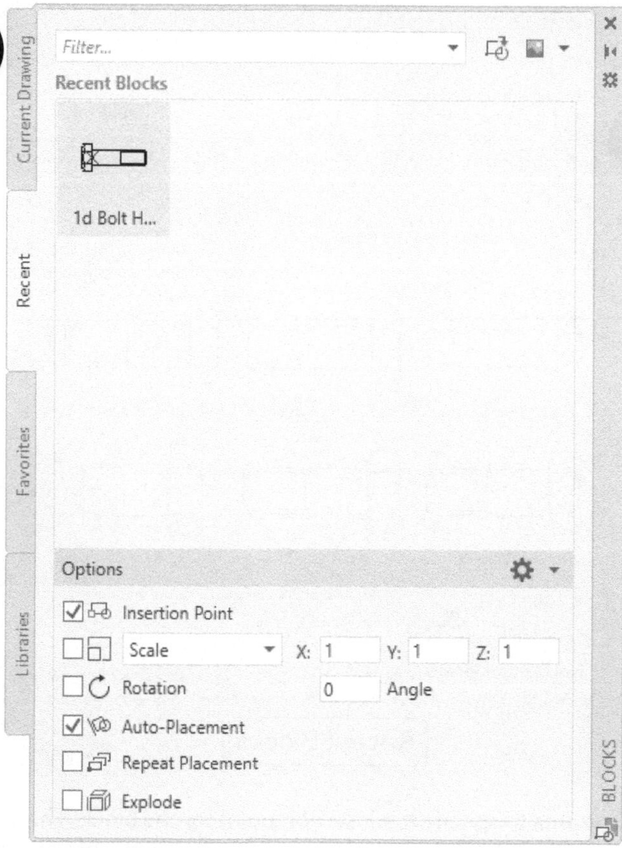

Scale

By default, the **Scale** check box is cleared in the **Options** area of the **BLOCKS** palette. As a result, you can specify non-uniform or uniform scale value for the block to be inserted by selecting the **Scale** or **Uniform Scale** option in the **Scale** drop-down list, respectively. When the **Scale** option is selected in the **Scale** drop-down list, you can specify the scale in the X, Y, and Z axes of the block in the respective fields. When the **Uniform Scale** option is selected, you can specify the uniform scale value in the field that appears.

If you select the **Scale** check box in the **Options** area of the **BLOCKS** palette, then you will be prompted to specify the scale for the block in the drawing area after you specify the insertion point of the block. Note that you can specify a non-uniform or uniform scale in the drawing area depending upon the option selected in the **Scale** drop-down list.

Rotation

When the **Rotation** check box is cleared in the **Options** area of the **BLOCKS** palette, you can specify the rotational angle for the block in the **Angle** field that appears in the palette. When the **Rotation** check box is selected, you will be prompted to specify the rotational angle for the block in the drawing area after defining the insertion point.

Repeat Placement

By default, the **Repeat Placement** check box is cleared. As a result, the block is inserted only once at the specified insertion point in the drawing area. On selecting this check box, you can insert the block multiple times by defining insertion points in the drawing area one after the other. To exit the insertion of the block, press the ESC key.

Explode

By default, the **Explode** check box is cleared. As a result, the block is inserted as a single entity. On selecting this check box, the block gets exploded automatically into individual entities in the drawing area.

Similar to inserting the recently used blocks from the **Recent** tab of the **BLOCKS** palette, you can insert blocks of the current drawing, favorites, and block libraries by activating the **Current Drawing**, **Favorites**, and **Libraries** tabs of the **BLOCKS** palette, respectively. All these tabs are discussed next.

Current Drawing Tab

The **Current Drawing** tab displays a list of all the blocks that are created or are available in the currently opened drawing. The options in this tab are the same as discussed earlier.

Favorites Tab

The **Favorites** tab displays a list of all the blocks that are saved as a favorite. To save an existing block to the **Favorites** tab, right-click on it in the **BLOCKS** palette to display a shortcut menu, see Figure 10.13. In this shortcut menu, click on the **Copy to Favorites** option, see Figure 10.13. Similarly, to remove a block from the **Favorites** tab, right-click on it in the **Favorites** tab and then click on the **Remove from Favorites List** option in the shortcut menu that appears.

10.13

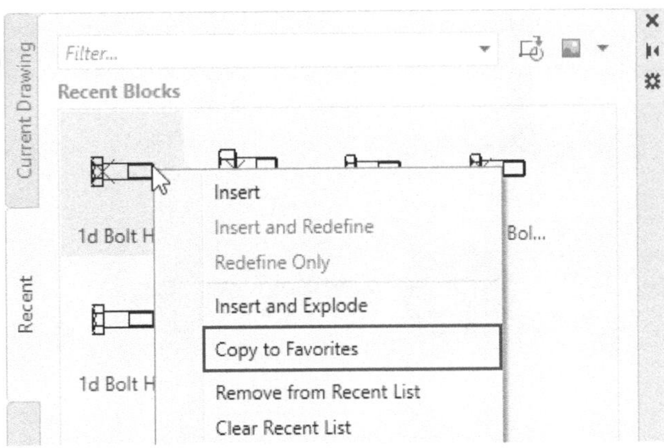

Libraries Tab

The **Libraries** tab is used for inserting a block from a block library or another drawing. To access the blocks of the other drawing, click on the button available in the **Libraries** tab, see Figure 10.14. The **Select a folder or file for Block Library** dialog box appears. In this dialog box, browse to the required location and then select a drawing file. Next, click on the **Open** button. The selected drawing file and all its blocks appear in the palette. Now, you can insert the block in the drawing area. You can also insert the entire drawing as a block in the current drawing. Note that a block library is a single file containing blocks. You can use the Autodesk block library from the web or create your own.

10.14

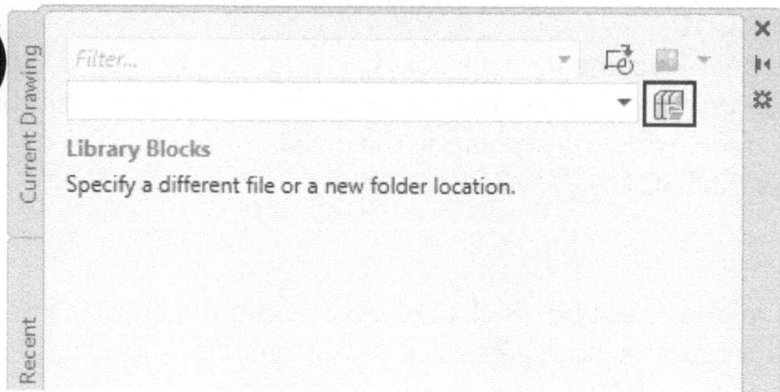

After specifying all the parameters for inserting the block in the **Options** area of the **BLOCKS** palette, click on the block to be inserted in the dialog box. The selected block gets attached to the cursor with its base/insertion point, which is specified while creating the block, see Figure 10.15. Also, you are prompted to specify the insertion point in the drawing area. Click to specify an insertion point for the block. The block gets inserted at the specified insertion point, see Figure 10.16. In this figure, the block is inserted by specifying the insertion point at location 1 as marked in Figure 10.15. Similarly, you can insert the same block several times in the drawing by selecting the **Repeat Placement** check box. Figure 10.17 shows a drawing in which 6 instances of the block are inserted into the drawing.

10.15

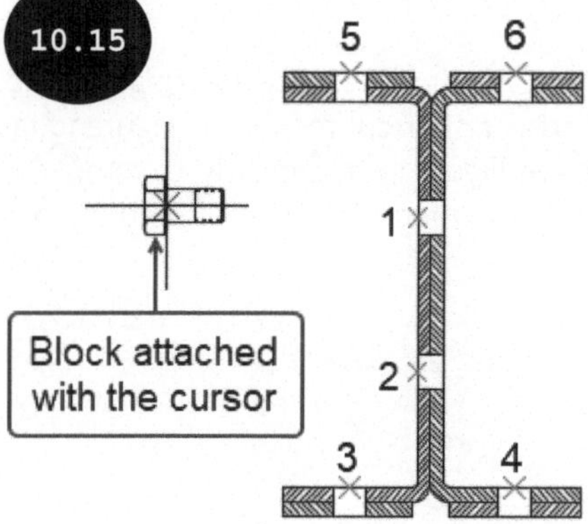

10.16

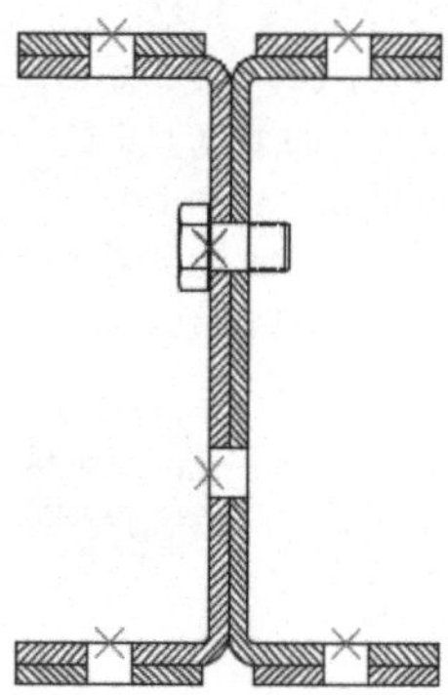

10.17

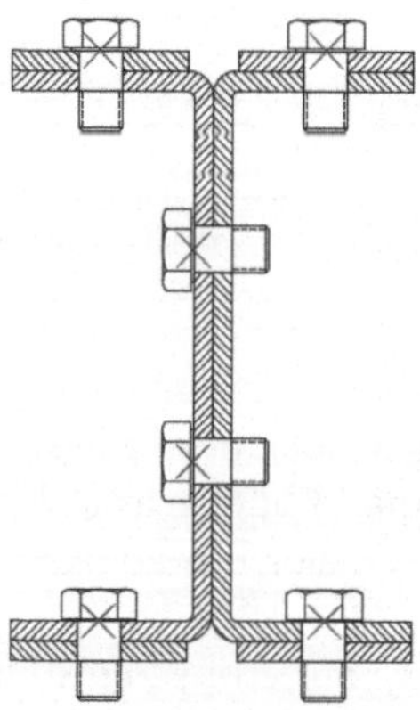

Tip: You can control the display of blocks as list, details, small icons, large icons, etc, in the **BLOCKS** palette by using the options available in the **Icon or List Style** drop-down list, see Figure 10.18.

10.18

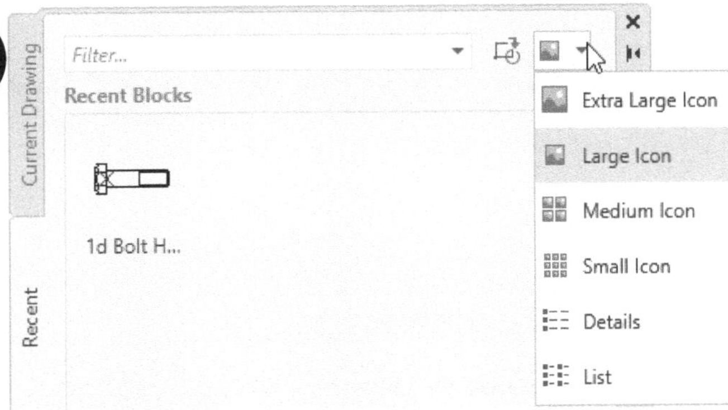

Creating a WBlock

A WBlock is a group of objects or an entire drawing that is saved as an external file and acts as a single object. In AutoCAD, WBlocks are same as the Blocks, with the only difference being that the WBlocks are saved as external files and can be inserted several times in any drawing, whereas the Blocks are saved in the same drawing in which they are created. You can create a WBlock either by using the **Write Block** tool or by using the WBLOCK command. To create a WBlock, click on the **Write Block** tool in the **Block** flyout of the **Block Definition** panel in the **Insert** tab, see Figure 10.19. The **Write Block** dialog box appears, see Figure 10.20. Alternatively, enter W in the Command Line window and then press ENTER. W is the shortcut of the WBLOCK command. The **Write Block** dialog box has two areas: **Source** and **Destination**. The options for both these areas are discussed next.

10.19

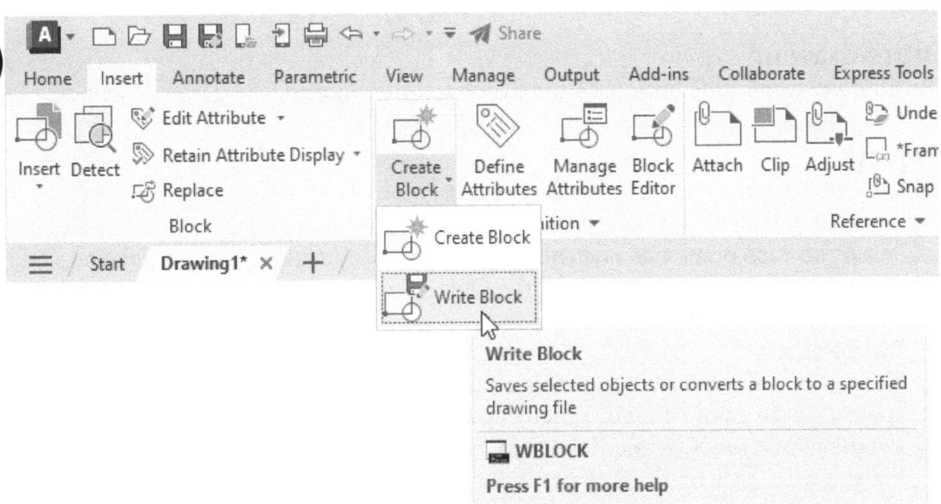

10.20

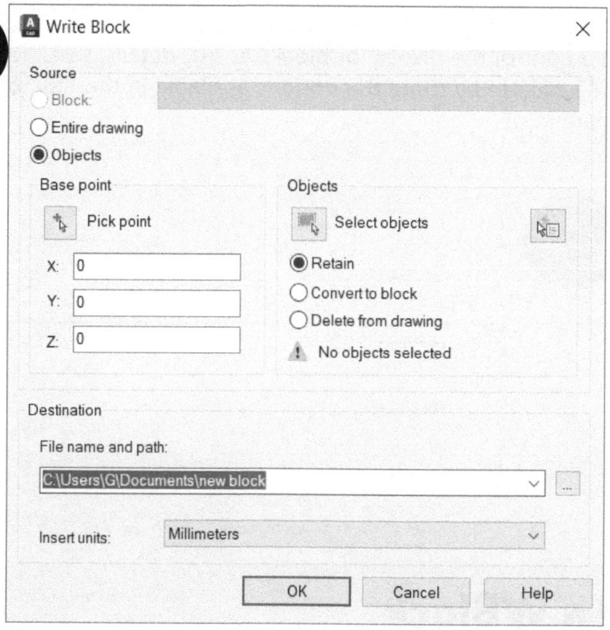

Source

The options in the **Source** area of the dialog box are used for specifying whether the block, the entire drawing, or objects of the drawing are to be converted into a WBlock. The options are discussed next.

Block

The **Block** radio button is used for selecting an existing block for converting into a WBlock. On selecting the **Block** radio button, the **Block** drop-down list gets enabled in front of this radio button. In this drop-down list, select the required Block to be converted into a WBlock. Note that the **Block** radio button is enabled only when the current drawing has existing Blocks available.

Entire drawing

The **Entire drawing** radio button is used to convert the whole drawing into a WBlock.

Objects

The **Objects** radio button is used for selecting a group of objects of the drawing to be converted into a WBlock. By default, this radio button is selected in the **Source** area of the dialog box. As a result, the options in the **Base point** area and the **Objects** area of the dialog box are enabled, see Figure 10.20. The options of the **Base point** area and the **Objects** area are discussed next.

Base Point

The options of the **Base point** area are used for selecting a base point for the WBlock. You can specify a base point either by specifying a point in the drawing area or by entering its X, Y, and Z coordinates in the **X**, **Y**, and **Z** fields of the dialog box, respectively. To specify a base point in the drawing area, click on the **Pick point** button in the **Base point** area of the dialog box. The **Write Block** dialog box gets closed, and you are prompted to specify an insertion base point. Click in the drawing area to specify the base point. The **Write Block** dialog box appears again, and the base point is specified.

Objects

The options of the **Objects** area are used for selecting a group of objects to be converted into a WBlock. To select objects, click on the **Select objects** button of this area. The **Write Block** dialog box gets closed, and you are prompted to select objects. Select objects in the drawing area by clicking the left mouse button or by using the Window/Cross Window selection method. After selecting the objects, press ENTER. The **Write Block** dialog box appears again, and the information about the number of objects selected appears at the bottom of this area, see Figure 10.21. Similar to this, the other options such as **Retain**, **Convert to block**, and **Delete from drawing** of this area are same as those discussed earlier while creating the Blocks using the **Create Block** tool.

10.21

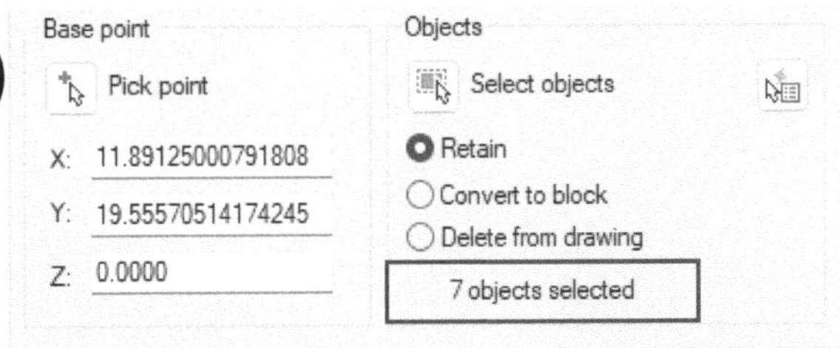

Destination

After specifying the source (block, entire drawing, or objects) for creating a WBlock, you need to define the name and the destination where you want to save the WBlock. You can specify a name and the destination for the WBlock by using the options in the **Destination** area of the dialog box. The options are discussed next.

File name and path

The **File name and path** field is used for specifying a name and the location where the WBlock has to be saved. To specify a name and a location for the WBlock, click on the [...] button to the right of this field. The **Browse for Drawing File** dialog box appears. In this dialog box, browse to the location where you want to save the WBlock and then enter a new name for the WBlock in the **File name** field of this dialog box. Next, click on the **Save** button. The **Browse for Drawing File** dialog box gets closed, and the specified location and the name appear in the **File name and path** field of the **Write Block** dialog box.

Insert units

The **Insert units** drop-down list is used for selecting the unit for the WBlock.

After specifying the source and destination, click on the **OK** button. The **Write Block** dialog box gets closed, and the WBlock is saved in the specified location.

Inserting a WBlock into a Drawing

You can insert a WBlock into any drawing by using the **Insert > Blocks from Libraries** tool of the **Block** panel in the **Insert** tab or by using the INSERT command. To insert a WBlock into a drawing, enter **I** in the Command Line window and then press ENTER. The **BLOCKS** palette appears. Next, click on the **Libraries** tab in the **BLOCKS** palette, see Figure 10.22.

10.22

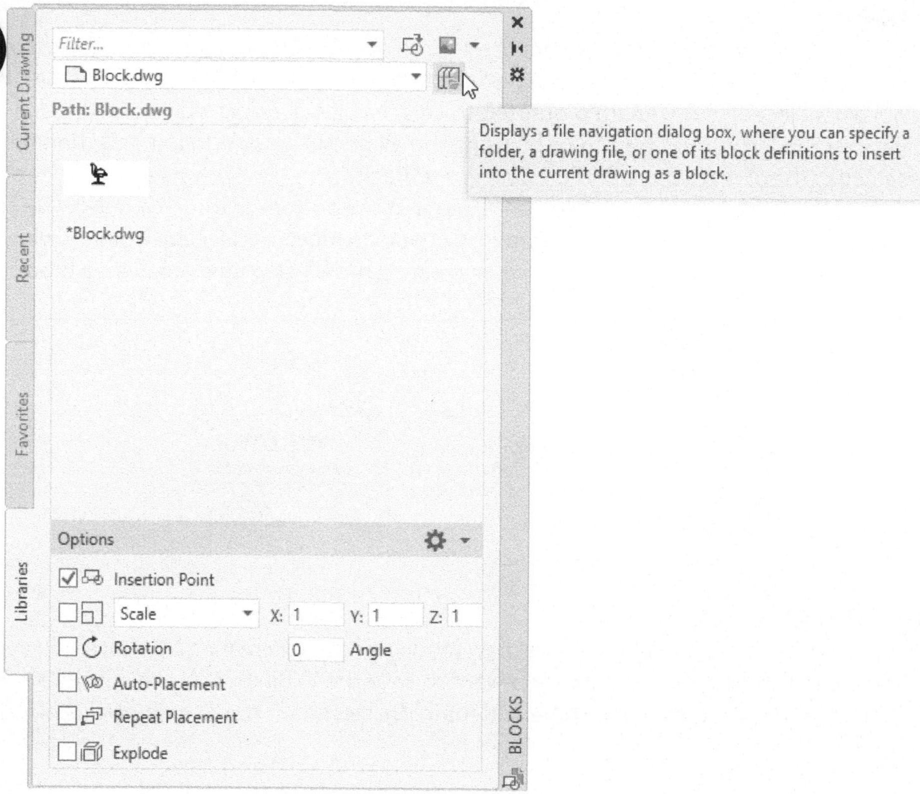

In the **BLOCKS** palette, click on the button, see Figure 10.22. The **Select a folder or file for Block Library** dialog box appears. In this dialog box, browse to the location where the WBlock has been saved and then click on the WBlock to insert it into the drawing. Next, click on the **Open** button in the dialog box. The **Select a folder or file for Block Library** dialog box gets closed, and the selected WBlock appears in the **BLOCKS** palette, see Figure 10.22. Next, specify other parameters such as scale and angle of rotation in the respective fields of the **Options** area on the **BLOCKS** palette. The options in the **BLOCKS** palette are the same as those discussed earlier. After specifying the parameters, click on the Wblock to be inserted. The selected WBlock gets attached to the cursor with the base point specified while creating it. Next, click to specify the insertion point in the drawing area. The WBlock gets inserted at the specified insertion point. Similarly, you can insert the WBlock several times in the drawing.

Editing a Block

In a drawing, you may need to edit or modify existing blocks. In AutoCAD, you can edit the existing blocks either by using the **Block Editor** tool or the BEDIT command. To edit a block, click on the **Block Editor** tool in the **Block Definition** panel of the **Insert** tab, see Figure 10.23. The **Edit Block Definition** dialog box appears, see Figure 10.24. It displays a list of all the blocks available in the current drawing. Alternatively, enter **BE** in the Command Line window and then press ENTER (BE is the shortcut for the BEDIT command).

10.23

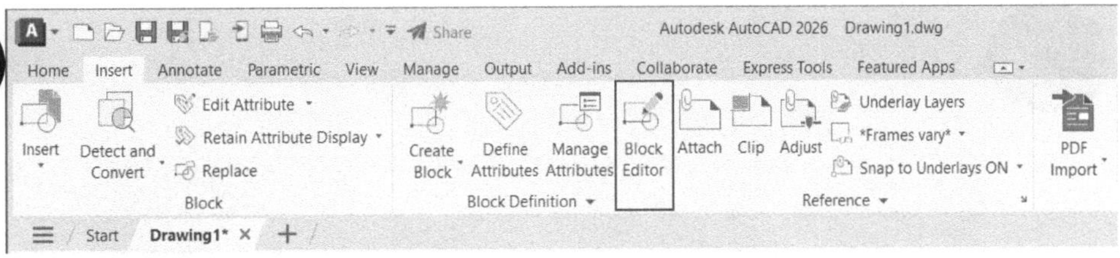

10.24

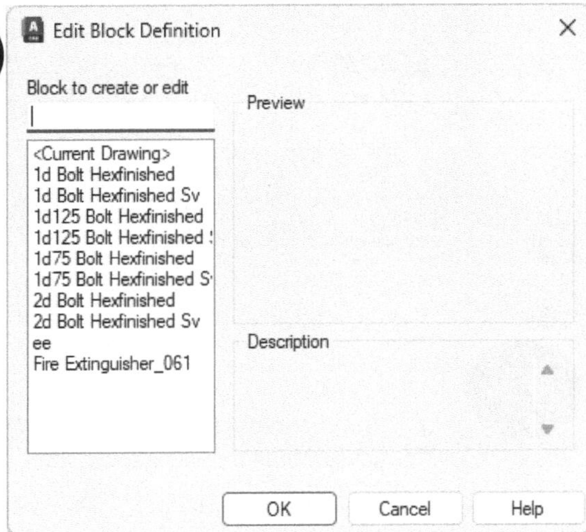

Click on the block to be edited in the **Edit Block Definition** dialog box. A preview of the selected block appears in the **Preview** area of the dialog box. Next, click on the **OK** button. The selected block is opened in the Block Editor, and the **Block Editor** tab appears in the **Ribbon**, see Figure 10.25. Now, you can make the changes in the block such as add new entities, delete existing entities, stretch, rotate, and so on, by using the tools of the **Home** tab in the **Ribbon**. The tools in the **Block Editor** tab are used to make the block dynamic. You will learn more about making a dynamic block later in this chapter. After making the necessary changes in the block, click on the **Save Block** tool in the **Open/Save** panel of the **Block Editor** tab. The changes made in the block get saved. Next, click on the **Close Block Editor** tool in the **Close** panel of the **Block Editor** tab to close the Block Editor. Note that if you have not saved the block after making the changes then by clicking the **Close Block Editor** tool, the **Block - Changes Not Saved** window appears, see Figure 10.26.

10.25

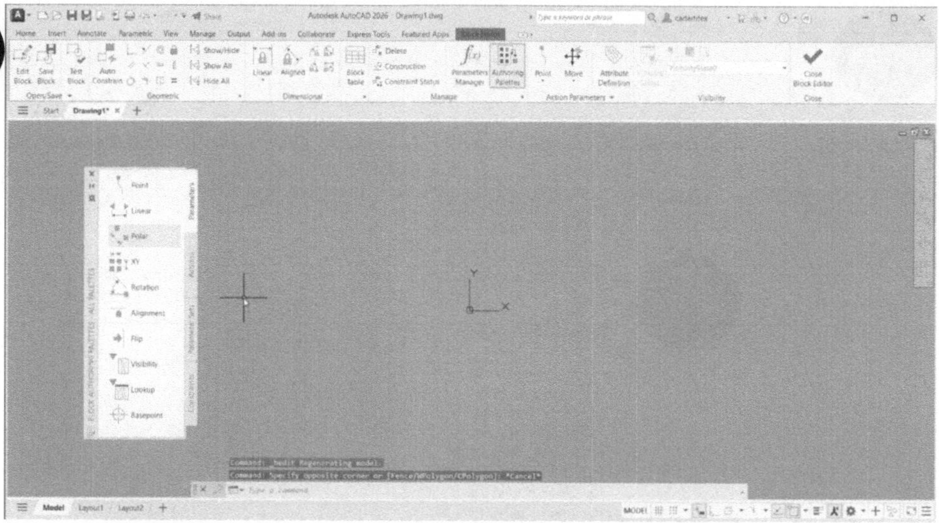

10.26

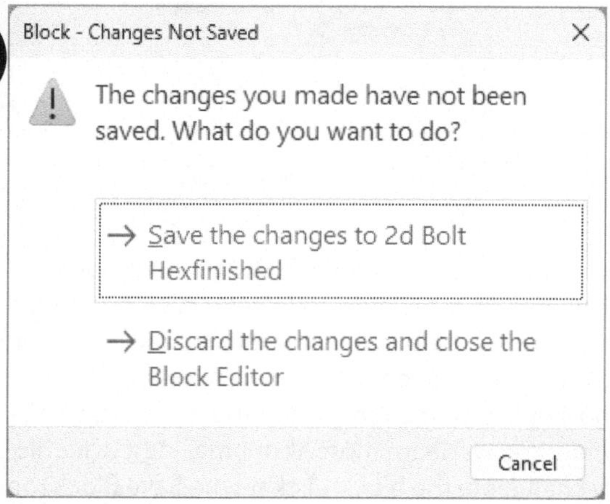

In the **Block - Changes Not Saved** window, click on **Save the changes to** *'the name of the block'* option to save the changes made in the Block Editor. To discard the changes made, click on **Discard the changes and close the Block Editor** option.

Making a Dynamic Block

A dynamic block is a block that can be modified dynamically in the drawing area. You can make a block dynamic by specifying the required parameters and actions using the tools in the **Block Editor** tab. To make a dynamic block, click on the **Block Editor** tool in the **Block Definition** panel of the **Insert** tab, see Figure 10.27. The **Edit Block Definition** dialog box appears. Alternatively, enter **BE** in the Command Line window and then press ENTER (BE is the shortcut of the BEDIT command).

10.27

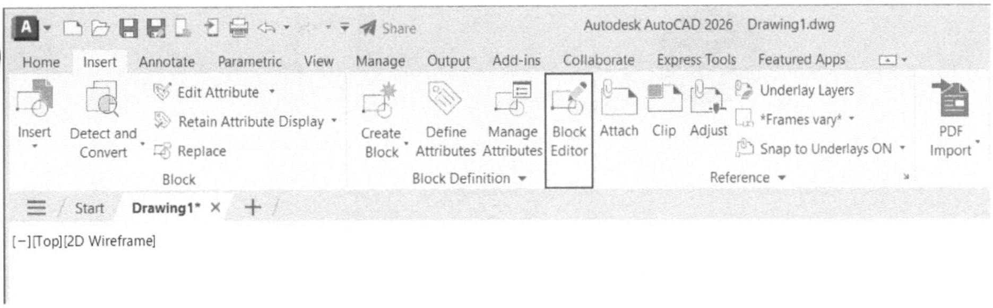

In the **Edit Block Definition** dialog box, select the block to be edited or converted into a dynamic block and then click on the **OK** button. The selected block gets opened in the Block Editor, and the **Block Editor** tab appears in the **Ribbon**, see Figure 10.28. In this figure, a rectangular block representing a table appears in the Block Editor.

10.28

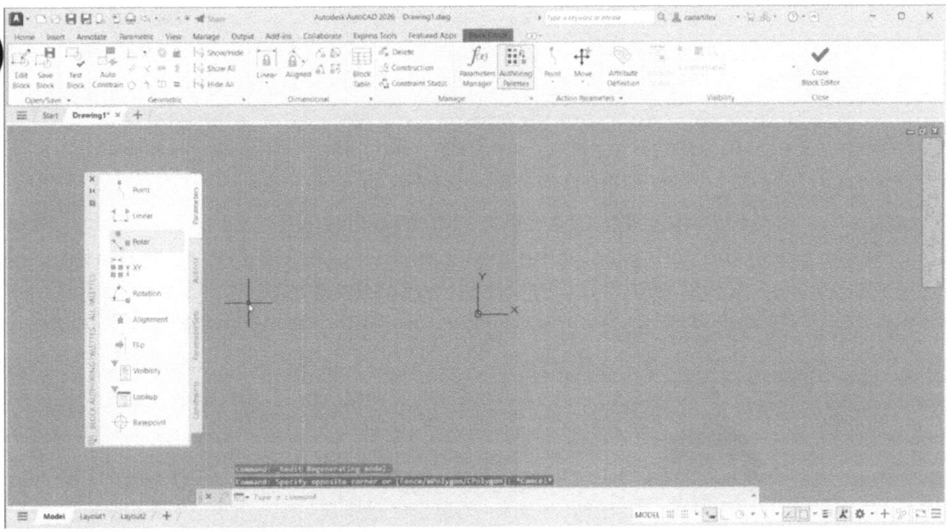

Once the block is opened in the Block Editor, you can make the block dynamic by specifying the required parameters and actions. To specify parameters for creating a dynamic block, click on the **Parameters** tab in the **BLOCK AUTHORING PALETTES**. The tools to specify parameters appear, see Figure 10.29. By using the tools of the **Parameters** tab, you can specify the parameters for the dynamic block.

For example, to specify a linear parameter, click on the **Linear** tool in the **Parameters** tab. You are prompted to specify the start point.

```
Specify start point or [Name Label Chain Description Base Palette
Value set]:
```

10.29

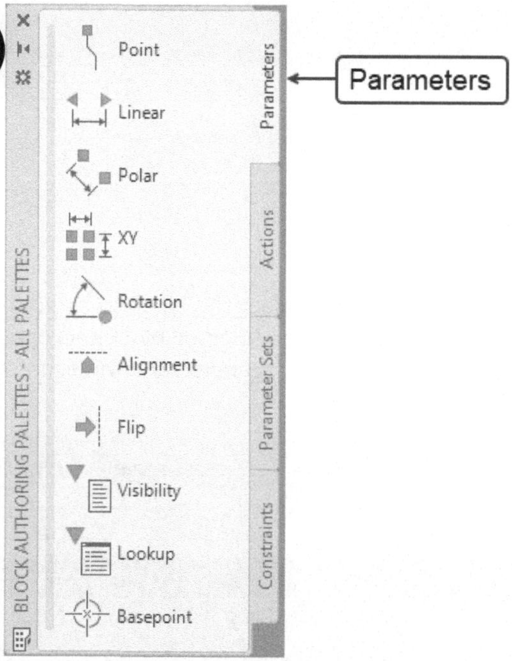

Next, click to specify the start point for the linear parameter, see Figure 10.30. In this figure, the midpoint of the upper horizontal line of the rectangle is defined as the start point. As soon as you specify the start point, a label is attached to the cursor, and you are prompted to specify the endpoint, see Figure 10.30.

```
Specify endpoint:
```

10.30

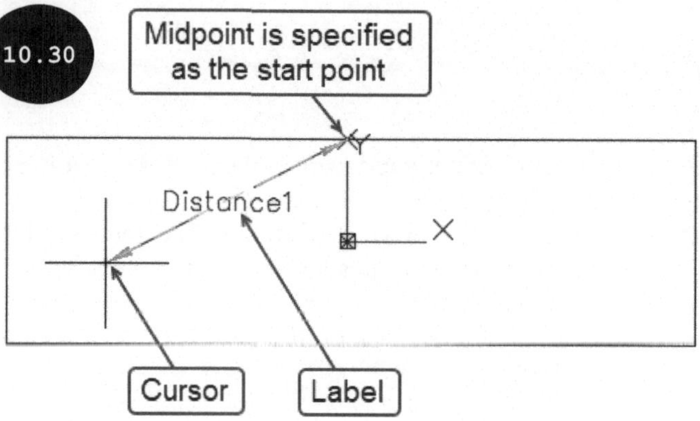

Next, click to specify the endpoint of the label, see Figure 10.31. You are prompted to specify the label location.

```
Specify label location:
```

Click to specify the label location. The label is placed in the specified location and the linear parameter is defined. Also, the grips appear at the specified midpoints, see Figure 10.32. The linear parameter allows you to modify the block in a linear fashion dynamically, by using the grips in the drawing area. However, only specifying the linear parameter does not make the block dynamic. You also need to specify the action such as stretch, scale, or move for the linear parameter.

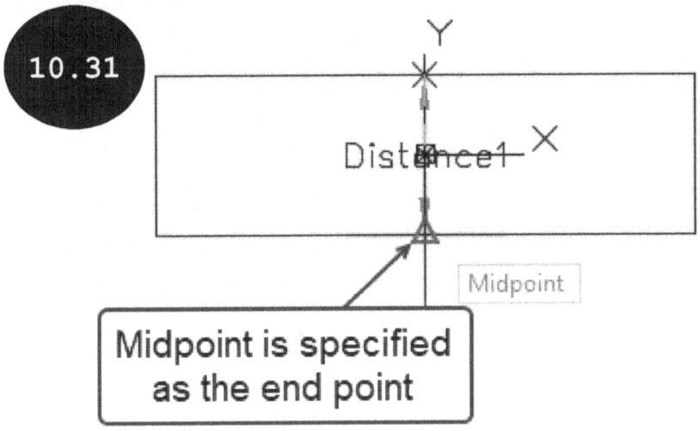

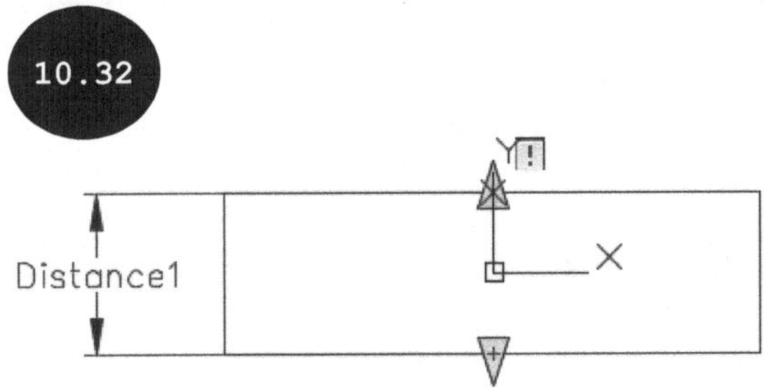

To specify the action for the parameter, click on the **Actions** tab in the **BLOCK AUTHORING PALETTES**. The tools to specify actions for the parameter such as **Move, Scale, Stretch,** and **Flip** appear in the **Actions** tab, see Figure 10.33.

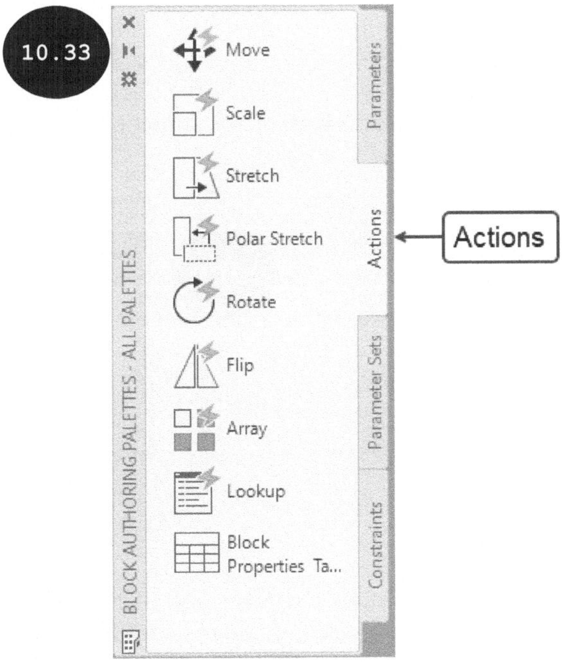

For example, to specify a stretch action for the linear parameter, click on the **Stretch** tool in the **Actions** tab of the **BLOCK AUTHORING PALETTES**. You are prompted to select a parameter for specifying the action.

```
Select parameter:
```

Click on the parameter (linear parameter) for specifying the action. You can click on the label of the parameter to select it. As soon as you select the parameter (linear parameter), you are prompted to specify the parameter point to associate the action.

```
Specify parameter point to associate with action or enter [sTart
point Second point] <Second>:
```

Move the cursor over the grip, which is displayed at the midpoint of the upper horizontal line. The cursor snaps to the midpoint and a cross mark appears, see Figure 10.34. Next, click on the midpoint of the upper horizontal line as the parameter point to associate the action. You are prompted to specify the first corner of the stretch frame. Note that the stretch frame is used for defining the objects to be stretched by using the grips in the drawing area, dynamically. You can create a stretch frame by specifying its two diagonally opposite corners.

```
Specify first corner of stretch frame or [CPolygon]:
```

Click to specify the first corner of the stretch frame, see Figure 10.34. You are prompted to specify the opposite corner of the stretch frame.

```
Specify opposite corner:
```

Move the cursor diagonally and then click to specify the second corner of the stretch frame, see Figure 10.35. You are prompted to select objects to be stretched.

```
Select objects:
```

10.34

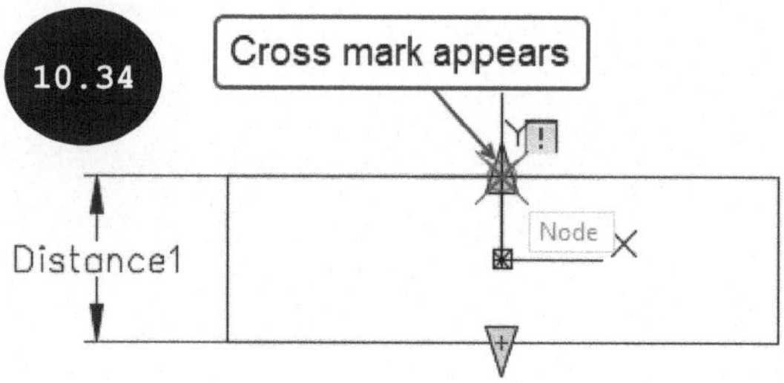

10.35

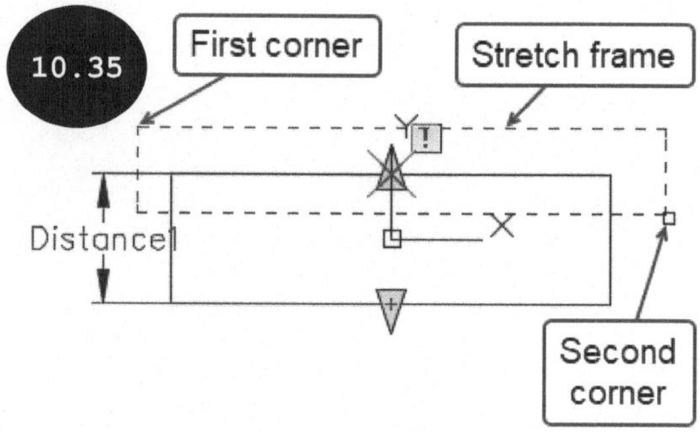

Click on the rectangle as the object to be stretched. Next, press ENTER. The stretch action is assigned to the upper selected grip of the rectangle. Similarly, assign the stretch action to the grip, which appears at the midpoint of the lower horizontal line of the block (rectangle). After assigning the parameter and the required action to it, click on the **Close Block Editor** tool in the **Close** panel of the **Block Editor** tab. The **Block - Changes Not Saved** window appears, see Figure 10.36. Click on **Save the changes to** *'name of the block'* in the **Block - Changes Not Saved** window. The changes made in the Block Editor are saved and the Block Editor gets closed. Also, the block becomes a dynamic block.

10.36

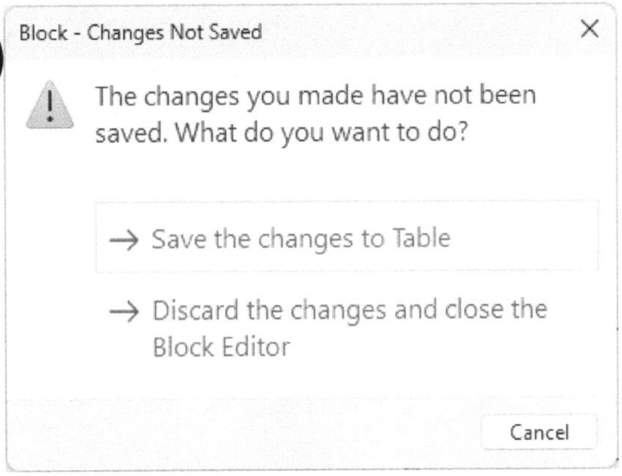

Now, if you select the block (dynamic block) in the drawing area, the grips of the dynamic block appear, see Figure 10.37. By using these grips, you can stretch the block, dynamically in the drawing.

10.37

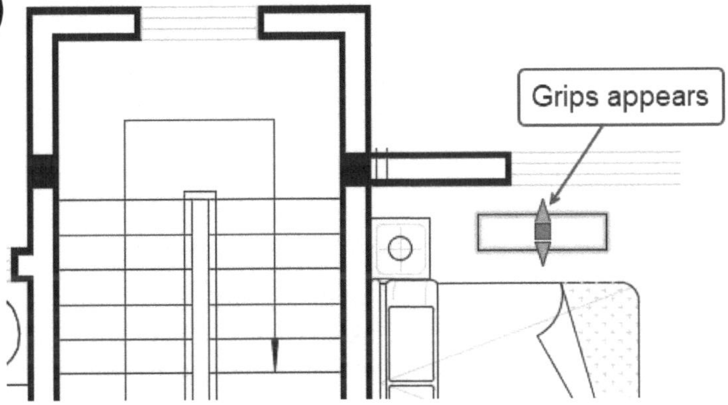

Working with External References (Xrefs)

In AutoCAD, external references (Xrefs) are the drawings that are linked or attached to the current drawing, externally. External references (Xrefs) drawings are not a permanent part of the drawing and are connected externally to the drawing. The external references (Xrefs) drawings are most widely used in large assembly drawings, which have multiple parts. You can create drawings of all parts as individual drawings and then assemble them in the main drawing as external references (Xrefs). External references also allow multiple users (CAD Engineers or Operators) to work on a single project (drawing) and then assemble all the drawings created by different users as external references to the main drawing. You can attach external references to a drawing by using the **EXTERNAL REFERENCES** Palette. To invoke the **EXTERNAL REFERENCES** Palette, click on the **External References Palette** tool in the **Palettes** panel of the **View** tab, see Figure 10.38. The **EXTERNAL REFERENCES** palette appears, see Figure 10.39. Alternatively, enter **XREF** in the Command Line window and then press ENTER to invoke this palette.

10.38

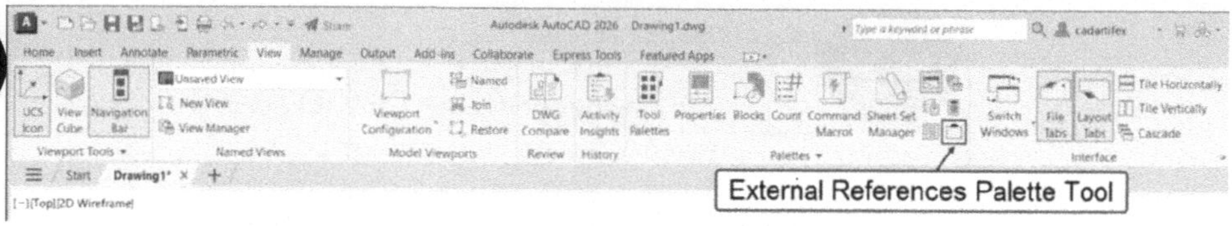

10.39

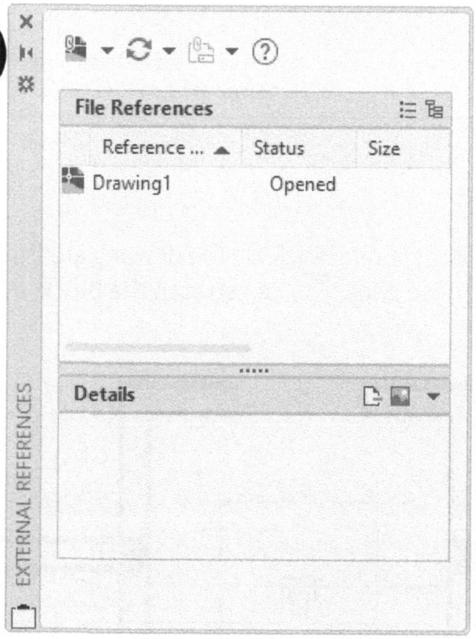

The **EXTERNAL REFERENCES** palette is used for attaching a new Xref, detaching an existing Xref, unloading the attached Xref and reloading the unloaded Xref. Also, the **EXTERNAL REFERENCES** Palette displays the current status of each Xref that is attached in the current drawing.

To attach an Xref in the current drawing, click on the arrow in the **Attach** tool of the **EXTERNAL REFERENCES** palette. The **Attach** flyout appears, see Figure 10.40. By using the tools of this flyout, you can attach DWG, Image, DWF, DGN, PDF, Point Cloud, and Coordination Model files. For example, to attach a DWG file, click on the **Attach DWG** tool in the **Attach** flyout. The **Select Reference File** dialog box appears. In this dialog box, browse to the location where the file to be attached is saved. Next, select the DWG file and then click on the **Open** button. The **Attach External Reference** dialog box appears, see Figure 10.41.

10.40

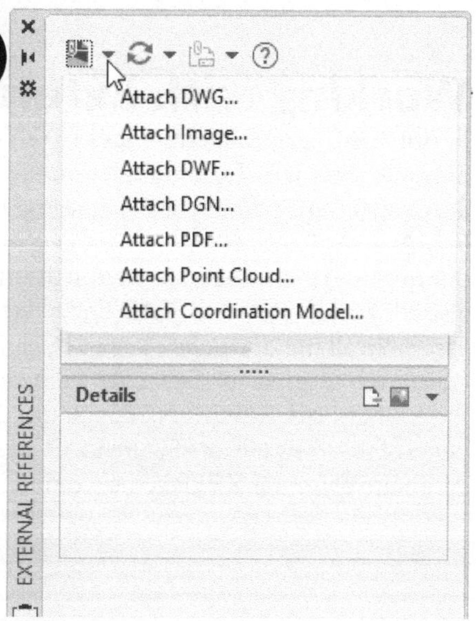

10.41

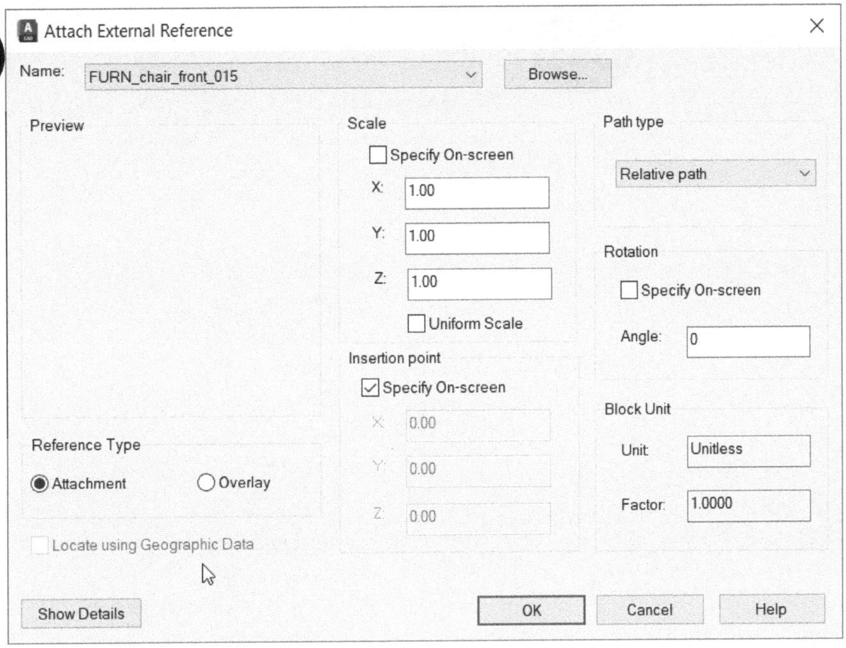

In the **Attach External Reference** dialog box, specify the parameters such as scale, insertion point, reference type, and rotation for attaching the external reference. Next, click on the **OK** button. The selected DWG file is attached to the cursor at its base point and you are prompted to specify the insertion point.

```
Specify insertion point or [Scale X Y Z Rotate PScale PX PY PZ
PRotate]:
```

Click to specify the insertion point in the drawing area. The selected drawing (DWG) is attached to the current drawing and placed at the specified insertion point. Also, the name of the attached drawing is listed in the **EXTERNAL REFERENCES** palette. Similarly, you can attach multiple files to the current drawing.

To detach an Xref, unload the attached Xref, reload the unloaded Xref, and so on, click on the Xref in the **EXTERNAL REFERENCES** palette and then right-click. A shortcut menu appears, see Figure 10.42. In this shortcut menu, click on the required option. For example, if you want to unload the Xref, click on the **Unload** option. The selected file gets unloaded and disappears from the current drawing. Also, a symbol of an arrow appears in front of the file name in the **EXTERNAL REFERENCES** palette. You can reload the unloaded file. To do so, click on the name of the drawing file to be reloaded in the current drawing and then right-click. A shortcut menu appears. In this shortcut menu, click on the **Reload** option. The file gets reloaded and is visible in the drawing area. Similarly, you can detach the existing Xrefs, change the Xref type, and so on. The **Details** area of the **EXTERNAL REFERENCES** palette displays the status of the selected Xref file.

10.42

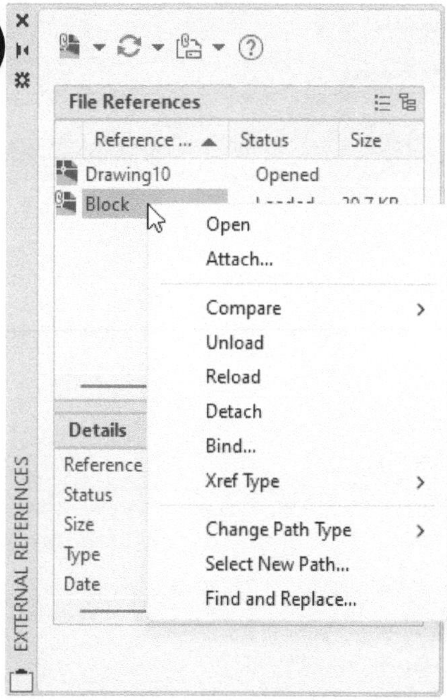

In AutoCAD, if any modification is made to an external reference file of a drawing, then on opening the drawing that has the modified external reference file, AutoCAD displays a message on the lower right corner of the screen informing about the changes made. Click on this message to view details of the changes. The **Xref Compare** appears and the differences in current and previous versions of that file are shown in different colors, see Figure 10.43. You can invoke the **Settings** drop-down list, which contains the color scheme for different sets of entities of both versions, see Figure 10.43. You can choose to display the required set of entities such as entities that are not in the updated version or only the entities that have been altered by choosing the required option from this drop-down list. In Figure 10.43, the entities in red show the earlier position of the bed and entities in green show the new position of the bed. After comparing the changes, exit the **Xref Compare** by clicking on the green tick-mark in the toolbar.

10.43

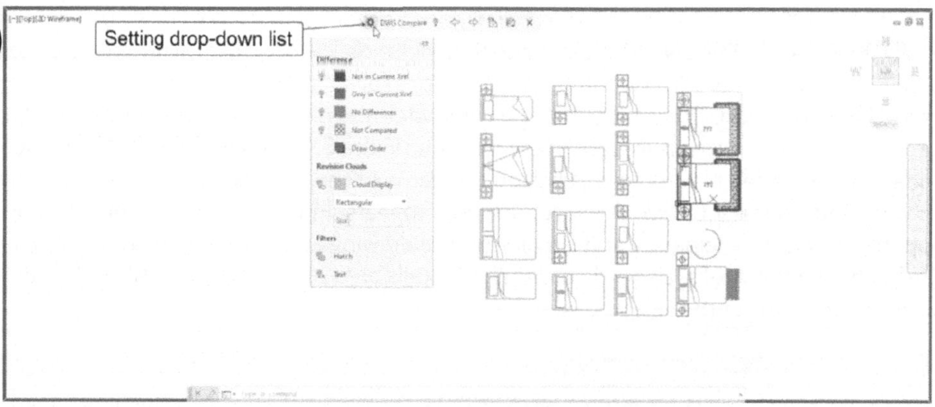

Tutorial 1

Create the objects: arrow, condenser, exchanger, boiler, pump, flux drum, and valve as shown in Figure 10.44, and then convert them into blocks. After creating the blocks, create the process flow diagram and insert the blocks in it, see Figure 10.45. Do not apply dimensions to the blocks. Also, you can assign the missing dimensions. You also need to add single line text in the flow diagram, see Figure 10.45.

10.44

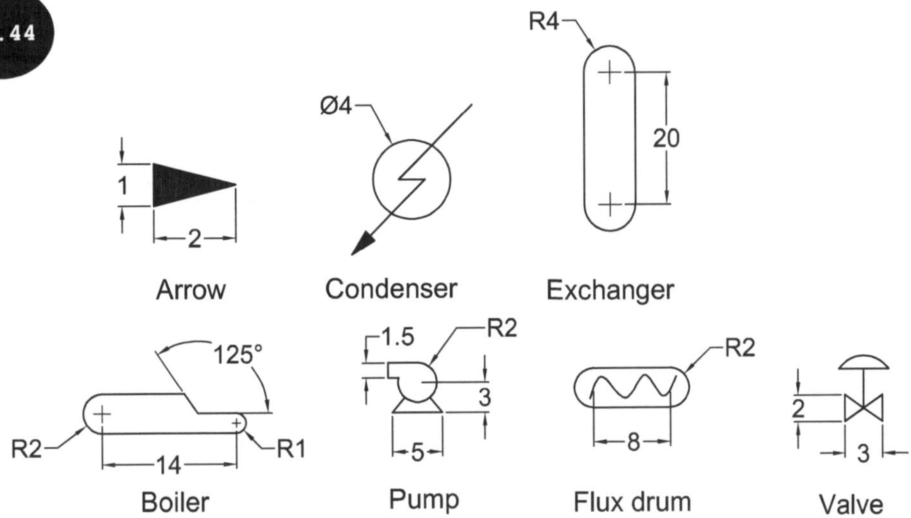

10.45

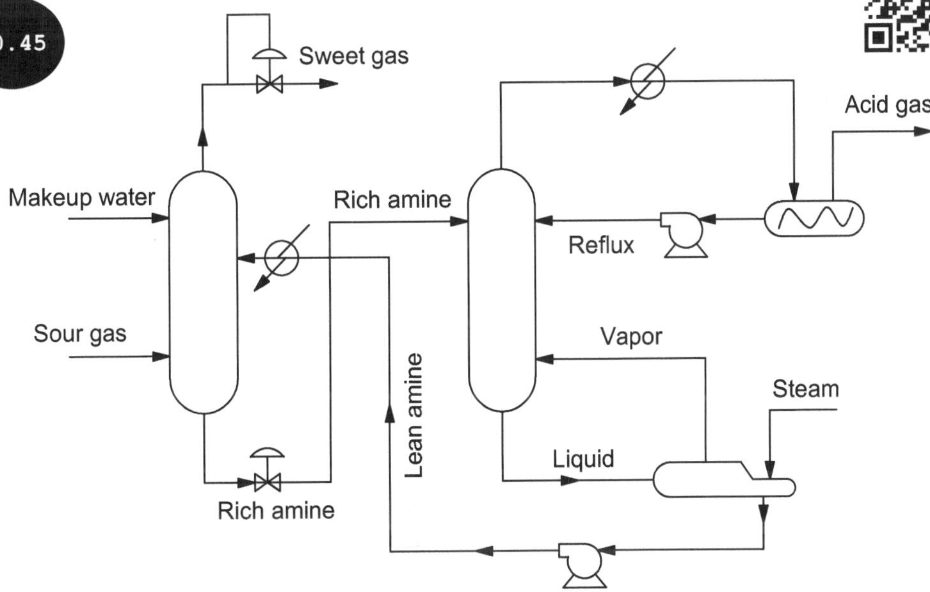

Section 1: Starting AutoCAD

1. Start AutoCAD and then open a new drawing file.

Section 2: Creating Blocks

1. Create the drawing of an arrow as shown in Figure 10.46, by using the **Line** tool. For the overall size of the arrow, refer to Figure 10.44.

2. Fill the enclosed area of the arrow with a solid hatch pattern by using the **Hatch** tool, see Figure 10.47.

10.46

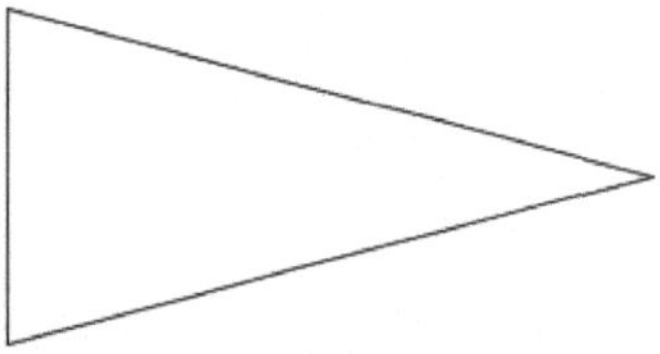

10.47

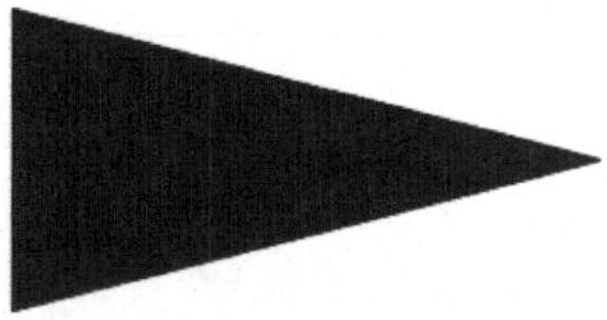

After creating the arrow, you need to convert it into a block.

3. Click on the **Insert** tab in the **Ribbon**. The tools of the **Insert** tab of the **Ribbon** appear, see Figure 10.48.

10.48

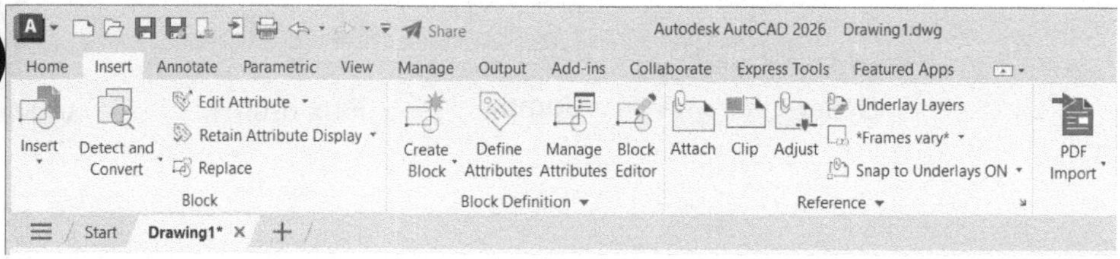

4. Click on the **Create Block** tool in the **Block Definition** panel of the **Insert** tab. The **Block Definition** dialog box appears, see Figure 10.49.

10.49

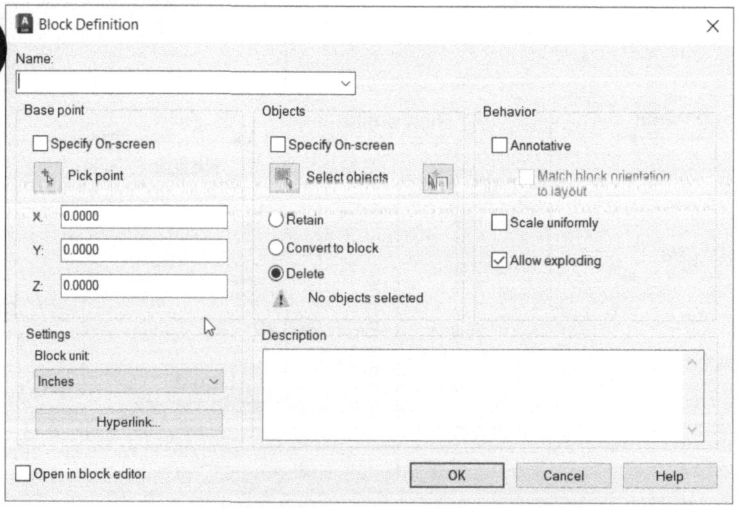

5. Enter **Arrow** as the name of the block in the **Name** field of the dialog box.

6. Click on the **Pick point** button in the **Base point** area of the dialog box. The dialog box disappears, and you are prompted to specify the insertion base point.

```
_block specify insertion base point:
```

7. Click on the tip of the arrow as the insertion base point of the block, see Figure 10.50. The base point is defined and the **Block Definition** dialog box appears again.

8. Click on the **Select objects** button in the **Objects** area of the dialog box. The dialog box disappears, and you are prompted to select objects.

```
Select objects:
```

9. Select all the entities of the arrow object including the hatch pattern in the drawing area by using the Window selection method, see Figure 10.51.

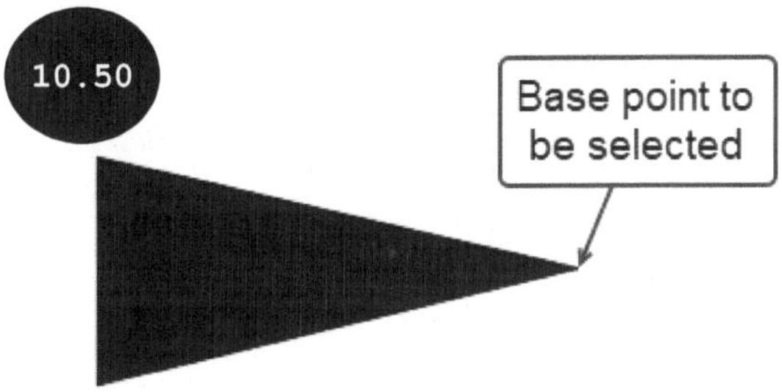

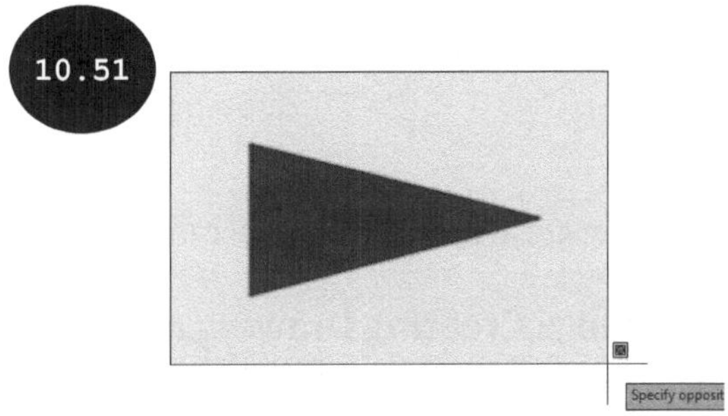

10. After selecting all the entities of the object, press ENTER. The entities are selected and the **Block Definition** dialog box appears again.

11. Select the **Delete** radio button in the **Objects** area of the dialog box to delete the selected entities (arrow) in the drawing area and to create the block in the drawing.

12. Click on the **OK** button in the **Block Definition** dialog box. The Arrow block is created and saved internally in the drawing. Also, it is deleted from the drawing area.

13. Similarly, create the remaining objects: condenser, exchanger, boiler, pump, flux drum, and valve and then convert them into blocks, see Figure 10.52. In this figure, the cross mark indicates the base point of the objects.

10.52

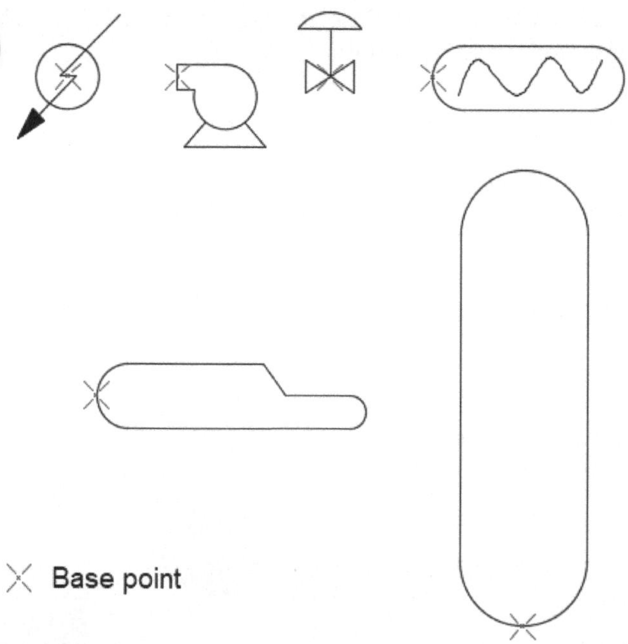

After creating the blocks, you can create the drawing and insert the blocks in it.

Section 3: Creating Drawing and Inserting Blocks

1. Click on the **Insert** tab in the **Ribbon**. The tools of the **Insert** tab of the **Ribbon** appears.

2. Click on the **Insert** tool in the **Block** panel of the **Insert** tab. The **Block** flyout appears with the display of all the blocks created in the drawing, see Figure 10.53. In this flyout, you may need to scroll the list to select the required block.

10.53

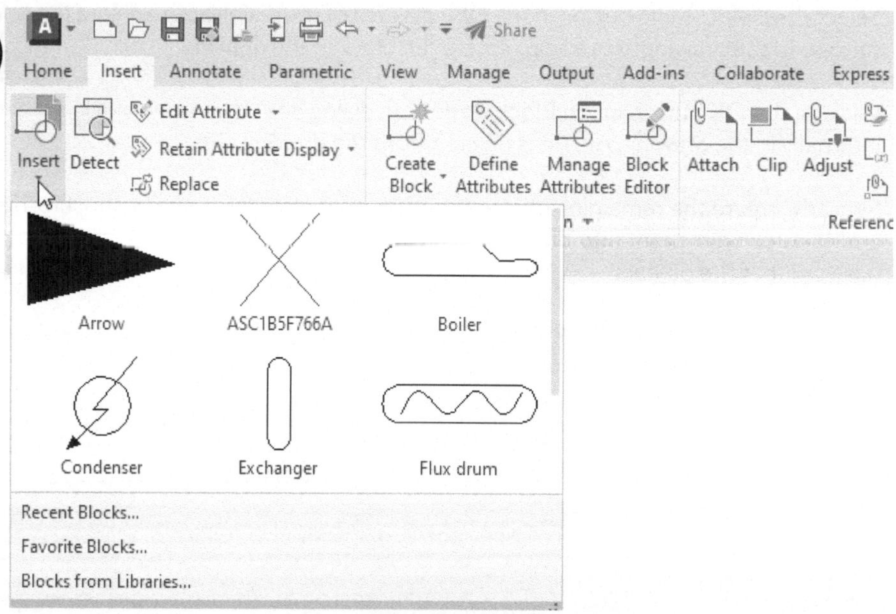

3. Click on the Exchanger block in the flyout that appears. The Exchanger block is attached to the cursor at its specified base point. Also, you are prompted to specify the insertion point.

```
Specify insertion point or [Basepoint Scale Rotate Explode REpeat]:
```

4. Click anywhere in the drawing area to specify the insertion point of the Exchanger block. The Exchanger block is placed at the specified location in the drawing area.

5. Similarly, insert another instance of the Exchanger block in the drawing area, see Figure 10.54. Note that you need to place the second instance of the Exchanger block inline with the first inserted Exchanger block by keeping some space between them, see Figure 10.54.

10.54

6. Invoke the **Line** tool and then create the line entities of the drawing as shown in Figure 10.55. You can assume the length of the lines. In the figure, the cross marks (P1 through P6) indicate the insertion points for the blocks in the drawing and are for your reference only.

10.55

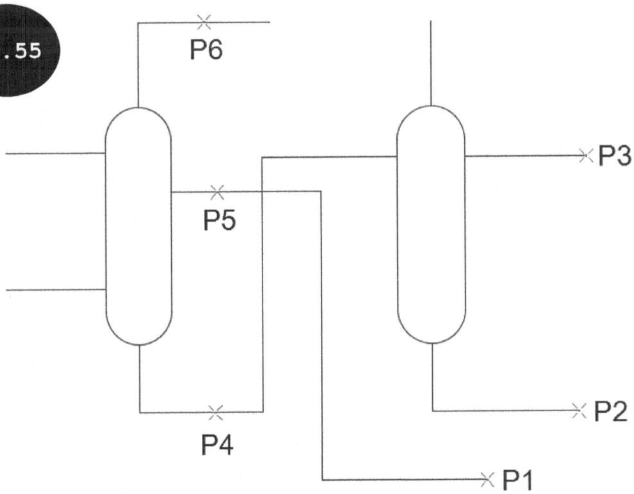

7. Click on the **Insert** tool in the **Block** panel of the **Insert** tab. The **Block** flyout appears. In this flyout, click on the Pump block. The Pump block is attached to the cursor at its specified base point. Also, you are prompted to specify an insertion point.

```
Specify insertion point or [Basepoint Scale Rotate Explode REpeat]:
```

8. Move the cursor toward the insertion point "P1" in the drawing, refer to Figure 10.55. Next, click to specify the insertion point for the Pump block. The Pump block is placed at the specified insertion point in the drawing area, see Figure 10.56.

10.56

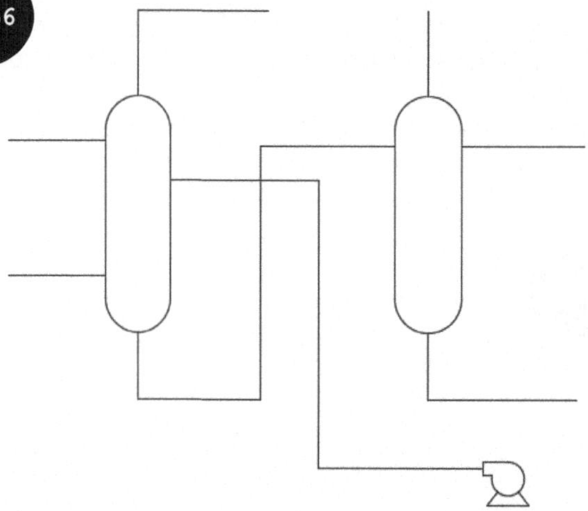

9. Similarly, insert a Boiler block at the insertion point "P2", a Pump block at the insertion point P3, a Valve block at the insertion point P4, a Condenser block at the insertion point P5, and a Valve block at the insertion point P6, see Figure 10.57.

10.57

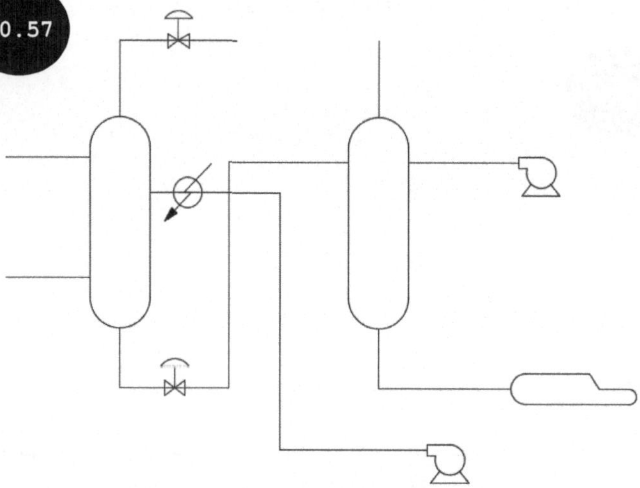

10. Create the line entities (L1 through L10) of the drawing by using the **Line** tool, see Figure 10.58. You can assume the length of the lines. Note that Figure 10.58 is numbered for your reference only.

10.58

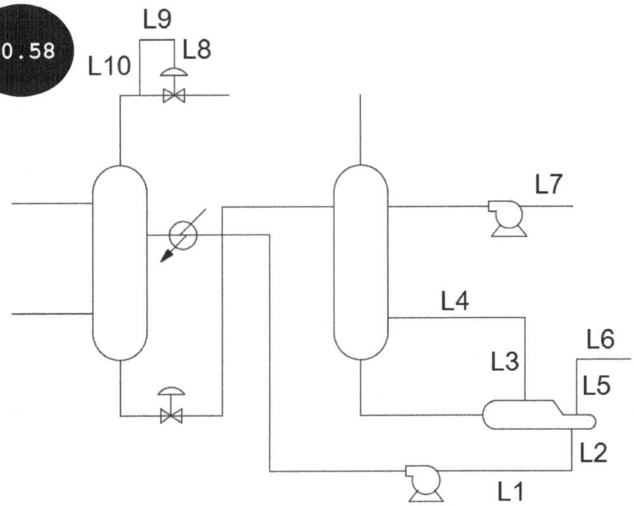

11. Insert the Flux drum block at the endpoint of the line "L7", see Figure 10.59.

10.59

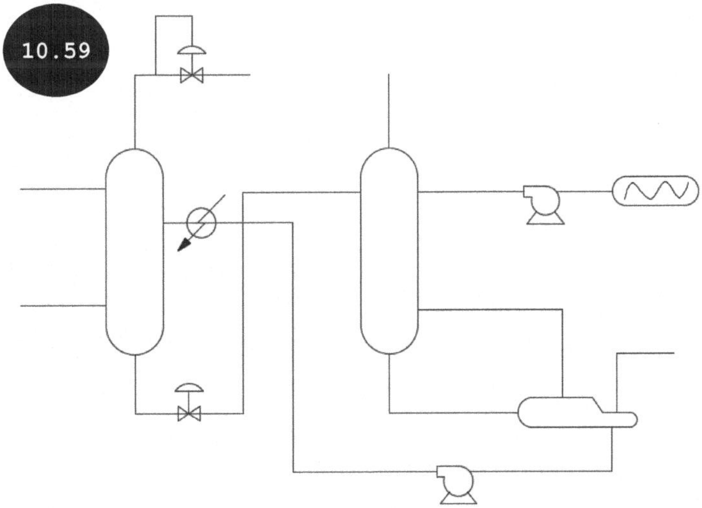

12. Create the line entities (L11 through L14) of the drawing by using the **Line** tool, see Figure 10.60. You can assume the length of the lines. Note that Figure 10.60 is numbered for your reference only.

10.60

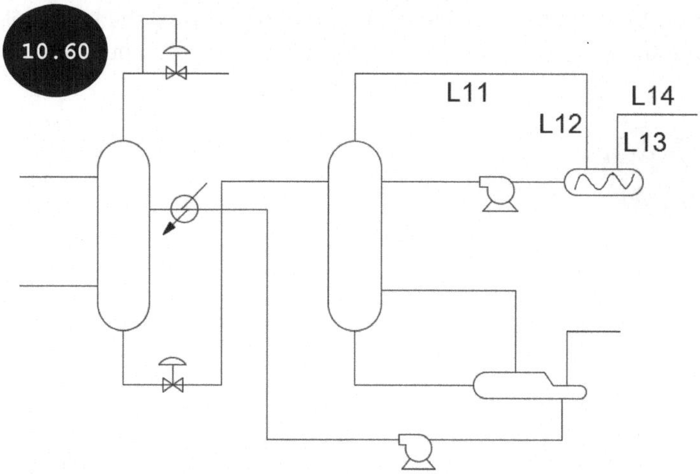

13. Insert the Condenser block at the midpoint of the Line "L11", see Figure 10.61.

10.61

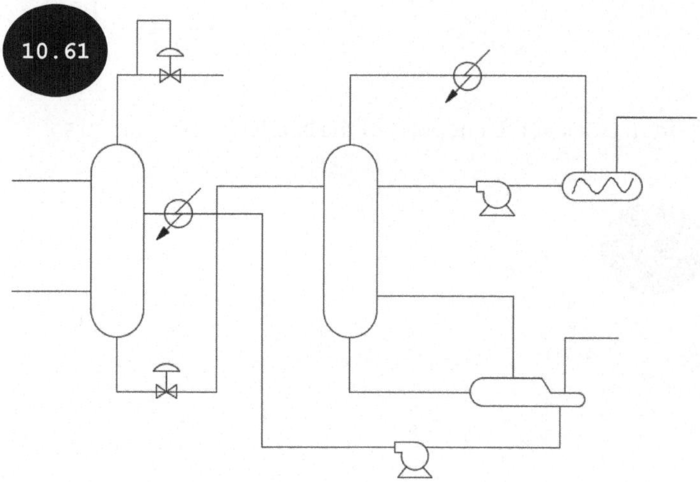

Now, you need to insert the Arrow blocks in the drawing to define the flow of the process in the drawing.

14. Click on the **Insert** tool in the **Block** panel of the **Insert** tab. The **Block** flyout appears. In this flyout, click on the Arrow block. The Arrow block gets attached to the cursor at its base point. Also, you are prompted to specify an insertion point.

```
Specify insertion point or [Basepoint Scale Rotate Explode REpeat]:
```

15. Move the cursor to the endpoint of the line "L14", refer to Figure 10.60. Next, click to specify the insertion point of the Arrow block when the cursor snaps to it. The Arrow block is inserted and placed at the specified insertion point, see Figure 10.62.

10.62

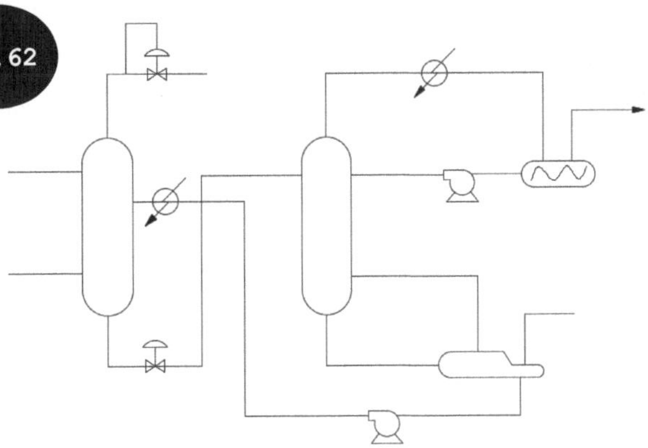

16. Again, invoke the **Block** flyout and then click on the Arrow block. The Arrow block gets attached to the cursor at its specified base point. Also, you are prompted to specify an insertion point.

```
Specify insertion point or [Basepoint Scale Rotate Explode REpeat]:
```

17. Click on the **Rotate** option in the command prompt. You are prompted to specify a rotation angle. Alternatively, enter **R** in the Command Line window and then press ENTER.

```
Specify rotation angle <0>:
```

18. Enter **-90** in the Command Line window and then press ENTER. The rotation angle of the attached Arrow block changes.

19. Move the cursor to the end point of the Line "L12", refer to Figure 10.60. Next, click to specify the insertion point of the Arrow block when the cursor snaps to it. The Arrow block is inserted and placed at the specified insertion point, see Figure 10.63.

20. Similarly, insert the Arrow blocks at the remaining locations of the drawing, see Figure 10.64. You can click on the **REpeat** option in the command prompt, when prompted to specify the insertion point, to insert multiple instances of the arrow having same orientation.

10.63

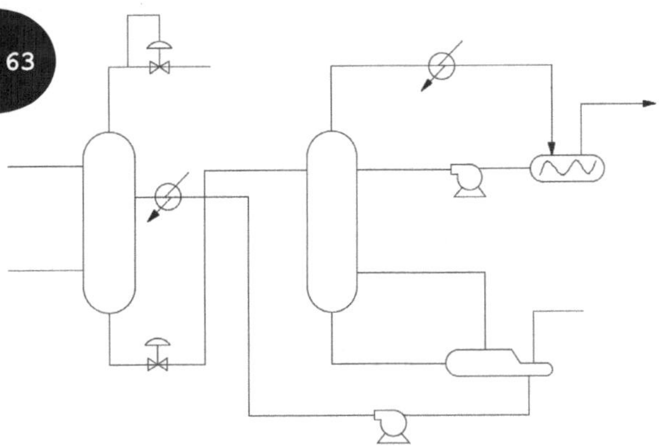

10.64

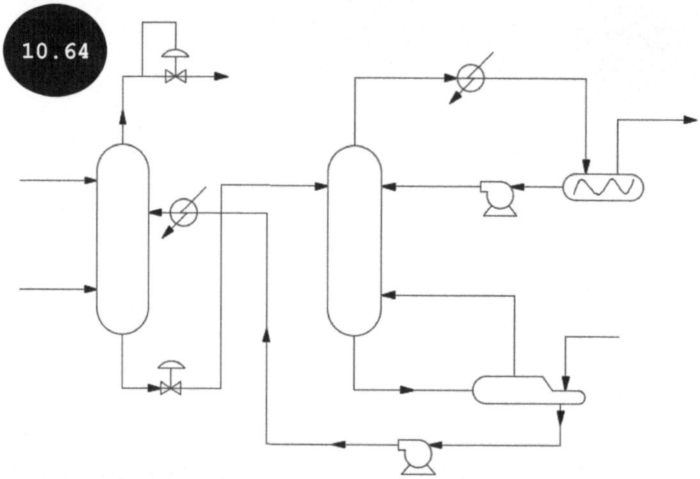

Section 4: Adding Single Line Text

1. Add the single line text in the drawing area by using the **Single Line** tool, see Figure 10.65.

10.65

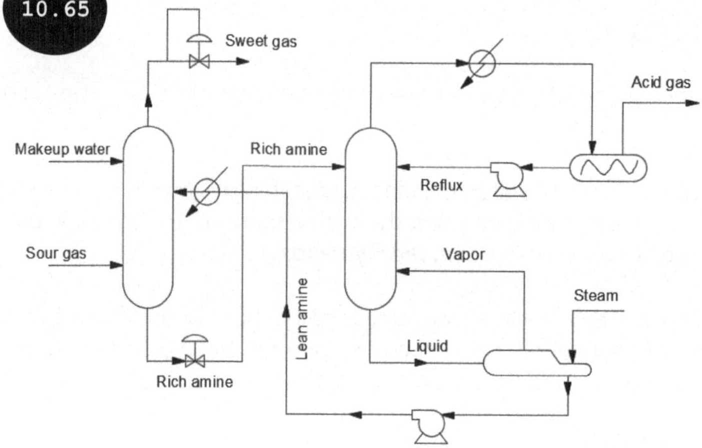

Section 5: Saving the Drawing

1. Click on the **Save** tool in the **Quick Access Toolbar**. The **Save Drawing As** dialog box appears.

2. Browse to the *AutoCAD* folder and then create a folder with the name *Chapter 10* inside the *AutoCAD* folder. Next, enter **Tutorial 1** in the **File name** field of the dialog box.

3. Click on the **Save** button. The drawing is saved with the name Tutorial 1 in the *Chapter 10* folder.

Hands-on Test Drive 1

Create the drawing template shown in Figure 10.66, and then convert it into WBlock (external block) by using the WBLOCK command so that you can insert the drawing template in any drawing as a block. Dimensions are for your reference only. You can assign the missing dimensions.

10.66

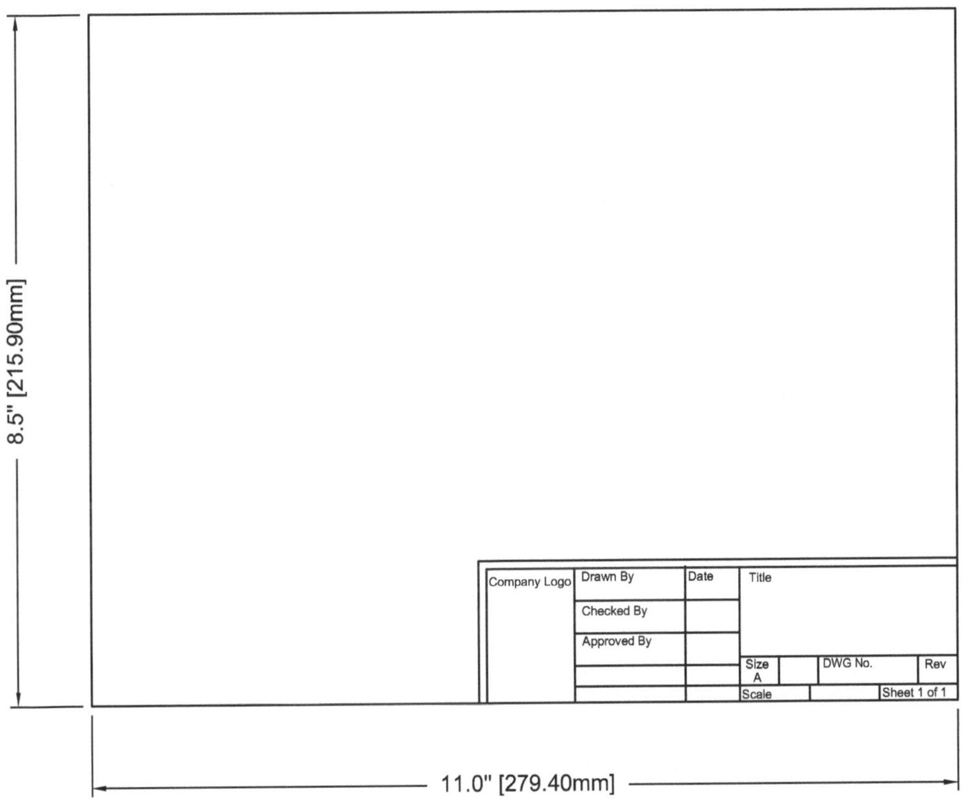

Summary

The chapter introduced methods for creating and inserting a Block and WBlock into a drawing. It also explained how to edit Blocks, make Dynamic Blocks, and how to work with external reference files (Xrefs).

Questions

Complete the following sentences:

- In AutoCAD, you can create a Block either by using the ________ tool or ________ command.
- ________ is the shortcut for the BLOCK command.
- The blocks created in the current drawing can be inserted into the drawing several times by using the ________ tool.
- You can create a WBlock either by using the ________ tool or ________ command.
- In AutoCAD, you can edit blocks either by using the ________ tool or ________ command.
- A ________ block can be modified dynamically in the drawing area.
- In AutoCAD, external reference files are known as ________ .
- You can attach external reference files to a drawing by using the ________ palette.
- To invoke the EXTERNAL REFERENCES Palette, click on the ________ tool.

CHAPTER

11

Working with Layouts

In this chapter, the following topics will be discussed:

- Getting Started with Paper Space/Layout
- Understanding Different Components of a Layout
- Setting up the Sheet/Paper Size for a Layout
- Adding, Renaming, and Deleting a Layout
- Working with Viewports
- Accessing the Model Space within a Viewport
- Clipping a Viewport
- Locking the Object Scale in a Viewport
- Controlling the Display of Objects in a Viewport
- Controlling Layer Properties for Viewports
- Switching to the Model Space
- Creating Viewports in the Model Space
- Joining Two Viewports
- Restoring Viewports

So far in this textbook, you have learned about creating drawings in Model space. AutoCAD is provided with two distinct working environments: Model space and Paper space. By default, when you start AutoCAD, the Model space is the activated environment for creating drawings. The drawing created in the Model space is in 1:1 scale and it represents the real-world size of the model, whereas the Paper space is used for plotting drawings and generating different drawing views. In the Paper space, you can create multiple viewports, which represent different drawing views. Paper space is nothing but a sheet of paper on which the final drawing can be printed or plotted. The Paper space is also known as the layout. You can switch between the Model space and Paper space by using the tabs: **Model**, **Layout1**, and **Layout2** available at the lower left corner of the drawing area, see Figure 11.1.

11.1

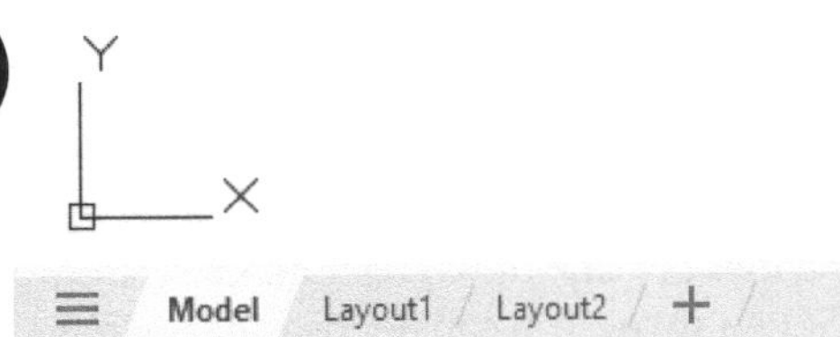

By default, two layouts: **Layout1** and **Layout2** are available as the Paper space. In these layouts, you can prepare your drawing for plotting and generate different drawing views. In addition to the default layouts, you can add multiple layouts, as required. You will learn about adding layouts later in this chapter.

Getting Started with Paper Space/Layout

As discussed, the Paper space is a sheet of paper, which is used to prepare drawings for plotting and printing. Drawings are used to fully and clearly communicate the requirements for manufacturing the end product. It is a language that conveys ideas and information about the product. You can either take the printout of the drawing on paper or create an electronic file to convey information about the product. The Design Web Format (DWF) is the most commonly used electronic file format to communicate information about a product. In AutoCAD, you can plot a drawing in both the working environments: Model space and Paper space (layout). However, it is recommended to use Paper space (layout) for plotting a drawing because the Paper space/layout gives you more flexibility to control the drawing for printing and allows you to generate different drawing views with different scales. Also, it gives the same appearance of the drawing as it is on the sheet of paper. By default, two layouts: **Layout1** and **Layout2** are available for plotting a drawing. In addition to the default layouts, you can add multiple layouts to generate different drawing views of an object on different layouts. In AutoCAD, each layout represents a sheet of paper having a standard size. You will learn about adding layouts later in this chapter.

To activate the Paper space, click on the **Layout1** tab in the lower left corner of the drawing area, see Figure 11.2. The Paper space gets activated, and the drawing created in the Model space appears in a default viewport. Also, the **Layout** tab appears in the **Ribbon**. You can create multiple viewports, delete and/or modify the existing viewports in a layout. However, before you learn about creating, deleting, and editing viewports, it is important to understand the different components of a layout and set up the sheet size for a layout.

11.2

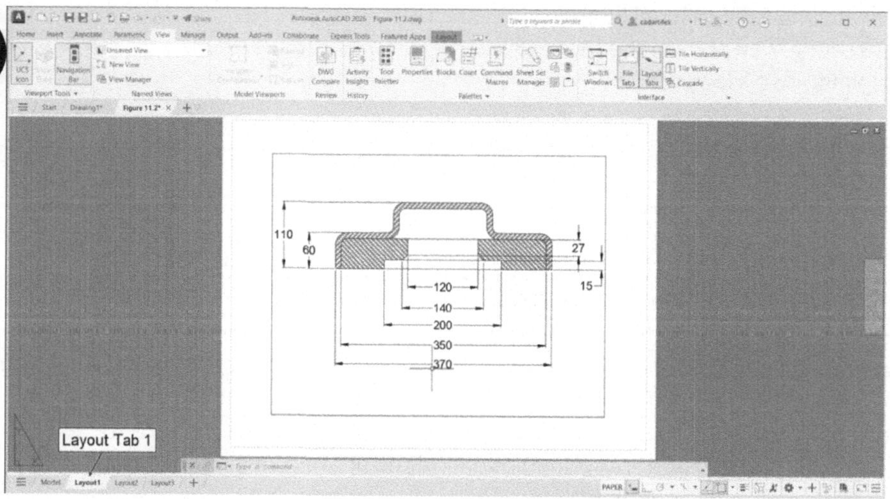

Understanding Different Components of a Layout

In AutoCAD, a layout has several components such as paper/sheet, plot area, viewport, and layout icon, see Figure 11.3. The paper of a layout has a standard size. By default, the paper size of layout1 is 8.5" X 11.0", which is an ISO A4 sheet. You can define the paper/sheet size of a layout, as required. You will learn about setting up the sheet size later in this chapter. The plot area of a layout is the maximum area of printing the drawing and is represented by dotted lines, see Figure 11.3. The viewports of a layout are used for creating different drawing views of a model. You can create multiple viewports in a layout. You will learn about creating viewports later in this chapter.

11.3

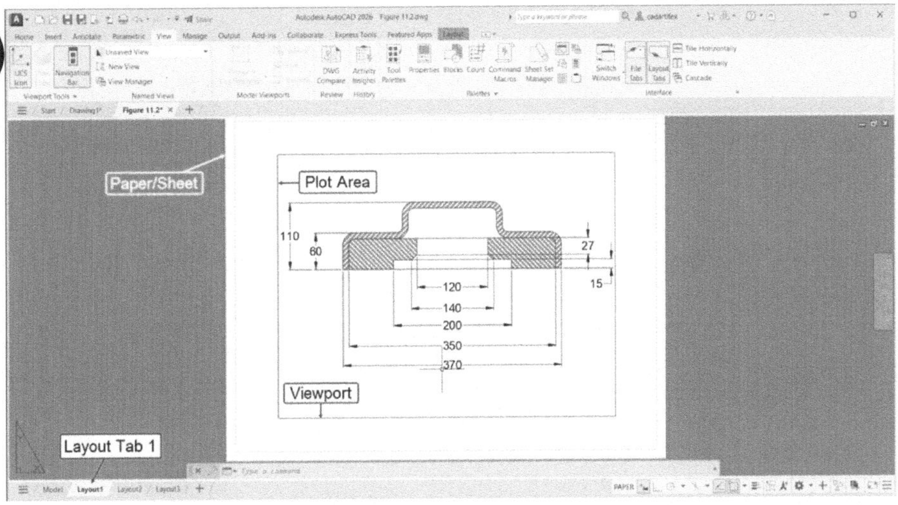

Setting up the Sheet/Paper Size for a Layout

In AutoCAD, the default layouts (Layout1 and Layout2) have default paper/sheet sizes assigned. You can change the default paper/sheet size for a layout, as per the requirement. To do so, activate the layout whose paper/sheet size is to be changed by clicking on its tab available at the lower left corner of the drawing area. Next, right-click on the activated layout tab. A flyout appears, see Figure 11.4. In this flyout, click on the **Page Setup Manager** option. The **Page Setup Manager** dialog box appears, see Figure 11.5. Alternatively, click on the **Page Setup** tool in the **Layout** panel of the **Layout** tab in the **Ribbon**. Note that the **Layout** tab appears in the **Ribbon** only when a layout is activated.

11.4

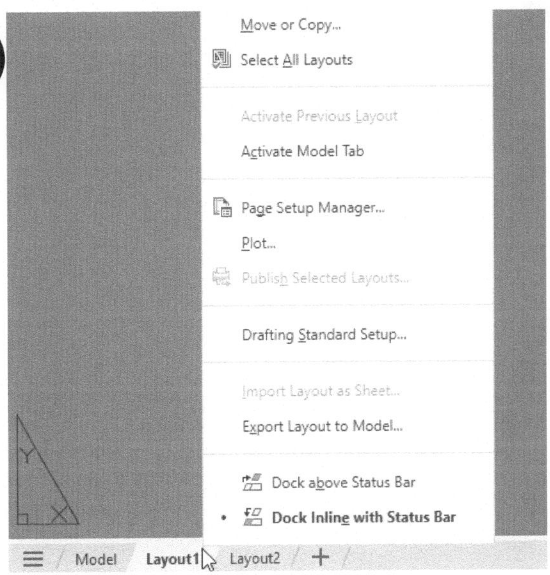

11.5

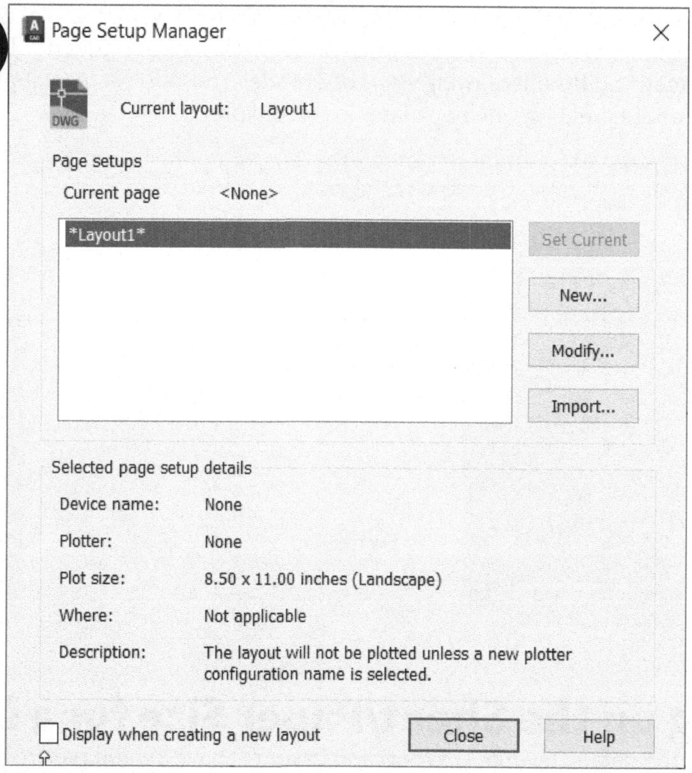

In the **Page Setup Manager** dialog box, the current activated layout is selected in the **Current page setup** area. Also, the details of the selected layout such as plot size and description are displayed in the **Selected page setup details** area of the dialog box. Click on the **Modify** button in the dialog box to modify the default page size of the selected layout. The **Page Setup** dialog box appears, see Figure 11.6.

11.6

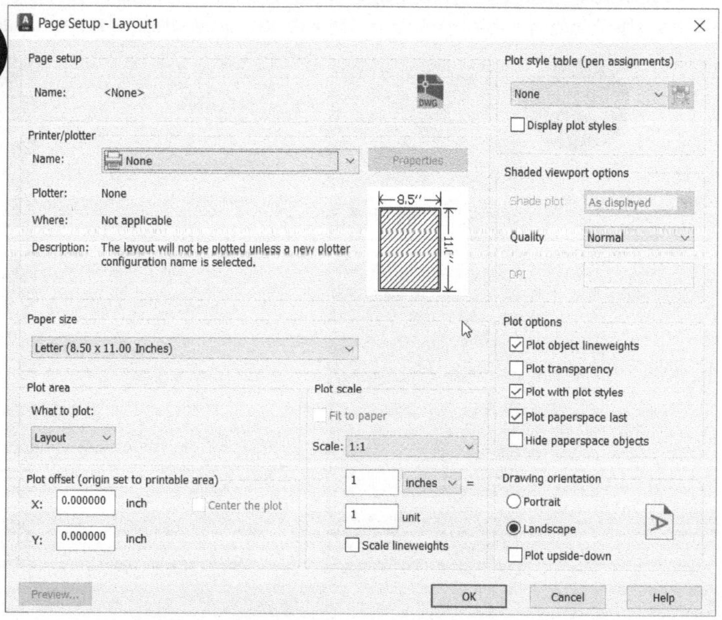

By using the **Paper size** drop-down list of the **Page Setup** dialog box, you can select the required paper size for the layout. You can also choose the orientation of the sheet: portrait or landscape by using the respective radio buttons in the **Drawing orientation** area of the dialog box. After selecting the required paper size and orientation of the layout, click on the **OK** button in the dialog box. The paper/sheet size for the selected layout is modified. Now, you can close the **Page Setup Manager** dialog box by clicking the **Close** button in the dialog box.

Adding, Renaming, and Deleting a Layout

As discussed, by default, two layouts: **Layout1** and **Layout2** are provided as Paper space to prepare the drawing for plotting and printing. Each layout represents a sheet of paper. However, in some of the drawings, these two layouts are not enough, you may need to add additional layouts for generating drawing views of a drawing. In AutoCAD, you can add multiple layouts for a drawing as required. To add additional layouts, right-click on a layout tab in the lower left corner of the drawing area. A flyout appears, see Figure 11.7. In this flyout, click on the **New Layout** option, see Figure 11.7. A new layout with a default name gets added, see Figure 11.8. In this figure, **Layout3** is the newly added layout. to Alternatively, you can click on the +sign available to the right of the last layout tab to add a layout the drawing, refer to Figure 11.8. You can also click on the **New** tool in the **Layout** panel of the **Layout** tab in the **Ribbon** to add a layout, see Figure 11.9.

11.7

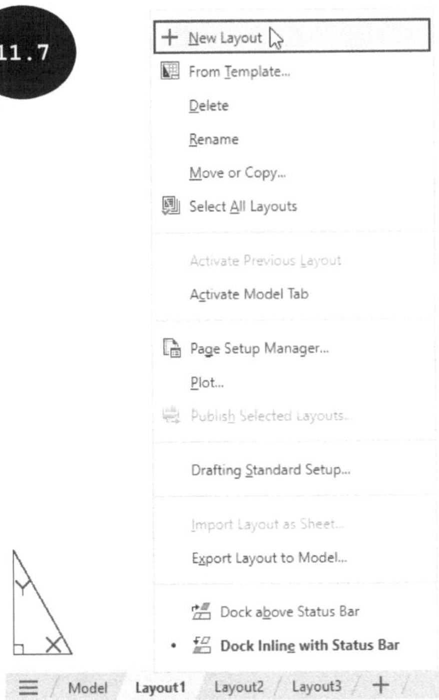

11.8

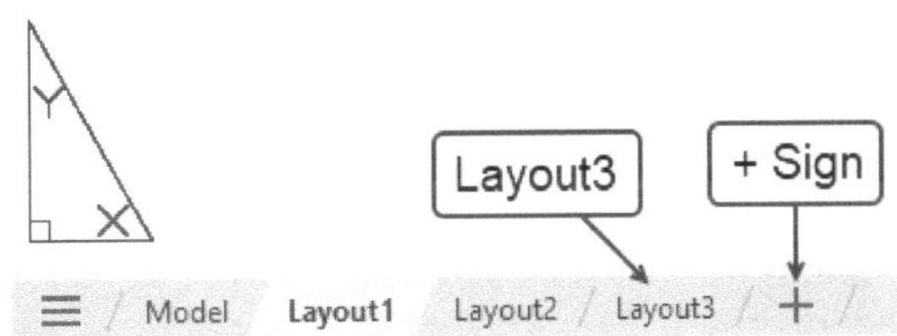

11.9

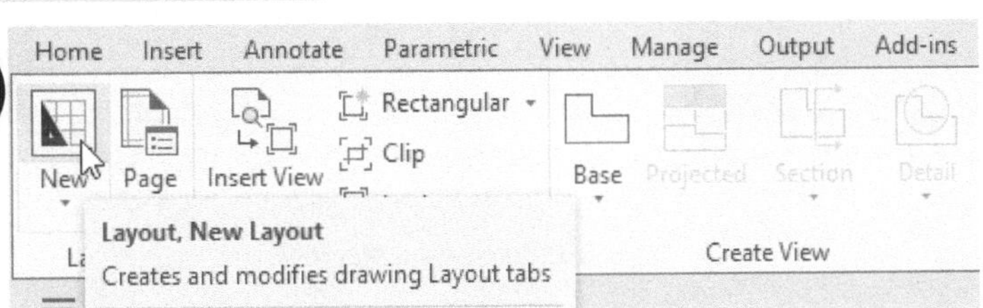

As discussed, on adding a layout, a default name is assigned to the newly added layout such as Layout3, Layout4, or Layout5. You can change the default assigned name of the newly added or an existing layout of the drawing. To do so, right-click on the layout tab whose name has to be changed. A flyout appears. In this flyout, click on the **Rename** option. The default name of the selected layout is displayed in an edit field, see Figure 11.10. In this edit field, enter the new name for the layout as required and then press ENTER. The name of the layout is changed as specified.

11.10

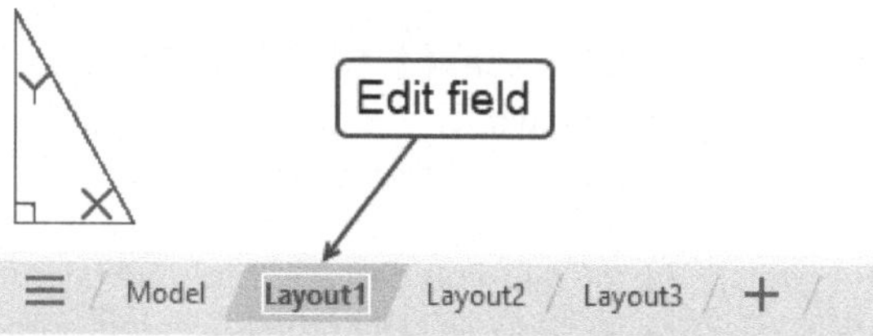

You can also delete a layout that was added by mistake or is no longer required to be a part of the drawing. To delete a layout, right-click on the layout tab which is to be deleted. A flyout appears. In this flyout, click on the **Delete** option. The selected layout gets deleted and is no longer a part of the current drawing.

Working with Viewports

When you activate a layout by clicking on its respective tab (Layout1 or Layout2) available at the lower left corner of the drawing area, the drawing created in the Model space appears in a default viewport, see Figure 11.11. A viewport is a rectangular area that displays the drawing created in the Model space. You can fit the entire drawing in a single viewport or create multiple viewports in the layout to display different views of the model at various scales. You can perform various editing operations on a viewport such as move, copy, rotate, scale, and stretch. Moreover, you can also delete an existing viewport of a drawing. The method for editing, deleting, and creating viewports is discussed next.

11.11

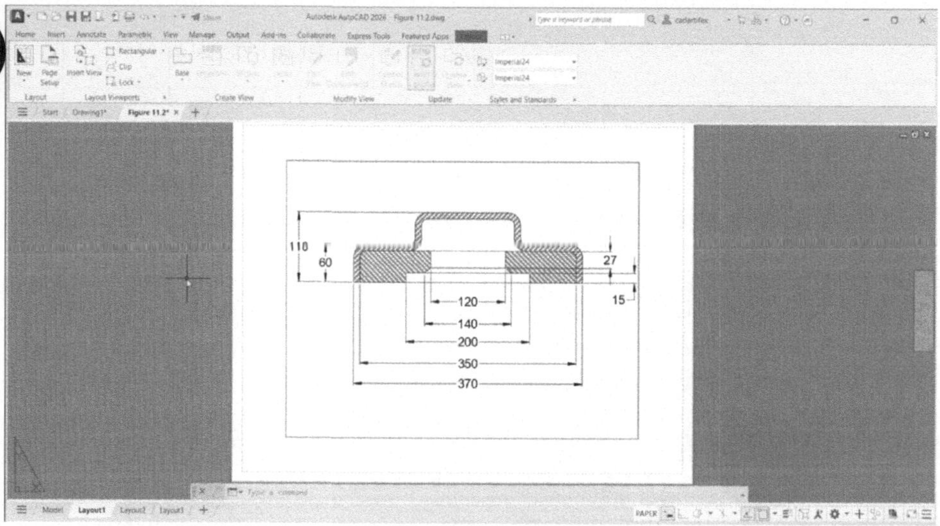

Editing a Viewport

In AutoCAD, similar to performing various editing operations on an entity such as line, rectangle, and circle, you can perform editing operations such as move, copy, rotate, scale, and stretch on a viewport of a layout. For example, to stretch a viewport, click on the viewport boundary to be stretched. The viewport boundary gets highlighted with the display of grips, see Figure 11.12. Now, by using the grips of the viewport boundary, you can stretch the viewport as required. Alternatively, you can also use the **Stretch** tool. Figure 11.13 shows a shrinking view of the viewport. Note that in this figure, after shrinking the viewport, the drawing view is not displayed completely inside the viewport. In such cases, you can access the model space within the viewport of a layout to zoom or pan the drawing such that it fits inside the viewport. You will learn about accessing the model space within the viewport of a layout later in this chapter.

11.12

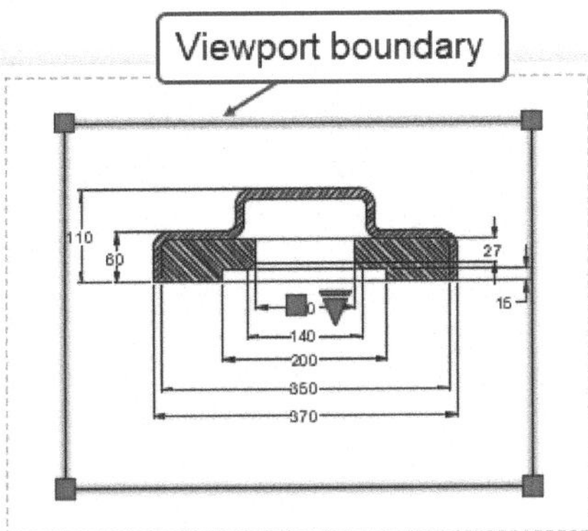

11.13

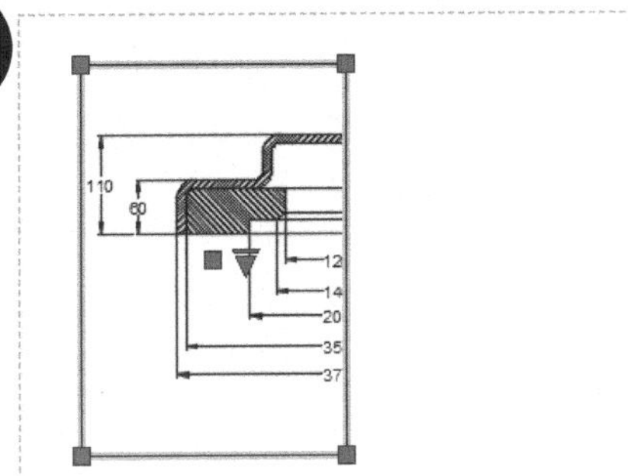

You can also move and scale the viewport by using the square and triangular grips, respectively that appear at the center of the viewport boundary, refer to Figures 11.12 and 11.13. When you click on the triangular grip, a list of predefined scale factors appears, see Figure 11.14. From this list, you can select the required scale factor for the layout. Note that on changing the scale of the viewport, the boundary of the viewport as well as the drawing gets scaled, accordingly. To move the viewport, click on the square grip that appears at the center of the viewport boundary and then click to specify the new position of the viewpoint in the drawing sheet.

11.14

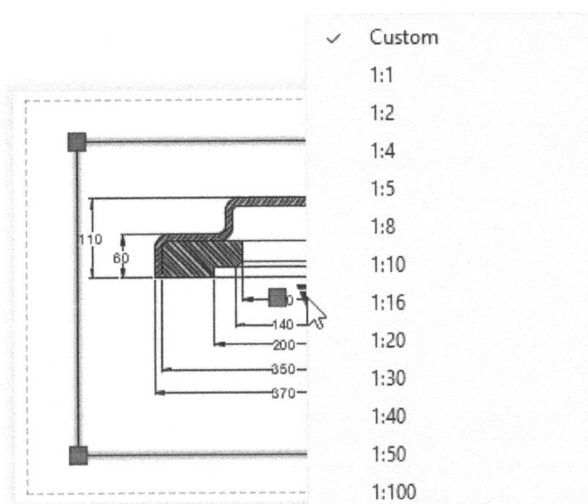

Deleting a Viewport

In AutoCAD, similar to deleting an entity such as line, rectangle, and circle, you can delete a viewport. To delete a viewport, click on it. Its boundary gets highlighted with the display of grips, refer to Figure 11.12. Next, press the DELETE key. The selected viewport gets deleted.

Creating Viewports

In addition to the default viewports, you can create multiple viewports in a layout for displaying different views of a model, see Figure 11.15. The viewports created in a layout are known as floating viewports as you can create viewports of any shape and size. Moreover, the viewports in a layout can be overlapped and edited.

11.15

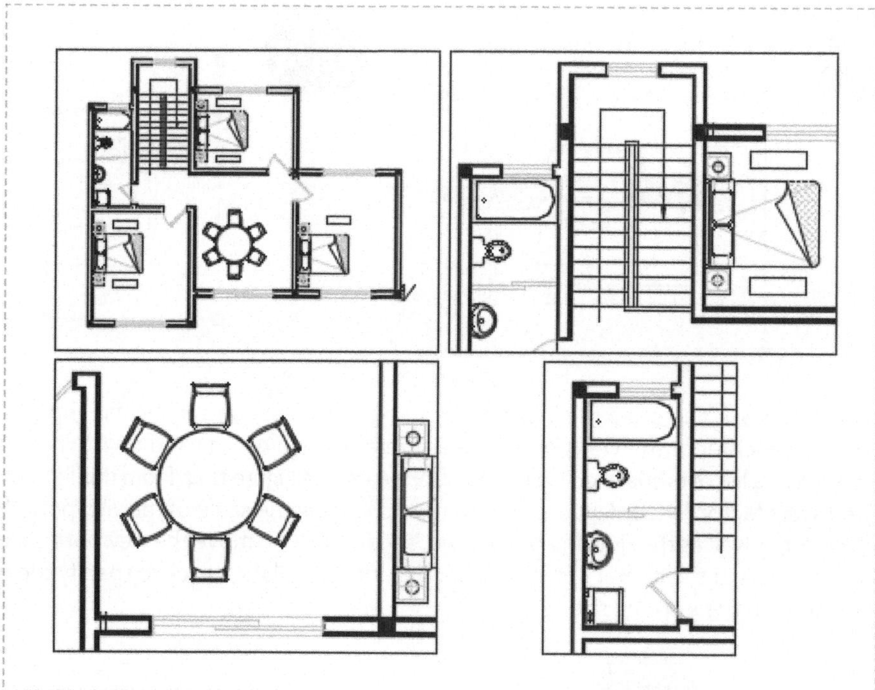

The tools for creating viewports are in the **Layout Viewports** panel of the **Layout** tab in the **Ribbon**, see Figure 11.16. You can create different types of viewports by using these tools. The methods for creating viewports are discussed next.

11.16

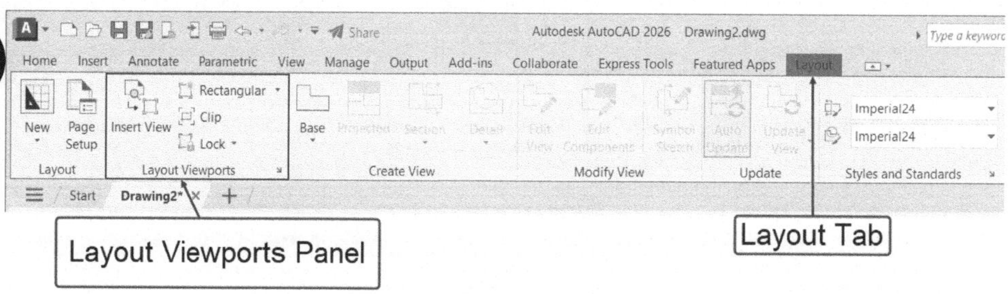

Creating a Rectangular Viewport

To create a rectangular viewport, click on the **Rectangular** tool in the **Layout Viewports** panel of the **Layout** tab, refer to Figure 11.16. You are prompted to specify the first corner of the viewport. Alternatively, enter **-VPORTS** in the Command Line window and then press ENTER to create a rectangular viewport.

```
Specify corner of viewport or [ON OFF Fit Shadeplot Lock NEw NAmed
Object Polygonal Restore LAyer 2 3 4] <Fit>:
```

Click to specify a corner of the viewport in the paper area of the layout, see Figure 11.17. You are prompted to specify the opposite corner of the viewport.

```
Specify opposite corner:
```

Click to specify the diagonally opposite corner of the viewport, see Figure 11.17. A rectangular viewport is created, and the drawing created in the Model space fits entirely inside the viewport, see Figure 11.17. Similarly, you can create multiple rectangular viewports in a layout. You can zoom, pan, or change the scale of the drawing view in a viewport by accessing the Model space within the viewport of a layout. You will learn about accessing the Model space within the viewport later in this chapter.

11.17

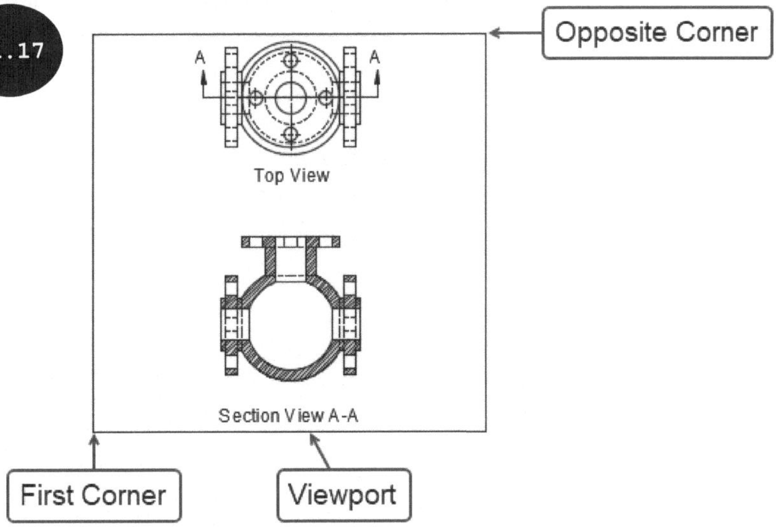

Note: You can also create rectangular viewports by using the MVIEW command. For doing so, enter **MV** in the Command Line window and then press ENTER. You are prompted to specify the first corner of the viewport. Specify the first and second/opposite corner of the viewport in a layout. A rectangular viewport is created. You can also create two, three, or four viewports together by using this command. For doing so, enter 2, 3, or 4 respectively, and then press ENTER when you are prompted to specify the first corner of the viewport. Next, you are prompted to specify the arrangement of the viewports "`Enter viewport arrangement [Horizontal Vertical Above Below Left Right] <Right>:`" Specify the arrangement for the viewports by clicking on their respective option in the command prompt. Next, specify the first and second/opposite corners that define the overall area/boundary for the viewports. The viewports are created.

Creating a Polygonal Viewport

To create a polygonal viewport, click on the **Layout** tab in the **Ribbon** and then click on the down arrow in the **Rectangular** tool of the **Layout Viewports** panel, see Figure 11.18. The **Viewport** flyout appears, see Figure 11.18. In the **Viewport** flyout, click on the **Polygonal** tool. You are prompted to specify the start point. Alternatively, enter **-VPORTS** in the Command Line window and then click on the **Polygonal** option in the command prompt.

```
Specify start point:
```

11.18

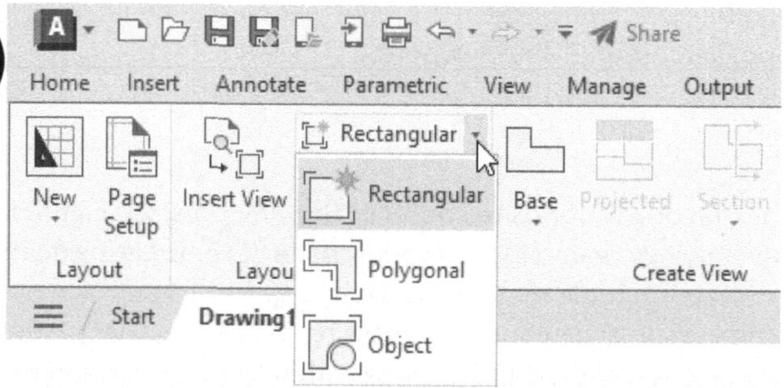

Click to specify the start point of the polygonal viewport in the paper/sheet area of the layout, see Figure 11.19. You are prompted to specify the next point for creating the polygonal viewport.

```
Specify next point or [Arc Length Undo]:
```

Click to specify the second point of the polygonal viewport, see Figure 11.19. You can also specify the length of the line or coordinates (X, Y) of the second point. As soon as you specify the second point, you are prompted to specify the third point for creating the polygonal viewport.

```
Specify next point or [Arc Close Length Undo]:
```

Similarly, you can continue to specify points in the paper/sheet area of the layout for creating a polygonal viewport. To close the viewport, either click on the **Close** option in the command prompt or enter **C** and then press ENTER. The closed polygonal viewport is created and the drawing views created in the Model space appear in it, see Figure 11.19. Note that the drawing views created in the Model space may not fit entirely inside the viewport. You can fit the drawing views in the viewport as well as zoom, pan, or change the scale by accessing the Model space within the viewport. You will learn about accessing the Model space within the viewport later in this chapter.

11.19

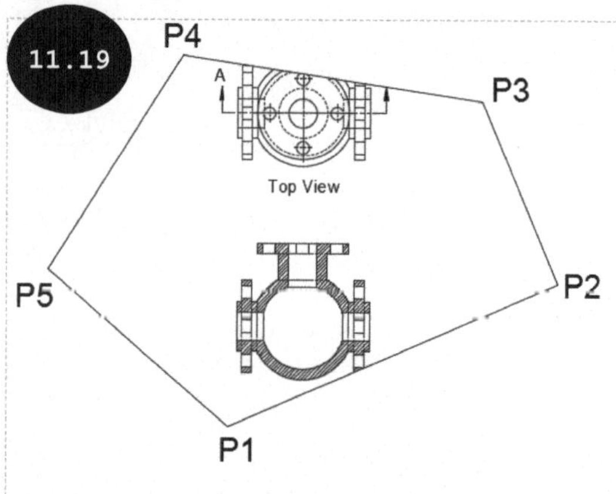

You can create a polygonal viewport having line entities or a combination of line and arc entities. To create a polygonal viewport having arc entities, you need to activate the arc mode either by clicking on the **Arc** option in the command prompt or by entering **A** in the Command Line window and then pressing ENTER. Note that once the arc mode is activated, you can create a chain of arc entities by specifying the arc endpoints. To activate the line mode again, either click on the **Line** option in the command prompt or enter **L** and then press ENTER. Figure 11.20 shows a polygonal viewport created by line and arc entities.

11.20

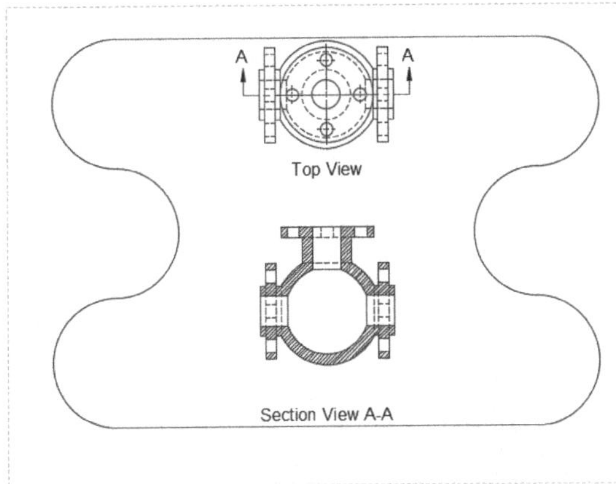

Creating a Viewport by using a Closed Object or Geometry

In addition to creating rectangular and polygonal viewports, you can convert an existing closed geometry into a viewport. Note that all entities of the closed geometry to be converted into a viewport must act as a single object. You can convert a rectangle created by using the **Rectangle** tool, a circle, an ellipse, a closed spline, or a group of closed polyline entities created by using the **Polyline** tool into a viewport. Note that the polyline entities should have been closed by using the **Close** option of the command prompt to convert them into a viewport. Figure 11.21 shows a closed spline and a group of polyline entities.

11.21

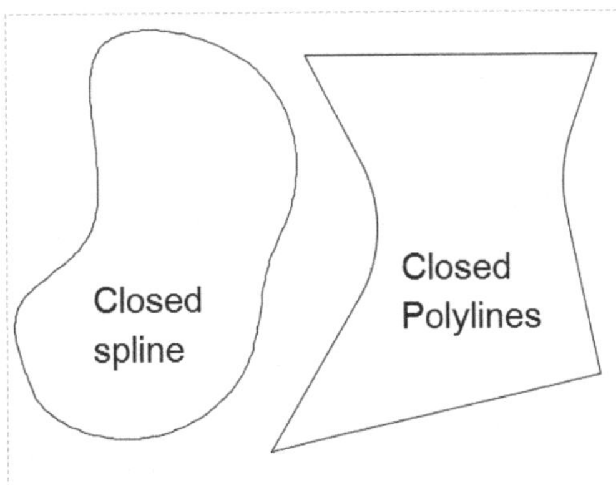

To convert a closed geometry into a viewport, click on the **Layout** tab in the **Ribbon** and then click on the down arrow in the **Rectangular** tool of the **Layout Viewports** panel, see Figure 11.22. The **Viewport** flyout appears, see Figure 11.22. In this flyout, click on the **Object** tool. You are prompted to select an object to convert into a viewport. Alternatively, enter **-VPORTS** in the Command Line window and then click on the **Object** option in the command prompt.

```
Specify corner of viewport or [ON OFF Fit Shadeplot Lock NEw NAmed
Object Polygonal Restore LAyer 2 3 4] <Fit>:_o Select object to clip
viewport:
```

11.22

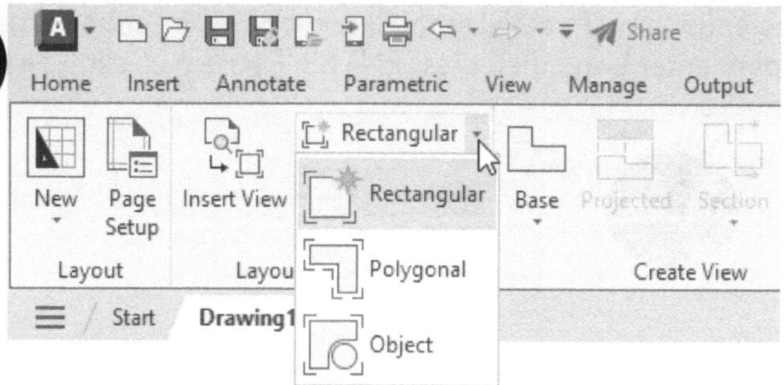

Click on the object to be converted into a viewport. The selected object gets converted into a viewport, and the drawing views created in the Model space appear inside the viewport, see Figure 11.23. Similarly, you can again invoke the **Object** tool and convert another closed object into a viewport, see Figure 11.24.

11.23

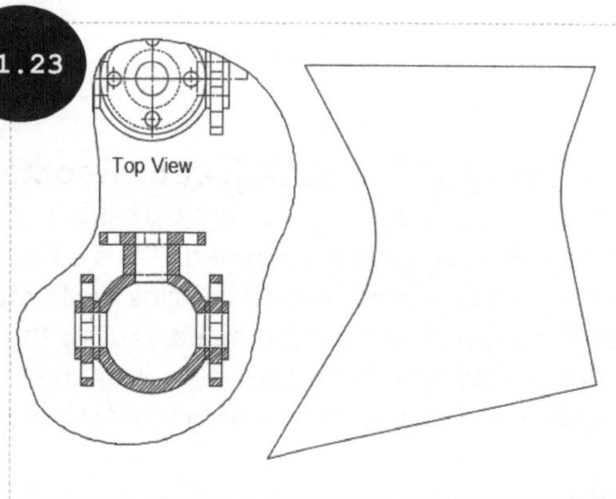

11.24

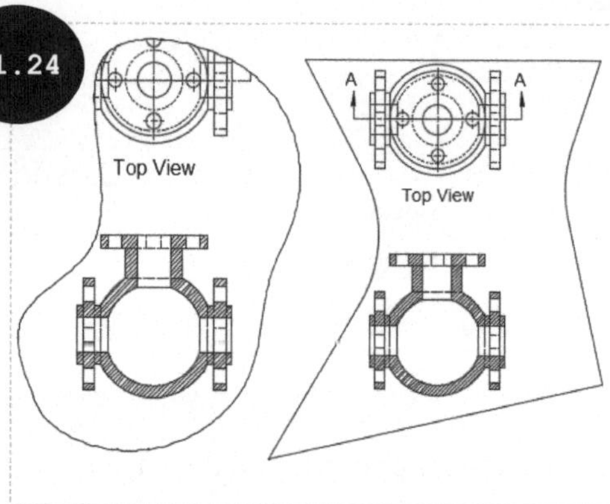

Creating Pre-Defined Standard Viewports

You can create pre-defined standard viewports in a layout by using the **Viewport** dialog box. To do so, click on the down arrow to the right of the **Layout Viewports** panel in the **Layout** tab, see Figure 11.25. The **Viewports** dialog box appears. In this dialog box, click on the **New Viewports** tab to display the list of standard viewports, see Figure 11.26. Alternatively, enter **+VPORTS** in the Command Line window and then press ENTER twice to invoke the **Viewports** dialog box.

11.25

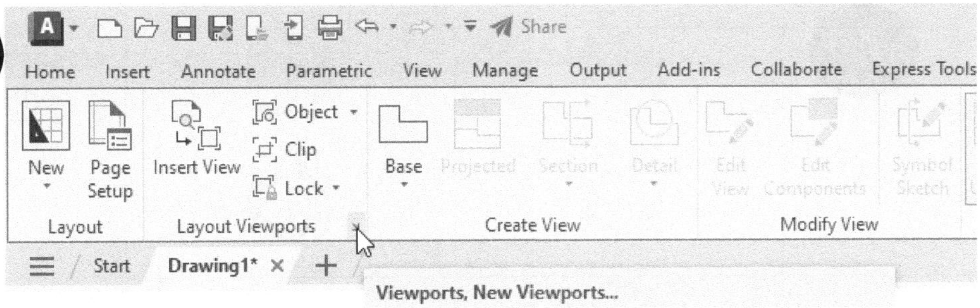

11.26

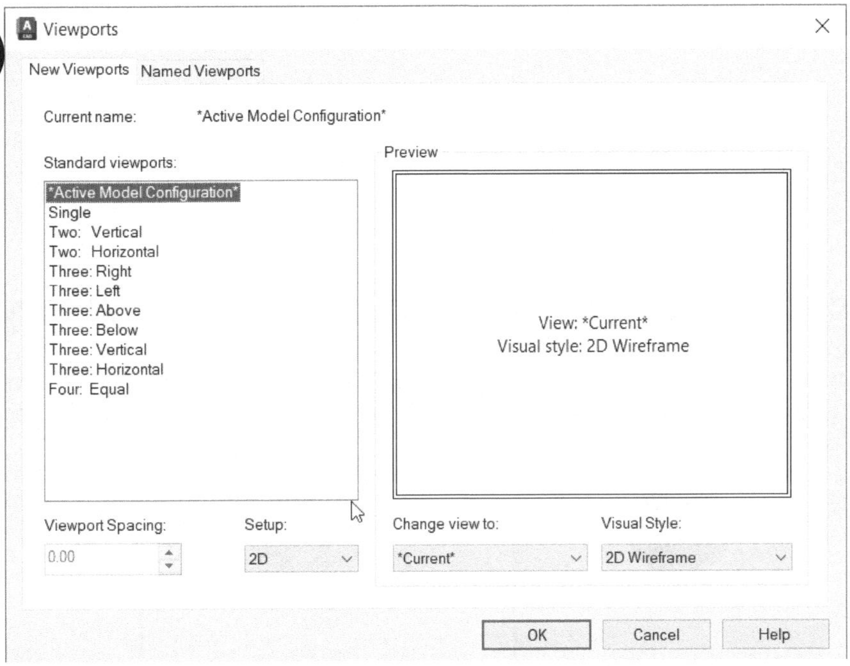

In the **Standard viewports** area of the dialog box, you can select the required standard viewports to be created. For example to create four rectangular viewports of equal sizes, select the **Four: Equal** option in the **Standard viewports** area. A preview of the selected viewports appears in the **Preview** area of the dialog box. After selecting the required standard viewports, click on the **OK** button in the dialog box. You are prompted to specify the first corner of a window which encloses the viewports.

```
Specify first corner or [Fit] <Fit>:
```

Click to specify the first corner of the window in the paper area of the layout, see Figure 11.27. You are prompted to specify the opposite corner of the window.

```
Specify opposite corner:
```

Click to specify the diagonally opposite corner of the window, see Figure 11.27. The viewports are created, see Figure 11.27. In this figure, four viewports of equal sizes are created in the layout.

11.27

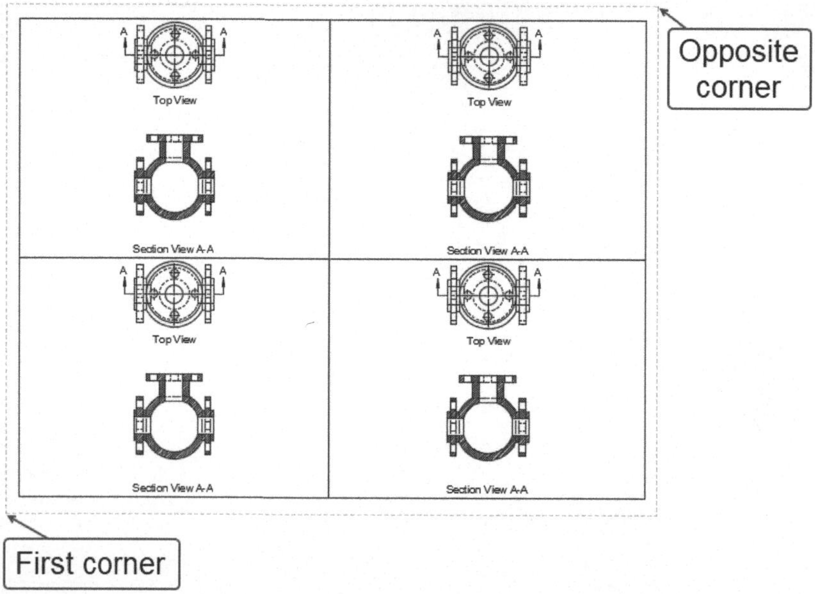

Accessing the Model Space within a Viewport

In AutoCAD, you can access the Model space within a viewport of a layout to perform the editing operations and changing the drawing display. To do so, double-click inside the viewport. The Model space gets activated, and the UCS icon appears inside the viewport, which indicates that the Model space is activated, see Figure 11.28.

11.28

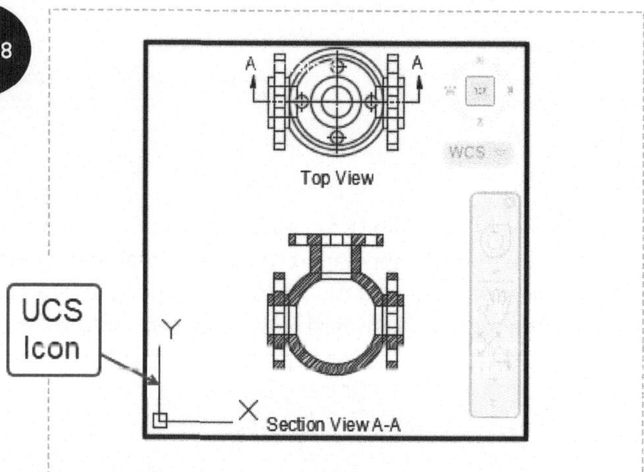

After accessing the Model space, you can zoom or pan the drawing to fit the drawing view inside the viewport. Also, you can change the scale of the drawing view by using the **Scale of the selected viewport** drop-down list in the Status Bar. To invoke the **Scale of the selected viewport** drop-down list, click on the **Scale of the selected viewport** button in the Status Bar, see Figure 11.29. Moreover, you can edit the properties of the drawing entities such as linetype scale, lineweight, and linetype in the Model space.

11.29

Alternatively, you can also access the Model space within a viewport by clicking on the **PAPER** button in the Status Bar (see Figure 11.30) or by using the MSPACE command. Note that if only one viewport is available in the layout then on clicking the **Paper** button or by entering the **MSPACE** command, the Model space gets activated within the available viewport. However, if more than one viewport is available in the layout, then the Model space gets activated within the last created or activated viewport of the layout. You can also click on the required viewport of the layout to access the Model space in it.

11.30

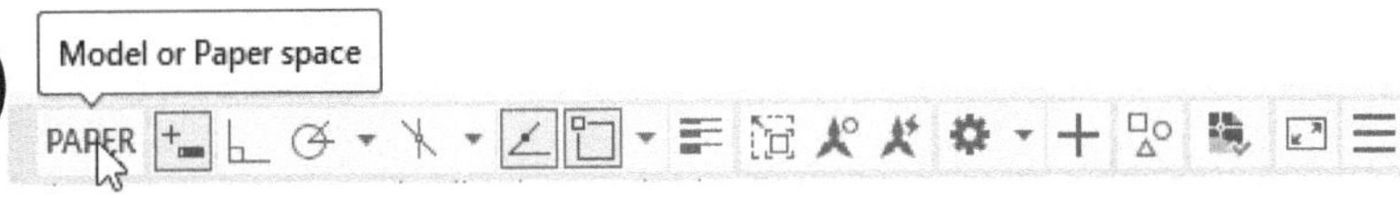

After making the necessary changes in the Model space, you need to switch back to the Paper space. To switch back to the Paper space, double-click anywhere outside the viewport. Alternatively, click on the **MODEL** button in the Status Bar (see Figure 11.31) or enter **PSPACE** and then press ENTER.

11.31

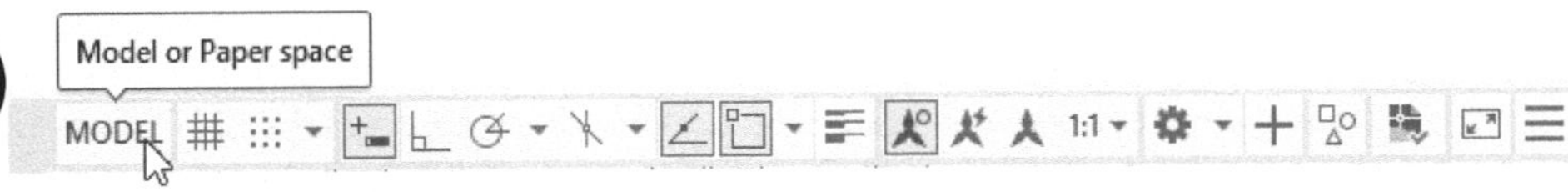

Clipping a Viewport

You can clip a viewport of a layout by using the **Clip** tool of the **Layout Viewports** panel in the **Layout** tab. To do so, you need to first create a closed object as the clipping object for clipping the viewport. The objects that can be used as clipping objects include a rectangle created by using the **Rectangle** tool, a circle, an ellipse, a closed spline, or a group of closed polyline entities created by using the **Polyline** tool (the polyline entities should have been closed by using the **Close** option of the command prompt).

To clip a viewport, click on the **Clip** tool in the **Layout Viewports** panel in the **Layout** tab, see Figure 11.32. You are prompted to select the viewport to be clipped. Alternatively, enter **VPCLIP** in the Command Line window and then press ENTER to invoke the **Clip** tool.

```
Select viewport to clip:
```

11.32

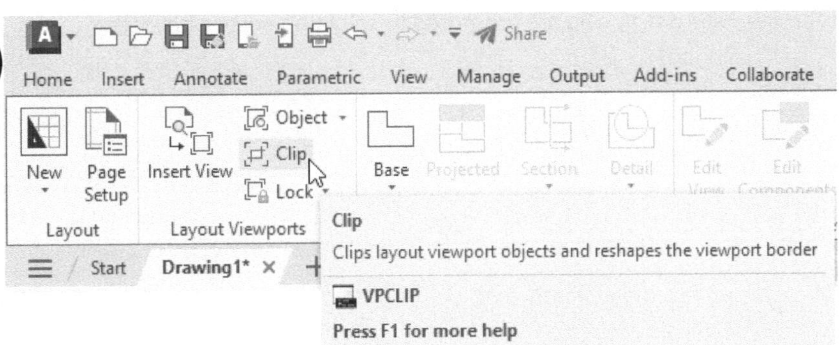

After invoking the **Clip** tool, click on the viewport to be clipped, see Figure 11.33. You are prompted to select a clipping object.

```
Select clipping object or [Polygonal] <Polygonal>:
```

Click on the clipping object, see Figure 11.33. The selected viewport gets clipped, see Figure 11.34.

11.33

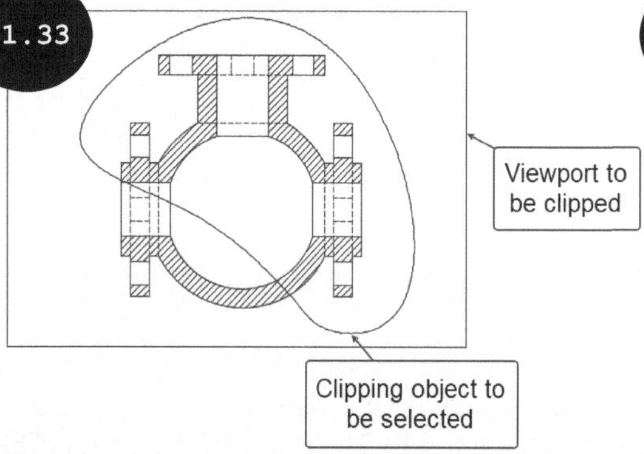

11.34

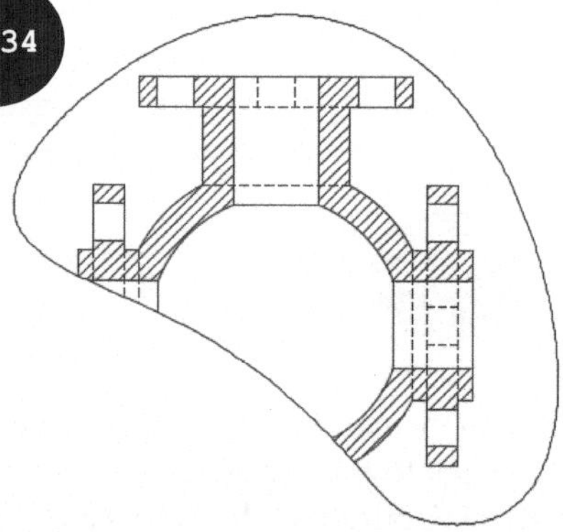

Note: You can also create a group of closed polyline entities by using the **Polyline** tool as the clipping object after invoking the **Clip** tool. For doing so, press the ENTER key when you are prompted to select the clipping object in the command prompt. As soon as you press ENTER, you are prompted to specify the start point of the polylines. After specifying all the points of the polylines, click on the **Close** option in the command prompt to create a closed loop of polylines. The selected viewport gets clipped by the polyline object created.

Locking the Object Scale in a Viewport

In AutoCAD, you can lock or unlock the scale (display) of objects in a viewport by using the **Lock** or **Unlock** tool of the **Layout Viewports** panel in the **Layout** tab, respectively. Note that once the objects of a viewport are locked, you cannot perform operations such as zoom and pan after accessing the Model space in the layout. Locking the scale of objects is useful if you want to prevent any modification by mistake.

To lock the scale of objects in a viewport, click on the **Lock** tool in the **Layout Viewports** panel of the **Layout** tab, see Figure 11.35. You are prompted to select objects to be locked.

```
Select objects:
```

11.35

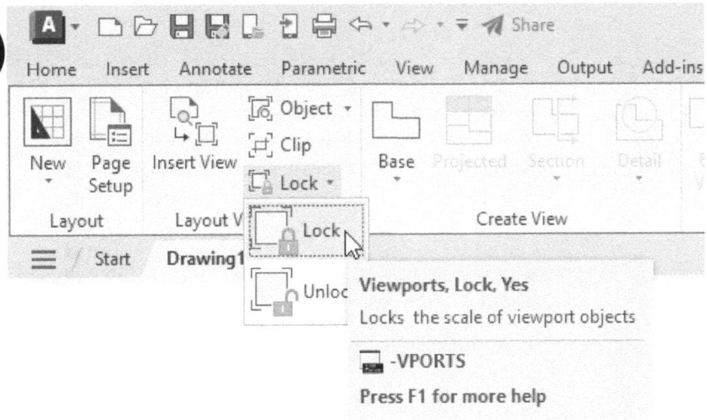

Click on the viewport whose objects/drawing views are to be locked. You can select multiple viewports one by one. Next, press ENTER. The display of the objects of the selected viewport is locked. Note that you can access the Model space within the locked viewport but cannot modify the display/scale of the objects. However, you can edit the properties of the objects such as linetype scale, linetype, and lineweight. Also, you can add or delete the entities in the locked viewport. To unlock the viewport, click on the arrow in the **Lock** tool of the **Layout Viewports** panel. A flyout appears, refer to Figure 11.35. In this flyout, click on the **Unlock** tool. Next, click on the viewport to be unlocked.

Alternatively, to lock the display or scale of objects of a viewport, click on the viewport to be locked and then right-click. A shortcut menu appears. In this shortcut menu, click on the **Display Locked > Yes**. Similarly, click on the **Display Locked > No** to unlock the display of objects of the selected viewport.

Controlling the Display of Objects in a Viewport

You can turn on or off the display of objects in a viewport. To turn off the display of objects in a viewport, click on the viewport and then right-click. A shortcut menu appears. In this shortcut menu, click on the **Display Viewport Objects > No**. The display of objects of the selected viewport turns off. To turn on the display of objects again, click on the viewport and then right-click. Next, click on the **Display Viewport Objects > Yes** in the shortcut menu that appears.

Controlling Layer Properties for Viewports

In AutoCAD, you can control the layer properties for viewports such as freeze/thaw the newly created viewports, freeze all viewports, viewport color, viewport linetype, and viewport lineweight by using the **LAYER PROPERTIES MANAGER**. The concept of working with layers has been discussed in chapter 3.

To control the layer properties for a viewport, double-click inside the viewport to access the Model space. Next, invoke the **LAYER PROPERTIES MANAGER** either by clicking on the **Layer Properties** tool in the **Layers** panel of the **Home** tab or by entering the **LA** in the Command Line window, see Figure 11.36. Most of the options of the **LAYER PROPERTIES MANAGER** have been discussed in chapter 3. The options that have not been discussed in chapter 3 are discussed next.

11.36

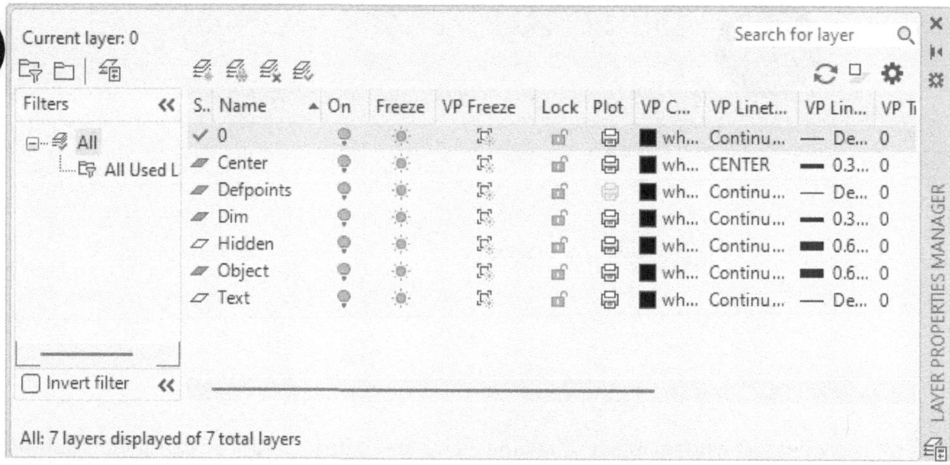

Viewport Freeze

The **VP Freeze** field of the **LAYER PROPERTIES MANAGER** is used for freezing the objects of the current viewport. To freeze objects of the current viewport, click on the **VP Freeze** field of the layer, see Figure 11.37. The layer gets frozen, and the objects assigned to the frozen layer become invisible in the currently active viewport. For example, if you click on the **VP Freeze** field of the Dimension layer (see Figure 11.37) then the Dimension layer gets frozen, and all dimensions assigned to the layer become invisible in the currently active viewport.

11.37

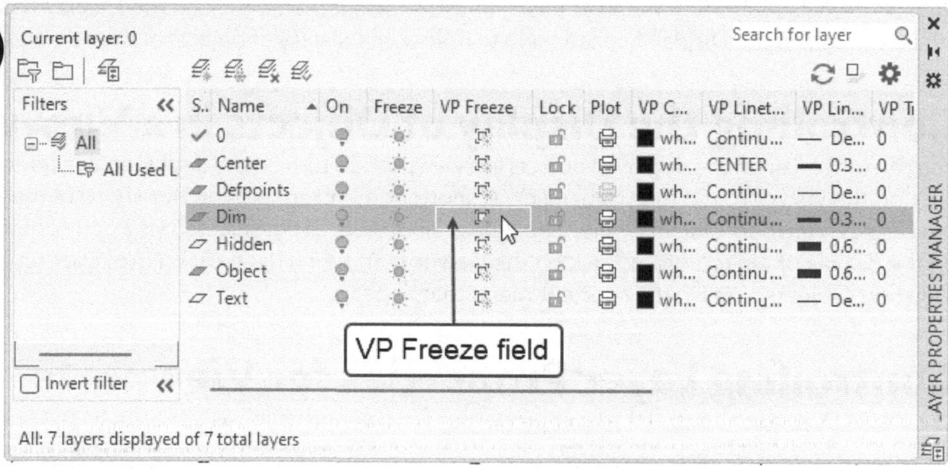

Viewport Color

You can change the color of objects in the current viewport by using the **VP Color** field of a layer. To change an object's color in the current viewport, click on the **VP Color** field of a layer, see Figure 11.38. The **Select Color** dialog box appears. In this dialog box, select the required color to be assigned to the respective objects of the layer. Next, click on the **OK** button to accept the change and close the dialog box. The color of the objects of the selected layer gets changed in the current viewport. For example, to change the color of the dimensions in the current viewport, click on the **VP Color** field of the Dimension layer (see Figure 11.38) and then select the required color in the **Select Color** dialog box that appears. Next, click **OK** in the **Select Color** dialog box. The color of the dimensions gets changed in the current viewport.

11.38

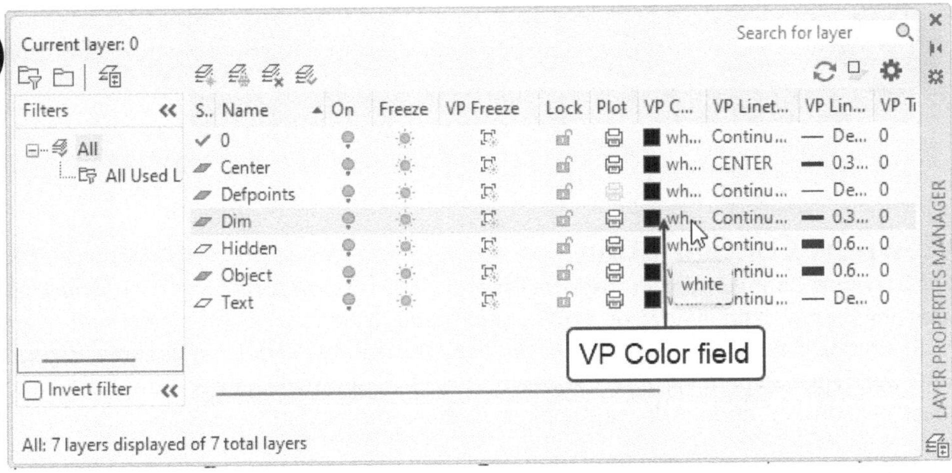

Similarly, you can change the linetype, lineweight, and transparency of the objects of a layer in the current viewport by using the VP Linetype, VP Lineweight, and VP Transparency fields of the layer, respectively in the **LAYER PROPERTIES MANAGER**.

Note: If none of the viewports is activated then on changing the viewport color, viewport linetype, viewport lineweight, and so on, only the boundary of the viewports in the layout gets affected by the change.

Switching to the Model Space

As discussed, you can switch between the Model space and Paper space (layout) anytime by using the tabs (**Model**, **Layout1**, and **Layout2**) available at the lower left corner of the drawing area, see Figure 11.39. The **Model** tab represents the Model space, and **Layout** tab represents the Paper space (layout) of a drawing.

11.39

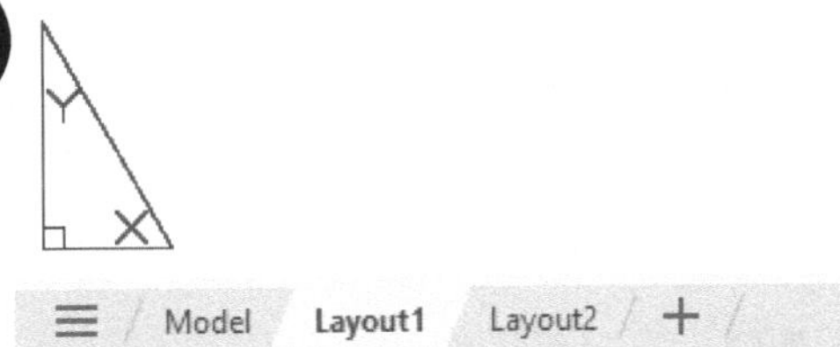

Creating Viewports in the Model Space

In AutoCAD, you can also create viewports in the Model space. The viewports created in the Model space are known as Tiled viewports. By default, when you start AutoCAD, a single viewport is displayed in the Model space. You can create multiple viewports in the Model space to display the different drawing views of an object. Creating viewports in the Model space is the same as dividing the work/drawing area into multiple areas. You can only create rectangular space viewports in the Model space by using the tools available in the **Model Viewports** panel of the **View** tab in the **Ribbon**, see Figure 11.40. The tools are discussed next.

11.40

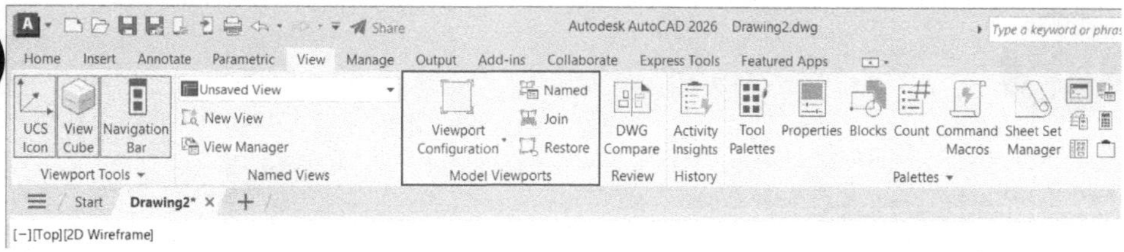

Viewport Configuration

The **Viewport Configuration** drop-down list of the **Model Viewports** panel of the **View** tab is used for selecting the pre-defined viewport configurations, see Figure 11.41. You can select the required viewport configuration in this drop-down list such as **Two: Vertical**, **Two: Horizontal**, **Three: Right**, **Three: Left**, and **Four: Equal**. Depending upon the viewport configuration selected, the drawing area of the Model space gets divided, and the drawing appears in all viewports.

11.41

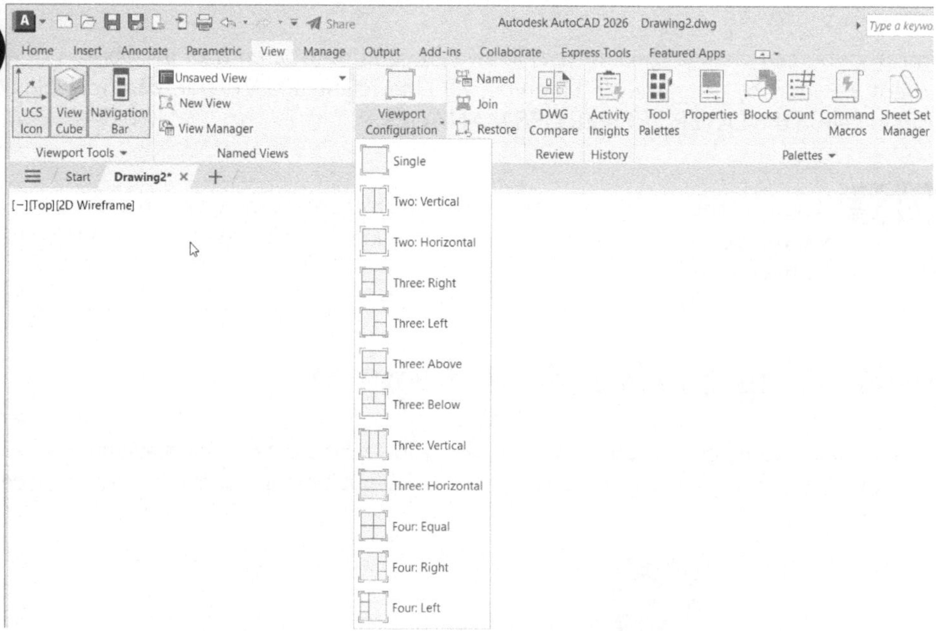

Similarly, you can create viewports in the Model space by using the **Named** tool in the **Model Viewports** panel of the **View** tab.

Joining Two Viewports

You can also merge or join two viewports by using the **Join** tool of the **Model Viewports** panel in the **View** tab. To join two viewports, click on the **Join** tool in the **Model Viewports** panel. You are prompted to select the dominant viewport.

```
Select dominant viewport <current viewport>:
```

Click on a viewport as the dominant viewport in the drawing area. You are prompted to select the viewport to be joined to the dominant viewport selected.

```
Select viewport to join:
```

Click on the viewport to be joined. The selected viewport gets joined to the selected dominant viewport.

Restoring Viewports

You can restore a multiple viewport configuration to a default single viewport in the Model space by using the **Restore** tool of the **Model Viewports** panel in the **View** tab. The **Restore** tool is used for toggling between a single viewport and the last multiple viewport configuration.

Tutorial 1

Create the drawing shown in Figure 11.42 in the Model space. After creating the drawing, create an elliptical viewport in a layout and set the drawing scale in the viewport to 1:50, see Figure 11.43. The major axis of the elliptical viewport is 7 inches (177.80 mm), and the minor axis of the elliptical viewport is 4 inches (101.60 mm) for your reference. All dimensions are in mm.

11.42

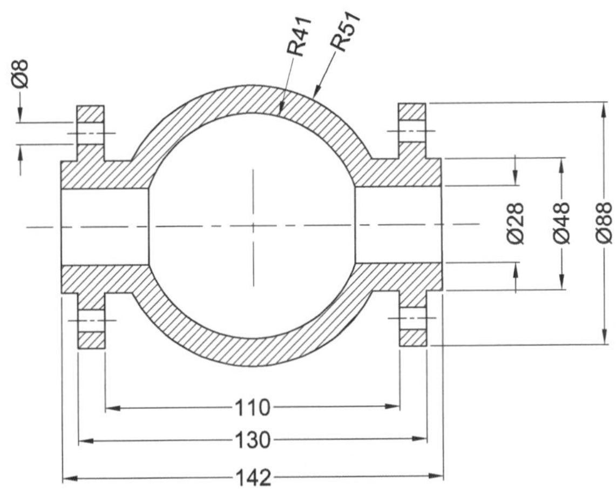

11.43

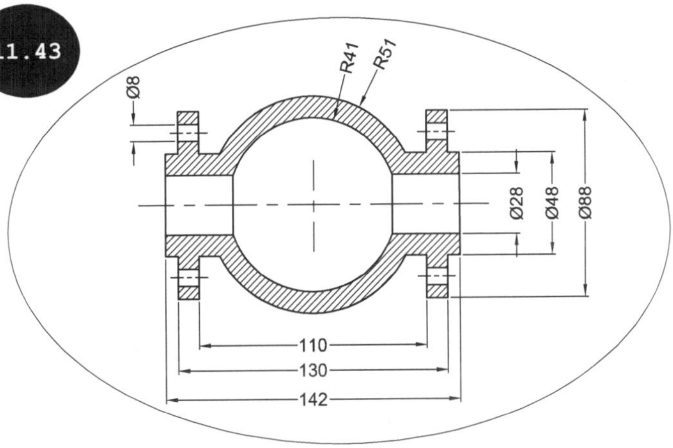

Section 1: Starting AutoCAD

1. Start AutoCAD and then open a new drawing file.

Section 2: Creating the Drawing and Applying Dimensions

1. Create the drawing as shown in Figure 11.44. You can refer to Figure 11.42 for dimensions. Also, you can assume the missing dimensions.

2. Apply the ANSI31 hatch pattern in the required enclosed areas of the drawing by using the **Hatch** tool in the **Draw** panel of the **Home** tab, see Figure 11.45. Note that you may need to adjust the hatch pattern scale so that the pattern appears similar to the one shown in Figure 11.45.

11.44

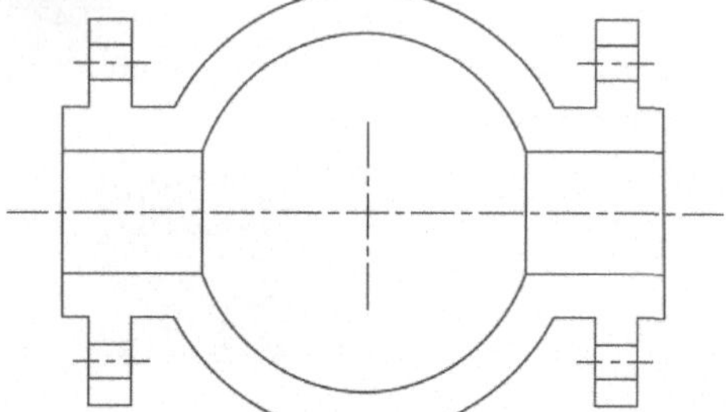

11.45

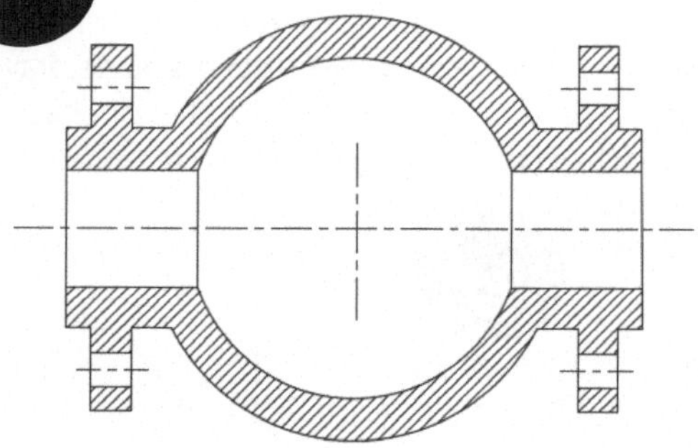

3. Apply dimensions to the drawing by using the dimension tools, see Figure 11.46. Note that you need to modify the dimension style properties such as text height, arrow size, extend beyond dimension lines, and offset from the origin by using the DIMSTYLE command.

11.46

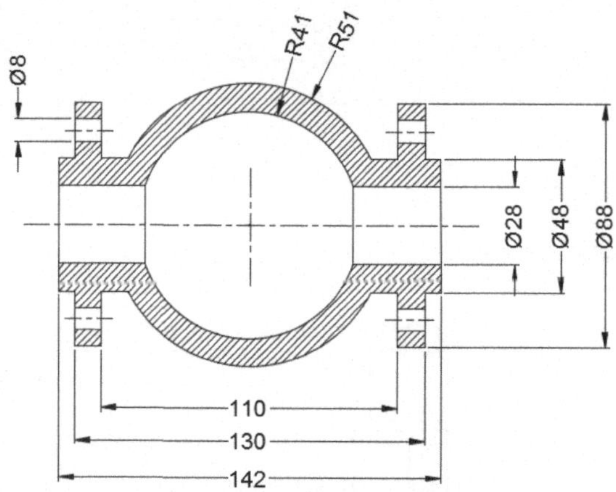

Section 3: Creating Elliptical Shaped Viewport in a Layout

1. Click on the **Layout1** tab in the lower left corner of the drawing area. The **Layout1** is activated, and the drawing created in the Model space appears in a default viewport, see Figure 11.47.

11.47

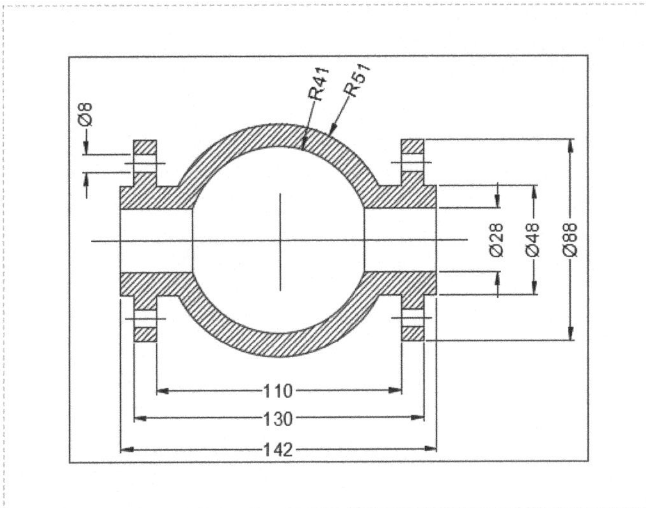

2. Click on the rectangular boundary of the viewport and then press the DELETE key to delete the default viewport.

   Now, you need to draw an ellipse as the boundary of the viewport.

3. Create an ellipse having a major axis of 7 inches (177.80 mm) and a minor axis of 4 inches (101.60 mm) on the sheet, see Figure 11.48. You can create an ellipse by using the **Center** tool of the **Ellipse** flyout in the **Draw** panel of the **Home** tab (see Figure 11.49) or by entering **EL** in the Command Line window. EL is the shortcut for the ELLIPSE command.

11.48

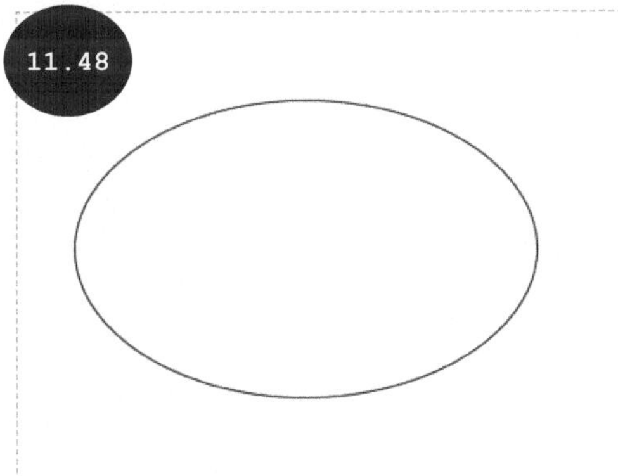

11.49

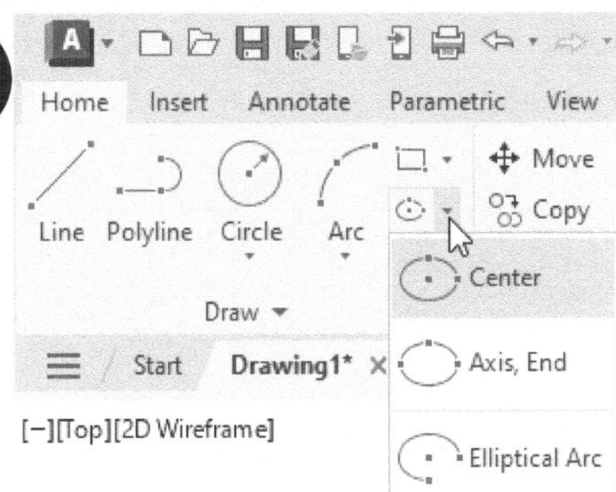

   After creating the ellipse, you can convert it into a viewport.

4. Click on the **Layout** tab in the **Ribbon** to display the tools and panels of the **Layout** tab.

5. Click on the down arrow in the **Rectangular** tool of the **Layout Viewports** panel in the **Layout** tab, see Figure 11.50. The **Viewport** flyout appears, see Figure 11.50. In this flyout, click on the **Object** tool. You are prompted to select the object to be converted into a viewport. Alternatively, enter **-VPORTS** in the Command Line window and then click on the **Object** option in the command prompt.

```
Specify corner of viewport or [ON OFF Fit Shadeplot Lock NEw NAmed
Object Polygonal Restore LAyer 2 3 4] <Fit>:_o Select object to
clip viewport:
```

6. Click on the ellipse drawn on the sheet as the object to be converted into a viewport. The ellipse gets converted into a viewport, and the drawing created in the Model space is displayed inside it with the default scale, see Figure 11.51.

11.50

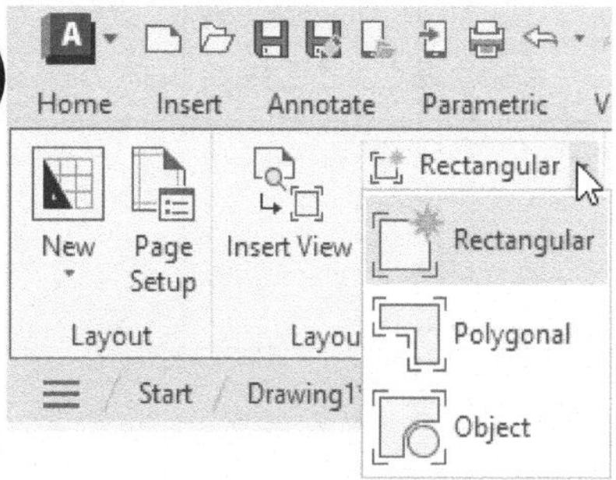

11.51

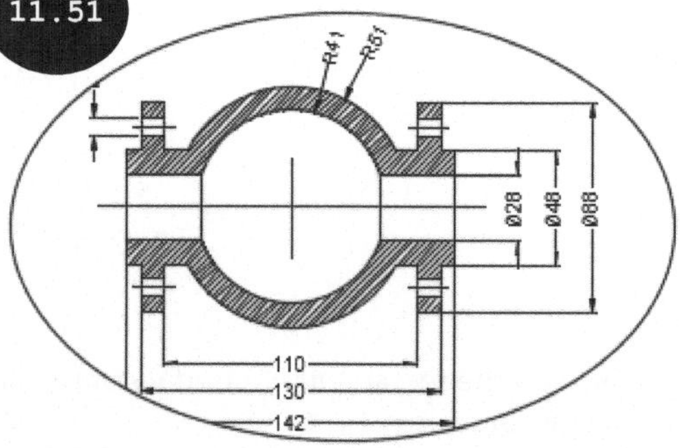

7. Double-click inside the elliptical viewport to access the Model space in the Layout. Next, select **1:50** as the scale of the viewport in the drop-down list which appears on clicking the **Scale of the selected viewport** tool in the **Status Bar**, see Figure 11.52.

11.52

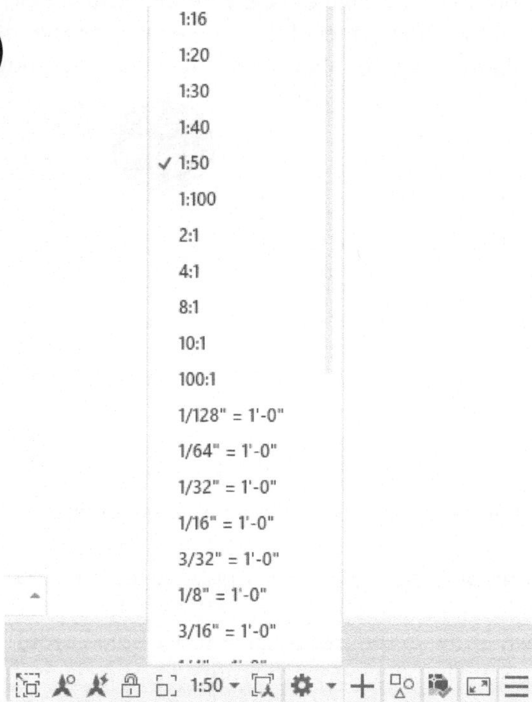

8. Double-click anywhere outside the elliptical viewport to switch back to the Paper space (layout). The scale of the selected viewport is changed to 1:50, see Figure 11.53.

11.53

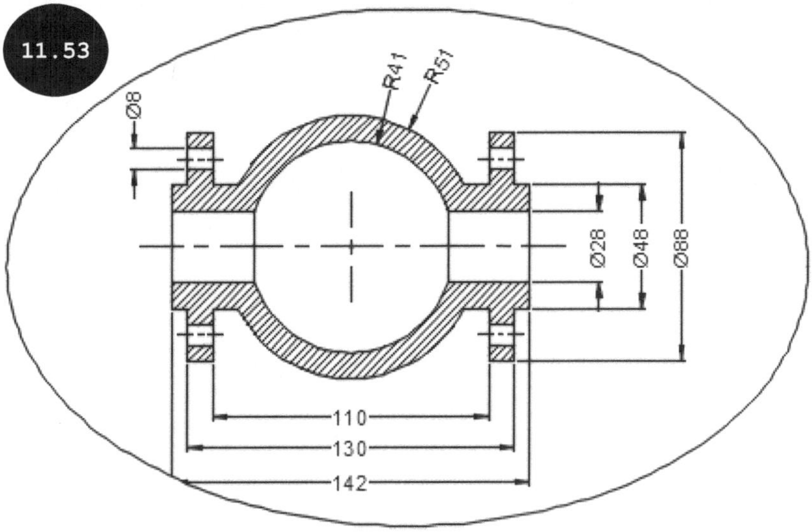

Section 4: Saving the Drawing

1. Click on the **Save** tool in the **Quick Access Toolbar**. The **Save Drawing As** dialog box appears.

2. Browse to the *AutoCAD* folder and then create a folder with the name *Chapter 11* inside the *AutoCAD* folder. Next, enter **Tutorial 1** in the **File name** field of the dialog box.

3. Click on the **Save** button. The drawing is saved with the name Tutorial 1 in the *Chapter 11* folder.

Hands-on Test Drive 1

Create the drawing in the Model space, see Figure 11.54. After creating the drawing, create two rectangular viewports in a layout, see Figure 11.55. In the first viewport, fit the drawing completely inside the viewport, see Figure 11.55 (a). In the second viewport, zoom the object such that it appears similar to the one shown in Figure 11.55 (b).

11.54

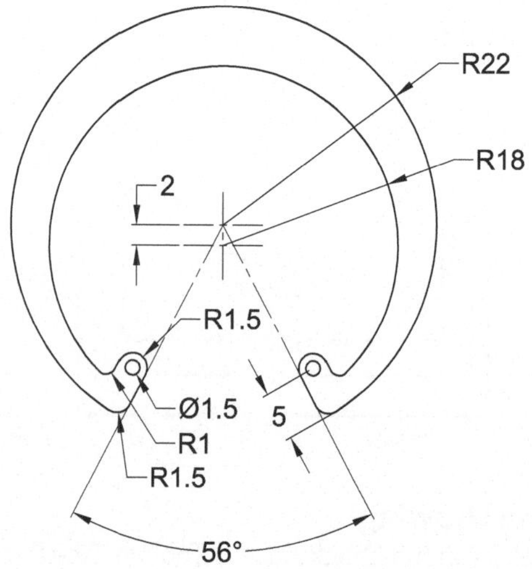

11.55

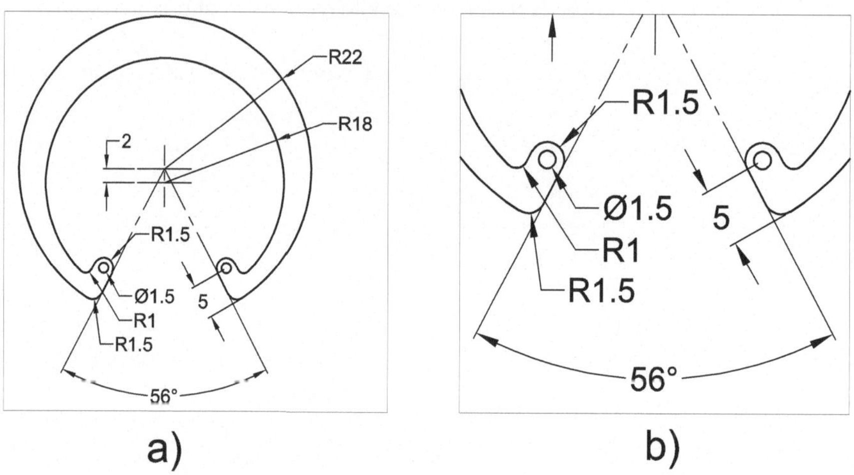

Hands-on Test Drive 2

Open the drawing created in Tutorial 2 of Chapter 7 and then create four rectangular viewports of equal sizes in a layout, see Figure 11.56. In these four viewports, adjust the drawing similar to the one shown in Figure 11.56.

11.56

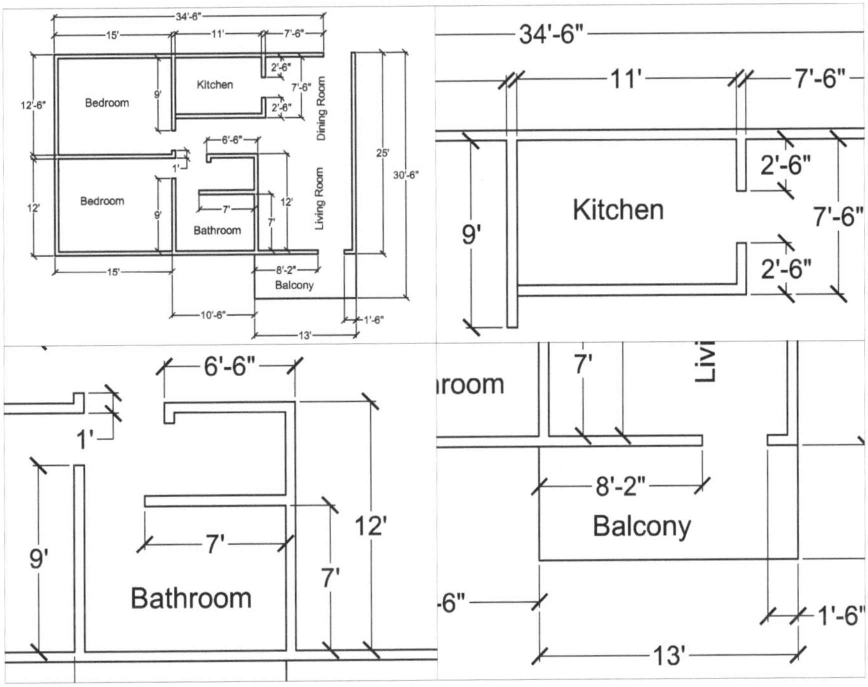

Summary

The chapter introduced how to get started with a Paper space/layout and the different components of a layout (Paper space). It also explained how to set up the sheet/paper size of a layout, and how to add, rename, and delete a layout in addition to working with viewports, accessing the Model space within a viewport, clipping a viewport, locking the object scale in a viewport, controlling the display of objects in a viewport, and controlling layer properties of a viewport. Additionally, it described methods for switching between the Model space and layout, and creating viewports in the Model space.

Questions

Complete the following sentences:

- AutoCAD is provided with two distinct working environments: ________ and ________.

- The ________ working environment of AutoCAD is used for plotting/printing drawings and generating different drawing views.
- The ________ tool in the **Layout** panel of the **Layout** tab is used for invoking the **Page Setup Manager** dialog box.
- A viewport created in a layout is known as ________ viewport.
- The ________ tool is used for creating rectangular viewports in a layout.
- The ________ tool is used for creating polygonal viewports in a layout.
- The ________ tool is used for converting a closed object into a viewport.
- The ________ tool is used for clipping the existing viewports of a layout.
- The ________ and ________ tools are used for locking and unlocking the scale (display) of objects in a viewport, respectively.
- The viewports created in the Model space are known as ________ viewports.
- The ________ tool is used for merging or joining two viewports in the Model space.

CHAPTER

12

Printing and Plotting

In this chapter, the following topics will be discussed:

- Configuring a Plotter (Output Device)
- Creating a Plot Style
- Setting up a Default Plot Style
- Plotting a Drawing

Printing/Plotting is a process of getting a hard-copy output of a drawing. The hard copy of a drawing is imperative to communicate ideas and information about the end product to the engineers working on the site. However, before you learn about plotting/printing a drawing in AutoCAD, it is important to understand how to configure a plotter (output device) and how to set up a plot style.

Configuring a Plotter (Output Device)

In AutoCAD, a plotter is used to send the output information to the system printer to get the hard copy of a drawing. To configure a plotter, click on the **Plotter Manager** tool in the **Plot** panel of the **Output** tab, see Figure 12.1. The **Plotters** system window appears, which displays the list of AutoCAD plotters, see Figure 12.2. Alternatively, enter **PLOTTERMANAGER** in the Command Line window and then press ENTER.

12.1

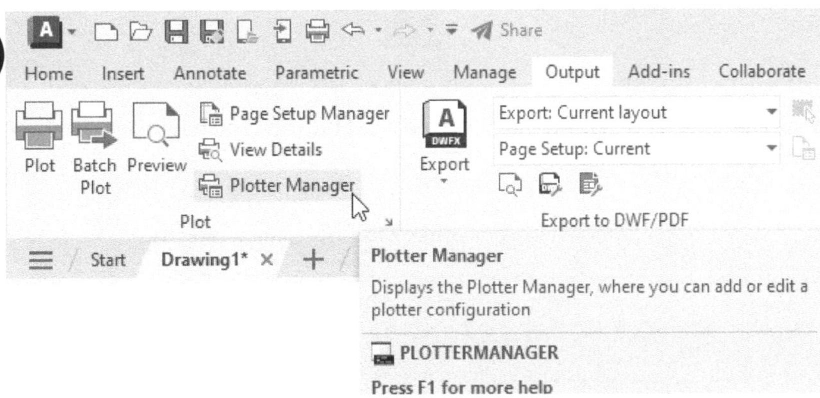

12.2

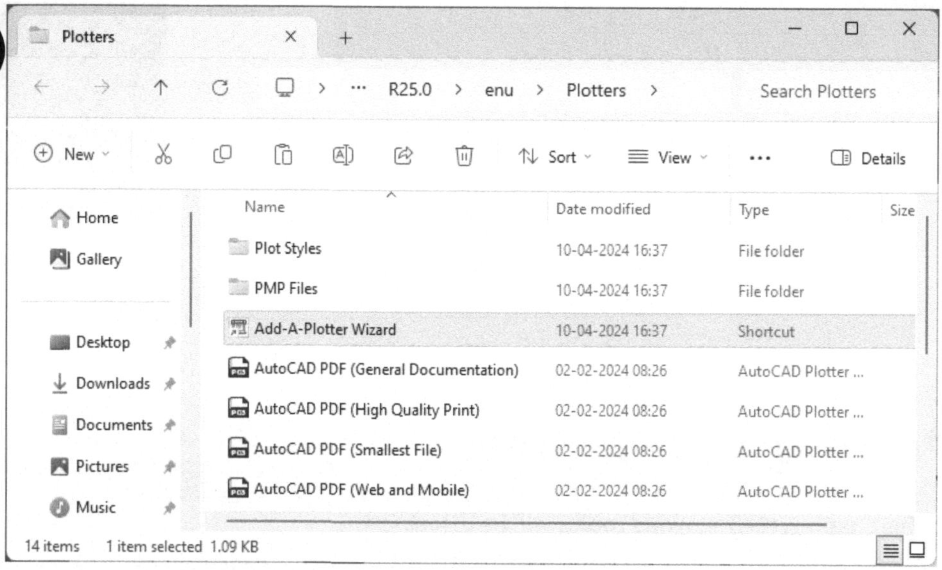

In the **Plotters** system window, double-click on the **Add-A-Plotter Wizard**. The **Add Plotter** dialog box is displayed with its **Introduction Page**, see Figure 12.3.

12.3

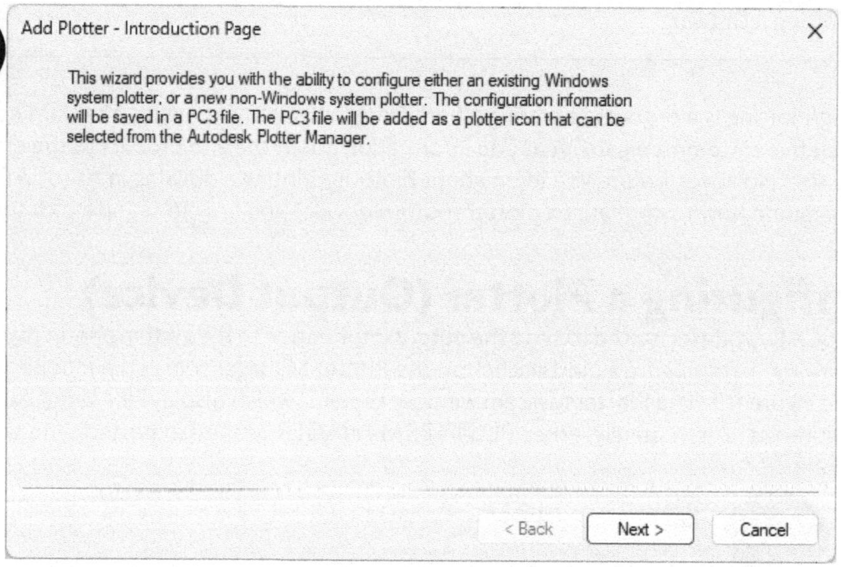

Next, in the **Add Plotter** dialog box, click on the **Next** button. The **Begin** page of the **Add Plotter** dialog box appears, see Figure 12.4.

12.4

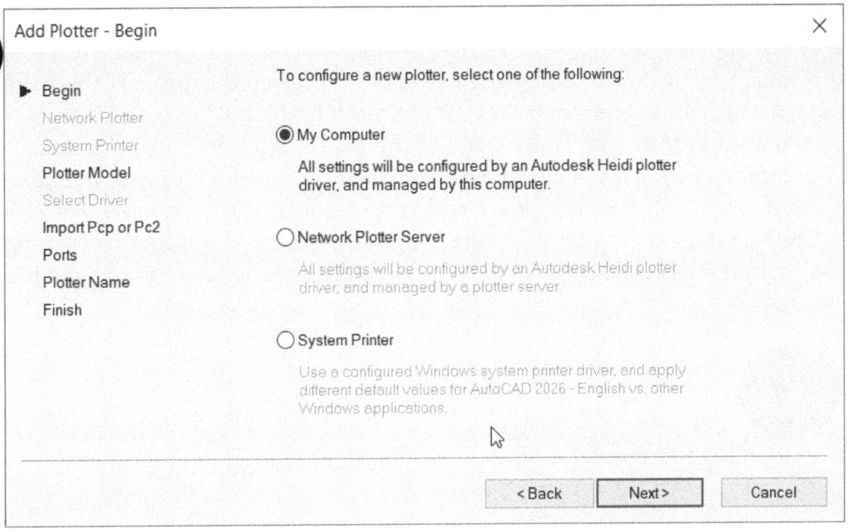

In the **Begin** page of the **Add Plotter** dialog box, select the **System Printer** radio button and then click on the **Next** button. The **System Printer** page of the **Add Plotter** dialog box appears, which displays the list of system printers installed on your system, see Figure 12.5. In Figure 12.5, the **HP LaserJet Pro MFP M126nw** is listed as the system printer installed on the system. In your case, the listed printers may differ depending on which printer drivers have been installed on your system. Note that if none of the printers are installed on your computer, then you need to install the printer first to add it as a plotter and to take the printout of the drawing. Select the system printer from the list of printers in the dialog box and then click on the **Next** button. The **Import Pcp or Pc2** page of the dialog box appears. This page is used to import a legacy PCP or PC2 file from older versions of AutoCAD.

12.5

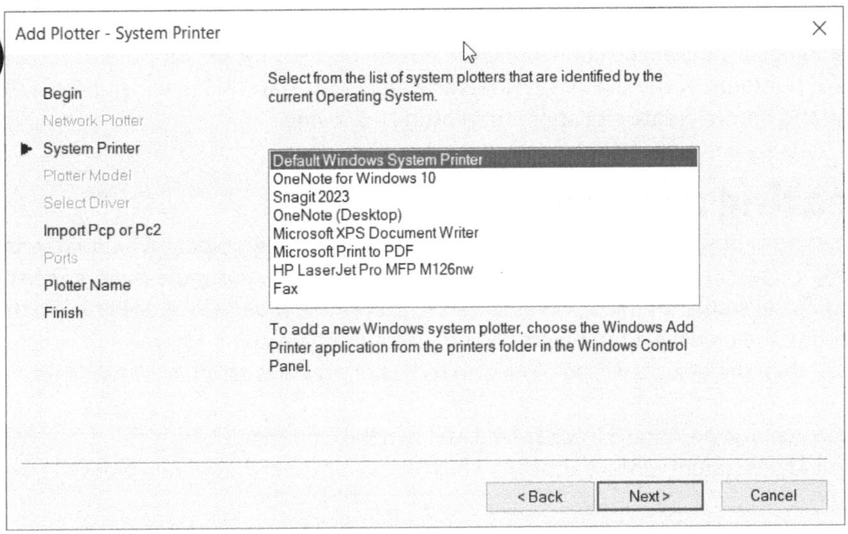

In the **Import Pcp or Pc2** page of the dialog box, click on the **Next** button. The **Plotter Name** page of the dialog box appears, see Figure 12.6. Enter the name of the plotter in the **Plotter Name** field of the **Plotter Name** page. By default, the name of the printer selected appears in this field. You can accept the default name or enter a new name for the plotter in this field. After entering the name of the plotter, click on the **Next** button. The **Finish** page of the **Add Plotter** dialog box appears. This page of the dialog box informs you that the plotter has been installed successfully with the default configuration settings. You can modify the default configuration settings of the installed plotter by using the **Edit Plotter Configuration** button on this page. Accept the default configuration settings for the plotter and then click on the **Finish** button in the dialog box. The dialog box is closed and the plotter is added in the AutoCAD.

12.6

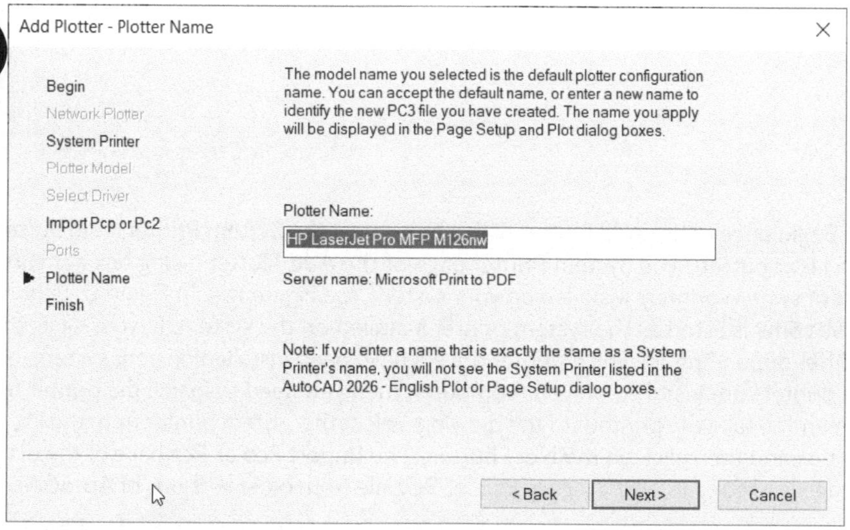

After adding the plotter and connecting the system printer to your computer through USB or wifi, you can take printouts of the drawing. However, before you start taking the printouts, it is important to understand how to create plot styles for plotting a drawing.

Creating a Plot Style

A plot style is used for defining the appearance of drawing objects which include color, linetype, lineweight, line end style, and so on. Note that the plot style overrides the layer properties of the drawing objects. For example, if red color is assigned to a layer and blue color is assigned to the plot style then on plotting the drawing, the objects will be plotted in blue color. However, if no plot style has been assigned then the objects will be plotted in red color, which is assigned to the layer.

To create a plot style, enter **STYLESMANAGER** in the Command Line window and then press ENTER. The **Plot Styles** system window appears, which displays a list of predefined plot style files, see Figure 12.7.

12.7

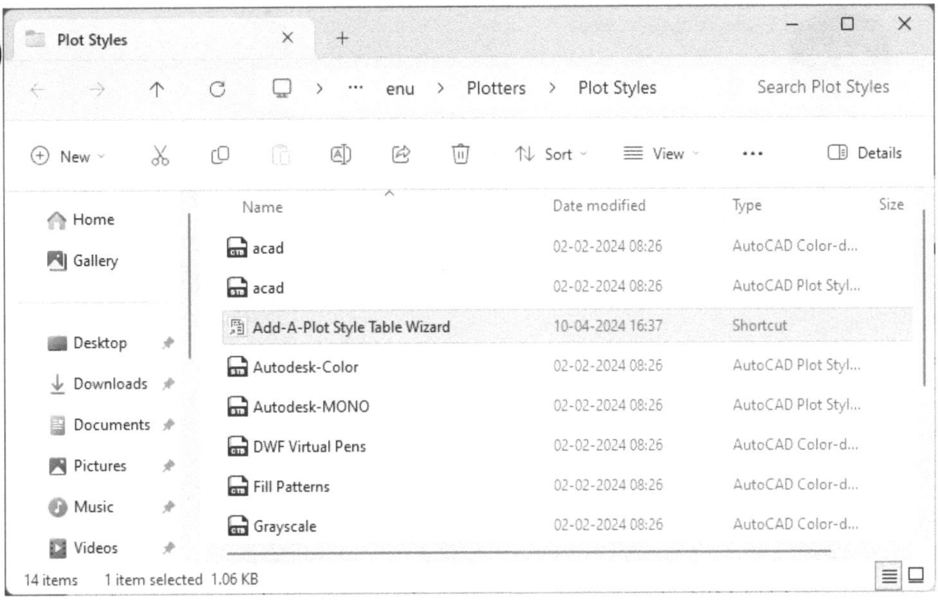

In this **Plot Styles** system window, double-click on the **Add-A-Plot Style Table Wizard**. The **Add Plot Style Table** dialog box appears, see Figure 12.8. Read the given information and then click on the **Next** button in the **Add Plot Style Table** dialog box. The **Begin** page of the **Add Plot Style Table** dialog box appears, see Figure 12.9.

12.8

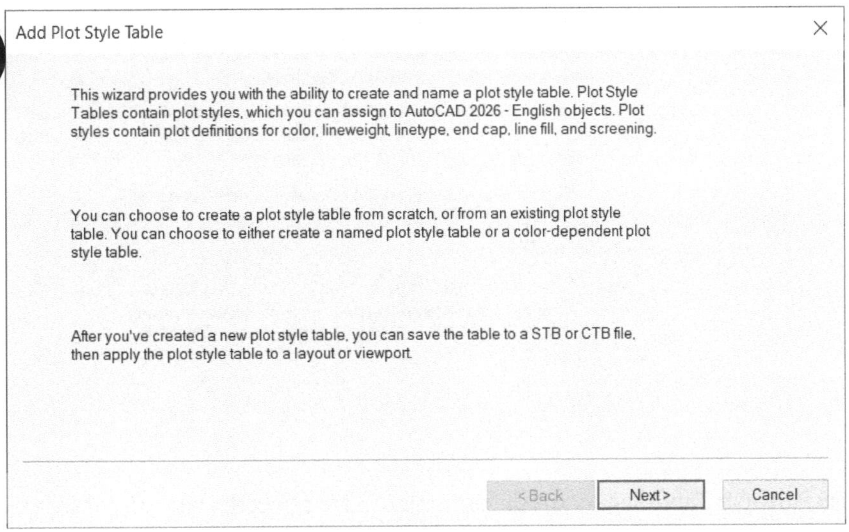

12.9

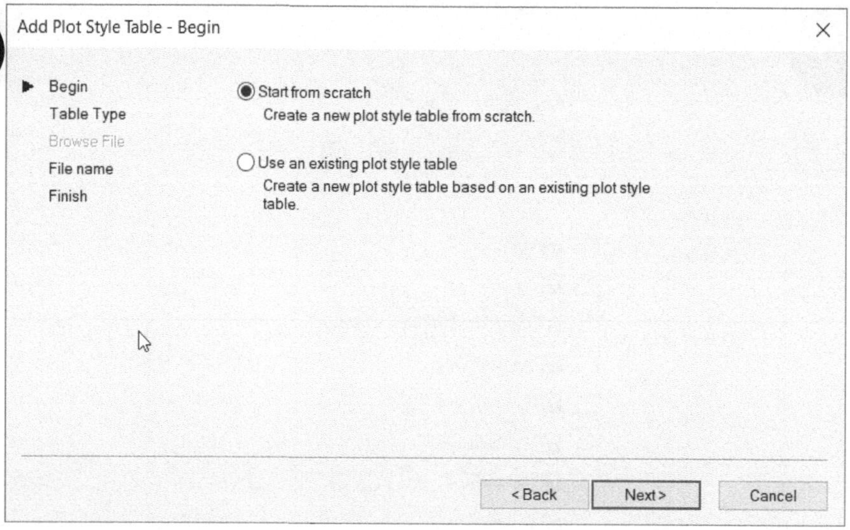

In the **Begin** page of the **Add Plot Style Table** dialog box, the **Start from scratch** radio button is selected by default. This radio button is used for creating a new plot style from scratch. On selecting the **Use an existing plot style table** radio button, you can select an existing plot style as the base style to create the new plot style. Select the **Start from scratch** radio button in the dialog box and then click on the **Next** button. The **Pick Plot Style Table** page of the dialog box appears, see Figure 12.10.

12.10

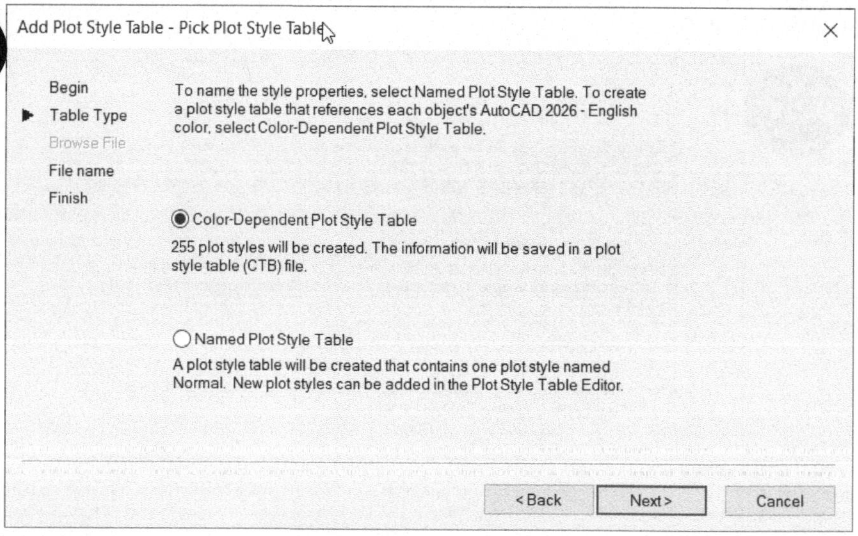

The **Pick Plot Style Table** page of the dialog box is used to select the type of plot style to be created. You can create two types of plot styles: color-dependent and named plot styles by choosing the respective radio buttons in the dialog box. The color-dependent plot style allows you to assign plot styles to the individual AutoCAD colors. For example, you can assign 0.5 mm width to the red objects of the drawing and 0.75 mm width to the blue objects of the drawing. In such a case, all red objects will plot with 0.5 mm width (pen) and the blue objects will plot with 0.75 mm width (pen). The color-dependent plot style is similar to the older method of highlighting the drawing objects with a particular physical pen whereas, the named plot style allows you to assign a plot style directly to objects or layers of the drawing instead of color only.

Select the required type of plot style in the dialog box by choosing the respective radio button (**Color-Dependent Plot Style Table** or **Named Plot Style Table**) and then click on the **Next** button. The **File name** page of the dialog box appears. Enter the name of the plot style in the **File name** field of the dialog box and then click on the **Next** button. The **Finish** page of the **Add Plot Style Table** dialog box appears, see Figure 12.11.

12.11

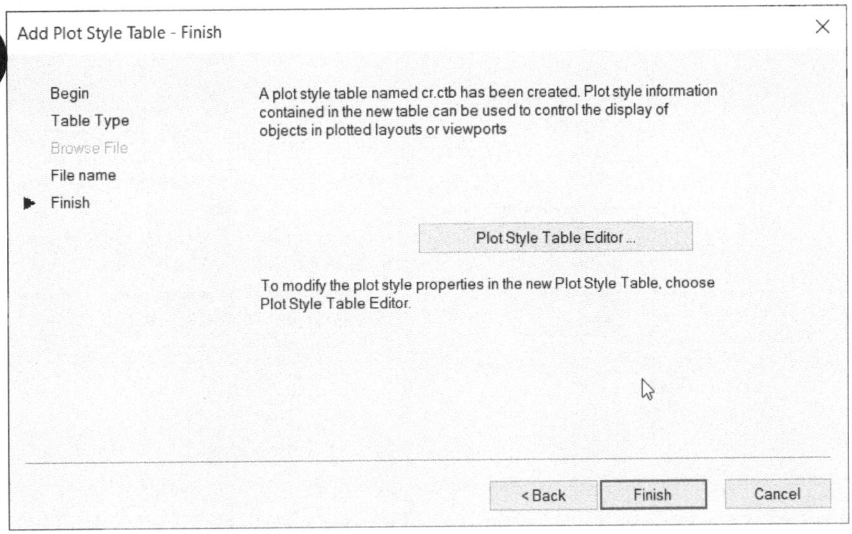

Note that the **Finish** page of the dialog box appears based on the type of plot style selected in the **Pick Plot Style Table** page of the dialog box. Figure 12.11 shows the **Finish** page when the **Color-Dependent Plot Style Table** radio button is selected as the plot style. The **Finish** page of the dialog box informs you that the plot style is created with the default settings. You can edit the default settings of the added plot style by using the **Plot Style Table Editor** button on the **Finish** page. When you click on the **Plot Style Table Editor** button, the **Plot Style Table Editor** dialog box appears. Note that the display of the **Plot Style Table Editor** dialog box depends on the type of plot style selected. Figure 12.12 shows the **Plot Style Table Editor** dialog box when the color-dependent plot style is selected, and Figure 12.13 shows the **Plot Style Table Editor** dialog box when the named plot style is selected.

12.12

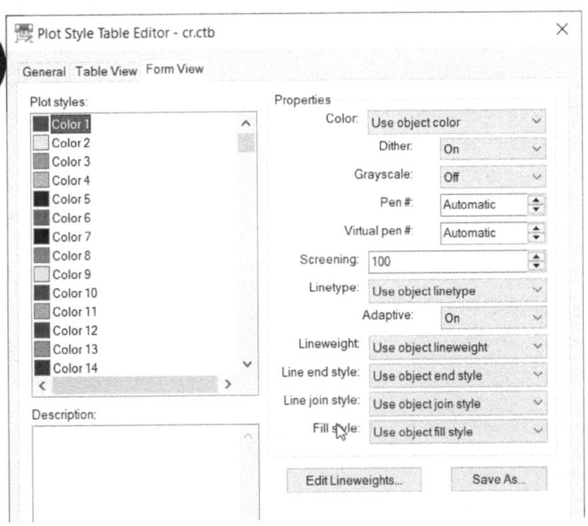

12.13

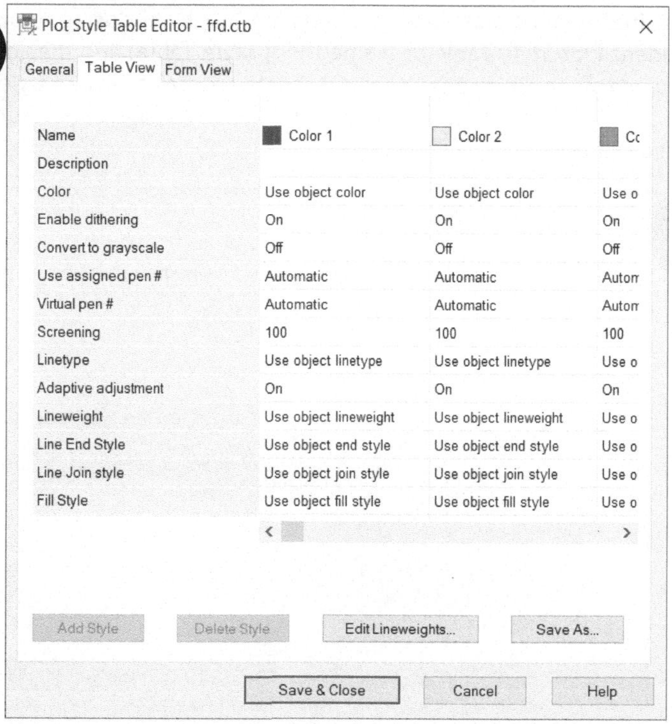

The **Plot Style Table Editor** dialog box has three tabs: **General**, **Table View**, and **Form View**. By using these tabs, you can edit all the properties of the plot style. The **General** tab of the dialog box displays information such as the name, path, scale factor, and description of the plot style. In this tab, all the information provided is read-only except the description.

The **Table View** tab of the dialog box displays all existing styles created in the plot style with their properties. In the case of a color-dependent plot style, the different color styles (**Color 1**, **Color 2**, **Color 3**, ... and **Color 255**) are displayed in the **Table View** tab of the dialog box. You can select a color style such as **Color 1**, **Color 2**, or **Color 3** in this tab of the dialog box and then edit its properties by using the respective fields or drop-down lists of the **Table View** tab in the dialog box. Whereas, in the case of a named plot style, the Normal style is the default created style and displayed in the **Table View** tab of the dialog box. You can edit the default style or add new styles by using the **Add Style** button of the dialog box, refer to Figure 12.13. On clicking the **Add Style** button in the **Table View** tab of the dialog box, a new column with the default style name "**Style 1**" is added to the dialog box. By using the fields or drop-down lists of the newly added column (Style 1), you can change the style name, and edit the style properties such as object color, linetype, lineweight, screening, and line end style.

The **Form View** tab of the **Plot Style Table Editor** dialog box displays a list of all the available styles. The available styles are displayed in the **Plot Styles** area of the dialog box and the properties of the selected style are displayed in the **Properties** area of the dialog box. You can select any style in the **Plot Styles** area and then edit its properties in the **Properties** area of the dialog box.

After editing the properties of the existing styles or creating new styles for the plot style in the **Plot Style Table Editor** dialog box, click on the **Save & Close** button to save the changes made and close the dialog box. Next, click on the **Finish** button in the **Add Plot Style Tabl**e dialog box. The plot style is created and saved as **.ctb* or **.stb* file in the **Plot Styles** directory of the local drive on your system. Note that the color-dependent plot style is saved with **.ctb* file extension, whereas the named plot style is saved with **.stb* file extension.

Setting up a Default Plot Style

After creating a plot style: color-dependent or named, you need to add the plot style in the drawing for plotting. You can add plot style by using the **Options** dialog box. To add a plot style for plotting the drawing, enter **OP** in the Command Line window and then press ENTER. The **Options** dialog box appears, see Figure 12.14. In the **Options** dialog box, click on the **Plot and Publish** tab. The options related to plotting and publishing the drawing appear in the dialog box, see Figure 12.14. Next, click on the **Plot Style Table Settings** button in the lower right of the dialog box. The **Plot Style Table Settings** dialog box appears, see Figure 12.15.

12.14

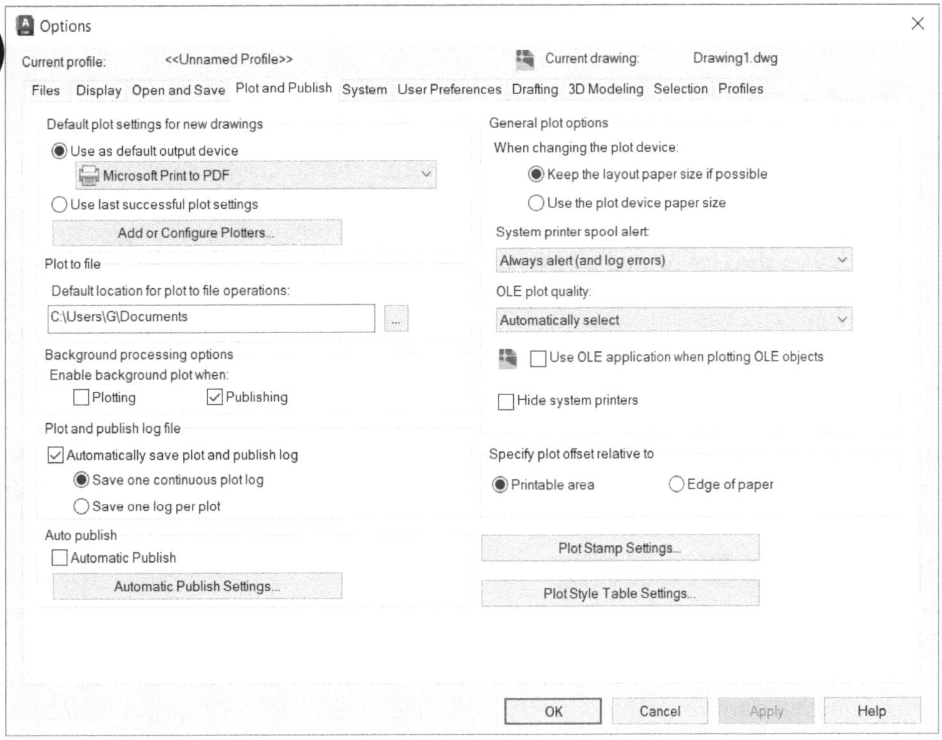

12.15

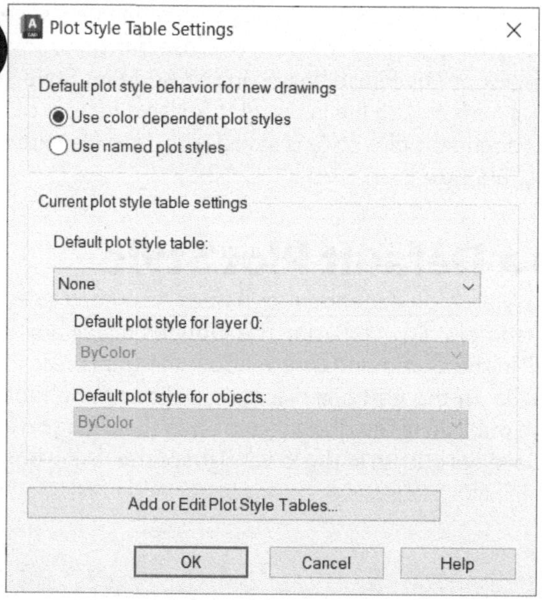

In the **Plot Style Table Settings** dialog box, the **Use color dependent plot styles** radio button is selected in the **Default plot style behavior for new drawings** area, and the **None** option is selected in the **Default plot style table** drop-down list, by default. As a result, the no color-dependent style is used as the default plot style for plotting the drawing. You can select a color-dependent plot style in the **Default plot style table** drop-down list as the default plot style. To define the named plot style as the default plot style, select the **Use named plot styles** radio button in the **Default plot style behavior for new drawings** area of the dialog box. Next, select a required named plot style in the **Default plot style table** drop-down list. Also, you can select the default plot style for the objects of layer 0 in the **Default plot style for layer 0** drop-down list and the default style for the drawing objects in the **Default plot style for objects** drop-down list of the dialog box. After specifying the default plot style (color-dependent or named), click on the OK button in the **Plot Style Table Settings** dialog box and then click on the **OK** button in the **Options** dialog box. The default plot style is specified. Note that the changes made in the **Plot Style Table Settings** dialog box are reflected in the new drawing only (not in the current drawing).

Plotting a Drawing

After adding the plotter and creating the plot style, as required, you can plot the drawing on a sheet of paper. You can plot drawings in the Model space as well as in the Paper space (layout). Plotting drawings in Model space is usually done to create a test plot. Whereas, the Paper space (layout) is the recommended environment for plotting drawings where you can display multiple scaled drawing views in different viewports. The methods for plotting a drawing in both environments (Model space and Paper space) are the same.

To plot a drawing, activate the required environment (Model space or Paper space) for plotting the drawing. To activate the Model space, click on the **Model** tab, whereas to activate the Paper space, click on the required layout tab (**Layout1, Layout2**, ...) in the lower left corner of the drawing area. Next, click on the **Plot** tool in the **Plot** panel of the **Output** tab, see Figure 12.16. The **Plot** dialog box appears, see Figure 12.17. Alternatively, press CTRL+ P to invoke the **Plot** dialog box. You can also right-click on the active **Model** tab or the active layout tab and then click on the **Plot** option in the shortcut menu that appears to invoke the **Plot** dialog box.

12.16

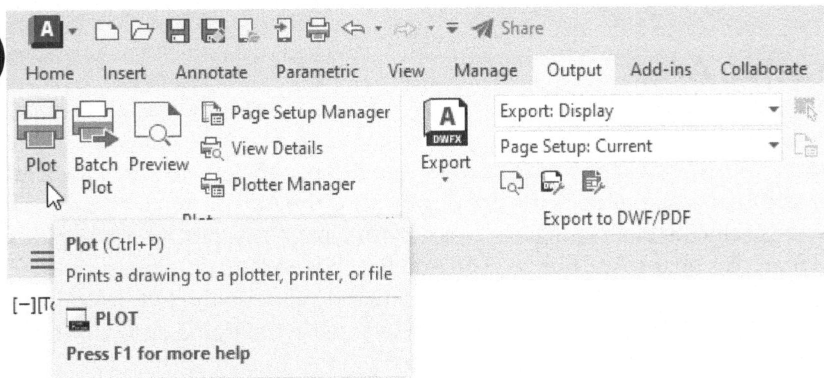

12.17

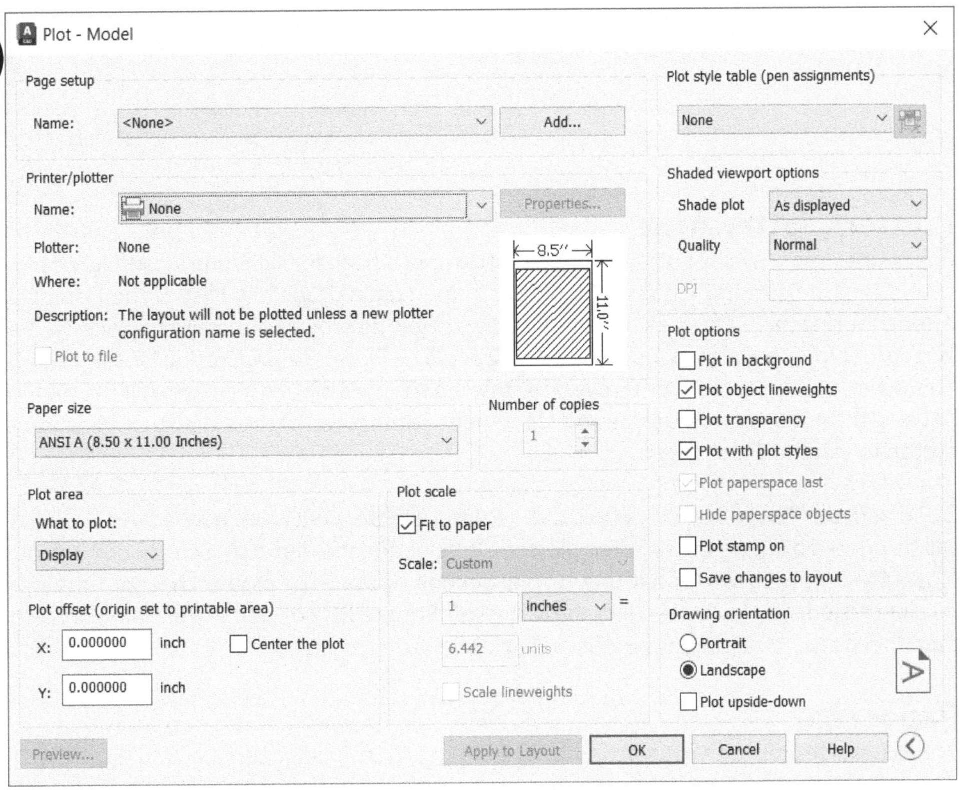

The options in the **Plot** dialog box are used for specifying plot settings such as a plotter, page size, plot area, plot scale, plot style, and drawing orientation. Some of the options of the **Plot** dialog box are discussed next.

Page setup Area

The **Page setup** area of the dialog box is used for selecting an already saved page setup. A page setup consists of plot settings such as a plotter, page size, plot area, plot scale, plot style, and drawing orientation. You can select an already saved page setup in the **Name** drop-down list of this area. You can also add a new page setup in the drawing by using the **Add** button in this area. To add a new page setup, first specify the plot settings such as a plotter, page size, plot area, and plot scale in the dialog box and then click on the **Add** button. The **Add Page Setup** dialog box appears, see Figure 12.18. In this dialog box, enter the name of the page setup and then click on the **OK** button. The new page setup with the specified plot settings gets added and selected in the **Name** drop-down list of the dialog box.

12.18

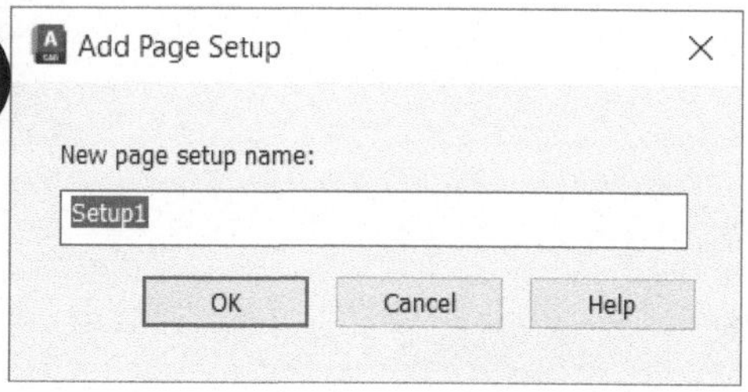

Printer/plotter Area

The **Name** drop-down list of the **Printer/plotter** area is used for selecting a configured plotting device for plotting the drawing. Choose the plotter in the **Name** drop-down list of the **Printer/plotter** area. After choosing the plotter, you can also edit or review its properties. To do so, click on the **Properties** button in the **Printer/plotter** area of the dialog box. The **Plotter Configuration Editor** dialog box appears. This dialog box displays the information about the selected plotter. You can edit the plotter properties by using the options in the **Device and Document Settings** tab of the dialog box. Next, click on the **OK** button to exit the dialog box.

By default, the **Plot to file** check box of the **Printer/plotter** area is unchecked. As a result, the drawing will be printed by using the selected plotter. On selecting the **Plot to file** check box, the output can be plotted to a file such as .dwf, .plt, .jpg, or .png depending upon the plotter chosen. You can also plot the output to a .pdf file. To do so, select the **Microsoft Print to PDF** option in the **Name** drop-down list and then specify the remaining plot settings. The options for specifying the plot settings are discussed next.

Paper size

The **Paper size** drop-down list is used for selecting the standard paper size for the selected plotter. This drop-down list displays a list of standard paper sizes. Note that the availability of paper sizes in this drop-down list depends upon the plotter selected in the **Name** drop-down list of the **Printer/Plotter** area in the dialog box. If the **None** option is selected in the **Name** drop-down list, then all the standard paper sizes are listed in this drop-down list.

Number of copies

The **Number of copies** field is used for specifying the number of copies to print. Note that if the **Plot to file** check box is selected in the **Printer/plotter** area, then the **Number of copies** field is disabled.

Plot area

The options in the **What to plot** drop-down list of the **Plot area** are used for specifying the portion of the drawing to print. The options in the **What to plot** drop-down list are displayed depending on whether you are plotting in Model space or Paper space (layout). Figure 12.19 shows the **What to plot** drop-down list when you are in Model space, and Figure 12.20 shows the **What to plot** drop-down list when you are in Paper space (layout). The options are discussed next.

12.19

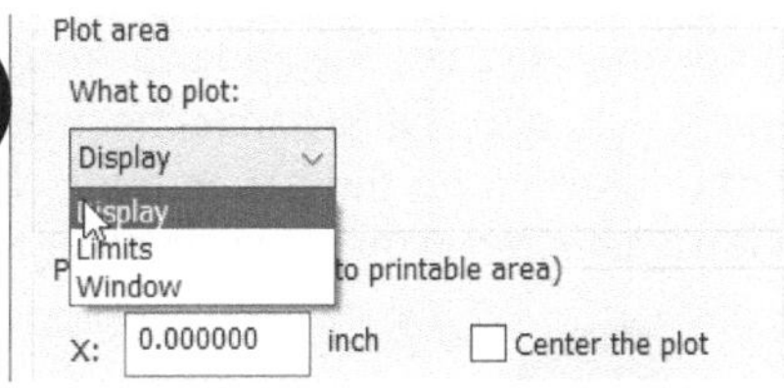

12.20

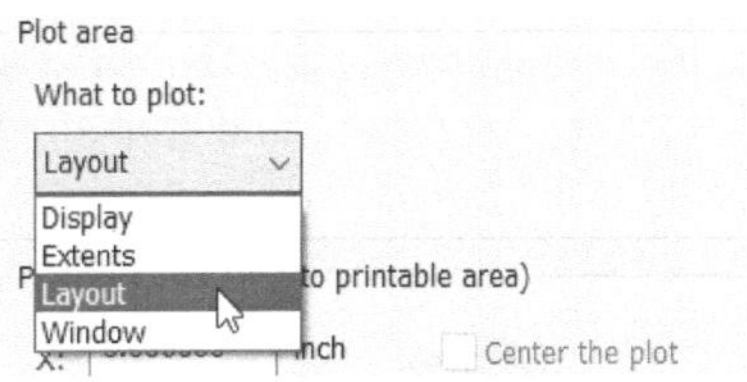

Display

The **Display** option of the **What to plot** drop-down list is used for plotting the portion of the drawing that is currently displayed on the screen.

Extents

The **Extents** option is used for plotting the portion of the drawing that contains objects. By using this option, you can plot the entire drawing even if some of its objects are not currently displayed on the screen.

Limits

The **Limits** option is used for plotting the complete area that is defined by the drawing limits. Note that this option is available only if you are plotting the drawing in the Model space.

Layout

The **Layout** option is used for plotting the drawing that lies within the printable area of the active layout. Note that this option is available only if you are plotting the drawing in the Paper space (layout).

Window

The **Window** option is used for defining a window around the area/portion of the drawing to print. On selecting the **Window** option, the **Plot** dialog box disappears, and you are prompted to specify the first corner of the window. Click to specify the first corner. You are prompted to specify the opposite corner of the window. Click to specify the opposite corner. The area to be plotted is defined by the window drawn, and the **Plot** dialog box appears again.

Plot offset (origin set to printable area)

The options in the **Plot offset (origin set to printable area)** area are used for specifying offset distances from the origin (0,0) to define the lower left corner of the printable area. By default, the origin (0,0) is defined as the lower left corner of the printable area, see Figure 12.21. You can specify the X and Y offset distances from the origin (0,0) to define the lower left corner of the printable area in the X and Y fields of this area, respectively.

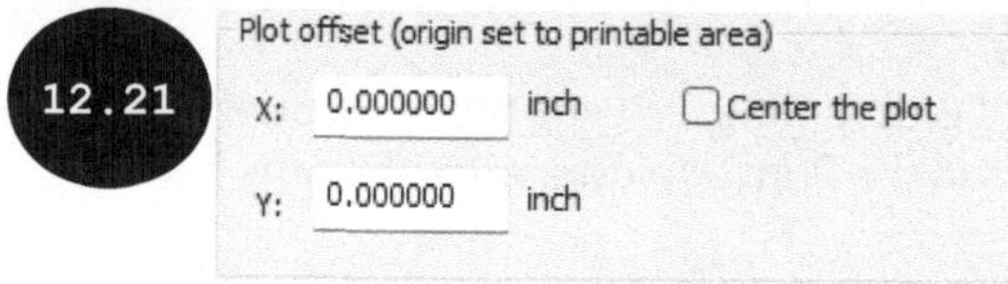

On selecting the **Center the plot** check box, AutoCAD automatically calculates the X and Y offset values to center the plot on the paper. Note that the **Center the plot** check box is not enabled when the **Layout** option is selected in the **What to plot** drop-down list of the **Plot** area.

Plot scale

The options in the **Plot scale** area are used for controlling the scale of the drawing concerning the plot area. By default, the scale is set to 1:1 in the **Scale** drop-down list, see Figure 12.22. You can specify a scale for the plot in the **Scale** drop-down list, as required. When the **Fit to paper** check box is selected, see Figure 12.23, AutoCAD automatically fits the entire drawing on the paper. Note that the **Fit to paper** check box is not enabled when the **Layout** option is selected in the **What to plot** drop-down list.

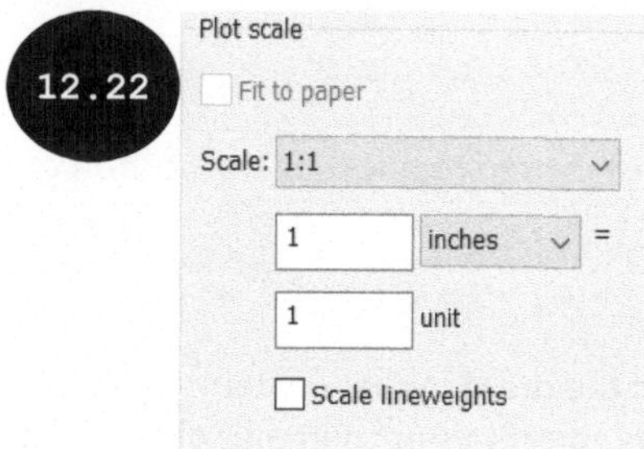

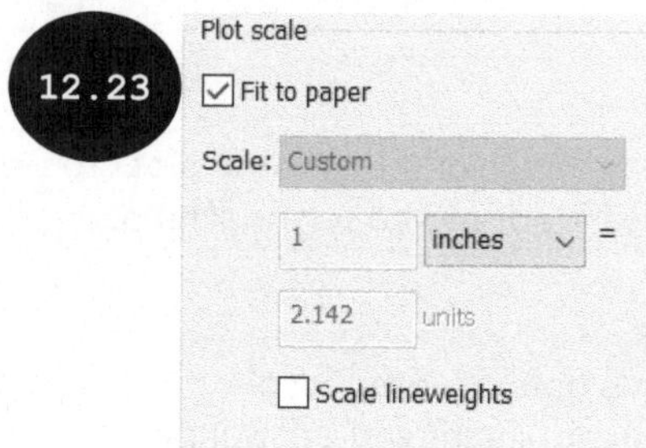

On selecting the **Scale lineweights** check box of this area, the lineweights of the objects to be plotted to get scaled in proportion to the specified plot scale. Note that this **Scale lineweights** check box is not enabled when you are plotting in the Model space.

Plot style table (pen assignments)

The **Plot style table (pen assignments)** area is used for selecting a plot style for plotting the drawing. The **Plot style table** drop-down list in this area displays a list of already created plot styles. You can select the required plot style in this drop-down list. By default, the **None** option is selected in the **Plot style table** drop-down list. As a result, no plot style is used for plotting the drawing and the drawing will plot as per the layers properties of the drawing objects. As discussed, a plot style overrides the layer properties of the drawing objects. Note that when you select a plot style in this drop-down list, the **Question** window may appear. In this window, click on the **Yes** button to assign the selected plot style to all the layouts of the drawing. If you want to assign the selected plot style only to the currently active layout, then click on the **No** button in this window.

Note: If you are working with default drawing template (*acad.dwt*), then the **Plot style table** drop-down list of the **Plot style table (pen assignments)** area displays a list of color-dependent plot styles. To display the default specified plot styles: named or color-dependent specified in the **Plot Style Table Settings** dialog box, you need to open the drawing without the default template. For doing so, click on the **New** tool in the **Quick Access Toolbar**. The **Select template** dialog box appears, see Figure 12.24. In this dialog box, select the **acad.dwt** template file and then click on the arrow next to the **Open** button in the dialog box. A flyout appears, see Figure 12.24. In this flyout, either click on the **Open with no Template - Imperial** or the **Open with no Template - Metric** option, as required. The new drawing file with no default template gets opened.

12.24

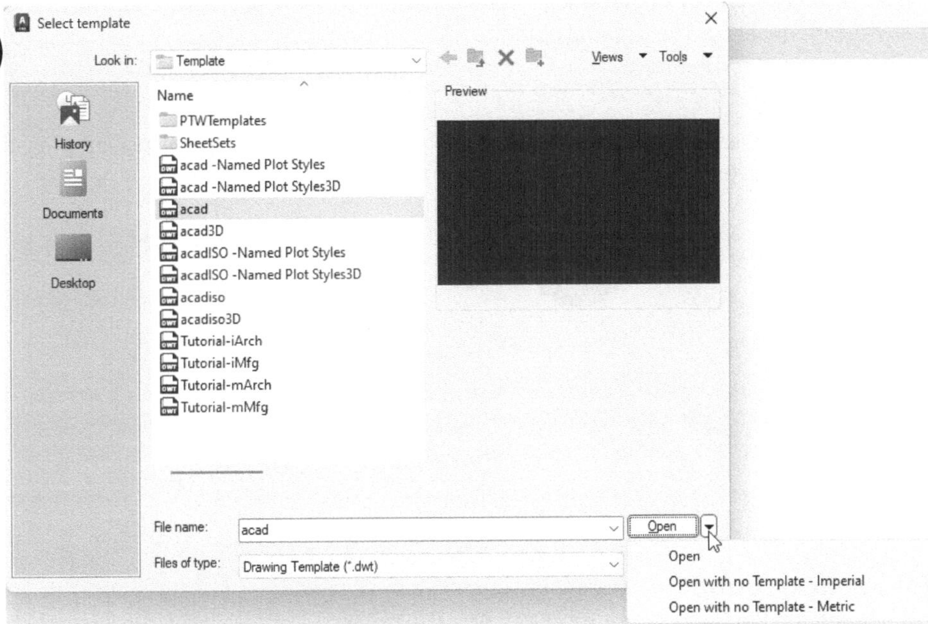

You can also edit or modify the properties of the selected plot style by using the **Edit** button available next to the **Plot style table** drop-down list in the **Plot style table (pen assignments)** area of the dialog box. On clicking the **Edit** button, the **Plot Style Table Editor** dialog box appears, which is used for editing the properties of the selected plot style. After making the changes in the selected plot style, you can click on the **Save & Close** button in the **Plot Style Table Editor** dialog box to save the changes made and to exit the dialog box.

Shaded viewport options

The options in the **Shaded viewport options** area of the dialog box are used for plotting a shaded or a rendered image of the drawing. By default, the **As displayed** option is selected in the **Shade plot** drop-down list, see Figure 12.25. As a result, the drawing objects are plotted as they appear on the screen. Note that the **Shade plot** drop-down list of this area is enabled if you are plotting the drawing in Model space.

12.25

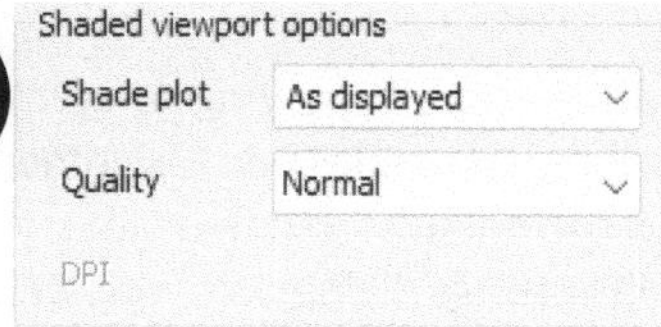

On selecting an option in the **Shade plot** drop-down list, the drawing gets plotted with the respective display style. The options include **Legacy wireframe**, **Legacy hidden**, **Conceptual**, **Hidden**, **Realistic**, **Shaded**, **Shaded with edges**, **Shades of Gray**, **Sketchy**, **Wireframe**, **X-Ray**, **Rendered**, **Low**, **Medium**, and **High**.

The options in the **Quality** drop-down list of the **Shaded viewport options** area are used for selecting the printing quality/resolution at which shaded and rendered drawing objects are to be plotted. You can select the **Draft**, **Preview**, **Normal**, **Presentation**, **Maximum**, or **Custom** option in the drop-down list as the plot quality of the drawing objects.

Plot options

The **Plot options** area is provided with additional options to control the display of drawing objects in print, see Figure 12.26. The options are discussed next.

12.26

Plot in background

On selecting the **Plot in background** check box, the process of plotting the drawing takes place in the background only.

Plot object lineweights

By default, the **Plot object lineweights** check box is selected in this area. As a result, the objects are plotted as per the lineweights assigned to the objects and layers.

Plot transparency

On selecting the **Plot transparency** check box, the objects are plotted with specified transparency.

Plot with plot styles

By default, the **Plot with plot styles** check box is selected in this area. As a result, the objects are plotted with the specified plot style.

Plot paperspace last

The **Plot paperspace last** check box is enabled if you are plotting the drawing in a layout. By default, this check box is selected. As a result, the Model space geometry is plotted first, followed by the Paper space geometry.

Hide Paperspace Objects

The **Hide Paperspace Objects** check box is enabled if you are working on a layout. On selecting the **Hide Paperspace Objects** check box, the 3D model drawn in a layout is plotted with hidden lines removed display style. You can copy and paste the 3D model drawn in Model space to a layout.

Plot stamp on

On selecting the **Plot stamp on** check box, the display of the plot stamp is turned on in the plot. The plot stamp settings can be specified in the **Plot Stamp** dialog box. A plot stamp is used for adding a logo or additional information about the current drawing such as drawing name, layout name, date and time, and paper size. To invoke the **Plot Stamp** dialog box, click on the **Plot stamp on** check box. The **Plot Stamp Settings** button appears, see Figure 12.27. Next, click on this button to invoke the **Plot Stamp** dialog box. Alternatively, you can invoke the **Plot Stamp** dialog box for specifying the plot stamp settings by clicking on the **Plot Stamp Settings** button in the **Plot and Publish** tab of the **Options** dialog box.

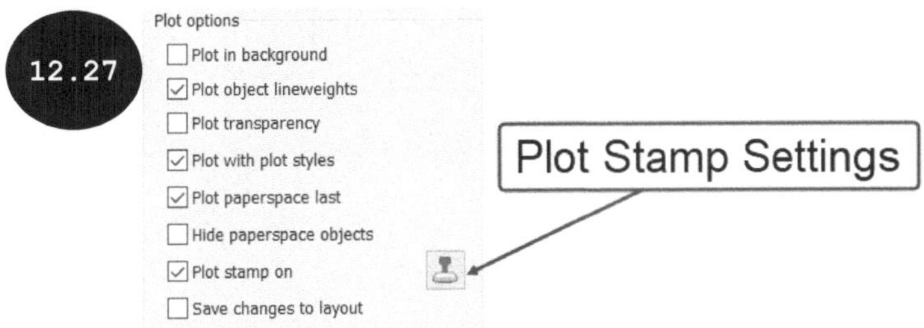

Save changes to layout

On selecting the **Save changes to layout** check box, the changes made in the **Plot** dialog box get saved with the current layout.

Drawing orientation

The options in the **Drawing orientation** area are used for specifying the orientation (portrait or landscape) of the drawing on the paper, see Figure 12.28. You can select the **Portrait** or **Landscape** radio button as per the requirement to specify the orientation of the drawing. The **Plot upside-down** check box is used for flipping the orientation of the plot upside down depending upon whether the **Portrait** or **Landscape** radio button is selected.

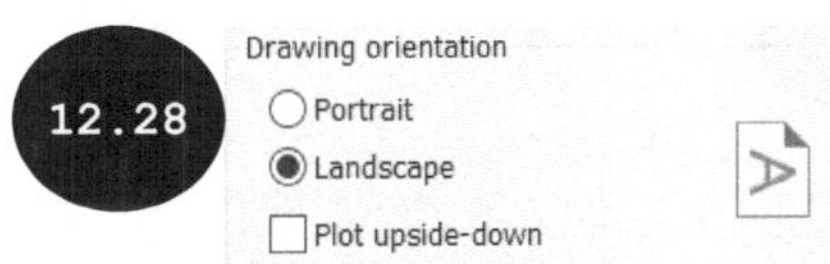

OK

After specifying all the plot settings/parameters in the **Plot** dialog box, click on the **OK** button. The **Plot Job Progress** window appears, which indicates that the process of plotting the drawing is in progress. Once the process of plotting the drawing is completed, the **Plot Job Progress** window gets closed, and you get the plotter output of the drawing.

Tutorial 1

Create the drawing shown in Figure 12.29 in the Model space. After creating the drawing, take the printout of the drawing on a sheet of paper with the default settings.

12.29

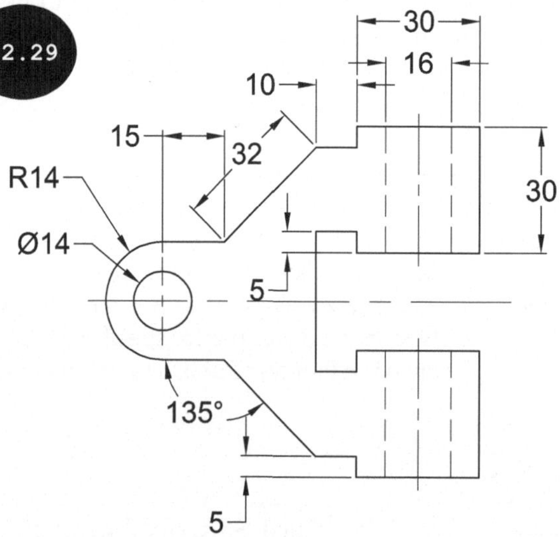

Section 1: Starting AutoCAD

1. Start AutoCAD and then open a new drawing file.

Section 2: Creating Drawing

1. Create the drawing and apply dimensions, see Figure 12.30.

Note: To create the drawing, you need to create different layers for hidden lines, centerlines, object entities, and dimensions. Also, for dimensions, you need to change the settings such that the dimension text, arrow, and so on, are visible clearly in the drawing. You can control the dimension settings either by creating a new dimension style or by editing an existing style using the **Dimension Style Manager** dialog box, as discussed in earlier chapters.

12.30

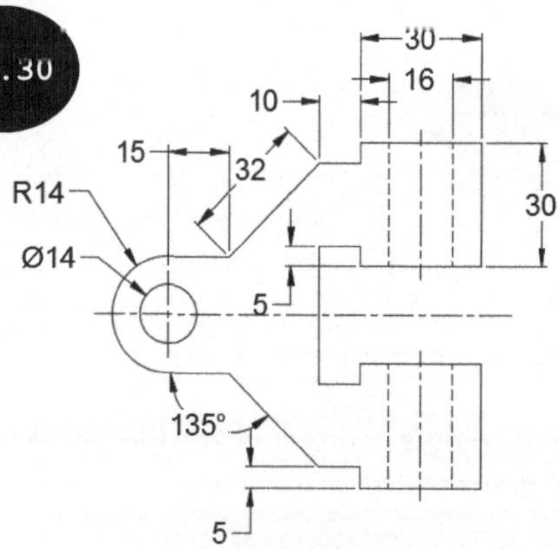

Section 3: Configuring/Adding Plotter

1. Ensure that a plotter is configured in your system. Before configuring a plotter, ensure that the system printer (output device) is installed on your computer.

   To configure a plotter, enter **PLOTTERMANAGER** in the Command Line window and then press ENTER. The **Plotters** system window appears. Alternatively, click on the **Plotter Manager** tool in the **Plot** panel of the **Output** tab in the **Ribbon** for invoking the **Plotters** system window. Next, double-click on **Add-A-Plotter Wizard** in the **Plotters** system window. The **Introduction Page** of the **Add Plotter** dialog box appears, see Figure 12.31.

   12.31

   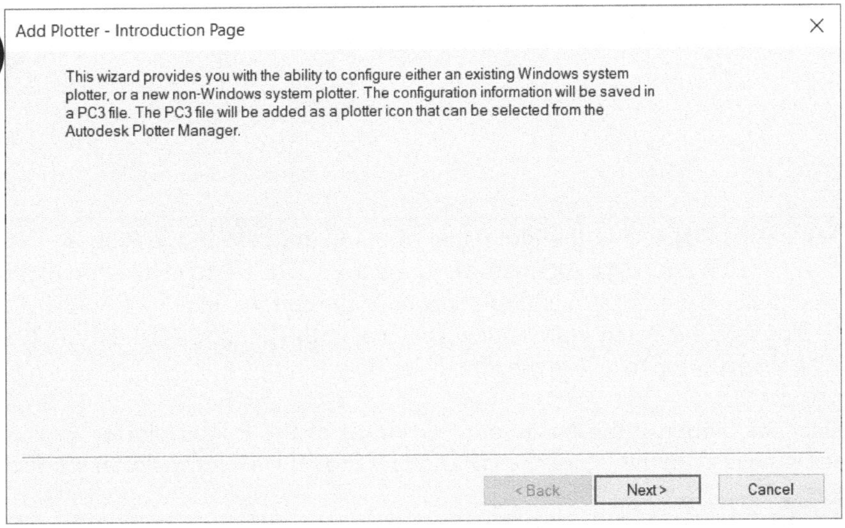

   Next, read the information given in the **Introduction Page** of the **Add Plotter** dialog box and then click on the **Next** button. The **Begin** page of the dialog box appears. In the **Begin** page, select the **System Printer** radio button and then click on the **Next** button. The **System Printer** page of the dialog box appears. On this page, choose the system printer. If the system printer is not listed on this page, then you need to install the printer drivers in your system first. After selecting the system printer, click on the **Next** button. The **Import Pcp or Pc2** page appears. Click on the **Next** button in the **Import Pcp or Pc2** page. The **Plotter Name** page appears. Enter the name of the plotter on this page and then click on the **Next** button. The **Finish** page of the dialog box appears. Next, click on the **Finish** button. The plotter gets configured in the system.

2. Ensure that the system printer is connected to your computer through USB, Wifi, or any other mode.

Section 4: Plotting/Printing Drawing

1. Click on the **Layout1** tab in the lower left corner of the drawing area. The **Layout1** tab gets activated, and the drawing created in the Model space appears in the default viewport of the layout, see Figure 12.32. You can also delete the default viewport and create a new viewport as per your requirement by using the MV command or by using the tools in the **Layout Viewports** panel of the **Layout** tab in the **Ribbon**.

12.32

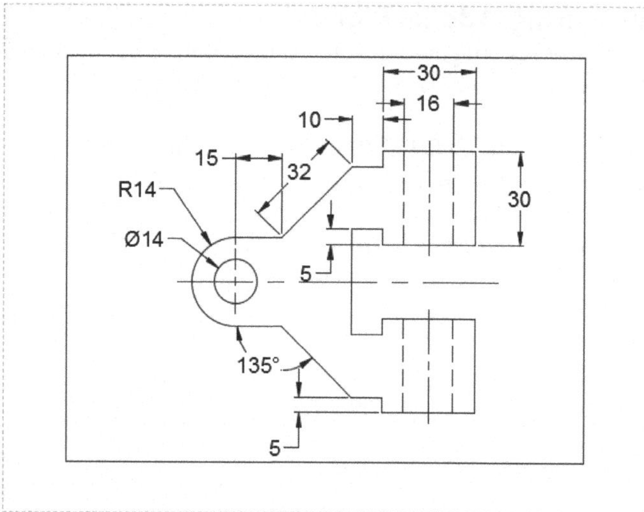

2. Click on the **Plot** tool in the **Plot** panel of the **Output** tab in the **Ribbon**. The **Plot** dialog box appears, see Figure 12.33. Alternatively, press the CTRL + P to invoke the **Plot** dialog box. Note that if multiple drawings/layouts are opened in the current session of AutoCAD then on clicking the **Plot** tool, the **Batch Plot** window appears. In this window, click on the **Continue to plot a single sheet** button to invoke the **Plot** dialog box.

3. Select the plotter in the **Name** drop-down list of the **Printer/plotter** area in the dialog box, see Figure 12.33. In this figure, the **HP LaserJet Pro MFP M126nw** plotter is selected.

12.33

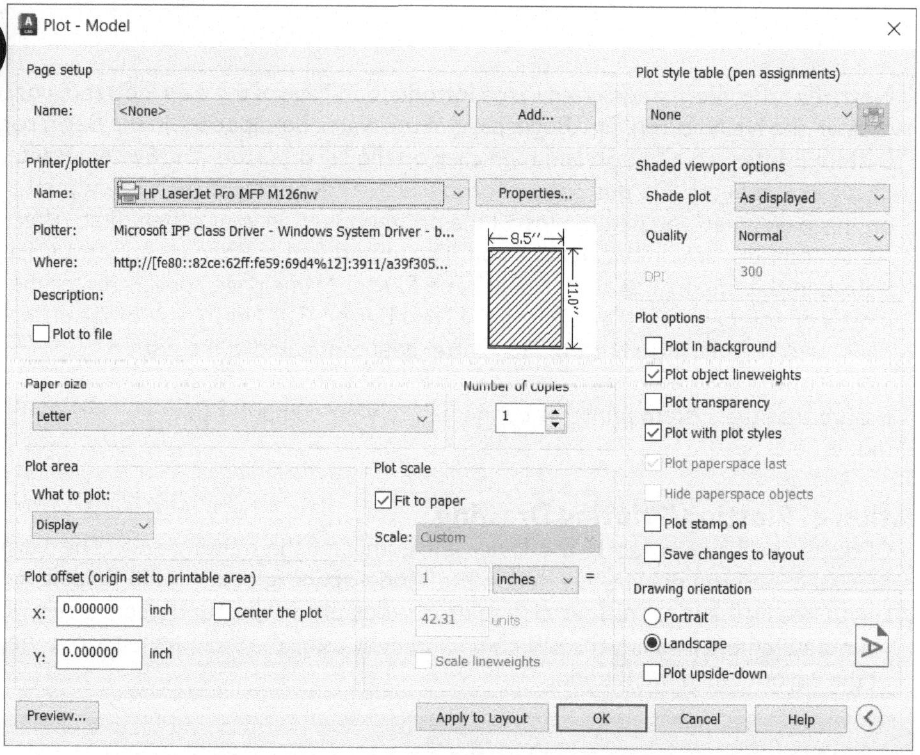

4. Select the **A4** paper size in the **Paper size** drop-down list of the dialog box.

5. Select the **Window** option in the **What to plot** drop-down list of the **Plot area** in the dialog box. The **Plot** dialog box disappears, and you are prompted to specify the first corner of the plot window.

```
Specify first corner:
```

Note: If the **Window** option is selected by default in the **What to plot** drop-down list, then you need to click on the **Window** button that appears next to the **What to plot** drop-down list.

6. Click to specify the first corner of the plot window. Note that the plot window defines the area of the drawing to be printed. You are prompted to specify the opposite corner of the window.

```
Specify first corner: Specify opposite corner:
```

7. Click to specify the opposite corner of the plot window. The plottable area is defined, and the **Plot** dialog box appears again.

8. Ensure that the **Center the plot** and **Fit to paper** check boxes of the dialog box are selected.

9. Accept the remaining default plot settings in the dialog box and then click on the **OK** button. The **Plot Job Progress** window appears, and the process of plotting starts. Once the process of plotting the drawing is completed, the **Plot Job Progress** window disappears, and the drawing gets plotted on a sheet of paper. Ensure that your printer device is connected to your computer through USB or wifi before taking the printout of the drawing. To view the preview of the plot before taking the print, click on the **Preview** button of the dialog box.

Section 5: Saving the Drawing

1. Click on the **Save** tool in the **Quick Access Toolbar**. The **Save Drawing As** dialog box appears.

2. Browse to the *AutoCAD* folder and then create a folder with the name *Chapter 12* inside the *AutoCAD* folder. Next, enter **Tutorial 1** in the **File name** field of the dialog box and then click on the **Save** button. The drawing is saved with the name Tutorial 1 in the *Chapter 12* folder.

Tutorial 2

Create the drawing as shown in Figure 12.34 in the Model space. You need to assign a blue color to hidden lines, a magenta color to dimensions, a black color to objects entities, and a cyan color to the reference lines of the drawing. You can assign these different colors to the drawing entities by creating different layers. Note that in Figure 12.34, the reference lines are turned off. After creating the drawing with different colors, you need to take a printout of the drawing by creating a color-dependent plot style named 'My Color Plot Style' such that all drawing entities are printed in black color on a sheet of paper. Also, assign the 0.8 mm lineweight to the object entities, 0.65 mm lineweight to the dimensions, and 0.53 mm lineweight to hidden lines in the color-dependent plot style for taking a printout of the drawing.

12.34

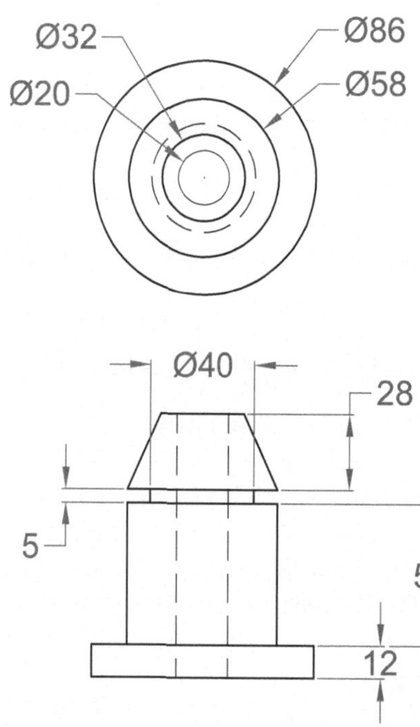

Section 1: Starting AutoCAD

1. Start AutoCAD and then open a new drawing file.

Section 2: Creating Layers

1. Invoke the **LAYER PROPERTIES MANAGER** and then create four layers with the names: **Object**, **Dimension**, **Hidden**, and **Reference**. Next, assign a magenta color to the **Dimension** layer, a blue color to the **Hidden** layer, and a cyan color to the **Reference** layer. Also, assign the **CENTER** linetype to the **Reference** layer, the **HIDDEN** linetype to the **Hidden** layer, and accept the remaining default parameters of the layers, see Figure 12.35.

2. Double-click on the **Object** layer to make it the current layer of the drawing. A green color tick mark appears in front of the name of the **Object** layer in the **LAYER PROPERTIES MANAGER**, which indicates that the **Object** layer is now the current layer of the drawing, see Figure 12.35.

12.35

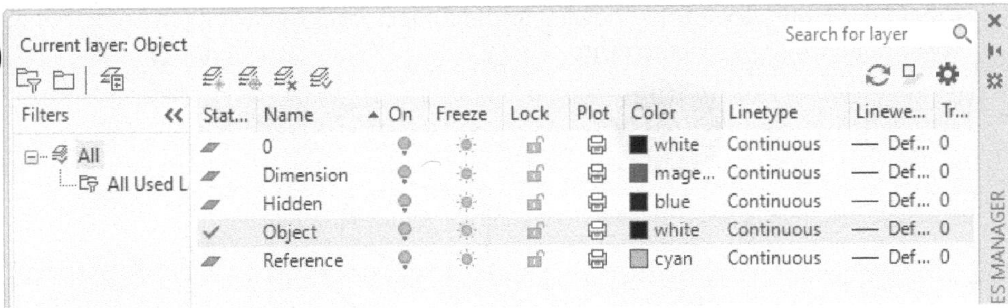

3. After creating the layers, close the **LAYER PROPERTIES MANAGER.**

   Now, you can create the drawing.

Section 3: Creating the Drawing

1. Create five circles as the Top view of the drawing, see Figure 12.36. For the diameter dimensions of the circles, refer to Figure 12.34.

12.36

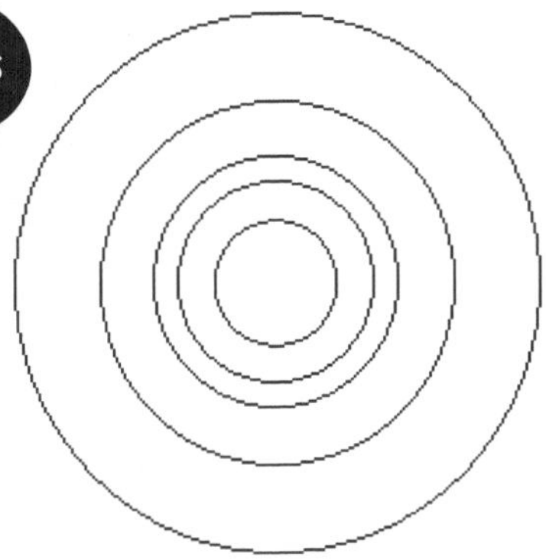

2. After creating the Top view of the drawing, activate the **Reference** layer by selecting it in the **Layer** drop-down list of the **Layers** panel in the **Home** tab, see Figure 12.37. Next, create vertical construction lines passing through the left and right quadrants, and the center of the circles as the reference entities to create the Front view of the drawing, see Figure 12.38.

12.37

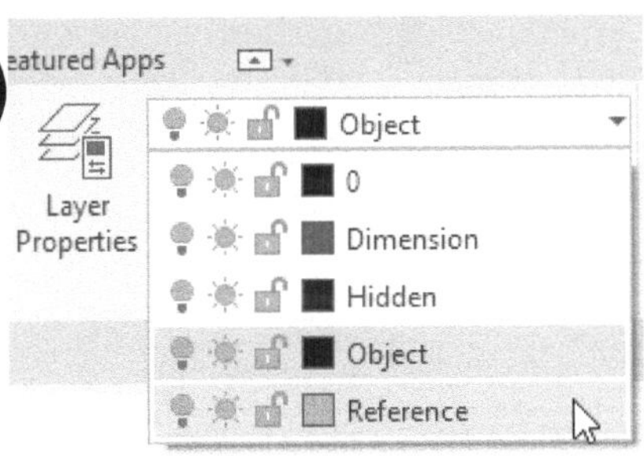

12.38

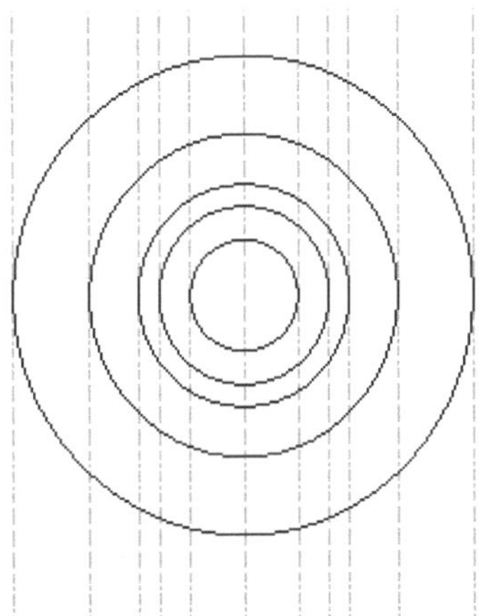

3. Create the Front view of the drawing in the **Object** layer by taking reference from the vertical construction lines, see Figure 12.39.

12.39

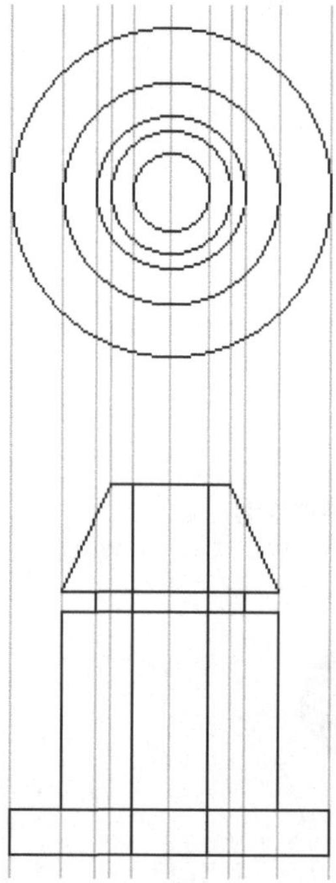

4. Assign the hidden entities of the drawing to the Hidden layer, see Figure 12.40. Next, hide the Reference layer, see Figure 12.41.

12.40

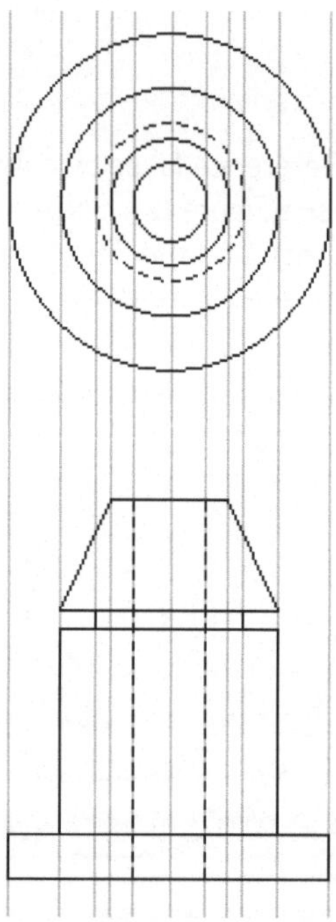

12.41

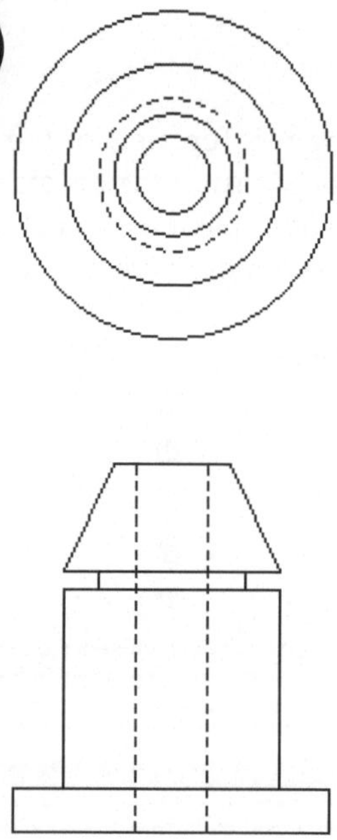

Now, you need to apply dimensions to the drawing.

5. Make the **Dimension** layer the current layer of the drawing and then apply dimensions to the drawing, see Figure 12.42. Note that you need to change the dimension settings such that the dimension text, dimension arrow, and other dimension components are visible clearly in the drawing area either by creating a new dimension style or by editing the existing dimension style. You can create or edit the dimension style by using the **Dimension Style Manager** dialog box as discussed in earlier chapters.

12.42

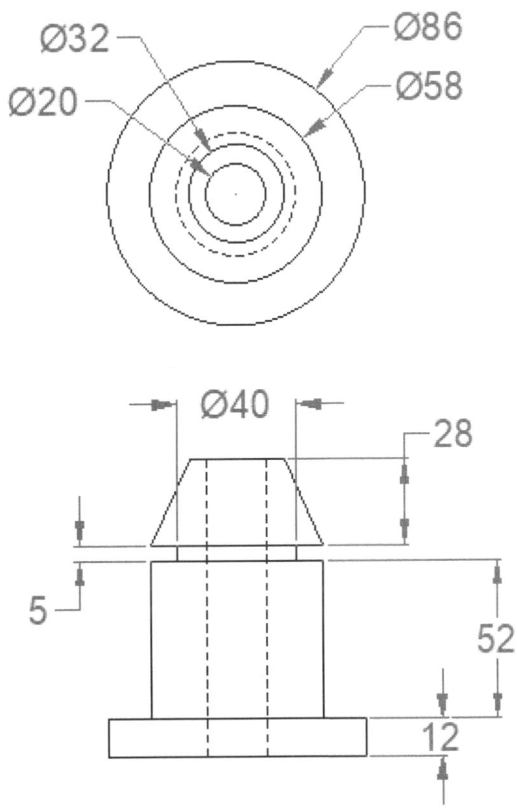

Section 4: Configuring/Adding Plotter

1. Ensure that a plotter is configured in your system. Note that before configuring a plotter, you need to ensure that the system printer (output device) drivers are installed on your computer.

   To configure a plotter, enter **PLOTTERMANAGER** in the Command Line window and then press ENTER. The **Plotters** system window appears. Alternatively, click on the **Plotter Manager** tool in the **Plot** panel of the **Output** tab in the **Ribbon**. Next, double-click on **Add-A-Plotter Wizard** in the **Plotters** system window. The **Introduction Page** of the **Add Plotter** dialog box appears, see Figure 12.43.

Next, read the information given in the **Introduction Page** of the **Add Plotter** dialog box and then click on the **Next** button. The **Begin** page of the dialog box appears. In the **Begin** page, select the **System Printer** radio button and then click on the **Next** button. The **System Printer** page of the dialog box appears. On this page, choose the system printer. If the system printer is not listed on this page, then you need to install the printer drivers in your system first. After selecting the system printer, click on the **Next** button. The **Import Pcp or Pc2** page appears. Click on the **Next** button in the **Import Pcp or Pc2** page. The **Plotter Name** page appears. Enter the name of the plotter on this page and then click on the **Next** button. The **Finish** page of the dialog box appears. Next, click on the **Finish** button. The plotter gets configured in the system.

2. Ensure that the system printer is connected to your computer through USB or Wifi.

12.43

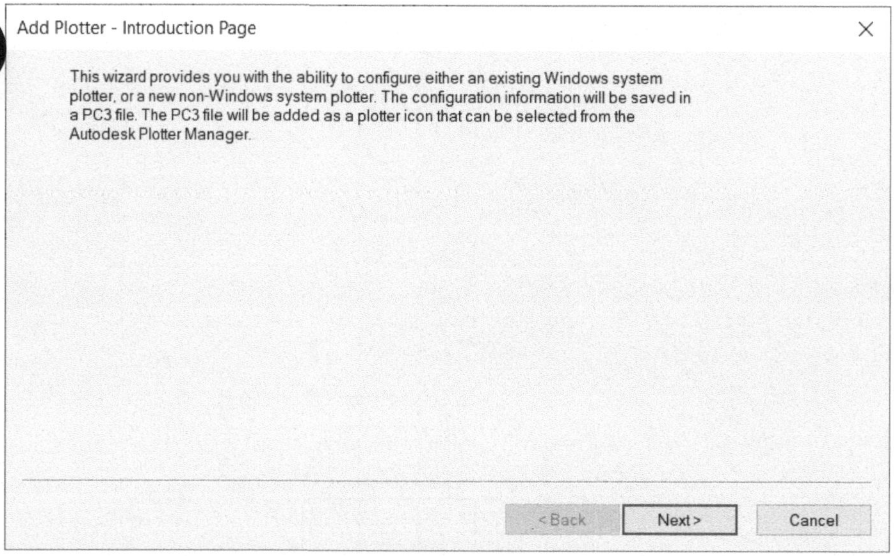

Section 5: Creating Color-Dependent Plot Style

1. Enter **STYLESMANAGER** in the Command Line window and then press ENTER. The **Plot Styles** system window appears, which displays the list of predefined plot style files.

2. Double-click on **Add-A-Plot Style Table Wizard** in the **Plot Styles** system window. The **Add Plot Style Table** dialog box appears. Read the information on this page and then click on the **Next** button. The **Begin** page of the **Add Plot Style Table** dialog box appears, see Figure 12.44.

12.44

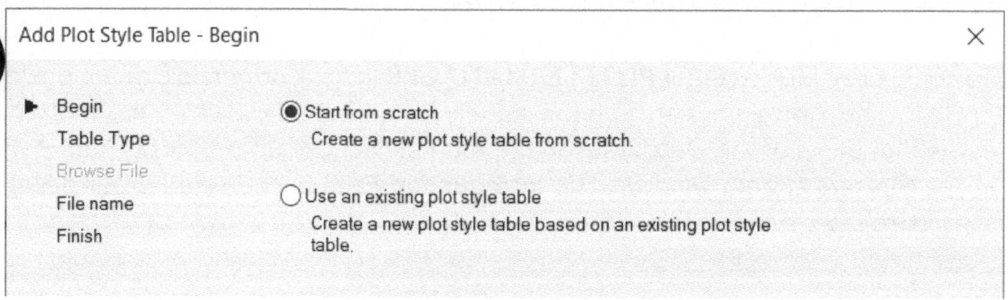

3. Ensure that the **Start from scratch** radio button is selected on the **Begin** page of the dialog box, see Figure 12.44. Next, click on the **Next** button. The **Pick Plot Style Table** page of the dialog box appears.

4. Ensure that the **Color-Dependent Plot Style Table** radio button is selected in the **Pick Plot Style Table** page of the dialog box. Next, click on the **Next** button. The **File name** page of the dialog box appears, see Figure 12.45.

5. Enter **My Color Plot Style** in the **File name** field as the name of the plot style, see Figure 12.45. Next, click on the **Next** button. The **Finish** page of the dialog box appears.

12.45

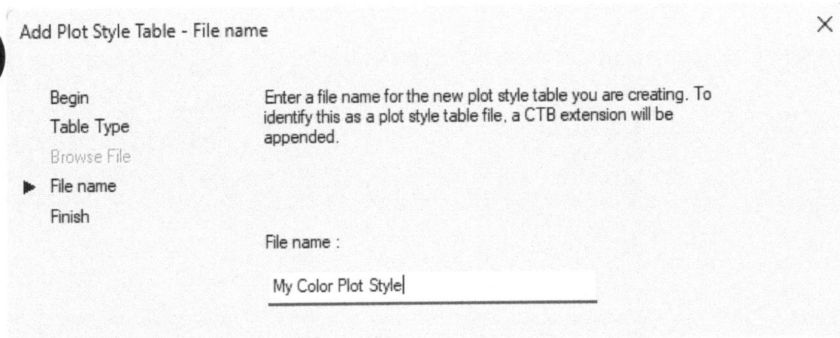

6. Click on the **Plot Style Table Editor** button on the **Finish** page of the dialog box. The **Plot Style Table Editor** dialog box appears, see Figure 12.46.

12.46

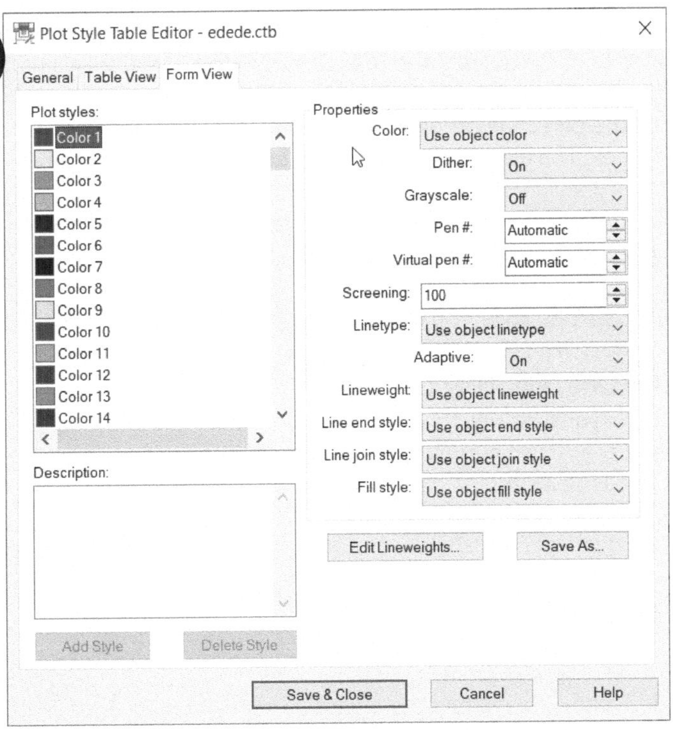

7. Ensure that the **Form View** tab of the **Plot Style Table Editor** dialog box is activated, see Figure 12.47.

8. Select the **Color 5** (blue color) in the **Plot styles** area of the dialog box. All the properties of the **Color 5** plot style appear in the **Properties** area of the dialog box, see Figure 12.47.

9. Select the **Black** color in the **Color** drop-down list and the **0.5300 mm** in the **Lineweight** drop-down list of the **Properties** area of the dialog box, see Figure 12.47.

12.47

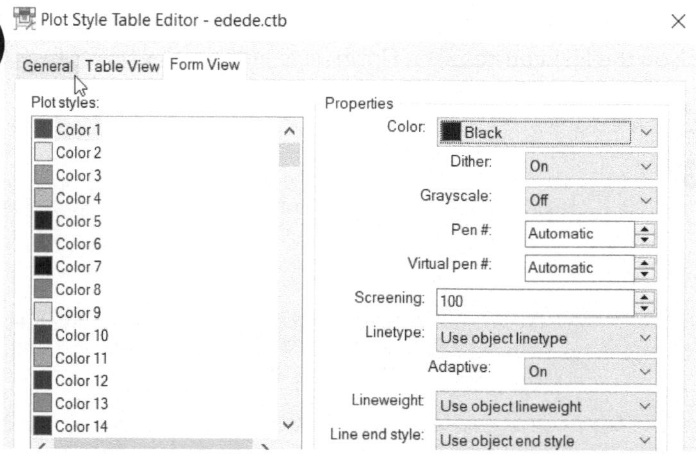

10. Similarly, change the properties of the **Color 6** (magenta color) and **Color 7** (black color) plot styles. For the **Color 6** plot style, select black color as the print color of the objects and 0.65 mm as the print lineweight of the objects. For the **Color 7** (black color) plot style, select the black color as the print color of the objects and the 0.8 mm as the print lineweight of the objects.

11. After editing the plot style properties, click on the **Save & Close** button of the **Plot Style Table Editor** dialog box. The dialog box gets closed, and the plot style properties are modified.

12. Click on the **Finish** button in the **Add Plot Style Table** dialog box. The color-dependent plot style with the name **My Color Plot Style** is created.

    After creating the plot style, you can print the drawing as per the newly created plot style.

Section 6: Plotting/Printing Drawing

1. Click on the **Layout1** tab in the lower left corner of the drawing area. The **Layout1** tab gets activated and the drawing created in the Model space appears in the default viewport in the layout, see Figure 12.48.

12.48

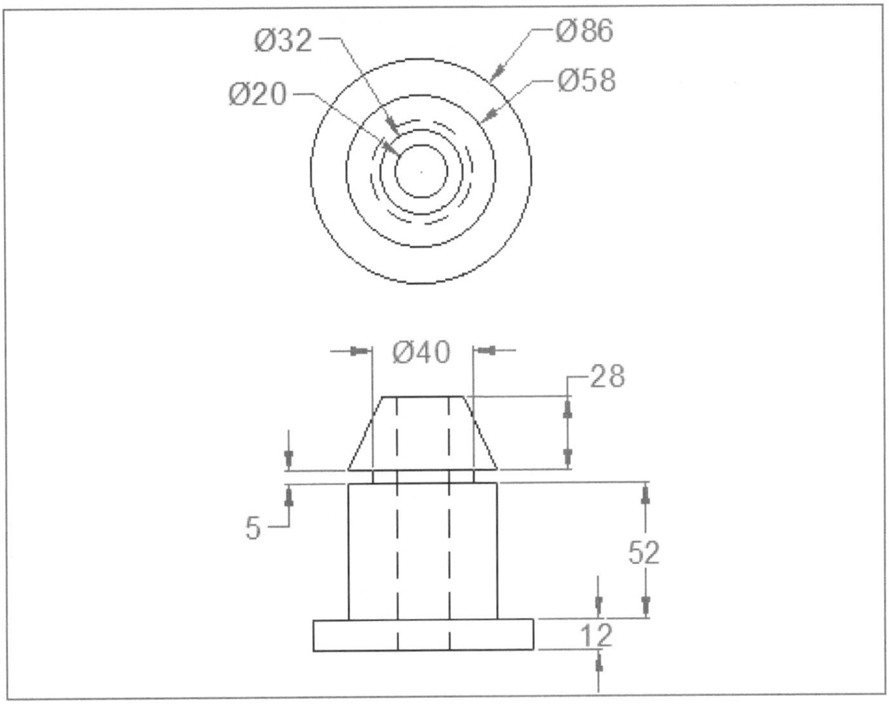

2. Click on the **Plot** tool in the **Plot** panel of the **Output** tab in the **Ribbon**. The **Plot** dialog box appears, see Figure 12.49. Alternatively, press CTRL + P to invoke the **Plot** dialog box. Note that if multiple drawings/layouts are opened in the current session of AutoCAD then on clicking the **Plot** tool, the **Batch Plot** window appears. In this window, click on the **Continue to plot a single sheet** button to invoke the **Plot** dialog box.

3. Select the plotter from the **Name** drop-down list of the **Printer/plotter** area of the dialog box, see Figure 12.49. In this figure, the **HP LaserJet Pro MFP M126nw** plotter is selected.

12.49

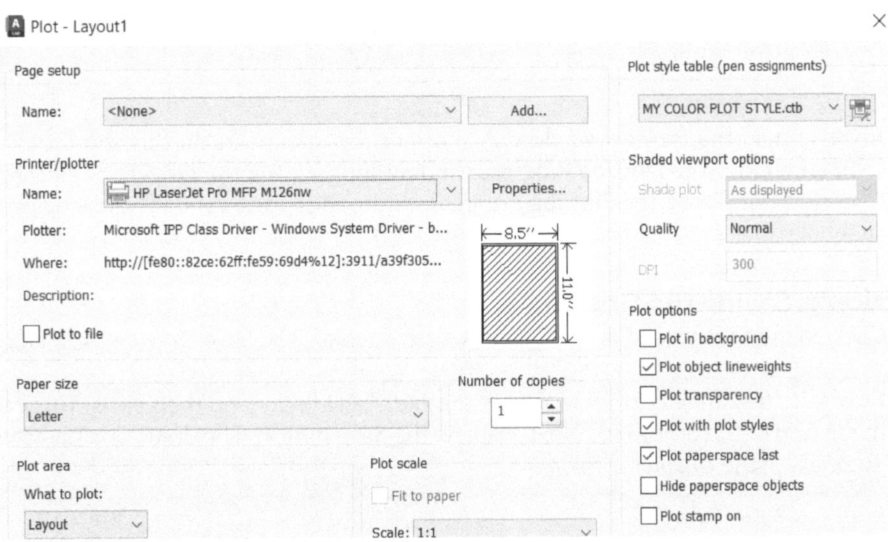

4. Ensure that the **Letter** option is selected in the **Paper size** drop-down list and the **Layout** option is selected in the **What to plot** drop-down list of the **Plot** area in the dialog box, see Figure 12.49.

5. Select the *My Color Plot Style.ctb* plot style in the **Plot style table** drop-down list of the **Plot style table (pen assignments)** area.

6. Ensure that the **Plot with plot styles** check box is selected in the **Plot options** area of the dialog box.

7. Accept the remaining default settings and then click on the **Preview** button in the dialog box. The plot preview of the drawing appears in the **Preview** window, see Figure 12.50.

12.50

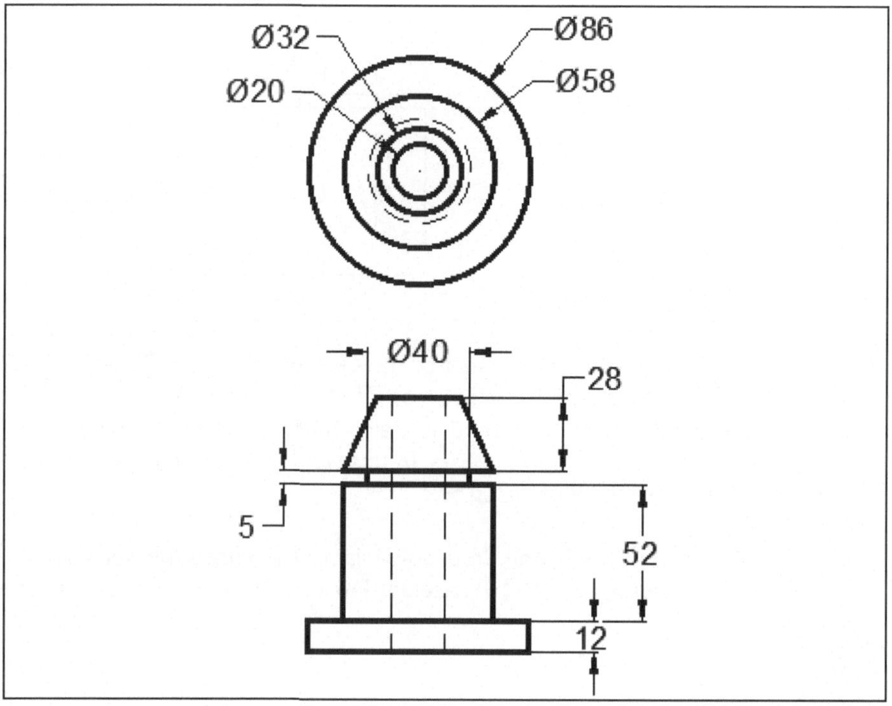

8. Right-click in the **Preview** window. A shortcut menu appears. In this shortcut menu, click on the **Plot** option. The **Plot Job Progress** window appears, and the process of plotting gets started. Once it is completed, the **Plot Job Progress** window disappears and the drawing gets plotted on a sheet of paper.

Section 7: Saving the Drawing

1. Click on the **Save** tool in the **Quick Access Toolbar**. The **Save Drawing As** dialog box appears.

2. Browse to the *Chapter 12* folder inside the *AutoCAD* folder and then enter **Tutorial 2** in the **File name** field of the dialog box. Next, click on the **Save** button. The drawing is saved with the name Tutorial 2 in the *Chapter 12* folder.

Hands-on Test Drive 1

Open the drawing created in the Hands-on Test Drive 2 of Chapter 6 (see Figure 12.51) and then take two copies of the print on A4 size sheets.

12.51

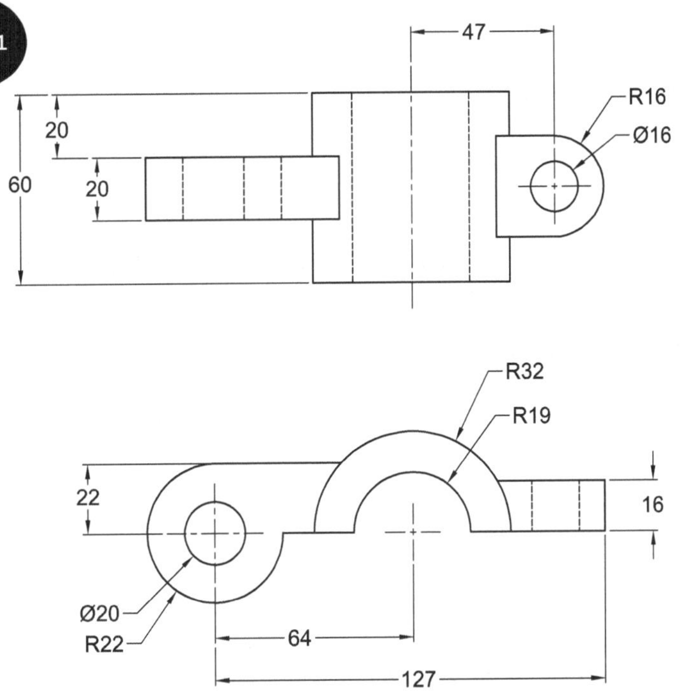

Hands-on Test Drive 2

Open the drawing created in Tutorial 1 of Chapter 9, see Figure 12.52, and then take the printout of the drawing in the Model space.

12.52

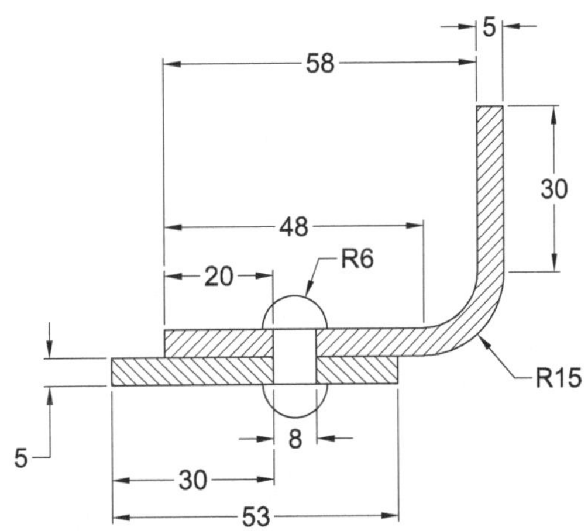

Summary

The chapter introduced how to configure a plotter (output device) in AutoCAD. It also explained how to create a plot style, set up the default plot style for plotting/printing and how to plot/print drawings in AutoCAD.

Questions

Complete the following sentences:

- The ________ tool and the ________ command are used for invoking the **Plotters** system window for configuring a plotter in AutoCAD.
- The ________ command is used for invoking the **Plot Styles** system window for creating a plot style.
- In AutoCAD, you can create two types of plot styles: ________ and ________ .
- The ________ tool is used for invoking the **Plot** dialog box for plotting/printing a drawing.
- The options in the ________ drop-down list of the **Plot** area in the **Plot** dialog box are used for specifying the portion of the drawing to print.
- The ________ option is used for plotting the portion of the drawing that is currently displayed on the screen.
- The ________ option is used for defining a window around the portion of the drawing to be printed.
- The ________ style is used for overriding the layer properties of the drawing objects while plotting/printing.
- The ________ radio button in the **Begin** page of the **Add Plot Style Table** dialog box is used for creating a new plot style from scratch.
- The ________ plot style allows you to assign plot styles to the individual AutoCAD colors.
- The ________ plot style allows you to assign plot style directly to objects or layers of a drawing.
- The ________ dialog box is used for setting up a default plot style for plotting/printing a drawing.

CHAPTER

13

Introducing 3D Basics and Creating 3D Models

In this chapter, the following topics will be discussed:

- Invoking the 3D Modeling/3D Basics Workspace
- Creating 3D Primitives
- Creating 3D Models
- Working with World Coordinate System (WCS)
- Working with User Coordinate System (UCS)
- Setting Work Plane to Predefined Orthographic View
- Working with Dynamic UCS
- Controlling the Display of the UCS
- Creating an Extrude Feature
- Converting a Closed Sketch into a Region
- Creating a Revolve Feature
- Creating a Sweep Feature
- Creating a Loft Feature
- Working with Presspull Tool
- Creating a 3D Wall-like Polysolid
- Performing Boolean Operations
- Checking Interference between Bodies
- Copying Edges of a Solid Feature
- Performing Modifying Operations

In this chapter, you will learn about creating 3D models. In AutoCAD, you can create three types of 3D models: solid, surface, and mesh. A solid model is filled with material and has mass properties, see Figure 13.1. It represents a real-world component. A surface model is a thin shell model that does not have mass or volume, see Figure 13.2. It is mainly used to achieve complex shapes of a design. A mesh model is a polygonal representation of a 3D shape that does not have mass properties, see Figure 13.3. In this chapter, you will learn about creating 3D solid models. In AutoCAD, you can create 3D models in the **3D Modeling** or **3D Basics** workspace. The method for invoking the **3D Modeling** or **3D Basics** workspace is discussed next.

13.1

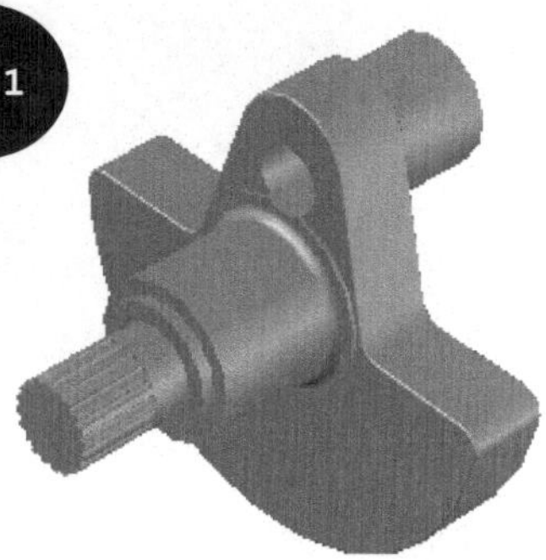

13.2

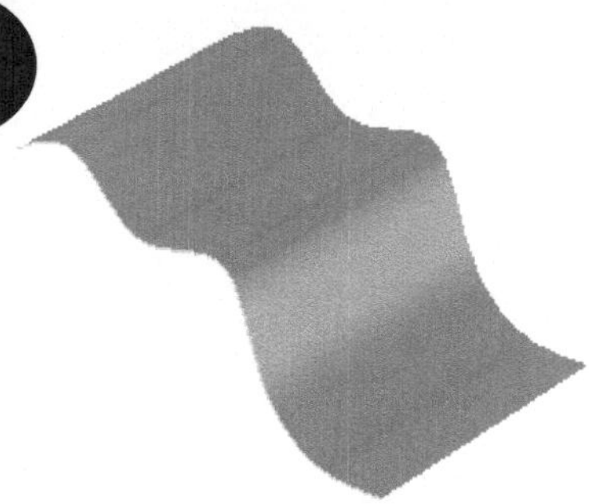

13.3

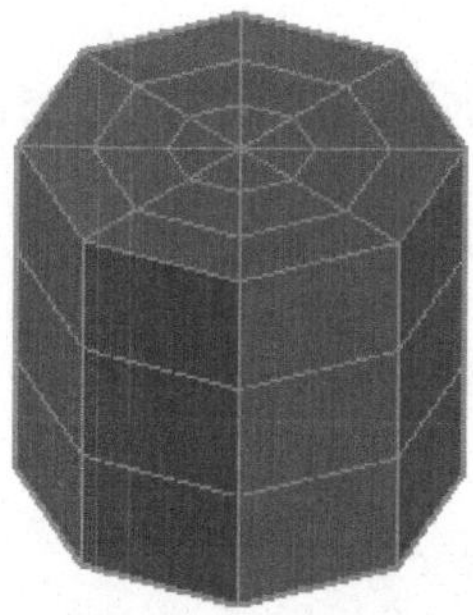

Invoking the 3D Modeling/3D Basics Workspace

To create 3D models in AutoCAD, you need to switch to the **3D Modeling** or **3D Basics** workspace. The **3D Modeling** workspace consists of all the tools that are required to create a 3D model, whereas the **3D Basics** workspace consists of only the important or basic tools for creating a 3D model. To switch to the **3D Modeling** workspace, click on the **Workspace Switching** button in the Status Bar. The **Workspace Switching** flyout appears, see Figure 13.4. It displays a list of all the available workspaces. Next, click on the **3D Modeling** workspace in this flyout. The **3D Modeling** workspace is invoked and the startup user interface appears, see Figure 13.5. Now, you can create a 3D model by using the various 3D modeling tools available in the **Ribbon**. Alternatively, you can directly start a new drawing file in the **3D Modeling** workspace by using the *acad3D.dwt, acadiso3D.dwt, acad -Named Plot Styles3D.dwt,* or *acadISO -Named Plot Styles3D.dwt* template. To do so, click on the **New** tool in the **Quick Access Toolbar.** The **Select template** dialog box appears. In this dialog box, select the required template to invoke the **3D Modeling** workspace and then click on the **Open** button.

13.4

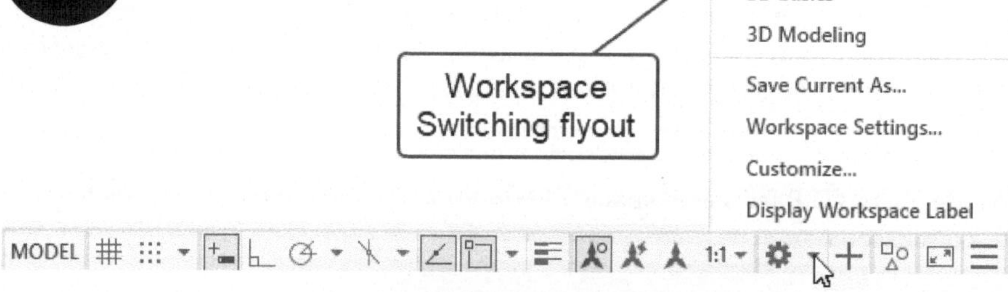

13.5

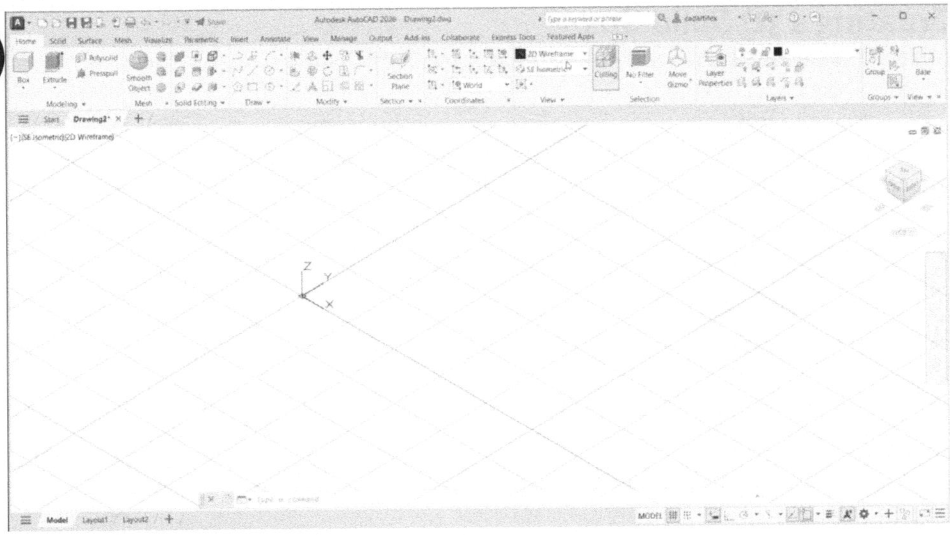

Creating 3D Primitives

In AutoCAD, you can create various predefined 3D solid primitives such as Box, Cylinder, Cone, Sphere, Pyramid, Wedge, and Torus. The tools to create various primitives are available in the **Primitive** flyout of the **Modeling** panel in the **Home** tab, see Figure 13.6. You can also access these tools in the **Primitive** panel of the **Solid** tab in the **Ribbon**, see Figure 13.7. The methods for creating various 3D primitives are discussed next.

13.6

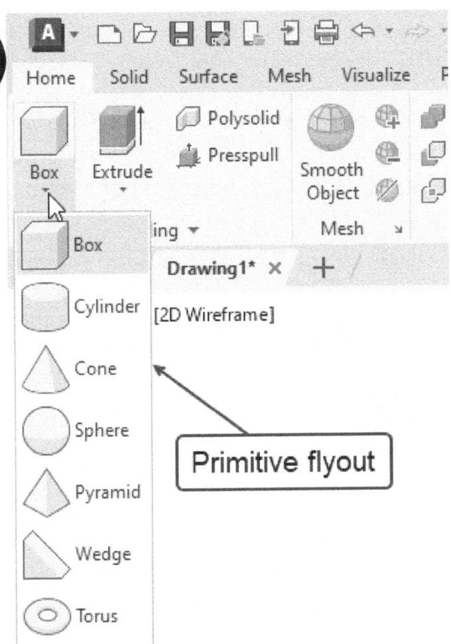

13.7

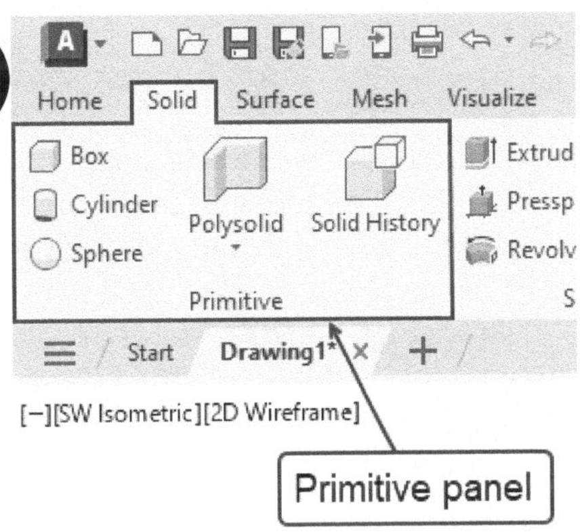

Creating a 3D Solid Box

You can create a 3D solid box by using the **Box** tool, which is discussed below:

1. Click on the **Box** tool in the **Modeling** panel of the **Home** tab, see Figure 13.8. You are prompted to specify the first corner of the box. Alternatively, you can enter **BOX** in the Command Line window and then press ENTER to activate this tool.

```
Specify first corner or [Center]:
```

13.8

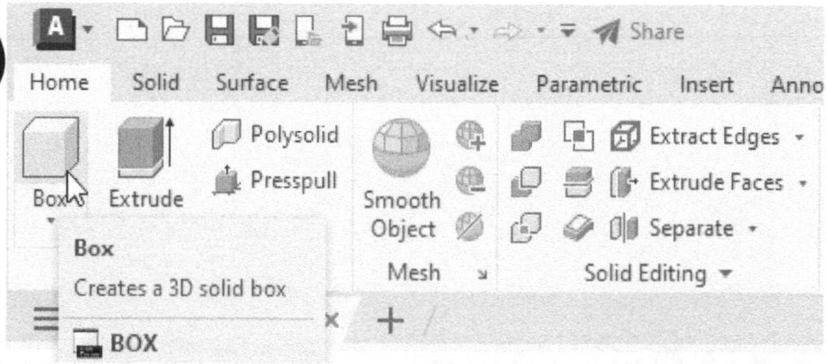

2. Change the orientation of the drawing view to isometric by clicking on the **Home** icon of the ViewCube.

3. Click to specify the first corner of the box in the drawing area. You are prompted to specify the other corner of the box. You can also enter X and Y coordinates to specify the first corner of the box.

```
Specify other corner or [Cube Length]:
```

4. Click to specify the diagonally opposite corner of the box in the drawing area. The preview of the 3D solid box appears (see Figure 13.9), and you are prompted to specify its height. You can also specify the length and width values of the box to specify the second corner of the box.

```
Specify height or [2Point] <2.0000>:
```

5. Enter the height of the box and then press ENTER. A 3D solid box of the specified height is created, see Figure 13.10.

13.9

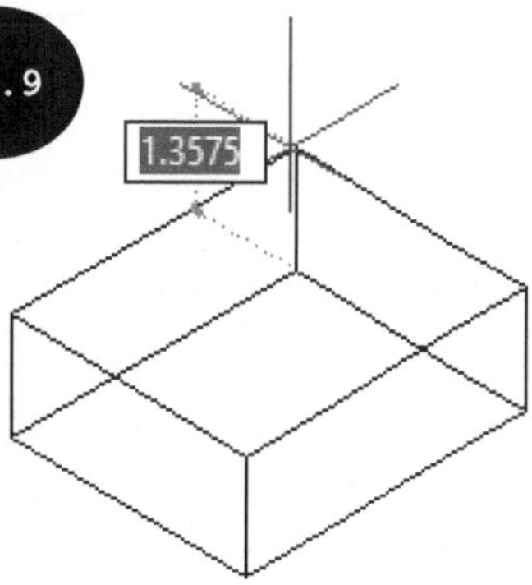

13.10

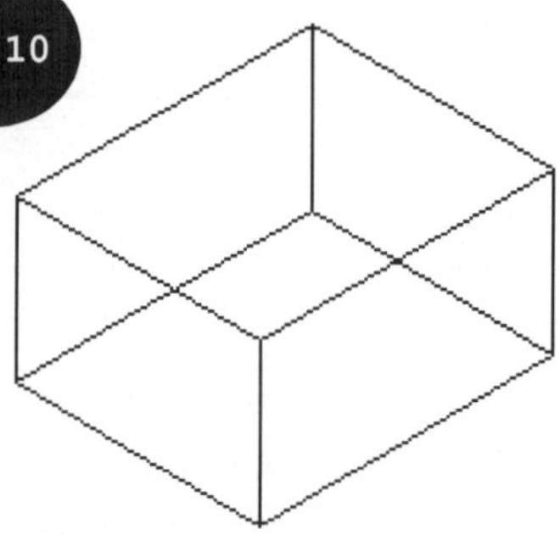

Note: By default, the visual style for a 3D model is defined as a 2D Wireframe. As a result, a 3D model appears in the 2D Wireframe visual style in the drawing area, see Figure 13.10. You can change the visual style of the model to Conceptual, Hidden, Shaded, Shaded with Edges, Shades of Gray, Wireframe, and so on by using the **Visual Styles** flyout of the **View** panel in the **Home** tab, see Figure 13.11.

13.11

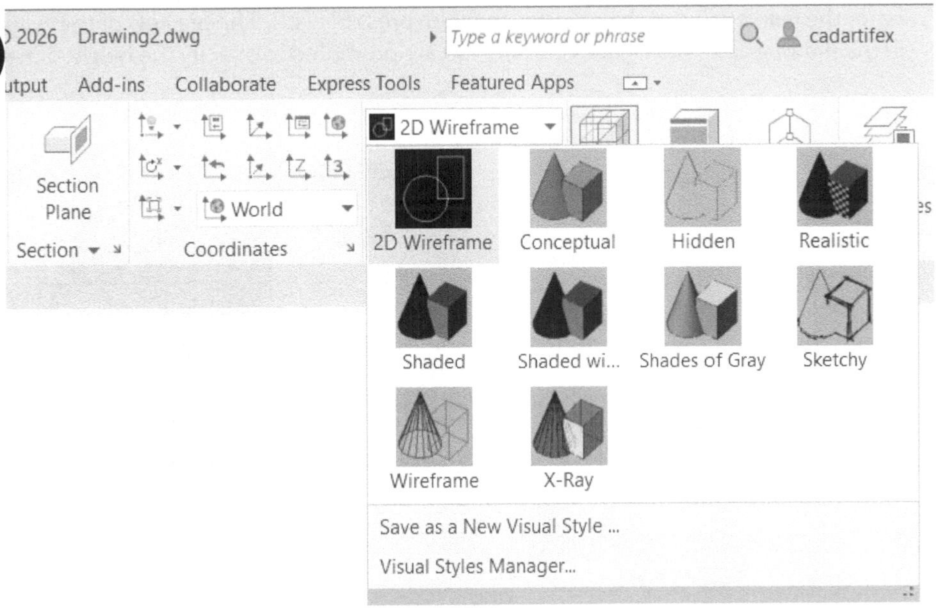

6. Change the visual style of the model to "shades of gray" visual style by clicking on the **Shades of Gray** tool in the **Visual Styles** flyout of the **View** panel in the **Home** tab, see Figure 13.12.

13.12

Creating a 3D Solid Cylinder

You can create a 3D solid cylinder by using the **Cylinder** tool, which is discussed below:

1. Invoke the **Primitive** flyout in the **Modeling** panel of the **Home** tab and then click on the **Cylinder** tool, see Figure 13.13. You are prompted to specify the center point of the cylinder base. Alternatively, you can enter **CYL** in the Command Line window and then press ENTER to activate this tool.

```
Specify center point of base or [3P 2P Ttr Elliptical]:
```

2. Click to specify the center point of the cylinder base in the drawing area. The center point is specified and you are prompted to specify its radius. You can also specify the coordinates (X,Y) to specify the center point of the cylinder base.

```
Specify base radius or [Diameter]:
```

3. Enter the radius value of the cylinder and then press ENTER. The preview of the cylinder appears in the drawing area, see Figure 13.14 and you are prompted to specify the height of the cylinder.

```
Specify height or [2Point Axis endpoint] <1.0000>:
```

13.13

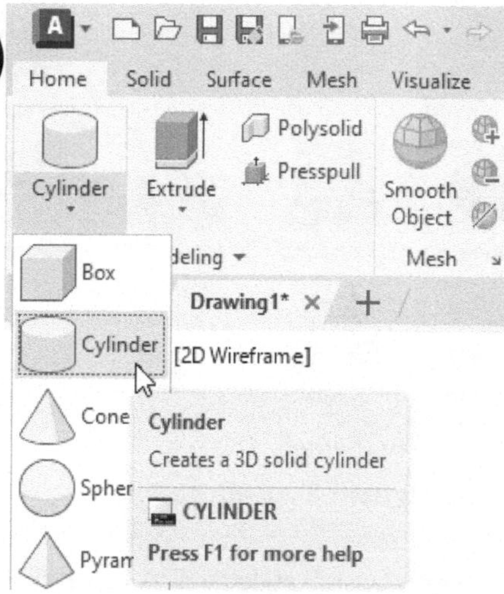

13.14

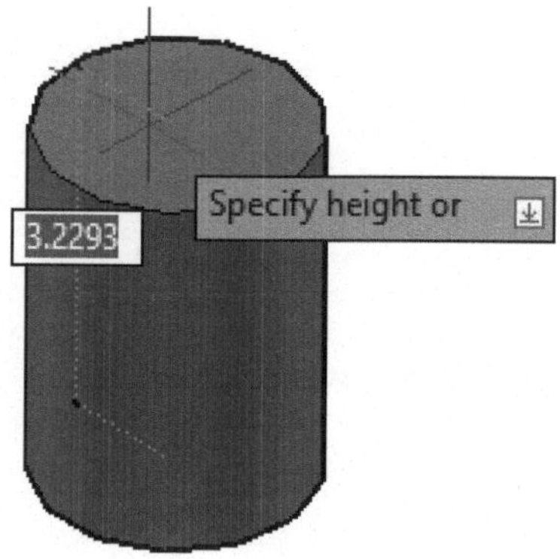

4. Enter the height of the cylinder and then press ENTER. A 3D solid cylinder of the specified height is created, see Figure 13.15.

13.15

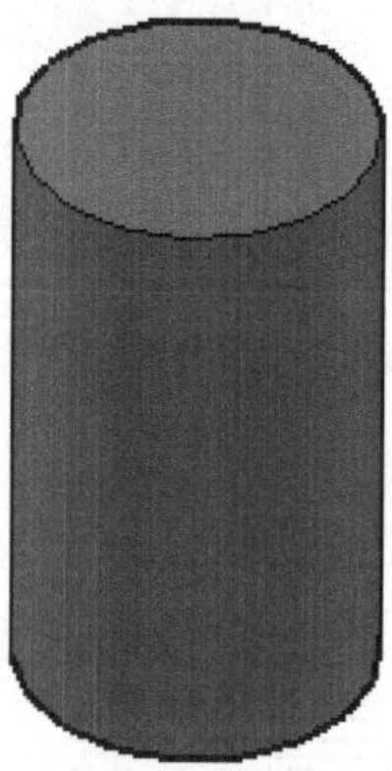

Note: In Figures 13.14 and 13.15, the default visual style of the model is changed to "shades of gray" visual style.

Creating a 3D Solid Cone

You can create a 3D solid cone by using the **Cone** tool, which is discussed below:

1. Invoke the **Primitive** flyout and then click on the **Cone** tool. You are prompted to specify the center point of the cone base. Alternatively, you can enter **CONE** in the Command Line window and then press ENTER to activate this tool.

```
Specify center point of base or [3P 2P Ttr Elliptical]:
```

2. Click to specify the center point of the cone base in the drawing area. The center point is specified and you are prompted to specify its radius. You can also specify the coordinates (X,Y) to specify the center point of the cone base.

```
Specify base radius or [Diameter] <1.0000>:
```

3. Enter the radius value of the cone base and then press ENTER. The preview of the cone appears in the drawing area, see Figure 13.16 and you are prompted to specify the height of the cone.

```
Specify height or [2Point Axis endpoint Top radius] <4.0000>:
```

4. Enter the height of the cone and then press ENTER. A 3D solid cone of the specified height is created, see Figure 13.17.

13.16

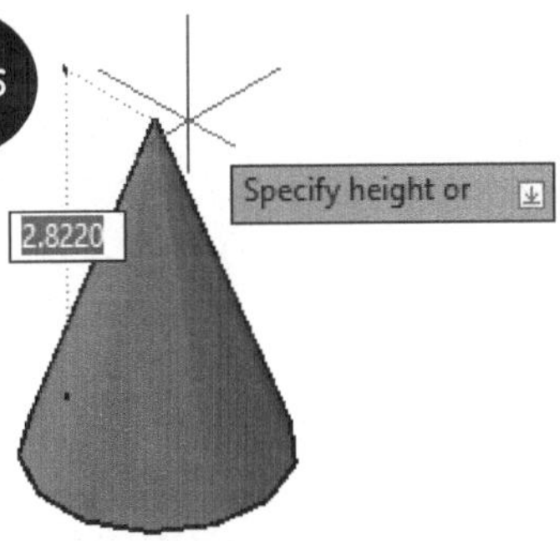

13.17

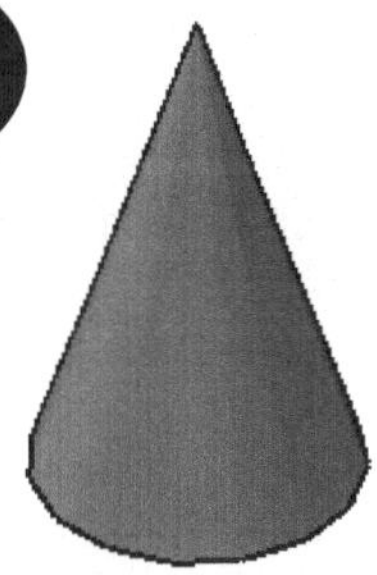

Creating a 3D Solid Sphere

You can create a 3D solid sphere by using the **Sphere** tool, which is discussed below:

1. Invoke the **Primitive** flyout and then click on the **Sphere** tool. You are prompted to specify the center point of the sphere. Alternatively, you can enter **SPHERE** in the Command Line window and then press ENTER to activate this tool.

```
Specify center point or [3P 2P Ttr]:
```

2. Click to specify the center point of the sphere in the drawing area. The center point is specified and you are prompted to specify its radius. You can also specify the coordinates (X,Y) to specify the center point of the sphere.

```
Specify radius or [Diameter] <1.0000>:
```

3. Enter the radius value of the sphere and then press ENTER. A 3D solid sphere of the specified radius is created, see Figure 13.18.

13.18

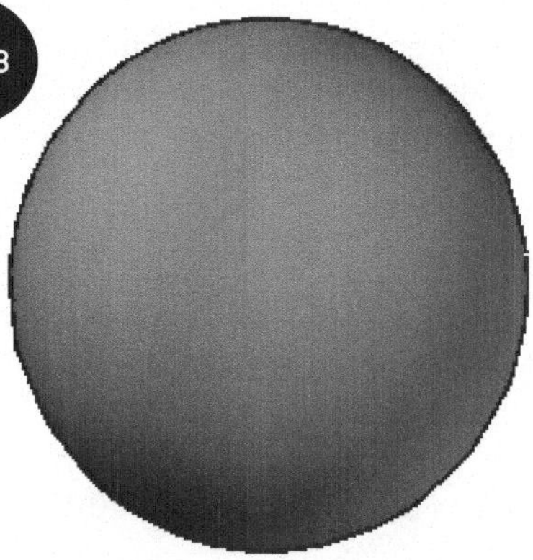

Creating a 3D Solid Pyramid

You can create a 3D solid pyramid by using the **Pyramid** tool, which is discussed below:

1. Invoke the **Primitive** flyout and then click on the **Pyramid** tool. You are prompted to specify the center point of the pyramid base. Alternatively, you can enter **PYR** in the Command Line window and then press ENTER to activate this tool.

```
Specify center point of base or [Edge Sides]:
```

2. Click to specify the center point of the pyramid base in the drawing area. The center point is specified and you are prompted to specify the radius of an imaginary circle to create a circumscribed pyramid base. You can also specify the coordinates (X,Y) to specify the center point of the pyramid base.

```
Specify base radius or [Inscribed] <1.0000>:
```

Note: You can create a circumscribed or an inscribed pyramid base. The circumscribed pyramid base is created outside an imaginary circle such that the midpoints of the pyramid sides touch the imaginary circle. The inscribed pyramid base is created inside an imaginary circle such that its vertices touch the imaginary circle. By default, you are prompted to specify the radius of an imaginary circle to create the circumscribed pyramid base. To create the inscribed pyramid base, click on the **Inscribed** option in the command prompt.

3. Enter the radius value of an imaginary circle to create the circumscribed pyramid base and then press ENTER. A preview of the pyramid appears and you are prompted to specify the height of the pyramid.

```
Specify height or [2Point Axis endpoint Top radius] <1.0000>:
```

4. Enter the height of the pyramid and then press ENTER. A 3D solid pyramid of the specified height is created, see Figure 13.19.

13.19

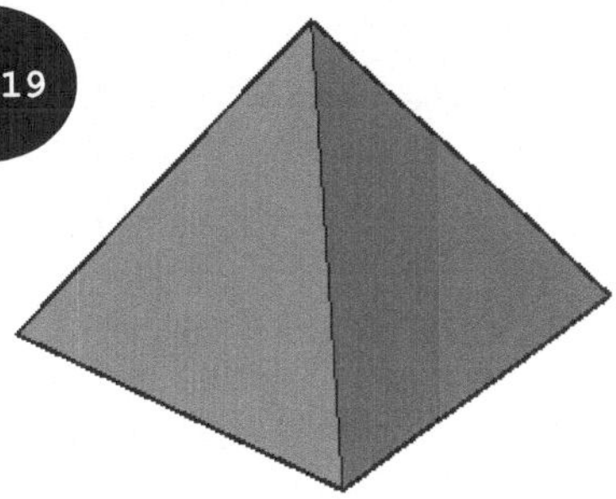

Creating a 3D Solid Wedge

You can create a 3D solid wedge by using the **Wedge** tool, which is discussed below:

1. Invoke the **Primitive** flyout and then click on the **Wedge** tool. You are prompted to specify the first corner of the wedge. Alternatively, you can enter **WE** in the Command Line window and then press ENTER to activate this tool.

   ```
   Specify first corner or [Center]:
   ```

2. Click to specify the first corner of the wedge in the drawing area. You are prompted to specify the other corner of the wedge.

   ```
   Specify other corner or [Cube Length]:
   ```

3. Click to specify the diagonally opposite corner of the wedge in the drawing area. A preview of the 3D solid wedge appears, see Figure 13.20 and you are prompted to specify its height. Note that the sloped side of the wedge is always opposite to the first corner specified.

   ```
   Specify height or [2Point] <1.0000>:
   ```

4. Enter the height of the wedge and then press ENTER. A 3D solid wedge of the specified height is created, see Figure 13.21.

13.20

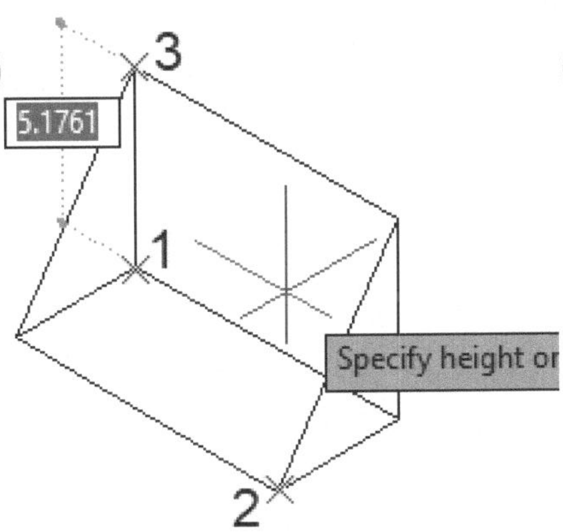

13.21

Creating a 3D Solid Torus

You can create a 3D solid torus by using the **Torus** tool, which is discussed below:

1. Invoke the **Primitive** flyout and then click on the **Torus** tool. You are prompted to specify the center point of the torus. Alternatively, you can enter **TOR** in the Command Line window and then press ENTER to activate this tool.

    ```
    Specify center point or [3P 2P Ttr]:
    ```

2. Click to specify the center point of the torus in the drawing area. The preview of a circle appears and you are prompted to specify its radius.

    ```
    Specify radius or [Diameter] <4.0000>:
    ```

3. Enter the radius value of the torus circle and then press ENTER. The preview of a torus appears and you are prompted to specify the tube radius of the torus.

    ```
    Specify tube radius or [2Point Diameter]:
    ```

4. Enter the tube radius of the torus and then press ENTER. A torus of a specified tube radius is created, see Figure 13.22.

13.22

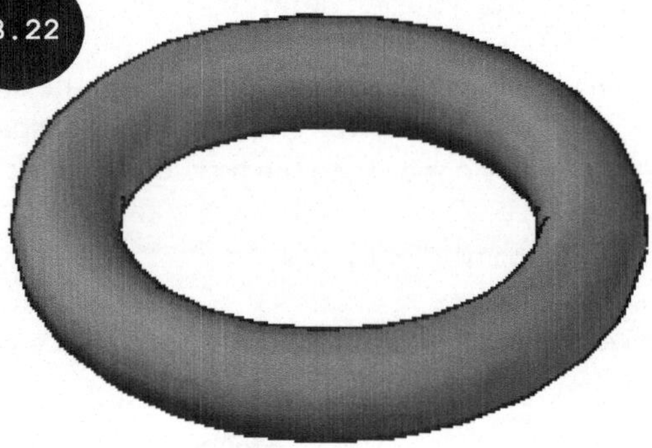

Creating 3D Models

In addition to creating predefined 3D solid primitives such as box, cylinder, cone, sphere, pyramid, wedge, and torus, you can create user-defined 3D features of a model by using the solid modeling tools such as **Extrude**, **Revolve**, **Sweep**, and **Loft**. In AutoCAD, to create a 3D solid model, you need to create all its features one after the other by using solid modeling tools, see Figure 13.23. The first created feature of a model is known as the base or parent feature of the model. However, before you start creating the base or parent feature of a model, it is important to understand the world coordinate system (WCS) and user coordinate system (UCS).

13.23

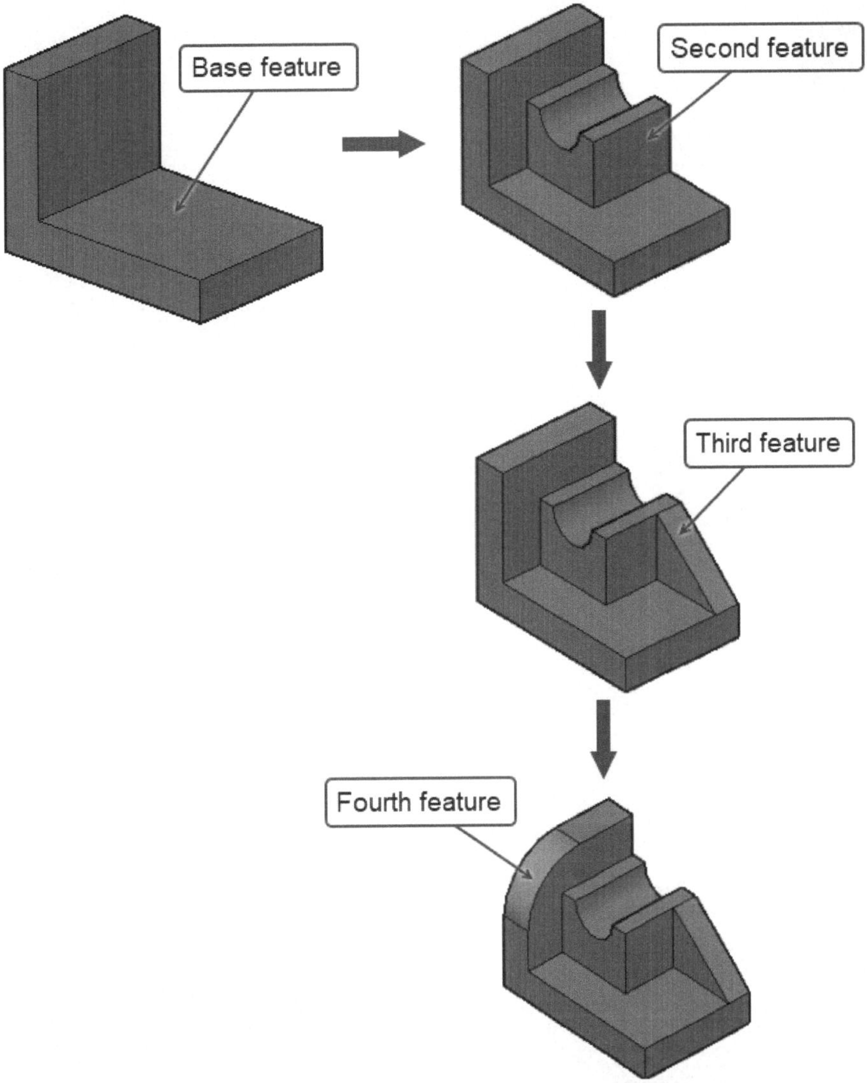

Working with World Coordinate System (WCS)

By default, when you start a new drawing file, the world coordinate system (WCS) is provided at the lower left corner of the screen, see Figure 13.24. The WCS allows you to create the 2D sketch of a feature on the fixed Top plane (XY plane) and add material along the Z axis only, see Figure 13.25. However, to create a real-world 3D model, you also need to create features other than the default Top plane (XY plane), which is not possible using the WCS. For example, you cannot create a feature such that its 2D sketch is created on the Front plane and material is added along its normal direction by using the WCS, see Figure 13.26. Similarly, you cannot create a feature on the right side of the existing model as shown in Figure 13.27 by using the WCS.

13.24

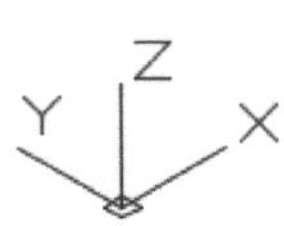

13.25

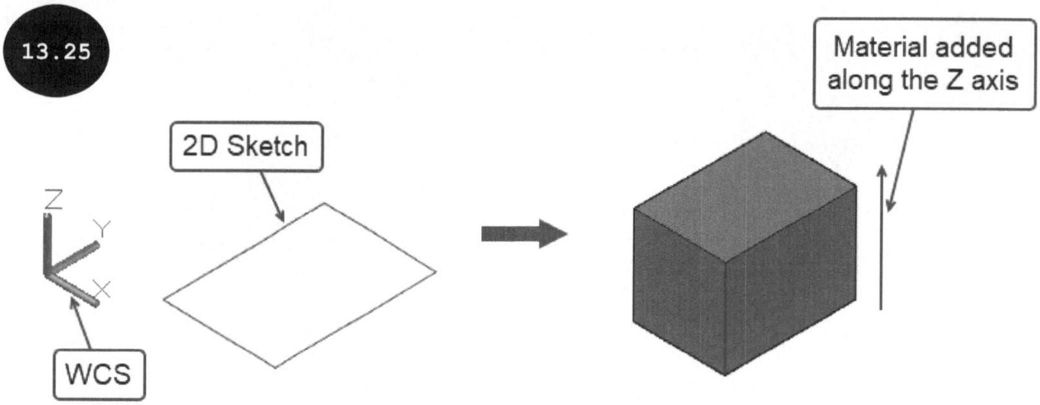

13.26

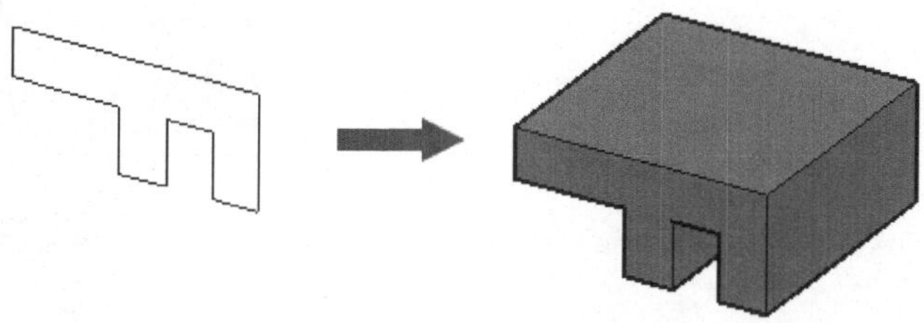

13.27

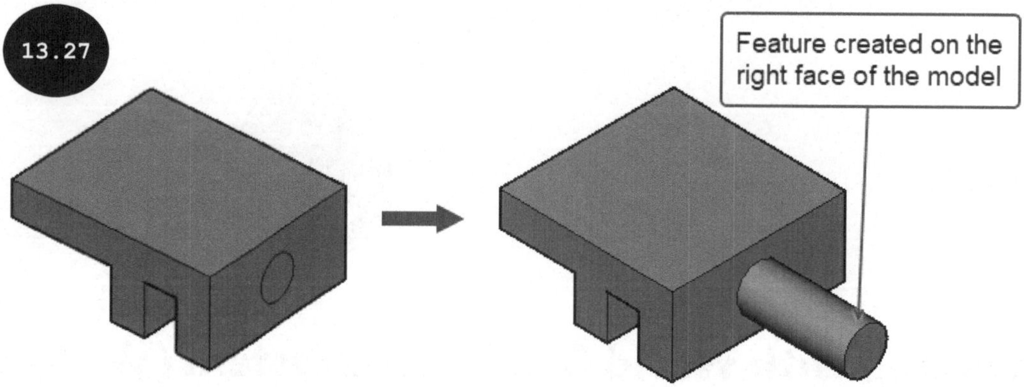

To overcome these situations, you can create a user coordinate system (UCS), as per your requirement, which is discussed next.

Working with User Coordinate System (UCS)

User coordinate system (UCS) is a movable coordinate system that allows you to change the position of the origin and the orientation of the X, Y, and Z axes to establish the work plane (XY plane) as per your requirement. Tools for controlling the UCS are available in the **Coordinates** panel of the **Home** tab (see Figure 13.28) and are discussed next.

13.28

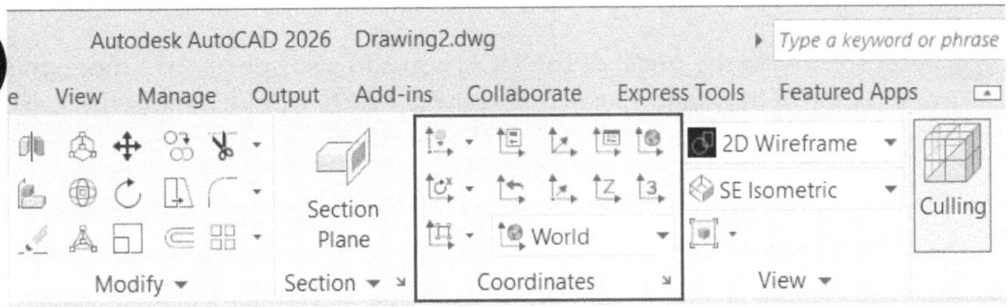

UCS

The **UCS** tool is used to create a new user coordinate system by specifying the UCS origin to the desired location. The method for creating a new user coordinate system by using the **UCS** tool is discussed below:

1. Click on the **UCS** tool in the **Coordinates** panel of the **Home** tab, see Figure 13.29. A preview of the UCS is attached to the cursor and you are prompted to specify the origin of the UCS. Alternatively, you can enter the **UCS** in the Command Line window and then press ENTER to activate this tool.

13.29

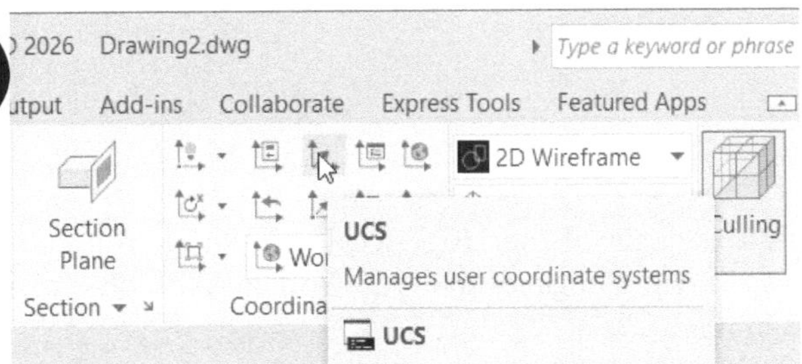

2. Click to specify the origin of the UCS, see Figure 13.30. You can also enter the X and Y coordinates to specify the origin of the UCS. You are prompted to specify a point on X-axis.

3. Press the ENTER key. The UCS is created in the specified position without changing the orientation of the X, Y, and Z axes, see Figure 13.31. Now, you can create the object on the XY plane of the UCS.

13.30

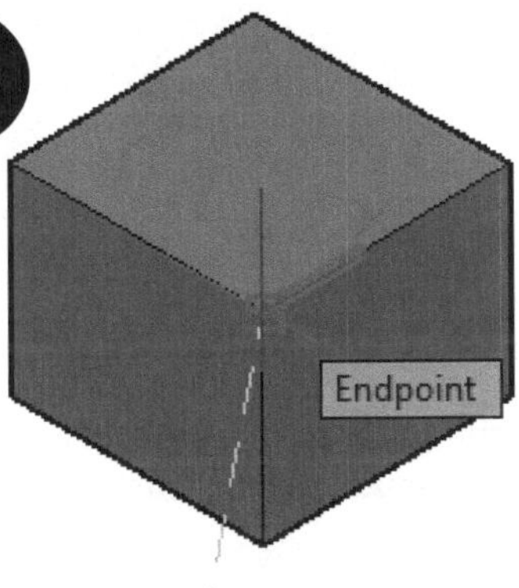

13.31

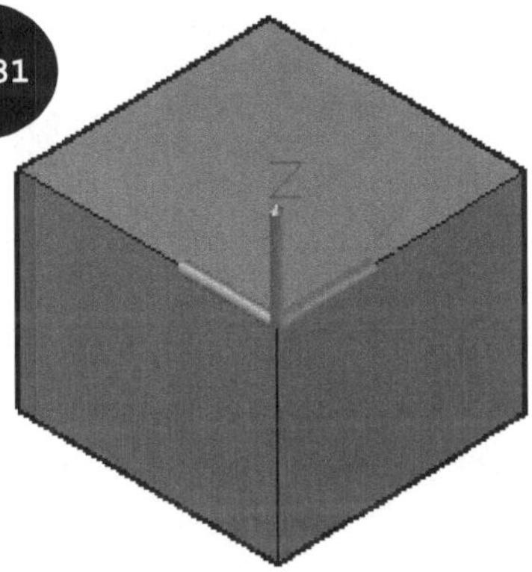

Note: After specifying the origin of the UCS, you can also specify two more points to define the orientation of the X and Y axes, respectively. The first point defines the X axis and the second point defines the Y axis of the UCS. The method for creating a new UCS by specifying three points is discussed next.

3 Point

The **3 Point** tool is used for creating a user coordinate system by specifying three points. The method for creating a UCS by using this tool is discussed below:

1. Click on the **3 Point** tool in the **Coordinates** panel of the **Home** tab, see Figure 13.32. A preview of the UCS is attached to the cursor and you are prompted to specify a new origin point.

13.32

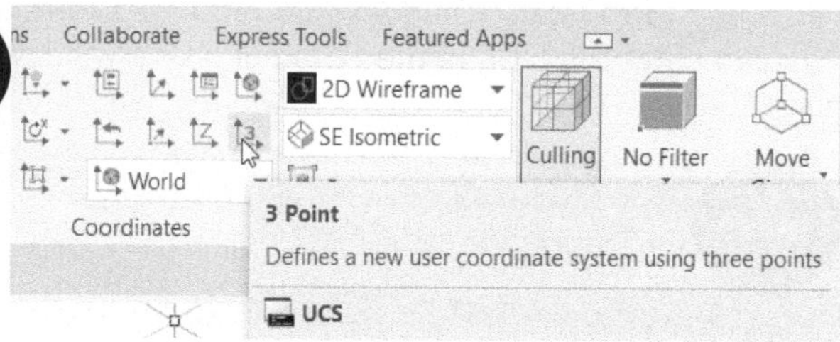

2. Click to specify the origin of the UCS, see Figure 13.33. You can also enter the X, Y, and Z coordinates to specify the origin of the UCS. You are prompted to specify a point to define the positive X-axis of the UCS.

3. Click to specify a point to define the positive X-axis of the UCS, see Figure 13.34. The positive X axis of the UCS is defined and you are prompted to specify a point to define the positive Y-axis.

13.33

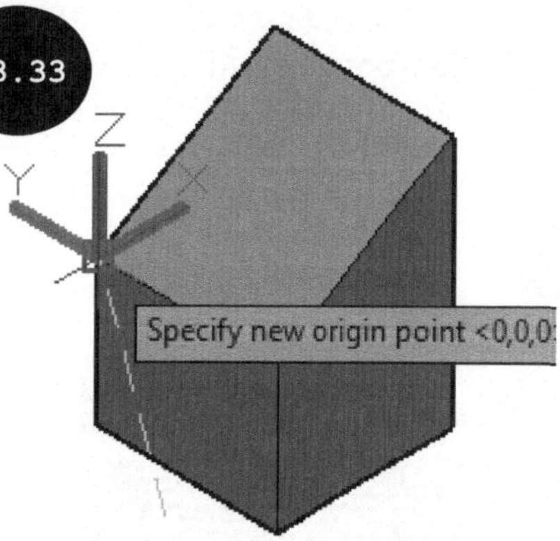

13.34

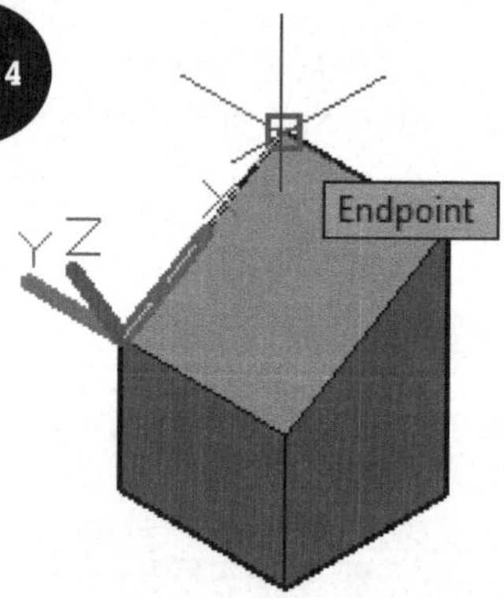

4. Click to specify a point to define the positive Y-axis of the UCS, see Figure 13.35. The UCS is created, see Figure 13.36. Now, you can create the object on the XY plane of the UCS.

13.35

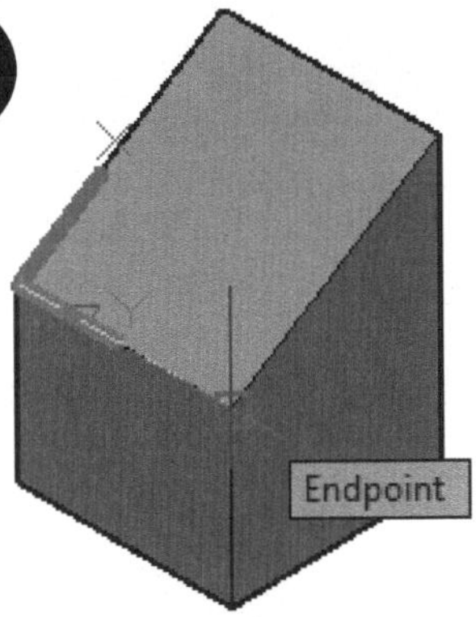

13.36

UCS, Previous

The UCS, **Previous** tool is used for restoring the previous position of the user coordinate system. To do so, click on the **UCS, Previous** tool, see Figure 13.37. The previously created UCS is restored. Alternatively, enter **UCS** in the Command Line window and then press ENTER. Next, click on the **Previous** option in the command prompt. You can undo/restore the last 10 UCS created in the current session of AutoCAD by using this tool.

13.37

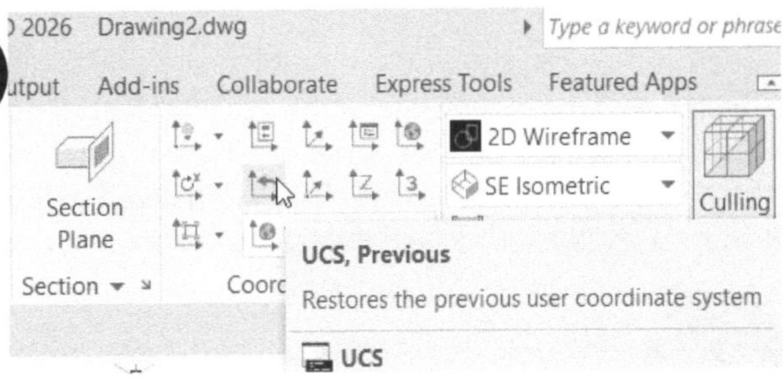

Origin

The **Origin** tool is used for shifting the user coordinate system to a new location by specifying its origin in the desired location. To do so, click on the **Origin** tool, see Figure 13.38, and then click to specify the position of the origin. The user coordinate system is created in the specified position without changing the orientation of its X, Y, and Z axes. Alternatively, you can use the **UCS** tool/command to create a new user coordinate system by specifying its origin, as discussed earlier.

13.38

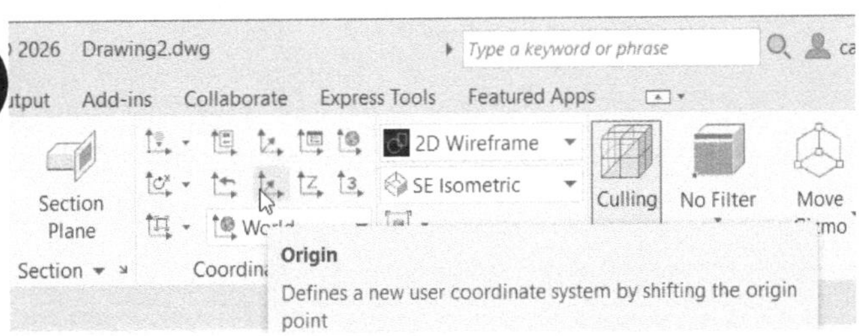

Z-Axis Vector

The **Z-Axis Vector** tool is used for creating a new user coordinate system by specifying its origin and the positive Z axis positions. To do so, click on the **Z-Axis Vector** tool, see Figure 13.39, and then click to specify the origin of the UCS. Next, click to define the positive Z axis of the UCS, see Figure 13.40. Alternatively, enter the **UCS** in the Command Line window and then press ENTER. Next, click on the **ZAxis** option in the command prompt to create the UCS by specifying its origin and the positive Z axis positions.

13.39

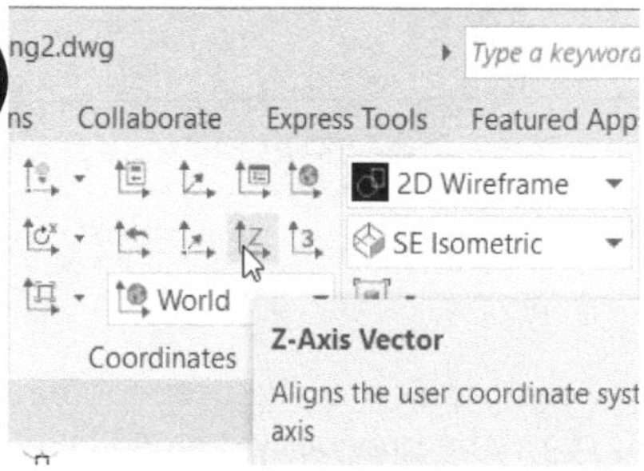

13.40

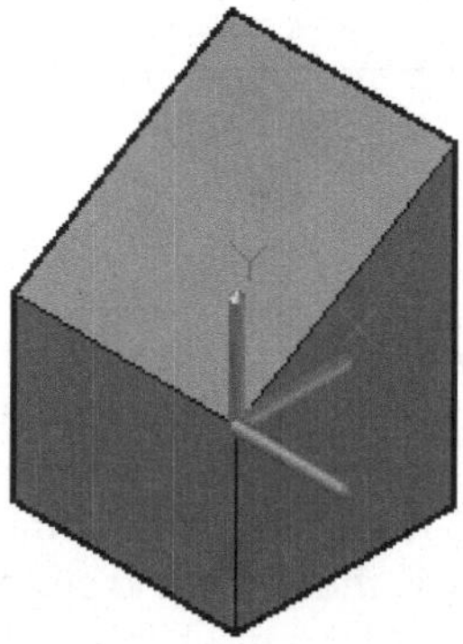

X

The **X** tool is used for changing the orientation of the existing UCS by rotating it around its X-axis. To do so, click on the **X** tool in the **Coordinates** panel, see Figure 13.41. Next, specify the rotation angle of the UCS about the X-axis and then press ENTER. Alternatively, enter **UCS** in the Command Line window and then press ENTER. Next, click on the **X** option in the command prompt to activate this tool.

13.41

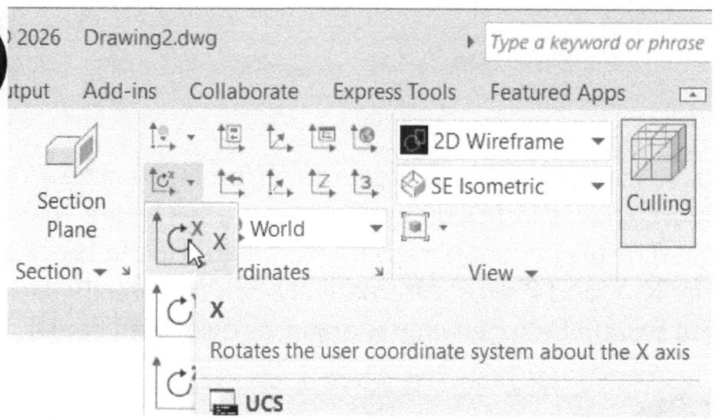

Y and Z

Similar to the **X** tool, the **Y and Z** tools are used for rotating the UCS about the Y-axis and Z-axis, respectively.

View

The **View** tool is used for aligning the XY plane (work plane) of the UCS parallel to the screen. To do so, click on the **View** tool in the **Coordinates** panel, see Figure 13.42. The XY plane of the UCS becomes parallel to the screen. Alternatively, enter **UCS** in the Command Line window and then press ENTER. Next, click on the **View** option in the command prompt to activate this tool.

Object

The **Object** tool is used for creating a new UCS aligned to an object. To do so, click on the **Object** tool in the **Coordinates** panel, see Figure 13.43, and then move the cursor over the object. A preview of the UCS appears aligned to the object. Next, click to specify the origin of the UCS. The UCS is created such that its Z-axis is perpendicular to the face of the object selected. Alternatively, enter **UCS** in the Command Line window and then press ENTER. Next, click on the **Object** option in the command prompt to activate this tool.

13.42

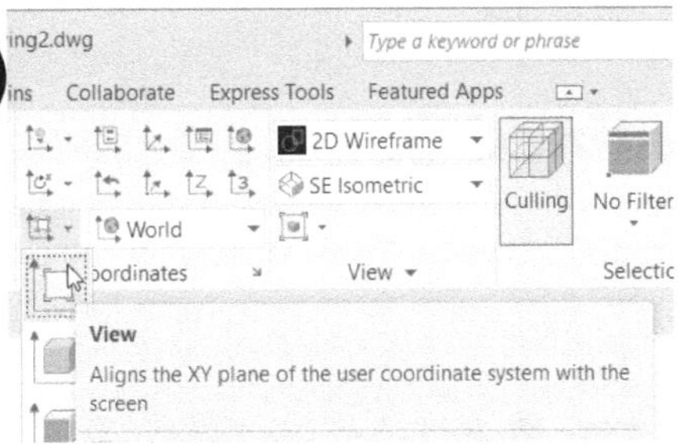

13.43

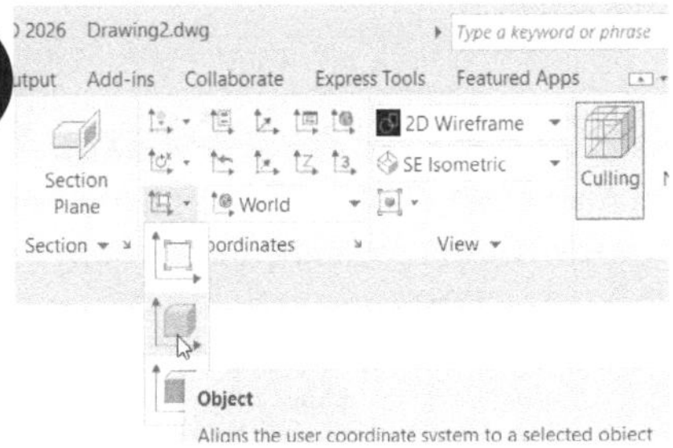

Face

The **Face** tool is used for creating a new UCS aligned to a face. To do so, click on the **Face** tool in the **Coordinates** panel, see Figure 13.44, and then move the cursor over a Face. The preview of the UCS appears aligned to the face, see Figure 13.45. Next, click to specify the origin of the UCS. Next, press ENTER to accept the default orientation of the UCS or select **Next**, **Xflip**, or **Yflip** option in the command sequence or in the flyout that appears on the screen. The **Next** option is used to place the UCS on the adjacent face. The **Xflip** and **Yflip** options are used for rotating the UCS by 180 degrees around the X and Y axes, respectively. The UCS is created such that its XY plane is aligned to the selected face. Alternatively, enter **UCS** in the Command Line window and then press ENTER. Next, click on the **Face** option in the command prompt to activate this tool.

13.44

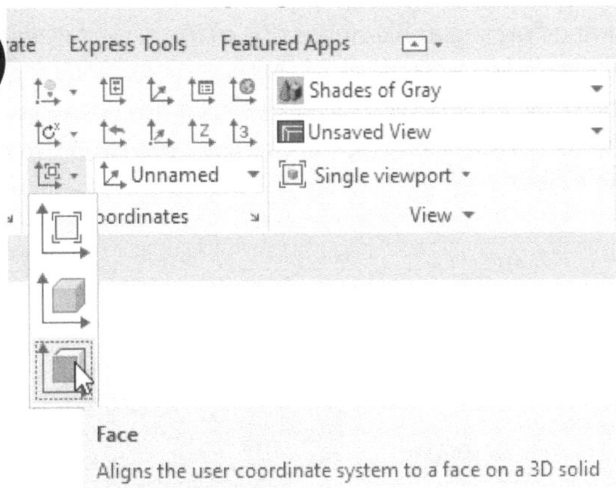

13.45

UCS, World

The **UCS, World** tool is used for positioning the user coordinate system to the default world coordinate system. For doing so, click on the **UCS, World** tool, see Figure 13.46. The user coordinate system is located in the default world coordinate system. Alternatively, enter **UCS** in the Command Line window and then press ENTER. Next, click on the **World** option in the command prompt to activate this tool.

13.46

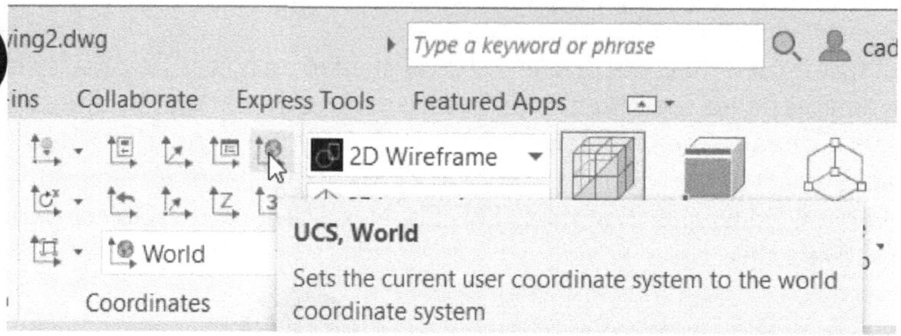

Setting Work Plane to Predefined Orthographic View

In AutoCAD, you can also set the work plane (XY plane) of the UCS to predefined orthographic views such as Top, Front, Left, and Right by using the **Named UCS Combo Control** flyout of the **Coordinates** Panel, see Figure 13.47.

13.47

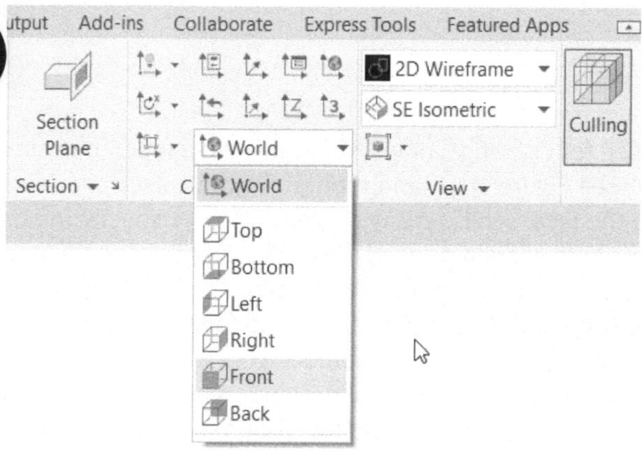

Setting the work plane (XY plane) to a predefined orthographic view is one of the easiest ways to manage the work plane for creating a 3D object. For example, to create an object on the front view, click on the **Front** tool in the **Named UCS Combo Control** flyout. The work plane (XY plane) of the UCS is set to the front view for creating an object, see Figure 13.48. In this figure, the work plane (XY plane) of the UCS is set to the front view for creating the object.

13.48

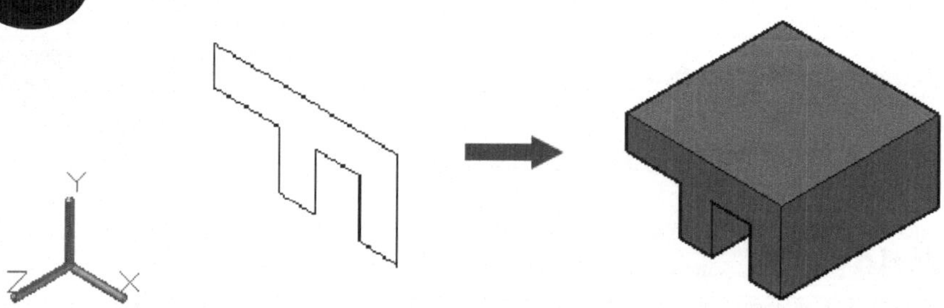

Similarly, you can set the work plane (XY plane) of the UCS to other orthographic views by clicking on the respective tool in this flyout.

Working with Dynamic UCS

Dynamic UCS is a temporary UCS that appears automatically when you move the cursor over the face of a 3D solid object. For example, to create a circle on the face of an existing object, activate the **Center, Radius** tool and then move the cursor over the face of the object. The face of the object gets highlighted and the Dynamic UCS appears, see Figure 13.49 which allows you to create the circle on the highlighted face of the object. Note that the XY plane (work plane) of the Dynamic UCS aligns with the face of the existing object. To activate or deactivate the **Dynamic UCS** mode, click on the **Dynamics UCS** tool in the Status Bar, see Figure 13.50. Note that if the **Dynamics UCS** tool is not available in the Status Bar, then you need to add it. To do so, click on the **Customization** tool in the Status Bar and then click on the **Dynamics UCS** tool in the **Customization** menu that appears, see Figure 13.51.

13.49

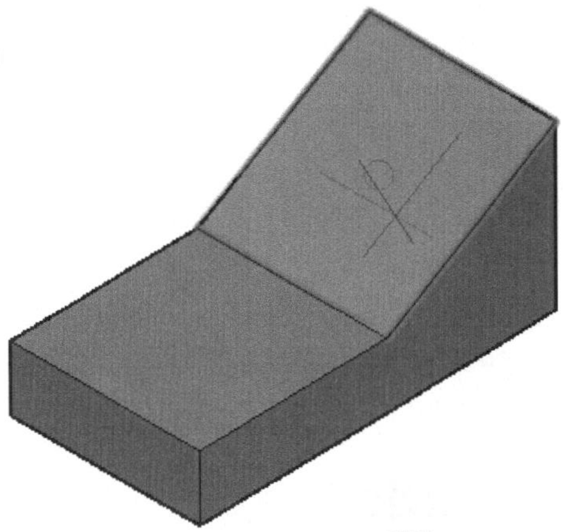

13.50

13.51

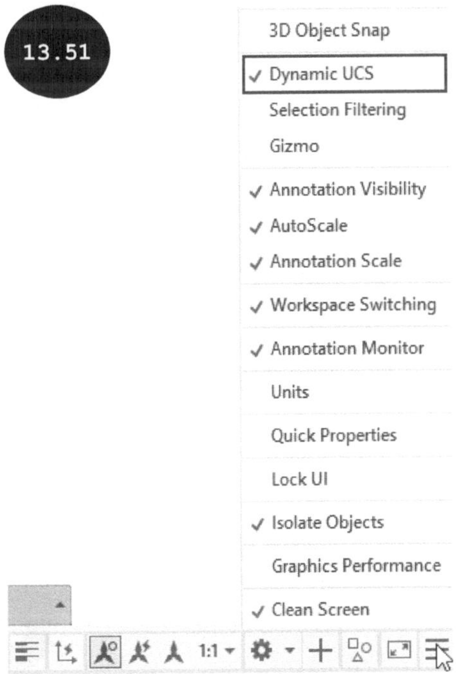

You can also activate or deactivate the Dynamic UCS mode by using the UCSDETECT command or by pressing the F6 key.

Controlling the Display of the UCS

In AutoCAD, you can control the display of the UCS icon in the drawing area by using the **Show UCS Icon at Origin**, **Show UCS Icon**, and **Hide UCS Icon** tools of the **Coordinates** Panel, see Figure 13.52. Alternatively, you can also control the display of the UCS icon by using the UCSICON command.

13.52

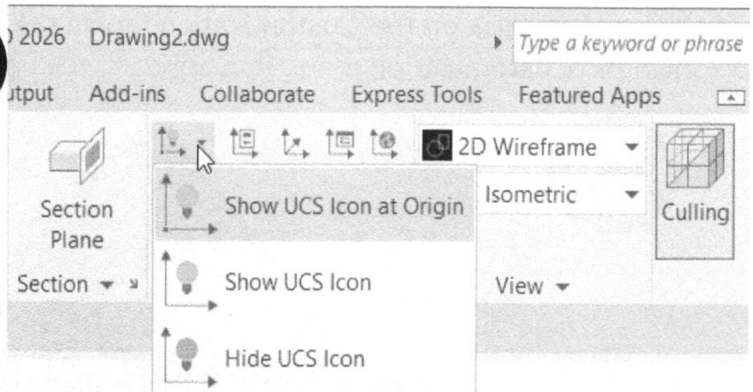

The **Show UCS Icon at Origin** tool is used for displaying the UCS icon at the origin (0,0) in the drawing. The **Show UCS Icon** tool is used for displaying the UCS icon at the lower left corner of the drawing area. The **Hide UCS Icon** tool is used for hiding the display of the UCS icon in the drawing area.

Creating an Extrude Feature

An extrude feature is created by adding material, normal to the work plane (XY). Note that the sketch of the extrude feature defines its geometry. Figure 13.53 shows different extrude features that are created from the respective sketches. In AutoCAD, you can create an extrude feature by adding material, to a closed sketch or a region, along the Z-axis using the **Extrude** tool. The method for creating an extrude feature is discussed below:

13.53

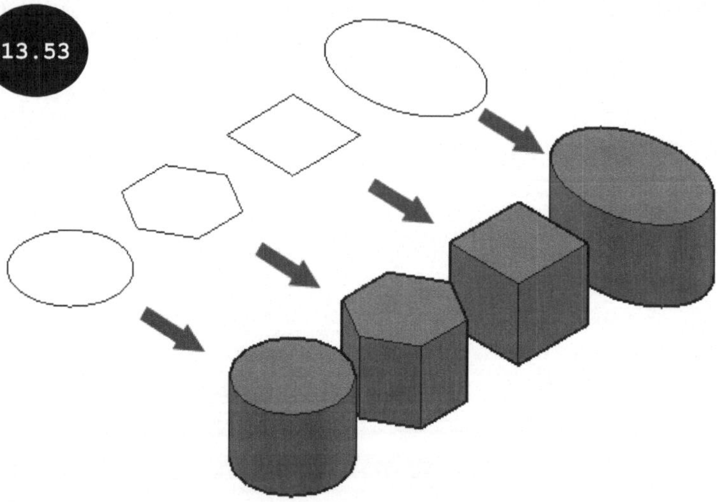

1. Create a closed sketch on the work plane (XY plane) by using the drawing tools available in the **Draw** panel of the **Home** tab, see Figure 13.54. In this figure, the closed sketch is created by using the **Polyline** tool. Note that before you create a sketch, you need to set the work plane (XY plane), as required by creating a new UCS.

13.54

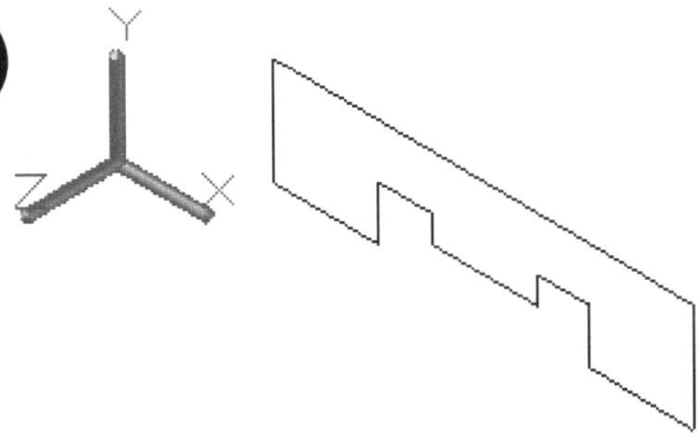

Note: If the closed sketch is created by using the **Line** tool, then first you need to convert it into a region by using the **Region** tool or REG command to create a 3D solid extrude feature. You will learn about converting a closed sketch into a region later in this chapter.

2. Click on the **Extrude** tool in the **Modeling** panel of the **Home** tab, see Figure 13.55. You are prompted to select an object to extrude.

```
Select objects to extrude or [MOde]:
```

13.55

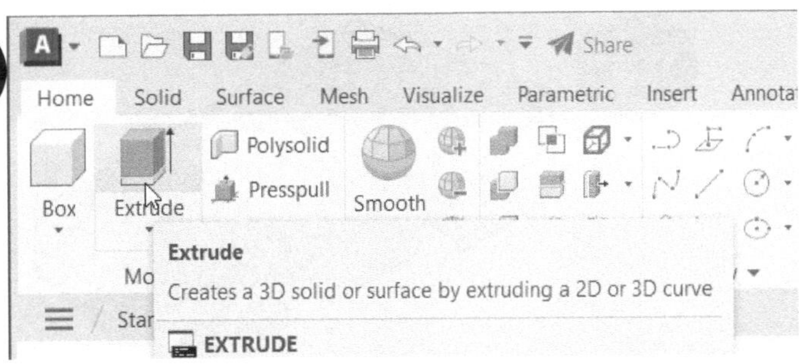

3. Click on the closed sketch as the object to be extruded and then press ENTER. A preview of the extrude feature appears and you are prompted to specify the height of the extrusion.

```
Specify height of extrusion or [Direction Path Taper angle Expression]
<4.0000>:
```

4. Move the cursor on either side of the work plane to define the direction of extrusion.

5. Enter the height of the extrusion and then press ENTER. The extrude feature is created by adding material of a specified height along the Z-axis, see Figure 13.56.

13.56

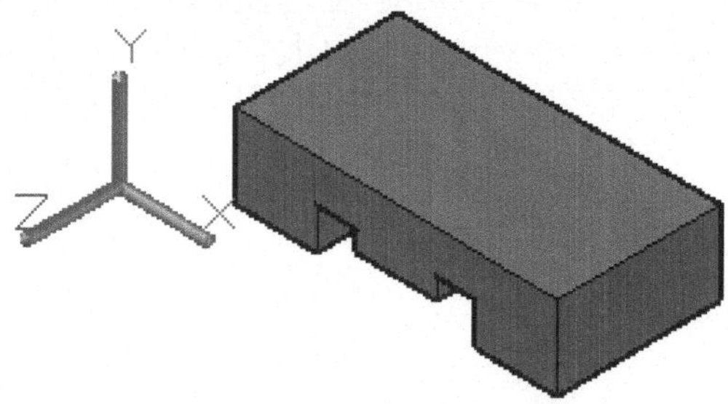

Note: You can also add tapering to the extrude feature, specify the direction of extrusion other than Z-axis, or extrude along a path by using the **Taper angle**, **Direction**, and **Path** options, respectively that appear in the command prompt when you are prompted to specify the height of extrusion. To add tapering to the extrude feature, click on the **Taper angle** option in the command prompt and then specify the taper angle. Next, press ENTER. A preview of the extrude feature with a specified taper angle appears. Next, specify the height of extrusion and then press ENTER. The extrude feature having tapering on all its sides is created, see Figure 13.57.

To specify the direction of extrusion other than the Z-axis, click on the **Direction** option in the command prompt and then specify two points to define the direction of extrusion. To extrude the feature along a path, click on the **Path** option in the command prompt and then select an entity as the path to create the extrude feature.

13.57

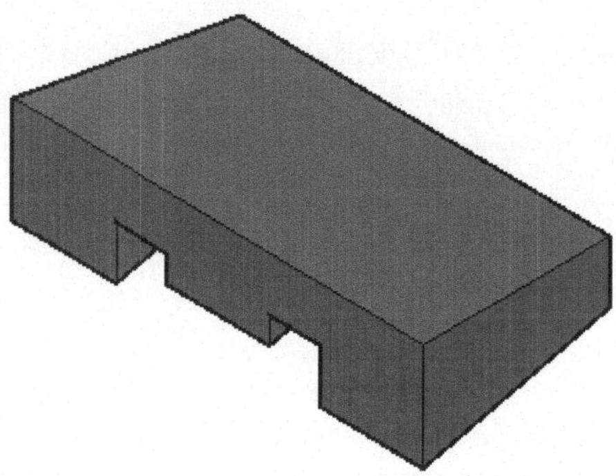

Converting a Closed Sketch into a Region

In AutoCAD, if a closed sketch is created by using tools such as **Line** and **Arc**, then you need to convert it into a region for creating a 3D solid feature. This is so because, the entities of such a sketch act as individual entities and cannot be used to create a solid feature. In AutoCAD, the individual entities or open sketch are used for creating a surface feature. Figure 13.58 shows a closed sketch that is created by using the **Line** and **Arc** tools and Figure 13.59 shows the resultant surface feature created by extruding all its entities. The method for converting a sketch into a region is discussed below:

13.58

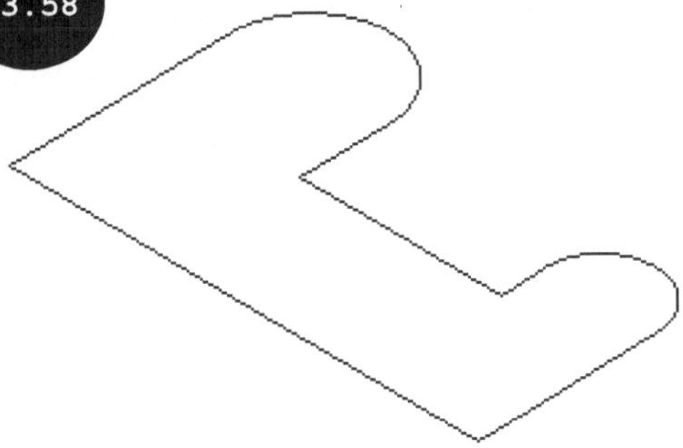

13.59

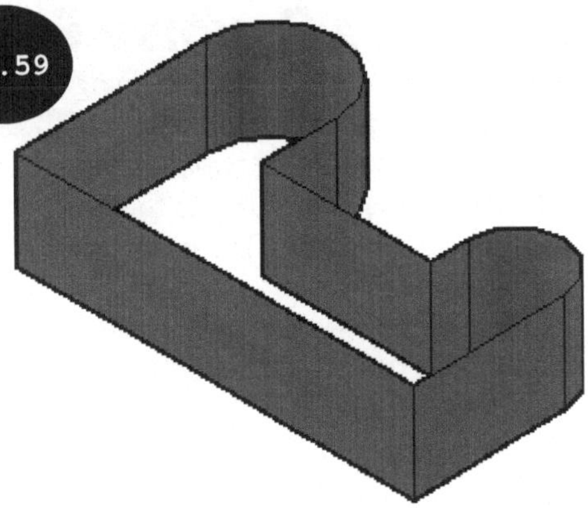

1. Click on the **Region** tool in the expanded **Draw** panel of the **Home** tab, see Figure 13.60. Alternatively, enter **REG** in the Command Line window and then press ENTER to activate this tool. You are prompted to select objects.

13.60

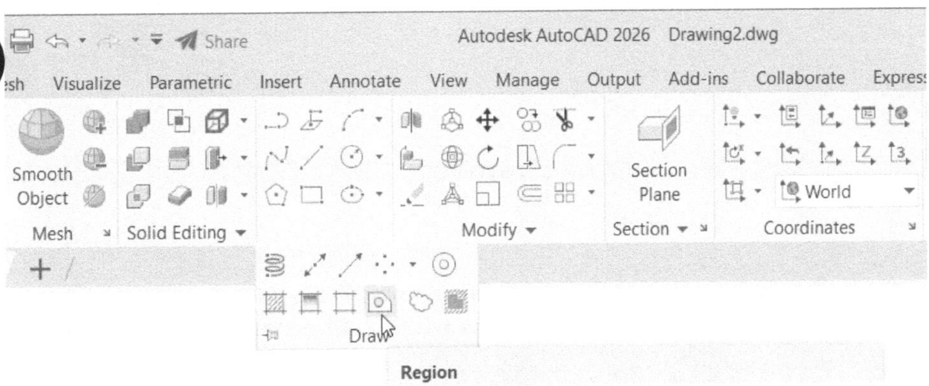

2. Select all entities of the closed sketch one after the other by clicking the left mouse button. You can also draw a window around the entities to be selected.

13.61

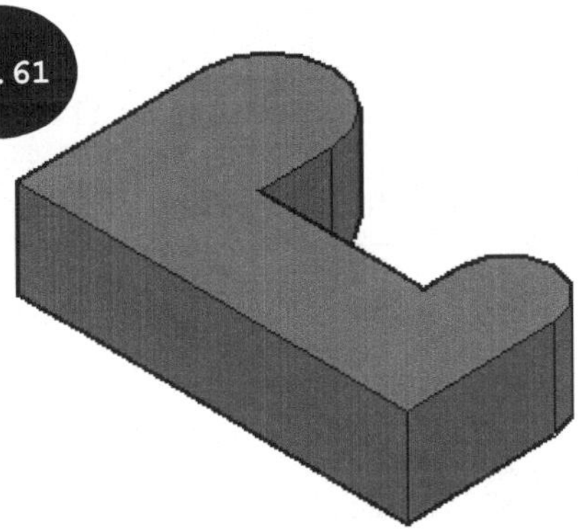

3. After selecting the entities, press ENTER. The selected entities are converted into a region and act as a single object. Now, you can extrude the sketch to create a solid feature, see Figure 13.61.

Tip: In the case of an open sketch, you can use the JOIN command to merge all the individual entities of the sketch and convert them into a single object.

Creating a Revolve Feature

A revolve feature is created by revolving the sketch around an axis of revolution. Note that the sketch to be revolved should be on either side of the axis of revolution, see Figure 13.62. You can define the axis of revolution by specifying two points in the drawing area or by selecting a linear entity. You can also use the X or Y axis of the UCS as the axis of revolution. In AutoCAD, you can create a revolve feature by using the **Revolve** tool. The method for creating a revolve feature is discussed below:

1. Click on the **Revolve** tool in the **Modeling** panel of the **Home** tab, see Figure 13.63. You are prompted to select objects to revolve. Alternatively, enter **REV** in the Command Line window and then press ENTER to activate this tool.

13.62

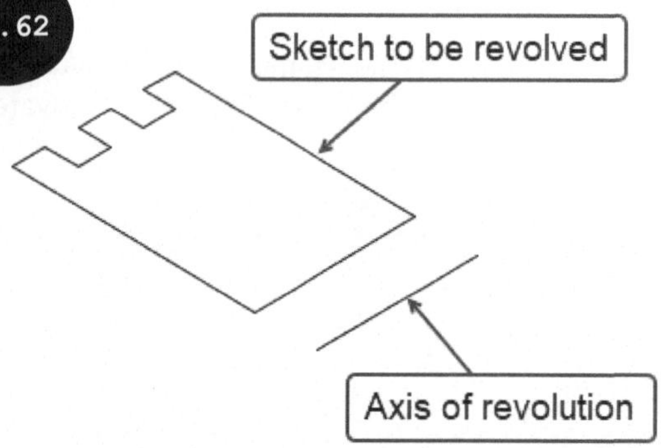

13.63

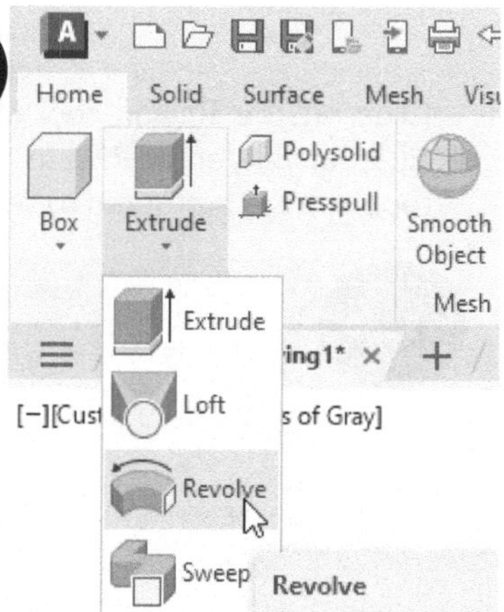

2. Select the sketch to be revolved and then press ENTER. You are prompted to specify the start point of the axis or select an object as the axis to revolve the selected sketch.

```
Specify axis start point or define axis by [Object X Y Z] <Object>:
```

3. Click to specify the start and end points in the drawing area to define the axis of revolution one after another and then press ENTER. A preview of the revolve feature appears and you are prompted to specify the angle of revolution. By default, the direction of rotation is defined by using the right-hand thumb rule, where the right hand thumb points toward the axis of rotation and the curled fingers define the positive direction of rotation.

```
Specify angle of revolution or [STart angle Reverse EXpression]
<360>:
```

Note: To select an object as the axis of revolution, click on the **Object** option in the command prompt and then select an object as the axis of revolution. You can also revolve the sketch around the X, Y, or Z axis by using the **X**, **Y**, or **Z** option that appears in the command prompt.

4. Click on the **Reverse** option in the command prompt to reverse the direction of rotation, if needed.

5. Enter the angle of revolution and then press ENTER. The revolve feature is created by revolving the sketch around the axis of revolution, see Figure 13.64.

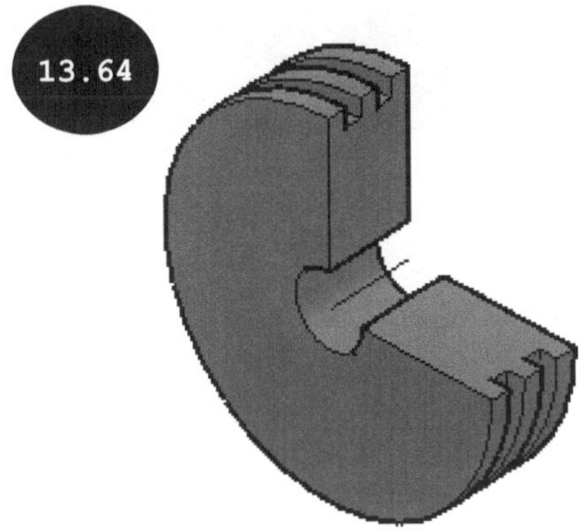

Creating a Sweep Feature

A sweep feature is created by sweeping a profile along a path. Figures 13.65 and 13.66 show a profile and a path as well as the resultant sweep feature created by sweeping the profile along the path. Note that the profile defines the cross-section of the sweep feature and the path defines the route followed by the profile for creating the feature. The profile and path can be open or closed. However, if the profile is closed, a solid feature will be created, and if the profile is open, a surface feature will be created. Figure 13.65 shows a closed profile and an open path. Figure 13.66 shows an open profile and path. The method for creating a sweep feature is discussed below:

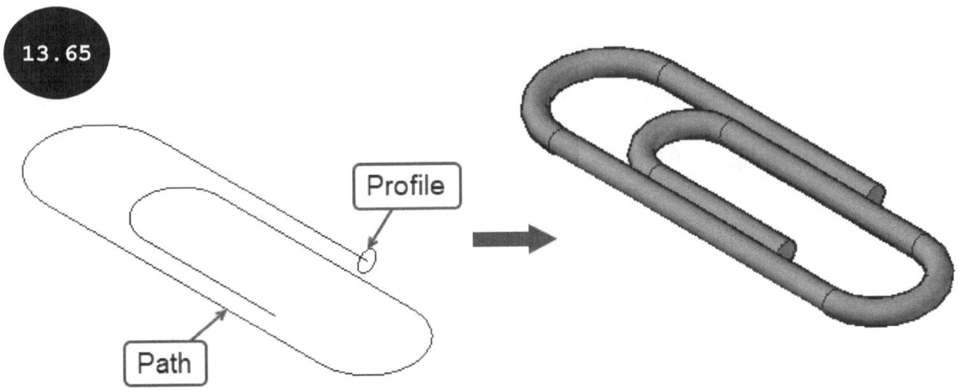

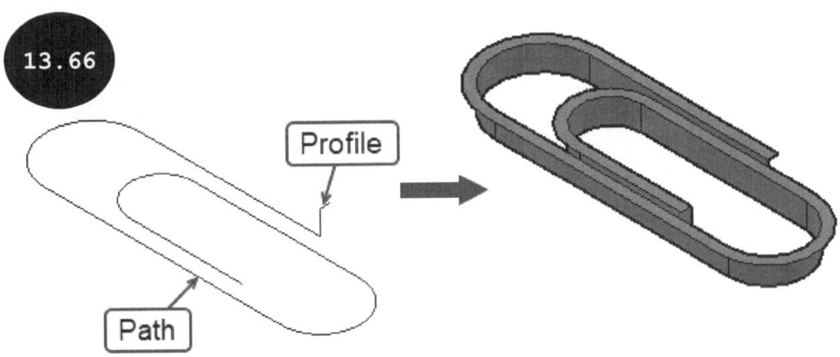

1. Click on the **Sweep** tool in the **Modeling** panel of the **Home** tab, see Figure 13.67. You are prompted to select objects to sweep. Alternatively, enter **SWEEP** in the Command Line window and then press ENTER to activate this tool.

13.67

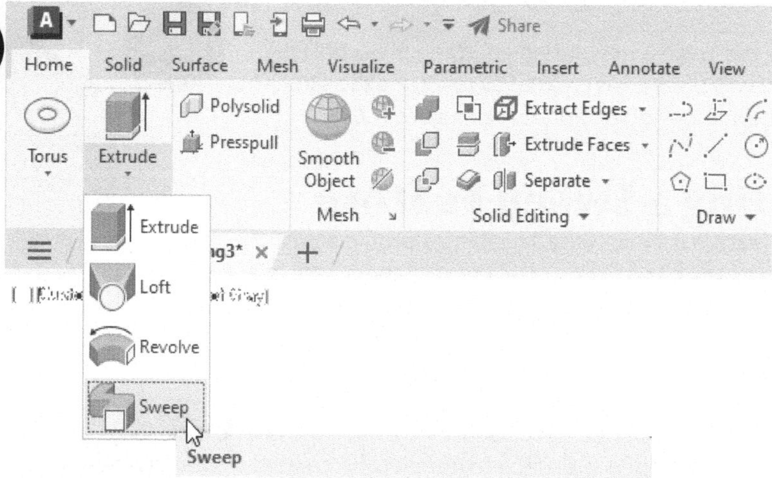

2. Select an object as the profile and then press ENTER. You are prompted to select a sweep path. Note that you can select single or multiple objects to sweep along the path. However, all the objects must be created on the same work plane.

Note: You can also twist a profile along a path by specifying the twist angle using the **Twist** option that appears in the command prompt. You can also specify the base point for the sweep feature by using the **Base point** option that appears in the command prompt. By default, the center point of the profile is used as the base point of the sweep feature. Moreover, by using the **Scale** option of the command prompt, you can scale the profile along the path.

3. Select a sweep path in the drawing area. The sweep feature is created, see Figure 13.68. Note that all entities or segments of the path must act as a single object. In Figure 13.68, the path is created by using the **Polyline** tool. Also, the profile, the path, and the resultant sweep feature must not self-intersect.

13.68

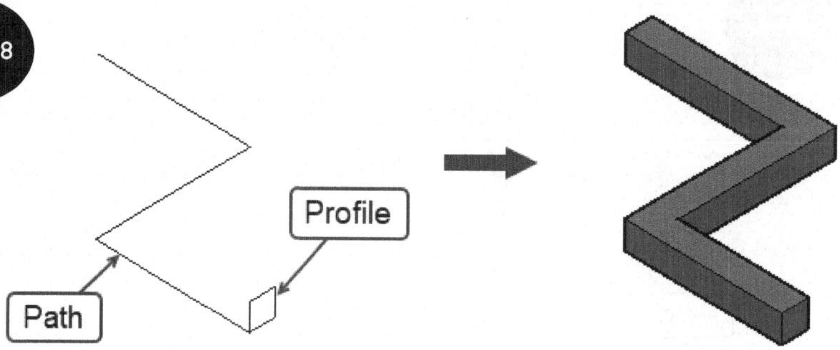

Creating a Loft Feature

A loft feature is created by lofting two or more than two profiles (sections) such that the cross-sectional shape of the loft feature transits from one profile to another. Figure 13.69 shows three profiles created on different work planes having offset distance between each other or at different elevations. Figure 13.70 shows the resultant loft feature created.

13.69

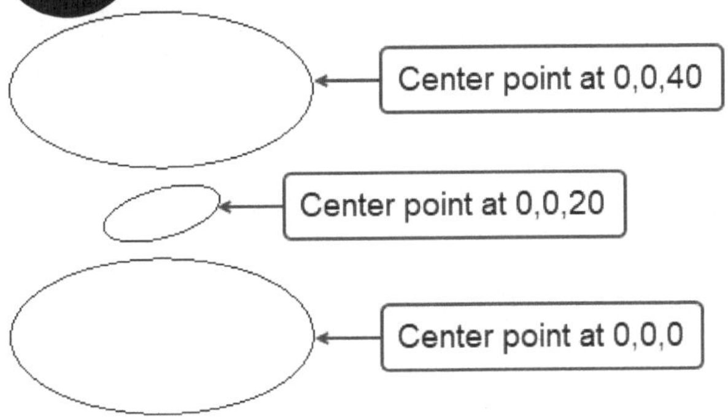

13.70

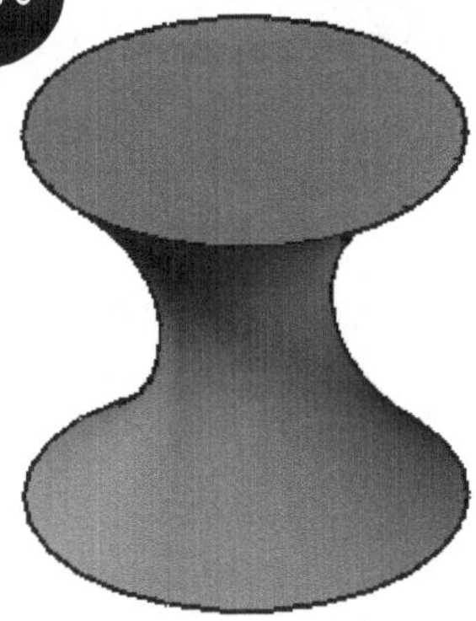

In AutoCAD, you can select all opened or closed profiles to create a loft feature. Note that if all profiles are opened, then the surface loft feature will be created, whereas if all profiles are closed, then the solid loft feature will be created. The method for creating a loft feature is discussed below:

1. Click on the **Loft** tool in the **Modeling** panel of the **Home** tab, see Figure 13.71. You are prompted to select cross sections in lofting order. Alternatively, enter **LOFT** in the Command Line window and then press ENTER to activate this tool.

2. Select all the profiles of the loft feature one by one in an order. The preview of the loft feature appears, see Figure 13.72. Next, press ENTER. You are prompted to select an option: **Guides**, **Path**, **Cross section only**, or **Settings** for creating the loft feature. The options are discussed next.

```
Enter an option [Guides Path Cross sections only Settings] <Cross
sections only>:
```

13.71

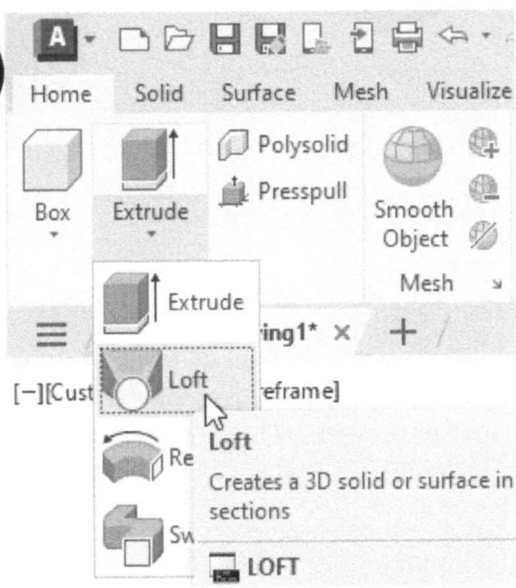

13.72

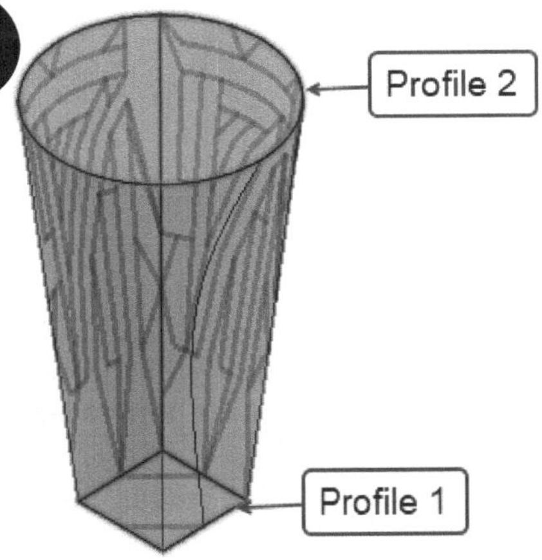

Guides: The **Guides** option allows you to create a loft feature with profiles and guide curves. Guide curves are used for guiding the cross-sectional shape of the loft feature, see Figure 13.73. In this figure, one guide curve is selected to guide the cross-section shape of the loft feature. You can select single or multiple guide curves for controlling the shape of the loft feature. To do so, click on the **Guides** option and then select the guide curves.

13.73

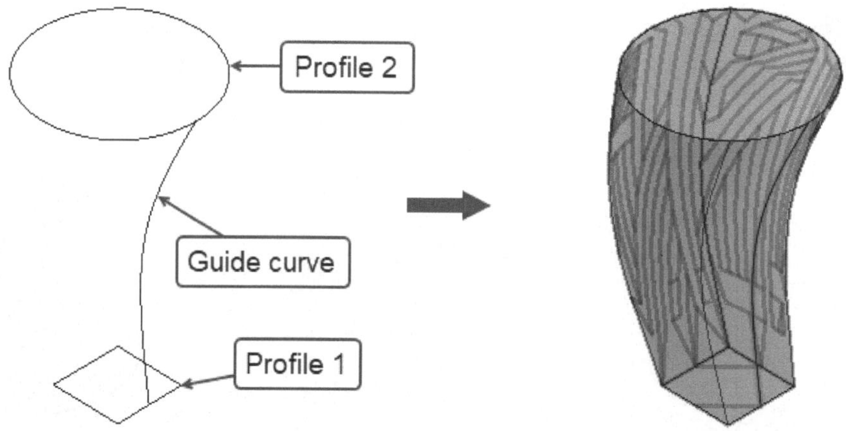

Path: The **Path** option is used for maintaining the neutral axis of the loft feature and consistent transition between the profiles, see Figure 13.74. To do so, click on the **Path** option and then select the path of the loft feature in the drawing area. Note that all entities or segments of the path must act as a single object. In Figure 13.74, the entities/segments of the path are merged together by using the JOINT command. You can only select one path to create the loft feature.

13.74

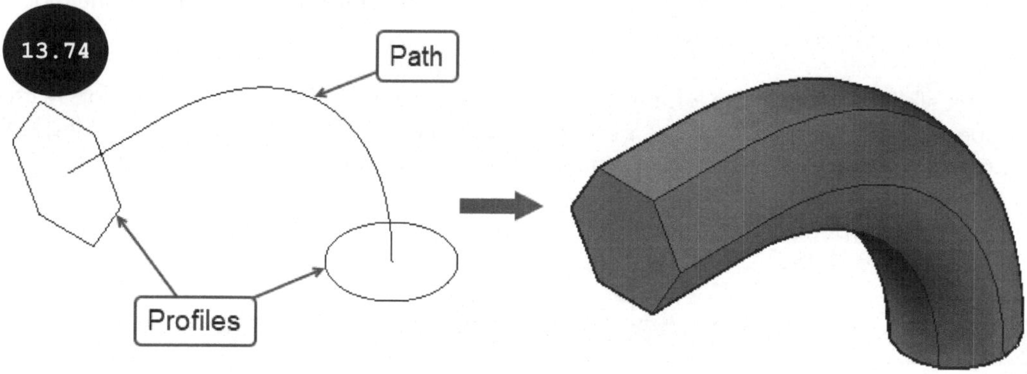

Cross sections only: The **Cross sections only** option is used for creating a loft feature only with profiles. By default, this option is selected. As a result, to create a loft feature only with profiles, press the ENTER key.

Settings: The **Settings** option is used for specifying settings such as start continuity and end continuity for creating the loft feature. To do so, click on the **Settings** option. The **Loft Settings** dialog box appears. The **Ruled** radio button of the dialog box is used for maintaining the straight transition between the profiles of the loft feature, see Figure 13.75. The **Smooth Fit** radio button is used to maintain a smooth transition between the profiles, see Figure 13.76.

13.75

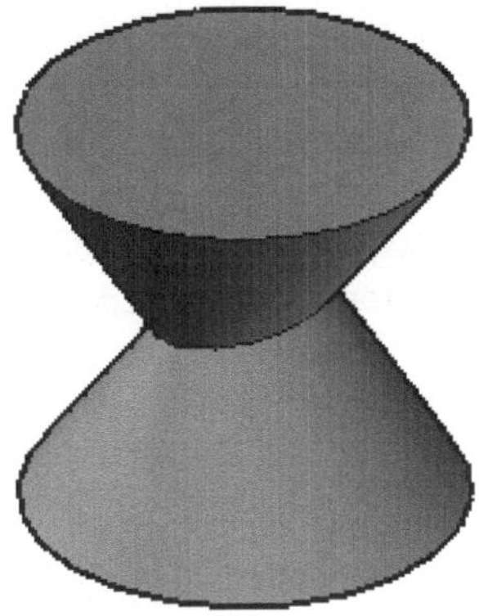

13.76

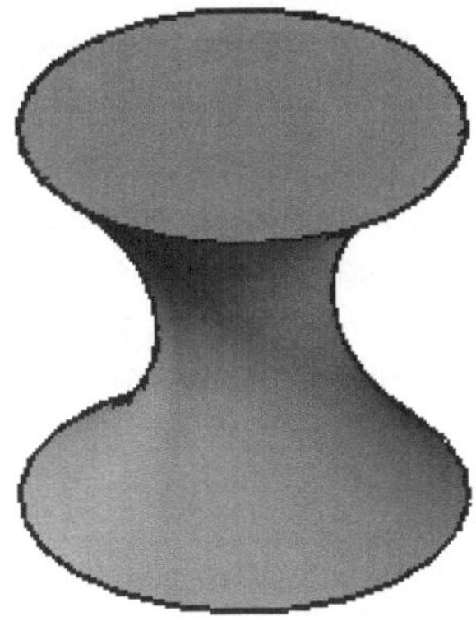

The **Normal to** radio button of the **Loft Settings** dialog box is used for creating a loft feature, normal to the profiles/cross-sections. You can create a loft feature normal to all cross-sections, start cross-section, end cross-section, or start and end cross-sections by selecting the respective option in the **Normal to** drop-down list of the dialog box. The **Draft angles** radio button is used for specifying the start and end draft angles and magnitude in the respective fields of the dialog box.

The **Close surface or solid** check box is used for creating a closed loft feature such that the start and end profiles/cross-sections of the feature connect with each other, see Figures 13.77 and 13.78. Figure 13.77 shows the preview of a loft feature when the **Close surface or solid** check box is cleared and Figure 13.78 shows the preview of a loft feature when the **Close surface or solid** check box is selected. To create a closed loft feature, a minimum of three sections/profiles are required. Also, the total angle between the start and end sections should be more than 120 degrees.

13.77

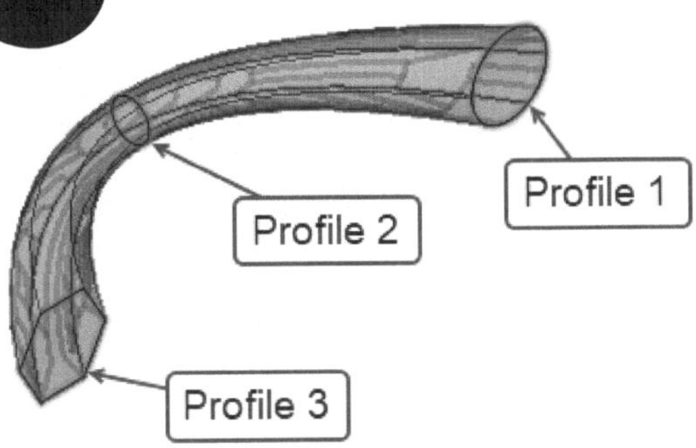

13.78

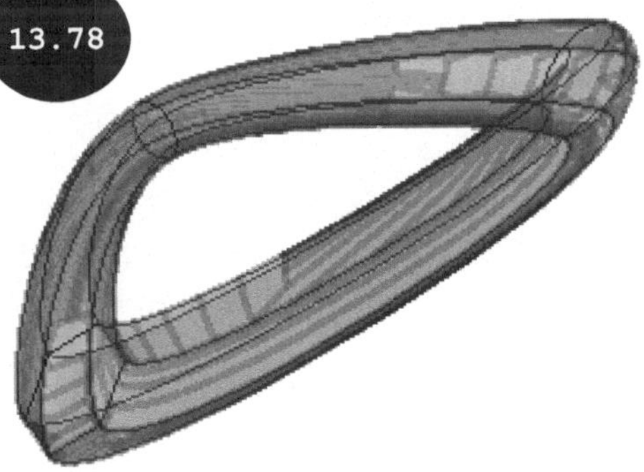

3. Select the required option **Guides**, **Path**, **Cross sections only**, or **Settings** to create the loft feature, as required.

4. Press the ENTER key to create the loft feature.

Working with Presspull Tool

The **Presspull** tool is one of the most powerful tools for quickly and dynamically creating or modifying a solid model. This tool is used for creating or editing a 3D solid model by adding or removing material depending on whether you perform a press or pull operation on a closed region of a sketch. If you pull a closed region, it adds material, see Figure 13.79 (a), whereas if you press a closed region of an existing 3D model, it removes material, see Figure 13.79 (b). The method for adding or removing material by using the **Presspull** tool is discussed below:

13.79

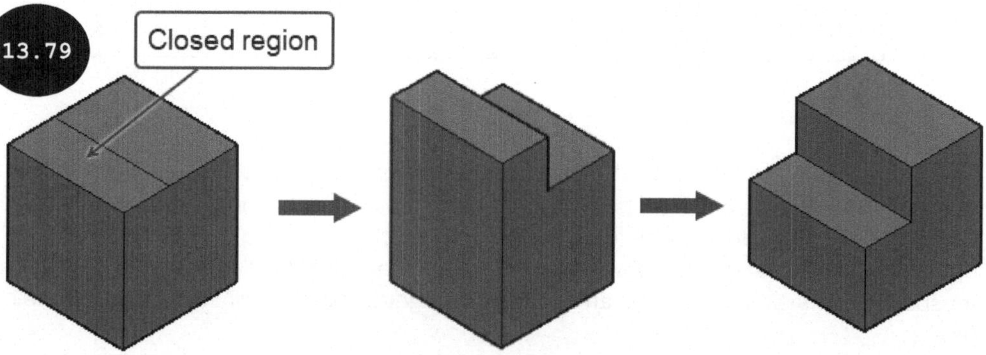

a) Material added b) Material removed

1. Click on the **Presspull** tool in the **Modeling** panel of the **Home** tab, see Figure 13.80. You are prompted to select an object or boundary area.

13.80

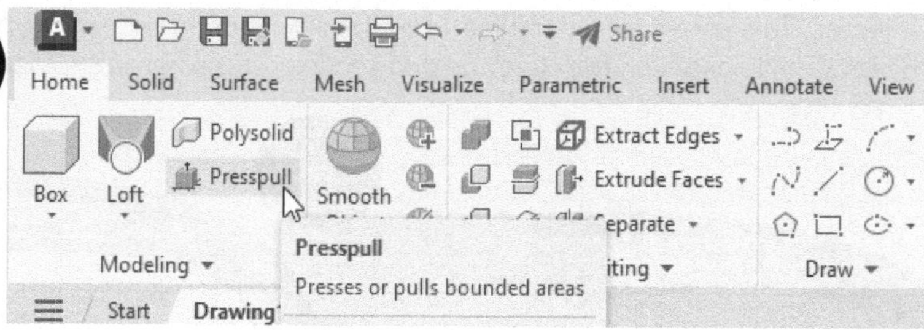

2. Select an object or a closed region (boundary area) of a sketch, see Figure 13.81. A preview of the feature appears and you are prompted to specify the height of extrusion.

3. Move the cursor in the required direction (press or pull). Next, enter the height of the extrusion and then press ENTER. The material is added to or removed from the selected region of the sketch, see Figure 13.82. In this figure, the material is added to the selected region of the sketch.

13.81

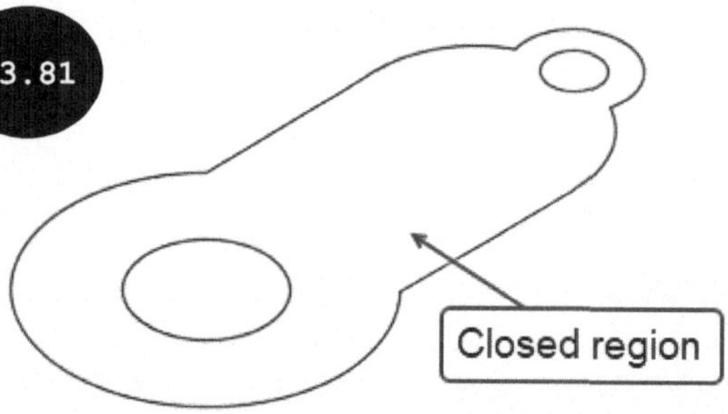

13.82

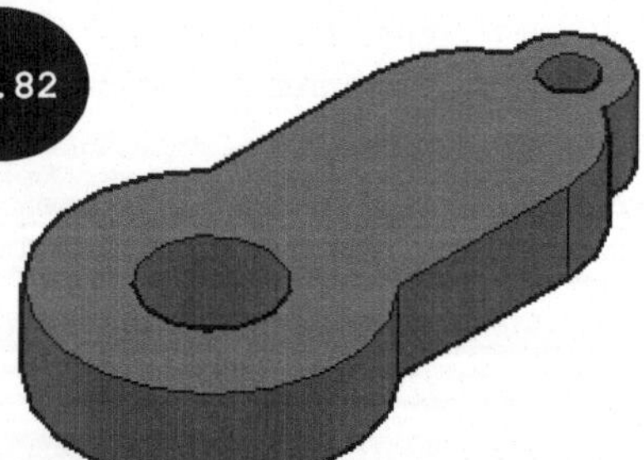

Note: You can select a closed sketch consisting of lines, circles, arcs, and polylines. You can also select a region or a face of a 3D model to add or remove material by using the **Presspull** tool, see Figures 13.83 and 13.84. In Figure 13.83, the top face of the model is divided into two regions by creating a line and Figure 13.84 shows the model after removing the material by pressing a region of the top face using the **Presspull** tool.

13.83

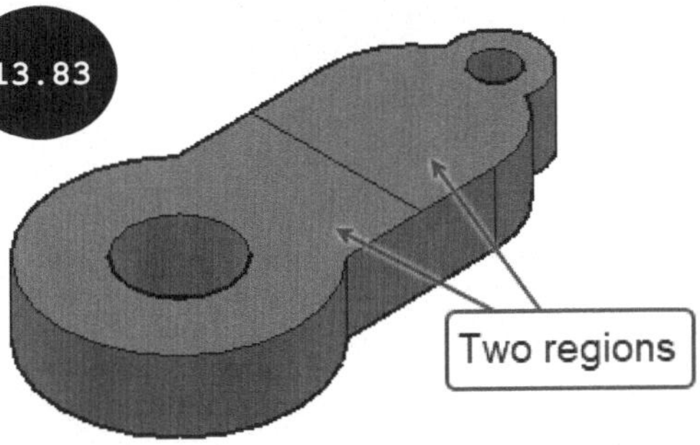

13.84

Creating a 3D Wall-like Polysolid

In AutoCAD, you can create a 3D wall-like polysolid feature by using the **Polysolid** tool. The method for creating a 3D wall-like polysolid feature is discussed below:

1. Click on the **Polysolid** tool in the **Modeling** panel of the **Home** tab, see Figure 13.85. You are prompted to specify the start point of the wall.

```
Specify start point or [Object Height Width Justify] <Object>:
```

2. Click on the **Height** option in the command prompt, type the height of the wall and then press ENTER.

3. Click on the **Width** option in the command prompt, type the width of the wall and then press ENTER.

Note: If you do not specify the height and width of the wall then the wall will be created with default height and width.

After specifying the height and width of the wall, you can start creating the wall.

4. Click to specify the start point of the wall in the drawing area, see Figure 13.86. A preview of the wall with specified height and width appears and you are prompted to specify the next point.

5. Click to specify the second point in the drawing area, see Figure 13.86. A wall is created and you are prompted to specify the next point of the wall.

6. Similarly, click to specify other points in the drawing area one by one to create the wall and then press ENTER to finish the creation of the wall.

13.85

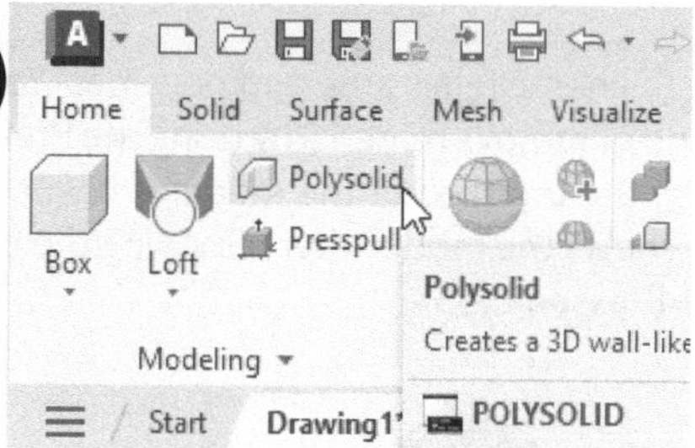

13.86

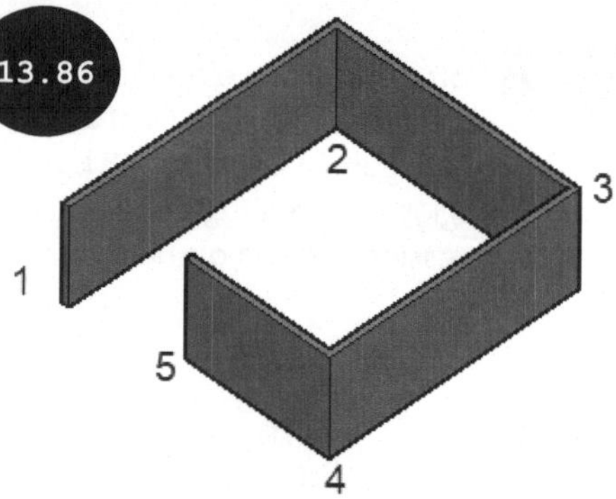

Note: Instead of specifying points in the drawing area for creating a wall of specified height and width, you can select an object (a line, a polyline, an arc, or a circle) to create the wall. To do so, click on the **Object** option in the command prompt when you are prompted to specify the start point of the wall. Next, select the object to create the wall.

Performing Boolean Operations

In AutoCAD, you can perform boolean operations such as combine, subtract, or intersect two or more than two solid features by using the **Solid, Union**, **Solid, Subtract**, or **Solid, Intersect** tools, respectively. The tools for performing boolean operations are available in the **Solid Editing** panel of the **Home** tab. The methods for performing different boolean operations are discussed next.

Combining Solid Bodies

You can combine two or more than two solid features/bodies together and form a single body by using the **Solid, Union** tool, and the method for doing so is discussed below:

1. Click on the **Solid, Union** tool in the **Solid Editing** panel of the **Home** tab, see Figure 13.87 to combine two or more than two solid features/bodies together. You are prompted to select objects. You can also activate this tool by using the UNION or UNI command.

13.87

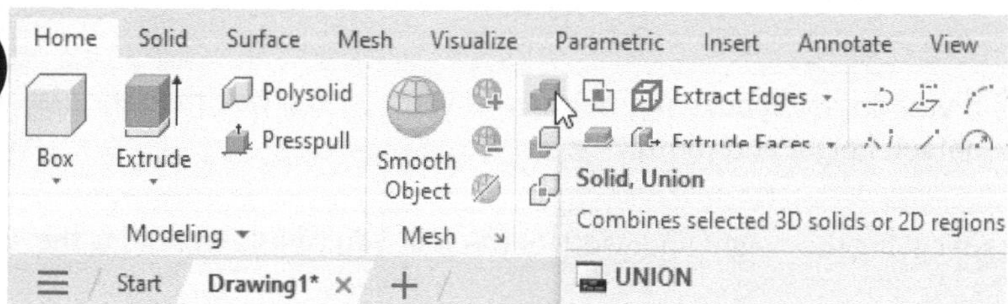

2. Select two or more than two solid features/bodies in the drawing area one by one, see Figure 13.88. Next, press ENTER. The selected bodies get combined together and act as a single body, see Figure 13.89.

13.88

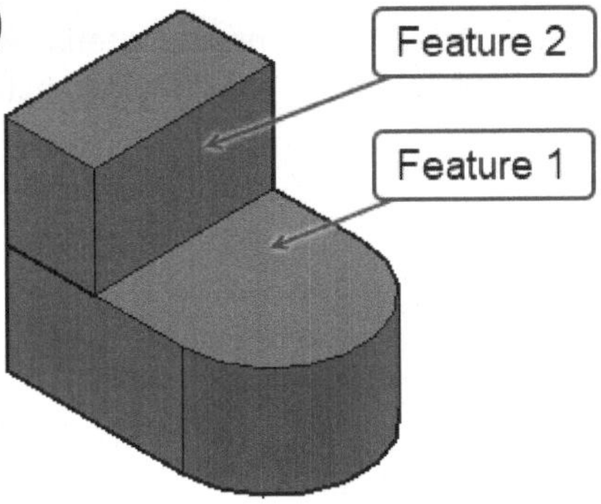

13.89

Subtracting Solid Bodies

You can subtract single or multiple bodies/features from another body by using the **Solid, Subtract** tool, and the method for doing so is discussed below:

1. Click on the **Solid, Subtract** tool, see Figure 13.90 or type SUBTRACT command and then press ENTER. You are prompted to select objects as tool bodies.

13.90

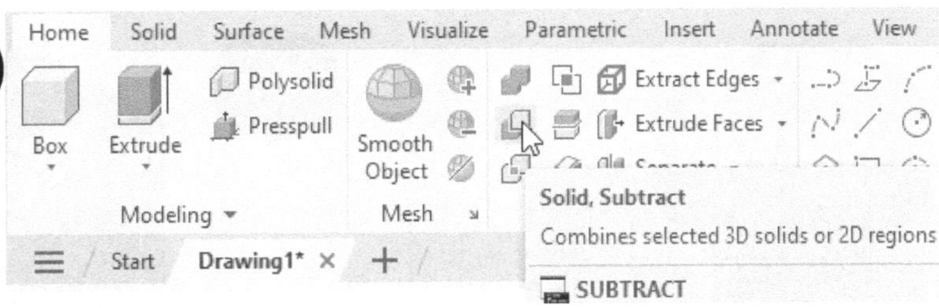

2. Select two or more than two solid features/bodies in the drawing area to subtract from, see Figure 13.91. Next, press ENTER. You are prompted to select objects.

3. Select one or more bodies in the drawing area to subtract and then press ENTER. The second set of bodies gets subtracted from the first selected set, see Figure 13.92.

13.91

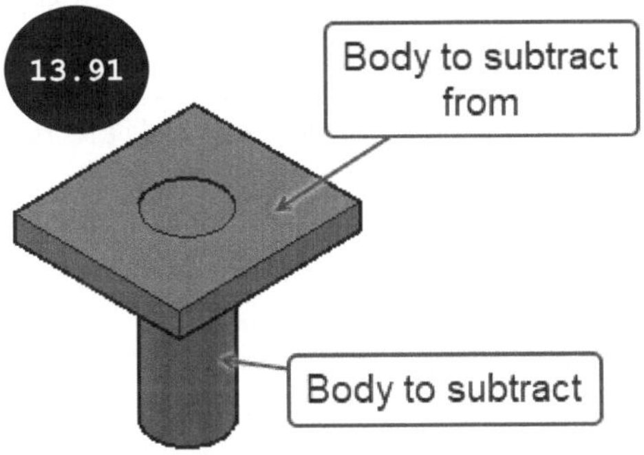

13.92

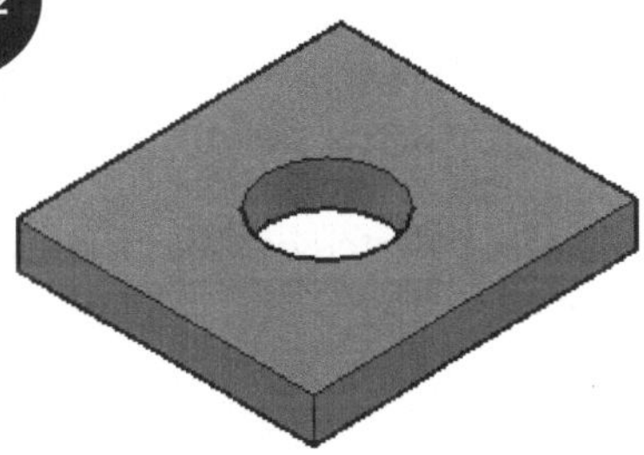

Intersecting Solid Bodies

You can create a composite solid body by only keeping the intersecting/common material between the existing bodies using the **Solid, Intersect** tool and the method for doing so is discussed below:

1. Click on the **Solid, Intersect** tool, see Figure 13.93 or type INTERSECT or IN command and then press ENTER. You are prompted to select objects.

13.93

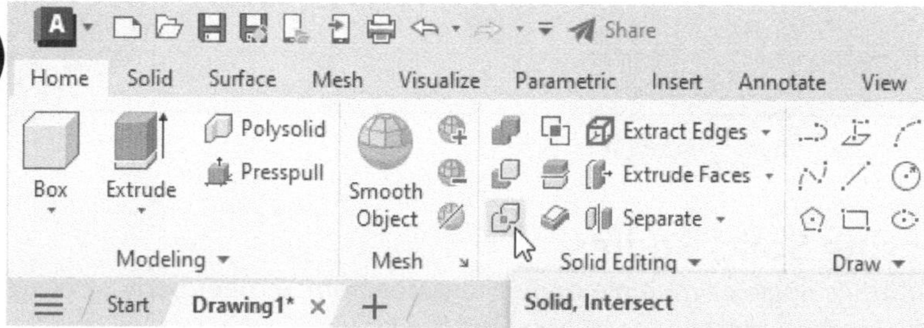

2. Select bodies in the drawing area and then press ENTER. A new composite solid body is created by only keeping the intersecting/common material between the selected bodies, see Figures 13.94 and 13.95.

13.94

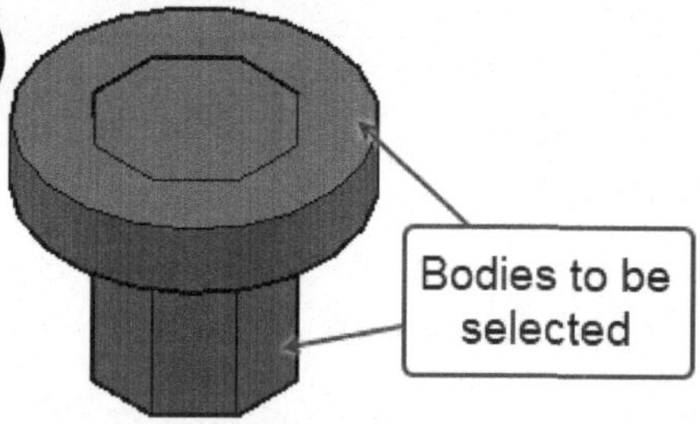

13.95

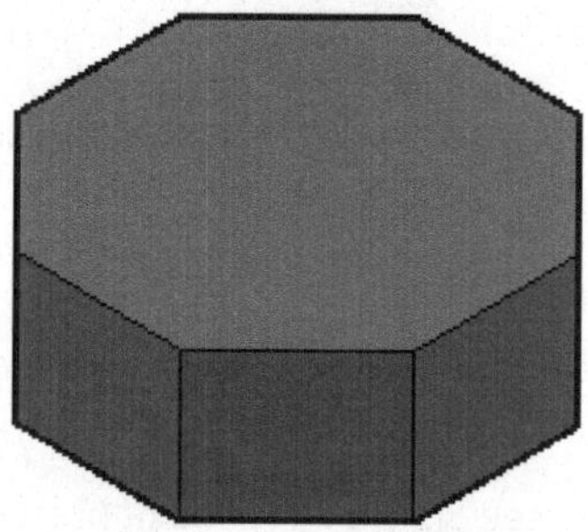

Checking Interference between Bodies

In AutoCAD, you can also check the Interference between two or more than two bodies by using the **Interfere** tool. For doing so, click on the **Interfere** tool in the **Solid Editing** panel of the **Home** tab (see Figure 13.96) or type **INTERFERE** in the Command Line window and then press ENTER. You are prompted to select the first set of objects. Select the first set of bodies and then press ENTER. You are prompted to select a second set of bodies. Select the second set of bodies and press ENTER. The **Interference Checking** dialog box appears which displays the results, see Figure 13.97. Also, the interference that is detected between the selected sets of bodies gets highlighted in the graphics area. After reviewing the interference, click on the **Close** button in the dialog box to exit it.

13.96

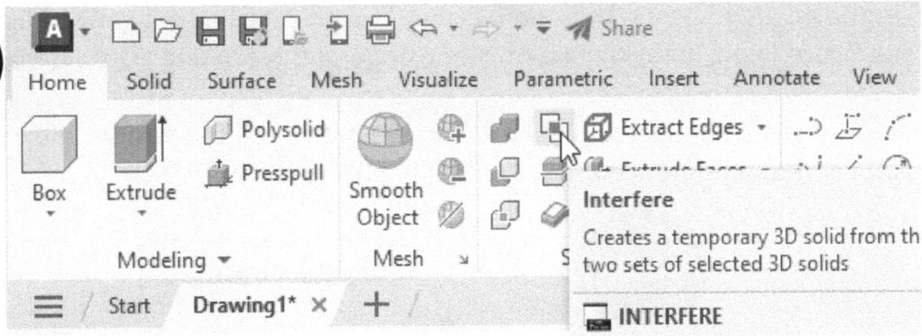

13.97

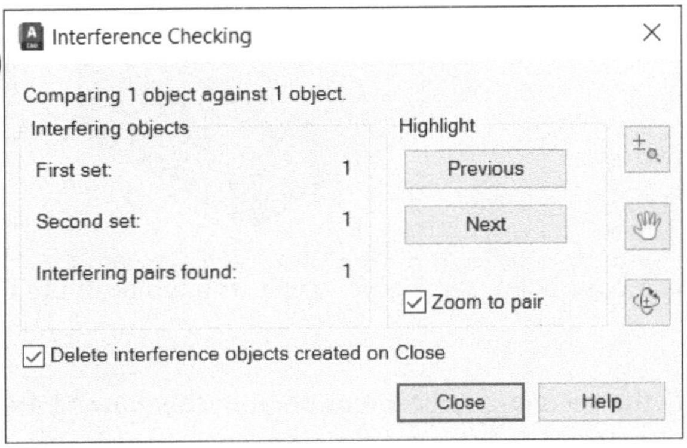

Copying Edges of a Solid Feature

In AutoCAD, you can copy the edges of an existing 3D solid feature by using the **Copy Edges** tool. The copied edges can be used for modifying a feature or creating a new 3D solid feature. The method for copying the edges of an existing 3D solid feature is discussed below:

1. Click on the **Copy Edges** tool in the **Solid Editing** panel of the **Home** tab, see Figure 13.98. You are prompted to select edges. Alternatively, enter **SOLIDEDIT** in the Command Line window and then press ENTER. Next, click on the **Edge** option and then the **Copy** option in the command prompt to copy the edges.

13.98

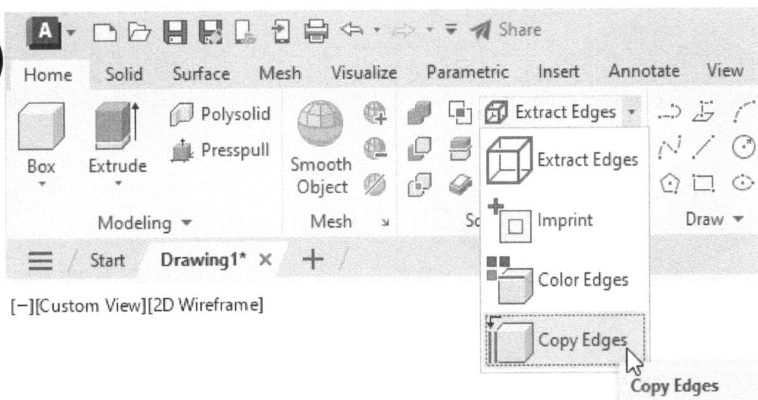

2. Click on the edges to be copied one by one. The selected edges get highlighted in the drawing area, see Figure 13.99. In this figure, only one edge of the existing 3D solid feature is selected.

3. After selecting the edges, press ENTER. You are prompted to specify a base point. Note that the base point acts as a reference point for copying the selected edges.

13.99

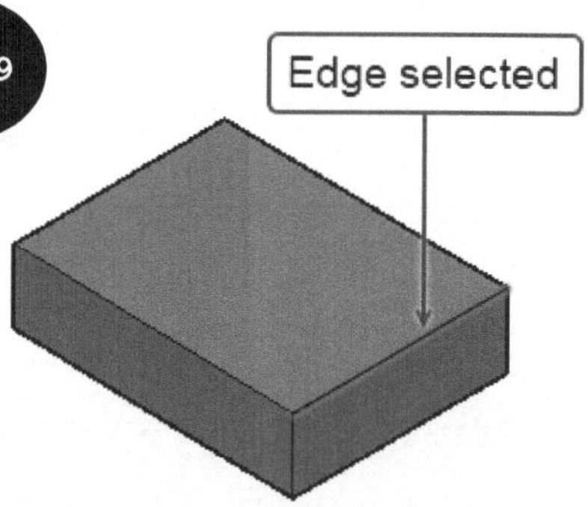

4. Click to specify a base point, see Figure 13.100. You are prompted to specify a second point of displacement.

5. Click to specify the second/displacement point in the drawing area, see Figure 13.100. You can also enter the displacement distance value and then press ENTER. You are prompted to select an option: **Copy**, **Color**, **Undo**, or **Exit**.

```
Enter an edge editing option [Copy coLor Undo eXit] <eXit>:
```

6. Press ENTER twice to exit the tool. The selected edge gets copied in the specified location, see Figure 13.101. Now, you can add or remove material by using the **Presspull** tool, see Figure 13.102. In this figure, material is added by pulling a region of the top face of the model which is created by the copied edge.

13.100

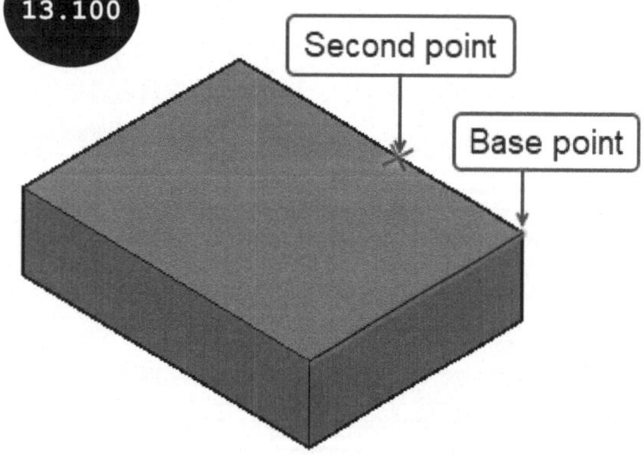

13.101

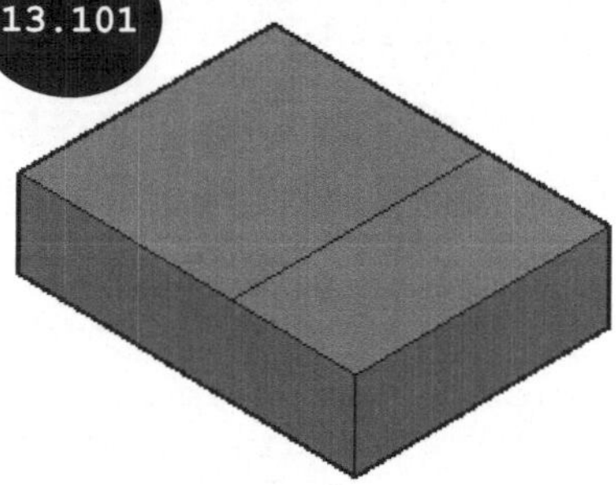

Note: If you click on the **Copy** option, the **Copy Edges** tool remains activated and you are prompted to select another set of edges to be copied. The **Color** option is used for coloring the selected edges of the existing model. The **Undo** option is used for undoing the previously performed operation.

13.102

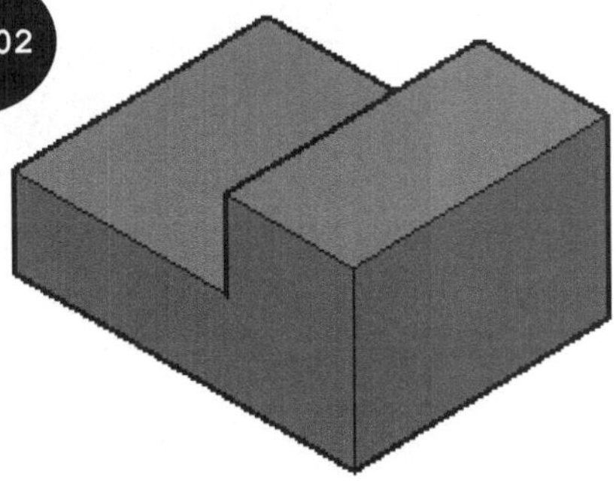

Performing Modifying Operations

In AutoCAD, you can perform various modifying operations such as move, rotate, scale, copy, array, mirror, and fillet by using the modifying tools available in the **Modify** panel of the **Home** tab, see Figure 13.103. The methods for performing various modifying operations are the same as discussed earlier while creating 2D drawings.

13.103

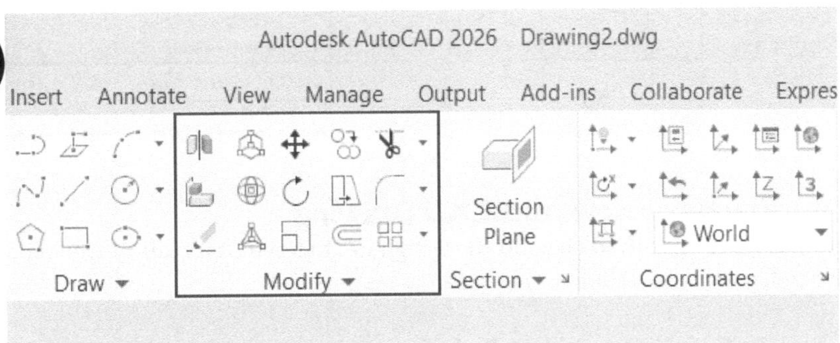

Tutorial 1

Create the 3D model, as shown in Figure 13.104.

13.104

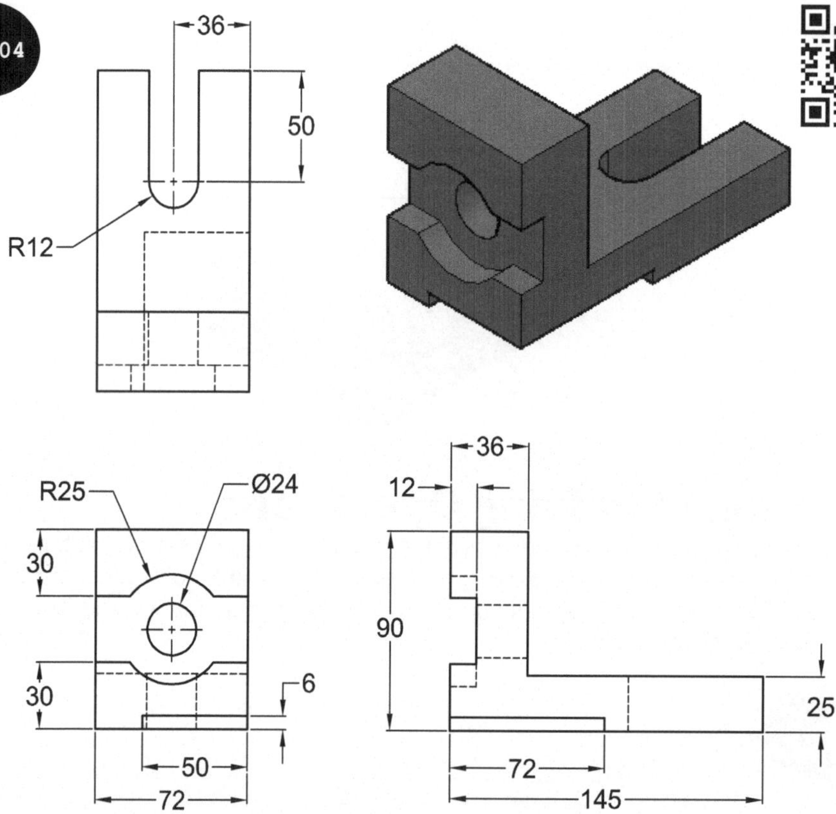

Section 1: Starting a new AutoCAD Drawing

1. Start AutoCAD and then click on the + sign next to the **Start** tab of the initial screen. The new drawing file with the default drawing template gets invoked.

Section 2: Defining Drawing Limits

1. Follow the command sequence given below to define the limits of the drawing.

```
Command: LIMITS (ENTER)
Specify lower left corner or [ON/OFF]<0.0000,0.0000>: 0,0 (ENTER)
Specify upper right corner <12.0000,9.0000>: 250,150 (ENTER)
```

Section 3: Selecting the Workspace

Now, you need to activate the 3D Modeling workspace to create the 3D model.

1. Click on the **Workspace Switching** button in the Status Bar. A flyout appears, see Figure 13.105.

2. Click on the **3D Modeling** option in the flyout to activate the 3D Modeling workspace.

13.105

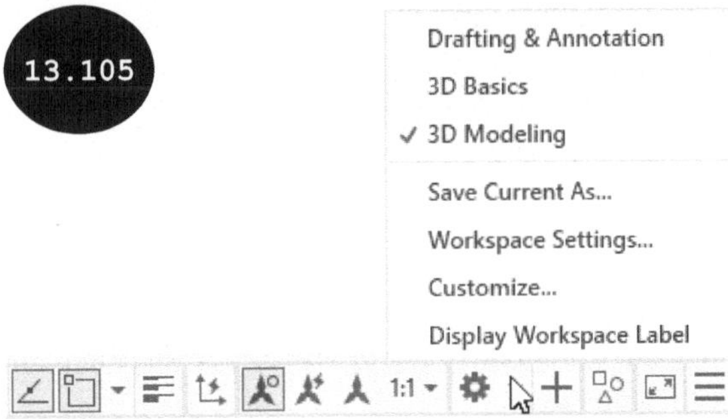

Section 4: Creating the Base Feature of the 3D Model

Now, you need to create the base feature of the 3D model. The base feature of the model is an extrude feature.

1. Turn off the display of grids in the drawing area by clicking on the **Display drawing grid** button in the Status Bar.

2. Change the view orientation of the drawing to SE isometric by clicking on the **SE Isometric** tool in the **View** flyout of the **View** panel in the **Home** tab, see Figure 13.106.

13.106

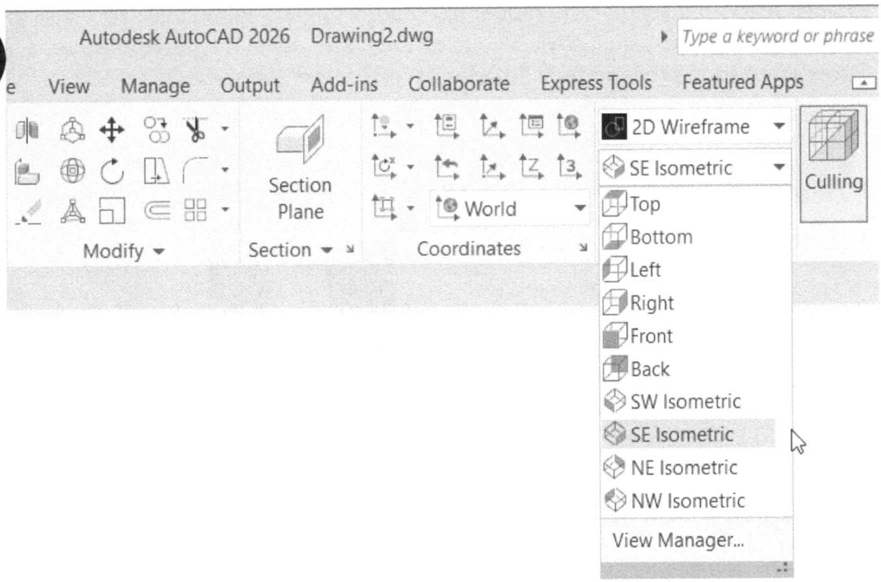

3. Ensure that the Ortho mode is turned on. You can turn on or off the Ortho mode by clicking on the **Ortho Mode** button in the Status Bar or by pressing the F8 key.

4. Ensure that the Dynamic Input mode is activated. You can turn on or off the Dynamic Input mode by clicking on the **Dynamic Input** button in the Status Bar.

5. Draw a rectangle of length 72 units and width 145 units by using the **Rectangle** tool in the drawing area, see Figure 13.107.

Now, you need to create a 3D solid feature by extruding the rectangle.

6. Click on the **Extrude** tool in the **Modeling** panel of the **Home** tab or type **EXT** and then press ENTER. The **Extrude** tool gets activated and you are prompted to select objects to extrude.

7. Select the rectangle in the drawing area and then press ENTER. A preview of the extrude feature appears and you are prompted to specify the height of the extrusion.

8. Enter **25** units as the height of the extrusion and then press ENTER. An extrude feature of 25 units in height is created, see Figure 13.108.

13.107

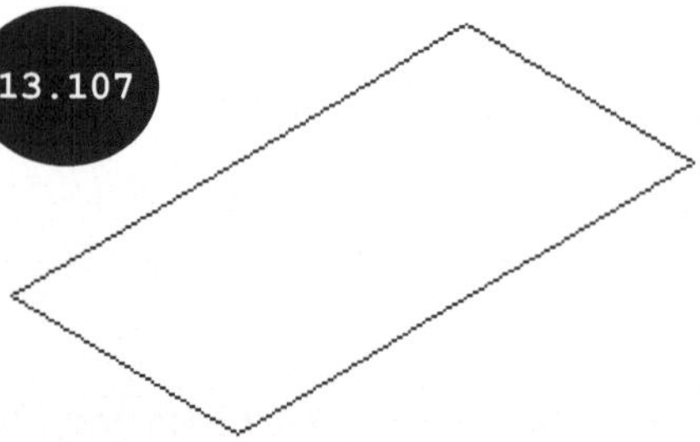

13.108

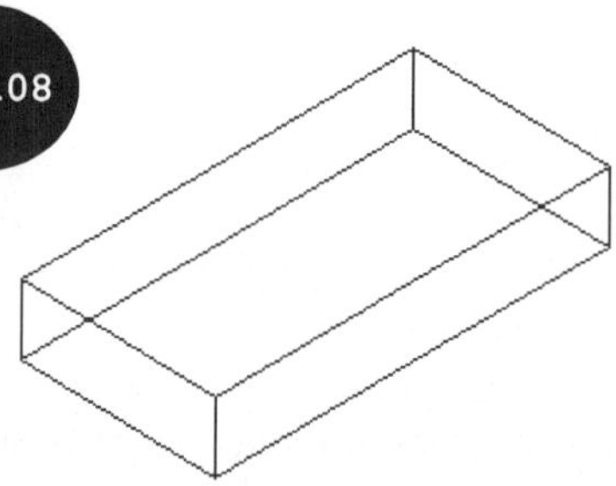

9. Change the visual style of the model to "shades of gray" visual style by clicking on the **Shades of Gray** tool in the **Visual Style** flyout of the **View** panel in the **Home** tab, see Figure 13.109. Figure 13.110 shows the model in "shades of gray" visual style.

13.109

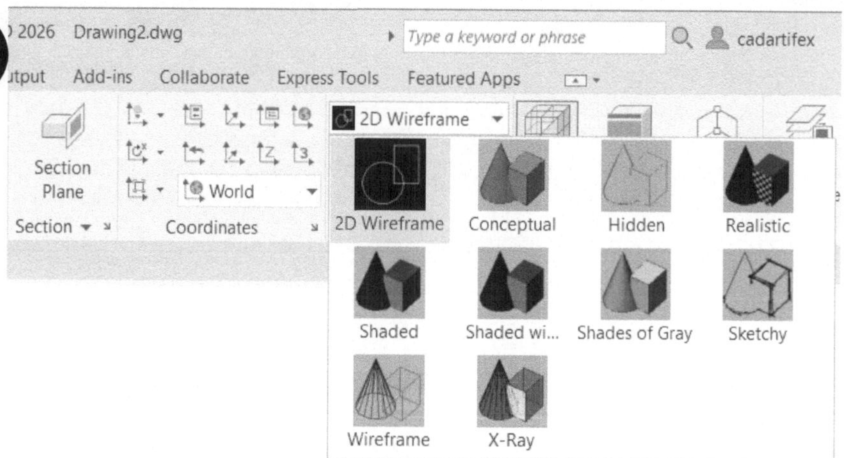

13.110

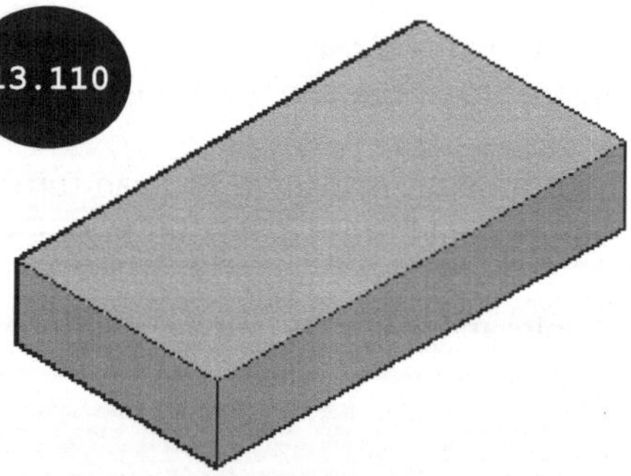

Section 5: Creating the Second Feature

Now, you need to create the second feature of the model.

1. Click on the **Copy Edges** tool in the **Solid Editing** panel of the **Home** tab, see Figure 13.111. You are prompted to select edges to be copied.

2. Click on the front edge of the top planar face of the base feature. The edge gets selected, see Figure 13.112. Next, press ENTER. You are prompted to select a base point.

13.111

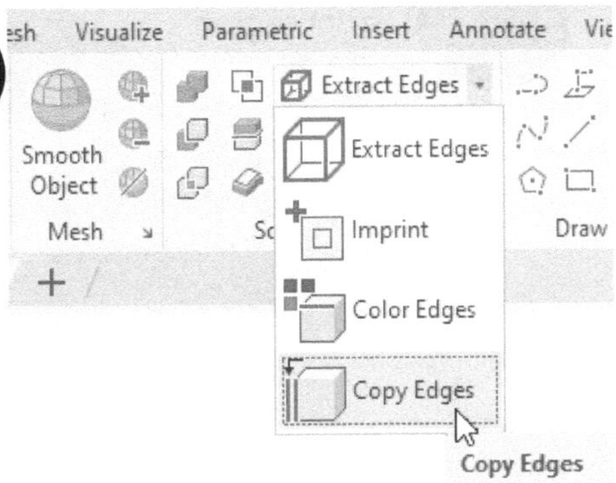

13.112

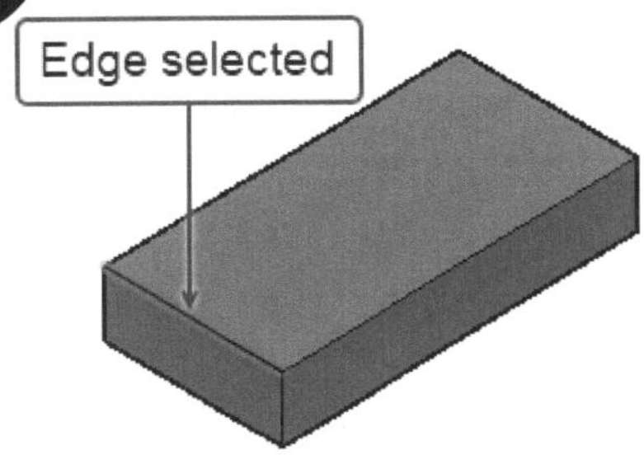

3. Click anywhere in the drawing area to specify the base point, see Figure 13.113. You are prompted to specify a second point of displacement.

4. Move the cursor horizontally along the positive Y-axis direction, see Figure 13.113.

5. Type **36** and then press ENTER. The selected edge is copied on the top planar face of the base feature at an offset distance of 36 units, see Figure 13.114. Next, press ESC to exit the tool.

13.113

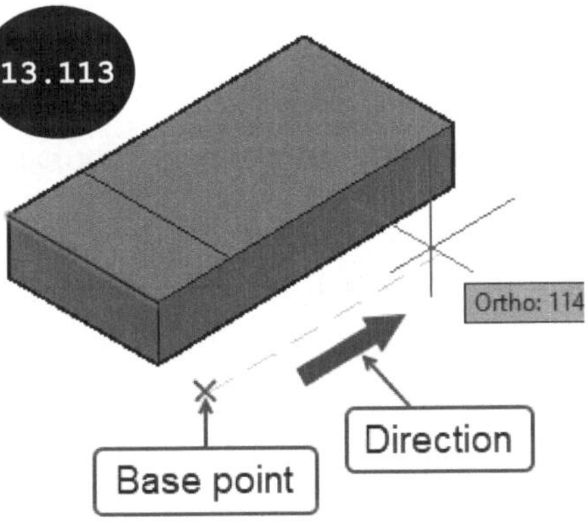

13.114

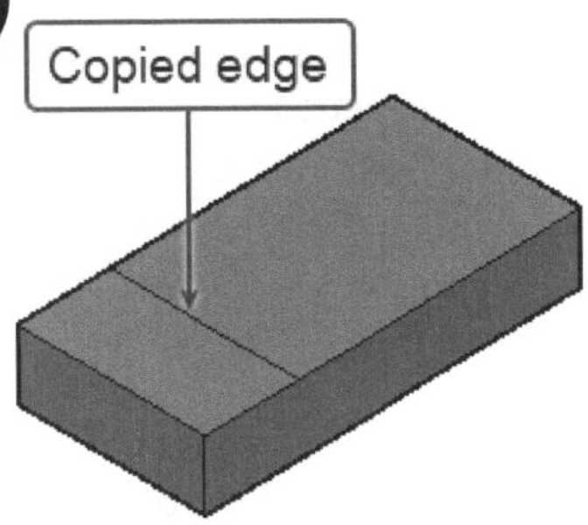

Now, you can create the second feature by adding material.

6. Click on the **Presspull** tool in the **Modeling** panel, see Figure 13.115 or enter PRESSPULL in the Command Line window and then press ENTER. The **Presspull** tool gets activated and you are prompted to select an object or a bounded area.
7. Click on the front enclosed region of the top planar face of the base feature, see Figure 13.116. A preview of the second feature appears and you are prompted to specify the extrusion height.

13.115

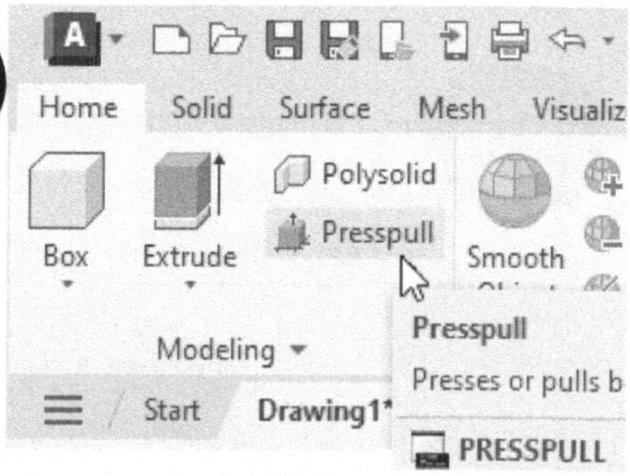

13.116

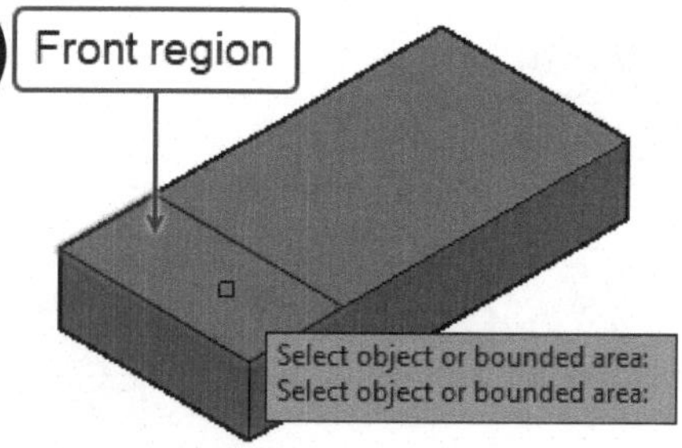

8. Move the cursor vertically upward. Next, type 65 and then press ENTER. The second feature is created by adding material to the height of 65 units, see Figure 13.117.

13.117

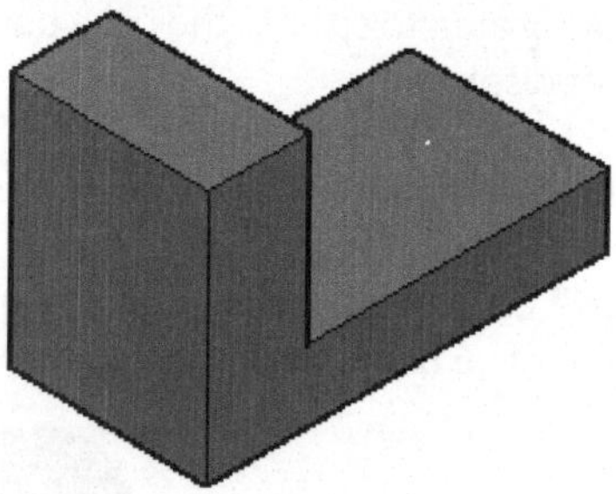

Section 6: Creating the Third Feature

Now, you need to create the third feature of the model. The third feature of the model is created by removing the material.

1. Click on the **Copy Edges** tool in the **Solid Editing** panel of the **Home** tab. You are prompted to select edges to be copied.

2. Click on the front vertical edge of the model, see Figure 13.118 and then press ENTER. You are prompted to select a base point.

3. Click anywhere in the drawing area to specify the base point. You are prompted to specify a second point of displacement.

4. Move the cursor horizontally along the negative X-axis direction, see Figure 13.119. Next, type 36 and then press ENTER. The selected edge is copied on the front face of the model at an offset distance of 36 units, see Figure 13.120. Next, press ESC to exit the tool.

13.118

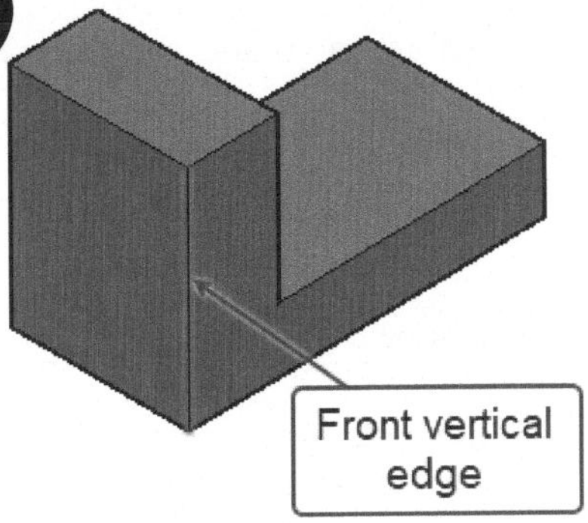

13.119

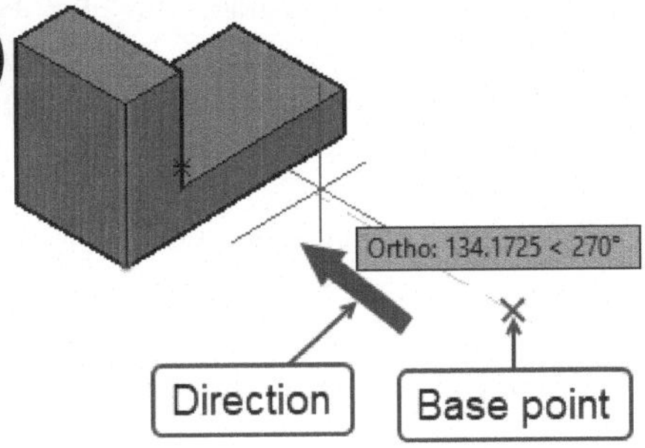

13.120

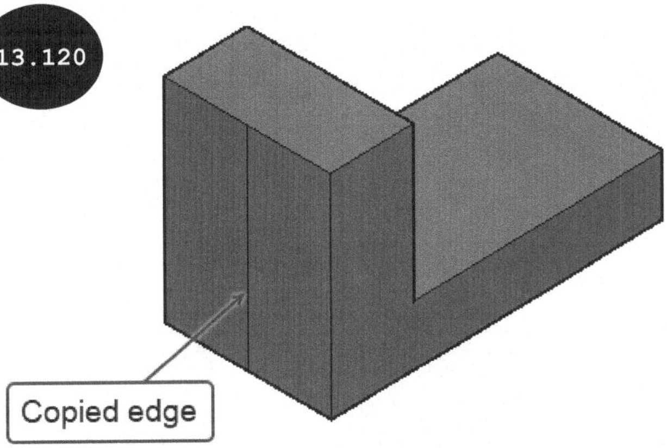

Now, you need to change the work plane (XY) to the Front view of the drawing.

5. Invoke the **Named UCS Combo Control** flyout in the **Coordinates** panel of the **Home** tab and then click on the **Front** tool to set the work plane (XY) to the Front view of the drawing, see Figure 13.121.

6. Click on the **Center, Radius** tool in the **Draw** panel of the Home tab and then draw a circle of radius 25 units whose center point is at the midpoint of the previously copied edge, see Figure 13.122.

13.121

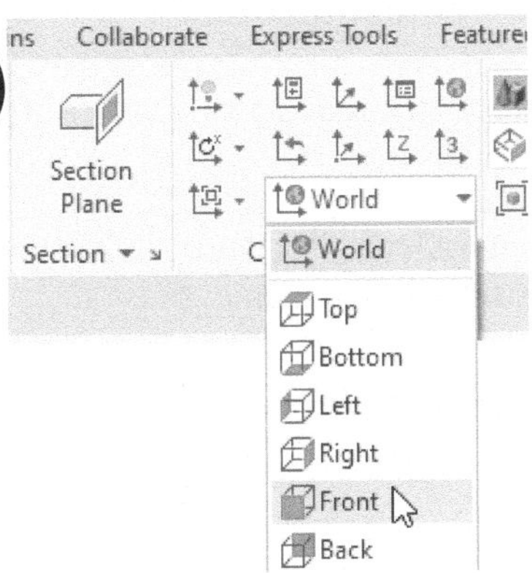

13.122

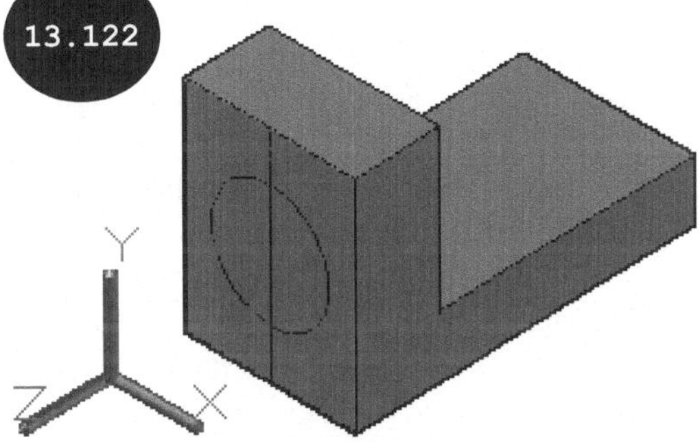

After creating the circle, you can erase/delete the copied edge.

7. Type **E** and then press ENTER. The Erase command gets activated and you are prompted to select objects to be erased.

8. Select the copied edge by clicking the left mouse button and then press ENTER. The selected edge gets erased, see Figure 13.123.

   Now, you can create the third feature by removing the material.

9. Click on the **Presspull** tool in the **Modeling** panel or enter PRESSPULL in the Command Line window and then press ENTER. The **Presspull** tool gets activated and you are prompted to select an object or a bounded area.

10. Click inside the previously drawn circle as the region to remove the material from. A preview of the feature appears and you are prompted to specify the extrusion height.

11. Move the cursor along the negative Z-axis direction. Next, enter **12** as the height of extrusion and then press ENTER. The third feature is created by removing the material, see Figure 13.124.

13.123

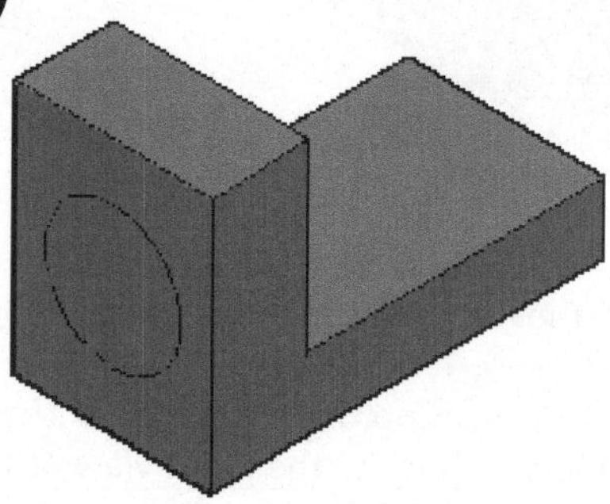

13.124

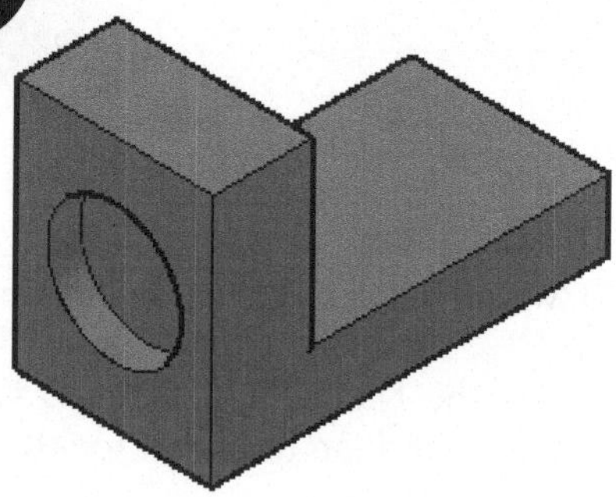

Section 7: Creating the Fourth Feature

Now, you need to create the fourth feature of the model. The fourth feature of the model is created by removing material.

1. Copy the top and bottom edges of the front planar face of the model to a distance of 30 units, by using the **Copy Edges** tool, see Figure 13.125.

2. Invoke the **Presspull** tool and then press and hold the SHIFT key. Next, select two enclosed regions one by one by clicking the left mouse button, see Figure 13.126.

3. Release the SHIFT key and then press ENTER. You are prompted to specify the height of the extrusion.

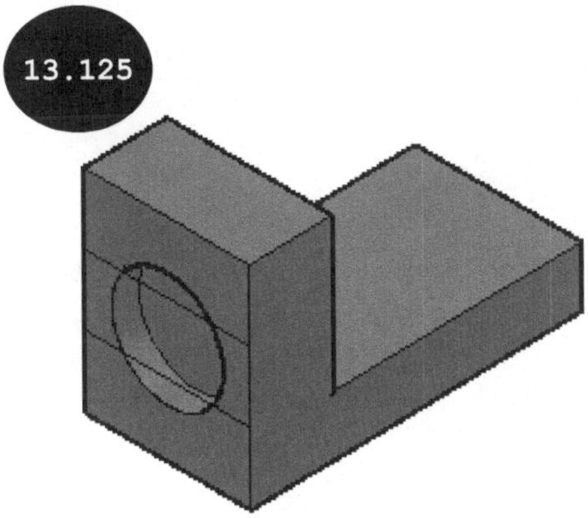

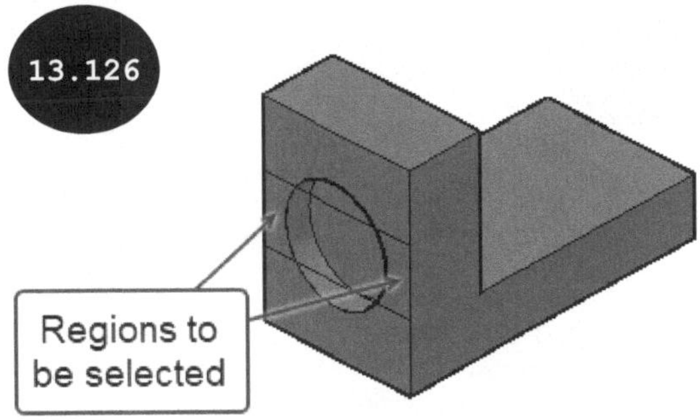

4. Move the cursor backward and then type 12. Next, press ENTER. The fourth feature is created by removing material from the model, see Figure 13.127.

5. After creating the fourth feature, you can erase the copied edges by using the ERASE command.

Section 8: Creating the Fifth Feature

Now, you need to create the fifth feature of the model. The fifth feature of the model is created by removing material.

1. Ensure that the work plane (XY) is set to the Front view.

2. Invoke the **Center, Radius** tool and then click to specify the center point of the circle when the cursor snaps to the center of the back semi-circular edge of the model, see Figure 13.128. You are prompted to specify the radius of the circle.

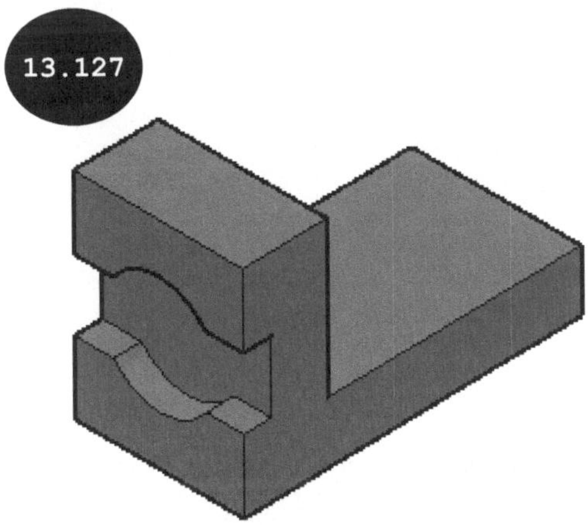

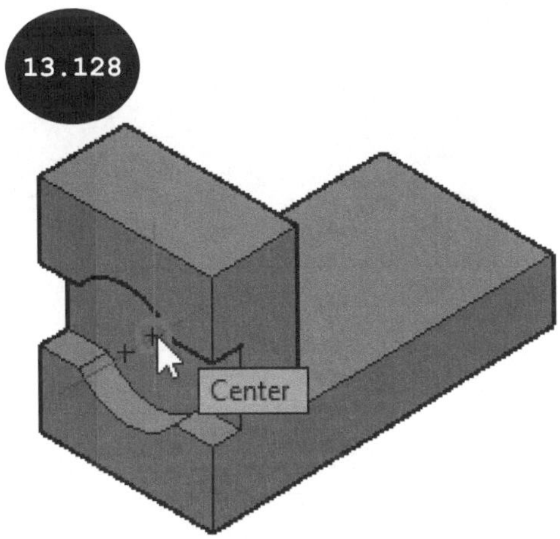

3. Type **12** and then press ENTER. A circle of radius 12 units is created, see Figure 13.129.

4. Invoke the **Presspull** tool and then remove the material by selecting the enclosed region of the previously created circle to create a through hole, see Figure 13.130.

13.129

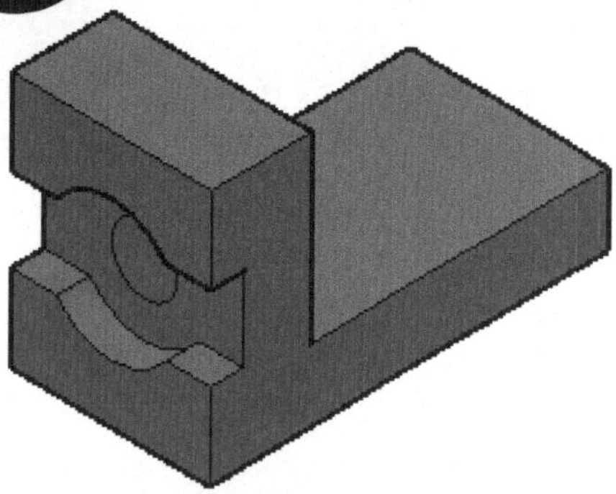

13.130

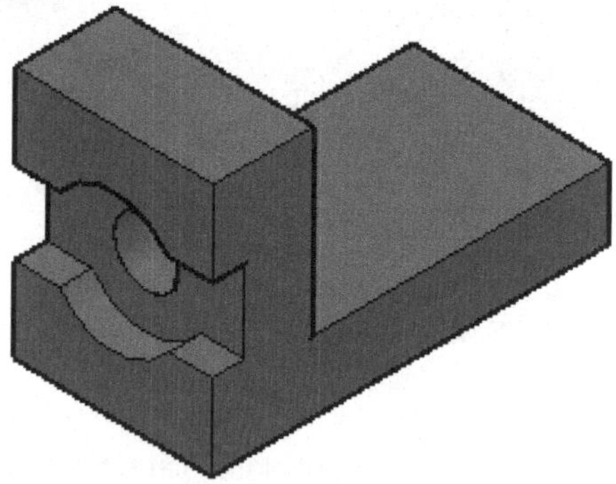

Section 9: Creating the Sixth Feature

Now, you need to create the sixth feature of the model.

1. Copy the edge of the top planar face of the base feature to a distance of 50 units by using the **Copy Edges** tool, see Figure 13.131.

2. Invoke the **Named UCS Combo Control** flyout in the **Coordinates** panel of the **Home** tab and then click on the **Top** tool to set the work plane (XY) to the Top view for creating the sketch on the top planar face of the base feature, see Figure 13.132.

13.131

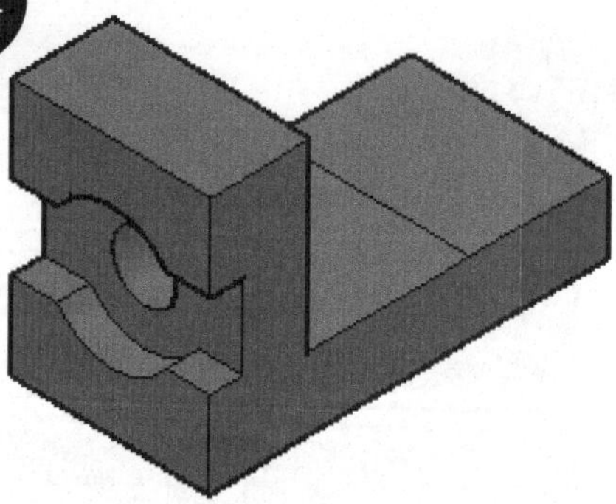

13.132

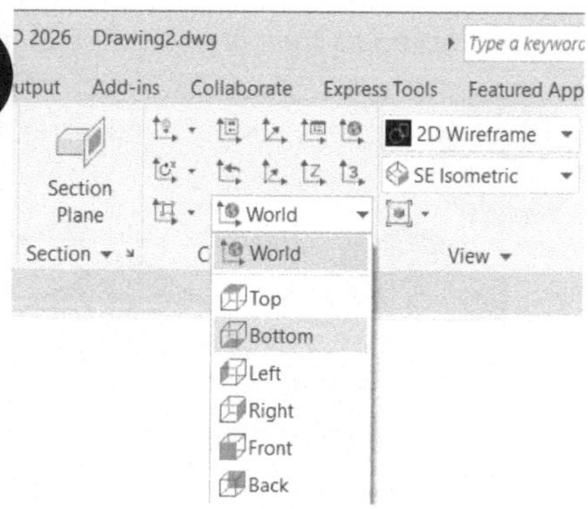

3. Draw a sketch of the sixth feature by using the **Circle, Radius** and **Line** tools, see Figure 13.133. Note that the center point of the circle is at the midpoint of the copied edge and its radius is 12 units.

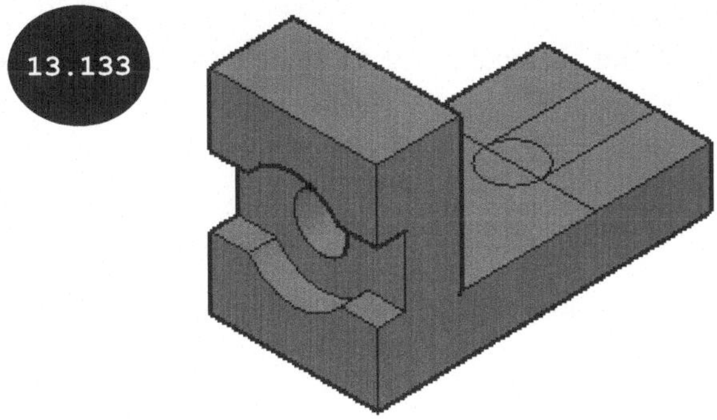

4. Erase the copied edge by using the ERASE command and trim the unwanted entities of the sketch by using the **Trim** tool. Figure 13.134 shows the final sketch of the sixth feature.

5. Invoke the **Presspull** tool and then remove the material throughout the entire model by selecting the enclosed region of the sketch. Figure 13.135 shows the model after creating the sixth feature by removing the material.

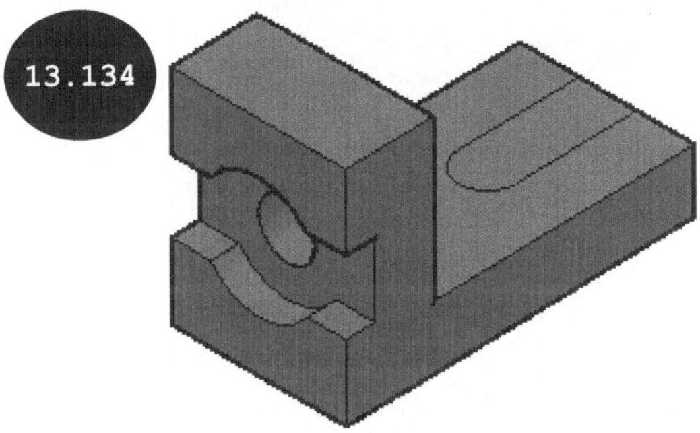

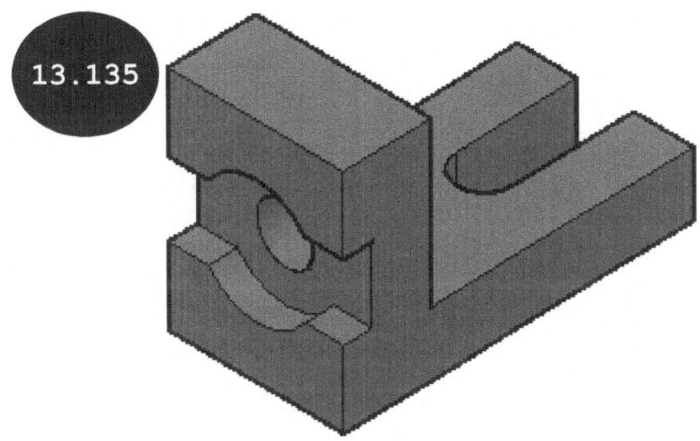

Section 10: Creating the Seventh Feature

1. Create the seventh feature by copying the edges of the model (see Figure 13.136) and then removing the material by using the **Presspull** tool to a depth of 50 units, see Figure 13.137. You can refer to Figure 13.104 for dissensions or distance for the copied edges. After creating the feature, erase the copied edges. Figure 13.137 shows the final model after creating all its features.

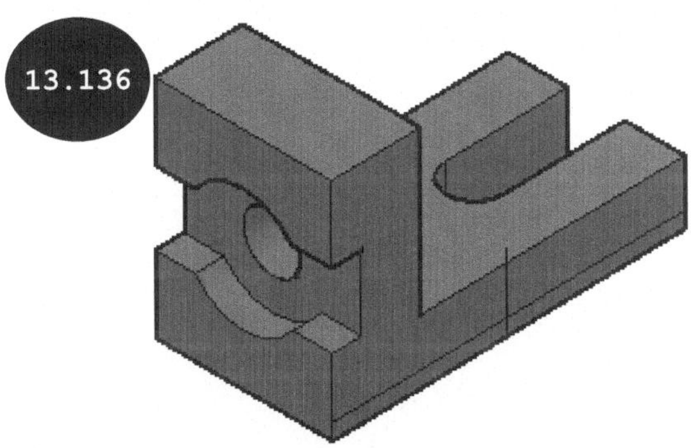

Section 11: Saving the Model

1. Save the model with the name "Tutorial 1" in the *Chapter 13* folder. You need to create this folder inside the *AutoCAD* folder.

Hands-on Test Drive 1

Create the 3D model, as shown in Figure 13.138. The different views and dimensions are given in the same figure.

13.138

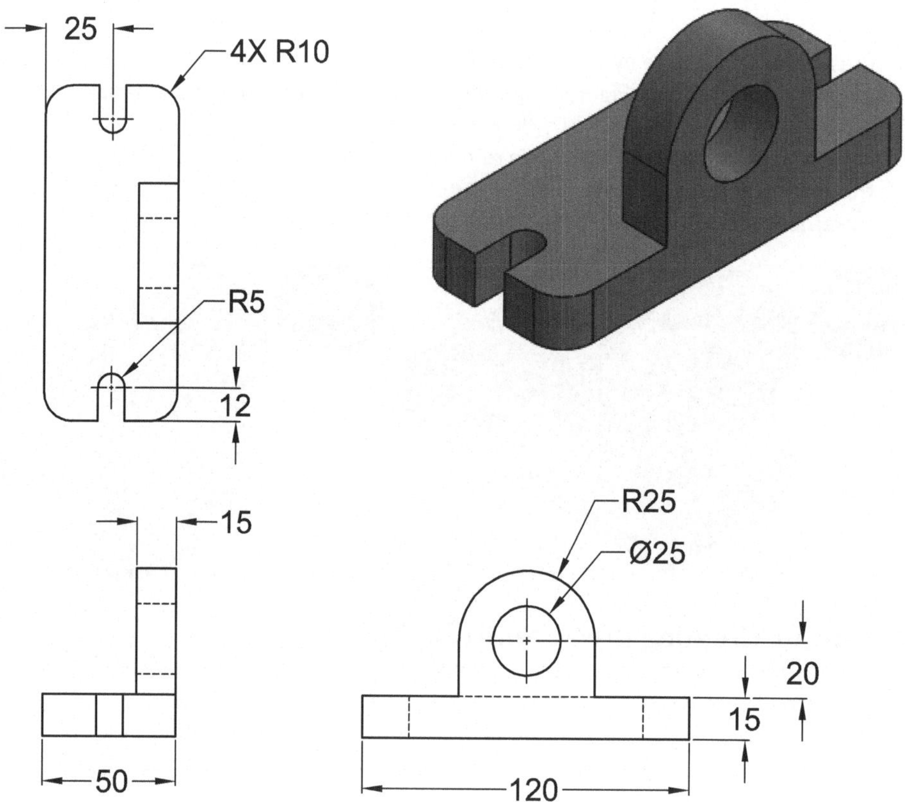

Hands-on Test Drive 2

Create the 3D model, as shown in Figure 13.139.

13.139

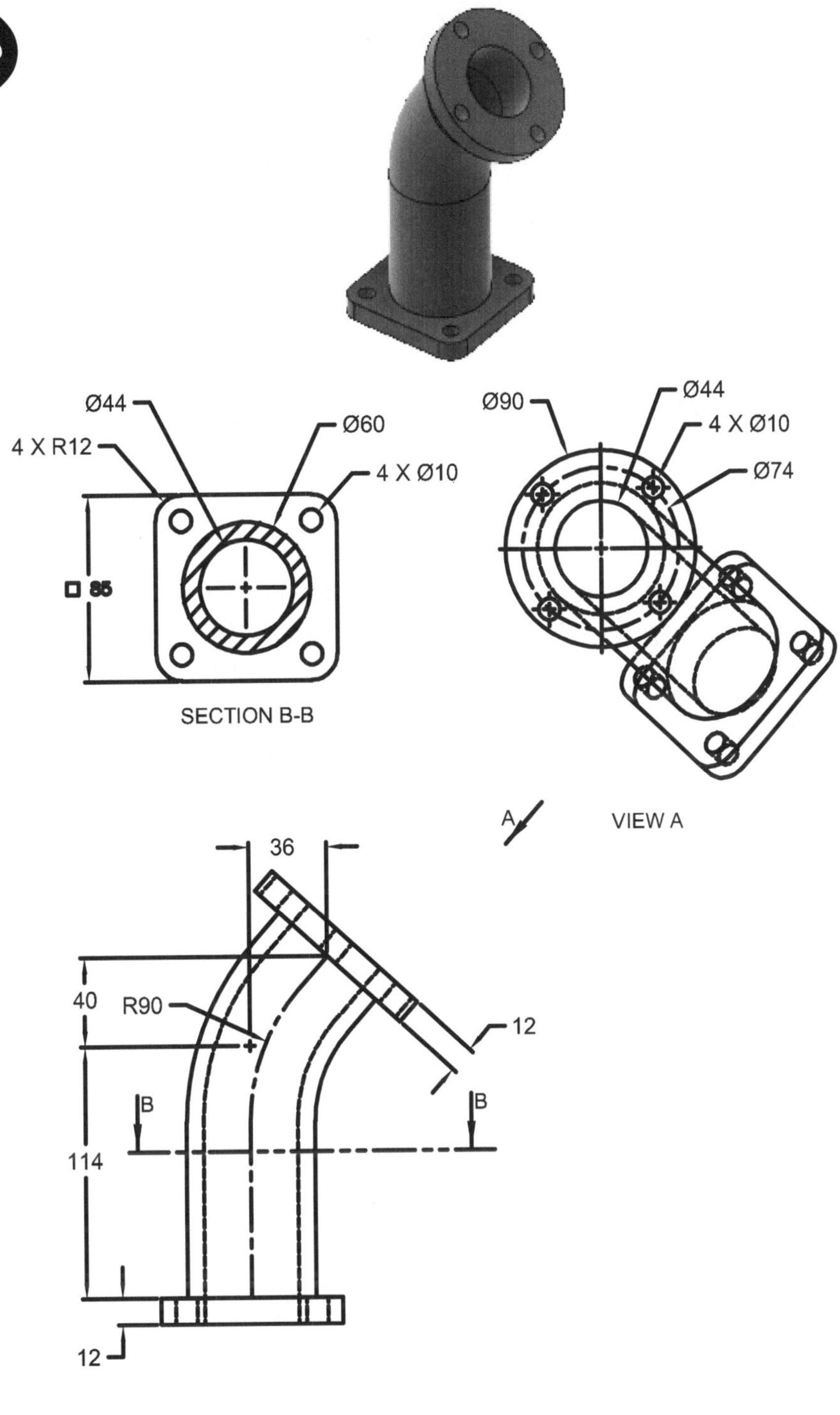

Hands-on Test Drive 3

Create the 3D model, as shown in Figure 13.140. The different views and dimensions are given in the same figure.

13.140

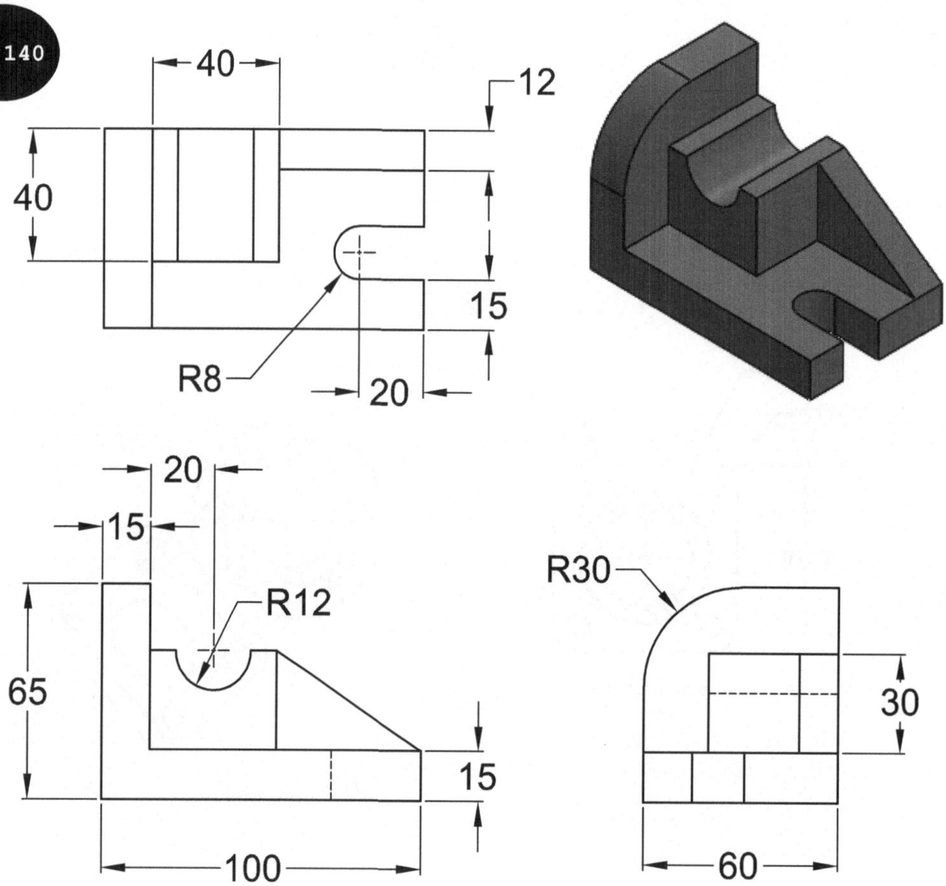

Summary

The chapter discussed about creating 3D Models in the 3D Modeling workspace including various 3D primitives such as box, cylinder, sphere, cone, and torus. It described the World Coordinate System (WCS) and User Coordinate System (UCS) and introduced how to set the work plane to a predefined orthographic view, work with Dynamic UCS, and control the display of UCS. Besides, the chapter explained how to create extrude, revolve, sweep, loft, and 3D wall-like polysolid features of a 3D model. It also explained how to perform various boolean operations, check interference, and copy edges of a solid feature.

Questions

Complete the following sentences:

- In AutoCAD, you can create 3D models in the _________ or _________ workspace.
- The tools in the _________ flyout of the **View** panel in the **Home** tab are used for controlling the visual style for the 3D model.
- The _________ is a movable coordinate system that allows you to change the position of the origin and the orientation of the X, Y, and Z axes to establish the work plane (XY plane) as per your requirement.
- The _________ tool is used for creating a user coordinate system by specifying three points.
- The _________ tool is used for restoring the previous position of the user coordinate system.
- The tools in the _________ flyout of the **Coordinates** panel in the **Home** tab are used to set the work plane (XY) of the UCS to the predefined orthographic views such as Top, Front, Left, and Right.
- In AutoCAD, the _________ is a temporary UCS that appears automatically when you move the cursor over the face of a 3D solid object.
- The _________ tool is used for converting the individual entities of a closed sketch into a region for creating a 3D solid feature.
- The _________ tool is used for creating a sweep feature.
- A _________ feature is created by lofting two or more than two profiles (sections) such that the cross-sectional shape of the loft feature transits from one profile to another.
- The _________ tool is used for creating or editing a 3D solid model by adding or removing material depending on whether you perform a press or pull operation.

- The _________ tool is used for creating a 3D wall-like polysolid feature.
- The _________ tool is used for checking the interference between two or more than two bodies.
- The _________ tool is used for copying the edges of an existing 3D solid feature.

INDEX

Symbols

A

B

C

D

E

F

G

H

I

N

O

P

T

U

V

W

X

Y

Z

Other Publications by CADArtifex

Some of the other Publications by CADArtifex are given below:

AutoCAD Textbooks

AutoCAD 2026: A Power Guide for Beginners and Intermediate Users
AutoCAD 2025: A Power Guide for Beginners and Intermediate Users
AutoCAD 2024: A Power Guide for Beginners and Intermediate Users
and more

AutoCAD For Architectural Design Textbooks

AutoCAD 2023 for Architectural Design: A Power Guide for Beginners and Intermediate Users
AutoCAD 2022 for Architectural Design: A Power Guide for Beginners and Intermediate Users
AutoCAD 2021 for Architectural Design: A Power Guide for Beginners and Intermediate Users
and more

Autodesk Fusion 360 Textbooks

Autodesk Fusion 360: A Power Guide for Beginners and Intermediate Users (7th Edition)
Autodesk Fusion 360: A Power Guide for Beginners and Intermediate Users (6th Edition)
Autodesk Fusion 360: A Power Guide for Beginners and Intermediate Users (5th Edition)
and more

Autodesk Fusion 360 Surface and T-Spline Textbooks

Autodesk Fusion 360 Surface Design and Sculpting with T-Spline Surfaces (7th Edition)
Autodesk Fusion 360 Surface Design and Sculpting with T-Spline Surfaces (6th Edition)
and more

Autodesk Inventor Textbooks

Autodesk Inventor 2026: A Power Guide for Beginners and Intermediate Users
Autodesk Inventor 2025: A Power Guide for Beginners and Intermediate Users
Autodesk Inventor 2024: A Power Guide for Beginners and Intermediate Users
and more

FreeCAD Textbooks

FreeCAD 1.0: A Power Guide for Beginners and Intermediate Users
FreeCAD 0.21: A Power Guide for Beginners and Intermediate Users
FreeCAD 0.20: A Power Guide for Beginners and Intermediate Users

Onshape Textbooks
Onshape 2025: A Power Guide for Beginners and Intermediate Users

PTC Creo Parametric Textbooks
Creo Parametric 11.0: A Power Guide for Beginners and Intermediate Users
Creo Parametric 10.0: A Power Guide for Beginners and Intermediate Users
Creo Parametric 9.0: A Power Guide for Beginners and Intermediate Users
and more

SOLIDWORKS Textbooks
SOLIDWORKS 2025: A Power Guide for Beginners and Intermediate User
SOLIDWORKS 2024: A Power Guide for Beginners and Intermediate User
SOLIDWORKS 2023: A Power Guide for Beginners and Intermediate User
SOLIDWORKS 2021: A Power Guide for Beginners and Intermediate User
and more

SOLIDWORKS Sheet Metal and Surface Design Textbooks
SOLIDWORKS Sheet Metal and Surface Design 2025 for Beginners and Intermediate Users
SOLIDWORKS Sheet Metal and Surface Design 2024 for Beginners and Intermediate Users
and more

SOLIDWORKS Simulation Textbooks
SOLIDWORKS Simulation 2025: A Power Guide for Beginners and Intermediate User
SOLIDWORKS Simulation 2024: A Power Guide for Beginners and Intermediate User
SOLIDWORKS Simulation 2023: A Power Guide for Beginners and Intermediate User
SOLIDWORKS Simulation 2022: A Power Guide for Beginners and Intermediate User
and more

Exercises Books
Some of the exercises books are given below:

100 AutoCAD Exercises - Learn by Practicing (2 Edition)
Autodesk Inventor Exercises - Learn by Practicing
Autodesk Fusion 360 Exercises Learn by Practicing (2023-24)
SOLIDWORKS Exercises - Learn by Practicing (3 Edition)

New Project-Based eBook/Video Courses*

- Autodesk Fusion 360 Project-Based eBook/ Video Courses Bundle
- SOLIDWORKS Project-Based eBook/Video Courses Bundle

**For more information, visit: cadartifex.com > PROJECTS*
